# 24th International Conference on Computational Linguistics

# (COLING 2012)



**Demonstrations**

## Mumbai, India
## 8-15 December 2012

**Editors:**

**Martin Kay**
**Christian Boitet**

ISBN: 978-1-62748-391-9

**Printed from e-media with permission by:**

Curran Associates, Inc.
57 Morehouse Lane
Red Hook, NY 12571

CURRAN ASSOCIATES INC. proceedings.com

**Some format issues inherent in the e-media version may also appear in this print version.**



Printed by Curran Associates, Inc. (2013)



Association for Computational Linguistics
209 N. Eighth Street
Stroudsburg, Pennsylvania 18360

Phone: 1-570-476-8006
Fax: 1-570-476-0860

acl@aclweb.org

**Additional copies of this publication are available from:**

Curran Associates, Inc.
57 Morehouse Lane
Red Hook, NY 12571 USA
Phone: 845-758-0400
Fax: 845-758-2634
Email: curran@proceedings.com
Web: www.proceedings.com

COLING 2012

# 24th International Conference on Computational Linguistics

# Proceedings of COLING 2012: Demonstration Papers

Program chairs:
Martin Kay and Christian Boitet

8-15 December 2012
Mumbai, India

## Diamond sponsors

Tata Consultancy Services
Linguistic Data Consortium for Indian Languages (LDC-IL)

## Gold Sponsors

Microsoft Research
Beijing Baidu Netcon Science Technology Co. Ltd.

## Silver sponsors

IBM, India Private Limited
Crimson Interactive Pvt. Ltd.
Yahoo
Easy Transcription & Software Pvt. Ltd.

# Table of Contents

# Complex Predicates in Telugu: A computational perspective

*Rahul BALUSU*
EFL University, India
kodiguddu@gmail.com

ABSTRACT
Complex predicates raise the question of how to encode them in computational lexicons. Their computational implementation in South Asian languages is in its infancy. This paper examines in detail the variety of complex predicates in Telugu revealing the syntactic process of their composition and the constraints on their formation. The framework used is First Phase Syntax (Ramchand 2008). In this lexical semantic approach that ties together the constraints on the meaning and the argument structure of complex predicates, each verb breaks down into 3 sub-event heads which determine the nature of the verb. Complex predicates are formed by one verb subsuming the sub-event heads of another verb, and this is constrained in principled ways. The data analysed and the constraints developed in the paper are of use to linguists working on computational solutions for Telugu and other languages, for design and development of predicate structure functions in linguistic processors.

KEYWORDS: Complex Predicates, Dravidian, First Phase Syntax, Argument Structure, Telugu.

*Proceedings of COLING 2012: Demonstration Papers*, pages 1–8,
COLING 2012, Mumbai, December 2012.

# 1 Introduction

Complex predicates are predicates that are multi-headed; they are composed of more than one grammatical element (either morphemes or words), each of which contributes part of the information ordinarily associated with a head (Alsina *et al.* 1997). They exhibit word-like properties in terms of argument structure composition and in sometimes having lexicalised meanings (Lapointe 1980). They exhibit phrase-like properties in allowing certain syntactic operations, such as movement, to manipulate their internal structure (Bresnan and Mchombo 1995). While complex predicates have two or more heads, these heads function as a single predicate in a monoclausal configuration. Computationally, we need a mapping procedure in order to account for the full set of predicate meanings that can be associated with monoclausal structures, which derives both 'word-like' meanings, and 'phrase-like' meanings (Mohanan 2007).

# 2 Theoretical Framework: A super quick guide to First Phase Syntax

In First Phase Syntax (Ramchand 2008) terms, the verbal domain decomposes into 3 distinct heads or subevent projections: init[iation]P, proc[ess]P, and res[ult]P. Each subevent head enters in a predicational relation with its specifier position. InitP introduces the causation event and licenses the external argument – the Initiator. ProcP specifies the process or the nature of the change and licenses the internal argument – the Undergoer. ResP introduces the result state and licenses the holder of the result state – the Resultee. Depending on which subevent heads a verb lexicalizes, it belongs to a particular verb class – <init, proc, res>, <proc,res>, etc. Activities are <init, proc>. Achievements are <init, proc, res>. Unergatives have co-indexed <init, proc>. Unaccusatives lack <init>. The DP argument can occupy two or more specifier positions. For example, Initiator-Undergoer in *John ran*, Undergoer-Resultee in *The vase broke*, and Initiator-Undergoer-Resultee in *John arrived*. Composite thematic roles are encoded in the lexical entry of the verb – the verb determines whether a DP will raise from one specifier to another or not. An event head can have verbal or non-verbal material (DP, AP, PP, etc.) occupying its complement position – Rheme. Rhemes are not subjects of events but part of the description of the predicate. A DP in the rheme position builds one joint predication with the verb. A DP in the specifier position of a subevent head is a verbal argument.

# 3 Verbal Complex Predicates in Telugu

There are 3 aspectual/completive light verbs in Telugu, shown in (1).

| | | | |
|---|---|---|---|
| (1) | **poo 'go'** | **veyyi 'throw'** | **paDa.veyyi 'throw down'** |
| | Sita paD.i.pooindi | Sita pustakam cadi.veesindi | Sita pustakam cadiv.i.paDesindi |
| | Sita fall.perf.went | Sita book read.perf.throw | Sita book read.perf.throwdown |
| | 'Sita fell (fully)' | 'Sita read the book (fully)' | 'Sita read the book (totally)' |

Complex predicates like these have been analyzed in First Phase Syntax terms as underassociation of the main or heavy verb features under the light verb. This is shown for the Telugu data that is given above in (2). The light verb bears tense and agreement. The heavy verb appears as a perfective/conjunctive participle with the marker *-i*. The light verb has a very abstract semantics. The semantic content of the complex predicate comes from the heavy verb. The subevent feature specification of the light verb is the same as the subevent specification of that verb when it is used as a heavy verb (Butt's Generalization; see Butt 1997, 2003). The heavy verb lexicalizes or occupies the rheme position. Together they form one joint predication.

(2)

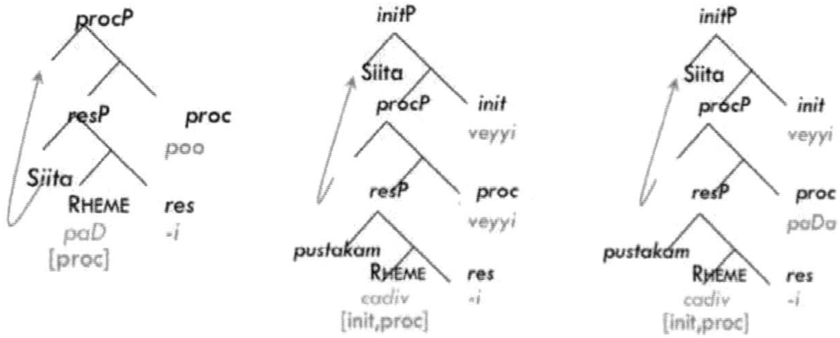


Of the 3 aspectuals in Telugu, *poo* is an unaccusative verb (<init>-less in First Phase terms) and selects for other unaccussative verbs. The other two have an <init> head and select for verbs with <init>. The <init>-less light verb cannot select <init> verbs and the <init> light verb cannot select <init>-less verbs as shown in (3). This further strengthens the selectional restrictions of light verbs that Ramchand (2008) identifies from Bangla data.

(3)

| **poo + <init>** | **veyyi + <init>less** | **paDa.veyyi + <init>less** |
|---|---|---|
| *Sita cadives.i.poindi | *Sita USA vell.i.veesindi | *Sita USA vell.i.paDeesindi |
| Sita read.perf.went | Sita USA go.perf.threw | Sita USA go.perf.throwdown |
| Intended: 'Sita read' | Intended: 'Sita went to USA' | Intended: 'Sita went to USA' |

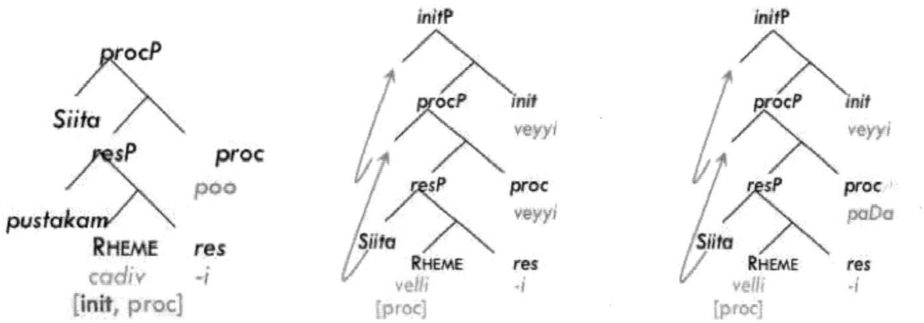


The constraints on underassociation that Ramchand (2008) derives from analyzing complex predicates in Bangla and Hindi are the following: 1) Underassociation of category features of any 'main verb' is possible, constrained by Agree. 2) Agreeing categorial features must unify their conceptual content. This means that if the heavy verb is specified for [init] but the light verb is not, the structure will not converge.

Among the 3 aspectual light verbs, *paDa.veyyi* is a complex light verb and involves 'double' complex predication of two verbs *paDu* and *veyyi* as shown in (4).

(4)

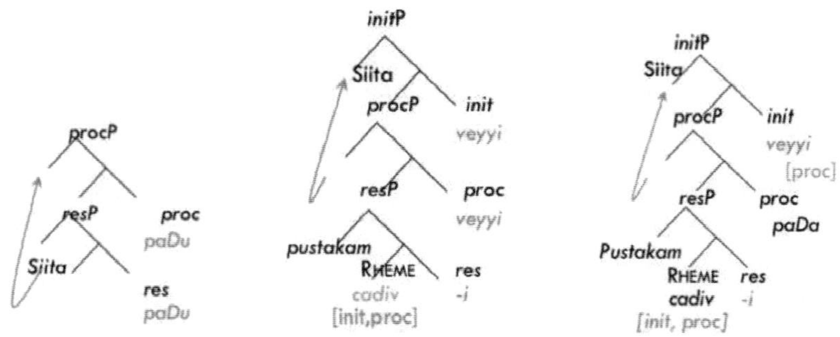

The causative suffix in Telugu is *-inc* or *-imp* as shown in (5)a. An unaccusative verb can be transitivized using the causative as shown in (5)b. It can causativize further with underassociation as shown in (5)c.

(5) a.

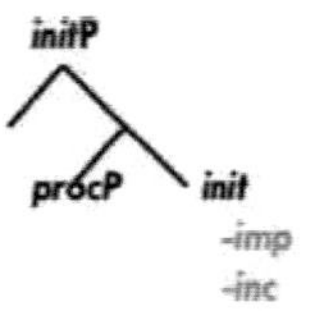


b.

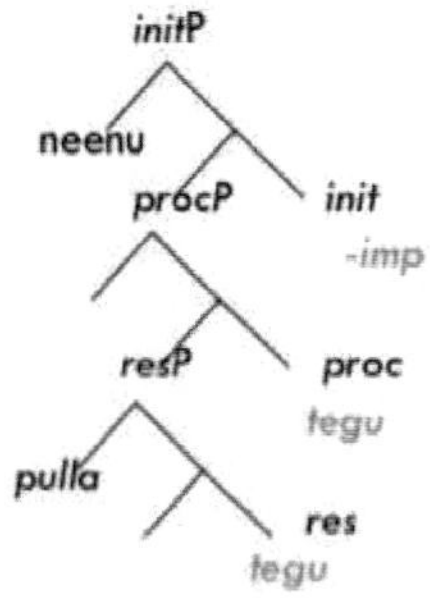


c.

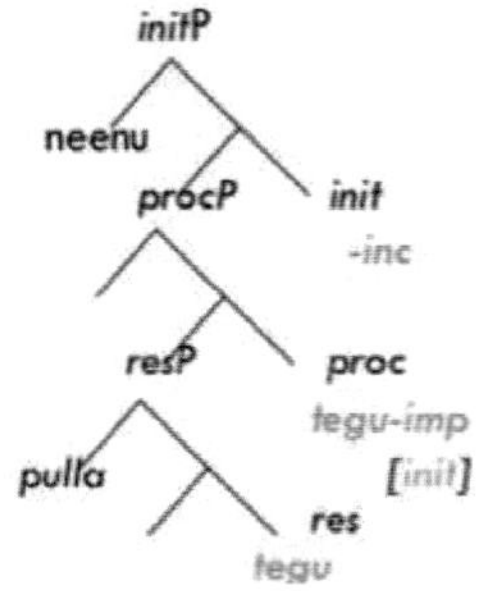


But the causative cannot co-occur with an unaccusative (<init>less) light verb, as shown in (6). This is because the [init] feature of *-inc* cannot underassociate with the <init>less light verb, whereas it can underassociate with <init> light verbs, as predicted by the constraints on underassociation.

(6) *karig-inci-poo vs. karig-inci-veyyi     *karig-inci-poo vs. karig-inci-veyyi
[init]     [init]-[init]

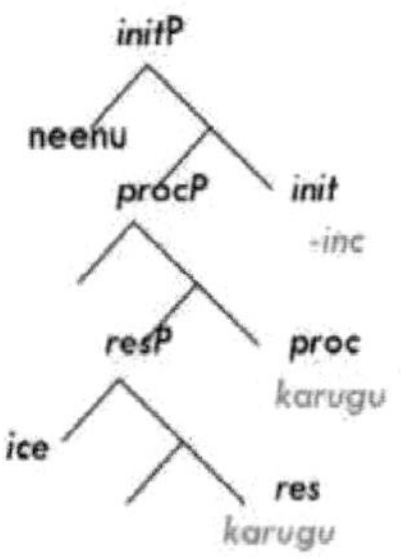


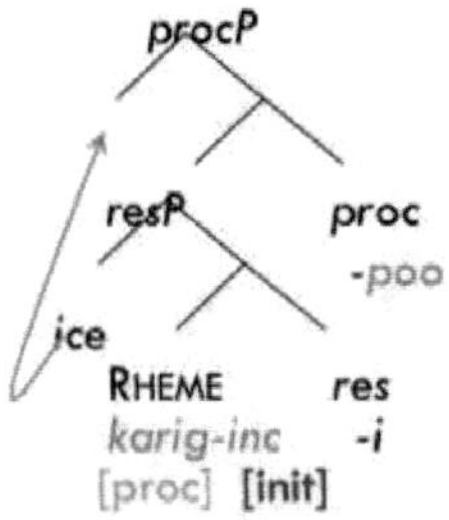


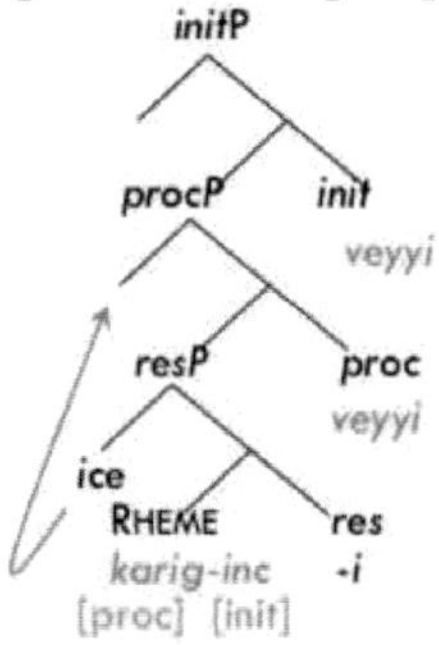


The benefactive light verb in Telugu is *peTTu* 'put'. In most languages it is 'give'. It is an applicative light verb. It always increase the valency, as shown in (7).

(7) Sita pustakam akkaDa peTTindi
Sita book there put
'Sita put the book there'

Sita Raviki cadiv.i.peTTindi
Sita Ravi read.PERF.put
'Sita read for Ravi (out loud or for his sake)'

The permissive light verb in Telugu is *an + ivvu – aN* is the infinitival marker, *ivvu* is 'give'. It is also an applicative light verb. But it doesn't increase the valency, as shown in (8).

(8) Sita pustakam Raviki iccindi
Sita book Ravi give
'Sita gave the book to Ravi'

Sita Ravini cadav.an.iccindi
Sita Ravi read.inf.give
'Sita let Ravi read'

In summary, there are three aspectuals in Telugu – one of these light verbs is itself complex. There are three Transitivizers – light verbs with direct lexicalization. They provide inceptual meaning. Non-aspectuals compose differently from aspectuals. There are other interesting beasts in the Telugu light verb jungle. Causativization with light verbs differs syntactically and semantically from that with the causative morpheme. Unlike the aspectual light verbs, the applicative light verbs can combine with <init> and <init>less verbs.

## 4 Nominal Complex Predicates in Telugu

In nominal complex predication, the light verb lexicalizes the subevent heads and provides the argument structure skeleton (Pantcheva 2007 *et seq.*). The light verb has a very abstract semantics. The semantic content of the complex predicate comes from the preverb (Lazard 1957). The preverb lexicalizes the rheme. Together they form one joint predication. This is shown in (9).

(9)

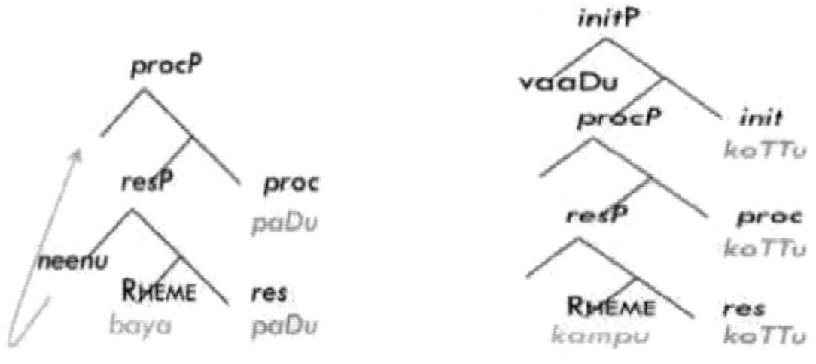


As the light verb lexicalizes the verbal heads, the argument structure depends entirely on the categorial specification of the light verb. Karimi-Doostan (1997) divides Persian light verbs into two classes: initiatory and transition light verbs. Telugu light verbs also fall into these two groups as shown in (10). In First Phase Syntax terms, initiatory light verbs have <init> specification, transitory light verbs do not have an <init> subevent head.

(10) **<init> light verbs**

ceyyi 'make' ivvu 'give'
peTTu 'put' tiyyi 'remove'
koTTu 'hit' aaDu 'play'
veyyi 'throw' cuupincu 'show'

**<init>less light verbs**

paDu 'fall' avvu 'happen'
kalugu 'arose' tegu 'break'
poo 'go' digu 'go down'
ekku 'go up' maaru 'change'

When the <init> light verbs compose with a nominal element, they have an initiatory meaning with an external argument. When the <init>less light verbs combine with a nominal element, they have an experiential meaning only. This is shown in (11) and (12).

(11) **paDu**

neenu booltaa paDDaanu
I flip fell
'I flipped'

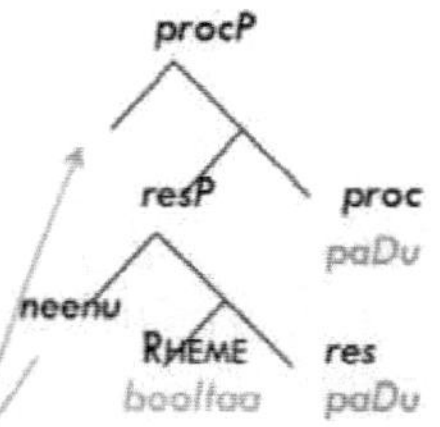


**koTTu**

neenu booltaa koTTeenu
I flip hit
'I did a cartwheel'

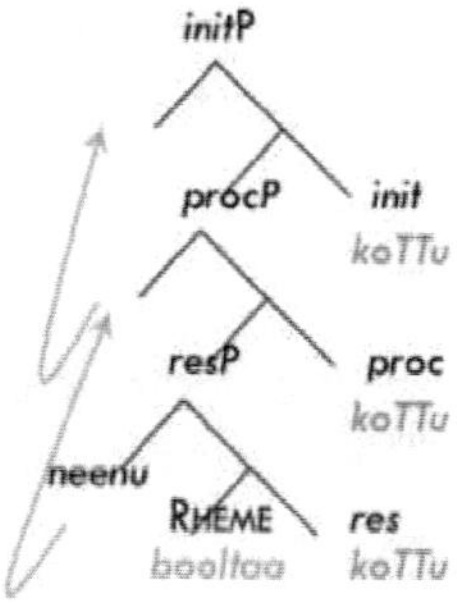


(12) **<init>less = experiential**

baya paDu 'get scared'
pedda avvu 'grow up'
muuta paDu 'closed down'

**<init> = initiatory**

baya peTTu 'scare someone'
pedda ceyyi 'bring up'
muuta veyyi 'close something down'

Loan words productively enter into nominal complex predicate formation. The loan words are overwhelmingly verbs in the language they are borrowed from. But in the nominal complex predicates they enter as rhemes. This is shown in (13).

| | | |
|---|---|---|
| (13) | **Loanwords with <init> light verbs** | **Loanwords with <init>less** |
| | ***ceyyi*** *'make',* ***koTTu*** *'hit',* ***ivvu*** *'give'* | **light verb** ***avvu*** *'happen'* |
| | print/phone/call/defeat/post/apply | surprise/shock/excite/ |
| | hurt/help/type/madad/ready/brush | defeat/begin/irritate/ |

In sum, in nominal complex predicates in Telugu, the verb determines the argument structure. The lexical-encyclopaedic information is smeared from the nominal element onto this skeleton. <init>less to <init> change in light verb changes meaning from undergoer to initiator. The nominal complex predicate behaves syntactically like the light verb that constitutes it.

Nominal predicates enter into constructions only with corresponding verbal predicates. This is shown in (14). The nominal complex predicate behaves syntactically like the light verb that constitutes it. A mismatch is not allowed in terms of sub-event heads. This is shown in (15).

| | | | |
|---|---|---|---|
| (14) | **poo 'go'** | **veyyi 'throw'** | **paDa.veyyi 'throw down'** |
| | Sita bay.paD.i.poindi | Sita guraka.peTT.i.veesindi | Sita sutti.koTT.i.paDeesindi |
| | Sita fear.fell.perf.went | Sita snore.put.perf.threw | Sita hammer.hit.perf.fall.threw |
| | 'Sita got afraid' | 'Sita snored away' | 'Sita talked boringly' |

| | | |
|---|---|---|
| (15) | **<init>less NomCPr + <init> verb** | **<init> NomCPr + <init>less verb** |
| | *Siita baya.paD.i.veesindi | *Siita sutti.koTT.i.pooindi |
| | Sita fear.fell.perf.threw | Sita hammer.hit.perf.went |
| | Intended: 'Sita got afraid' | Intended: 'Sita talked boringly' |

A comparison of nominal and verbal complex predicate formation in Telugu is given in (16).

| | | |
|---|---|---|
| (16) | **Nominal Complex Predication** | **Verbal Complex Predication** |
| | a. No underassociation | a. Underassociation |
| | b. No inceptual meanings | b. Inceptual meanings |
| | c. Less compositional meaning (partly from N, partly from V) | c. More compositional meaning ('skeletal' light verb) |
| | d. Nominal is without any wrapping. | d. Heavy V has perfective wrapping |

## Conclusion and perspectives

This detailed analysis of complex predicates of all types, verbal and nominal, in Telugu, shows that underlying their superficial differences and display of variety, they can be fruitfully analyzed in a lexical decompositional approach like First Phase Syntax in a unified manner, which along the way reveals the syntactic process of their composition and the constraints on their formation. This is of interest to computational linguists working on languages that heavily employ complex predicates in designing and developing solutions for predicate and argument structure and function in linguistic processors. The data presented here is an initial exploration of the approach towards a lexical semantic implementation of complex predicates together with the constraints on the composition of their argument structure and meaning.

## References

Alsina, A., Bresnan, J., and Sells, P. (1997). Complex predicates: structure and theory. In Alsina, A., Bresnan, J., and Sells, P., editors, *Complex predicates*, pages 1–12. Center for the Study of Language and Information, Stanford.

Bresnan, J. and Mchombo, S. A. (1995). The lexical integrity principle: Evidence from Bantu. *Natural Language and Linguistic Theory*, 13(2):181–254.

Butt, M. (1997). Complex predicates in Urdu. In Alsina, A., Bresnan, J., and Sells, P., editors, *Complex Predicates*, pages 107–150. Center for the Study of Language and Information, Stanford.

Butt, M. (2003). The light verb jungle. In Aygen, G., Bowern, C., and Quinn, C., editors, *Workshop on Multi-Verb Constructions*, volume 9 of *Harvard Working Papers in Linguistics*, pages 1–49. Papers from the GSAS/Dudley House workshop on light verbs.

Karimi-Doostan, G. (1997). *Light verb constructions in Persian*. PhD thesis, University of Essex.

Lapointe, S. (1980). A lexical analysis of the English auxiliary verb system. *Lexical grammar*, pages 215–254.

Lazard, G. (1957). *Grammaire du Persan contemporain*. Librairie C. Klincksiek, Paris.

Mohanan, T. (2007). Grammatical verbs (with special reference to light verbs). *The Blackwell Companion to Syntax*, pages 459–492.

Pantcheva, M. (2007). *Assembling Persian Complex Predicates*. Handout, ConSole XVI, Paris.

Pantcheva, M. (2008). Noun preverbs in Persian complex predicates. *Tromsø Working Papers on Language and Linguistics: Nordlyd*, 35:19–45.

Pantcheva, M. (2010). First phase syntax of Persian complex predicates: Argument structure and telicity. *Journal of South Asian Linguistics*, 2(1).

Ramchand, G. C. (2008). *Verb Meaning and the Lexicon*. Cambridge Studies in Linguistics. Cambridge University Press, Cambridge, United Kingdom.

# Heloise — An Ariane-G5 compatible environment for developing expert MT systems online

*Vincent Berment*[1] *Christian Boitet*[2]
(1) INaLCO, Place du Maréchal de Lattre de Tassigny - 75775 Paris cedex 16
(2) GETALP, LIG-campus, 385, avenue de la Bibliothèque - 38041 Grenoble cedex 9

*Vincent.Berment@imag.fr, Christian.Boitet@imag.fr*

ABSTRACT

Heloise is a reengineering of the specialised languages for linguistic programming (SLLPs) of Ariane-G5 running both Linux and Windows. Heloise makes the core of Ariane-G5 available to anyone willing to develop "expert" (i.e. relying on linguistic expertise) operational machine translation (MT) systems in that framework, used with success since the 80's to build many prototypes and a few systems of the "multilevel transfer" and "interlingua" architecture. This initiative is part of the movement to reduce the digital divide by providing easily understandable tools that allow the development of lingware for poorly-resourced languages (π-languages). This demo article presents Heloise and provides some information about ongoing development using it.

KEYWORDS: machine translation, specialised languages for linguistic programming, SLLP, MT lingware, online lingware building, collaborative lingware building, Ariane-G5, Heloise, under-resourced languages

TITRE ET RÉSUMÉ EN FRANÇAIS

## Héloïse — Un environnement compatible Ariane-G5 pour développer des systèmes de TA experte

Héloïse est une réingénierie des langages spécialisés (LSPL) d'Ariane-G5 tournant sous Linux et Windows. Héloïse rend le cœur d'Ariane-G5 accessible à toute personne désirant réaliser par elle-même des systèmes de traduction automatique (TA) experts (s'appuyant sur une expertise linguistique) opérationnels dans cet environnement, qui a été utilisé avec succès depuis les années 80 pour construire de nombreux prototypes et quelques systèmes adoptant une architecture de "transfert multiniveau" et d'"interlingua". Cette démarche s'inscrit dans le mouvement visant réduire la fracture numérique par la mise à disposition d'outils facilement appropriables, et permettant de développer des linguiciels pour des langues peu dotées (langues-π). Cet article démo présente Héloïse et fournit quelques informations sur les développements actuels réalisés avec Héloïse.

MOTS-CLÉS EN FRANÇAIS : traduction automatique, langages spécialisés pour la programmation linguistique, LSPL, linguiciels de TA, construction en ligne de linguiciels, Ariane-G5, Héloïse, langues peu dotées.

# 1 Introduction

Ariane-G5 is a generator of machine translation systems developed and improved by the GETA group[1] during the years 1970 and 1980. This framework, despite the numerous publications and cooperative projects that made it widely known, remains of difficult access because of the "mainframe" environment under which it runs (zVM/CMS on z390). Ariane-G5 can be accessed either natively through a 3270 terminal emulator or using CASH, a portable "meta-environment" (written in Revolution) which contains the source files (lingware, corpus), and which communicates with Ariane-G5 that performs all the treatments (compilations and executions of "translation chains").

Heloise is a reengineering of compilers and "engines" of Ariane-G5's Specialized Languages for Linguistic Programming (SLLPs), running both Linux and Windows. The aim of its author when he developed this new version of Ariane-G5 SLLPs, was to make this system available to anyone wishing to design his own operational expert MT system (i.e. an MT system relying on linguistic expertise, as opposed to systems based on statistical properties of languages). This approach is part of the movement aiming at reducing the digital divide through the provision of tools, usable by non-specialists, and enabling them to develop their own language services.

This demo article aims at presenting Heloise and provides some information about ongoing development using it.

# 2 Ariane-G5

## 2.1 General principles

Ariane-G5 is a generator of machine translation systems. It uses an expert approach (including a description of the languages handled) and the generated systems are generally based on a multilevel transfer linguistic architecture, and developed using a heuristic programming approach. It has also been used for "abstract pivot" approaches (IF semantico-pragmatic formulas for speech MT in the CSTAR and Nespole! projects in 1995-2003, and UNL linguistic-semantic graphs since 1997).

Ariane-G5 relies on five Specialized Languages for Linguistic Programming (SLLPs) operating on decorated trees. The specificity of an SLLP is that it offers high-level data structures (decorated trees or graphs, grammars, dictionaries) and high-level control structures (1-ary or N-ary non-determinism, pattern-matching in trees, guarded iteration).

A minimal translation system produced by Ariane-G5 includes 6 phases (MA, SA, LT, ST, SG, MG), grouped two by two into 3 steps:

- Morphological Analysis and Structural Analysis (analysis step),
- Lexical Transfer and Structural Transfer (transfer step),
- Structural Generation and Morphological Generation (generation step).

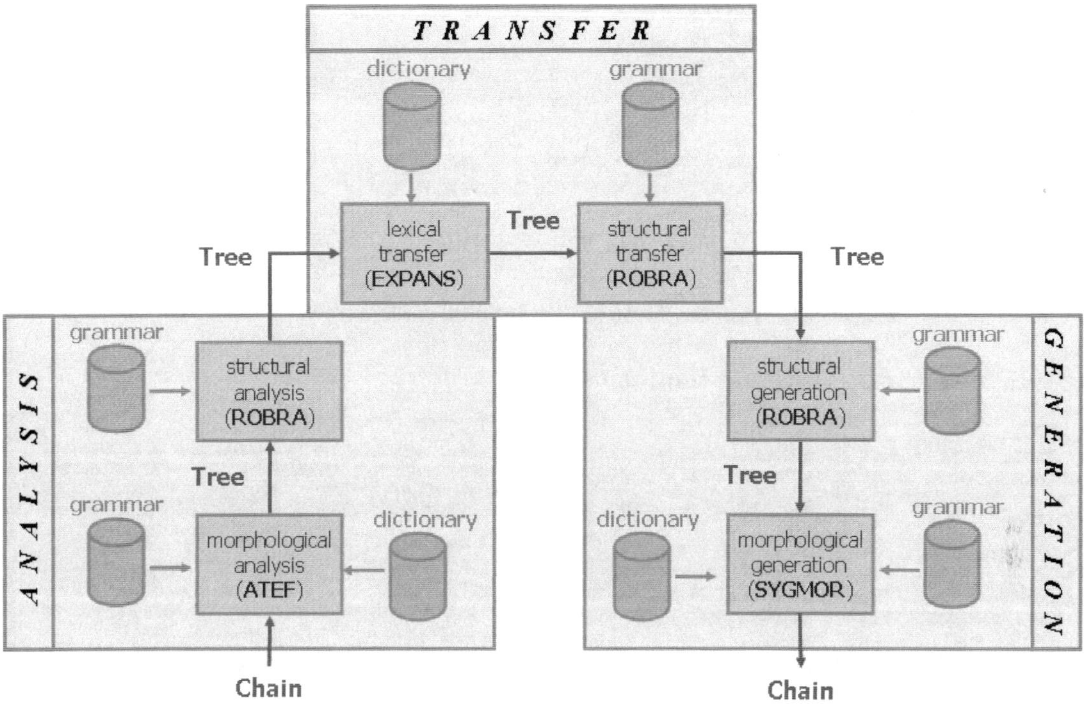


FIGURE 1 – Ariane: analysis, transfer et generation.

## 2.2 Lingware available to L-developers

The following lingware source is available under BSD license[2] since September 2010. This code greatly facilitates the implementation of new systems[3]. These lingware modules include:

- Large-scale prototype systems
  - Russian-French: RU5-FR5
  - French-English: BV-aéro/FE
  - English-French: B'VITAL
- Mockup systems
  - English-French teaching mockup: BEX-FEX
  - French-English teaching mockup: FEX-BEX
  - French-English (DGT, Telecommunications)
  - Portuguese-English
  - French-Russian (LIDIA)
  - French-German (LIDIA)
  - French-English (LIDIA)
  - UNL-Chinese: WNL-HN3
  - UNL-French: UNL-FR5

[2] See http://en.wikipedia.org/wiki/BSD_licenses.
[3] These lingware modules will soon be available for download.

- French-UNL : FR6-UNL
    - English-Malay: ANG-MAL
    - English-Thai: IN4-TH4
    - English-(Chinese, Japanese, Arabic)
    - Chinese-(English, French, German, Russian, Japanese)
    - German-French
- Steps or groups of isolated phases
    - Analysis of Portuguese: AMPOR+ASPOR
    - Analyses of German: AMALX...
    - Analysis of Japanese (Annick Laurent's PhD thesis)

# 3 Heloise, screenshots and comments

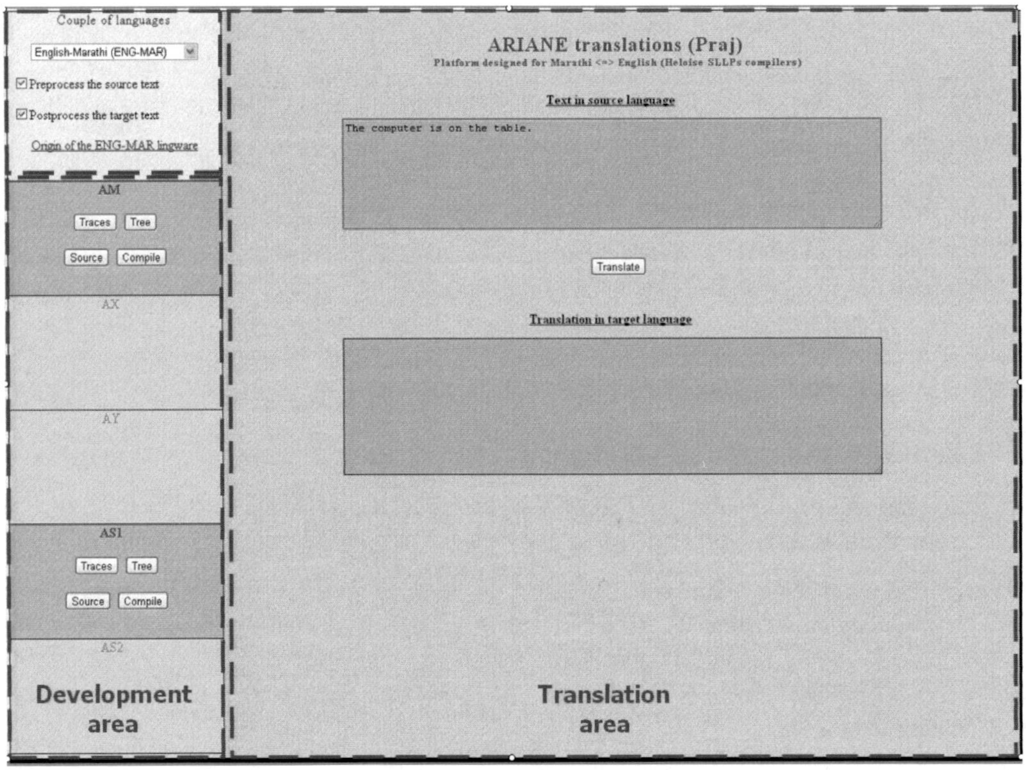


FIGURE 2 – Lingware development environment of Heloise

Heloise is an on-line tool available from any browser. The lingware developer (L-developer) is offered three areas as shown in figure 2:

- A "Selection" area in which he can select the current pair of languages,
- A "Development" area from which he controls the compiling and testing process,
- A "Translation" area in which he can make his translation trials.

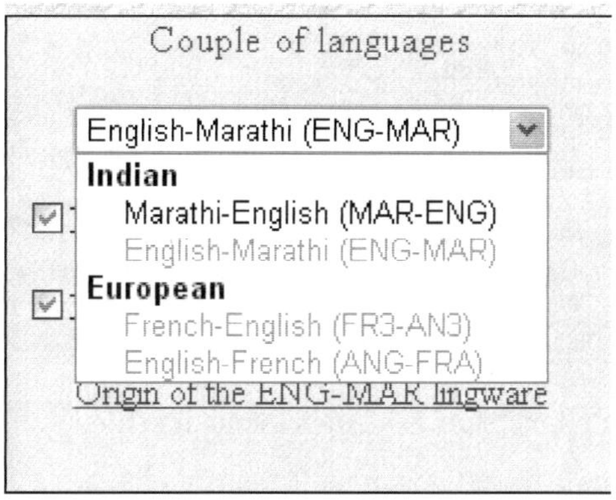


FIGURE 3 – Selection area

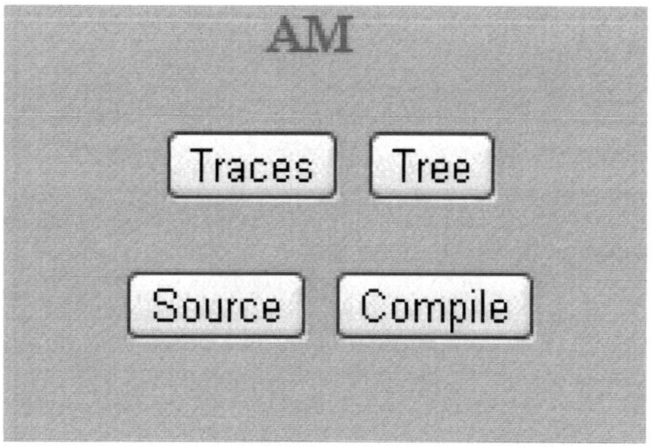


FIGURE 4 – Development area

The "Development" area provides four commands to the L-developer for each phase:

- The "Source" button, to get access and to manage the lingware files,
- The "Compile" button, to compile the lingware of the phase,
- The "Traces" button, to see the logs of a translation trial for the phase,
- The "Tree" button, to display the output tree of a translation for the phase.

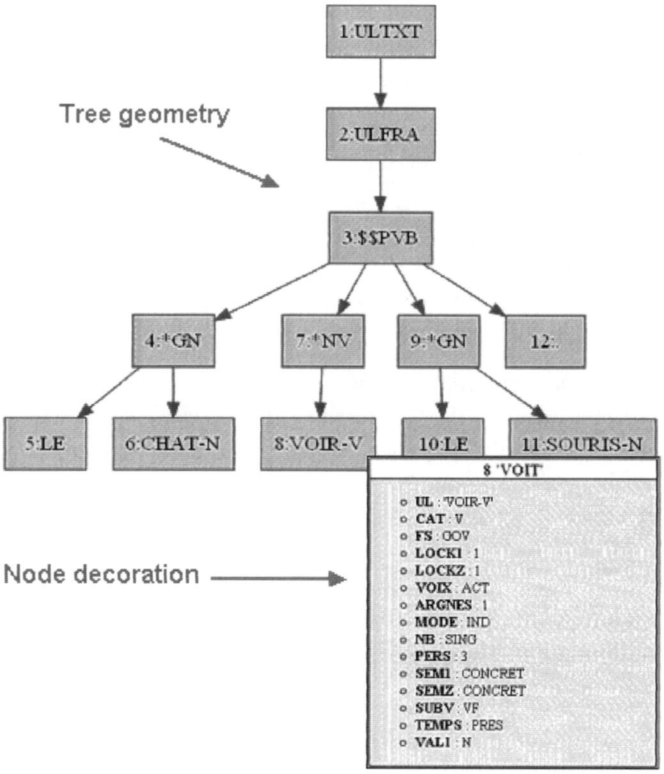


FIGURE 5 –Geometry and node decorations of an output tree

| Source files of the Praj directory | | |
|---|---|---|
| **File name** | **Heloise => Local** | **Local => Heloise** |
| FILASENG.FMATA.txt | Download | Choisissez un fichier Aucun fichier choisi Upload |
| FILASENG.GRAM1.txt | Download | Choisissez un fichier Aucun fichier choisi Upload |
| FILASENG.VARBG.txt | Download | Choisissez un fichier Aucun fichier choisi Upload |

FIGURE 6 – From this table, the L-developer downloads and uploads his lingware source files

## Conclusion

L-development works are currently undertaken for several pairs of languages, including:

- Several π-languages (under-resourced languages) such as Khmer, Lao and Marathi,
- European languages, such as English, French and German.

The quality reached for the MT systems is the one obtained with Ariane-G5's methodology and tools, but without the size limitations of Ariane-G5 (~50 pages input text, 64Knodes trees…).

## References


Bachut D., Le projet EUROLANG : *une nouvelle perspective pour les outils d'aide à la traduction*, Actes de TALN 1994, journées du PRC-CHM, Université de Marseille, 7-8 avril 1994.

Bachut D., Verastegui N., *Software tools for the environment of a computer aided translation system*, COLING-1984, Stanford University, pages 330 à 333, 2-6 juillet 1984.

Berment V., *Méthodes pour informatiser les langues et les groupes de langues peu dotés*, Thèse de doctorat, Grenoble, 18 mai 2004.

Boitet C., *Le point sur Ariane-78 début 1982 (DSE-1), vol. 1, partie 1, le logiciel*, rapport de la convention ADI n° 81/423, avril 1982.

Boitet C., Guillaume P., Quézel-Ambrunaz M., *A case study in software evolution: from Ariane-78.4 to Ariane-85*, Proceedings of the Conference on Theoretical and Methodological Issues in Machine Translation of Natural Languages, Colgate University, Hamilton, New York, 14-16 août 1985.

Boitet C., *Current machine translation systems developed with GETA's methodology and software tools*, conférence Translating and the Computer 8, 13-14 novembre 1986.

Boitet C., *La TAO à Grenoble en 1990, 1980-90 : TAO du réviseur et TAO du traducteur*, partie des supports de l'école d'été de Lannion organisée en 1990 par le LATL et le CNET, 1990.

Boitet C., *A research perspective on how to democratize machine translation and translation aids aiming at high quality final output*, MT Summit VII, Kent Ridge Digital Labs, Singapour, pages 125 à 133, 13-17 septembre 1999.

Boitet C., *A roadmap for MT: four « keys » to handle more languages, for all kinds of tasks, while making it possible to improve quality (on demand)*, International Conference on Universal

Knowledge and Language (ICUKL 2002), Goa, 25-29 novembre 2002.

Boitet C., *Les architectures linguistiques et computationnelles en traduction automatique sont indépendantes*, TALN 2008, Avignon, 9-13 juin 2008.

Del Vigna C., Berment V., Boitet C., *La notion d'occurrence de formes de forêt (orientée et ordonnée) dans le langage ROBRA pour la traduction automatique, Approches algébrique, logique et algorithmique*, Journée thématique ATALA sur la traduction automatique, ENST Paris, 1er décembre 2007.

Guillaume P., Ariane-G5 : *Les langages spécialisés TRACOMPL et EXPANS*, document GÉTA, juin 1989.

Guilbaud J.-P., Ariane-G5 : *Environnement de développement et d'exécution de systèmes (linguiciels) de traduction automatique*, Journée du GDR I3 co-organisée avec l'ATALA, Paris, novembre 1999.

Nguyen H.-T., *Des systèmes de TA homogènes aux systèmes de TAO hétérogènes*, Thèse de doctorat, Grenoble, 18 décembre 2009.

Vauquois B., *Aspects of mechanical translation in 1979*, Conference for Japan IBM Scientific program, juillet 1979.

Vauquois B., *Computer aided translation and the Arabic language*, First Arab school on science and technology, Rabat, octobre 1983.

# Keyphrase Extraction in Scientific Articles: A Supervised Approach

*Pinaki BHASKAR*[1] *Kishorjit NONGMEIKAPAM*[2] *Sivaji BANDYOPADHYAY*[1]
(1) Department of Computer Science and Engineering, Jadavpur University, Kolkata – 700032, India
(2) Department of Computer Science and Engineering, Manipur Institute of Technology, Manipur University, Imphal, India
pinaki.bhaskar@gmail.com, kishorjit.nogmeikapa@gmail.com, sivaji_cse_ju@yahoo.com

ABSTRACT

This paper contains the detailed approach of automatic extraction of Keyphrases from scientific articles (i.e. research paper) using supervised tool like Conditional Random Fields (CRF). Keyphrase is a word or set of words that describe the close relationship of content and context in the document. Keyphrases are sometimes topics of the document that represent the key ideas of the document. Automatic Keyphrase extraction is a very important module for the automatic systems like query or topic independent summarization, question-answering (QA), information retrieval (IR), document classification etc. The system was developed for the Task 5 of SemEval-2. The system is trained using 144 scientific articles and tested on 100 scientific articles. Different combinations of features have been used. With combined keywords i.e. both author-assigned and reader-assigned keyword sets as answers, the system shows a precision of 32.34%, recall of 33.09% and F-measure of 32.71% with top 15 candidates.

---

KEYWORDS : Keyphrase Extraction, Topic Extraction, Information Extraction, Summarization, Question Answering (QA), Document Classification.

---

*Proceedings of COLING 2012: Demonstration Papers*, pages 17–24,
COLING 2012, Mumbai, December 2012.

## 1 Introduction

Keyphrase is a word or set of words that describe the close relationship of content and context in the document. Keyphrases are sometimes simple nouns or noun phrases (NPs) that represent the key ideas of the document i.e. topic. Keyphrases can serve as a representative summary of the document and also serve as high quality index terms (Kim and Kan, 2009). Keyphrases can be used in various natural language processing (NLP) applications such as summarization (Bhaskar et al., 2012a, 2012b, 2010a, 2010b), information retrieval (IR) (Bhaskar et al., 2010c), question answering (QA) (Bhaskar et al., 2012c, 2012d; Pakray et al., 2011), document classification etc. Specially for the query or topic independent summarization system, it's a must needed module. Keyphrase extraction also plays an important role in Search engines.

Works on identification of keyphrase using noun phrase are reported in (Barker and Cornacchia, 2000). Noun phrases are extracted from a text using a base noun phrase skimmer and an off-the-shelf online dictionary.

Keyphrase Extraction Algorithm (KEA) was proposed in order to automatically extract keyphrase (Witten et al., 1999). The supervised learning methodologies have also been reported (Frank et al, 1999).

Some works have been done for automatic keywords extraction using CRF technique. A comparative study on the performance of the six keyword extraction models, i.e., CRF, SVM, MLR, Logit, BaseLine1 and BaseLine2 has been reported in (Chengzhi et al., 2008). The study shows that CRF based system outperforms SVM based system.

The CRF based Keyphrase extraction system is presented in Section 3. The system evaluation and error analysis are reported in Section 4 and the conclusion is drawn in the next section.

## 2 Preparing the System

### 2.1 Features Identification for the System

Selection of features is important in CRF. Features used in the system are,

**F = {*Dependency, POS tag(s), Chunk, NE, TF range, Title, Abstract, Body, Reference, Stem of word,* $W_{i-m}, \ldots, W_{i-1}, W_i, W_{i+1}, \ldots, W_{i-n}$ }**

The features are detailed as follows:

i) **Dependency parsing:** Some of the keyphrases are multiword. So relationship of verb with subject or object is to be identified through dependency parsing and thus used as a feature.

ii) **POS feature:** The Part of Speech (POS) tags of the preceding word, the current word and the following word are used as a feature in order to know the POS combination of a keyphrase.

iii) **Chunking:** Chunking is done to mark the Noun phrases and the Verb phrases since much of the keyphrases are noun phrases.

iv) **Named Entity (NE):** The Named Entity (NE) tag of the preceding word, the current word and the following word are used as a feature in order to know the named entity combination of a keyphrase.

v) **Term frequency (TF) range:** The maximum value of the term frequency (max_TF) is divided into five equal sizes (*size_of_range)* and each of the term frequency values is mapped to the appropriate range (0 to 4). The term frequency range value is used as a feature. i.e.

$$\text{size\_of\_range} = \frac{\text{max\_TF}}{5},$$

Thus, Table 1 shows the range representation. This is done to have uniformed values for the term frequency feature instead of random and scattered values.

| **Class** | **Range** |
|---|---|
| *0 to size_of_range* | *0* |
| *size_of_range + 1 to 2*size_of_range* | *1* |
| *2*size_of_range + 1 to 3*size_of_range* | *2* |
| *3*size_of_range + 1 to 4*size_of_range* | *3* |
| *4*size_of_range + 1 to 5*size_of_range* | *4* |

TABLE 1 – Term frequency (TF) range

vi) **Word in Title:** Every word is marked with T if found in the title else O to mark other. The title word feature is useful because the words in title have a high chance to be a keyphrase.

vii) **Word in Abstract:** Every word is marked with A if found in the abstracts else O to mark other. The abstract word feature is useful because the words in abstracts have a high chance to be a keyphrase.

viii) **Word in Body:** Every word is marked with B if found in the body of the text else O to mark other. It is a useful feature because words present in the body of the text are distinguished from other words in the document.

ix) **Word in Reference:** Every word is marked with R if found in the references else O to mark other. The reference word feature is useful because the words in references have a high chance to be a keyphrase.

x) **Stemming:** The Porter Stemmer algorithm is used to stem every word and the output stem for each word is used as a feature. This is because words in keyphrases can appear in different inflected forms.

xi) **Context word feature:** The preceding and the following word of the current word are considered as context feature since keyphrases can be a group of words.

## 2.2 Corpus Preparation

Automatic identification of keyphrases is our main task. In order to perform this task the data provided by the SEMEVAL-2 Task Id #5 is being used both for training and testing. In total 144 scientific articles or papers are provided for training and another 100 documents have been marked for testing. All the files are cleaned by placing spaces before and after every punctuation mark and removing the citations in the text. The author names appearing after the paper title was removed. In the reference section, only the paper or book title was kept and all other details were deleted.

## 3 CRF based Keyphrase Extraction System

### 3.1 Extraction of Positional Feature

One algorithm has been defined to extract the title from a document. Another algorithm has been defined to extract the positional feature of a word, i.e., whether the word is present in title, abstracts, body or in references.

**Algorithm 1:** Algorithm to extract the title.

**Step 1:** Read the line one by one from the beginning of the article until a '.'(dot) or '@' found in the line. ('.'(dot) occurs in author's name and '@' occurs in author's mail id).

**Step 2:** If '.' found first in a line then each line before it is extracted as Title and returned.

**Step 3:** If '@' found first in a line then extract all the line before it.

**Step 4:** Check the extracted line one by one from beginning.

**Step 5:** Take a line; extract all the words of that line. Check whether all the words are not repeated in the article (excluding the references) or not. If not then stop and extract all the previous lines as Title and return.

**Algorithm 2:** Algorithm to extract the Positional Features.

**Step 1:** Take each word from the article.

**Step 2:** Stem all the words.

**Step 3:** Check the position of the occurrence of the words.

**Step 4:** If the word occurs in the extracted title (using algorithm 1) of the article then mark it as 'T' else 'O' in title feature column.

**Step 5:** If the word occurs in between the word ABSTRACT and INTRODUCTION then mark it as 'A' else 'O' in abstracts feature column.

**Step 6:** If the word occurs in between the word INTRODUCTION and REFERENCES then mark it as 'B' else 'O' in body feature column.

**Step 7:** If the word occurs after the word REFERENCES then mark it as 'R' else 'O' in references feature column.

### 3.2 Generating Feature File for CRF

The features used in the keyphrase extraction system are identified in the following ways.

**Step 1:** The dependency parsing is done by the Stanford Parser[1]. The output of the parser is modified by making the word and the associated tags for every word appearing in a line.

**Step 2:** The same output is used for chunking and for every word it identifies whether the word is a part of a noun phrase or a verb phrase.

**Step 3:** The Stanford POS Tagger[2] is used for POS tagging of the documents.

---

[1] http://nlp.stanford.edu/software/lex-parser.shtml

**Step 4:** The term frequency (*TF*) range is identified as defined before.

**Step 5:** Using the algorithms described in Section 3.1 every word is marked as *T* or *O* for the title word feature, marked as *A* or *O* for the abstract word feature, marked as *B* or *O* for the body word feature and marked as *R* or *O* for the reference word feature.

**Step 6:** The Porter Stemming Algorithm[3] is used to identify the stem of every word that is used as another feature.

**Step 7:** In the training data with the combined keyphrases, the words that begin a keyphrase are marked with *B-KP* and words that are present intermediate in a keyphrase are marked as *I-KP*. All other words are marked as *O*. But for test data only *O* is marked in this column.

### 3.3 Training the CRF and Running Test Files

A template file is created in order to train the system using the feature file generated from the tanning set following the above procedure described in the Section 3.2. After training the C++ based CRF++ 0.53 package[4] which is readily available as open source for segmenting or labeling sequential data, a model file is produced. The model file is required to run the test files.

The feature file is again created from the test set using the above steps as outlined in Section 3.2 except the step 7. For test set the last feature column i.e. Keyphrase column, is marked with 'O'. This feature file is used with the C++ based CRF++ 0.53 package. After running the Test files into the system, the system produce the output file with the keyphrases marked with *B-KP* and *I-KP*. All the Keyphrases are extracted from the output file and stemmed using Porter Stemmer.

## 4 Evaluation and Error Analysis

The evaluation results of the CRF based keyphrase extraction system are shown in Table 3, where *P, R* and *F* mean micro-averaged precision, recall and F-scores. In second column, *R* denotes the use of the reader-assigned keyword set as gold-standard data and *C* denotes the use of combined keywords i.e. both author-assigned and reader-assigned keyword sets as answers. There are three sets of score. First set of score i.e. Top 5 candidates, is obtained by evaluating only top 5 keyphrases from evaluated data. Similarly Top 10 candidates set is obtained by evaluating top 10 keyphrases and Top 15 Candidates set result is obtained by evaluating all 15 keyphrases.

| **Team** | **By** | **Top 5 Candidates** | | | **Top 10 candidates** | | | **Top 15 candidates** | | |
|---|---|---|---|---|---|---|---|---|---|---|
| | | **P** | **R** | **F** | **P** | **R** | **F** | **P** | **R** | **F** |
| *JU_CSE* | R | 36.33% | 15.09% | 21.33% | 27.41% | 22.76% | 24.87% | 22.54% | 28.08% | 25.01% |
| | C | 52.08% | 17.77% | 26.49% | 39.69% | 27.07% | 32.18% | 32.34% | 33.09% | **32.71%** |

TABLE 3 – Result for JU_CSE system with CRF

2 http://nlp.stanford.edu/software/tagger.shtml
3 http://tartarus.org/~martin/PorterStemmer/
4 http://crfpp.sourceforge.net/

The scores for the top 5 candidates and top 10 candidates of keyphrases extracted show a better precision score since the keyphrases are generally concentrated in the title and abstracts. The recall shows a contrast improvement from 17.77% to 33.09% as the number of candidate increases since the coverage of the text increases. The F-score is 32.71% when top 15 candidates are considered which is 17.61% i.e. 2.17 times better from the best baseline model with F-score of 15.10%. Different features have been tried and the best feature we have used in the system is:

**F = {*Dependency, $POS_{i-1}$, $POS_i$, $POS_{i+1}$, $NE_{i-1}$, $NE_i$, $NE_{i+1}$, chunking, TF range, Title, Abstract, Body, Reference, Stem of word, $W_{i-1}$, $W_i$, $W_{i+1}$*}**

Here, $POS_{i-1}$, $POS_i$ and $POS_{i+1}$ are the POS tags of the previous word, the current word and the following word respectively. Similarly $W_{i-1}$, $W_i$ and $W_{i+1}$ denote the previous word, the current word and the following word respectively. This $POS_i$ and $W_i$ give a contrasting result when only the word and the POS of the word are considered.

A better result could have been obtained if Term Frequency * Inverse Document Frequency (*TF*IDF)* range is included (Frank et al., 1999; Witten et al., 1999). *TF*IDF* measures the document cohesion. The maximum value of the *TF*IDF* (max_*TF_IDF)* can be divided into five equal size (*size_of_range)* and each of the *TF*IDF* values is mapped to the appropriate range (0 to 4). i.e.

$$\textbf{size\_of\_range} = \frac{\textbf{max\_TF\_IDF}}{\textbf{5}},$$

We have used the Unigram template in the template file CRF++ 0.53 package but the use of bigram could have improved the score.

## Conclusion and Perspectives

A CRF based approach to keyphrase extraction has been attempted in the present task for scientific articles. Proper cleaning of the input documents and identification of more appropriate features could have improved the score.

In future we will use MWE as a feature in CRF. Most of the cases the keyphrases are multi-word. We also like to port our system in different domains like news, tourism, health or general.


## Acknowledgment

The work has been carried out with support from Department of Electronics and Information Technology (DeitY), MCIT, Govt. of India funded Project Development of "Cross Lingual Information Access (CLIA)" System Phase II.


## References


Barker. K. and Cornacchia. N. (2000). Using noun phrase heads to extract document keyphrases. In *the 13th Biennial Conference of the Canadian Society on Computational Studies of Intelligence: Advances in Artificial Intelligence*, pages 40-52, Canada.

Bhaskar. P. and Bandyopadhyay. S. (2012a). Language Independent Query Focused Snippet Generation. In *the proceedings of CLEF 2012 Conference and Labs of the Evaluation Forum*, pages 140–142, Rome, Italy, T. Catarci et al. (Eds.): CLEF 2012, LNCS 7488, 2012, Springer-Verlag Berlin Heidelberg 2012.

Bhaskar. P. and Bandyopadhyay. S. (2012b). Cross Lingual Query Dependent Snippet Generation. In *International Journal of Computer Science and Information Technologies (IJCSIT)*, pages 4603 – 4609, ISSN: 0975-9646, Vol. 3, Issue 4.

Bhaskar. P., Banerjee. S., Neogi. S. and Bandyopadhyay. S. (2012c). A Hybrid QA System with Focused IR and Automatic Summarization for INEX 2011. In *Focused Retrieval of Content and Structure: 10th International Workshop of the Initiative for the Evaluation of XML Retrieval, INEX 2011*, Shlomo Geva, Jaap Kamps, and Ralf Schenkel, editors. Saarbruecken, Germany, Revised and Selected Papers. Volume 7424 of Lecture Notes in Computer Science. Springer Verlag, Berlin, Heidelberg.

Bhaskar. P. and Bandyopadhyay. S. (2012d). Answer Extraction of Comparative and Evaluative Question in Tourism Domain. In *International Journal of Computer Science and Information Technologies (IJCSIT)*, pages 4610 – 4616, ISSN: 0975-9646, Vol. 3, Issue 4.

Pakray. P., Bhaskar. P., Banerjee. S., Pal. B., Gelbukh. A. and Bandyopadhyay. S. (2011). A Hybrid Question Answering System based on Information Retrieval and Answer Validation. In *the proceedings of Question Answering for Machine Reading Evaluation (QA4MRE) at CLEF 2011*, Amsterdam.

Bhaskar. P. and Bandyopadhyay. S. (2010a). A Query Focused Automatic Multi Document Summarizer. In *the proceeding of the 8th International Conference on Natural Language Processing (ICON 2010)*, pages 241-250, IIT, Kharagpur, India.

Bhaskar. P. and Bandyopadhyay. S. (2010b). A Query Focused Multi Document Automatic Summarization. In *the proceedings of the 24th Pacific Asia Conference on Language, Information and Computation (PACLIC 24)*, Tohoku University, Sendai, Japan.

Bhaskar. P., Das. A., Pakray. P. and Bandyopadhyay. S. (2010c). Theme Based English and Bengali Ad-hoc Monolingual Information Retrieval in FIRE 2010. In *the proceedings of the Forum for Information Retrieval Evaluation (FIRE) – 2010*, Gandhinagar, India.

Davanzo. E. and Magnini. B. (2005). A Keyphrase-Based Approach to Summarization:the LAKE System at DUC-2005. In *the Document Understanding Conferences*.

Frank. E., Paynter. G., Witten.I., Gutwin. C. and Nevill-Manning. G. (1999). Domain-specific keyphrase extraction. In *the Sixteenth International Joint Conference on Artificial Intelligence (IJCAI-99)*, pages 668-673, California.

Kim. S. N. and Kan. M. Y. (2009). Re-examining Automatic Keyphrase Extraction Approaches in Scientific Articles. In *the 2009 Workshop on multiword Expressions, ACL-IJCNLP 2009*, pages 9-16, Suntec, Singapore.

Lafferty. J., McCallum. A. and Pereira. F. (2001). Conditional Random Fields: Probabilistic Models for Segmenting and Labeling Sequence Data. In *the 18th International Conference on Machine Learning (ICML01)*, pages 282-289, Williamstown, MA, USA.

Turney. P. (1999). Learning to Extract Keyphrases from Text. In *the National Research Council, Institute for Information Technology, Technical Report ERB-1057*. (NRC \#41622).

Witten. I., Paynter. G., Frank. E., Gutwin. C. and Nevill-Manning. G. (1999). KEA:Practical Automtic Key phrase Extraction. In *the fourth ACM conference on Digital libraries*, pages 254-256.

Zhang, C., Wang, H., Liu, Y., Wu, D., Liao, Y. and Wang, B. (2008). Automatic keyword Extraction from Documents Using Conditional Random Fields. In *Journal of Computational Information Systems*, 4:3, pages 1169-1180.

# IKAR: An Improved Kit for Anaphora Resolution for Polish

*Bartosz Broda Łukasz Burdka Marek Maziarz*
Institute of Informatics, Wroclaw University of Technology, Poland
{bartosz.broda, marek.maziarz}@pwr.wroc.pl, luk.burdka@gmail.com

ABSTRACT
This paper presents Improved Kit for Anaphora resolution (IKAR) – a hybrid system for anaphora resolution for Polish that combines machine learning methods with hand written rules. We give an overview of anaphora types annotated in the corpus and inner workings of the system. The preliminary experiments evaluating IKAR resolution performance are discussed. We have achieved promising results using standard measures employed in evaluation of anaphora and coreference resolution systems.

KEYWORDS: Anaphora Resoulution, Coreference, Polish.

*Proceedings of COLING 2012: Demonstration Papers*, pages 25–32,
COLING 2012, Mumbai, December 2012.

## 1 Introduction

The basic definition of anaphora says that it links two expressions which point to the same entity in real world (Huang, 2010). Anaphora Resolution (AR) is a difficult and important problem for Natural Language Processing (NLP). The difficulty not only comes from the computational point of view, but also from wide range of linguistic issues For extensive review of both the theoretical aspect and approaches used see (Poesio et al., 2010).

In this paper we present IKAR (*Improved Kit for Anaphora Resolution*), a hybrid toolkit for AR for Polish. We combine Machine Learning (ML) and rule based methods. This approach is an extension of our preliminary experiments which was exclusively based on ML. As we need an AR for solving practical NLP problems (e.g., question answering), after initial ML experiments we observed that some phenomena can be easily tackled with rule based component. The combination of both in IKAR is guided by a ML classifier, which allows for further extensions of both typical features used by ML in the problem domain as well as adding more rules.

The work on AR is relatively sparse for Polish. There have been some early approaches, but they were limited in scope, e.g., (Marciniak, 2002; Matysiak, 2007). Recently, the field has been invigorated with baseline work on both rule-based and ML approaches to AR (Kopeć and Ogrodniczuk, 2012; Ogrodniczuk and Kopeć, 2011a,b). Their approach differs from ours in two important ways. First, the definition of anaphora is different and the dataset is smaller than employed in this work. See Sec. 2 for the subtypes of anaphora that we deal with in this work. Second, they evaluate rule-based system and statistical system independently.

## 2 Anaphora in KPWr

Coreference is a type of anaphora. It links two expressions which point to the same referent (or denote the same class of entieties) in real world (Huang, 2010; Stede, 2012). Out of different types of anaphora distinguished by semanticists, cf. (Halliday and Ruqaiya, 1976; Cornish, 1986; King, 2010), and computational linguists, (Mitkov et al., 2000; NP4, 2010; Poesio, 2004; ACE, 2010), we have chosen those phenomena which can be roughly named after (Mitkov, 2003) a *direct anaphora*. We distinguish: (a) coreference between nominal and pronominal expressions (Larson and Segal, 1996; King, 2010), (b) coreference between two nominal phrases (either based on identity of reference or on lexical synonymy/hyponymy/hypernymy (Mitkov, 2003)). We add to this group also (c) *zero anaphora* - i.e., anaphora of omitted subject. In order to further limit issues connected with coreference recognition we have decided to annotate only coreferential relations to proper nouns. The KPWr Corpus (Broda et al., 2012) was annotated by two annotators which worked on separated documents. The annotators were supported with precise guidelines (Maziarz et al., 2011a), during annotation process they were encouraged to ask a superior linguist anytime they needed and to modify this document. Because of the procedure the inter-annotator agreement could not be checked[1]. The KPWr Corpus is avaiable under the CC BY 3.0 licence (Broda et al., 2012).

(1) **Coreference between two proper names** (PN-PN type).

This relation type links occurrences of coreferent proper names. Majority of the relation instances are instances of the same proper name:[2]

[1a] (...) chcę być tylko bliżej *Loty*, oto cały sekret. (...) moje i *Loty* serca rozumieją się tak doskonale. ['(...) I only

[1] In near future we are aiming at annotating 10% of the annotated corpus in order to check the kappa

[2] All examples are taken from KPWr

wish to be closer to *Charlotte*, —that is the secret. (...) my heart and *Charlotte's* understand each other so perfectly.']

Seldom the same referent is named with different names:

[1b] Uniwersytet tworzy się z *Filii Uniwersytetu Warszawskiego w Białymstoku*. (...) zatrudnieni w *Filii w Białymstoku* stają się pracownikami Uniwersytetu. ['The University forms from *the Branch of Warsaw University in Białystok*. (...) employees hired at *the Branch in Białystok* become employees of the University.']

**(2) Coreference between a proper name and an agreed noun phrase** (PN-AgP type)

With PN-AgP link we capture coreference between a proper name and an agreed noun phrase based on hyponymy/hypernymy, i.e. common noun denoting a class of entities which includes a referent of a proper noun). Under *agreed noun phrase* we understand nominal phrase built on syntactic agreement on number, gender and case:[3]

[2a] (...) ataki na schorowanego generała *Jaruzelskiego*. To przecież Jarosław Kaczyński porównał *generała* do Adolfa Eichmanna ['(...) attacks on ailing general *Jaruzelski*. It was Jarosław Kaczyński who compared *the general* to Adolf Eichmann.']

Here *generał* 'general' is a class which includes general Jaruzelski.

We have annotated not only cases of anaphora, but also of cataphora. In [2b] a usual direction of anaphora is reversed: a common noun *człowiek* 'a man' – a head of AgP *człowiek... nieco otyły* 'a little bit obese man' – is a class of entities which *Napoleon* belongs to:

[2b] (...) jechał na białym koniu *człowiek-1* średniego wieku, *1-nieco otyły* (...). Pierwszym z tych jeźdźców był *Napoleon*, drugim byłem ja ['(...) *a little bit obese man* of the medium age rode a white horse (...). From these riders *Napoleon* was first, I was second.']

**(3) Coreference between a pronoun and a proper name** (PN-Pron type):

The main subclass of PN-Pron corefrence links a *personal* pronoun with a proper name. In [3a] a pronoun of the third person – *jej* (ona:ppron3:sg:dat:f)[4] – points to a name of a former female-treasurer of a municipal council – *Aniela T.*:

[3a] (...) wieloletnia była skarbnik gminy *Aniela T.* Wójt (...) kazał *jej* opuścić budynek ['*Aniela T.*, a long-standing treasurer (...). The borough leader (...) ordered *her* to leave the building.']

In KPWr we annotate also coreference between demonstrative pronouns and proper names. In [3b] the pronoun *tam* 'there' refers to the Internet:

[3b] (...) *internet* jest nie dla nich, że nie ma *tam* miejsc, które mogłyby ich zainteresować (...) ['(...) *the Internet* is not for them and *there* are not sites interesting for them']

**(4) Zero anaphora - coreference between a proper noun and zero-subject** (PN-$\phi$ type)

In Polish subject is often omitted. We wanted to link coreferent proper name and zero-subject; to avoid introducing into text artificial units, we have decided to establish links to verbs with zero-subjects, like in this example:

[4a] *Toronto Dominion Centre* - kompleks handlowo-kulturalny (...). *Składa się* z 3 czarnych budynków (...). ['*The Toronto-Dominion Centre* - is a cluster of buildings (...) of commercial and cultural function. (It) *consists* of three black buildings (...)']

---

[3]For further details and definitions please see (Radziszewski et al., 2012)

[4]The tags come from (Woliński, 2003)

## 3 An Improved Kit for Anaphora Resolution

The aim of our experiment with IKAR[5] (Improved Kit for Anaphora Resolution) is to mark pairs of annotations joined by the anaphora relation. Such a pair always consists of a mention and its antecedent. We recognize so far these relations that point backwards, i.e., pairs that consist of a mention and its antecedent (so cases of cataphora were excluded). A mention can be a proper name (PN), a pronoun or an AgP. The antecedent is always a PN. We leave recognizing zero-subjects for further works.

### 3.1 Experimental Settings

The idea of the whole experiment is as follows: we create a list of annotation pairs on the basis of the annotated corpus, extract features from these pairs and classify if they should be joined by the anaphora relation. Then we compare the outcome with real relation instances.

The learning sequence has to contain positive and negative examples. The selection of positive examples is straightforward, i.e., they consists of coreference annotation pairs. The selection of negative examples needs more attention. We use different approaches and features for each one of the three recognized relation types (PN-PN, PN-AgP, PN-Pron).

(1) **Coreference between two proper names** (PN-PN type). For each entity referred to by a proper name a chain of references is created. Then each PN is linked to the nearest PN referring to the same entity that occurred in the text before. These pairs constitute positive PN-PN examples. For each mention, negative pairs are created by that mention and its false 'antecedents' from certain range between original mention and its real antecedent. This procedure guarantees that they will not point to actually the same entity. We produced 3006 positive and 14676 negetive examples using this approach.

For each relation type a distinct set of features is established for classification purposes. The PN-PN recognition appeared to be the easiest one. The PN-PN classifier is based mostly on similarity of both PN phrases. Following features are extracted in order to determine if two annotations should be joined. *CosSimilarity*: it measures how much both phrases are formed by the same set of words. Base forms of each token are compared. *TokenCountDiff*: difference in number of tokens forming each PN. *SameChannName*: feature indicating if both PNs share the same type of proper name. *Number*: feature indicating if both PNs share the same grammatical number. *Gender*: feature indicating if both PNs share the same gender. We employ C4.5 decision trees (Quinlan, 1993) in the experiments.

(2) **Coreference between an agreed noun phrase and a proper name** (PN-AgP type). Similarly to PN-PN case, all AgPs in KPWr are related to the first occurrence of a given entity. It is more natural to see the anaphora between an AgP and the nearest PN (of course, if it points to the very same entity). We generate positive PN-AgP examples taking an AgP and its antecedent PN from the same coreference chain. Negative examples are generated in a different way than for PN-PN. For each mention, we choose any proper name that occurred in the text earlier not further than 50 tokens. We take just up to two negative 'antecedents' for each mention. This way we have obtained 1077 positive and 1833 negative examples.

Unlike in a PN-PN case, both annotations (i.e., a PN and an AgP) does not need to sound similar or even share the same gender. Thus, to tell whether an AgP refers to a given PN we

[5]Will be released on GPL `http://nlp.pwr.wroc.pl/en/tools-and-resources/ikar`

need to focus on semantic similarity of AgP's head and a semantic category of a particular PN. We use only one feature called SemanticLink to determine if the relation is present. It is more complex than PN-PN set of features so it needs a closer look. SemanticLink takes advantage of the Polish WordNet (Piasecki et al., 2009) to rate the semantic similarity.

**Semantic Link algorithm (For a pair of AgP head name category)** For each name category a representative synset from the wordnet was selected manually. Then the procedure is following: First, find matching synset for AgP's head. Search is capped up to 10 similarity, hypernym and holonym edges. If it cannot be found, switch places of category's synset and head's synset and search again. (In case the head's synset is more general than that of category's.) If it cannot be found, the distance is minimal number of edges separating head and the category synset. (Note that a head usually gets more than one synset, because its meaning is not disambiguated.) The score: 1/distance can be interpreted as how well AgP's head can refer to PN from a given category. If there is no better antecedent candidate between AgP and a given PN then it is a positive match.

(3) **Coreference between a pronoun and a proper name** (PN-Pron type). When recognizing pronoun-PN relations the important thing we have to focus on is the distance, sharing the mention and its antecedent. In Polish language a pronoun often refers to the latest entity that shares number and gender with it (this observation is supported by the results of our experiments). However, it can happen that a pronoun refers directly to an AgP instead of a PN. Then, we check if a given AgP refers to the same PN. If so we should assume that this PN is in fact coreferent to the pronoun. Again, we use a single binary feature called Pronoun Link. Negative examples were generated like in PN-AgP case. We have obtained 450 positive and 596 negative examples.

**Pronoun Link algorithm** Check if there is an AgP between a pronoun and a PN that meets Semantic Link criteria for a given PN and gender and number for a given pronoun and there in no closer AgP which meets these criteria. If the condition is fulfilled there is a link between that pronoun and a PN. Otherwise, check if a pronoun and a PN share the same gender and number and if there is no closer PN that meets these criteria. If the condition is fulfilled there is a Pronoun Link.

## 3.2 Resolution process in IKAR

When given a plain text the process of anaphora resolution requires a few additional steps. The text needs to be divided into tokens and sentences. Next, we need to perform morphologicall analysis (Radziszewski and Śniatowski, 2011) and a morpho-syntactic disambiguation (Radziszewski and Śniatowski, 2011). We find proper names using Liner2 (Marcińczuk et al., 2011). Finally, the text is chunked (Maziarz et al., 2011b).

All possible mentions have to be annotated in the text. All pronouns are considered to be mentions and those AgPs which heads are on the list of possible mention keywords. Such list is created by IKAR during the learning process. Finally, the resolution process can be initiated.

**PN-PN Resolution** For PN possible antecedents are PNs that appeared previously. After the classification is done it is possible that one mention was classified to have more than one antecedent (which in fact may be the same entity).

All mentions that are classified to have an antecedent are being processed in order starting from the beginning of the text. If a mention refers to only one antecedent then it is checked if that antecedent refers to any other word. If so then the relation is rerouted to that word which is thought to be the first occurrence of this entity in the text. Now, any already processed mention points to the first occurrence of the entity.If a mention refers to more than one antecedent it is checked if it refers to the same entity. If there are more than one entities - an entity with greater number of references is chosen. If all of them are referenced by the same number of relations the one that occurred in a text closer to the mention is chosen. At the end of the process every PN is matched with the same entity.

**PN-AgP Resolution** When PNs are already matched with certain entities the possible PN-AgP relations can be determined. If there are a lot of PNs referring to the same entity the possible antecedent is the one closest to the mention. It is also possible that for one mention more than one PN were classified as antecedents. The Semantic Link score is calculated for each of them and the one with the best score is chosen as an antecedent. If there are two candidates with the same score the one closer to the mention is chosen.

**PN-Pronoun Resolution** Possible relations between pronouns and PNs are determined the same way as PN-AgP relations. If there is more than one antecedent for a given mention the closest is chosen. However, we allow only one relation for each pronoun. Also PN-AgP relations are already resolved at this point so if a pronoun refers directly to an AgP it is clear to which PN it really refers to.

## 4 IKAR Evaluation

There are three classifiers dedicated for each relation type. Therefore we evaluate each of them separately. We also use SemEval Scorer for calculating $B^3$, BLANC and MUC measures. The scorer compares a classified file with a source file. We employ 10-fold cross-validation in both evaluation settings. The ZeroR classifier was used as a baseline.

The F-measure of Weka-based evaluation for C.45 are on average higher by 0.12 pp. than the baseline (we omit detailed results for brevity). The results of Scorer evaluation are shown in the Tab. 1. Also, the results are higher than the baseline. The achieved results are higher than other contemporary systems presented for Polish (Kopeć and Ogrodniczuk, 2012; Ogrodniczuk and Kopeć, 2011a,b). Alas, those results are not directly comparable as the guidelines for annotation of corpora differ and the size of the dataset used in this paper is larger.

| Measure | Classifier | Precision | Recall | F-measure |
|---|---|---|---|---|
| $B^3$ | ZeroR | 99.98% | 71.34% | 83.27% |
| $B^3$ | C4.5 | 98.37% | 89.81% | 93.89% |
| MUC | ZeroR | 0.00% | 0.00% | 0.00% |
| MUC | C4.5 | 95.16% | 74.65% | 83.67% |
| BLANC | ZeroR | 47.67% | 49.99% | 48.81% |
| BLANC | C4.5 | 94.34% | 77.32% | 83.61% |

Table 1: SemEval evaluation

## 5 Conclusions and Further Works

In this paper we have presented an Improved Kit for Anaphora Resolution (IKAR) for Polish. The system was evaluated on the data annotated in the KPWr Corpus. The types of anaphora annotated in the KPWr were also described. The evaluation was performed using two independent methodologies. Its outcome indicates that described approaches are promising for the anaphora resolution. We are planning to compare the outcome of our work to GATE's ANNIE IE and other applications developed for Polish.

## References

(2010). Annotation of cross-document coreference: A pilot study.

(2010). Automatic content extraction.

Broda, B., Marcińczuk, M., Maziarz, M., Radziszewski, A., and Wardyński, A. (2012). Kpwr: Towards a free corpus of polish. In Chair), N. C. C., Choukri, K., Declerck, T., Doğan, M. U., Maegaard, B., Mariani, J., Odijk, J., and Piperidis, S., editors, *Proceedings of the Eight International Conference on Language Resources and Evaluation (LREC'12)*, Istanbul, Turkey. European Language Resources Association (ELRA).

Cornish, F. (1986). *Anaphoric Relations in English and French: A Discourse Perspective*. Croom Helm Ltd.

Halliday, M. A. K. and Ruqaiya, H. (1976). *Cohesion in English*. Longman, London.

Huang, Y. (2010). Coreference: Identity and similarity. In Brown, K., editor, *Concise Encyclopedia of Philosophy of Language and Linguistics*. Elsevier.

King, J. (2010). Anaphora: Philosophical aspects. In Barber, A. and Stainton, R. J., editors, *Concise Encyclopedia of Philosophy of Language and Linguistics*. Elsevier.

Kopeć, M. and Ogrodniczuk, M. (2012). Creating a coreference resolution system for polish. In Chair), N. C. C., Choukri, K., Declerck, T., Doğan, M. U., Maegaard, B., Mariani, J., Odijk, J., and Piperidis, S., editors, *Proceedings of the Eight International Conference on Language Resources and Evaluation (LREC'12)*, Istanbul, Turkey. European Language Resources Association (ELRA).

Larson, R. and Segal, G. (1996). *Knowledge of Meaning: An Introduction to Semantic Theory*. The MIT Press.

Marciniak, M. (2002). Anaphora binding in Polish. Theory and implementation. In *Proceedings of DAARC2002*, Lisbon.

Marcińczuk, M., Stanek, M., Piasecki, M., and Musiał, A. (2011). Rich Set of Features for Proper Name Recognition in Polish Texts. In *Proceedings of the International Joint Conference Security and Intelligent Information Systems, 2011*, Lecture Notes in Computer Science (to be published). Springer.

Matysiak, I. (2007). Information extraction systems and nominal anaphora analysis needs. In *Proceedings of the International Multiconference on Computer Science and Information Technology*.

Maziarz, M., Marcińczuk, M., Piasecki, M., Radziszewski, A., Nowak, J., Wardyński, A., and Wieczorek, J. (2011a). Wytyczne do znakowania koreferencji [guideliness for coreference annotation].

Maziarz, M., Radziszewski, A., and Wieczorek, J. (2011b). Chunking of Polish: guidelines, discussion and experiments with Machine Learning. In *Proceedings of the LTC 2011*.

Mitkov, R. (2003). Anaphora resolution. In *The Oxford Handbook of Computational Linguistics*, chapter 14. Oxford University Press.

Mitkov, R., Evans, R., Orasan, C., Barbu, C., Jones, L., and Sotirova, V. (2000). Coreference and anaphora: developing annotating tools, annotated resources and annotation stages. In *Proceedings of DAARC2000*, pages 49–58.

Ogrodniczuk, M. and Kopeć, M. (2011a). End-to-end coreference resolution baseline system for Polish. In Vetulani, Z., editor, *Proceedings of the 5th Language & Technology Conference: Human Language Technologies as a Challenge for Computer Science and Linguistics*, pages 167–171, Poznań, Poland.

Ogrodniczuk, M. and Kopeć, M. (2011b). Rule-based coreference resolution module for Polish. In *Proceedings of the 8th Discourse Anaphora and Anaphor Resolution Colloquium (DAARC 2011)*, pages 191–200, Faro, Portugal.

Piasecki, M., Szpakowicz, S., and Broda, B. (2009). *A wordnet from the ground up*. Oficyna wydawnicza Politechniki Wroclawskiej.

Poesio, M. (2004). The mate/gnome proposals for anaphoric annotation (revisited). In *Proceedings of the 5th SIGdial Workshop on Discourse and Dialogue*, pages 154–162, Boston.

Poesio, M., Ponzetto, S. P., and Versley, Y. (2010). Computational models of anaphora resolution: A survey.

Quinlan, J. R. (1993). *C4. 5: programs for machine learning*. Morgan Kaufmann.

Radziszewski, A., Maziarz, M., and Wieczorek, J. (2012). Shallow syntactic annotation in the Corpus of Wrocław University of Technolog. *Cognitive Studies*, 12.

Radziszewski, A. and Śniatowski, T. (2011). Maca — a configurable tool to integrate Polish morphological data. In *Proceedings of the Second International Workshop on Free/Open-Source Rule-Based Machine Translation*.

Radziszewski, A. and Śniatowski, T. (2011). A Memory-Based Tagger for Polish. In *Proceedings of the LTC 2011*. Tagger available at http://nlp.pwr.wroc.pl/redmine/projects/wmbt/wiki/.

Stede, M. (2012). *Discourse Processing*. Morgan & Claypool Publishers.

Woliński, M. (2003). System znaczników morfosyntaktycznych w korpusie ipi pan. *Polonica*, 12:39–55.

# Intention Analysis for Sales, Marketing and Customer Service

*Cohan Sujay Carlos*[1] *Madhulika Yalamanchi*[1]
(1) Aiaioo Labs, India
cohan@aiaioo.com, madhulika@aiaioo.com

ABSTRACT

In recent years, social media has become a customer touch-point for the business functions of marketing, sales and customer service. We aim to show that intention analysis might be useful to these business functions and that it can be performed effectively on short texts (at the granularity level of a single sentence). We demonstrate a scheme of categorization of intentions that is amenable to automation using simple machine learning techniques that are language-independent. We discuss the grounding that this scheme of categorization has in speech act theory. In the demonstration we go over a number of usage scenarios in an attempt to show that the use of automatic intention detection tools would benefit the business functions of sales, marketing and service. We also show that social media can be used not just to convey pleasure or displeasure (that is, to express sentiment) but also to discuss personal needs and to report problems (to express intentions). We evaluate methods for automatically discovering intentions in text, and establish that it is possible to perform intention analysis on social media with an accuracy of 66.97% ± 0.10%.

KEYWORDS: intention analysis, intent analysis, social media, speech act theory, sentiment analysis, emotion analysis, intention.

*Proceedings of COLING 2012: Demonstration Papers*, pages 33–40,
COLING 2012, Mumbai, December 2012.

# 1 Introduction

In this paper and the accompanying demonstration, we present and attempt to demonstrate the effectiveness of a method of categorization of intentions that is based on the needs of the marketing, sales and service functions of a business which are, according to Smith et al. (2011), the functions most impacted by social media. The categories of intention that we use are *purchase, inquire, complain, criticise, praise, direct, quit, compare, wish* and *sell*. We also use an *other* category consisting of sentences that do not express intentions.

In the demonstration, we show that the intention categories *purchase, sell* and *wish* are valuable to sales, that the *inquire* category can be used for outbound marketing, that *criticise, compare* and *praise* can be used for inbound marketing, and that *complain, direct* and *quit* can be used for customer service.

This does not mean that these categories are only of use to business. The intention to *complain* and the intention to *quit* have been studied extensively by Hirschman (1970) in the context of a wide range of social, political and economic phenomena. A game theoretic framework for the work of Hirschman (1970) has been proposed by Gehlbach (2006) and used to model the mechanism of collapse of communism in East Germany.

In Section 2 we describe the theoretical underpinnings of the present work and in Section 3 we go over related research. In Section 4 we discuss the quantity of social media messages that contain the categories of intentions that are the subject of the present study (we compare the quantities of intentions expressed with the quantities of expressions of sentiment). In Section 5 we describe and evaluate machine learning algorithms for automated intention analysis.

# 2 Background

## 2.1 Speech Act Theory

Austin (1975), in the theory of *speech acts*, distinguished between utterances that are statements (whose truth or falsity is verifiable) and utterances that are not statements. He observed that, "there are, traditionally, besides (grammarians') statements, also questions and exclamations, and sentences expressing commands or wishes or concessions."

In our work we deal with certain types of speech acts that can be called 'intentions' according to one common dictionary definition of the word 'intention', which is, "an aim or plan". In particular, we focus on the ten categories of intention (excluding *other*) in Table 1.

Another concept from speech act theory (Searle, 1983) is the 'direction of fit' of a speech act or *intentional state*. The direction of fit is said to be 'mind-to-world' if through the performance of the speech act, a mental state is established, revealed or altered. The direction of fit of a speech act or intentional state is said to be 'world-to-mind' if the performance of the speech act alters the state of the world.

Seven of the ten categories of intentions in our annotation scheme have the world-to-mind direction of fit (they are desires or intentions) and three have the mind-to-world direction of fit (beliefs). The three categories that have the mind-to-world direction of fit correspond to categories used in opinion mining (namely 'praise', 'criticize' and 'compare').

## 2.2 Discourse Theory

In the introducton to the collection "Intentions in Communication" Cohen et al. (1990) suggest that any theory that purports to explain communication and discourse "will have to place a strong emphasis on issues of *intention*". To illustrate the point, they offer a sample dialog between a customer looking for some meat and a butcher selling the same:

- Customer: "Where are the chuck steaks you advertised for 88 cents per pound?"
- Butcher: "How many do you want?"

The butcher's response would be perfectly natural in a scenario where the steaks are behind the counter where customers are not allowed, and the plausibility of this conversation shows that people infer intention, just as the butcher infers the intention of the customer to be a purchase intention (in this case, possibly as much from the context as from the language).

Georgeff et al. (1999) discuss the Belief-Desire-Intention (BDI) Model of Agency based on the work of Bratman (1987). In the present work, the term "intentions" loosely corresponds to the sense of "desire" as well as "intention" in the BDI model.

# 3 Related Research

## 3.1 Wishes in Reviews and Discussions

Goldberg et al. (2009) developed a corpus of wishes from a set of New Year's Day wishes and through evaluation of learning algorithms for the domains *'products'* and *'politics'*, showed that even though the content of wishes might be domain-specific, the manner in which wishes are expressed is not entirely so. The definition of the word 'wish' used by Goldberg et al. (2009) is "a desire or hope for something to happen".

The wish to *purchase* and the wish to *suggest* improvements are studied in Ramanand et al. (2010). Ramanand et al. (2010) propose rules for identifying both kinds of wishes and test the collection of rules using a corpus that includes product reviews, customer surveys and comments from consumer forums. In addition, they evaluate their system on the *WISH corpus* of Goldberg et al. (2009). Wu and He (2011) also study the wish to suggest and the wish to purchase using variants of Class Sequential Rules (CSRs).

## 3.2 Requests and Promises in Email

Lampert et al. (2010) study the identification of requests in email messages and obtain an accuracy of 83.76%. A study of email communications by Carvalho and Cohen (2006) and Cohen et al. (2004) focuses on discovering speech acts in email, building upon earlier work on illocutionary speech acts (Searle, 1975; Winograd, 1987).

## 3.3 Speech Acts in Conversations

Bouchet (2009) describes the construction of a corpus of user requests for assistance, annotated with the illocutionary speech acts *assertive*, *commissive*, *directive*, *expressive*, *declarative*, and an *other* category for utterances that cannot be classified into one of those. Ravi and Kim (2007) use rules to identify threads that may have unanswered questions and therefore require instructor attention. In their approach, each message is classified as a *question*, *answer*, *elaboration* and *correction*.

## 3.4 Sentiment and Emotion

Three of the intentions in the present study, namely the intention to *praise* something, to *criticize* something, and to *compare* something with something else, have been studied by researchers in connection with sentiment analysis.

The detection of comparisons in text has been studied by Jindal and Liu (2006), and the use of comparative sentences in opinion mining has been studied by Ganapathibhotla and Liu (2008). Yang and Ko (2011) proposed a method to automatically identify 7 categories of comparatives in Korean. Li et al. (2010) used a weakly supervised method to identify comparative questions from a large online question archive. Different perspectives might be reflected in contrastive opinions, and these are studied by Fang et al. (2012) in the context of political texts using the Cross-Perspective Topic model.

The mining of opinion features and the creation of review summaries is studied in Hu and Liu (2006, 2004). A study of sentiment classification is reported in Pang et al. (2002), and the use of subjectivity detection in sentiment classification is reported in Pang and Lee (2004).

Studies to detect emotions in internet chat conversations have been described in Wu et al. (2002); Holzman and Pottenger (2003); Shashank and Bhattacharyya (2010). Minato et al. (2008) describe the creation of an emotions corpus in the Japanese language. Vidrascu and Devillers (2005) attempt to detect emotions in speech data from call center recordings.

# 4 Distribution of Intentions

Table 1 lists the categories of intentions that are the subject of the present study, their mapping to concepts from speech act theory, namely direction of fit, intentional state (desire/belief) and illocutionary point, and their counts in a corpus of sentences from social media.

| Intention | Direction of fit | Des/Bel | Illocution | Business Fn | Count |
|---|---|---|---|---|---|
| wish | mind-to-world | desire | directive | marketing | 543 |
| purchase | mind-to-world | desire | directive | sales | 2221 |
| inquire | mind-to-world | desire | directive | marketing | 2972 |
| compare | world-to-mind | belief | representative | research | 508 |
| praise | world-to-mind | belief | representative | research | 1574 |
| criticize | world-to-mind | belief | representative | research | 2031 |
| complain | mind-to-world | desire | representative | service | 2107 |
| quit | mind-to-world | desire | commissive | service | 744 |
| direct | mind-to-world | desire | directive | service | 706 |
| sell | mind-to-world | desire | directive | procurement | 524 |
| other | | | | | 2775 |

Table 1: Categories annotated in the corpus.

Only 4113 sentences belonged to categories related to opinion (praise, criticize and compare), demonstrating that other speech acts are prevalent on social media in certain contexts.

# 5 Experimental Evaluation

A set of experiments was performed using naive bayes classification, maximum entropy classification, and support vector machine classification to see if intention analysis could be automated, and to see what features might be used to tell categories of intentions apart.

## 5.1 Corpus Slices

The experiments were performed using three slices of categories from the corpus. The first slice (Slice 1) consisted of the categories purchase, inquire, complain, criticize, praise and other, (6 categories) all of which number greater than 1500 in the corpus. The second slice (Slice 2) consisted of direct and quit (both of which have more than 700 each in the corpus) in addition to the above categories, for a total of 8 categories. The last slice (Slice 3) consisted of sell, compare and wish (which have more than 500 occurrences each in the corpus) in addition to the 8 categories mentioned above, for a total of 11 categories.

## 5.2 Automatic Classification

Naive bayesian (NB) classifiers, maximum entropy (ME) classifiers, and support vector machine (SVM) classifiers were evaluated on the corpus of intentions. The features used were n-grams (all n-grams containing keywords used to crawl the social media text were discarded).

| **Features** | **NB** | **ME** | **SVM (RBF)** |
|---|---|---|---|
| unigrams | $60.97 \pm 0.01$ | $68.24 \pm 0.02$ | $68.96 \pm 0.02$ |
| bigrams | $60.07 \pm 0.02$ | $65.38 \pm 0.01$ | $65.19 \pm 0.01$ |
| **unigrams+bigrams** | $64.07 \pm 0.02$ | $70.43 \pm 0.02$ | $69.37 \pm 0.02$ |

Table 2: Average five-fold cross-validation accuracies on Slice 1 (sentence order randomized).

| **Features** | **NB** | **ME** | **SVM (RBF)** |
|---|---|---|---|
| unigrams | $51.18 \pm 0.02$ | $53.06 \pm 0.01$ | $58.96 \pm 0.02$ |
| bigrams | $52.14 \pm 0.02$ | $54.89 \pm 0.01$ | $52.96 \pm 0.01$ |
| unigrams+bigrams | $56.66 \pm 0.02$ | $60.71 \pm 0.02$ | $57.95 \pm 0.01$ |

Table 3: Average five-fold cross-validation accuracies on Slice 2 (sentence order randomized).

| **Features** | **NB** | **ME** | **SVM (RBF)** |
|---|---|---|---|
| unigrams | $46.40 \pm 0.01$ | $53.06 \pm 0.01$ | $52.99 \pm 0.02$ |
| bigrams | $46.94 \pm 0.01$ | $50.01 \pm 0.01$ | $48.18 \pm 0.02$ |
| unigrams+bigrams | $51.45 \pm 0.01$ | $55.43 \pm 0.02$ | $52.62 \pm 0.02$ |

Table 4: Average five-fold cross-validation accuracies on Slice 3 (sentence order randomized).

Accuracy scores for Slices 1, 2 and 3 are listed in Table 2, Table 3 and Table 4 and Table 5.

# 6 Demonstration

We will demonstrate the use of intention analysis in a number of usage scenarios to establish its value to sales, marketing and customer service.

## 6.1 Identifying Leads for Sales

The ability to find customers who have a need for a particular product or service is valuable to the sales function of a business. We demonstrate how customers who wish to buy certain products may be identified by monitoring conversations on social media.

| Features | NB | ME | SVM (RBF) |
|---|---|---|---|
| unigrams | $57.91 \pm 0.10$ | $65.27 \pm 0.11$ | $65.96 \pm 0.09$ |
| bigrams | $56.61 \pm 0.06$ | $62.22 \pm 0.08$ | $61.78 \pm 0.09$ |
| unigrams+bigrams | $59.97 \pm 0.08$ | $66.97 \pm 0.10$ | $65.57 \pm 0.09$ |

Table 5: Average 5-fold cross-validation accuracies on Slice 1 of the unshuffled corpus.

## 6.2 Identifying Needs for Marketing

Marketing can use inquiries on social media to identify interested persons and educate them about pertinent offerings. Political teams can use inquiries to educate voters. They can also use intentions expressed on social media to identify needs and wants. In this segment of the demonstration, we show how inquiries about a product or service, and expressions of interest may be detected.

## 6.3 Identifying Issues for Customer Service

Customer service might be able to better respond to criticism and complaints if it can spot customers who are dissatisfied or have problems. In this segment of the demonstration, we show how complaints and criticism of a product or a service may be detected.

# 7 Conclusion

In this study, we have proposed a way of categorizing text in terms of the intentions expressed. We have argued that such a set of categories might be useful to numerous business functions. We have shown that these categories are encountered frequently on social media, and demonstrated the value of using intention analysis in marketing, sales and customer service scenarios. Furthermore, we have shown that it is possible to achieve an accuracy of $66.97\% \pm 0.10\%$ at the task of classifying sentence-length texts into the intention categories described in this paper.


# Acknowledgements

We are very grateful to the team of Chakri J. Prabhakar, Jonas Prabhakar, Noopura Srihari and Shachi Ranganath for their patient, careful and painstaking (and underpaid and very under-rewarded) development of the corpus that was used in these experiments. We are also in the debt of Vijay Ramachandran and Rohit Chauhan, the founders of WisdomTap.com, for paying us to start working on intention analysis, for sharing with us a number of novel ideas on the subject of purchase intention analysis and its applications, and for their help and support of our research work and our efforts to build a corpus for intention analysis. We are also sincerely grateful to the anonymous reviewers of an earlier and longer version of this paper for their valuable comments and suggestions.


# References


Austin, J. L. (1975). *How to Do Things With Words*. Harvard University Press, Cambridge, MA.

Bouchet, F. (2009). Characterization of conversational activities in a corpus of assistance requests. In Icard, T., editor, *Proceedings of the 14th Student Session of the European Summer School for Logic, Language, and Information (ESSLLI)*, pages 40–50.

Bratman, M. E. (1987). *Intention, Plans, and Practical Reason*. Harvard University Press, Cambridge, MA.

Carvalho, V. R. and Cohen, W. W. (2006). Improving email speech act analysis via n-gram selection. In *Proceedings of the HLT/NAACL 2006 (Human Language Technology conference - North American chapter of the Association for Computational Linguistics) - ACTS Workshop*, New York City, NY.

Cohen, P. R., Pollack, M. E., and Morgan, J. L. (1990). *Intentions in Communication*. The MIT Press.

Cohen, W. W., Carvalho, V. R., and Mitchell, T. M. (2004). Learning to classify email into "speech acts". In Lin, D. and Wu, D., editors, *Proceedings of EMNLP 2004*, pages 309–316, Barcelona, Spain. Association for Computational Linguistics.

Fang, Y., Si, L., Somasundaram, N., and Yu, Z. (2012). Mining contrastive opinions on political texts using cross-perspective topic model. In Adar, E., Teevan, J., Agichtein, E., and Maarek, Y., editors, *WSDM*, pages 63–72. ACM.

Ganapathibhotla, M. and Liu, B. (2008). Mining opinions in comparative sentences. In Scott, D. and Uszkoreit, H., editors, *COLING*, pages 241–248.

Gehlbach, S. (2006). A formal model of exit and voice. *Rationality and Society*, 18(4):1043–4631.

Georgeff, M., Pell, B., Pollack, M., Tambe, M., and Wooldridge, M. (1999). The belief-desire-intention model of agency. pages 1–10. Springer.

Goldberg, A. B., Fillmore, N., Andrzejewski, D., Xu, Z., Gibson, B., and Zhu, X. (2009). May all your wishes come true: a study of wishes and how to recognize them. In *NAACL '09 Proceedings of Human Language Technologies: The 2009 Annual Conference of the North American Chapter of the Association for Computational Linguistics*, pages 263–271, Stroudsburg, PA. Association for Consumer Research.

Hirschman, A. O. (1970). *Exit, Voice, and Loyalty - Responses to Decline in Firms, Organizations, and States*. Harvard University Press, Cambridge, MA.

Holzman, L. E. and Pottenger, W. M. (2003). Classification of emotions in internet chat: An application of machine learning using speech phonemes. 2003. available on www: www.lehigh.edu/ leh7/papers/emotionclassification.p df. Technical report, Lehigh University.

Hu, M. and Liu, B. (2004). Mining and summarizing customer reviews. In Kim, W., Kohavi, R., Gehrke, J., and DuMouchel, W., editors, *KDD*, pages 168–177. ACM.

Hu, M. and Liu, B. (2006). Opinion feature extraction using class sequential rules. In *AAAI Spring Symposium: Computational Approaches to Analyzing Weblogs*, pages 61–66.

Jindal, N. and Liu, B. (2006). Mining comparative sentences and relations. In *AAAI*, pages 1331–1336. AAAI Press.

Lampert, A., Dale, R., and Paris, C. (2010). Detecting emails containing requests for action. In *HLT '10 Human Language Technologies: The 2010 Annual Conference of the North American Chapter of the Association for Computational Linguistics*, Stroudsburg, PA.

Li, S., Lin, C.-Y., Song, Y.-I., and Li, Z. (2010). Comparable entity mining from comparative questions. In Hajic, J., Carberry, S., and Clark, S., editors, *ACL*, pages 650–658. The Association for Computer Linguistics.

Minato, J., Bracewell, D. B., Ren, F., and Kuroiwa, S. (2008). Japanese emotion corpus analysis and its usefor automatic emotion word identification. *Engineering Letters*, 16(1):172–177.

Pang, B. and Lee, L. (2004). A sentimental education: Sentiment analysis using subjectivity summarization based on minimum cuts. In Scott, D., Daelemans, W., and Walker, M. A., editors, *ACL*, pages 271–278. ACL.

Pang, B., Lee, L., and Vaithyanathan, S. (2002). Thumbs up? sentiment classification using machine learning techniques. *CoRR*, cs.CL/0205070.

Ramanand, J., Bhavsar, K., and Pedanekar, N. (2010). Wishful thinking: finding suggestions and 'buy' wishes from product reviews. In *CAAGET '10 Proceedings of the NAACL HLT 2010 Workshop on Computational Approaches to Analysis and Generation of Emotion in Text*, Stroudsburg, PA.

Ravi, S. and Kim, J. (2007). Profiling student interactions in threaded discussions with speech act classifiers. In *Proceedings of the 2007 Conference on Artificial Intelligence in Education: Building Technology Rich Learning Contexts That Work*, pages 357–364, Amsterdam, The Netherlands. IOS Press.

Searle, J. R. (1975). A taxonomy of illocutionary acts. *Language, Mind and Knowledge*, pages 344–369.

Searle, J. R. (1983). *Intentionality: An Essay in the Philosophy of Mind*. Cambridge University Press, Cambridge, MA.

Shashank and Bhattacharyya, P. (2010). Emotion analysis of internet chat. In *In the Proceedings of the ICON Conference 2010*.

Smith, N., Wollen, R., and Zhou, C. (2011). *The Social Media Management Handbook*. John Wiley and Sons, Inc., Hoboken, NJ.

Vidrascu, L. and Devillers, L. (2005). Detection of real-life emotions in call centers. In *INTERSPEECH*, pages 1841–1844. ISCA.

Winograd, T. (1987). A language/action perspective on the design of cooperative work. *Human-Computer Interaction*, 3(1):3–30.

Wu, T., Khan, F. M., Fisher, T. A., Shuler, L. A., and Pottenger, W. M. (2002). Posting act tagging using transformation-based learning. In *In the Proceedings of the Workshop on Foundations of Data Mining and Discovery, IEEE International Conference on Data Mining*.

Wu, X. and He, Z. (2011). Identifying wish sentence in product reviews. *Journal of Computational Information Systems*, 7(5):1607–1613.

Yang, S. and Ko, Y. (2011). Extracting comparative entities and predicates from texts using comparative type classification. In Lin, D., Matsumoto, Y., and Mihalcea, R., editors, *ACL*, pages 1636–1644. The Association for Computer Linguistics.

# Authorship Identification in Bengali Literature: a Comparative Analysis

*Tanmoy Chakraborty*
Department of Computer Science & Engineering
Indian Institute of Technology, Kharagpur
India
its_tanmoy@cse.iitkgp.ernet.in

ABSTRACT

Stylometry is the study of the unique linguistic styles and writing behaviors of individuals. It belongs to the core task of text categorization like authorship identification, plagiarism detection etc. Though reasonable number of studies have been conducted in English language, no major work has been done so far in Bengali. In this work, We will present a demonstration of authorship identification of the documents written in Bengali. We adopt a set of fine-grained stylistic features for the analysis of the text and use them to develop two different models: statistical similarity model consisting of three measures and their combination, and machine learning model with Decision Tree, Neural Network and SVM. Experimental results show that SVM outperforms other state-of-the-art methods after 10-fold cross validations. We also validate the relative importance of each stylistic feature to show that some of them remain consistently significant in every model used in this experiment.

KEYWORDS: Stylometry, Authorship Identification, Vocabulary Richness, Machine Learning.

*Proceedings of COLING 2012: Demonstration Papers*, pages 41–50,
COLING 2012, Mumbai, December 2012.

# 1 Introduction

Stylometry is an approach that analyses text in text mining e.g., novels, stories, dramas that the famous author wrote, trying to measure the author's style, rhythm of his pen, subjection of his desire, prosody of his mind by choosing some attributes which are consistent throughout his writing, which plays the linguistic fingerprint of that author. Authorship identification belongs to the subtask of Stylometry detection where a correspondence between the predefined writers and the unknown articles has to be established taking into account various stylistic features of the documents. The main target in this study is to build a decision making system that enables users to predict and to choose the right author from a specific anonymous authors' articles under consideration, by choosing various lexical, syntactic, analytical features called as ***stylistic markers***. Wu incorporate two models—(i) statistical model using three well-established similarity measures- cosine-similarity, chi-square measure, euclidean distance, and (ii) machine learning approach with Decision Tree, Neural Network and Support Vector Machine (SVM).

The pioneering study on authorship attributes identification using word-length histograms appeared at the very end of nineteen century (Malyutov, 2006). After that, a number of studies based on content analysis (Krippendorff, 2003), computational stylistic approach (Stamatatos et al., 1999), exponential gradient learn algorithm (Argamon et al., 2003), Winnow regularized algorithm (Zhang et al., 2002), SVM based approach (Pavelec et al., 2007) have been proposed for various languages like English, Portuguese (see (Stamatatos, 2009) for reviews). As a beginning of Indian language Stylometry analysis, (Chanda et al., 2010) started working with handwritten Bengali texts to judge authors. (Das and Mitra, 2011) proposed an authorship identification task in Bengali using simple n-gram token counts. Their approach is restrictive when considering authors of the same period and same genre. The texts we have chosen are of the same genre and of the same time period to ensure that the success of the learners would infer that texts can be classified only on the style, not by the prolific discrimination of text genres or distinct time of writings. We have compared our methods with the conventional technique called *vocabulary richness* and the existing method proposed by (Das and Mitra, 2011) in Bengali. The observation of the effect of each stylistic feature over 10-cross validations relies on that fact that some of them are inevitable for authorship identification task especially in Bengali, and few of the rare studied features could accelerate the performance of this mapping task.

# 2 Proposed Methodology

The system architecture of the proposed stylometry detection system is shown in Figure 1. In this section, we briefly describe different components of the system architecture and then analytically present the set of stylistic features.

## 2.1 Textual analysis

Basic pre-processing before actual textual analysis is required so that stylistic markers are clearly viewed to the system for further analysis. Token-level markers discussed in the next subsection are extracted from this pre-processed corpus. Bengali Shallow parser[1] has been used to separate the sentence and the chunk boundaries and to identify parts-of-

[1]http://ltrc.iiit.ac.in/analyzer/bengali

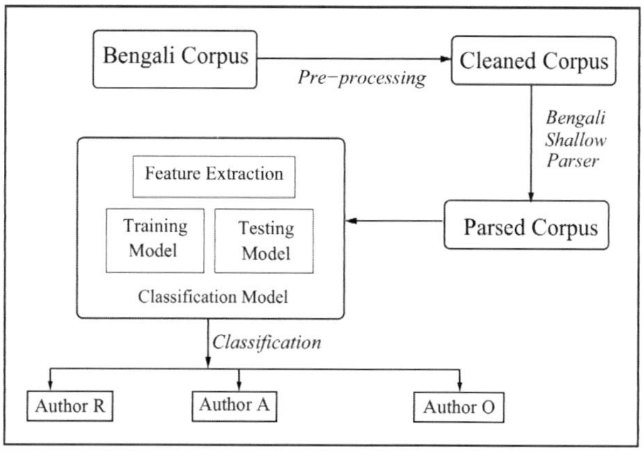


Figure 1: System architecture

speech of each token. From this parsed text, chunk-level and context-level markers are also demarcated.

## 2.2 Stylistic features extraction

Stylistic features have been proposed as more reliable style markers than for example, word-level features since the stylistic markers are sometime not under the conscious control of the author. To allow the selection of the linguistic features rather than n-gram terms, robust and accurate text analysis tools such as lemmatizers, part-of-speech (POS) taggers, chunkers etc are needed. We have used the Shallow parser, which gives a parsed output of a raw input corpus. The stylistic markers which have been selected in this experiment are discussed in Table 1. Most of the features described in Table 1 are self-explanatory. However, the problem occurs when identifying keywords (KW) from the articles of each author which serve as the representative of that author. For this, we have identified top fifty high frequent words (since we have tried to generate maximum distinct and non-overlapped set of keywords) excluding stop-words in Bengali for each author using $TF * IDF$ method. Note that, all the features are normalized to make the system independent of document length.

## 2.3 Building classification model

Three well-known statistical similarity based metrics namely Cosine-Similarity (COS), Chi-Square measure (CS) and Euclidean Distance (ED) are used to get their individual effect on classifying documents, and their combined effort (COM) has also been reported. For machine-learning model, we incorporate three different modules: Decision Trees (DT)[2], Neural Networks (NN)[3] and Support Vector Machine (SVM). For training and classification phases of SVM, we have used YamCha[4] toolkit and TinySVM- 0.07[5] classifier respectively with pairwise multi-class decision method and the polynomial kernel.

[2]See5 package by Quinlan, http://www.rulequest.com/see5-info.html
[3]Neuroshell – the commercial software package, http://www.neuroshell.com/
[4]http://chasen-org/ taku/software/yamcha/
[5]http://cl.aist-nara.ac.jp/taku-ku/software/TinySVM

| | No. | Feature | Explanation | Normalization |
|---|---|---|---|---|
| Token Level | 1. | L(w) | Average length of the word | Avg. len.(word)/ Max len.(word) |
| | 2. | $KW(R)$ | Intersection of the keywords of Author R and the test document | $\lvert KW(doc) \bigcap KW(R) \rvert$ |
| | 3. | $KW(A)$ | Intersection of the keywords of Author A and the test document | $\lvert KW(doc) \bigcap KW(A) \rvert$ |
| | 4. | $KW(O)$ | Intersection of the keywords of Author O and the test document | $\lvert KW(doc) \bigcap KW(O) \rvert$ |
| | 5. | HL | Hapex Legomena (No of words with frequency=1) | count(HL)/count(word) |
| | 6. | Punc. | No of punctuations | count(punc)/count(word) |
| Phrase Level | 7. | NP | Detected Noun Phrase | count(NP)/count of all phrase |
| | 8. | VP | Detected Verb Phrase | count(VP)/count of all phrase |
| | 9. | CP | Detected Conjunct Phrase | count(CP)/count of all phrase |
| | 10. | UN | Detected unknown word | count(POS)/count of all phrase |
| | 11. | RE | Detected reduplications and echo words | count(RDP+ECHO)/count of all phrase |
| Context Level | 12. | Dig | Number of the dialogs | Count(dialog)/ No. of sentences |
| | 13. | L(d) | Average length of the dialog | Avg. words per dialog/ No. of sentences |
| | 14. | L(p) | Average length of the paragraph | Avg. words per para/ No. of sentences |

Table 1: Selected features used in the classification model

# 3 Experimental Results

## 3.1 Corpus

Resource acquisition is one of the challenging obstacles to work with electronically resource constrained languages like Bengali. However, this system has used 150 stories in Bengali written by the noted Indian Nobel laureate Rabindranath Tagore[6]. We choose this domain for two reasons: firstly, in such writings the idiosyncratic style of the author is not likely to be overshadowed by the characteristics of the corresponding text-genre; secondly, in the previous research (Chakaraborty and Bandyopadhyay, 2011), the author has worked on the corpus of Rabindranath Tagore to explore some of the stylistic behaviors of his documents. To differentiate them from other authors' articles, we have selected 150 articles of Sarat Chandra Chottopadhyay and 150 articles[7] of a group of other authors (excluding previous two authors) of the same time period. We divide 100 documents in each cluster for training and validation purpose and rest for testing. The statistics of the entire dateset is tabulated in Table 2. Statistical similarity based measures use all 100 documents for making representatives the clusters. In machine learning models, we use 10-fold cross validation method discussed later for better constructing the validation and testing submodules. This demonstration focuses on two topics: (a) the effort of many authors on feature selection

[6]http://www.rabindra-rachanabali.nltr.org

[7]http://banglalibrary.evergreenbangla.com/

and learning and (b) the effort of limited data in authorship detection.

| Clusters | Authors | No. of documents | No. of tokens | No. of unique tokens |
|---|---|---|---|---|
| Cluster 1 | Rabindranath Tagore (Author R) | 150 | 6,862,580 | 4,978,672 |
| Cluster 2 | Sarat Chandra Chottopadyhay (Author A) | 150 | 4,083,417 | 2,987,450 |
| Cluster 3 | Others (Author O) | 150 | 3,818,216 | 2,657,813 |

Table 2: Statistics of the used dataset

## 3.2 Baseline system (BL)

In order to set up a baseline system, we use traditional lexical-based methodology called *vocabulary richness* (VR) (Holmes, 2004) which is basically the type-token ratio ($V/N$), where $V$ is the size of the vocabulary of the sample text and $N$ is the number of tokens which forms the simple text. By using nearest-neighbor algorithm, the baseline system tries to map each of the testing documents to one author. We have also compared our approach with the state-of-the-art method proposed by (Das and Mitra, 2011). The results of the baseline systems are depicted using confusion matrices in Table 3.

| | Vocabulary richness (VR) | | | | (Das and Mitra, 2011) | | | |
|---|---|---|---|---|---|---|---|---|
| | R | A | O | e(error) in % | R | A | O | e(error) in % |
| R | *26* | 14 | 10 | 48% | *31* | 9 | 10 | 38% |
| A | 17 | *21* | 12 | 58% | 18 | *30* | 2 | 40% |
| O | 16 | 20 | *14* | 72% | 10 | 6 | *34* | 32% |
| Avg. error | | | | 56% | Avg. error | | | 36.67% |

Table 3: Confusion matrices of two baseline system (correct mappings are italicized diagonally).

## 3.3 Performances of two different models

The confusion matrices in Table 4 describe the accuracy of the statistical measures and the results of their combined voting. The accuracy of the majority voting technique is 67.3% which is relatively better than others. Since the attributes tested are continuous, all the decision trees are constructed using the fuzzy threshold parameter, so that the knife-edge behavior for decision trees is softened by constructing an interval close to the threshold. For neural network, many structures of the multilayer network were experimented with before we came up with our best network. Backpropogation feed forward networks yield the best result with the following architecture: 14 input nodes, 8 nodes on the first hidden layer, 6 nodes on the second hidden layer, and 6 output nodes (to act as error correcting codes). Two output nodes are allotted to a single author (this increases the Hamming distance between the classifications - the bit string that is output with each bit corresponding to one author in the classification- of any two authors, thus decreasing the possibility of misclassification). Out of 100 training samples, 30% are used in the validation set which determines whether over-fitting has occurred and when to stop training. It is worth noting that the reported results are the average of 10-fold cross validations. We will discuss the comparative results of individual cross validation phase in the next section. Table 5 reports the error rate of individual model in three confusion matrices. At a glance, machine learning approaches especially SVM (83.3% accuracy) perform tremendously well compared to the other models.

| | Statistical similarity models | | | | | | | | | | | | | | | |
|---|---|---|---|---|---|---|---|---|---|---|---|---|---|---|---|---|
| | Cosine similarity (COS) | | | | Chi-square measure (CS) | | | | Euclidean distance (ED) | | | | Majority voting (COM) | | | |
| | R | A | O | e(%) | R | A | O | e(%) | R | A | O | e(%) | R | A | O | e(%) |
| R | *30* | 12 | 8 | 40 | *34* | 9 | 7 | 32 | *27* | 15 | 8 | 46 | *34* | 7 | 9 | 28 |
| A | 15 | *27* | 8 | 46 | 14 | *30* | 6 | 40 | 18 | *26* | 6 | 48 | 11 | *32* | 7 | 36 |
| O | 12 | 9 | *29* | 42 | 9 | 8 | *33* | 34 | 17 | 6 | *27* | 46 | 6 | 11 | *33* | 34 |
| | Avg. error | | | 42.7 | Avg. error | | | 35.3 | Avg. error | | | 46.6 | Avg. error | | | 32.7 |

Table 4: Confusion matrices of statistical similarity measures on test set.

| | Machine Learning models | | | | | | | | | | | |
|---|---|---|---|---|---|---|---|---|---|---|---|---|
| | Decision Tree | | | | Neural Networks | | | | Support Vector Machine | | | |
| | R | A | O | e(%) | R | A | O | e(%) | R | A | O | e(%) |
| R | *35* | 8 | 6 | 28 | *38* | 9 | 3 | 24 | *44* | 3 | 3 | 12 |
| A | 7 | *37* | 6 | 26 | 10 | *35* | 5 | 30 | 8 | *40* | 2 | 20 |
| O | 6 | 5 | *39* | 22 | 9 | 5 | *36* | 28 | 2 | 7 | *41* | 18 |
| | Avg. error | | | 25.3 | Avg. error | | | 27.3 | Avg. error | | | 16.7 |

Table 5: Confusion matrices of machine learning models on test set (averaged over 10-fold cross validations).

### 3.4 Comparative analysis

The performance of any machine learning tool highly depends on the population and divergence of training samples. Limited dataset can overshadowed the intrinsic productivity of the tool. Because of the lack of large number of dataset, we divide the training data randomly into 10 sets and use 10-fold cross validation technique to prevent overfitting for each machine learning model. The boxplot in Figure 2(a) reports the performance of each model on 10-fold cross validation phrase with mean accuracy and variance. In three cases, since the notches in the box plots overlap, we can conclude, with certain confidence, that the true medians do not differ. The outliers are marked separately with the dotted points. The difference between lower and upper quartiles in SVM is comparatively smaller than the others that shows relative low variance of accuracies in different iterations.

We also measure the pairwise agreement in mapping three types of authors using Cohen's Kappa coefficient (Cohen, 1960). In Figure 2(b), the high correlation between Decision Tree and Neural Network models, which is considerably high compared to the others signifies that the effects of both of these models in author-document mapping task are reasonably identical and less efficient compared to SVM model.

As a pioneer of studying different machine learning models in Bengali authorship task, it is worth measuring the relative importance of individual feature in each learning model that gets some features high privilege and helps in feature ranking. We have dropped each

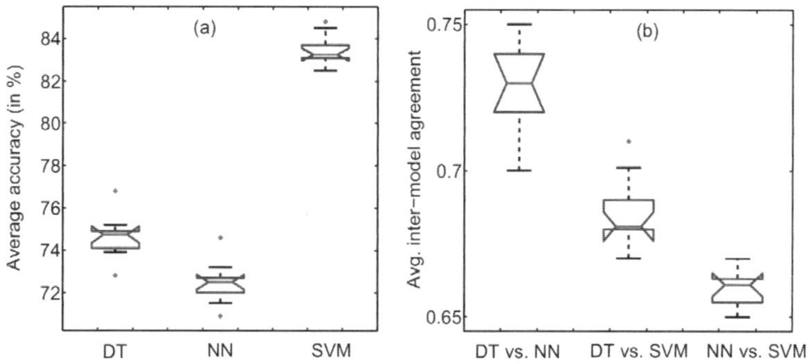


Figure 2: (a) Boxplot of average accuracy (in %) of three machine learning modules on 10-fold cross validations; (b) pair-wise average inter-model agreement of the models using Cohen's Kappa measure.

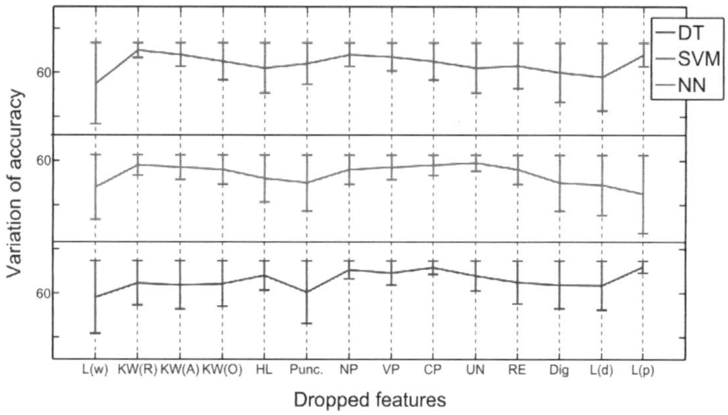


Figure 3: (Color online) Average accuracy after deleting features one at a time (the magnitude of the error bar indicates the difference of the accuracies before and after dropping one feature for each machine learning model).

feature one by one and pointed out its relative impact on accuracy over 10-fold cross validations. The points against each feature in the line graphs in Figure 3 show percentage of accuracy when that feature is dropped, and the magnitude of the corresponding error bar measures the difference between final accuracy (when all features present) and accuracy after dropping that feature. All models rely on the high importance of length of the word in this task. All of them also reach to the common consensus of the importance of KW(R), KW(A), KW(O), NP and CP. But few of the features typically reflect unpredictable signatures in different models. For instance, length of the dialog and unknown word count show larger significance in SVM, but they are not so significant in other two models. Similar characteristics are also observed in Decision tree and Neural network models.

Finally, we study the responsibility of individual authors for producing erroneous results. Figure 4 depicts that almost in every case, the system has little overestimated the authors of documents as author R. It may occur due to the acquisition of documents because the documents in cluster 2 and cluster 3 are not so diverse and well-structured as the documents of Rabindranath Tagore. Developing appropriate corpus for this study is itself a separate research area specially when dealing with learning modules, and it takes huge amount of time. The more the focus will be on this language, the more we expect to get diverge corpus of different Bengali writers.

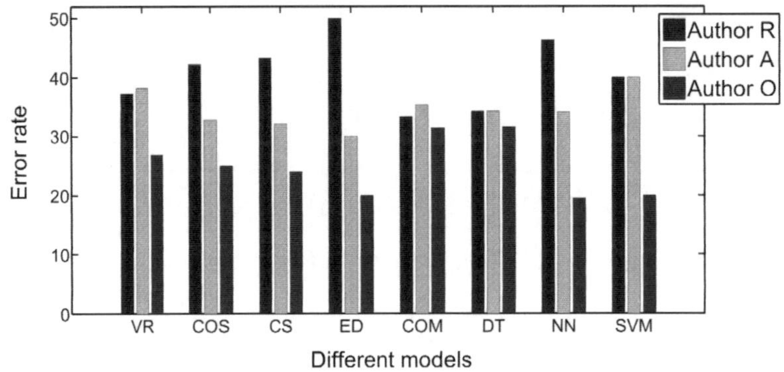


Figure 4: (Color online) Error analysis: percentage of error occurs due to wrong identified authors.

## 4 Conclusion and Future work

This paper attempts to demonstrate the mechanism to recognize three authors in Bengali literature based on their style of writing (without taking into account the author's profile, genre or writing time). We have incorporated both statistical similarity based measures and three machine learning models over same feature sets and compared them with the baseline system. All of the machine learning models especially SVM yield a significantly higher accuracy than other models. Although the SVM yielded a better numerical performance, and are considered inherently suitable to capture an intangible concept like style, the decision trees are human readable making it possible to define style. While more features could produce additional discriminatory material, the present study proves that artificial intelligence provides stylometry with excellent classifiers that require fewer and relevant input variables than traditional statistics. We also showed that the significance of the used features in authorship identification task are relative to the used model. This preliminary study is the journey to reveal the intrinsic style of writing of the Bengali authors based upon which we plan to build more robust, generic and diverge authorship identification tool.

## References


Argamon, S., Šarić, M., and Stein, S. S. (2003). Style mining of electronic messages for multiple authorship discrimination: first results. In *KDD '03: Proceedings of the ninth ACM SIGKDD international conference on Knowledge discovery and data mining*, pages 475–480. ACM.

Chakaraborty, T. and Bandyopadhyay, S. (2011). Inference of fine-grained attributes of bengali corpus for stylometry detection. pages 79–83.

Chanda, S., Franke, K., Pal, U., and Wakabayashi, T. (2010). Text independent writer identification for bengali script. In *Proceedings of the 2010 20th International Confer-*

*ence on Pattern Recognition*, ICPR '10, pages 2005–2008, Washington, DC, USA. IEEE Computer Society.

Cohen, J. (1960). A Coefficient of Agreement for Nominal Scales. *Educational and Psychological Measurement*, 20(1):37–46.

Das, S. and Mitra, P. (2011). Author identification in bengali literary works. In *Proceedings of the 4th international conference on Pattern recognition and machine intelligence*, PReMI'11, pages 220–226, Berlin, Heidelberg. Springer-Verlag.

Holmes, D. (2004). Review: Attributing authorship: An introduction. *LLC*, 19(4):528–530.

Krippendorff, K. (2003). *Content Analysis: An Introduction to Its Methodology.* SAGE Publications.

Malyutov, M. B. (2006). General theory of information transfer and combinatorics. chapter Authorship attribution of texts: a review, pages 362–380. Springer-Verlag, Berlin, Heidelberg.

Merriam, T. (1998). Heterogeneous authorship in early shakespeare and the problem of henry v. *Literary and Linguistic Computing*, 13(1):15–27.

Pavelec, D., Justino, E. J. R., and Oliveira, L. S. (2007). Author identification using stylometric features. *Inteligencia Artificial, Revista Iberoamericana de Inteligencia Artificial*, 11(36):59–66.

Rudman, J. (1997). The State of Authorship Attribution Studies: Some Problems and Solutions. *Computers and the Humanities*, 31(4):351–365.

Stamatatos, E. (2009). A survey of modern authorship attribution methods. *J. Am. Soc. Inf. Sci. Technol.*, 60(3):538–556.

Stamatatos, E., Fakotakis, N., and Kokkinakis, G. (1999). Automatic authorship attribution. In *Proceedings of the ninth conference on European chapter of the Association for Computational Linguistics*, pages 158–164. Association for Computational Linguistics.

Vapnik, V. N. (1995). *The nature of statistical learning theory.* Springer-Verlag New York, Inc., New York, NY, USA.

Zhang, T., Damerau, F., and Johnson, D. (2002). Text chunking based on a generalization of winnow. *Journal of Machine Learning Research*, 2:615–637.

# Word Root Finder: a morphological segmentor based on CRF

*Joseph Z. Chang Jason S. Chang*
National Tsing Hua University, No. 101, Section 2, Kuang-Fu Road, Hsinchu, Taiwan
joseph.nthu.tw@gmail.com, jason.jschang@gmail.com

ABSTRACT
Morphological segmentation of words is a subproblem of many natural language tasks, including handling out-of-vocabulary (OOV) words in machine translation, more effective information retrieval, and computer assisted vocabulary learning. Previous work typically relies on extensive statistical and semantic analyses to induce legitimate stems and affixes. We introduce a new learning based method and a prototype implementation of a knowledge light system for learning to segment a given word into word parts, including prefixes, suffixes, stems, and even roots. The method is based on the Conditional Random Fields (CRF) model. Evaluation results show that our method with a small set of seed training data and readily available resources can produce fine-grained morphological segmentation results that rival previous work and systems.

KEYWORDS: morphology, affix, word root, CRF.

*Proceedings of COLING 2012: Demonstration Papers*, pages 51–58,
COLING 2012, Mumbai, December 2012.

# 1 Introduction

Morphological segmentation is the process of converting the surface form of a given word to the lexical form with additional grammatical information such as part of speech, gender, and number. The lexical form (or lemma) is the entries found in a dictionary or a lexicon. The conversion may involve stripping some prefixes or suffixes off the surface form.

For example, in *The Celex Morphological Database* (Baayen et al., 1996), the word *abstraction* is segmented into a stem *abstract* and a suffix *ion*. Celex provides additional grammatical information (e.g., the suffix *ion* in *abstraction*turns verb into noun. Our goal is to produce even more fine-grained segmentation, e.g., splitting the word *abstraction* into three meaningful units: *abs*, *tract* and *ion*, respectively meaning "*away*", "*draw*", and "*noun of verbal action*".

Constructing a fine-grained morphological system can potentially be beneficial to second language learners. Nation (2001) points out that an important aspect of learning vocabulary in another langauge is knowing how to relate unknown words and meanings to known word parts. English affixes and word roots are considered helpful for learning English. Understanding the meaning of affixes and roots in new words can expedite learning, a point emphasized in many prep books for standardized test such as GRE and TOEFL.

Many existing methods for morphological analysis rely on human crafted data, and therefore have to be redone for special domains. An unsupervised or lightly supervised method has the advantage of saving significant time and effort, when the need to adopt to new domains arises.

The problem can be approached in many ways. Most work in the literature focuses on inducing the morphology of a natural language, discovering the stems and affixes explicitly. An alternative approach is to build a morphological segmenter of words without having to produce a complete list of word parts including prefixes, suffixes, and stems (or roots).

The rest of the paper is organized as follows. In the next section, we survey the related work, and point out the differences of the proposed method. In Section 3, we describe in detail our method and a prototype system. Finally in Section 4, we report the evaluation results.

# 2 Related Work

Much research has investigated morphological analysis along the line of two level model proposed by Koskenniemi (1983). Recently, researchers have begun to propose methods for automatic analysis based on morphology knowledge induced from distributional statistics based on a corpus (Gaussier, 1999; Goldsmith, 1997) . In particular, Goldsmith (2001) shows that it is possible to generate legitimate stems and suffixes with an accuracy rate of 83% for English. More recently, Schone and Jurafsky (2000) propose to use word semantics from derived Latent Semantic Analysis (LSA) in an attempt to correct errors in morphology induction.

Morphological models or morphological segmenters can be used to keep the entries in a dictionary to a minimal by taking advantage of morphological regularity in natural language. Woods (2000) proposes a method that aggressively applies morphology to broaden the coverage a lexicon to make possible more conceptual and effective indexing for information retrieval. The author used around 1,200 morphological rules. Similarly, Gdaniec and Manandise (2002) show that by exploiting affixes, they can extend the lexicon of a machine translation system to cope with OOV words. We use a similar method to expand our seed training data.

More recently, Creutz and Lagus (2006) present Morfessor, an unsupervised method for segmenting words into frequent substrings that are similar to morphemes. The method is based on

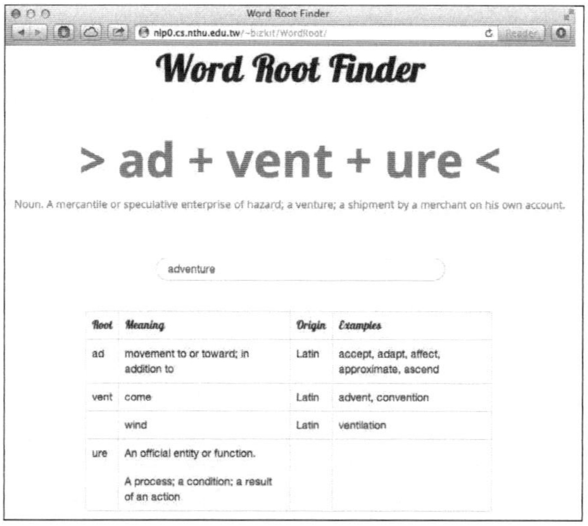


Figure 1: A system screen shot.

the principle of minimal description length (MDL), not unlike previous work such as Brent et al. (1995) and Goldsmith (2001). Additionally, Morfessor is enhanced by HMM states of *prefix*, *stems*, *suffix*, and *noise* based on morpheme length and successor/predecessor perplexity.

The system described in this paper differs from previous work in a number of aspects:

1. Previous work has focused mostly on two way splitting into stem and suffix (or amalgam of suffixes), while we attempt to split into Latin/Greek roots often found in English words.
2. We use a small set of words with hand annotation of prefixes, suffixes, and roots.
3. We experimented with several lists of affixes and a comprehensive lexicon (i.e., the Princeton WordNet 3.0) to expand the seed training data for better results.
4. We employ CRF with features from external knowledge sources to generalize from a small training set, without producing an explicit representation of morphology.

## 3 Method

In this section, we describe our method that comprises of three main steps. First, we automatically generate a training dataset by expanding a small set of seed annotated words (Section 3.1). In Step 2, we describe how to train a CRF model for word part segmentation (Section 3.2). Finally, we use the trained CRF model to construct a web-based system (Section 3.3).

### 3.1 Generate training data from seed data

To achieve reasonable coverage, supervised methods need a large training corpus. However, corpus annotated with fine-grained word parts is hard to come by. Here we describe two strategies that use a small set of annotated words to automatically generate a larger training set. The method is not unlike Woods (2000) or Gdaniec and Manandise (2002).

#### 3.1.1 Expanding training data using prefix and suffix lists

Many words in English consist of stem, roots, and affixes. For examples, *finite* and *in+finite*, *senior* and *senior+ity*, *nation* and *inter+nation+al+ism*. Affix lists are not as difficult to come by, comparing to word lists with fine-grained morphological annotations. With a list of affixes, we can iteratively and recursively attach prefixes and suffixes to words in the seed data, potentially forming a new annotated word. Since these expansions from a known word (e.g., *danger*) can be real words (e.g., *danger-ous*) as well as non-words (e.g., *danger-al*), we need to check each expansion against a dictionary to ensure the correctness. For example, with the list of affixes, "*in-, de-, -ness*", we can expand *fin+ite* into *fin+ite+ness, de+fin+ite, in+fin+ite, in+de+fin+ite, in+de+fin+ite+ness*.

#### 3.1.2 Expanding training data using The Celex Database

Word lists annotated with more coarse-grained morphological annotations are also readily available, such as *The Celex Morphological Database*. Morphological annotations used in *The Celex Morphological Database* comprises of affixes and words, e.g., *abstract+ion*, while our target is to segment words into affixes and *word roots*, e.g., *abs+tract+ion*. By further segmenting the words in *The Celex Morphological Database* using the seed data, we can effectively generate more words for training. For example, with the seed word *abs+tract* and the *Celex* entry *abstract+ion*, we can successfully produce *abs+tract+ion*, an annotated word not found in the seed data.

### 3.2 Training a CRF model

After generating the training data, we treat each characters as a token, and generate several features using readily available affix lists. Our feature each token includes:

1. the character itself
2. whether the character is a vowel
3. does the remaining characters match a known suffix
4. does the preceding characters match a known prefix

We use two symbols for outcomes to represent segmentation: "+" indicates the character is the first character of the next word part, and "-" indicates otherwise. For example, if we want to segment the word *abstraction* into three parts: *abs, tract* and *ion*, the outcome sequence would be "- - - + - - - - + - -". Base on the generated features and annotations, we train a CRF model.

### 3.3 Runtime system

As the user of this system types in a word, the system continuously update the segmentation results on screen. A screen shot of our prototype [1] is shown in Figure 1, indicating that the user has entered the word *adventure*, and the system displays segmentation results, "*ad + vent + ure*", along with Wiktionary[2] definition. Additionally, information (based on Wiktionary and Wikipedia [3] of word parts, including definitions, origins, and examples are also displayed.

## 4 Evaluation and Discussion

We collected a total of 579 words (*Bennett-579*) with segmentation annotation from the book *Word Building with English Word Parts* by *Andrew E. Bennett* published by *Jong Wen Books Co.* in 2007. From the book, we randomly select 10%, or 60, annotated words for evaluation, identified in this paper as *Bennett-60*. The the remaining 90% forms a separate set of 519

[1] morphology.herokuapp.com
[2] en.wiktionary.org
[3] en.wikipedia.org/wiki/List_of_Greek_and_Latin_roots_in_English (as of Aug 22th, 2012)

| training set | Bennett-60 test set | | | Bennett+XC-117 test set | | |
|---|---|---|---|---|---|---|
| | tag prec. | tag rec. | word acc. | tag prec. | tag rec. | word acc. |
| Bennett-519 | .85 | .82 | .80 | .84 | .57 | .49 |
| +XB | .88 | .93 | **.87** | .89 | .87 | .76 |
| +XW | .81 | .87 | .78 | .88 | .80 | .65 |
| +XC | .85 | .95 | .83 | .87 | .80 | .66 |
| +XB+XW | .85 | .87 | .82 | .89 | .87 | .76 |
| +XB+XW+XC | .83 | .87 | .78 | .92 | .90 | **.81** |

Table 1: Evaluation results.

annotated words used for training, identified as *Bennett-519*. To more effectively evaluate the proposed method, we use *The Celex Morphology Database* with the method described in Section 3.1.2 to expand *Bennett-60* to *Bennett+XC-117* with 57 additional annotated words as the second test set. The Princeton WordNet 3.0 (Fellbaum, 1998) is used in the expansion process as a dictionary to ensure that the expanded words are legitimate.

Table 1 shows the evaluation results. We evaluate our system using three metrics: **tagging precision** and **tagging recall** indicate the tagging performance of the "+" tag. For example, if there are a total of 100 "+" tags in all outcome sequences, and the system tagged 50 tokens with the "+" tags, and 40 of them are correct. The tagging precision would be *80%*, and the tagging recall would be *40%*. **Word accuracy** is defined by the number of correctly tagged sequences, or words, divided by total number of test words. A sequence of outcomes for a word is considered correct, only when all the "+" and "-" tags are identical with the answer.

We explore the performance differences of using different resources to generate training data, the 6 systems evaluated are trained using the following traning sets repectively:

- **Bennett-519** : The system trained with the 519 annotated words from a book.
- **+XB** : A list of 3,308 annotated words expanded from **Bennett-519** with a list of 200 affixes collected from the same book.
- **+XW** : A list of 4,341 annotated words expanded from **Bennett-519** with a list of 1,421 affixes collected from Wikipedia.
- **+XC** : A list of 970 annotated words expanded by matching **Bennett-519** and *Celex*.
- **+XB+XW** : A list of 5,141 annotated words by combining **+XB** and **+XW**.
- **+XB+XW+XC** : A list of 5,366 annotated words by combining **+XB**, **+XW** and **+XC**.

As shown in Table 1, all six systems yield better performance on the *Bennett-60* test set than on the *Bennett+XC-117* test set, indicating the latter is a more difficult task. Further examining the two test sets, we found the everage number of segments per word is 2.7 for the *Bennett+XC-117* test set, and 2.0 for the *Bennett-60* test set. This is to be expected, since we generated *Bennett+XC-117* by extending words in *Bennet-60*. The **+XB** system performed the best on *Bennett-60*, with 87% word accurarcy. The **+XC** system ranked second, with 83% word accurarcy. For the *Bennett+XC-117* test set, the **+XB+XW+XC** system with all available traning data performed best with 81% word accurarcy, a 32% improvement comparing to the **Bennett-519** system trained using only the seed data.

In Tables 2 and 3, we list all 60 annotated words in the *Bennet-60* test set. The two tables respectively show the errornous/correct results of running **+XB** on the test set of *Bennett-60*.

By using supervised learning, we had to pay the price of preparing hand annotated training

| answer | matri+x | sen+il+ity | ultra+violet | corp+se |
|---|---|---|---|---|
| **result** | matrix | senil+ity | ultra+vio+let | cor+pse |

| **answer** | loqu+acious | domi+cile | verit+able | mand+atory |
|---|---|---|---|---|
| **result** | loqu+aci+ous | dom+ic+ile | ver+it+able | mand+at+ory |

Table 2: The 8 incorrect results and answers of running the **+XB** system on *Bennett-60* test set.

| | | | | | |
|---|---|---|---|---|---|
| cycl+ist | endo+plasm | miss+ive | popul+ar | sub+scribe | with+stand |
| counter+point | dys+topia | milli+liter | poly+glot | son+ar | with+draw |
| con+fuse | doct+or | matri+mony | phonet+ics | sen+ior | voy+age |
| carn+al | dis+tort | lustr+ous | per+suade | se+cede | ver+ity |
| by+pass | dis+course | kilo+meter | patron+ize | re+tain | vent+ure |
| amphi+boly | dia+lect | in+pire | ob+struct | re+cline | tele+scope |
| ambi+ance | dextr+ity | hydr+ant | non+sense | pro+vide | tele+graph |
| de+flect | fin+ite | nomin+al | pre+view | sur+face | |
| de+cline | en+voy | nat+ion | pre+mature | super+vise | |

Table 3: The 52 correct result of running the **+XB** system on *Bennett-60* test set.

data and lists of affixes, but we try to keep that to a minimum and used many existing resources to expand the dataset. However, the system does not require an internal lexicon at runtime and is capable of finding morphemes that is unseen in the training set and the affix lists. For example, many correcly identified morphemes shown in Table 3 such as *boly*, *topia*, *mony*, and *glot* are unseen morphemes. This shows by leveraging the set of rich features, the system provides a surprisingly high level of generality based on a relatively small training set.

## Future work and summary

Many future research directions present themselves. We could handle cases where suffixes and words are not simply concatenated. For that, appending *ous* to *carnivore* should produces *carnivorous* instead of *carnivoreous*. A set of rules can be learned by using the manually annotated *Celex*. The same set of rules can also be used in runtime, to restore the segmented word roots to its original form. For example, after segmenting *advocation* into *ad+voc+at+ion*, we could modify *at+ion* into *ate+ion*, so that we can look up the meaning of the root *ate* in a affix dictionary. Additionally, an interesting direction to explore is incorporating more features in the CRF model. Statistics related to a prefix and the next letters (e.g., Prefix conditional entropy), or a suffix and preceding letter could be used as additional features in an attempt to improve accuracy. Yet another direction of research would be to disambiguate the meaning of affixes and roots, based on the definition or translation of the word, using known derivatives of affixes and word roots.

In summary, we have proposed a new method for constructing a fine-grained morphological word segmenter. The method comprises of three main parts, namely generating training data using a set of annotated seed data, generating features and label for training a CRF model for fine-grained word part segmentation, and a web-based prototype system. By combining two sets of manually annotated word lists, namely *Celex-2* and *Bennett-579*, we automatically produced enlarged training and test sets for more effective training and rigourous evaluation. Our system trained with all available training data is able to segment eight out of ten test words correctly. With the trained CRF model, we construct a web-base runtime system, a service that is potentially beneficial to English learners.

## References

Baayen, R., Piepenbrock, R., and Gulikers, L. (1996). The CELEX Morphological Database, second edition.

Brent, M. R., Murthy, S. K., and Lundberg, A. (1995). Discovering morphemic suffixes a case study in MDL induction. In *The Fifth International Workshop on AI and Statistics*, pages 264–271.

Creutz, M. and Lagus, K. (2006). Morfessor in the morpho challenge. In *Proceedings of the PASCAL Challenge Workshop on Unsupervised Segmentation of Words into Morphemes*.

Fellbaum, C. (1998). *WordNet: An Electronic Lexical Database*. Language, Speech, and Communication. MIT Press.

Gaussier, E. (1999). Unsupervised learning of derivational morphology from inflectional lexicons. In *Proceedings of ACL Workshop on Unsupervised Learning in Natural Language Processing*.

Gdaniec, C. and Manandise, E. (2002). Using word formation rules to extend mt lexicons. In *Proceedings of the 5th Conference of the Association for Machine Translation in the Americas on Machine Translation: From Research to Real Users*, AMTA '02, pages 64–73, London, UK. Springer-Verlag.

Goldsmith, J. (1997). *Unsupervised learning of the morphology of a natural language*. University of Chicago.

Goldsmith, J. (2001). Unsupervised learning of the morphology of a natural language. *Computational Linguistics*, 27(2):153–198.

Koskenniemi, K. (1983). *Two-level morphology: a general computational model for word-form recognition and production*. Publications (Helsingin yliopisto. Yleisen kielitieteen laitos). University of Helsinki, Department of General Linguistics.

Nation, P. (2001). *Learning Vocabulary in Another Language*. The Cambridge Applied Linguistics Series. Cambridge University Press.

Schone, P. and Jurafsky, D. (2000). Knowledge-free induction of morphology using latent semantic analysis. In *Proceedings of the 2nd workshop on Learning language in logic and the 4th conference on Computational natural language learning - Volume 7*, ConLL '00, pages 67–72, Stroudsburg, PA, USA. Association for Computational Linguistics.

Woods, W. A. (2000). Aggressive morphology for robust lexical coverage. In *Proceedings of the sixth conference on Applied natural language processing*, ANLC '00, pages 218–223, Stroudsburg, PA, USA. Association for Computational Linguistics.

# An Efficient Technique for De-noising Sentences using Monolingual Corpus and Synonym Dictionary

Sanjay Chatterji*, Diptesh Chatterjee, Sudeshna Sarkar
Department of Computer Sc. & Engineering, Indian Institute of Technology, Kharagpur, India
e-mail: {schatt, diptesh, sudeshna}@cse.iitkgp.ernet.in

ABSTRACT
We describe a method of correcting noisy output of a machine translation system. Our idea is to consider different phrases of a given sentence, and find appropriate replacements of some of these from the frequently occurring similar phrases in the monolingual corpus. The frequent phrases in the monolingual corpus are indexed by a search engine. When looking for similar phrases we consider phrases containing words that are spelling variations of or are similar in meaning to the words in the input phrase. We use a framework where we can consider different ways of splitting a sentence into short phrases and combining them so as to get the best replacement sentence that tries to preserve the meaning meant to be conveyed by the original sentence.

## 1 Introduction

A sentence may contain a number of mistakes in the word level, phrase level and sentence level. These mistakes may be referred to as noise. Spelling mistakes, wrong lexical usage, use of inappropriate function words (like determiner, preposition, article, etc.), grammatical errors, wrong ordering of words in a sentence are some of the commonly encountered noises.

Noisy sentences are widely prevalent both in human generated sentences as well as sentences generated by a Natural Language Processing (NLP) system. The generation of noisy sentences by humans may be due to carelessness, lack of good language writing ability or lack of knowledge of spelling, vocabulary or grammar of the language. The systems which return natural language sentences as output, for example Machine Translation (MT) systems often make mistakes in the sentence. In this work, we have used a method to handle spelling errors, word choice errors, extra or missing word errors and reordering errors in the sentence using a monolingual corpus, a synonym dictionary, and a stemmer.

We have incorporated this method as a post-processing system for our Bengali to Hindi and Hindi to Bengali machine translation systems. Our base translation systems are imperfect and generate imperfect sentences. We analyzed the outputs of these systems and observed that a lot of noise can be corrected by applying this method. The evaluation results show that we are able to improve the performance of machine translation systems.

## 2 Related Work

Some work have also been done on the correction of errors of noisy sentence by finding the most appropriate replacement for each word or phrase. Willett and Angell (1983) have

*The author and the work are partially supported by Indian Language to Indian Language Machine Translation project sponsored by MCIT, DIT, Govt. of India.

*Proceedings of COLING 2012: Demonstration Papers*, pages 59–66,
COLING 2012, Mumbai, December 2012.

corrected the spellings of the words by finding the closest replacement candidate from the dictionary. The closeness of the dictionary word and the misspelled word is calculated using the count of the common trigram characters. Yannakoudakis and Fawthrop (1983) have divided the misspelled words into elements of spellings and replaced wrong elements by corrected elements.

Dahlmeier and Ng (2011) used Alternating Structure Optimization (ASO) technique for correcting grammatical errors in English article and preposition. Helping Our Own(HOO) shared task has been carried out in 2010, 2011 and 2012 to correct some particular classes of words like article, preposition, determiner, etc. of the English text and is reported by Dale and Kilgarriff (2010, 2011) and Dale et al. (2012).

The correction module has been used as pre-processing and post-processing stages of some machine translation systems. The rule based post-editing module proposed by Knight and Chander (1994) has used online resources for learning rules to correct the output of a Japanese-English machine translation system. Xia and Mccord (2004) has used automatically learned reordering rules in a hybrid English-French machine translation system.

## 3 Motivation

For correcting noisy sentences, similar to the approaches used in Statistical Machine Translation (SMT) systems, e.g., the IBM model (Brown et al., 1993; Koehn et al., 2003), may be used. But the development of a parallel corpus of noisy phrases and corresponding correct phrases is a time consuming task. However, instead of developing a parallel corpus, we wish to use monolingual corpus to improve the fluency of noisy sentences. For faithfulness, a synonym dictionary, a stemmer and phonetic mappings may be used in finding the phrases which preserves the actual meaning of the noisy phrases. The algorithm should have the ability to account for different classes of errors such as, Preposition, Postpossition or suffix errors, Spelling errors, Word form, Redundancy, Missing Word, Word Choice, Word ordering, etc.

## 4 Our Approach

Our approach to correcting noise in the sentences consists of correcting noise in the phrases of the sentence. For this, we split the sentence into small phrases. We make use of a n-gram language model obtained from a monolingual corpus. Frequent phrases in the language model that are similar to an input phrase are considered as candidates replacement for that phrase.

The function used to split the sentence into small phrases and for combining their candidates is discussed in Subsection 4.1 and the searching of the suitable candidate phrases in the corpus for the small phrases of the sentence is discussed in Subsection 4.2.

### 4.1 Spliting and Combining Phrases

Consider a sentence of $N$ words: $S = w_1 w_2 \ldots w_N$; where $w_i$ is the $i^{th}$ word of the sentence. A phrase in the sentence is of the form $P_{ij} = w_i w_{(i+1)} \ldots w_j$, where $1 \leq i \leq j \leq n$. The length of $P_{ij}$ phrase is $(j - i + 1)$. This phrase can be split into two phrases $P_{il}$ and $P_{(l+1)j}$ in different ways for $i \leq l < j$. A $m$-word phrase can thus be split in 2 sub-phrases in $m - 1$ ways. Each of these sub-phrases may be further split in the same way.

While considering each phrase of the sentence if the phrase is a short phrase its replacement candidates (candidates) can be found from the language model created from the monolingual corpus. For any phrase (short or long), we also consider combining the candidates of sub-phrases of every possible decompositions of that phrase. All these possible candidates will be considered for selecting the best candidate of the phrase. This module can be implemented using a dynamic programming method and a triangular matrix data structure. Each cell in the triangular matrix is a placeholder of a phrase of the sentence. An example triangular matrix for a four word sentence is shown in Figure 1.

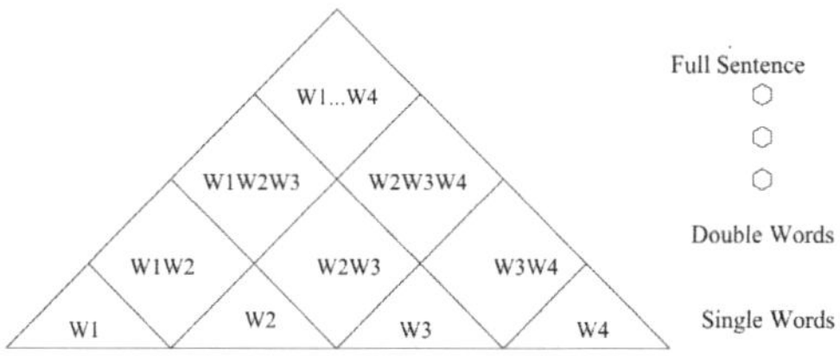


Figure 1: Triangular Matrix for a 4-word Sentence.

In the cell corresponding to a phrase, we store a list of candidates for that phrase. Candidate lists for lower length phrases of the sentence are stored at the lower level. In our bottom-up approach, members of the lower level cells are used to find the members of higher level cells. The basic algorithm is presented in Algorithm 1.

**Algorithm 1** DynamicFind(Sentence) // Finds corrected forms of the Sentence.

**INPUT:** Sentence $S = w_1, w_2, ..., w_N$
**Data Structure:** $R$ = Upper Triangle of a Square Matrix, $K = 5$
**for** $n$=1 to $N$ **do** {/*n indicates the length of the phrase*/}
  **for** start=1 to $N - n + 1$ **do** {/*start is the starting index of the n length phrase*/}
    **if** $n == 1$ **then** {/* Phrase of length 1 */}
      R[start][start] = FIND_BEST_SUB(($P_{start,start}$, $K$); /* Returns K candidates of $P_{start,start}$ phrase */
    **else**
      end = start+$n$ − 1; /* end is the ending index of the n length phrase */
      **if** $n \leq k$ **then** {/*Short phrase*/}
        R[start][end] ← FIND_BEST_SUB($P_{start,end}$, $K$)
      **end if**
      **for** j=start to end-1 **do**
        P1 ← R[start][j]; P2 ← R[j+1][end]; P3 ← COMBINE(P1,P2)
        R[start][end] ← KBEST(P3, R[start][end],K)
      **end for**
    **end if**
  **end for**
**end for**
Return R[1][N]

COMBINE(P1,P2): Concatenates all the phrases of $P1$ with all the phrases of $P2$ and combine their corresponding values.
KBEST($L_1$,$L_2$,K): Finds K best members among the members of two lists: $L_1$ and $L_2$.

In this algorithm, $S$ is an input noisy sentence of $N$ words. $P_{start,end}$ is a phrase, where *start* and *end* are starting and ending indices in the sentence. $n$ is the length of the phrase, where $n = end - start + 1$. For each short phrases the candidates along with their values computed by the substitute method discussed in the next subsection are stored in the corresponding bottom level cells of $R$.

Each multi word phrase is broken into a pair of sub-phrases. The variable $j$ indicates the intermediate point or partition point of the phrase. So, two sub-phrases of $P_{start,end}$ are: one of index *start* to $j$ and another of index $j + 1$ to *end*. A pair of candidate lists for each pair of sub-phrases are taken from previous level cells of the triangular matrix and stored in $P1$ and $P2$, respectively. The `COMBINE` function concatenates all the members of $P1$ with all the members of $P2$ and combine their values and store in $P3$.

For each short multi-word phrases, two candidate lists computed by substitute method and `COMBINE` function are sorted and top $K$ are selected by the `KBEST` function. These are stored into the corresponding cells of the $R$ matrix. The algorithm returns the members of the top cell of the $R$ matrix as the most relevant corrected sentence.

## 4.2 Computing the Phrase Substitutes

All phrases of length 1 to K of monolingual corpus are stored in a language model along with their frequencies. Given a short phrase from the noisy sentence, we have to search for the short phrases in the language model which are frequent and similar to the noisy sentence phrase. These searched phrases are candidates of the noisy sentence phrase.

### 4.2.1 Scoring Function

For each short phrase of the sentence, we define the following scoring function, based on the practical scoring function defined by Hatcher et al. (2010) in Lucene search engine, to find suitable candidate phrases from the language model.

$$score(q,p) = coord(q,p) \sum_{t \in q} \{tf(t,p)\ idf(t)^2\}\ BoostValue(p,l) \tag{1}$$

Here, $q$ is the query phrase of the sentence. $p$ is a phrase of length $l$ in language model, which is being considered currently. The components of equation 1 are explained below.

(i) Coordination factor $coord(q,p)$ indicates how many of query terms (words) are found in $p$. Length of query phrases and values of this function are both between 1 to $k$.

(ii) For term frequency $tf(t,p)$ we use square root of frequency of the query term $t$ in $p$.

(iii) For inverse document frequency $idf(t)$ we have used the inverse of the number of phrases in which the query term $t$ appears.

(iv) As we have mentioned earlier, we want to find those similar phrases which have highest frequency in the language model. So, we want to boost the score according to the frequency of the phrase. However, frequencies of the shorter phrases are not directly comparable with that of the longer phrases. Therefore, boost of a phrase is calculated with the help of the frequency of that phrase in the corpus and the length of the phrase.

### 4.2.2 Handling Variations

For finding suitable candidate phrases for each short phrase of noisy sentence, it does not suffice to only search for the frequent exact phrases in the language model which are similar to the input phrase. We need to search other variations of the words of this short phrase, e.g., spelling variation, morphological variation and lexical variation. We have developed a unified approach to handle all these effectively. This approach consisting of indexing several variations of each input phrase, and considering these variations for retrieval.

**Indexing**
This is done by indexing each phrase at several different levels, apart from indexing the original phrase. At the phonetic level, a phrase consisting of phonetically normalized words of the original phrase is indexed. At the morphological level, the phrase consisting of stemmed words of the original phrase is indexed, and at the lexical level, the phrase consisting of the synonym group IDs of the words in the original phrase is indexed.

**Retrieval**
Given an input phrase, $K$ similar phrases are retrieved at various levels – unaltered, morphological, phonetic, and lexical. We define four coefficients: $c_{word}$, $c_{stem}$, $c_{pm}$ and $c_{id}$ for these four searches, respectively and multiplied the scores of the searches with the corresponding coefficients. The top K phrases at each level are identified by using the scoring function shown in equation 1.

# 5 Experimental Results

In our experiments, we have considered that the length of short phrases is between 1 and 5. Further, the length of the indexed phrases is between 1 and 5. The values of $c_{word}$, $c_{stem}$, $c_{pm}$ and $c_{id}$ coefficients are experimentally set as 10, 8, 6, and 6, respectively. The value of $K$ is considered as 10.

## 5.1 Experimental Setup

The proposed approach is implemented for Hindi and Bengali languages. We have used following resources and modules for this task.

(i) Hindi and Bengali monolingual corpus crawled from the web and cleaned. The size of these two corpus are 300K and 430K sentences, respectively.

(ii) Hindi and Bengali synonym dictionaries divide words into some groups of synonyms.

(iii) Hindi and Bengali longest suffix stripper for stemming.

(iv) Hindi and Bengali words to phonetic word map table similar to the one proposed by UzZaman and Khan (2005).

## 5.2 Analysis with example

We now show how the system performed on some Hindi written sentences. The Hindi sentences are represented in itrans format with the word by word translation in square bracket. For every Hindi sentence, we show the English translation of the intended sentence. Then, the final sentence output by our system is given where the correct modifications are shown in boldface, and the incorrect modifications are underlined. Finally, we present a summary of the modifications.

1. **Original Hindi sentence (OH) :** mujhe le.DakA **ko** pasanda AYA. [To-Me Boy To Like Came]
   **Intended meaning in English (E) :** I liked the boy.
   **Final sentence (FH) :** mujhe le.DakA pasanda **AyA**. [To-Me Boy Like Came ]
   **Summary of Modifications(SM) :** Deleted postposition 'ko'. Changed spelling of 'AYA'.

2. **OH:** merA hindI AchchhA nahI. [My Hindi Good Not]
   **E:** My Hindi is not good.
   **FH:** merA ye hindI **achchhA** nahI **hai.** [My This Hindi Good Not is]
   **SM:** Inserted pronoun 'ye' and verb 'hai'. Changed spelling of 'AchchhA'.

3. **OH:** mere yahA.N Ane kA kAraNa hai mai.N khAnA chAhatA hai. [My Here Come 's Reason Is I Eat Want Is]
   **E:** The reason why I came here is I wanted to eat something.
   **FH:** mere yahA.N Ane kA kAraNa **yaha** hai **ki** jo mai.N khAnA chAhatA **thA**. [My Here Come 's Reason This Is That What I Eat Want Was]
   **SM:** Inserted 'yaha', 'ki' and 'jo'. Replace 'hai' by 'thA'.

### 5.3 An Application to postprocessing of sentences obtained through Machine Translation

The proposed approach is applied to correct the output of two imperfect transfer based Machine Translation systems, the BHMT system translates Bengali sentences to Hindi, whereas the HBMT system translates from Hindi to Bengali. The proposed approach has improved the quality of the output of both the systems in terms of both perplexity and BLEU scores. The results can be seen in Table 1.

| | BHMT system | Modified System | HBMT system | Modified System |
|---|---|---|---|---|
| Perplexity | 34.243 | 27.811 | 39.612 | 35.862 |
| BLEU | 0.232 | 0.243 | 0.218 | 0.227 |

Table 1: Scores of MT output and proposed modifications.

## 6 Conclusion

We have presented a unified approach for correcting different types of noise in a sentence. We are able to handle major classes of noise, though we are not able to handle long range re-orderings. This approach is general and can be used for any language. The resources needed are minimal and can be easily obtained.

There is a need for more experiments, better tuning of the scoring model, and testing on different sources of noisy sentences.

**Acknowledgments**
We would like to thank all the annotators of Communication Empowerment Lab, IIT Kharagpur, for their active participation in the development of corpus. We extend special thanks to Dr. Rajendra Prasath for helping in data mining related tasks.

## References


Brown, P. F., Pietra, V. J., Pietra, S. A. D., and Mercer, R. L. (1993). The mathematics of statistical machine translation: Parameter estimation. *Computational Linguistics*, 19:263–311.

Dahlmeier, D. and Ng, H. T. (2011). Grammatical error correction with alternating structure optimization. In *ACL*, pages 915–923.

Dale, R., Anisimoff, I., and Narroway, G. (2012). Hoo 2012: A report on the preposition and determiner error correction shared task. In *Proceedings of the Seventh Workshop on Building Educational Applications Using NLP*, pages 54–62, Montréal, Canada. Association for Computational Linguistics.

Dale, R. and Kilgarriff, A. (2010). Helping Our Own: Text massaging for computational linguistics as a new shared task. In *Proceedings of the 6th International Natural Language Generation Conference*, pages 261–266, Dublin, Ireland.

Dale, R. and Kilgarriff, A. (2011). Helping Our Own: The HOO 2011 pilot shared task. In *Proceedings of the 13th European Workshop on Natural Language Generation*, pages 242–249, Nancy, France.

Hatcher, E., Gospodnetic, O., and McCandless, M. (2010). *Lucene in Action*. Manning, 2nd revised edition.

Knight, K. and Chander, I. (1994). Automated postediting of documents. In *AAAI*, pages 779–784.

Koehn, P., Och, F. J., and Marcu, D. (2003). Statistical phrase-based translation. In *Proceedings of the 2003 Conference of the North American Chapter of the Association for Computational Linguistics on Human Language Technology - Volume 1*, pages 48–54, Stroudsburg, PA, USA. Association for Computational Linguistics.

UzZaman, N. and Khan, M. (2005). A double metaphone encoding for bangla and its application in spelling checker. In *Proc. 2005 IEEE International Conference on Natural Language Processing and Knowledge Engineering*.

Willett, P. and Angell, R. (1983). Automatic spelling correction using a trigram similarity measure. *Information Processing & Management 19*, pages 255–261.

Xia, F. and Mccord, M. (2004). Improving a Statistical MT System with Automatically Learned Rewrite Patterns. In *Proceedings of Coling 2004*, pages 508–514, Geneva, Switzerland. COLING.

Yannakoudakis, E. J. and Fawthrop, D. (1983). The rules of spelling errors. *Information Processing And Management*, 19(2):87–99.

# An Example-based Japanese Proofreading System for Offshore Development

***Yuchang CHENG  Tomoki NAGASE***
Speech & Language Technologies Laboratory of Media Processing Systems Laboratories
FUJITSU LABORATORIES LTD.
4-1-1 Kamikodanaka, Nakahara-ku, Kawasaki, Kanagawa 211-8588, Japan
**cheng.yuchang**@jp.fujitsu.com, **nagase.tomoki**@jp.fujitsu.com

ABSTRACT

More than 70% of Japanese IT companies are engaged in the offshore development of their products in China. However, a decrease in the quality of the accompanying Japanese engineering documentation has become a serious problem due to errors in Japanese grammar. A proofreading system is therefore required for offshore development cases. The goal of this research is to construct an automatic proofreading system for the Japanese language that can be used in offshore development. We considered an example-based proofreading approach that can effectively use our proofreading corpus and simultaneously process multiple types of error. There are three main steps in the proofreading system. They are the search step, the check step and the replace step. We will make a demostration for the proofreading system and simulated the use of our example-based approach. The results show that using the entire corpus can reduce the errors by over 66%.

Title and abstract in another language (Japanese)

# オフショア開発向けの日本語自動校正システム

概要

近年，日本企業からのオフショア開発が増加傾向にある．オフショア開発では，外国人の執筆する日本語文書の品質確保が課題であり，校正作業がコストを押し上げている．そのため，自動校正システムの実用化が期待されている．本研究ではオフショア開発向けの日本語自動校正システムの開発を目的として，校正履歴コーパスを効果的に利用して，1文中で複数の誤用を同時に検出できる事例ベースの校正手法を提案した．事例ベースの校正システムは校正履歴コーパスを持つ．校正処理は，まず，処理対象文の単語依存構造をキーとし，校正履歴コーパスに同じ単語依存構造を持つ事例を検索する．その後，検索結果の適用候補事例に対し，単語の表記と意味概念情報を用いて事例が処理対象文の校正に適用できるかどうかを確認する．最後は，チェックされた適用事例候補を用いて，校正事例の修正方法と同様に処理対象文を校正する．提案手法の効果を検証するため，本デモはは事例ベースの自動校正手法を展示し、その効果をシミュレーションした．その結果，校正履歴コーパス全体を事例として本手法を適用することにより，誤り全体の66%を校正できることを示す．

---

KEYWORDS : Error correct system, proofread system, offshore development, detect the misuse in Japanese
KEYWORDS IN $L_2$ : 文章校正，日本語誤用の検出，オフショア開発

---

## 1 Condensed Version in L2－オフショア開発向けの日本語自動校正システム

本稿では，オフショア開発向けの日本語自動校正システムの開発を目的として，校正履歴コーパスを効果的に利用して，1文中で複数の誤用を同時に検出できる事例ベースの校正手法を提案した．

我々は中国人技術者の執筆した日本語技術文書の校正履歴をもとに，外国語母語話者による日本語誤用パターンの分析を行った(Cheng, 2012)．TABLE 2に誤り分類の種類と定義をまとめる．技術文書の校正において，最も誤りの頻度が高い助詞変更の校正が最重要課題である．しかし，助詞の校正が文の他の部分に影響を受ける場合や語彙誤用など校正方法が文脈に依存する場合，人手で誤りのパターンを一般化して校正ルールを作成することが困難である．そこで，我々は校正履歴をそのままシステムが読み込んで文書校正が動作する事例ベースの校正手法を考案した．事例ベースの校正手法では大量の校正例が必要であるが，実際のオフショア開発会社において業務の中で蓄積された大量の校正履歴を入手することにより，この校正手法を実現できる．

デモを行う事例ベースの校正システム（FIGURE **1**参照）はTABLE 1のような事例からなる校正履歴コーパスを持つ．校正処理は，1) 事例の検索，2) 事例のチェック，および 3) 対象文の書き直しのステップからなる．

まず，ステップ 1) では，処理対象文の単語依存構造をキーとし，校正履歴コーパスに同じ単語依存構造を持つ事例を検索する．検索条件によって複数の事例が適用候補になることがある．

ステップ 2) では，ステップ1の検索結果の適用候補事例に対し，事例が処理対象文の校正に適用できるかどうかを確認する．この場合は，処理対象文と校正事例（修正前の文）との共通部分が事例中の校正部分に似ているかどうかを確認する．適用可否を判定する際，単語の表記と意味概念情報を用いて対応部分の一致度を計算する．一致度の計算には単語の表記と意味概念情報に関する係数があり，係数は会社や業種に依存する．文の重複部分に修正が含まれない候補事例は処理対象文の校正に適用できないと判断され，適用事例候補から削除される．

ステップ 3) では，ステップ 2でチェックされた適用事例候補を用いて，校正事例の修正方法と同様に処理対象文を校正する．

事例ベースの校正手法の最大効果を調べるため，事例ベース手法の再現率に関するシミュレーションを行った（TABLE 3，TABLE 4参照）．異なる事例数をランダムで選択し，校正ステップに従いテスト事例に対する再現率を測った結果，校正コーパス全体を使用すると，誤用の66%が校正できることが判明した．

| | |
|---|---|
| Before proofreading sentence: | 引数<u>*の*</u>エンコード<u>*転換は*</u>されていない<br>(There is no code-converting of the argument.) |
| After proofreading sentence: | 引数<u>*が*</u>エンコード<u>*変換[DELETE]*</u>されていない<br>(The argument is not code-converted.) |

TABLE 1 – a proofreading example of the corpus.(校正履歴の例)

| Category | Definitions of the proofreading types(校正の分類) | Count |
|---|---|---|
| Category 1<br>Proofreading the errors that are interfere with understanding context (文脈の理解に支障が出る誤りの校正)<br>(Total count: 1060 / 8404 = 11%) | Erratum and omission of a word (誤字，脱字) | 316 |
| | Alphabet misspelling (スペルミス) | 49 |
| | The ambiguity between Chinese and Japanese (日中混同) | 142 |
| | Voiced sound, long vowel, and mis-pronunciation (濁音，長音，誤発音) | 239 |
| | Semantic mistake of words (意味誤り) | 255 |
| | Kana-kanji conversion mistake (かな変換誤り) | 59 |
| Category 2<br>Proofreading the errors that Chinese native speakers usually commit (中国語母語話者が犯しやすい誤りの校正)<br>(Total count: 5096 / 8404 = 53%) | Particle addition (助詞追加) | 720 |
| | Particle deletion (助詞削除) | 401 |
| | Particle change (助詞変更) | 2907 |
| | Verb tense and aspect (動詞時制とアスペクト) | 205 |
| | Active and passive of verbs (能動と受動) | 290 |
| | Confusion of noun phrase and phrasal verb (名詞句と動詞句の混同) | 573 |
| Category 3<br>Proofreading inappropriate expressions in engineering documents (技術文書として不適切な表現の校正)<br>(Total count: 2223 / 8404 = 23%) | Chinese character, hiragana, and declensional kana ending (漢字，ひらがな，送り仮名) | 674 |
| | Colloquialism (口語) | 187 |
| | Figure and unit (数字と単位) | 123 |
| | Formal speech/Casual speech (敬体常体) | 76 |
| | Technical terms (専門語) | 267 |
| | Vocabulary meaning (語彙意味) | 896 |
| Category 4<br>Proofreading the incomprehensible sentence structure and logic (文構造と論理の校正)(Total count: 1265 / 8404 = 13%) | Shortening of verbose text (冗長短縮) | 350 |
| | Sentence structure correction (文構造修正) | 809 |
| | Information addition (情報追加) | 106 |

TABLE 2 – proofreading types and the count of correction history. (誤り分類の定義と頻度)

| Category | distribution |
|---|---|
| Category 1 | 11% |
| Category 2 | 51% |
| Category 3 | 21% |
| Category 4 | 17% |

TABLE 3 – the distribution of the testing data (テストデータの分布)

| Corpus size | Sim 1 | Sim 2 | Sim 3 | Sim 4 | Sim 5 |
|---|---|---|---|---|---|
| 0 | 0.0% | 0.0% | 0.0% | 0.0% | 0.0% |
| 1000 | 33.3% | 32.7% | 30.1% | 34.2% | 36.3% |
| 3000 | 49.7% | 53.2% | 47.1% | 55.8% | 52.9% |
| 5000 | 57.6% | 58.5% | 57.3% | 62.3% | 59.9% |
| 8082 | 65.8% | 65.8% | 65.8% | 65.8% | 65.8% |

TABLE 4 – the result of the simulation (シミュレーション結果)

## 2 Introduction

With the advancement of corporate globalization, the outsourcing of system development to foreign countries (i.e., offshore development) has increased in IT companies. More than 70% of Japanese IT companies currently have the offshore development of their products in China. With respect to offshore development in China, there is an increase in cases where native Chinese engineers are employed by the offshore vendor in both the software development phase and the design phase. This means that a large proportion of the engineering documentation, such as the specifications and technical reports, are created in Japanese by Chinese native engineers. Generally, the engineers who prepare the documentation are very proficient in Japanese. However, this has been accompanied by a decrease in the quality of the engineering documentation due to misuse of the language used by the purchaser, and the purchaser is required to manually proofread the engineering documentation. To reduce the cost of manually proofreading, there is a need for the development of a "document proofreading system" that automatically proofreads the documentation in the language of the purchaser. The goal of this research is to construct an automatic proofreading system for Japanese which can be utilized for offshore development.

Recently, proofreading technologies (or error detection, correction) have been considered as applied technologies for the machine translation and the language education. Many recent studies have focused on proofreading for English as a Second Language (ESL) learners (Izumi et al., 2003; Han et al., 2006; Gamon et al., 2008; Gamon, 2010). Other researches (Oyama and Matsumoto, 2010; Imaeda et al., 2003; Nampo et al., 2007; Suzuki and Toutanova, 2006; Mizumoto et. al, 2011) focus on errors that are more common to Japanese learners, such as case particles. The error correcting corpora used in previous works (regarding Japanese as a Second Language (JSL)) was acquired from essays, examinations, and social network services. These corpora include all types of error made by all levels of Japanese "learners." It is impractical to cover all such in the construction of a proofreading system. We assume that there are limited types of error made by the native Chinese engineers, and concentrate on some specific categories (because the engineers are not Japanese "learners").

We had analyzed a Japanese proofreading corpus that provides a history of proofreading for offshore development in China (Cheng, 2012). According to our findings, most types of errors mentioned in the proofreading corpus relate to the misuse of particles. However, the misuse of particles usually occurs together with other types of errors in the same sentence (see TABLE 1), and it is difficult to define general rules for the proofreading of these multiple types of errors. In this demo, we will make a demostration of an example-based proofreading approach for the multiple types of errors. This example-based approach requires a sample collection, and our proofreading corpus can be directly used for the example-based approach. We can adopt the example-based approach in English or any other language, as long as there is a proofreading corpus in the language.

## 3 An introduction of Japanese proofreading corpus in offshore development

We had analyzed the Chinese native engineers' misuse tendency of Japanese in the proofreading corpus (Cheng, 2012). The corpus is a history of proofreading written by a native Japanese proofreader who has experience in the correction of engineering documents prepared by native Chinese engineers in offshore development. Our proofreading corpus includes 8404 examples, which were collected from 519 documents. These documents were prepared by 20 engineers who have successfully passed the N1 level of the Japanese-Language Proficiency Test (JLPT:

http://www.jlpt.jp/e/guideline/testsections.html). We assume that the error tendencies noted in these documents normally occur in all of the engineering documentation in the offshore development industry.

A proofreading example contained in the proofreading corpus is shown in TABLE 1. The proofreading example includes the before proofreading sentence and the result after manual proofreading. Many of the proofreading examples involved multiple types of error like this example in the proofreading corpus. We classified the proofreading examples and investigated the distribution of the proofreading types in the corpus.

TABLE 2 shows the distribution of the proofreading corpus. The largest category of the proofreading is Category 2 that occupies about 53% (5096/9644) more than the entire half. Category 2 includes the proofreading of particles and the verb. This observation is similar to previous work (Oyama, 2010), but we found that the ratio of this type of error in the proofreading corpus is more than in Japanese learner's error data. The next largest is Category 3 that occupies the entire 23% (2223/9644). Category 4 accounts for 13% of the whole, and Category 1 accounts for 11% of the whole. Because Category 2 errors occur most frequently, we know that although the engineers have high Japanese proficiency, it is difficult to become proficient in the usage of particles and verbs.

## 4 The Demostrating System – An Example-based proofreading approach

Many examples of our proofreading corpus include multiple types of errors in a single sentence. It is difficult to introduce rules for proofreading multiple types of errors. By contrast, our corpus is not large enough for normal machine learners, because some proofreading examples occur only once and it causes the data sparse problem. To effectively use our proofreading corpus, we considered an example-based proofreading approach instead of using the machine-learning approach.

### 4.1 The system flowchart

FIGURE **1** shows the system flowchart and the process of proofreading. This system includes a proofreading corpus, which includes the original sentence (it includes error or misuse) and the proofreading result. The system proofreads wide types of errors and misuse by searching the corpus to find the useful examples. There are three main steps in the proofreading system. They are the search step (the part ③ in FIGURE **1**), the check step (the part ④ in FIGURE **1**) and the replace step (the part ⑤ in FIGURE **1**). The flow of the proofreading approach is described as the following paragraph.

The target proofreading documents are inputted into the system, and then the system divides the document to sentences and processes the sentences respectively (the part ① in FIGURE **1**). Then the system will do several processes to require information for proofreading (the part ② in FIGURE **1**).

These processes include morphological analysis, dependency parsing and the Semantic analysis. In the part ③ (search step), the system searches the proofreading corpus to find the useful examples for the proofreading, here the system will use the morphological and dependency information to search. The search results possibly have more than one example.

In the part ④, the system checks the search example in search step by estimating the similarity of the words in the target sentence and the proofreading examples. If there is no similar example in part ③ and ④ (after check step, it is possible that the searching results are rejected), the system will back to the part ② to process the next target sentence. If the search results pass the check step, the proofreading example can be used to proofread the target sentence.

In part ⑤ (replace step), the system will refer to the before sentence and the after sentence of the proofreading example to proofreading the target sentence. This means that the system will do "similar" proofreading to the target as the proof-reader was done in the example. Then the system outputs the proofreading results of the target sentence. In next section, we describe more detail about the main steps of the proofreading system.

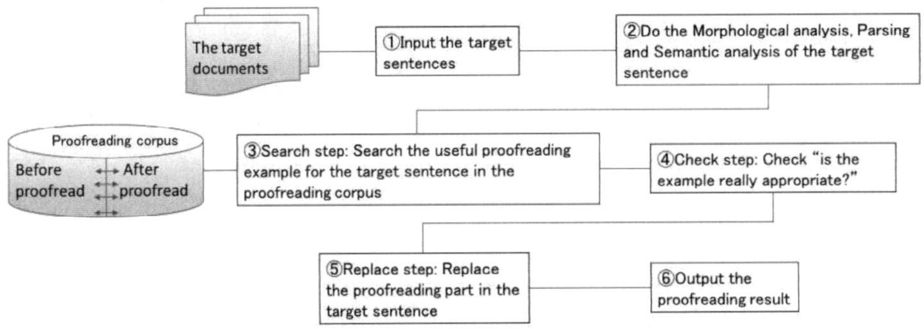


FIGURE 1 – The flowchart of our example-based proofreading system.

## 4.2 The main steps of the example-based approach

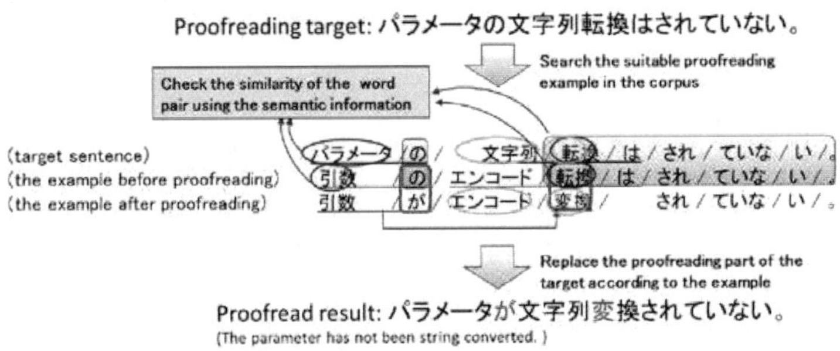


FIGURE 2 – an example of the example-based proofreading approach

FIGURE 2 shows an example of the example-based proofreading approach. The input sentence "パラメータの文字列転換はされていない. (The parameter has not been string converted.)" is the proofreading target. The system analysed the target sentence, than searched the corpus and found a possibly useful example "Before: 引数のエンコード転換はされていない → After: 引数がエンコード変換されていない(The argument is not converted the encoding.)". Then the system proofread the target sentence using the similar replacement in the example. That is, changing the particle "の(no)" in the target to the particle "が(ga)", changing the word "転換(convert)" to the word "変換(convert)", and deleting the particle "は(ha)". Therefore, the target sentence became to "パラメータが文字列変換されていない(The parameter has not been string converted. )". In our approach, if the proofreading example occurs once in the corpus, the system can use the example to proofread a new "similar" sentence. Therefore this approach can use the proofreading corpus efficiency.

**Search Step: "Is there any useful proofreading example for the target sentence in the proofreading corpus?"**

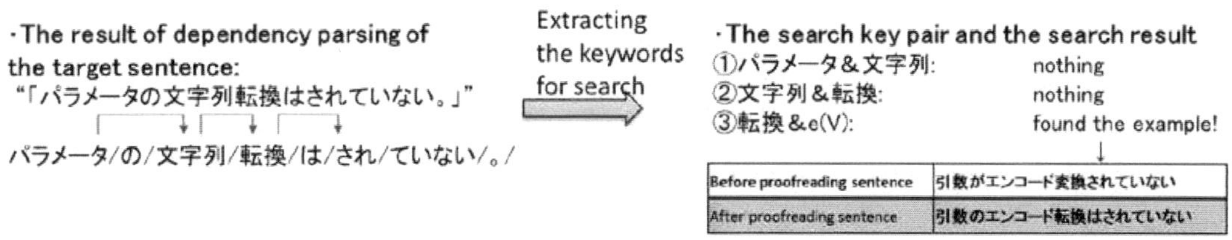


FIGURE **3** – The search key word of the target sentence and its rearch results

In this step, the system uses the dependency analysis results of the target sentence. FIGURE **3** shows the search keywords and the search result. The system used the substantives and the declinable words that have dependency relations in the target sentence to search the corpus. The proofreading examples in the corpus should also be analyzed with respect to the dependency structure and semantic structure. It should be noted that the system does not only search the string of the keywords, but also searches the morphological information and semantic information of words, such as the keyword pair ③. If the before proofreading sentence has a dependency relation that is similar to the keyword pair, the example is selected as a candidate for proofreading the target sentences. FIGURE **3** has only one search result, which is the example in TABLE 1. If there is no search result, the system reverts to part ② in FIGURE **1** to process the next target sentence.

**Check Step: "Is the example really appropriate?"**

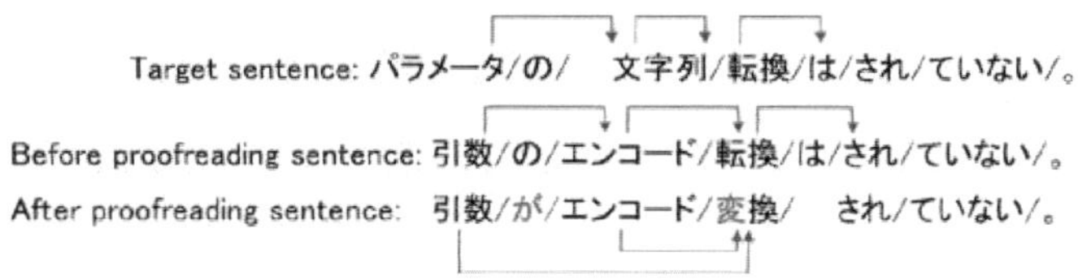


FIGURE **4** – The dependency structure of target, and before / after sentences

After searching the corpus, some (possibly) useful examples for proofreading were found. However, not all of these examples are useful for proofreading. In this step, the system checks two conditions regarding the example. The conditions are "Is the example similar to the target sentence?" and "Can the target replace the example?" Considering the example in FIGURE **4**, the target sentence should be similar to the before proofreading sentence. Also, there should be parts of the target sentence that can be replaced to change the before proofreading sentence to the after proofreading sentence.

For checking the first condition, the system considers the similarity of the corresponding words in the dependency structure between the target sentence and the before proofreading sentence. In this case, the system checked the word pair "パラメータ (parameter) / 引数 (argument)" and "文字列 (string) / エンコード (encoding)". The similarity of the word pair is calculated according to the following equation:

- $\text{Similarty} = \alpha \times \text{Txt} \div \text{WordLen} + \beta \times \text{Syn} + \gamma \times \text{Sem}$

Where:

- α, β, γ : The coefficients that can be changed for different proofreading corpus and manual tuning
- Txt: The edit distance between the words
- WordLen: The count of the character of the words
- Syn: The distance between the words in the dependency structure.
- Sem: The distance of the semantic class between the words, it can be tuning manually

If the similarity is smaller than a threshold value, the proofreading example will be excluded. The threshold value can be set manually for different situation, such as the different industry, company or project. In this case, the word pair "パラメータ (parameter) / 引数 (argument)" and "文字列 (string) / エンコード (encoding)" have similar usage in this offshore vendor.

To check the second condition, the system compares the morphological sequences of the before proofreading sentence and the after proofreading sentence. In FIGURE **4**, the sub-sequence "引数 (argument) / の(no) /" is changed to "引数(argument) / が(ga)/", and the sub-sequence "転換 (convert) / は(ha) /" is changed to "変換(convert)". Then, the system can use the sub-sequence in before proofreading sentence to rewrite the sub-sequence in the target sentence. If there is no need for the rewritten sub-sequence in the proofreading example, this example will be excluded.

**Replace Step: Replace the proofreading part in the target sentence**

After the checking step, the remaining examples can be used to proofread the target sentence. The sub-sequence that is rewritten in the proofreading example can be used for proofreading. Considering the case in FIGURE **2**, the system can proofread the words "パラメータ/の/" to "パラメータ/が/", and the sub-sequence "引数 (argument)/の(no)/" is changed to "引数/が(ga)/". Then, the system replaces all replaceable sub-sequences and outputs the proofreading result "パラメータが文字列変換されていない. (The parameter has not been string converted)."

## 5 System performance – a simulation

As described in section 4.2, the system requires several coefficients for the check step. However, the coefficients and threshold value need to be tuned, but this is currently difficult, as more examples are required for tuning. In this paper, we made a simulation that can estimate the upper limit of the recall. This simulation followed the approach that we described in section 4, but the check step is performed manually. That is, when the system checked the similarity between words, we judge the word pair manually.

The testing data, which includes 324 examples, is a part of our proofreading corpus. The distribution of the testing data is shown in TABLE 3 and is similar to the distribution of the whole corpus. The remaining part of the corpus (8080 examples) is used to proofread the testing data.

We repeated the simulation five times, and the results are shown in TABLE 4 (from the column "Sim 1" to "Sim 5"). To investigate the relationship between the scope of the proofreading and the size of the proofreading corpus, we randomly selected sentences in several sizes from the proofreading corpus in each simulation. The sizes are shown in the first column in TABLE 4. TABLE 4 shows that use of the entire corpus can reduce 66% of the errors. The proofreading result obtained by using a random part of the corpus is homogeneous. We can consider that the distribution of the entire corpus is also homogeneous.

## References


Yuchang, Cheng and Tomoki, nagase. (2012). Analysis of proofreading history intended for Japanese engineering document that foreign language speaker written (In Japanese). In *Proceedings of the 18rd Annual Meeting of the Association for Natural Language Processing,* pages 34–37, The Association for Natural Language Processing (Japan)

Elghafari, A., Meurers, D., & Wunsch, H. (2010). Exploring the data-driven prediction of prepositions in English. In *Proceedings of the 23rd International Conference on Computational Linguistics: Posters, (COLING'10),* pages 267–275, Stroudsburg, PA, USA, Association for Computational Linguistics.

De Felice, R., & Pulman, S. G. (2008). A Classifier-Based Approach to Preposition and Determiner Error Correction in L2 English. In *Proceedings of the 22nd International Conference on Computational Linguistics (Coling 2008),* pages 169–176, Manchester, UK: Coling 2008 Organizing Committee.

Gamon, M., Gao, J., Brockett, C., & Klementiev, R. (2008). Using contextual speller techniques and language modeling for ESL error correction. In *Proceedings of 4th International Joint Conference on Natural Language Processing (IJCNLP 2008),* pages 449-456, Hyderabad, India, Asian Federation of Natural Language Processing.

Han, N.-R., Chodorow, M., & Leacock, C. (2006). Detecting errors in English article usage by non-native speakers. *In Journal Natural Language Engineering archive, Vol. 12, Issue 2*, pages 115-129, Cambridge University Press New York, NY, USA

Koji Imaeda, Atsuo Kawai, Yuji Ishikawa, Ryo Nagata, and Fumito Masui. (2003). *Error Detection and Correction of Case particles in Japanese Learner's Composition (in japanese).* In Proceedings of the Information Processing Society of Japan SIG, pages 39–46.

Hiromi Oyama and Yuji Matsumoto. (2010). *Automatic Error Detection Method for Japanese Case Particles in Japanese Language Learners.* In Corpus, ICT, and Language Education, page 235–245.

Hiromi Oyama. (2010). Automatic Error Detection Method for Japanese Particles. Polyglossia Volume 18, (p 55-63).

IPA (2012). *the Annual report of IT Human Resources Development in 2012 (in Japanese)* , http://www.ipa.go.jp/jinzai/jigyou/docs/ITjinzai2012_Hires.pdf

Izumi, E., Uchimoto, K., Saiga, T., Supnithi, T., & Isahara, H. (2003). Automatic error detection in the Japanese learners' English spoken data. In *Proceedings of the 41st Annual Meeting on Association for Computational Linguistics (ACL'03)*, pages 145–148, Stroudsburg, PA, USA.

Mizumoto, T., Komachi, M., Nagata, M., & Matsumoto, Y. (2011). Mining Revision Log of Language Learning SNS for Automated Japanese Error Correction of Second Language Learners. In *Proceedings of 5th International Joint Conference on Natural Language Processing (IJCNLP 2011),* pages 147–155, Chiang Mai, Thailand: Asian Federation of Natural Language Processing.

Suzuki, H., & Toutanova, K. (2006). Learning to predict case markers in Japanese. In *Proceedings of the 21st International Conference on Computational Linguistics and the 44th annual meeting of the Association for Computational Linguistics (ACL'06)*, pages 1049–1056,

Stroudsburg, PA, USA, Association for Computational Linguistics.

Tetreault, J., Foster, J., & Chodorow, M. (2010). Using parse features for preposition selection and error detection. In *Proceedings of the ACL 2010 Conference Short Papers (ACLShort'10)*, pages 353–358, Stroudsburg, PA, USA, Association for Computational Linguistics.

# DomEx: Extraction of Sentiment Lexicons for Domains and Meta-Domains

*Ilia Chetviorkin*[1] *Natalia Loukachevitch*[2]
(1) Faculty of Computational Mathematics and Cybernetics,
Lomonosov Moscow State University,
Moscow, Leninskiye Gory 1, Building 52
(2) Research Computing Center,
Lomonosov Moscow State University,
Moscow, Leninskiye Gory 1, Building 4
ilia.chetviorkin@gmail.com, louk_nat@mail.ru

ABSTRACT

In this paper we describe a DomEx sentiment lexicon extractor, where a new approach for domain-specific sentiment lexicon extraction is implemented. Sentiment lexicon extraction is based on the machine learning model comprising a set of statistical and linguistic features. The extraction model is trained in the movie domain and then can be utilized to other domains. The system can work with various domains and languages after part of speech tagging. Finally, the system gives possibility to combine the sentiment lexicons from similar domains to obtain one general lexicon for the corresponding meta-domain.

TITLE AND ABSTRACT IN RUSSIAN

# DomEx: Извлечение Оценочной Лексики для Различных Предметных Областей и Мета-Областей

В данной работе мы описываем систему для извлечения оценочных слов DomEx, в которой реализован новый подход для формирования оценочного словаря. Извлечение оценочной лексики основано на машинном обучении с использованием набора статистических и лингвистических признаков. Модель для извлечения обучается в предметной области о фильмах и затем может быть использована в других предметных областях. Система может работать с различными предметными областями и языками после этапа морфологической обработки. Наконец, система дает возможность комбинировать списки оценочных слов из похожих предметных областей для формирования одного, общего словаря для соответствующей мета-области.

KEYWORDS : Sentiment Analysis, Sentiment Lexicon, Domain Adaptation

KEYWORDS IN RUSSIAN: Анализ Тональности, Оценочные слова, Адаптация к Предметной Области

*Proceedings of COLING 2012: Demonstration Papers*, pages 77–86,
COLING 2012, Mumbai, December 2012.

В последнее время большие усилия были направлены на решение задачи анализа мнений в различных предметных областях. Автоматизированные подходы к анализу тональности могут быть полезны для государственных органов и политиков, компаний и простых пользователей. Одной из важнейших задач, являющейся основой для анализа мнений в текстах, написанных на различных языках, является создание словарей оценочных слов.

В данной демонстрационной работе мы представляем ***DomEx***, систему по извлечению оценочных слов, которая использует обученную модель для извлечения оценочных слов в различных предметных областях и на различных языках, а также позволяет пользователям создавать общий словарь оценочной лексики для группы похожих областей.

Работа системы основана на нескольких текстовых коллекциях: коллекции отзывов о продуктах с оценками пользователей, коллекции описаний продуктов и контрастной коллекции (например, новостная коллекция). Такие коллекции могут быть автоматически сформированы для разных предметных областей. Кроме того, мы предположили, что можно выделить некоторые части корпуса мнений (например, о фильмах), в которых концентрация оценочных слов выше: предложения, заканчивающиеся на «!» или «...»; короткие предложения не более чем из 7 слов; предложения, содержащие слово «фильм» без других существительных. Условно назовем это корпус – малый корпус.

Для каждого слова в коллекции отзывов мы вычисляем набор лингвистических и статистических признаков:

- Частотные: частотность в коллекции (т.е. сколько раз слово встретилось во всей коллекции); документная частотность; частотность слов с большой буквы; «странность» (Ahmad et al., 2009); TFIDF.
- На основании оценки пользователя: отклонение от средней оценки; дисперсия оценки слова; вероятность встретить заданное слово с каждой из оценок.

Также был добавлен набор из лингвистических признаков, так как они играют важную роль в улучшении качества извлечения оценочных слов:

- Четыре бинарных признака для частей речи (существительное, прилагательное, глагол и наречие).
- Два бинарных признака, первый, отражающий неоднозначность части речи (т.е. слово может употребляться в разных частях речи, в зависимости от контекста), и второй, отражающий присутствие слова в словаре морфологического анализатора.
- Заранее заданный список приставок (например приставки “*не*”, “*бес*”, “*без*” и т.д.). Этот признак являтеся важным индикатором оценочных слов, начинающихся с отрицания.

Для обучения алгоритмов нам необходимо было размеченное множество слов. Для этого мы вручную разметили множество всех слов с частотой выше трех из предметной области о фильмах (18362 слова). Мы относили слово к категории оценочных в случае если могли представить его в каком-либо оценочном контексте.

Мы решали задачу классификации на два класса: разделение всех слов на оценочные и неоценочные. Для этих целей использовались следующие алгоритмы: *Logistic Regression*, *LogitBoost* и *Random Forest*. Все параметры алгоритмов были выставлены в соответствии с их значениями по умолчанию.

Используя данные алгоритмы, мы получили списки слов, упорядоченные по вероятности оценочности слов. Для оценки качества этих списков использовалась мера *Precision@n*. Для сравнения качества работы системы в разных предметных областях мы использовали значение n = 1000.

Мы заметили, что извлеченные списки оценочных слов существенно различаются в зависимости от алгоритма. Поэтому мы решили вычислить среднее от значений вероятностей в каждом из списков. В результате качество автоматического извлечения оценочных слов в области фильмов *Precision@1000* составило 81.5%.

Для использования системы в новой предметной области необходимо собрать аналогичный набор коллекций, как и предметной области о фильмах. Наши эксперименты в адаптации модели к другим предметным областям (книги, компьютерные игры) описаны в (Chetviorkin & Loukachevitch, 2011). Оценка качества переноса показала, что модель достаточно устойчива для использования в других областях.

Для использования нашей системы с другими языками нужно сделать несколько небольших изменений:

1. Все входные данные должны быть обработаны морфологическим анализатором для соответствующего языка. Все соответствующие тэги должны быть изменены в системе.
2. Необходимо изменить ключевое слово для извлечения потенциальных оценочных предложений при составлении малого корпуса.
3. Необходимо изменить список приставок в соответствии с обрабатываемым языком.

После таких изменений система без какого-либо дополнительного обучения может быть использована для обработки других языков.

Мы применили нашу систему для предметной области о фильмах на английском языке. Для этого использовались отзывы и описания с IMDb и новостная коллекция Reuters-21578. Используя эти коллекции, DomEx формирует вектора признаков для каждого слова и применяет модель, обученную на русскоязычных отзывах о фильмах. Качество работы системы после оценки составило 70.5% в соответствии с метрикой P@1000. Наиболее вероятными извлеченными английскими словами являются: *remarkable, recommended, overdo, understated, respected, overlook, lame*, и др. Некоторые из этих слов (например, *overlook*) являются оценочными словами только в предметной области о фильмах.

## 1 Introduction

Over the last few years a lot of efforts were made to solve sentiment analysis tasks in different domains. Automated approaches to sentiment analysis can be useful for state bodies and politicians, companies, and ordinary users. One of the important tasks, considered as a basis for sentiment analysis of documents written in a specific language, is a creation of its sentiment lexicon (Abdul-Mageed et al., 2011; Peres-Rosas et al., 2012).

Usually authors try to gather general sentiment lexicons for their languages (Mihalcea et al., 2007; Banea et al., 2008; Clematide & Klenner, 2010; Steinberger et al., 2011). However a lot of researchers stress the differences between sentiment lexicons in specific domains. For example, "must-see" is a strongly opinionated word in the movie domain, but neutral in the digital camera domain (Blitzer et al., 2007). For these reasons, supervised learning algorithms trained in one domain and applied to other domains demonstrate considerable decrease in the performance (Ponomareva & Thelwall, 2012; Read & Carroll, 2009; Taboada et al., 2011).

In many studies domain-specific sentiment lexicons are created using various types of propagation from a seed set of words, usually a general sentiment lexicon (Kanayama & Nasukawa, 2007; Lau et al., 2011; Qiu et al., 2011). In such approaches an important problem is to determine an appropriate seed lexicon for propagation, which can heavily influence the quality of the results. Besides, the propagation often lead to unclear for a human sentiment lists. So, for example, in (Lau et al., 2011) only 100 first obtained sentiment words are evaluated by experts, *precision@100* was around 80%, what means that the intrinsic quality of the extracted 4000 lexicon (as announced in the paper) can be quite low.

The sentiment lexicon extraction system presented in this demo exploits a set of statistical and linguistic measures, which can characterize domain-specific sentiment words from different sides. We combined these features into a single model using machine learning methods and trained it in the movie domain. We argue that this model incorporated into our system can be effectively transferred to other domains for extraction of their sentiment lexicons.

Stressing the differences in sentiment lexicons between domains, one should understand that domains can form clusters of similar domains. So a lot of sentiment words relevant to various product domains are not relevant to the political domain or the general news domain and vice versa. For example, such words as *evil* or *villain* are not applicable to all product domains. Therefore we suppose that gathering a specialized sentiment lexicon for meta-domains comprising several similar domains can be useful for researchers and practitioners.

In this demo paper we present ***DomEx*** sentiment lexicon extractor, which utilizes the trained extraction model to different domains and different languages and allows users to create a joint sentiment lexicon for a group of similar domains.

## 2 Training Model for Extraction of Sentiment Lexicon in a Specific Domain

Training of the sentiment lexicon model is based on several text collections, which can be automatically formed for many domains, such as: a collection of product reviews with authors' evaluation scores, a text collection of product descriptions and a contrast corpus (for example, a general news collection). For each word in the review collection we calculate a set of linguistic and statistical features using the aforementioned collections and then apply machine learning algorithms for term classification.

Our method does not require any seed words, and is rather language-independent, however, lemmatization (or stemming) and part-of speech tagging are desirable. Working with Russian language, we use a dictionary-based morphological processor, including unknown word processing. Below in the text we will say only about lemmatized words.

The basic model is constructed for the movie domain. We collected 28, 773 movie reviews of various genres from the online recommendation service *www.imhonet.ru*. For each review, user's score on a ten-point scale was extracted. We called this collection the **review collection**. We also required a contrast collection of texts for our experiments. In this collection the concentration of opinions should be as little as possible. For this purpose, we collected 17, 680 movie descriptions. This collection was named the **description collection**. One more contrast corpus was a collection of two million news documents. We had calculated a document frequency of each word in this collection and used only this frequency list further. This list was named the **news corpus**.

We also suggested that it was possible to extract some fragments of reviews from the review collection, which had higher concentration of sentiment words. These fragments may include: sentences ending with a "!"; sentences ending with a "..."; short sentences (no more than seven word length); sentences containing the word «movie» without any other nouns. We called this collection the **small collection**.

Our aim is to create a high quality list of sentiment words based on the combination of various discriminative features. We utilize the following set of features for each word:

- Frequency-based: collection frequency $f(w)$ (i.e. number of occurrences in all documents in the collection); document frequency; frequency of capitalized words; weirdness (Ahmad et al., 2009); TFIDF.
- Rating-based: deviation from the average score; word score variance; sentiment category likelihood for each *(word, category)* pair.

Some linguistic features were also added to our system because they can play crucial role in improving the sentiment lexicon extraction.

- Four binary features indicating word part of speech (noun, verb, adjective and adverb).

- Two binary features reflecting POS ambiguity (i.e. word can have various parts of speech depending on a context) and feature indicationg if this word is recognized by the POS tagger.
- Predefined list of prefixes of a word (for example, Russian prefixes "*ne*", "*bes*", "*bez*" etc. similar to English "*un*", "*in*", "*im*" etc.). This feature is a strong predictor for words starting with negation.

To train supervised machine learning algorithms we needed a set of labeled sentiment words. For our experiments we manually labeled words with the frequency greater than three in the movie review collection (18362 words). We marked up a word as a sentiment one in case we could imagine it in any opinion context in the movie domain.

We solved the two class classification problem: to separate all words into sentiment and neutral categories. For this purpose Weka[1] data mining tool was used. We considered the following algorithms: *Logistic Regression*, *LogitBoost* and *Random Forest*. All parameters in the algorithms were set to their default values.

Using this algorithms we obtained word lists, ordered by the predicted probability of their opinion orientation. To measure the quality of these lists the *Precision@n* metric was used. This metric was very convenient for measuring the quality of list combinations and it could be used with different thresholds. To compare quality of the algorithms in different domains we chose n = 1000. This level was not too large for the manual labeling and demonstrated the quality in an appropriate way. We noticed that the lists of sentiment words extracted by the algorithms differ significantly. So we decided to average word probability values in these three lists. Combining three classifiers we obtained Precision@1000 = 81.5%

As the baseline for our experiments we used the lists ordered by frequency in the review collection and deviation from the average score. *Precision@1000* in these lists was 26.9% and 35.5% accordingly. Thus our algorithms gave significant improvements over the baselines.

## 3 Model Adaptation. Meta-Domain Sentiment Lexicon

To adapt the model to a new domain it is necessary to collect similar data as for the movie domain. Our experiments in adaptation of the model to other domains (books, computer games) are described in (Chetviorkin & Loukachevitch. 2011). For all words in a particular field (excluding low frequent ones) we compute feature vectors and construct a domain word-feature matrix using them. We applied our classification model, which was trained in the movie domain, to these word-feature matrixes and manually evaluated the first thousand of the most probable sentiment words in each domain. The results of the evaluation showed that the sentiment lexicon extraction model is robust enough to be transferred to other domains.

Many domains can form groups with similar lexicons. So many similar sentiment words can be applied to various products. Therefore it is useful to generate sentiment lexicon for such a joint domain – meta-domain.

---

[1] http://www.cs.waikato.ac.nz/ml/weka/

Constructing the general sentiment lexicon from several extracted domain-specific lexicons we want to boost words that occur in many different domains and have high weights in each of them. We propose the following function for the word weight in the resulting list:

$$R(w) = \max_{d \in D}( prob_d(w)) \cdot \sum_{d \in D} \frac{1}{|D|} \cdot \left(1 - \frac{pos_d(w)}{|d|}\right)$$

where $D$ – is the domain set with five domains, $d$ is the sentiment word list for a particular domain and $|d|$ is the total number of words in this list. Functions $prob_d(w)$ and $pos_d(w)$ are the sentiment probability and position of the word in the list $d$.

The meta-domain list of sentiment words created in such a way consists of words really used in users' reviews and its creation does not require any dictionary resources.

## 4 System Functionality and Architecture

Thus ***DomEx*** extractor has the following functionality:

- Extraction of domain-specific sentiment lexicon (see Figure 1).
- Construction of a joint lexicon for several similar domains.
- Application of the model to other languages.

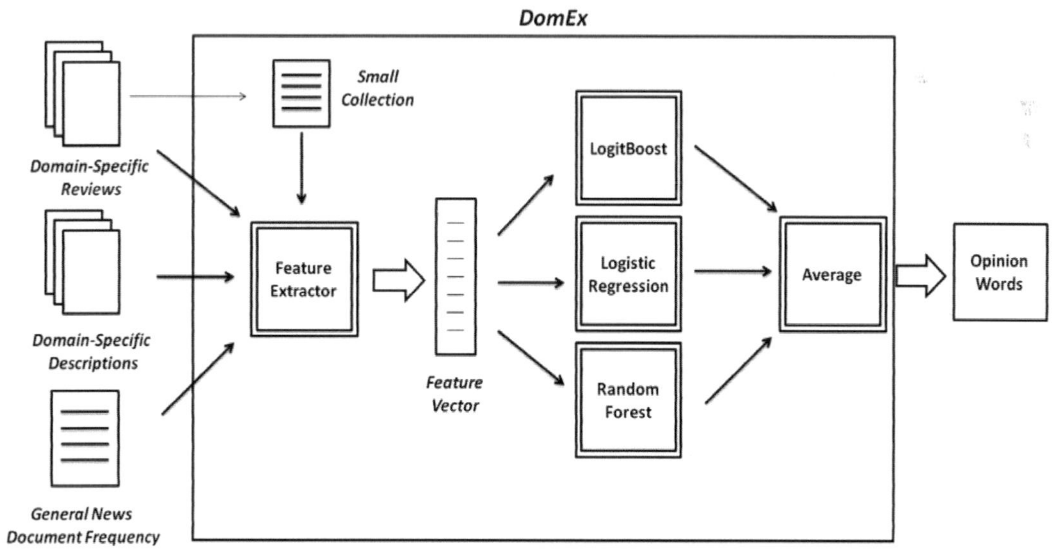


FIGURE 1 –System Overview. Double boxed items are system components and single boxed items are text files

To utilize our system for another language some minor changes should be made:

1. All input data collections should be pre-processed with corresponding POS tagger and change appropriate tags in the system.

2. Changing the key word for extracting potential opinion-bearing sentences during the construction of the small collection (see Section 2).
3. The list of sentiment-bearing prefixes should be specified for a specific language. These prefixes should indicate potential opinion words, for example "*un*", "*in*", "*im*" in English.

After such changes our system without any additional learning can be transformed to process texts in other languages. The most difficult part is to collect appropriate amount of reviews and descriptions of entities in the specific domain and language.

As an example, we utilized our system for English language in the movie domain. We use the review dataset from (Blitzer et al., 2007), but take only reviews from the movie domain. As contrast collections we used plot dataset freely available on the IMDb[2] and Reuters-21578[3] news collection. Using these datasets DomEx computed the word-feature matrix following the previously described procedure and applied our model trained on the Russian movie reviews. The evaluated quality of obtained lexicon was 70.5% according to P@1000 measure.

The most probable extracted English sentiment words in the movie domain were as follows: *remarkable, recommended, overdo, understated, respected, overlook, lame*, etc. Some of these words (for example *overlook*) are opinion words only in the movie domain.

## Conclusion and Perspectives

In this paper we presented DomEx sentiment lexicon extractor, in which a new approach for domain-specific sentiment lexicon extraction is implemented. Sentiment lexicon extraction is based on the machine learning model comprising a set of statistical and linguistic features. The extraction model is trained in the movie domain and then can be utilized to other domains. The experiments showed that the model can be transferred to other domains and had good generalization abilities. The system can work with various domains and languages after a part of speech tagging.

Finally, the system gives possibility to combine the sentiment lexicons from similar domains to obtain one general lexicon for the corresponding meta-domain.

## Acknowledgments

This work is partially supported by RFBR grant N11-07-00588-a.

## References

Abdul-Mageed M., Diab M., Korayem M. (2011). Subjectivity and Sentiment Analysis of Modern Standard Arabic. In *Proceedings of the 49th Annual Meeting of the Association for Computational Linguistics*, number 3, pp. 587-591.

Ahmad K., Gillam L., Tostevin L. (1999). University of Surrey participation in Trec8: Weirdness indexing for logical documents extrapolation and retrieval *In the Proceedings of Eigth Text Retrieval Conference (Trec-8).*

[2] Information courtesy of The Internet Movie Database (http://www.imdb.com). Used with permission.
[3] http://www.daviddlewis.com/resources/testcollections/reuters21578

Banea C., Mihalcea R., Wiebe J. and Hassan S. (2008). Multilingual subjectivity analysis using machine translation. In *Proceedings of the Conference on Empirical Methods in Natural Language Processing (EMNLP).*

Blitzer J., Dredze M., Pereira F. (2007) Biographies, bollywood, boom-boxes and blenders: Domain adaptation for sentiment classification. In *Proceedings of ACL 2007*, pp. 440–447.

Chetviorkin I. and Loukachevitch N. (2011). Extraction of Domain-specific Opinion Words for Similar Domains. In *Proceedings of the Workshop on Information Extraction and Knowledge Acquisition held in conjunction with RANLP 2011*, pp. 7–12.

Clematide S., Klenner S. (2010) Evaluation and extension of a polarity lexicon for German. In *WASSA-workshop held in conjunction with ECAI-2010*, pp 7-13.

Kanayama H. and Nasukawa T. (2006). Fully automatic lexicon expansion for domain-oriented sentiment analysis. In *EMNLP '06*, pp. 355–363, Morristown, NJ, USA.

Lau R., Lai C., Bruza P. and Wong K. (2011). Pseudo Labeling for Scalable Semi-supervised Learning of Domain-specific Sentiment Lexicons. In *20th ACM Conference on Information and Knowledge Management.*

Mihalcea R., Banea C. and Wiebe J. (2007). Learning multilingual subjective language via cross-lingual projections. In *Proceedings of the 45$^{th}$ Annual Meeting of the Association of Computational Linguistics*, pp. 976–983, Prague, Czech Republic.

Perez-Rosas V., Banea C. and Mihalcea R. (2012). Learning Sentiment Lexicons in Spanish. In *Proceedings of the Eight International Conference on Language Resources and Evaluation (LREC'12).*

Ponomareva N. and Thelwall M. (2012): Bibliographies or blenders: Which resource is best for cross-domain sentiment analysis? In *Proceedings of the 13th Conference on Intelligent Text Processing and Computational Linguistics.*

Qiu G., Liu B., Bu J. and Chen C. (2011). Opinion word expansion and target extraction through double propagation. *Computational Linguistics*, 37(1).

Read J., Carroll J. (2009). Weakly Supervised techniques for domain independent sentiment classification. In *Proceedings of the first International CIKM Workshop on Topic-Sentiment Analysis for Mass Opinion Measurement*, pp. 45-52.

Steinberger J., Lenkova P., Ebrahim M., Ehrmann M., Hurriyetogly A., Kabadjov M., Steinberger R., Tanev H., Zavarella V. and Vazquez S. (2011). Creating Sentiment Dictionaries via Triangulation. In *Proceedings of the 2nd Workshop on Computational Approaches to Subjectivity and Sentiment Analysis, ACL-HLT 2011*, pp. 28–36,

Taboada M., Brooke J., Tofiloski M., Voll K. and Stede M. (2011). Lexicon-based methods for Sentiment Analysis. *Computational linguistics*, 37(2).

# On the Romanian rhyme detection

Alina Maria CIOBANU, Liviu P. DINU
University of Bucharest, Faculty of Mathematics and Computer Science,
Centre for Computational Linguistics, Bucharest, Romania
alinamaria.ciobanu@yahoo.com, ldinu@fmi.unibuc.ro

ABSTRACT

In this paper we focus on detecting Romanian words without rhymes, using knowledge about stressed vowels and syllabification. We also investigate quantitative aspects and the etymological origins of the Romanian words without rhymes.

KEYWORDS : Romanian language, syllables, rhyme

*Proceedings of COLING 2012: Demonstration Papers*, pages 87–94,
COLING 2012, Mumbai, December 2012.

## 1 Introduction

Rhyme represents the correspondence of final sounds of words, beginning with the rightmost stressed vowel. Hence, two words rhyme if their final stressed vowels and all following phonemes are identical (Reddy and Knight 2011).

In Romanian language the accent is variable and therefore cannot be determined in a deterministic manner. It can differentiate between words ("mozaic" – adjective, "mozaic" - noun) and grammatical forms (DOOM dictionary). Syllabification is a challenging and important task, considering that a rigorous research on syllable structure and characteristics cannot be achieved without a complete database of the syllables in a given language (Dinu and Dinu 2006, Dinu and Dinu 2009). Some attempts have been made for the automation of syllabification. Dinu and Dinu (2005) proposed a parallel manner of syllabification for Romanian words, using some parallel extensions of insertion grammars, and in (Dinu, 2003) is proposed a sequential manner of syllabification, based on a Marcus contextual grammar.

Identifying words without rhyme is an important problem for poets and especially for automatic or assisted poetry translation. Reddy and Knight (2011) emphasize another related research area – historical linguistics, as rhymes of words in poetry can provide valuable information about dialect and pronunciation at a given time. We propose an instrument which can provide rhyming words for a given input word and offers other features as well, such as detection of words without rhymes and clustering words based on syllable number. These tools contribute to determination of rhythm and metrics. This instrument can be very useful in identifying words with sparse rhyme. Reddy and Knight (2011) affirm that repetition of rhyming pairs is inevitable in collections of rhyming poetry and is partially caused by sparsity of rhymes. In addition, we focus on identifying the etymological origins for input words in a given language. This feature proves especially useful for words without rhyme.

## 2 Related work

To our knowledge, there are two sites that focus on finding rhymes for Romanian words (http://www.webdex.ro/online/dictionar/rime and http://www.spunetiparerea.ro/dictionar-de-rime/cauta-rime.php). Both of them accept an input word and identify rhyming words. However, both systems determine rather the longest common suffix than rhyme. To our knowledge, they do not provide the other features that we discussed: the ability to automatically identify all words without rhymes from the dictionary and clustering words based on syllable number.

## 3 On the rhyme detection

The dataset we used is a Romanian language resource containing 525528 words, including all inflectional forms (Barbu, 2008). For each word, the following pieces of information are provided: syllabification, type of syllabification (based on pronunciation or structure), position of the stressed vowels and inflectional form. Below is represented a word entry in our dataset. The "obs" field indicates that the word is syllabified based on its structure.

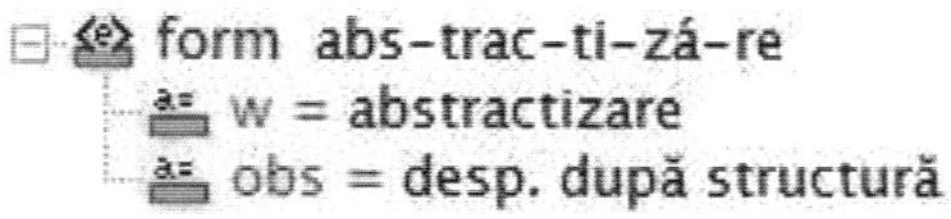


FIGURE 1 – word entry in database

In order to determine the words that do not rhyme with other words, we focused on clustering them based on their rhymes.

1. For polysyllabic words, which had stressed vowels marked, we considered the substring beginning with the rightmost stressed vowel.
2. For monosyllabic words, which did not have stressed vowels marked, we had to focus on the position of the vowels within diphthongs and triphthongs in order to correctly determine the rhymes.
   2.1. Therefore, for ascendant diphthongs we considered the substring beginning with the second character of the structure and for descendant diphthongs we considered the substring beginning with the first character of the structure.
   2.2. We applied similar rules for triphthongs, considering the substring beginning with the third character of the structure for ascendant triphthongs and the substring beginning with the second character of the structure for balanced triphthongs.
3. Once all the words in the dataset were clustered based on their rhymes, we easily identified those that did not have any correspondent words and were, hence, without rhyme.

We identified 8851 different rhymes, among which the most frequent is "áţi", having 8142 corresponding words. 10808 words of our database (2.05%) do not have rhyme.

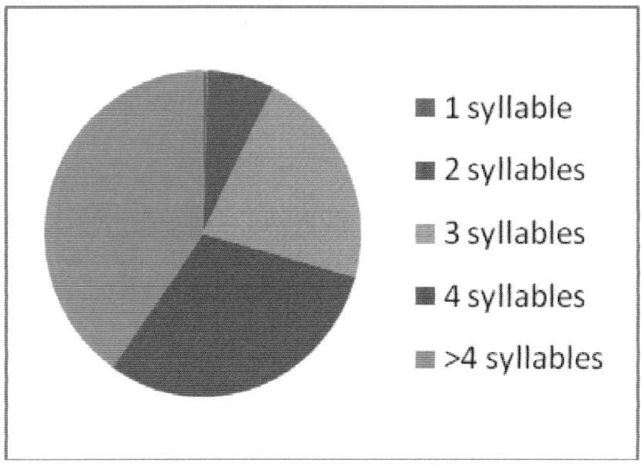


FIGURE 2 – Words with rhymes

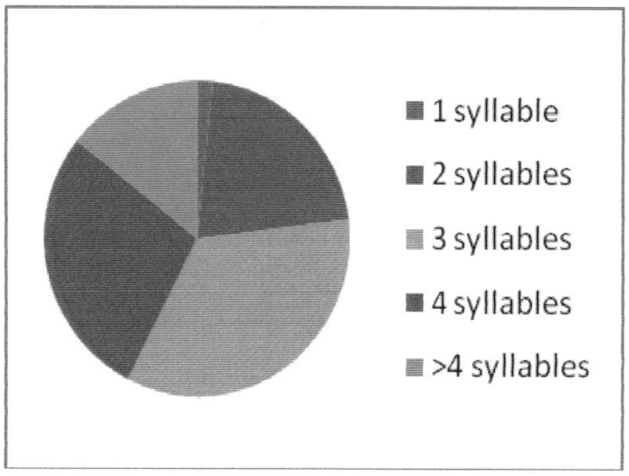


FIGURE 3 – Words without rhymes

Some observations can be derived from these charts. Most words with rhymes have more than four syllables, while most words without rhymes have three syllables. The number of monosyllabic words that do not have rhyme is small, only 174 out of 2894 do not rhyme with any other word. For each syllable cluster, the number of rhyming words is greater than the number of words without rhymes. The percentages in Table 1 do not add up to 100% because of the rounding.

| | Dictionary | | Words with rhymes | | Words without rhymes | |
|---|---|---|---|---|---|---|
| 1 syllable | 2894 | 0.55% | 2720 | 0.51% | 174 | 0.03% |
| 2 syllables | 37235 | 7.08% | 34923 | 6.64% | 2312 | 0.43% |
| 3 syllables | 116806 | 22.22% | 113073 | 21.51% | 3733 | 0.71% |
| 4 syllables | 159911 | 30.42% | 156877 | 29.85% | 3034 | 0.57% |
| >4 syllables | 208682 | 39.70% | 207127 | 39.41% | 1555 | 0.29% |

TABLE 1– words distributed by number of syllables

Once we detected which words of the dataset rhyme with other words, we could implement the other features stated above. Our tool provides rhyming words for a given input, relevant in automatic or assisted poetry translation. Below are selected words that rhyme with the monosyllabic word "strict", whose rhyme is "íct". The output words are syllabified and their stressed vowels are marked. It can be easily observed that all retrieved words have the same rhyme as the input word.

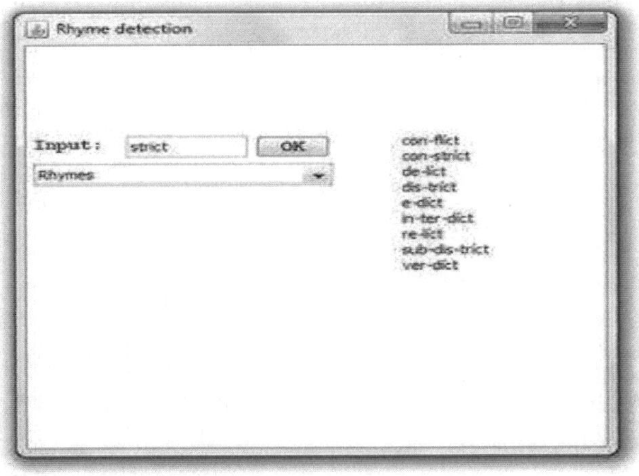


FIGURE 4 – Detecting word rhymes

Another important feature of our tool is the capability of clustering words based on their number of syllables. This feature proves very useful in identifying rhythm and metrics for poetry. In Figure 5 our tool identified words having an equal number of syllables with the Romanian word "geotip", which is formed by three syllables ("ge-o-típ").

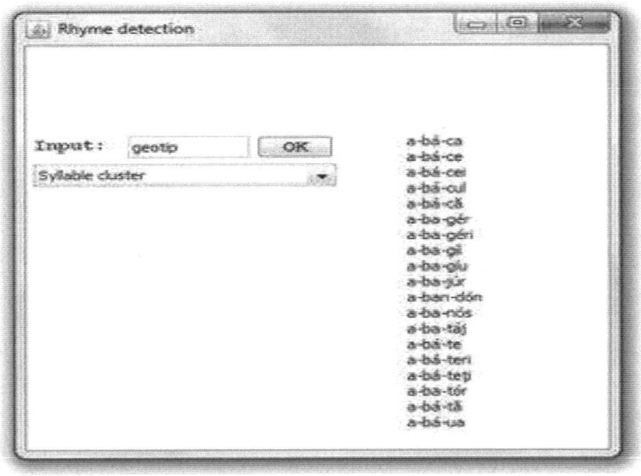


FIGURE 5 – Clustering words based on number of syllables

Our tool is able to identify words without rhymes, based on the algorithm we described above. In addition, the number of syllables can be selected, in order to retrieve only words without rhyme having the desired number of syllables. This feature is demonstrated below by selecting words without rhymes formed by four syllables.

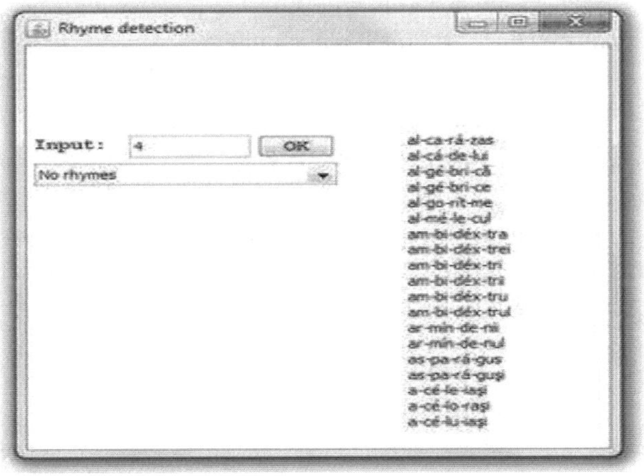


FIGURE 6 – Retrieving words without rhyme

After identifying words without rhymes, we were interested in establishing their etymological origin. In order to automatically detect this information, we used the dexonline.ro database (Copyright (C) 2004-2012 DEX online (http://dexonline.ro)), which gathers information from numerous Romanian dictionaries. We were thus able to determine the origins of the words in our dataset. This feature is valuable especially for words without rhymes. In Figure 7 our tool detected the origin of the word "legumă" and provided the Latin corresponding word ("legumen").

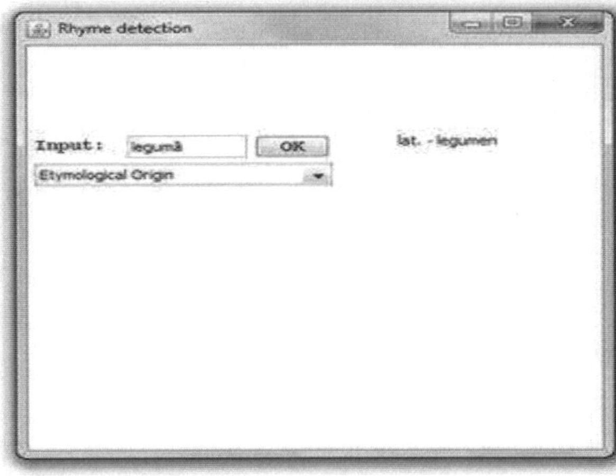


FIGURE 7 – Determining word's etymological origin

## Conclusion and perspectives

In this paper we present a method of identifying words without rhyme using knowledge regarding stressed vowels and syllabification applied on a dataset containing 525528 Romanian words, including all inflectional forms. Our main objective was to determine the words that do not have rhyme and to analyse their syllabic structure and etymological origin. The main result is that 2.05% of the words do not have rhyme. Most words with rhymes have more than four syllables, while most words without rhymes have three syllables.

Further, we presented a tool that is able to identify words without rhymes, to cluster words based on syllable number, to retrieve rhyming words for a given input and to identify etymological origins of the words. Being able to achieve all these pieces of information, our tool can be relevant in detection of words with sparse rhyme and automatic or assisted poetry translation. This research area has received attention in the past, but less effort has been spent on poetry analysis and translation until now (Greene et al 2010).

## Acknowledgments

The research of Liviu P. Dinu was supported by the CNCS, IDEI - PCE project 311/2011, "The Structure and Interpretation of the Romanian Nominal Phrase in Discourse Representation Theory: the Determiners." We want to thank to Solomon Marcus for the helpful comments. Note that the contribution of the authors to this paper is equal.

## References

Barbu, A.M. (2008): Romanian Lexical Data Bases: Inflected and Syllabic Forms Dictionaries, LREC 2008, May, 28-30, Marrakech, Marocco, 2008.

Dexonline.ro database - Copyright (C) 2004-2012 DEX online (http://dexonline.ro)

Dictionarul ortografic, ortoepic si morfologic al limbii romane (DOOM), Ed. Univers Enciclopedic Gold, Bucuresti, 2010.

Dinu, L.P. (2003). An approach to syllables via some extensions of Marcus contextual grammars. Grammars, 6(1), 1-12.

Dinu A. and Dinu L. P. (2005): A Parallel Approach to Syllabification, CICLing 2005, LNCS 3406, 83-87, 2005.

Dinu, A. and Dinu, L.P. (2006). On the data base of Romanian syllables and some of its quantitative and cryptographic aspects. In LREC 2006, May, 24-26, Genoa, Italy.

Dinu A. and Dinu L. P. (2009): On the behavior of Romanian syllables related to minimum effort laws. In C. Vertan, S. Piperidis, E. Paskaleva, M.Slavcheva (eds.): Proc. of Int. workshop on Multilingual resources, technologies and evaluation for central and Eastern European languages (workshop at RANLP 2009 conference), pp. 9-13, 14-16 September, 2009.

Greene E., Bodrumlu T. and Knight K. (2010): Automatic Analysis of Rhythmic Poetry with Applications to Generation and Translation. EMNLP 2010: 524-533.

Reddy S. and Knight K. (2011): Unsupervised Discovery of Rhyme Schemes. ACL (Short Papers) 2011: 77-82.

# Hierarchical Dialogue Policy Learning Using Flexible State Transitions and Linear Function Approximation

*Heriberto Cuayáhuitl*[1], *Ivana Kruijff-Korbayová*[2], *Nina Dethlefs*[1]
[1]Heriot-Watt University, Edinburgh, Scotland, United Kingdom
[2]German Research Center for Artificial Intelligence, Saarbrücken, Germany
h.cuayahuitl@hw.ac.uk, ivana.kruijff@dfki.de, n.s.dethlefs@hw.ac.uk

## Abstract
Conversational agents that use reinforcement learning for policy optimization in large domains often face the problem of limited scalability. This problem can be addressed either by using function approximation techniques that estimate an approximate true value function, or by using a hierarchical decomposition of a learning task into subtasks. In this paper, we present a novel approach for dialogue policy optimization that combines the benefits of hierarchical control with function approximation. The approach incorporates two concepts to allow flexible switching between sub-dialogues, extending current hierarchical reinforcement learning methods. First, hierarchical tree-based state representations initially represent a compact portion of the possible state space and are then dynamically extended in real time. Second, we allow state transitions across sub-dialogues to allow non-strict hierarchical control. Our approach is integrated, and tested with real users, in a robot dialogue system that learns to play Quiz games.

Keywords: spoken dialogue systems, reinforcement learning, hierarchical control, function approximation, user simulation, human-robot interaction, flexible interaction.

## 1 Introduction

The past decade has experienced important progress in spoken dialogue systems that learn their conversational behaviour. The Reinforcement Learning (RL) framework in particular has been an attractive alternative to hand-coded policies for the design of sophisticated and adaptive dialogue agents. An RL agent learns its behaviour from interaction with an environment, where situations are mapped to actions by maximizing a long-term reward signal (Sutton and Barto, 1998). While RL-based dialogue systems are promising, they still need to overcome several limitations to reach practical and wide-spread application. One of these limitations is the *curse of dimensionality*, the problem that the state space grows exponentially according to the variables taken into account. Another limitation is that attempts to address the first problem often involve rule-based reductions of the state space (Litman et al., 2000; Singh et al., 2002; Heeman, 2007; Williams, 2008; Cuayáhuitl et al., 2010b; Dethlefs et al., 2011) which can lead to reduced flexibility of system behaviour in terms of letting the user say and/or do anything at any time during the dialogue. Finally, even when function approximation techniques have been used to scale up in small-scale and single-task systems (Henderson et al., 2008; Li et al., 2009; Pietquin, 2011; Jurcícek et al., 2011), their application to more complex dialogue contexts has yet to be demonstrated.

Our motivation for increased *dialogue flexibility* in this paper is the assumption that users at times deviate from the system's expected user behaviour. In reduced state spaces this may lead to unseen dialogue states in which the system cannot react properly to the new situation, as is exemplified

*Proceedings of COLING 2012: Demonstration Papers*, pages 95–102,
COLING 2012, Mumbai, December 2012.

by dialogue 3S in Figure 1. So whilst a full state space represents maximal flexibility (according to the state variables considered), but is often not scalable, reducing the state space for increased scalability simultaneously faces a risk of reducing dialogue flexibility.

This paper presents a novel approach for dialogue policy optimization that increases both dialogue flexibility and scalability. It is couched within a Hierarchical Reinforcement Learning (HRL) framework, a principled and scalable model for optimizing sub-behaviours (Barto and Mahadevan, 2003). We extend an existing HRL-algorithm with the following features: (1) dynamic tree-based state representations that can grow during a dialogue, *during the course of the dialogue*, according to the state variables used in the interaction; and (2) rather than imposing strict hierarchical dialogue control, we allow users to navigate more flexibly across the available sub-dialogues. A further extension is the representation of the dialogue policy using function approximation in order to generalize decision-making even for unseen situations.

## 2 Proposed Learning Approach

This section proposes two extensions of the hierarchical RL framework presented in (Cuayáhuitl and Dethlefs, 2011b): (1) dynamic tree-based state representations that grow over the course of a dialogue; and (2) state transitions across sub-dialogues for flexible dialogue control. In addition, we make use of function approximation to support decision-making for unseen situations.

### 2.1 Dynamic Tree-based State Representations

We treat each multi-step action as a separate SMDP as described in (Cuayáhuitl et al., 2007; Cuayáhuitl, 2009). To allow compact state representations to grow over the course of a dialogue, we redefine such SMDP models as tuples $M_\beta^{(i,j)} = <S_\beta^{(i,j)}, A_\beta^{(i,j)}, T_\beta^{(i,j)}, R_\beta^{(i,j)}, L_\beta^{(i,j)}>$, where $S_\beta^{(i,j)}$ is a finite set of dynamic tree-based states that grow from $S_\beta^{(i,j)}$ to $S_{\beta'}^{(i,j)}$ after new states are encountered.[1] This principle is illustrated in Figure 1. Since the state space changes continuously, the actions per state $A_\beta^{(i,j)}$, the corresponding state transitions $T_\beta^{(i,j)}$, reward functions $R_\beta^{(i,j)}$, and context-free grammar $L_\beta^{(i,j)}$, which defines the tree-based state representations, are affected by these changes. When an unknown (or unseen) state is observed, the current subtask $M_\beta^{(i,j)}$ is updated to support that new state, where $\beta$ refers to the number of times the subtask $M^{(i,j)}$ has been updated. An update consists of the following steps:

1. extend the state space and corresponding grammar $L_\beta^{(i,j)}$ with the new states;
2. assign a set of actions to the new states, which satisfy pre-specified constraints (if any); and
3. extend the state transition function to support transitions to the new states.

Although our approach could also continuously extend the reward function to cover the new observed situations, we leave this point as future work. The solution to our redefined model consists in approximating or relearning an optimal policy for each agent in the hierarchy continuously often, i.e. whenever the state space has grown, according to

$$\pi_\beta^{*(i,j)}(s \in S_\beta^{(i,j)}) = \arg\max_{a \in A_\beta^{(i,j)}} Q_\beta^{*i,j}(s,a). \quad (1)$$

[1] No threshold is imposed on the growth of state spaces. In the worst case, it would represent all possible combinations of state variable values. Nevertheless, it is reasonable to assume that only a subset of it would be observed in real interactions.

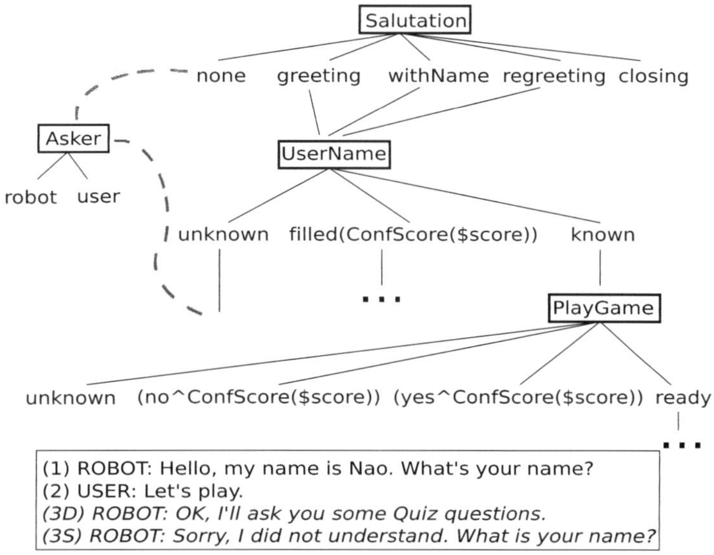


Figure 1: Fragment of our dialogue state space, where rectangles represent state variables that expand their domain values. A tree-branch (with expanded variables, here denoted as '$variable') is a unique dialogue state. The dashed lines illustrate a dynamically growing tree according to the example dialogue. Here, 3D represents a dialogue with dynamically growing state representations and 3S represents a dialogue with static state representations.

Note that the initial state space $S^{(i,j)}_{\beta=0}$ is compact so that unseen states can be observed during the agent-environment interaction from a knowledge-rich state $k$ that maintains the dialogue history. $k$ can also be seen as a knowledge base and is used to initialize states of each subtask, so that we can extend the state space for unseen states within a given set of state variables. We can approximate the optimal policies using linear function approximation. The policies are represented by a set of weighted linear functions expressed as

$$Q^{(i,j)}_{\theta}(s,a) = \theta^{(i,j)}_0 + \theta^{(i,j)}_1 f_1(s,a) + ... + \theta^{(i,j)}_n f_n(s,a) \quad (2)$$

with a set of state features $f_i \in F$ [2] and parameters $\theta^{(i,j)} = \{\theta^{(i,j)}_1, ...\theta^{(i,j)}_n\}$ for each agent in the hierarchy. A reinforcement learning agent can learn values for the parameters $\theta$, where the utility functions $Q^{(i,j)}_{\theta}$ approximate to the true utility functions.

## 2.2 Flexible Navigation across Sub-Dialogues

To allow flexible navigation across sub-dialogues, we extend the previous models with tuples $M^{(i,j)}_{\beta} = <S^{(i,j)}_{\beta}, A^{(i,j)}_{\beta}, T^{(i,j)}_{\beta}, R^{(i,j)}_{\beta}, L^{(i,j)}_{\beta}, G^{(i,j)}_{\beta}>$, where the new element $G^{(i,j)}_{\beta} = P(m'|m,s,a)$ is a stochastic model transition function that specifies the next model or subtask $m' \in \mu$ given model $m \in \mu$, state $s$ and action $a$. Here, $\mu$ refers to the set of all models. The new element $G^{(i,j)}_{\beta}$ is the mechanism to specify the currently active subtask for each state-action (see Figure 2). This is a relevant feature in dialogue agents in order to allow users to act freely at anytime and across

[2]A dialogue state is represented as a vector of binary features derived from the tree-based representations, where every possible variable-value pair in the tree is represented with 1 if present and 0 if absent.

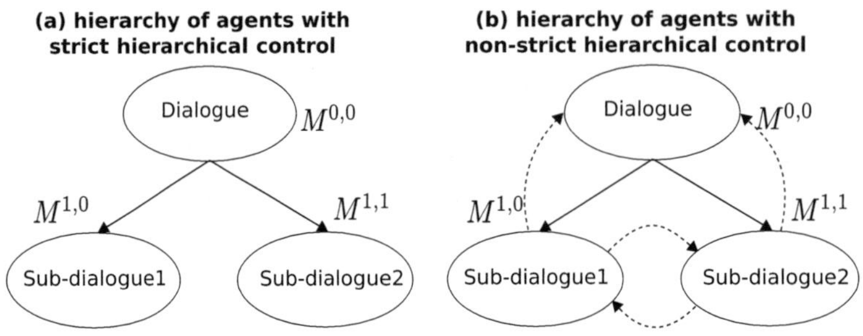


Figure 2: Hierarchies of agents with local and global state transitions.Whilst the straight arrows connecting models mean invoking a model and returning control after terminating its execution, the dashed arrows connecting models mean interrupting the execution of the current model and transition to another one to continue the interaction.

sub-dialogues, while dialogue agents should be able to react with appropriate actions. The goal of these extended SMDPs is to learn a similar mapping as in the previous section, expressed as

$$\pi_{\theta}^{*(i,j)}(s \in S_{\beta}^{(i,j)}) = \arg\max_{a \in A_{\beta}^{(i,j)}} Q_{\theta}^{*(i,j)}(s,a), \tag{3}$$

where we extend the HSMQ-learning algorithm (Dietterich, 2000; Cuayáhuitl et al., 2010b; Cuayáhuitl and Dethlefs, 2011a) to induce the action-value functions $Q_{\theta}$, one per SMDP model.

## 3 Experimental Setting

To test if our approach can generate more flexible interactions than a baseline, we use a robot dialogue system in the Quiz domain, where the robot[3] can ask the user questions, or vice-versa, the user can ask the robot questions. In addition, to allow flexibility, the user or robot can switch roles or stop playing at any point during the interaction (e.g. from any dialogue state).

### 3.1 Characterization of the Learning Agents

We use a compact hierarchy of dialogue agents with one parent and two children agents ('robot asks' and 'user asks'), which is shown in Figure 2. (Cuayáhuitl and Dethlefs, 2012)-Table 1 shows the set of state variables for our system, each one modelled as a discrete probability distribution with updated parameters at runtime. Dialogue and game features are included to inform the agent of situations in the interaction. Our action set consists of 80 meaningful combinations of speech act types[4] and associated parameters[5]. We constrained the actions per state based on the grammars $L_{\beta}^{(i,j)}$, i.e. only a subset of actions was allowed per dialogue state (constraints omitted due to space). While our HRL agent with tree-based states grows up to $10^4$ state-actions, a static, propositional representation (enumerating all variables and values) has $10^{12}$ state-action pairs. This makes the tree-based representation attractive for complex, large-scale systems.

[3] Our dialogue system has been fully implemented and tested using wizarded and speech-based user responses with the actual Nao humanoid robot. An evaluation with real users will be reported in a forthcoming paper.

[4] Set of speech act types: Salutation, Request, Apology, Confirm, Accept, SwitchRole, Acknowledgement, Provide, Stop, Feedback. Express, Classify, Retrieve, Provide.

[5] Greet, Closing, Name, PlayGame, Asker, KeepPlaying, GameFun, StopPlaying, Play, NoPlay, Fun, NoFun, GameInstructions, StartGame, Question, Answers, CorrectAnswer, IncorrectAnswer, GamePerformance, Answer, Success, Failure, GlobalGameScore, ContinuePlaying.

The **reward function** addressed efficient and effective interactions by encouraging to play and get the right answers as much as possible. It is defined by the following rewards for choosing action $a$ in state $s$: $+10$ for reaching a terminal state or answering a question correctly, $-10$ for remaining in the same state (i.e. $s_{t+1} = s_t$ or $s_{t+1} = s_{t-1}$), and 0 otherwise. The **user simulation** used a set of user dialogue acts as responses to the system dialogue acts (footnotes 4-5). The user dialogue acts were estimated using conditional distributions $P(a^{usr}|a^{sys})$ with Witten-Bell discounting from 21 wizarded dialogues (900 user turns). The attribute-values were distorted based on an equally distributed speech recognition error rate of 20%. The confidence scores of attribute values were generated from beta probability distributions with parameters ($\alpha$=2, $\beta$=6) for bad recognition and ($\alpha$=6, $\beta$=2) for good recognition.

## 3.2 The Robot Dialogue System

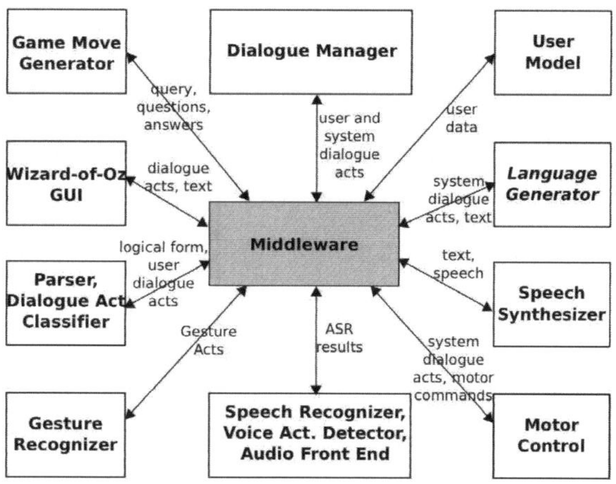


Figure 3: High-level architecture of the integrated system.

Our experiments were carried out using a dialogue system (Cuayáhuitl and Kruijff-Korbayová, 2012) running on the Nao robot [6]. The system integrates components for speech and gesture capture and interpretation, activity and interaction management, user modeling, speech and gesture production and robot motor control (see Figure 3). We use components developed by ourselves as well as off-the-shelf technologies such as Google speech recognition, OpenCV for gesture recognition, Acapela for speech synthesis, OpenCCG for language parsing and generation, and Weka and JavaBayes for maintaining a probabilistic personalized user profile. To bring all components together within a concurrent execution approach, we use the Urbi middleware (Baillie, 2005). More details on the system implementation are described in (Kruijff-Korbayová et al., 2012b,a).

During interactions, the user provided responses through a mobile device, which were processed by a Bayesian dialogue act classifier estimated from our Wizard-of-Oz data. Based on this, the next system action is selected by the Dialogue Manager component (as described in Sections 2 and 3). The dialogue act corresponding to the selected next system action is verbalized automatically by the Natural Language Generation component which produces text for the speech synthesizer. Nonverbal behavior planning and motor control are automatic communicative gestures assigned to specific types of dialogue acts (e.g., greetings, requests), and static key poses displaying emotions such as anger, sadness, fear, happiness, excitement and pride (Beck et al., 2010).

[6] www.aldebaran-robotics.com

Figure 4: Participants talking to the NAO robot through a smartphone while playing the Quiz game. The pieces of paper on the table are used by the users to ask the robot questions.

To summarize, the following features describe the system used in our experiments: (a) automatic speech and dialogue act recognition; (b) automatic system action selection; (c) user barge-ins in the form of interruptions of the robot's speech by an early user response; (d) automatically produced verbal output in English with many variations and expressive speech synthesis distinguishing sad, happy and neutral state; (e) automatically produced head and body poses and gestures; and (f) persistent user-specific interaction profile. This robot dialogue system has been evaluated with simulated and real users, see Figure 4. A comprehensive evaluation description and results analysis will be reported in a forthcoming paper.

## 4 Conclusion and Future Work

We have described a novel approach for optimizing dialogue systems by extending an existing HRL framework to support dynamic state spaces, non-strict hierarchical control, and linear function approximation. We evaluated our approach by incorporating it into a robot dialogue system that learns to play Quiz games. Our experimental results, based on simulation and experiments with human users (reported elsewhere), show that our approach is promising. It can yield more flexible interactions than a policy that uses strict control and is preferred by human users. We expect that our approach will represent an important step forward in the development of more sophisticated dialogue systems that combine the benefits of trainable, scalable and flexible interaction.

As future work, we suggest the following directions in order to equip spoken or multimodal dialogue systems with more flexible and adaptive conversational interaction: (1) to learn model state transition functions automatically so that the system can suggest how to navigate in the hierarchy of sub-dialogues; (2) to optimize dialogue control combining verbal and non-verbal behaviours (Cuayáhuitl and Dethlefs, 2012; Dethlefs et al., 2012b); (3) to optimize dialogue control jointly with natural language generation (Dethlefs and Cuayáhuitl, 2011b,a; Lemon, 2011); (4) to extend our approach with large hierarchies and partially observable SMDPs; (5) an application to situated dialogue systems (Cuayáhuitl et al., 2010a; Cuayáhuitl and Dethlefs, 2011a,b; Janarthanam et al., 2012); (6) an application to complex turn-taking phenomena in systems with multiple modalities for more natural and effective interactions (Chao and Thomaz, 2012); (7) an application to incremental dialogue processing (Schlangen and Skantze, 2009) using reinforcement learning (Dethlefs et al., 2012a), and (8) to induce the reward function during the course of the interaction for providing online adaptation.

## 5 Acknowledgments

Funding by the EU-FP7 projects ALIZ-E (ICT-248116, `www.aliz-e.org`) and Spacebook (270019, `http://www.spacebook-project.eu`) is gratefully acknowledged.

## References


Baillie, J. (2005). Urbi: Towards a universal robotic low-level programming language. In *2005 IEEE/RSJ International Conference on Intelligent Robots and Systems*, pages 3219–3224. IEEE.

Barto, A. and Mahadevan, S. (2003). Recent advances in hierarchical reinforcement learning. *Discrete Event Dynamic Systems: Theory and Applications*, 13(1-2):41–77.

Beck, A., Cañamero, L., and Bard, K. (2010). Towards an affect space for robots to display emotional body language. In *Ro-Man 2010*, pages 464–469, Viareggio, Italy.

Chao, C. and Thomaz, A. L. (2012). Timing in multimodal reciprocal interactions: control and analysis using timed petri nets. *Journal of Human-Robot Interaction*, 1(1):4–25.

Cuayáhuitl, H. (2009). *Hierarchical Reinforcement Learning for Spoken Dialogue Systems.* PhD thesis, School of Informatics, University of Edinburgh.

Cuayáhuitl, H. and Dethlefs, N. (2011a). Spatially-aware dialogue control using hierarchical reinforcement learning. *ACM Transactions on Speech and Language Processing*, 7(3):5:1–5:26.

Cuayáhuitl, H. and Dethlefs, N. (2012). Hierarchical multiagent reinforcement learning for coordinating verbal and non-verbal actions in robots. In *ECAI Workshop on Machine Learning for Interactive Systems (MLIS)*, pages 27–29, Montpellier, France.

Cuayáhuitl, H., Dethlefs, N., Frommberger, L., Richter, K.-F., and Bateman, J. (2010a). Generating adaptive route instructions using hierarchical reinforcement learning. In *Proc. of the International Conference on Spatial Cognition (Spatial Cognition VII)*, Portland, OR, USA.

Cuayáhuitl, H. and Dethlefs, N. a. (2011b). Optimizing situated dialogue management in unknown environments. In *INTERSPEECH*, pages 1009–1012, Florence, Italy.

Cuayáhuitl, H. and Kruijff-Korbayová, I. (2012). An interactive humanoid robot exhibiting flexible sub-dialogues. In *HLT-NAACL*, pages 17–20, Montreal, Canada.

Cuayáhuitl, H., Renals, S., Lemon, O., and Shimodaira, H. (2007). Hierarchical dialogue optimization using semi-Markov decision processes. In *INTERSPEECH*, pages 2693–2696, Antwerp, Belgium.

Cuayáhuitl, H., Renals, S., Lemon, O., and Shimodaira, H. (2010b). Evaluation of a hierarchical reinforcement learning spoken dialogue system. *Computer Speech and Language*, 24(2):395–429.

Dethlefs, N. and Cuayáhuitl, H. (2011a). Combining hierarchical reinforcement learning and Bayesian networks for natural language generation in situated dialogue. In *ENLG*, Nancy, France.

Dethlefs, N. and Cuayáhuitl, H. (2011b). Hierarchical reinforcement learning and hidden Markov models for task-oriented natural language generation. In *ACL-HLT*, pages 654–659, Portland, OR, USA.

Dethlefs, N., Cuayáhuitl, H., and Viethen, J. (2011). Optimising Natural Language Generation Decision Making for Situated Dialogue. In *SIGdial*, Portland, Oregon, USA.

Dethlefs, N., Hastie, H., Rieser, V., and Lemon, O. (2012a). Optimising Incremental Dialogue Decisions Using Information Density for Interactive Systems. In *Proceedings of the Conference on Empirical Methods in Natural Language Processing (EMNLP-CoNLL)*, Jeju, South Korea.

Dethlefs, N., Rieser, V., Hastie, H., and Lemon, O. (2012b). Towards optimising modality allocation for multimodal output generation in incremental dialogue. In *ECAI Workshop on Machine Learning for Interactive Systems (MLIS)*, pages 31–36, Montpellier, France.

Dietterich, T. (2000). An overview of MAXQ hierarchical reinforcement learning. In *Symposium on Abstraction, Reformulation, and Approximation (SARA)*, pages 26–44.

Heeman, P. (2007). Combining reinforcement learning with information-state update rules. In *Human Language Technology Conference (HLT)*, pages 268–275, Rochester, NY, USA.

Henderson, J., Lemon, O., and Georgila, K. (2008). Hybrid reinforcement/supervised learning of dialogue policies from fixed data sets. *Computational Linguistics*, 34(4):487–511.

Janarthanam, S., Lemon, O., Liu, X., Bartie, P., Mackaness, W., Dalmas, T., and Goetze, J. (2012). Integrating location, visibility, and Question-Answering in a spoken dialogue system for pedestrian city exploration. In *SEMDIAL*, pages 134–136, Paris, France.

Jurcícek, F., Thompson, B., and Young, S. (2011). Natural actor and belief critic: Reinforcement algorithm for learning parameters of dialogue systems modelled as POMDPs. *ACM Transactions on Speech and Language Processing*, 7(3):6.

Kruijff-Korbayová, I., Cuayáhuitl, H., Kiefer, B., Schröder, M., Cosi, P., Paci, G., Sommavilla, G., Tesser, F., Sahli, H., Athanasopoulos, G., Wang, W., Enescu, V., and Verhelst, W. (2012a). Spoken language processing in a conversational system for child-robot interaction. In *Workshop on Child-Computer Interaction (WOCCI)*, Portland, OR, USA.

Kruijff-Korbayová, I., Cuayáhuitl, H., Kiefer, B., Schröder, M., Csi, P., Paci, G., Sommavilla, G., Tesser, F., Sahli, H., Athanasopoulos, G., Wang, W., Enescu, V., and Verhelst, W. (2012b). A conversational system for multi-session child-robot interaction with several games. In *German Conference on Artificial Intelligence (KI), Saarbruecken, Germany.*

Lemon, O. (2011). Learning what to say and how to say it: Joint optimization of spoken dialogue management and natural language generation. *Computer Speech and Language.*

Li, L., Williams, J., and Balakrishnan, S. (2009). Reinforcement learning for dialog management using least-squares policy iteration and fast feature selection. In *INTERSPEECH*, Brighton, UK.

Litman, D., Kearns, M., Singh, S., and Walker, M. (2000). Automatic optimization of dialogue management. In *COLING*, pages 502–508, Saarbrucken, Germany.

Pietquin, O. (2011). Batch reinforcement learning for spoken dialogue systems with sparse value function approximation. In *NIPS Workshop on Learning and Planning from Batch Time Series Data*, Vancouver, Canada.

Schlangen, D. and Skantze, G. (2009). A General, Abstract Model of Incremental Dialogue Processing. In *EACL*, Athens, Greece.

Singh, S., Litman, D., Kearns, M., and Walker, M. (2002). Optimizing dialogue management with reinforcement learning: Experiments with the NJFun system. *JAIR*, 16:105–133.

Sutton, R. and Barto, A. (1998). *Reinforcement Learning: An Introduction.* MIT Press.

Williams, J. (2008). The best of both worlds: Unifying conventional dialog systems and POMDPs. In *INTERSPEECH*, Brisbane, Australia.

# Automated Paradigm Selection for FSA based Konkani Verb Morphological Analyzer

*Shilpa Desai Jyoti Pawar Pushpak Bhattacharya*
(1) Department of Computer Science and Technology, Goa University, Goa, India
(2) Department of Computer Science and Technology, Goa University, Goa, India
(3) Department of Computer Science and Engineering, IIT, Powai, Mumbai, India
sndesai@gmail.com, jyotidpawar@gmail.com, pb@cse.iitb.ac.in

ABSTRACT

A Morphological Analyzer is a crucial tool for any language. In popular tools used to build morphological analyzers like XFST, HFST and Apertium's lttoolbox, the finite state approach is used to sequence input characters. We have used the finite state approach to sequence morphemes instead of characters. In this paper we present the architecture and implementation details of a Corpus assisted FSA approach for building a Verb Morphological Analyzer. Our main contribution in this paper is the paradigm definition methodology used for the verbs in a morphologically rich Indian Language Konkani. The mapping of citation form of the verbs to paradigms was carried out using an untagged corpus for Konkani. Besides a reduction in human effort required an F-Score of 0.95 was obtained when the mapping was tested on a tagged corpus.

KEYWORDS: Verb Morphological Analyzer, Corpus, Hybrid Approach, Finite State Automata, Paradigm Mapping.

*Proceedings of COLING 2012: Demonstration Papers*, pages 103–110,
COLING 2012, Mumbai, December 2012.

## 1 Introduction

Morphological Analysis is a significant step in most Natural Language Processing (NLP) Applications. A Morphological Analyzer (MA) is a tool which retrieves the component morphemes of a given word and analyzes them. Some well known approaches used to build a Morphological Analyzer are Rule Based Affix Stripping Approach, Pure Unsupervised learning of Morphology (Hammarström, 2011), Finite State Approach (Beesley, 2003) and Semi-Supervised learning of Morphology (Lindén, 2009).

Rule based approaches use a set of rules in the language for stemming (Porter, 2000). The success of such approaches will depend on the rules incorporated which are vast for morphologically rich languages. In Pure Unsupervised learning of morphology (Freitag, 2005), (Goldsmith, 2001), (Hammarström, 2011), (Xanthos, 2007) corpus text of the concerned language is used to learn morphology of the language. The reported accuracy of such systems is relatively less as compared to the other methods.

Finite State Transducers is a computationally efficient, inherently bidirectional approach and can also be used for word generation. Many Indian Language groups use finite state tools for morphological analysis. Lttoolbox (Kulkarni, 2010) developed under Apertium is one such tool. The analysis process is done by splitting a word (e.g. cats) into its lemma 'cat' and the grammatical information <n><pl>. The major limitation of such a tool is that it requires a linguist to enter a large number of entries to create a morphological dictionary. It assumes that some form of *word and paradigm* (Hockett, 1954) model is available for the language. This approach to build Morphological Analyzer is time consuming when every word is manually listed in a morphological dictionary and mapped to a paradigm. A funded project to build a Morphological Analyzer using FST tools typically allocate 9 to 12 months for the work. In such Projects mapping of words to paradigms is done by a language expert manually.

In absence of a funded project, limited volunteer human experts are available to manually map words to paradigms. Hence we have made use of existing resources for the Konkani language namely Corpus and WordNet to reduce the human effort to map words to paradigms. For this we have designed our own paradigm structure and FSA based sequencing of morphemes which is used to generate word forms. Our approach builds a morphological dictionary which can be later exported to popular tools like XFST or lttoolbox. Our approach is an enhancement to the finite state approach which makes the implementation of FSA approach efficient with respect to time and linguistic effort. The rest of the paper is organized as follows - section 2 is on related work. Design and architecture of the FSA based approach using corpus for paradigm mapping is presented in section 3. Experimental results are presented in section 4 and finally we conclude the paper with remarks on scope for future work.

## 2 Related Work

Attempts to map a word to a paradigm computationally have been attempted earlier. Rule based systems which map words to paradigms have been attempted (Sánchez-Cartagena et al., 2012), these systems use POS information or some additional user input from native language speakers to map words to paradigms instead of a corpus alone. Functional Morphology (M Forsberg, 2007) have been used to define morphology for language like Swedish and Finnish and Tools based on Functional Morphology namely Extract (M Forsberg, 2006) which suggest new words for lexicon and map them to paradigms have been developed. Functional Morphology based tools use constraint grammars to map words correctly to paradigms. The morphology of the language has to be fitted into the Functional Morphology definition to be able to use a tool like extract. Our work is close to the paradigm selection by Linden (Lindén, 2009) which is implemented to choose the appropriate paradigm for a guesser program for unknown words. Our paradigm selector method is implemented for Konkani verbs to quicken the process of building a verb MA.

We have defined our own paradigm structure for Konkani which uses FSA based sequencing of morphemes and suffix classes which provides a compact way to define a paradigm. This feature of grouping suffixes into classes such that if one suffix in a class gets attached to the stem then all the suffixes of the same class can be attached to the same stem gives a convenient and compact method to define a paradigm.

## 3 Design and Architecture of FSA based approach using corpus for paradigm mapping

Generally a verb has a stem to which suffixes are attached. Ambiguity in Konkani verb stem formation which prompted us to have a relevant paradigm design are –

- Given ending characters of verb citation forms there is no single rule to obtain a stem. For example if verb citation form ends with वप[1] (vaph; ; ending characters of verb citation form) as in case of धांवप ( dhavap; to run; citation form of verb run), three rules can be applied. This gives rise to possible stems set with three entries namely {धांव, धांय, धां} ({dhav, dhayh, dha}; {run, not defined, not defined}; stems generated for verb run) of which only धांव (dhav; run; stem of verb run) is the correct stem. This is an ambiguity in stem formation for verbs. Hence simple rules based on verb citation form endings cannot be written to map verb citation forms to paradigms. Here a corpus is required to obtain support for the correct stem + suffix combination.
- A single verb citation form could give rise to more than one valid stem. Stems generated are such that two different stems of a single verb do not get attached to the same set of suffixes. For example verb आफडप (Aaphdaph; to touch; citation form of verb touch) gives rise to two stems namely आफुड (Aaphuda; touch; stem of verb touch) and आफड (Aaphd; ; stem of verb touch which has to be followed by appropriate suffix). An observation in such cases is that only one of these stems can exist as a valid verb form independently while the other stem has to be followed by some suffix and cannot appear as an independent verb form.
- Another case where there are more than one stem for a single verb citation form is when stems generated are alternatives to each other and one can be replaced by the other. Here unlike the above case, two stems of a single verb get attached with same set of suffixes. For example verb गावप (gavaph; to sing; citation form of verb sing) gives rise to two stems namely गाय (gayh; sing; stem of verb sing) and गा(ga; sing; stem of verb sing).

The Verb Morphological Analyzer has two main modules. It uses five resources as input and generates as output one crucial resource. Architecture of the FSA based Verb Morphological Analyzer using corpus for paradigm mapping is shown in FIGURE 1.

[1] A word in Konkani language is followed by transliteration in Roman Script, translation in English and gloss in brackets

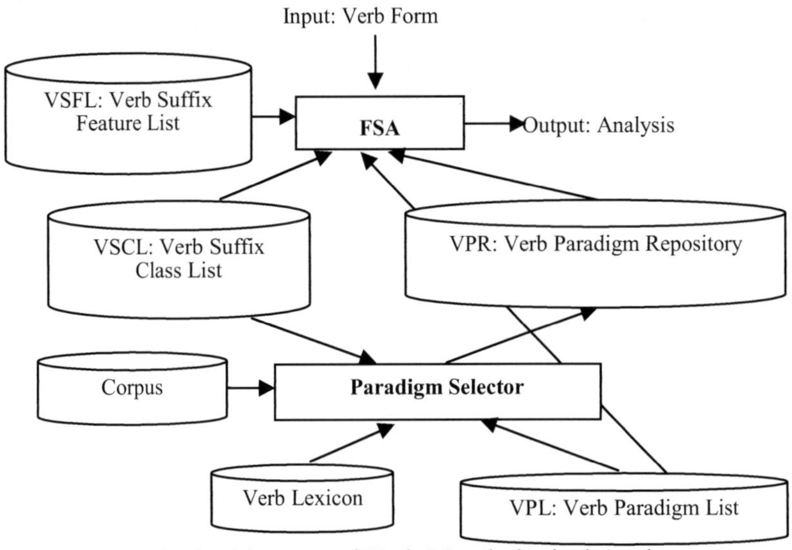


FIGURE 1 - Architecture of Verb Morphological Analyzer

The FSA module is used to sequence morphemes. It is used for both analysis and generation of word forms. Different verb forms in Konkani can be formed by attaching suffixes to stems of verbs (Sardessai, 1986). FIGURE 2 next shows the FSA constructed for Konkani Verb Analysis.

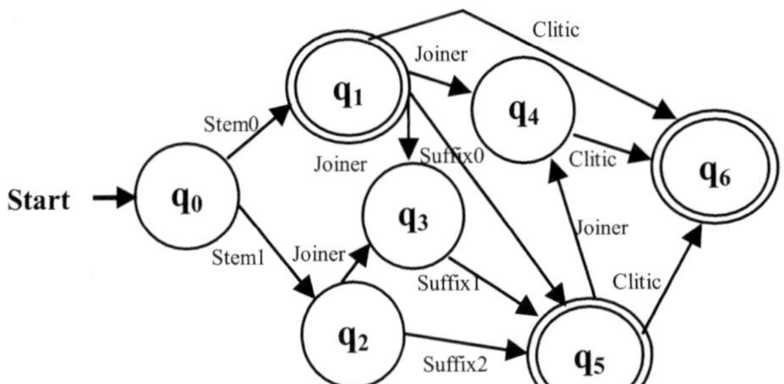


FIGURE 2 – FSA for Morphology of Konkani Verb

The other module is the Paradigm Selector module which maps a paradigm for an input verb and generates the crucial VPR resource. This module is run only when verbs not present in VPR are encountered.

The resources used in Verb Morphology Analyzer are -

- Verb lexicon: It contains citation form of a verb and Part of Speech category associated. This resource can be generated using the WordNet for the language.
- Corpus: Any standard corpus available in the language or a corpus generated by using any online newspaper of the language.
- Verb Suffix Feature List (VSFL): Verb Suffix Feature list has verb suffixes along with its associated morphological features.
- Verb Suffix Class List (VSCL): Here suffixes are grouped to form classes such that if one member of the class can be attached to a stem all other members of the same class can also be attached to the same stem.

- Verb Paradigm List (VPL): VPL has verb paradigms. It uses VSCL. We keep the following details of paradigm -
  - Paradigm-id: A unique identifier for each paradigm.
  - Root-Verb : A sample citation form of a verb which follows the paradigm
  - Stem-rule: A rule to obtain the stem for the given word. For example **delete,end,character#add,end,null** is a sample rule.
  - Suffix: A list of suffix classes, each class is followed by joiner property. Joiner property is used to accommodate changes which take place at morpheme boundary when two morphemes combine.

A word can have more than one stem in which case the stem-rule and suffix get repeated for each stem. The Paradigm Selector generates the Verb Paradigm Repository (VPR). VPR has an entire list of verbs in the language with the corresponding paradigm identifier of the paradigm it follows.

**Algorithm:** For every entry in verb lexicon, Paradigm Selector uses VPL Stem-rule to check compatibility of the verb with the paradigms. A verb may be compatible with more than one paradigm as the Stem-rule is same for those paradigms. The correct corresponding paradigm needs to be chosen from the compatible paradigm set. This is done with the help of a corpus. Assuming that each compatible paradigm is a valid paradigm, word variants are generated for that paradigm with the help of the FSA. The new generated words are then searched in the corpus. The paradigm corresponding to which maximum word variants are found is the correct paradigm corresponding to that word. Corresponding paradigm-id and sample paradigm, forms an entry in the generated output resource VPR.

## 4 Experimental Results

The implementation of the FSA based verb MA tool is done in Java using NetBeans IDE 6.9 on a Windows XP platform.

### 4.1 Results for Paradigm Selector Module

Data sets used by Paradigm Selector Module were the Konkani WordNet, the Asmitai corpus consisting of approximately 268,000 words, Verb Paradigm List and Verb Suffix Class List which were manually prepared. Experimental results for Paradigm Selector module are -

- Total number of Verbs used for the study after pruning the compound verbs was 1226.
- Total number of verbs for which paradigm were mapped by the program: 1003
  - Total number for which ambiguous paradigms (more than one) were mapped by the program: 159
  - Total number for which single paradigm were found by the program: 844
- Total number of verbs for which paradigms were not mapped by the program: 223
- Total number of verbs for which correct paradigms were found which was manually checked by linguist (true positives): 791
- Total number of verbs for which wrong paradigms were found which was manually checked by linguist (false positives): 53
- Total number of verbs for which ambiguous paradigms were found or no paradigm were found by the program (false negatives): 159+223 = 382

Precision = 0.93 Recall = 0.67 F-Score = 0.78

## 4.2 Results for FSA Module

The verbs for which no paradigm was selected were manually assigned paradigms. Verbs for which wrong paradigm was selected were corrected. This gave us an updated Verb-Paradigm Repository which was used by the FSA module.

Resources used as input was the tagged health and tourism domain corpus of ILCI used to obtain the verb variants, Verb Paradigm Repository generated, Verb Paradigm List, Verb Suffix Feature List and Verb Suffix Class List which were manually prepared. The corpus was partially validated at time of use.

Total number of unique verb variant forms used for the study was 8697 obtained from ILCI corpus by choosing the words tagged as verbs. Following results were obtained by the program -

- Total number of verb variants for which analysis was obtained: 7237
- Total number of verb variants for which analysis was not obtained: 1460

The verb variant for which analysis was not obtained was checked manually. We found the following three categories amongst the verb variants for which analysis was not obtained -

- Number of verb variants whose citation form was not present in the Lexicon(obtained from WordNet) thus was not present in Word Paradigm Repository: 632
- Number of verb variants which were tagged wrongly as verbs: 341
- Number of verb variants which were spelt wrongly in the corpus: 487

- Total number of verb variants for which correct analysis was obtained verified manually (true positives): 7183
- Total number of verb variants for which wrong analysis was obtained verified manually (false positives): 54
- Total number of verbs variants for which no analysis was obtained due to absence of citation form in Lexicon verified manually (false negatives): 632
- Total number of verb variants for which analysis was not obtained due to wrong tagging + wrong spelling verified manually (true negatives): 341+487 = 828

Precision =0.992 Recall = 0.919 F-Score = 0.954

## Conclusion and Perspectives

From the results obtained for paradigm selector module we can say that the corpus is a reasonably good source to select paradigms for verbs. Human resource building effort can be substantially reduced with the use of this method. If the corpus is augmented with more forms of the verb then it would improve the recall of the paradigm selector module. This method can also be applied to the other grammatical categories such as nouns, adverbs etc.

Precision of FSA module for verbs is good. Tagged corpus when used to test the efficiency of the FSA module, results in more paradigm discovery and enhancement of the suffix list. It also suggests a list of verb citation forms which were absent in the lexicon. In addition it identifies spelling errors and tagging errors if any in the tagged corpus and could be used to validate the quality of the tagged corpus. The recall of FSA module can be improved by adding the citation forms which are not found in the lexicon to the VPR.

## References


Amba Kulkarni, G UmaMaheshwar Rao, Building Morphological Analyzers and Generators for Indian Languages using FST, Tutorial for ICON 2010

D. Freitag, "Morphology induction from term clusters," In Proceedings of the ninth conference on computational natural language learning (CoNLL), pp. 128–135, 2005.

Goldsmith, John and Aris Xanthos, Learning phonological categories. Language, 85(1):4–38, 2009.

Harald Hammarström, Lars Borin,Unsupervised Learning of Morphology, Computational Linguistics June 2011, Vol. 37, No. 2: 309–350

Harris, Zellig S., Phoneme to morpheme. Language, 31(2):190–222, 1955.

John Goldsmith, Linguistica: An Automatic Morphological Analyzer, CLS 36 [Papers from the 36th Meeting of the Chicago Linguistics Society]Volume1: The Main Session. 2000.

John Goldsmith, Unsupervised Learning of the, Morphology of a Natural Language, Computational Linguistics June 2001, Vol. 27, No. 2: 153–198.

Jurafsky, D., & Martin, J. H. Speech and Language Processing. Prentice-Hall, 2000

Lindén, K. and Tuovila, J., Corpus-based Paradigm Selection for Morphological Entries. In *Proceedings of NODALIDA 2009*, Odense, Denmark, May 2009

M. Forsberg H. Hammarström A. Ranta, Morphological Lexicon Extraction from Raw Text Data, LNAI 4139, pp.488-499,FinTAL 2006.

M. Forsberg and A. Ranta. Functional morphology. http://www.cs.chalmers.se/~markus/FM, 2007.

M. Porter, "An algorithm for suffix stripping program," Vol. 14,pp. 130-137, 1980.

Madhavi Sardesai, Some Aspects of Konkani Grammar, M. Phil Thesis(1986).

Matthew Ameida, S.J, A Description of Konkani, Thomas Stephens Konknni Kendra, 1989

Suresh Jayvant Borkar, Konkani Vyakran, Konkani Bhasha Mandal, 1992.

Vícor M. Sánchez-Cartagena, Miquel Esplà-Gomis, Felipe Sánchez-Martínez, Juan Antonio Pérez-Ortiz, Choosing the correct paradigm for unknown words in rule-based machine translation systems, Proceedings of the Third International Workshop on Free/Open-Source Rule-Based Machine Translation, , Gothenburg, Sweden, June 13-15, 2012.

Wicentowski, Richard. 2002. Modeling and Learning Multilingual Inflectional Morphology in a Minimally Supervised Framework. Ph.D. thesis, Johns Hopkins University, Baltimore, MD.

Xanthos, Aris, Yu Hu, and John Goldsmith, Exploring variant definitions of pointer length in MDL. In Proceedings of the Eighth Meeting of the ACL Special Interest Group on Computational Phonology and Morphology at HLT-NAACL 2006.

# Hindi and Marathi to English NE Transliteration Tool using Phonology and Stress Analysis

*M L Dhore[1] S K Dixit[2] R M Dhore[3]*
(1)LINGUISTIC RESEARCH GROUP, VIT, Pune, Maharashtra, India
(2) LINGUISTIC RESEARCH GROUP, WIT, Solapur, Maharashtra, India
(3) LINGUISTIC RESEARCH GROUP, PVG COET, Pune, Maharashtra, India

manikrao.dhore@vit.edu, dixitsk@wit.edu, ruchidhore@pvg.edu

ABSTRACT

During last two decades, most of the named entity (NE) machine transliteration work in India has been carried out by using English as a source language and Indian languages as the target languages using grapheme model with statistical probability approaches and classification tools. It is evident that less amount of work has been carried out for Indian languages to English machine transliteration.

This paper focuses on the specific problem of machine transliteration of Hindi to English and Marathi to English which are previously less studied language pairs using a phonetic based direct approach without training any bilingual database. Our study shows that in depth knowledge of word formation in Devanagari script based languages can provide better results as compared to statistical approaches. Proposed phonetic based model transliterates Indian-origin named entities into English using full consonant approach and uses hybrid (rule based and metric based) stress analysis approach for schwa deletion.

KEYWORDS: Machine Transliteration, Named Entity, Full Consonant, Metrical Approach

*Proceedings of COLING 2012: Demonstration Papers*, pages 111–118,
COLING 2012, Mumbai, December 2012.

# 1. Introduction

Hindi is the official national language of the India and spoken by around 500 million Indians. Hindi is the world's fourth most commonly used language after Chinese, English and Spanish. Marathi is one of the widely spoken languages in India especially in the state of Maharashtra. Hindi and Marathi languages are derived from the Sanskrit and use the "Devanagari" script for writing. It is challenging to transliterate out of vocabulary words like names and technical terms occurring in the user input across languages with different alphabets and sound inventories. Transliteration is the conversion of a word from one language to another without losing its phonological characteristics (Padariya 2008). Hindi and Marathi to English NE transliteration is quite difficult due to many factors such as difference in writing script, difference in number of alphabets, capitalization of leading characters, phonetic characteristics, character length, number of valid transliterations and availability of the parallel corpus (Saha 2008).

# 2. Architecture of Transliteration System

The architecture of Hindi/Marathi to English transliteration system and its functional modules are shown in figure 1.

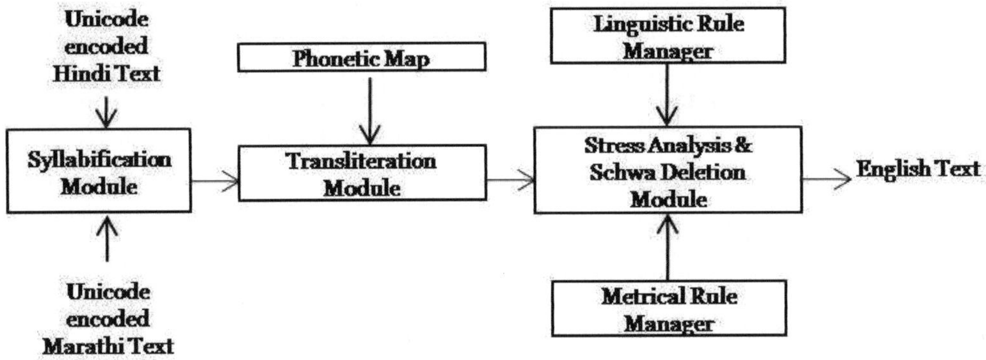


Figure 1. Architecture of Transliteration System

# 3. Phonetic Map for Hindi/Marathi to English

The possibility of different scripts between source and target languages is the problem that transliteration systems need to tackle. Hindi and Marathi use the Devanagari script whereas English uses the Roman script. Devanagari script used for Hindi and Marathi have 12 pure vowels, two additional loan vowels taken from the Sanskrit and one loan vowel from English. English has only five pure vowels but, the vowel sound is also associated with the consonants w and y (Koul 2008). There are 34 pure consonants, 5 traditional conjuncts, 7 loan consonants and 2 traditional signs in Devanagari script and each consonant have 14 variations through integration of 14 vowels while in Roman script there are only 21 consonants (Walambe 1990, Mudur 1999). Table 1 shows phonetic map for Devanagari to Roman transliteration along with their phonological mapping using full consonant approach. It is fully based on the National Library of

Kolkata and ITRANS of IIT Madras, India (Unicode 2007). The consonant /ळ/ is used only in Marathi language.

| Vowel | Matra | Vowel | Matra | Pure consonants | | | | |
|---|---|---|---|---|---|---|---|---|
| अ→a | | ॠ→RU | ◌ॄ | क→ka | ख→ kha | ग→ga | घ→gha | ङ→nga |
| आ→ A | ◌ा | ए→E | ◌े | च→cha | छ→chha | ज→ja | झ→jha | ञ→ya |
| इ→i | ि◌ | ऐ→ai | ◌ै | ट→Ta | ठ→Tha | ड→Da | ढ→dha | ण→Na |
| ई→ee | ◌ी | ओ→oo | ◌ो | त→ta | थ→tha | द→da | ध→Dha | न→na |
| उ→u | ◌ु | औ→au | ◌ौ | प→pa | फ→pha | ब→ba | भ→bha | म→ma |
| ऊ→U | ◌ू | अं→am | ◌ं/ ◌ँ | य→ya | र→ra | ल→la | व→va | श→sha |
| ऋ→Ru | ◌ृ | अ: →aH | ◌: | ष→Sha | स→sa | ळ→La | ह्→ha | |
| Conjucts,Symbols, Loan Letters → | | क्ष→ksha | ज्ञ→dnya | श्र→shra | द्य→dya | श्री | ॐ→om | क़→kxa |
| | | ढ़→Dhxa | ख़→khxa | ग़→gxa | ज़→jxa | फ़→phxa | ड़→Dxa | |

Table 1: Phonetic Map for Transliteration

## 4. Syllabification

Unicode encoded Hindi or Marathi named entity text input is given to the syllabification module which separates the input named entity into syllabic units. A syllabic unit is equivalent to one *'akshara' in* Devanagari where *'akshara'* is the minimal articulatory unit of speech in Hindi and Marathi. Few examples are

कैलाशनाथ → कै | ला | श | ना | थ and विजयराघवगढ़ → वि | ज | य | रा | घ | व | ग | ढ़

## 5. Transliteration Module

This module converts each syllabic unit in Devanagari into English by using phonetic map. Phonetic map is implemented by using the translation memory and mapping is done by writing the manual rules. It is to note that the first vowel /अ/ in Hindi/Marathi is mapped to English letter 'a' (short vowel) while the second vowel /आ/ is mapped to 'ā' (long vowel as per IPA) in English. The alphabet 'a' in English is a short vowel equivalent to /अ/ which is also a short vowel in Devanagari while /आ/ in Devanagari is a long vowel and mapped capital 'ā' or 'A' in our phonetic scheme. Unicode and ISCII character encoding standards for Indic scripts are based on full form of consonants (Singh 2006, BIS 1991). Few examples are

| Input | Transliteration | Observations |
|---|---|---|
| अनंता | anantA | Correct Transliteration |
| माणिक | mAnika | Last 'a' to be removed |
| कैलाशनाथ | kailashanatha | Schwa followed by 'sh' & last 'a' to be removed |
| विजयराघवगढ़ | vijayarAghavagaDha | Schwa followed by 'y', 'v' & last 'a' to be removed |

Table 2. Output of Transliteration Module

*Schwa* - The schwa is the vowel sound in many lightly pronounced unaccented syllables in words of more than one syllable. It is represented by /ə/ symbol (Naim 2009). The schwas remained in the transliterated output need to be deleted (Pandey 1990). The schwa identification and deletion is done by applying the manual rules and stress analysis. Instead of using either approach, it is better to combine both the approaches due to phonotactic constraints of Hindi and Marathi languages.

## 6. Rules for Schwa Retention and Deletion

From empirical observations the following six rules are applicable to all NEs (Choudhury 2004).

Rule 1: The schwa which occurs in isolation at the start of named entity never gets deleted. Example: amar (अमर, əmər) → [ə] : [mər]

Rule 2: The schwa preceding a full vowel never gets deleted to maintain lexical distinctions. Example: pawai (पवई, pəwəī) → [pə] : [wə] : [i]

Rule 3: The schwa which occurs in the first syllable never gets deleted if it is a consonant phoneme without any matra.

Rule 4: The schwa which occurs at the end of word always gets deleted. Example: gopal (गोपाल, gopAlə) → [go]:[pa] :[lə]

Rule 5: If the word ends in a consonant cluster or the rafar diacritic, then the schwa is retained. Example: atharva (अथर्व, əthərvə) → [ə]:[thərvə]

Rule 6: The schwa of the syllable immediately followed by a conjugate syllable should always be retained. Example: brahaspati (ब्रहस्पती, brahəspəti → [bra]:[hə]:[spa]:[ti]

## 7. Schwa Deletion Using Stress Analysis

Generally, the location of word stress in Hindi and Marathi is predictable on the basis of syllable stress. Stress is related both to the vowel length and the occurrence of postvocalic consonant. According to Hindi and Marathi phonology literature there are three classes of vowels used for stress analysis but it is possible to obtain the stress analysis using only two classes as shown below.

Class- I: Short vowels /a or ə/, /u/ and /i/ denoted by L (Light)

Class-II: Long vowels /ā/,/e/,/ī/,/o/,/ū/,/ai/, /au/ denoted by H (Heavy)

**Algorithm 1**: Schwa Deletion Using Stress Analysis

**If** last position has schwa **then**

    **If** last syllabic unit does not contains consonant cluster or the rafar diacritic **then**

        delete word-final schwa and resyllabify named entity

**endif**

**endif**

**foreach** syllabic unit in English **do** . assign metrical class ( L or H) **end foreach**

**foreach** syllabic unit and next syllabic unit **do** create metrical feet if any **end foreach**

**foreach** foot **do** find unstressed foot

    **if** the contexts of rule 1 to 4 from manual rules does not occur **then**

delete schwa(s) in unstressed foot and resyllabify foot

**endif**

**end foreach**

The process of combining syllables is carried out from right to left as schwa always appears to the right position (Naim 2009). With syllable stress and metrical feet, it is possible to find which syllable receives primary lexical stress. The stress information is used to decide whether the schwa is an unstressed syllable and to delete all such unstressed schwas. Few examples are shown in table 3.

| Named Entity | Metrical Assignments | Schwa Detection | Transliteration in English | Outcome |
|---|---|---|---|---|
| हेमवतीनंदन | HLLHHLL | heməvatinandan | hemvatinandan | Correct |
| त्रिलोकनारायण | HHLHHLL | trilokənArAyan | triloknArAyan | Correct |
| जगदंबाप्रसाद | LLHHHHL | jagədambAprasad | jagdambaprasAd | Correct |

Table 3. Schwa Deletion from Unstressed Syllables

## 8. Demonstration

We have developed real time application for a co-operative banking which allows user to enter data in Marathi or Hindi language and transliterate it into English. Figure 2 shows the snapshot from our experimentation for full name transliteration in English.

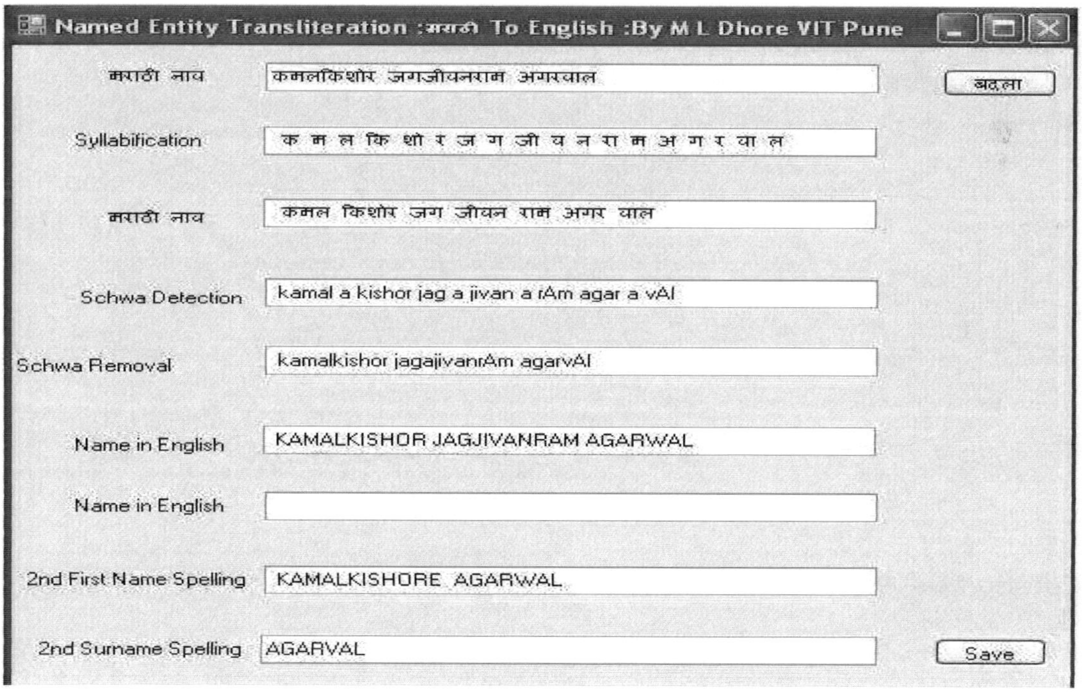


Figure 2. Transliteration Using Phonology and Stress Analysis

As there are more number of alphabets in Devanagari as compared to English, one alphabet in Devanagari can be mapped to multiple alphabets in English depending on the origin of word. Transliteration module maps the highest priority alphabet to generate the first candidate named entity. Table 4 is used to generate multiple transliteration candidates (Chinnakotla 2010).

| Hindi | क | ख | ग | ड | व | ई | श | क्ष | औ |
|---|---|---|---|---|---|---|---|---|---|
| English | k,c,q | k,kh | g, gh | d,dh | w,o,b,bh | i,e,ee,ey | sh,s | ksh,x | au,ou |

Table 4. Multiple Candidate Generation

Figure 3 shows the snapshot from our experimentation for personal profile of the bank account holder. It allows user to enter information in Marathi language and shows the corresponding transliterated record in English.

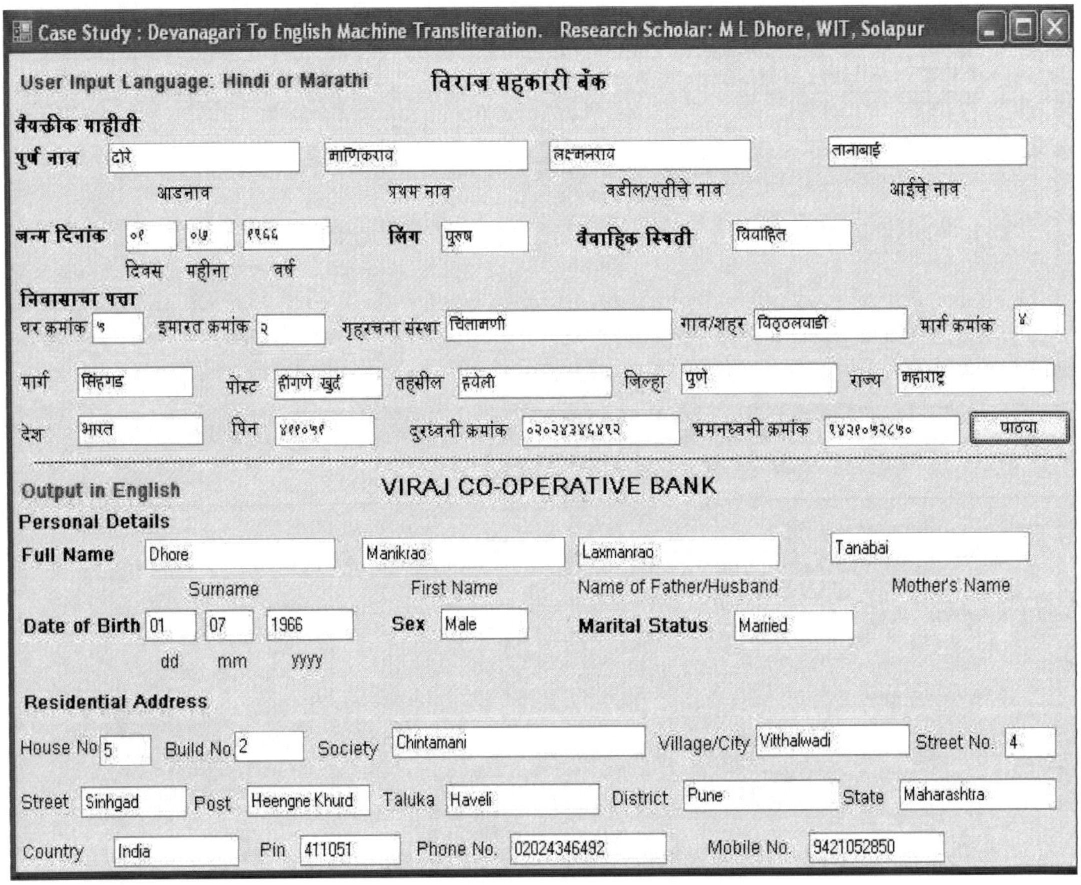


Figure 3. Account Holders Personal Information Form

## Conclusion

The use of machine transliteration in cross language applications is imminent and promising. Hindi and Marathi can be supported in all e-governance projects of the Government of India. As there is no need of bi-lingual and multilingual databases to be trained, this application can easily be ported on mobile devices. This application can help masses of India who do not know English.

## References

BIS (1991), Indian standard code for information interchange (ISCII), *Bureau Of Indian Standards*, New Delhi.

Chinnakotla Manoj K., Damani Om P., and Satoskar Avijit (2010), Transliteration for Resource-Scarce Languages, *ACM Trans. Asian Lang. Inform*,Article 14, pp 1-30.

Choudhury Monojit and Basu Anupam (2004), A rule based schwa deletion algorithm for Hindi, Indian Institute of Technology, Kharagpur,West Bengal, India.

Koul Omkar N. (2008), Modern Hindi Grammar, Dunwoody Press

Mudur S. P., Nayak N., Shanbhag S., and Joshi R. K. (1999), An architecture for the shaping of indic texts, *Computers and Graphics*, vol. 23, pp. 7–24.

Naim R Tyson and Ila Nagar (2009), Prosodic rules for schwa-deletion in Hindi Text-to-Speech synthesis, *International Journal of Speech Technology*, pp. 15–25

Padariya Nilesh, Chinnakotla Manoj, Nagesh Ajay, Damani Om P.(2008), Evaluation of Hindi to English, Marathi to English and English to Hindi, *IIT Mumbai CLIR at FIRE*.

Pandey Pramod Kumar (1990), Hindi schwa deletion, Department of Linguistics. South Gujarat University, Surat , India, *Lingua* 82, pp. 277-31

Saha Sujan Kumar, Ghosh P. S, Sarkar Sudeshna and Mitra Pabitra (2008), Named entity recognition in Hindi using maximum entropy and transliteration.

Singh Anil Kumar (2006), A computational phonetic model for Indian language scripts, Language Technologies Research Centre International Institute of Information Technology Hyderabad, India.

Unicode Standard 5.0 (2007) – Electronic edition, 1991–2007 Unicode, Inc. *Unicode Consortiums*, http://www.unicode.org.

Walambe M. R. (1990), Marathi Shuddalekhan, *Nitin Prakashan*, Pune

Walambe M. R. (1990), Marathi Vyakran, *Nitin Prakashan*, Pune

# Dealing with the grey sheep of the Romanian gender system, the neuter

*Liviu P. DINU, Vlad NICULAE, Maria ŞULEA*
University of Bucharest, Faculty of Mathematics and Computer Science,
Centre for Computational Linguistics, Bucharest
ldinu@fmi.unibuc.ro, vlad@vene.ro, mary.octavia@gmail.com

ABSTRACT
Romanian has been traditionally seen as bearing three lexical genders: masculine, feminine, and neuter, although it has always been known to have only two agreement patterns (for masculine and feminine). Previous machine learning classifiers which have attempted to discriminate Romanian nouns according to gender have taken as input only the singular form, either presupposing the traditional tripartite analysis, or using additional information from case inflected forms. We present here a tool based on two parallel support vector machines using n-gram features from the singular and from the plural, which distinguish the neuter.

KEYWORDS: Romanian morphology, neuter gender, noun class, SVM.

*Proceedings of COLING 2012: Demonstration Papers*, pages 119–124,
COLING 2012, Mumbai, December 2012.

# 1 The Romanian gender system

Recently, a big grammatical mistake made by a Romanian politician brought in attention the plural form of Romanian nouns. The traditional analysis (Graur et al., 1966; Rosetti, 1965, 1973; Corbett, 1991) identifies Romanian as the only Romance language bearing three lexical genders (masculine, feminine and neuter), whether the neuter was inherited from Latin (Constantinescu-Dobridor, 2001, p. 44), or redevelopped under the influence of Slavic languages (Rosetti, 1965; Petrucci, 1993). The first two genders generally have no problem regarding their plurals (follow a pattern more or less), the neuter gender being the one which poses some dificulties.These dificulties are not encompased only by politicians, but also for second language acquisition and; not to mention, in some cases, the long debates between linguists themselves. The problem occurs since the neuter gender has a masculine form for singular and a feminine form for plural (see Table 1 for examples). Since the language bears only two agreement markers (masculine and feminine), the three genders then need to be mapped onto the dual agreement, the way in which this mapping is done and on what basis also having been debated. However, under the premise that gender is expressed through agreement, the fact that Romanian neuter nouns lack their own marking and their own agreement pattern (they systematically and without exception follow the masculine agreement in the singular and the feminine in the plural as seen in Table 1) have lead Bateman and Polinsky (2010) and others to ask the question of whether Romanian has three genders, or two. Gender assignment thus becomes a burden not only for linguists to describe, but also for second language learners of Romanian to acquire.

| | singular | plural |
|---|---|---|
| masculine | băiat **frumos**<br>boy.M beautiful.M | băieți frumoși<br>boy.M beautiful.M |
| neuter | creion **frumos**<br>crayon.N beautiful.M | creioane **frumoase**<br>crayon.N beautiful.F |
| feminine | fată frumoasă<br>girl.F beautiful.F | fete **frumoase**<br>girl.F beautiful.F |

Table 1: Gender vs. agreement in Romanian

In our best knowledge, there are only two computational linguistics based approaches which attempted to discriminate Romanian nouns according to gender: Nastase and Popescu (2009) and (Cucerzan and Yarowsky, 2003). Our goal was, thus, to better -in comparison to Nastase and Popescu (2009)'s results- or successfully -in comparison to Cucerzan and Yarowsky (2003)'s experiment- distinguish these "neuter" nouns from feminines and masculines, by employing the minimum amount of information. We employed phonological information (coming from singular and plural noninflected nominative forms) as well as information coming from the feminine and masculine gender labels. In what follows we will present our tool for Romanian neuter nouns, which outperforms all previous attempts.

# 2 Our approach

We will look at singular and plural nominative indefinite forms (as specified by Bateman and Polinsky and used by Nastasescu and Popescu) and see if phonological features (endings) and information from masculine and feminine labels are sufficient to correctly classify Romanian neuter nouns as such. Another thing to take into consideration when looking at our classifier is the fact that, while Bateman and Polinsky (2010, p. 53-54) use both semantic and phonological features to assign gender, with the semantic features overriding the formal, we were unable use any semantic features, and used their phonological form as training examples.

## 2.1 Dataset

The dataset we used is a Romanian language resource containing a total of 480,722 inflected forms of Romanian nouns and adjectives. It was extracted from the text form of the morphological dictionary RoMorphoDict (Barbu, 2008), which was also used by Nastase and Popescu (2009) for their Romanian classifier, where every entry has the following structure:

```
form␣lemma␣description
```

Here, 'form' denotes the inflected form and 'description', the morphosyntactic description, encoding part of speech, gender, number, and case. For the morphosyntactic description, the initial dataset uses the slash ('/') as a disjunct operator meaning that 'm/n' stands for 'masculine or neuter', while the dash ('-') is used for the conjunct operator, with 'm-n' meaning 'masculine and neuter'. In the following, we will see that some of the disjunct gender labels can cause some problems in the extraction of the appropriate gender and subsequently in the classifier. Since our interest was in gender, we discarded all the adjectives listed and we isolated the nominative/accusative indefinite (without the enclitic article) form. We then split them into singulars and plurals; the defective nouns were excluded. The entries which were labeled as masculine or feminine were used as training and validation data for our experiment, while the neuters were left as the unlabeled test set. The training and validation set contained 30,308 nouns, and the neuter test set 9,822 nouns (each with singular and plural form).

## 2.2 Classifier and features

Our model consists of two binary linear support vector classifiers (Dinu et al., 2012), one for the singular forms and another one for the plural forms. Each of these has a free parameter $C$ that needs to be optimized to ensure good performance. We extracted character n-gram features vectors from the masculine and feminine nouns, separately. These vectors can represent counts of binary occurences of n-grams. We also considered that the suffix might carry more importance so we added the '$' character at the end of each inflected form. This allows the downstream classifier to assign a different weight to the $(n-1)$-grams that overlap with the suffix. Each possible combinations of parameters: n-gram length, use of binarization, addition of suffix, and the $C$ regularization parameter was evaluated using 10-fold cross-validation, for both singular and plurals. After the model has been selected and trained in this manner, the neuter nouns are plugged in and their singular forms are classified according to the singular classifier, while their plural forms are classified by the plural model. The experiment was set up and run using the *scikit-learn* machine learning library for Python (Pedregosa et al., 2011). The implementation of linear support vector machines used is *liblinear*.

# 3 Our results

The best parameters chosen by cross-validation are 5-gram features, append the suffix character, but don't binarize the feature vectors. On masculine-feminine singulars, this obtained an accuracy of 99.59%, with a precision of 99.63%, a recall of 99.80% and an $F_1$ score of 99.71%. The plural model scored an accuracy of 95.98%, with a precision of 97.32%, a recall of 97.05% and an $F_1$ score of 97.18%. We then moved on to check the classification results of the neuter forms, and performed error analysis on the results. Table 2a shows the distribution of neuter noun tuples (singular, plural) according to how our models classify their forms. Our hypothesis states that all of the mass should gather in the top-left corner, i.e. neuters should classify as masculine in the singular and feminine in the plural. There are more misclassifications in the plural form of neuter nouns than in their singular form. In what follows, we will briefly analyze the misclassifications and see if there is any room for improvement or any blatant mistakes that can be rectified.

| s/p | f | m |
|---|---|---|
| m | 8997 | 741 |
| f | 69 | 15 |

(a) With full training set

| s/p | f | m |
|---|---|---|
| m | 9537 | 201 |
| f | 83 | 1 |

(b) Misleading samples removed

Table 2: Distribution of neuters as classified by the system. In each table, the upper left corner shows nouns classified as expected (masculine in the singular, feminine in the plural), while the lower right corner shows completely misclassified nouns (nouns that seem to be feminine in the singular and masculine in the plural). The other two fields appropriately show nouns misclassified in only one of the forms.

### 3.1 Analyzing misclassifications

We first notice that 10 out of the 15 nouns that were completely misclassified are French borrowings which, although feminine in French, designate inanimate things. According to (Butiurca, 2005, p. 209), all feminine French nouns become neuter once they are borrowed into Romanian. The ones discussed here have the singular ending in 'é', written in Romanian without the accent, but retaining main stress as in French. Another of the 15, which also ends in an 'e' carrying main stress but not of French origin, is a noun formed from an acronym: *pefele* from *PFL*. There is also a noun (*coclaură–coclauri*) probably from the pre-Latin substratum, which is listed in Romanian dictionaries either as a pluralia tantum or as it is listed in the dataset. The others are feminine singular forms wrongly labeled in the original corpus as being neuter or neuter/feminine. Looking at the entries in the original dataset for two of the last five nouns completely misclassified (*levantin/levantină–levantinuri/levantine* and *bageac/bageacă–bageacuri/bageci*), we notice that the latter receives an 'n' tag for the singular form *bageacă*, which in (Collective, 2002) is listed as a feminine, and the former receives the 'n/f' tag, meaning *either a neuter, or a feminine* (Barbu, 2008, p. 1939), for both the neuter *levantin* and the feminine *levantină* singular form. We further notice that, when the gender tag 'n/f' accompanies a singular form, from the perspective of our system, a contradiction is stated. Seeing as Romanian has only two agreement patterns and that neuters agree like masculines in the singular and feminines in the plural, the feminine form levantină cannot be either neuter, and receive the masculine numeral *un* in the singular, or feminine, and receive the feminine numeral *o*. It can only be feminine. Through analoguous resoning, the tag 'n/m' accompanying a plural form is also "absurd". By eliminating the second gender from the two disjunct labels of the original dataset when extracting the nouns for our classifier, we correctly tagged the neuter variants with 'n', but also wrongly tagged 5 feminine singular forms with 'n' and 7 masculine plural forms with 'n'. There are other misclassified nouns, from the other two groups, whose misclasification is due to an error in their initial gender label, for instance *algoritm–algoritmi* is shown to be a masculine in (Collective, 2002), however in the corpus it is tagged as neuter (together with the neuter variant *algoritm–algoritme*) and it subsequently appears to be misclassified in the plural as a masculine, which in fact it is. Another problem causing the misclassification is represented by the hyphenated compound nouns, which are headed by the leftmost noun that also receives the number/gender inflection. Seeing as our classification system weighed more on the suffix, it was prone to fail in correctly clasifying them.

## Conclusion and perspectives

The results of our classifier make a strong case, in particular, for Bateman and Polinsky's analysis according to which class membership of nouns in Romanian is assigned based on form (nominative noninflected singular endings and plural markers), when semantic cues relating to natural gender (masculine and feminine) are absent, and, in general, for their two separate (for the singular and plural) dual-class division of the Romanian nominal domain. Furthermore, our classification model outperforms the two classifiers of Romanian nouns according to gender previously constructed in terms of correctly distinguishing the neuter.

## Acknowledgments

The research of Liviu P. Dinu was supported by the CNCS, IDEI - PCE project 311/2011, "The Structure and Interpretation of the Romanian Nominal Phrase in Discourse Representation Theory: the Determiners." Note that the contribution of the authors to this paper is equal.

## References

Barbu, A.-M. (2008). Romanian lexical databases: Inflected and syllabic forms dictionaries. In *Sixth International Language Resources and Evaluation (LREC'08)*.

Bateman, N. and Polinsky, M. (2010). *Romanian as a two-gender language*, chapter 3, pages 41–78. MIT Press, Cambridge, MA.

Butiurca, D. (2005). Influenţa franceză. In *European Integration-Between Tradition and Modernity (EITM), Volume 1*, pages 206–212.

Collective (2002). *Dicţionar ortografic al limbii române*. Editura Litera Internaţional.

Constantinescu-Dobridor, G. (2001). *Gramatica Limbii Române*. Editura Didactică şi Pedagogică Bucureşti.

Corbett, G. G. (1991). *Gender*. Cambridge University Press.

Cucerzan, S. and Yarowsky, D. (2003). Minimally supervised induction of grammatical gender. In *HLT-NAACL 2003*, pages 40–47.

Dinu, L. P., Niculae, V., and Şulea, O.-M. (2012). The romanian neuter examined through a two-gender n-gram classification system. In Calzolari, N., Choukri, K., Declerck, T., Doğan, M. U., Maegaard, B., Mariani, J., Odijk, J., and Piperidis, S., editors, *Proceedings of the*

*Eight International Conference on Language Resources and Evaluation (LREC'12)*, Istanbul, Turkey. European Language Resources Association (ELRA).

Graur, A., Avram, M., and Vasiliu, L. (1966). *Gramatica Limbii Române*, volume 1. Academy of the Socialist Republic of Romania, 2nd edition.

Nastase, V. and Popescu, M. (2009). What's in a name? in some languages, grammatical gender. In *EMNLP*, pages 1368–1377. ACL.

Pedregosa, F., Varoquaux, G., Gramfort, A., Michel, V., Thirion, B., Grisel, O., Blondel, M., Prettenhofer, P., Weiss, R., Dubourg, V., Vanderplas, J., Passos, A., Cournapeau, D., Brucher, M., Perrot, M., and Duchesnay, E. (2011). Scikit-learn: Machine learning in Python. *Journal of Machine Learning Research*, 12:2825–2830.

Petrucci, P. R. (1993). *Slavic features in the history of Romanian*. PhD thesis.

Rosetti, A. (1965). *Linguistica*. The Hague: Mouton.

Rosetti, A. (1973). *Breve Histoire de la Langue Rumain des Origines a Nos Jours*. The Hague: Mouton.

# Authorial studies using ranked lexical features

*Liviu P. DINU, Sergiu NISIOI*
University of Bucharest, Faculty of Mathematics and Computer Science,
Centre for Computational Linguistics, Bucharest
ldinu@fmi.unibuc.ro, sergiu.nisioi@gmail.com

ABSTRACT

The purpose of this article is to propose a tool for measuring distances between different styles of one or more authors. The main study is focused on measuring and visualizing distances in a space induced by ranked lexical features. We investigate the case of Vladimir Nabokov, a bilingual Russian - English language author.

KEYWORDS: stylometry, L1 distance, translationes, rankings, Nabokov.

*Proceedings of COLING 2012: Demonstration Papers*, pages 125–130,
COLING 2012, Mumbai, December 2012.

## 1 Introduction. Selecting the right features

The features generally considered to characterize the style of an author are function words - conjunctions, prepositions, pronouns, determiners, particles, etc.. These words consist of non-content words, mostly words without a semantic referent. Also they have a crucial role in the construction of a phrase, holding syntactic features and tying semantics together. These words form the closed class set of a language and can easily be extracted from Wiktionary (url), a database which is constantly being improved and provides a great source of linguistic knowledge for languages that do not usually have tools and resources. The function words can sometimes be a compound token composed from two function words, for example some Russian declensions requires two words (e.g. for masculine, singular, prepositional case of ves' is the token obo vsem). We have treated this case by analysing the occurrences of an expression. Selecting the right lexical features is difficult, on one hand, using the entire list of function words from a language to designate the style of author has the disadvantage of containing words that are hapax legomena or do not exist in the analysed corpus. On the other hand, this disadvantage can provide a spectrum of used and unused words of an author, this being a mark of style. Also, it is a fixed feature that belongs to the language and does not depend on additional decisions regarding the corpus. This type of procedure is also discussed by (Argamon and Levitan, 2005). In order to obtain features that are strictly related to the corpus, one can concatenate all the texts to be analysed and extract the first n (function) words (Burrows, 2002),(Argamon, 2008). The drawback of this procedure is that we can not always know if the value chosen for n is optimal with regard to the expected hypothesis. Cases appear when completely different values of n increase the accuracy of the result depending on the type of language and other factors discussed by (Rybicki et al., 2011). Our tools can handle both of these situations, for the first we can input a list of tokens, one on each line and for the second we are developing a special semi-automatic process. This, second list is constructed from the first n most frequent words which, agreeing with the study of (Jockers and Witten, 2012), have a *mean relative frequency of at least 0.05%*. We want to implement a special procedure that, given $n_1$ and $n_2$, two integers, computes the adjusted Rand index (Hubert and Arabie, 1985) between the cluster $i$ and the cluster $i-1$ with $n_1 < i \leq n_2$. The label for two clusters $A$ and $B$ to be joined will be given by $\min(A, B)$. This way we can label all the remaining clusters recursively. We were looking for a sequence of $i$ where the clustering becomes stable and the adjusted Rand index remains close to 1. Meaning that when adding new words to the list we obtain the same result. The sequence obtained can be trusted to offer one literary hypothesis from the entire set that is the most stable to the way an author uses his most common words.

All the token - function words retrieved from a document are stored in a trie structure, with small caps. In a normal trie in each node there will be an extra field to indicate that the respective node is an end of word. We have used this field to indicate the frequency of each token. After filling the trie structure we can traverse it to retrieve the entire list of tokens with the frequencies. Because frequencies are positive integers we have used Radix sort, a non-comparison, sorting method by least significant digit in order to obtain the rank-ordered list of words in linear complexity. Computing distances or measurements between documents is more efficient this way.

Our algorithms are based on the use of rankings induced by the frequencies of function words, e.g the most frequent word has rank one, the second most frequent rank two and so on. We call a tie the case when two or more frequencies are equal. In order to solve ties we apply the standard Spearman's rank correlation method. This means that if k objects claim the same rank (i.e. have the same frequency) and the first x ranks are already used by other objects then they will share the ranks and will receive the same rank number (the median from the k objects) which is in this case:

$$\frac{(x+1)+(x+2)+\cdots+(x+k)}{k} = x + \frac{(k+1)}{2} \tag{1}$$

Using rankings instead of raw frequencies has proved to offer better hypothesis regarding similarities between documents (Dinu et al., 2008).

## 2 Data visualisation

In order to inspect our results we have opted for a hierarchical clustering method based on the extension provided by (Szekely and Rizzo, 2005) for Ward's method. Their approach is concerned with increasing inner cluster homogeneity and inter-cluster heterogeneity. We have taken advantage of this joint-between within clustering method and we have adapted it for our $l1$ space to suit our purpose:

$$e_{l1}(A,B) = \frac{n_1 n_2}{n_1+n_2}\left(\frac{2}{n_1 n_2}\sum_{i=1}^{n_1}\sum_{j=1}^{n_2} \| a_i - b_j \|_1 - \frac{1}{n_1^2}\sum_{i=1}^{n_1}\sum_{j=1}^{n_1} \| a_i - a_j \|_1 - \frac{1}{n_2^2}\sum_{i=1}^{n_2}\sum_{j=1}^{n_2} \| b_i - b_j \|_1\right) \tag{2}$$

Where $A = \{a_1, \cdots, a_n\}$ and $B = \{b_1, \cdots, b_n\}$ are sets of size $n_1$ and $n_2$ respectively of m-dimensional vectors, $\| \cdot \|_1$ is the $l1$ norm. The Lance-Williams (Lance and Williams, 1967) parameters are exactly the same as for Ward's method (see (Szekely and Rizzo, 2005), Appendix):

$$d(C_i \cup C_j, C_k) = \frac{n_1+n_3}{n_1+n_2+n_3} d(C_i, C_k) + \frac{n_2+n_3}{n_1+n_2+n_3} d(C_j, C_k) - \frac{n_3}{n_1+n_2+n_3} d(C_i, C_j). \tag{3}$$

where $n_1, n_2, n_3$ are the sizes of cluster $C_i, C_j, C_k$ and becomes:

$$d_{(ij)k} := d(C_i \cup C_j, C_k) = \alpha_i\, d(C_i, C_k) + \alpha_j\, d(C_j, C_k) + \beta\, d(C_i, C_j) \tag{4}$$

where

$$\alpha_i = \frac{n_i + n_3}{n_1+n_2+n_3}, \qquad \beta = \frac{-n_3}{n_1+n_2+n_3}, \qquad \gamma = 0.$$

Many of the valuable $e$ properties proved only by coefficient handling like ultrametric property (Milligan, 1979) (i.e. $d_{ij} < \max\{d_{ik}, d_{jk}\}$) or space-dilatation (Everitt et al., 2009) (i.e $d_{k,(ij)} \geq \max\{d_{ki}, d_{kj}\}$) of the algorithm are inherited with this shift to $e_{l1}$. If $A$ and $B$ would be singletons, the $e_{l1}$ distance is proportional to Manhattan distance and is recommended to be used with it and not with an Euclidean distance. Such an algorithm is best suited for our ranked data.

## 3 Measurements

### 3.1 Manhattan Distance

The most natural measure to be applied on an $l1$ space is Manhattan distance. When used on rankings it is also called Spearman's foot-rule or Rank distance by (Dinu and Popescu, 2008). Given two tied ranked vectors $X = \{x_1, \cdots, x_n\}$ and $Y = \{y_1, \cdots, y_n\}$ the equation for Manhattan distance is:

$$D(X,Y) = \sum_{i=1}^{n} |x_i - y_i| \tag{5}$$

Notice that the distance remains the same if our tied ranked vectors are obtained by an ascending ordering relation (e.g. assign rank one to the most frequent function word, rank two to the second most frequent and so on) or by a descending ordering relation . This is simple to prove once we observe that for some frequencies $\{f_1 > f_2 > \cdots > f_n\}$, that generated an ascending tied rank $X_> = \{x_1, \cdots, x_n\}$, its descending tied rank can be obtained by the next equation from $X_>$:

$$X_< = (n - X_>) + 1 \tag{6}$$

This suggests that ranking the frequencies does not imply just a simple change of the weights, but rather a change of space in which distances between documents become more measurable and more stable.

## 4 Application

Considering the previous studies (Dinu et al., 2008) regarding the use of lexical ranked features we have used our tools to investigate further the case of Vladimir Nabokov, a bilingual Russian - English language author. The works after 1941 are written in English. Those before, are in Russian.

We have gathered a corpus consisting of his original works in English: *The Real Life of Sebastian Knight* (1941), *Bend Sinister* (1947), *Lolita* (1955), *Pnin* (1957), *Pale Fire* (1962) , *Ada or Ardor: A Family Chronicle* (1969), *Transparent Things* (1972), *Look at the Harlequins!* (1974) together with the Russian translation of each. And his original works in Russian: *Mashenka* (1926), *Korol' Dama Valet* (1928), *Zashchita Luzhina* (1930), *Podvig* (1932), *Kamera Obskura* (1933), *Otchayanie* (1934), *Priglasheniye na kazn* (1936), *Dar* (1938) together with the English translation of *Mary* (translation year: 1970) , *The (Luzhin) Defence* (translation year: 1964), *Laughter in the Dark* (translation year: 1938), *Invitation to a Beheading* (translation year: 1959).

In the first image (Figure 1) we observe that the translated Russian period novels *Mary*, *Luzhin Defence*, *Camera Obscura* and *Invitation to a Beheading* are clustered separately from the novels written after 1940 in English. In the second image (Figure 2) we are looking at the Russian translations of the novels. A similar result with the previous one is presented: two clusteres, one with the original works in Russian and one with the translated ones. Nabokov's last Russian novel *Dar* is clustered near the English period.

## Conclusion and perspectives

We have presented a reliable quantitative method with which we can measure distances between different styles of one or more authors. We have proved that, by using rankings,

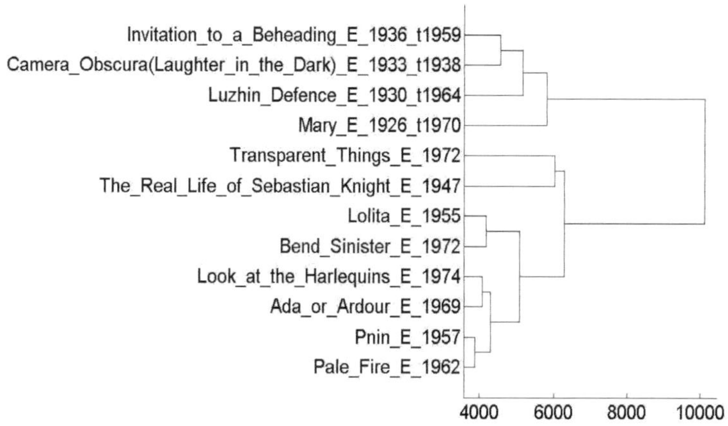


Figure 1: L1 distance applied with ranked lexical features of English.

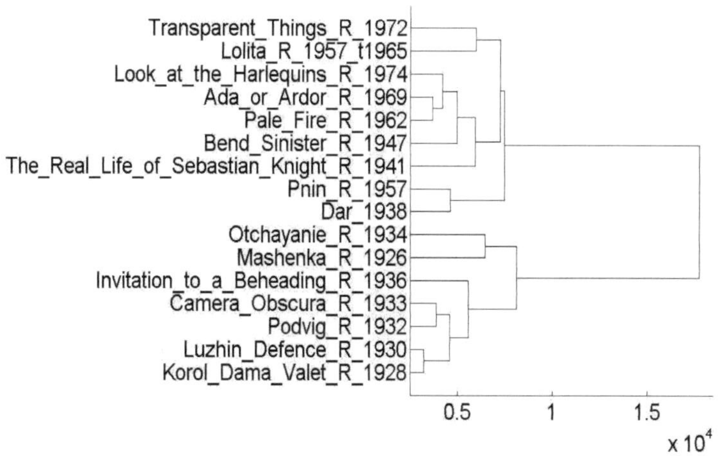


Figure 2: L1 distance applied with ranked lexical features of Russian.

Manhattan distance (or rank distance) was effective in distinguishing the style of an author. In future works we want to see if rankings can improve the accuracy of Burrows Delta (Burrows, 2002). Our $l1$ adapted clustering algorithm was able to distinguish between Nabokov's early Russian novels and his later English ones in both translation and original. Furthermore our results proved that on one hand Nabokov's style had changed significantly during his two literary periods and on the other hand that a translation affects a text in such a measure that stylistically it does not preserve the pattern of the original author. Therefore, although a method is oriented to simplicity, we can obtain significant results about an author's style if we rank an adequate set of lexical features. For further investigation we take into consideration the importance of pronouns in depicting an author's style. Moreover we intend to apply the methods on Samuel Beckett's and Milan Kundera's works and implicitly to draw comparisons between English and French, but also Czech and French. During the course of our study we have found an interesting coincidence. Manhattan distance, which is identical with the distance a rook makes between two squares on a chess table, proved to be suitable for the literary works of Nabokov, who was a chess composer.

## Acknowledgments

The research of Liviu P. Dinu was supported by the CNCS, IDEI - PCE project 311/2011, "The Structure and Interpretation of the Romanian Nominal Phrase in Discourse Representation Theory: the Determiners." We want to thank to Anca Bucur from the University of Bucharest for the helpful discussions. Note that the contribution of the authors to this paper is equal.

## References

Wiktionary. `ru.wiktionary.org/`.

Argamon, S. and Levitan, S. (2005). Measuring the usefulness of function words for authorship attribution. In *In Proceedings of the 2005 ACH/ALLC Conference*.

Argamon, S. E. (2008). Interpreting burrows' delta: Geometric and probabilistic foundations. *Literary and Linguistic Computing*, 23(2):131–147.

Burrows, J. F. (2002). Delta: A measure of stylistic difference and a guide to likely authorship. *Literary and Linguistic Computing*, 17(1):267–287.

Dinu, A., Dinu, L. P., and Popescu, M. (2008). Authorship identification of romanian texts with controversial paternity. pages 2871–2874, Marrakech, Maroc. LREC, ELRA.

Dinu, L. P. and Popescu, M. (2008). Rank distance as a stylistic similarity. pages 91–94, Manchester. Coling, ELRA.

Everitt, B. S., Landau, S., and Leese, M. (2009). *Cluster Analysis*. John Wiley & Sons.

Hubert, L. and Arabie, P. (1985). Comparing partitions. *Journal of Classification*, 2(1):193–218.

Jockers, M. L. and Witten, D. M. (2012). A comparative study of machine learning methods for authorship attribution. *Literary and Linguist Computing*, pages 215–223.

Lance, G. N. and Williams, W. T. (1967). A general theory of classificatory sorting strategies. *The Computer Journal*, 9(4):373–380.

Milligan, G. W. (1979). Ultrametric hierarchical clustering algorithms. *PSYCHOMETRIKA*, 44(3):343–346.

Rybicki, J., Eder, M., and Eder, M. (2011). Deeper delta across genres and languages: do we really need the most frequent words? pages 315–321.

Szekely, G. J. and Rizzo, M. L. (2005). Hierarchical clustering via joint between-within distances: Extending ward's minimum variance method. *Journal of Classification*, (22):151 – 183.

# ScienQuest: a treebank exploitation tool for non NLP-specialists

*Achille Falaise*[1], *Olivier Kraif*[2], *Agnès Tutin*[2], *David Rouquet*[1]
(1) LIG-GETALP, University of Grenoble, France
(2) LIDILEM, University of Grenoble, France
achille.falaise@imag.fr, olivier.kraif@u-grenoble3.fr,
agnes.tutin@u-grenoble3.fr, david.rouquet@imag.fr

ABSTRACT

The exploitation of syntactically analysed corpora (or treebanks) by non NLP-specialist is not a trivial problem. If the NLP community wants to make publicly available corpora with complex annotations, it is imperative to develop simple interfaces capable of handling advanced queries. In this paper, we present query methods developed during the Scientext project and intended for the general public. Queries can be made using forms, lemmas, parts of speech, and syntactic relations within specific textual divisions, such as title, abstract, introduction, conclusion, etc. Three query modes are described: an assisted query mode in which the user selects the elements of the query, a semantic mode which includes local pre-established grammars using syntactic functions, and an advanced search mode where the user create custom grammars.

# ScienQuest: un outil d'exploitation de corpus arborés pour les non spécialistes du TALN

RÉSUMÉ

L'exploitation de corpus analysés syntaxiquement (ou corpus arborés) pour le public non spécialiste du TALN n'est pas un problème trivial. Si la communauté du TALN souhaite mettre à la disposition des chercheurs non-informaticiens des corpus comportant des annotations linguistiques complexes, elle doit impérativement développer des interfaces simples à manipuler mais permettant des recherches fines. Dans cette communication, nous présentons les modes de recherche « grand public » développés dans le cadre du projet Scientext, qui met à disposition un corpus d'écrits scientifiques interrogeable par section textuelle, par partie du discours et par fonction syntaxique. Trois modes de recherche sont décrits : un mode libre et guidé, où l'utilisateur sélectionne lui-même les éléments de la requête, un mode sémantique, qui comporte des grammaires locales préétablies à l'aide des fonctions syntaxiques, et un mode avancé, dans lequel l'utilisateur crée ses propres grammaires.

KEYWORDS : corpus exploitation environments, treebanks, assisted grammar creation, visualization of linguistic information.

MOTS-CLÉS : environnement d'étude de corpus, corpus étiquetés et arborés, création de grammaires assistée, visualisation d'information linguistique.

*Proceedings of COLING 2012: Demonstration Papers*, pages 131–140,
COLING 2012, Mumbai, December 2012.

# 1 Version courte en français

## 1.1 Introduction

Les outils d'exploration de corpus annotés, en particulier de corpus arborés (c'est-à-dire comportant des relations syntaxiques), sont souvent complexes à utiliser, *a fortiori* pour des utilisateurs non initiés à la linguistique-informatique. L'ergonomie et la facilité d'utilisation des outils sont cependant des enjeux majeurs en TALN, surtout si l'on souhaite diffuser des traitements et des annotations linguistiques complexes dans la communauté des linguistes. Pour élargir le nombre d'utilisateurs des corpus annotés, il est essentiel de développer des outils d'exploration de corpus faciles à manipuler mais puissants. C'est ce qui nous a amenés à proposer un environnement de recherche simple, adapté aux linguistes, didacticiens, lexicographes ou épistémologues.

Nous présentons ici l'outil développé dans le cadre du projet Scientext[1], qui propose des modes de recherche simples pour non spécialistes du TALN sur un corpus d'écrits scientifiques analysé syntaxiquement. Il s'agit d'un outil d'étude en ligne de corpus arborés construit à partir d'un scénario de recherche simple : choix d'un corpus, recherche de phénomènes linguistiques, et enfin affichage des résultats. Ce scénario de base est facile à appréhender, et se décompose en plusieurs écrans simples qui peuvent s'enrichir de fonctions plus complexes « en douceur ».

Dans un premier temps, nous présentons les outils existants pour l'étude de corpus arborés, en particulier pour le français, rares et peu conviviaux. Nous détaillons ensuite les fonctionnalités de notre outil, et effectuons enfin un bilan de son utilisation.

## 1.2 Les corpus

Dans le cadre du projet Scientext, quatre corpus de textes scientifiques ont été collectés. Deux des corpus contiennent des textes anglais, et les deux autres des textes français. Ces corpus sont librement consultables sur le site du projet. D'autres corpus de textes littéraires et journalistiques en allemand, anglais, espagnol, français et russe ont été collectés dans le cadre du projet EMOLEX[2], mais ne sont pas consultables pour des raisons de droits. Tous ces corpus ont été annotés morpho-syntaxiquement, à l'aide de divers analyseurs (Syntex, Connexor, XIP, DeSR), et ont pu être exploités à l'aide de ScienQuest.

## 1.3 Les modes d'accès aux textes

Après avoir sélectionné un sous-corpus en fonction des genres et des sections textuelles désirés (figure 2), l'utilisateur peut effectuer des recherches sur le corpus selon trois modes, de complexité et d'expressivité croissante :

- **Un mode sémantique** permet d'accéder à des occurrences en corpus, à partir de grammaires prédéfinies. Les grammaires sont définies à l'aide d'un langage de requête existant (ConcQuest — Kraif, 2008), que nous avons étendu.

[1] http://scientext.msh-alpes.fr
[2] http://www.emolex.eu

- **Un mode simple et guidé** avec un assistant permet à l'utilisateur de sélectionner des formes, lemmes et/ou catégories, ainsi que les relations syntaxiques désirées (figures 4 et 5).
- **Un mode complexe** permet d'accéder à des occurrences en corpus, à partir de grammaires, utilisant les dépendances syntaxiques, les relations linéaires et des variables.

Une fois la requête effecutée, les occurrences trouvées sont affichées soit dans un concordancier (figure 6), soit sous forme de statistiques distributionnelles.

## 1.4 Conclusion

L'utilisation du système Scientext dépasse aujourd'hui le cadre du projet dont il est issu. Il est par exemple utilisé en didactique du FLE dans le cadre du projet FULS[3], et intègre de nouveaux corpus, traités avec des analyseurs différents, pour le projet EMOLEX.

Depuis le lancement public du site fin juin 2010, 9 021 requêtes ont été effectuées (en 1 474 sessions). Le mode guidé est utilisé pour 75% des requêtes, le mode sémantique (grammaires locales prédéfinies) pour 23% et le mode avancé pour 2% ; cela démontre bien selon nous l'intérêt de ces deux premiers modes de recherche. Malgré tout, il reste que les connaissances d'ordre syntaxique présentent une complexité inhérente qui freine quelque peu l'utilisation grand public de tels corpus, puisque seulement 47% des requêtes guidées comportaient des contraintes d'ordre syntaxique.

Plusieurs améliorations du système sont prévues : l'ajout de nouveaux corpus et l'ajout de fonctionnalités pour le mode guidé. Ces améliorations seront testées sur un ensemble d'utilisateurs non spécialistes du TALN.

[3] http://scientext.msh-alpes.fr/fuls

## 2 Introduction

Textual corpora are more and more often enriched with different types of linguistic annotations, such as structural and discursive annotations, lemmatisation, part-of-speech (POS) tagging, or syntactic tree structures. These annotations may be very appealing for non-NLP specialists, such as linguists, language teachers, lexicographers, and epistemologists. However, exploration tools for such corpora, especially treebanks (i.e. with syntactic relations) are often complex to use, a fortiori for users not familiar with computational linguistics. In order to broaden the scope of access to these annotations outside the NLP community, it is essential to develop tools that are both powerful, but easy to handle for corpus exploration. This objective led us to propose ScienQuest, a simple research environment suitable for non NLP-specialists.

ScienQuest was developed in the context of the Scientext project[4]. It is an online generic tool, which focuses on a GUI suitable for non NLP-specialists. It is based on the ConcQuest (Kraif, 2008) command-line search engine. ScienQuest was first used as part of the Scientext project, which includes several corpora of scientific texts, and then for several new corpora. ScienQuest is based on a simple search scenario. After building a sub-corpus based on the metadata of the texts in the corpus, user requests within this sub-corpus provide results displayed in two fashions: Key Word In Context (KWIC) and distributional statistics. This straightforward three-part baseline scenario is represented within the interface by the division into several simple screens.

In this paper, we first present the corpora currently operated within ScienQuest. Then, we describe briefly some of the existing tools for the study of treebanks. Finally, we detail the features of ScienQuest, and conclude with a review of its use.

## 3 Of corpora and users

The corpora of the Scientext project were collected to conduct a linguistic study on reasoning and positioning of authors, through phraseology, enunciative and syntactic markers related to syntactic causality. The corpora were parsed with Syntex (Bourigault, 2007). They consist of an English corpus of biology and medical articles (14M words), a corpus of argumentative texts of French learners of English (1M words), a French corpus of varied scientific texts (a range of genres and disciplines totalling 5M words), and a corpus of French scientific communication reviews (502 reviews, 35k words). These corpora are freely available within ScienQuest on the Scientext project website. A study is underway to draw upon these corpora using ScienQuest in the context of language courses.

ScienQuest has recently been integrated for the exploitation of the corpora of the EMOLEX[5] project, which aims to investigate the multilingual lexicon of emotions within five corpora of fiction and newspaper articles in English (200M words, analysed with XIP), French (230M words, analysed with Connexor), German (301M words, analysed with Connexor), Spanish (286M words, analysed with Connexor), and Russian (554k

[4] http://scientext.msh-alpes.fr
[5] http://www.emolex.eu

word, analysed with DeSR). For copyright issues, these corpora are unfortunately not publicly available yet.

ScienQuest was designed with usability in mind, and therefore was designed with user input in mind. A first survey was conducted in March 2008 with a group of researchers and students in linguistics, teaching, and communication from four different laboratories. A first prototype was built based on this first survey. A second survey was then conducted, with both new participants and researchers involved in the previous survey.

## 4 A brief overview of annotated corpora exploration tools

There are several environments for the study of linguistically annotated corpora. These environments are based on query languages; they sometimes come with a graphical environment, usually limited to a graphical query editor. This type of graphical environment can improve the readability compared to a query language used alone, but still maintains the same conceptual complexity. These tools require a familiarity with computer science basics such as logical operators and regular expressions that are often poorly mastered by non-specialists, who therefore are often reluctant to use these tools.

Most corpus research tools do not integrate the syntactic level. The Corpus Query Processor (CQP – Christ, 1994), developed at the *Institut für Maschinelle Sprachverarbeitung* of Stuttgart, has become a standard element in the community of NLP. A graphical interface for CQP, CQPWeb[6], is available. This GUI, has an interesting *simple mode*, where the user can type a sequence of word forms or lemmas ; however, it does not provide a simple way for more advanced searches involving POS or morphological features, for users who do not know the CQP language. In contrast, the rather less known GUI employed for the lemmatized and POS-tagged corpus Elicop (Mertens, 2002) was a source of inspiration for our interface. It is based on an easy-to-complete form and does not require prior knowledge of a query language (see Figure 1). The system does not, however, permit one to build a subcorpora and is also limited to four words without syntactic relations.

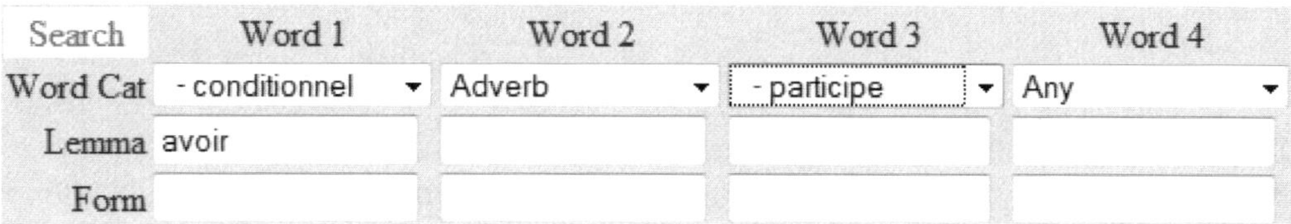


FIGURE 1 – Elicop search GUI.

TIGERSearch (Lezius and König, 2000) is one of the few graphic (off-line) environments for querying treebanks (of syntagmatic structure), but the tool is no longer maintained. This GUI is mostly a query editor, which makes querying more readable (especially for complex queries), but is not easier to master for users unfamiliar with computer science and NLP.

In conclusion, we can only deplore the lack of user-friendly online environments, especially those that incorporate treebanks. This gap is one of the reasons that led to the creation of ScienQuest.

[6] http://cwb.sourceforge.net/

## 5 ScienQuest features

Using Scientext consists of three main steps: sub-corpus construction, research, and finally the display of results. Unless otherwise stated, the examples given below are based on the corpus of English scientific texts.

### 5.1 Sub-corpus selection

By default, ScienQuest exploits the entire corpus. The first step is to simply accept this default choice or to select a sub-corpus. It is possible to group texts according to various criteria (e.g. text type, discipline, and textual section). For corpora with structural annotations (e.g. abstract, introduction, titles, etc.), it is also possible to restrict the sub-corpus according to these elements.

FIGURE 2 – Subcorpus selection GUI in ScienQuest for the French scientific texts corpus.

### 5.2 Search

Once the corpus is defined, the user is prompted to choose between three research modes. Whichever method chosen, the result of the user interaction will be a local grammar (local grammars are presented later in this paper). This grammar is compiled into the local query language used by the search engine, ConcQuest (Kraif, 2008) which performs searches within the corpus (see Figure 3).

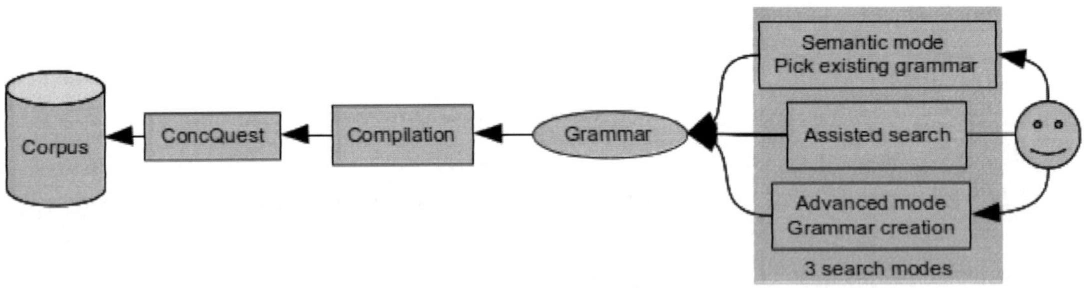

FIGURE 3 – Internal search process.

### 5.2.1 Semantic search: using a predetermined local grammar

A set of local grammars has been developed to enable semantic search within texts, so that the user is not encumbered by the complexity of queries. Fifteen local grammars were developed by (Tutin et al., 2009), primarily around the theme of reasoning and positioning of authors. The development of more local grammars is planned concerning other themes, especially to look for stereotypical expressions in a perspective of language teaching.

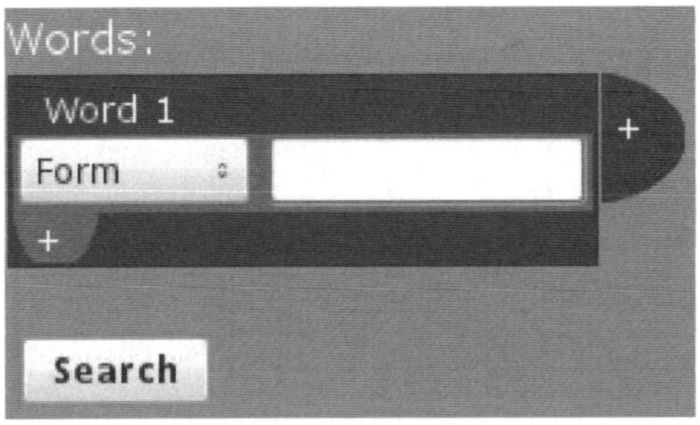


FIGURE 4 – Initial assisted search form.

### 5.2.2 Assisted search : an assistant for free searches

In assisted search mode, the interface first contains minimal content, with a single input field (search for one word, see Figure 4). Buttons allow the user to add words and constraints on form, lemma, part of speech (and possibly sub-category, e.g. proper noun, tensed verb, etc.). For more advanced users, regular expressions are accepted. By default, there are no syntactic relations between words, and their linear order is taken into account.

When several words are present, it is possible to specify a syntactic relation between these words. If a relation is selected, the word order is no longer taken into account (see Figure 5).

The form data are automatically converted into a local grammar in the back office. This mode is designed to satisfy most of the needs of medium-skilled users; however, it is deliberately limited to only a subset of features that can be easily intuitively understood, without the need of consulting the user guide. To use the full expressiveness of the search tool, one must switch to the advanced search option.

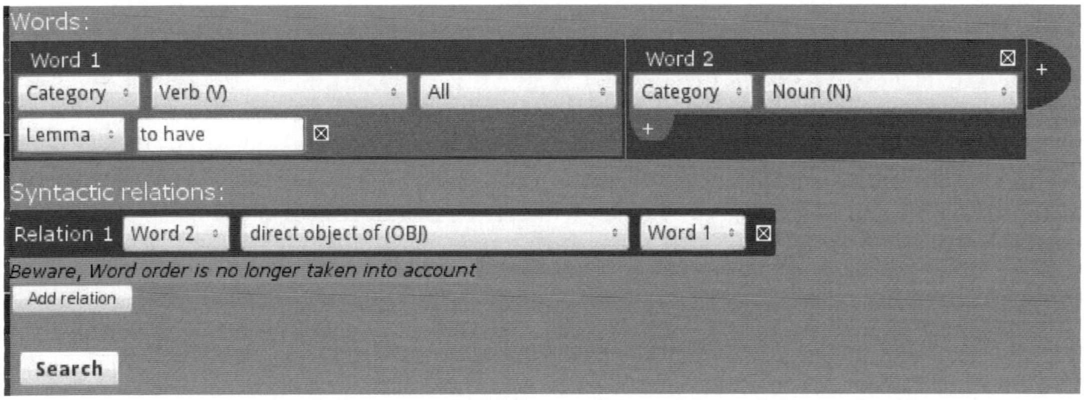


FIGURE 5 – Search for nouns which are direct object of the verb *to have.*

### 5.2.3 Advanced search: a local grammar language for treebanks querying

In the advanced search mode, the user can directly create a local grammar. This mode is dedicated to specialists, therefore we present only the main features here. The local grammar language is used to specify constraints on the words (form, lemma, part of speech, flexion), order, and syntactic relations between words. It is also possible to specify a list of words and variables.

Some innovative features of this language are specific to the treatment of treebanks, in particular the possibility to extend the syntactic relations encoded in the corpus. For example, the syntactic analyser Syntex, used for the Scientext corpora performs a shallow analysis, and thus creates no direct dependency relation between a verb in a perfect tense and its subject, but instead creates a relation SUBJ (subject) between the subject and auxiliary, and a relationship AUX (auxiliary) between the auxiliary and the verb. With ScienQuest local grammar language, it is possible to define a new generic relation or "deep subject" that takes into account this construction, as in the example grammar below. This grammar presents a set of rules detecting opinion verbs and their subject in deep syntax (e.g. the syntactic relation between [*I* or *we*] and [*to think*] in the sentence *we have thought* or *we can think*).

```
(SUBJINF,#2,#1) = (SUJ,#3,#1)(OBJ,#3,#2)    // For infinitive syntactic structures
(SUBJAUX,#2,#1) = (SUJ,#3,#1) (AUX,#3,#2)    // For syntactic structures with auxilliaries
(SUBJGENERIC,#2,#1) = (SUBJINF,#2,#1) OR (SUBJ,#1,#2) OR (SUBJAUX,#2,#1) // New syntactic rel.
$pron_author = we, I   // Pronouns refering to the author
$v_opinion = adhere, admit, adopt, affirm, forward, hold, contradict, agree, criticize, suggest, defend,
denounce, doubt, expect, estimate, judge, justify, think, postulate, prefer, favor, recognize, reject, refute, regret,
reject, wish, stress, subscribe, support, suggest   // Opinion verbs
Main = <lemma=$v_opinion,#1> && <lemma=$pron_author,#2> :: (SUBJGENERIC,#1,#2)
```

In order to help users to switch from semantic and assisted mode to the more complex advanced mode, all advanced queries can be initiated in semantic and assisted mode, and then enriched in advanced mode.

## 5.3 Visualisation of results

The search results are then browsable in a KWIC display (Figure 6), which includes information about the type of text, textual section, etc. In this view, the user can also remove the incorrect results, which will not appear in exports and statistics. This is very useful for fine-tuning results and for annotation error removal. These results can be exported in CSV and XLS formats as well as in HTML tables. It is also possible to broaden the context for a given line and to consult the syntactic dependencies.

Statistics on the occurrences found are available in both tabular and chart display: number of occurrences, percentage of lemmas and forms and their distribution by discipline, and text type or textual section. This type of functionality is still rarely available in tools dedicated to corpus study and is particularly interesting for the study of rhetorical structures in scientific writing.

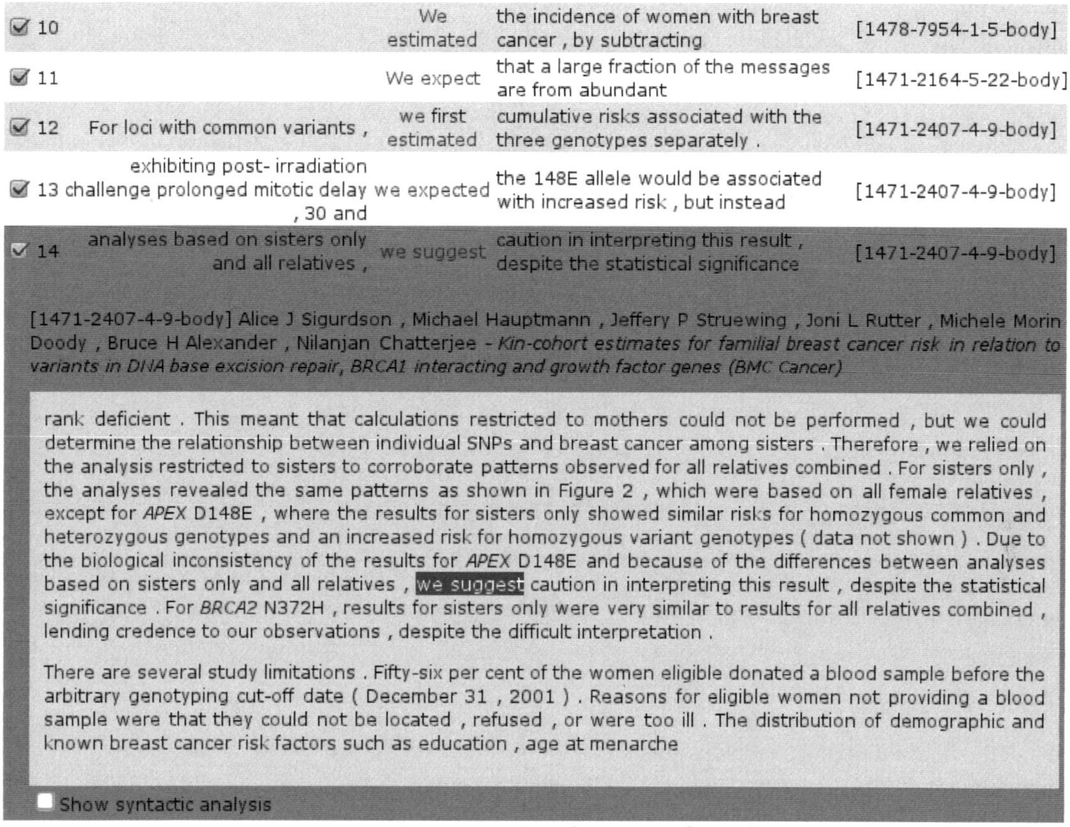


FIGURE 6 : KWIC visualisation of results.

## 6 First results and conclusion

Since the beginning of the public launch of ScienQuest in late June 2010, 9,021 requests were made during 1,474 sessions. Assisted search is used for 75% of the queries, semantic mode (predefined local grammars) for 23%, and advanced mode for the remaining 2%. We believe this demonstrates the importance of these first two search modes, which were introduced in ScienQuest. Nevertheless, the fact remains that syntactic knowledge has inherent complexity which hampers to a certain extent the use of treebanks, since only 47% of the assisted searches contained guided syntactic constraints.

The use of ScienQuest now exceeds the Scientext[7] project, from which it originated. It is for example used in the teaching of French as a foreign language in the FULS[8] project and incorporates new corpora for the EMOLEX[9] project.

Several system improvements are planned, such as adding new corpora and features for the assisted search. However, the ConcQuest search engine on which ScienQuest is based is rather slow ; we will envetually replace it with the new and faster ConcQuest 2.

[7] http://scientext.msh-alpes.fr
[8] http://scientext.msh-alpes.fr/fuls
[9] http://www.emolex.eu

## References


Abeillé, A.; Clément, L.; Toussenel, F. (2003). Building a treebank for French. In Abeillé A. (ed) *Treebanks*. Dordrecht, Germany : Kluwer.

Bick, Eckhard (2004). Parsing and evaluating the French Europarl corpus. In Paroubek, Patrick; Robba, Isabelle and Vilnat, Anne (ed.): *Méthodes et outils pour l'évaluation des analyseurs syntaxiques* (Journée ATALA, 15 mai 2004). pp. 4-9. Paris, France: ATALA.

Bick, Eckhard (2005). Live use of Corpus data and Corpus annotation tools in CALL: Some new developments in VISL. In Holmboe, Henrik (ed.), *Nordic Language Technology, Årbog for Nordisk Sprogteknologisk Forskningsprogram 2000-2004* (Yearbook 2004), pp.171-186. Copenhagen, Danemark : Museum Tusculanum.

Bourigault, Didier (2007). *Un analyseur syntaxique opérationnel : SYNTEX*. Mémoire de HDR. Toulouse, France.

Christ, Oli (1994). A modular and flexible architecture for an integrated corpus query system. In *COMPLEX'94*, Budapest, Hungary.

Christ, Oli and Schulze, B.M. (1995). Ein flexibles und modulares Anfragesystem für Textcorpora. *Tagungsbericht des Arbeitstreffen Lexikon + Text*. Tübingen, Germany : Niemeyer.

Kraif, Olivier (2008), Comment allier la puissance du TAL et la simplicité d'utilisation ? l'exemple du concordancier bilingue ConcQuest. In Actes des *9ème Journées d'analyse statistique des données textuelles*, JADT 2008, pp. 625-634. Lyon, France: Presses universitaires de Lyon.

Lezius, Wolfgang and König, Esther (2000). Towards a search engine for syntactically annotated corpora. In Schukat-Talamazzini, Ernst G. and Zühlke, Werner (ed.): *KONVENS-2000 Sprachkommunikation*, pp. 113-116. Ilmenau, Germany : VDE-Verlag.

Mertens, Piet (2002). Les corpus de français parlé ELICOP : consultation et exploitation. In Binon, Jean; Desmet, Piet; Elen, Jan; Mertens, Piet; Sercu, Lies (ed.) *Tableaux vivants, Opstellen over taal- en onderwijs, aangeboden aan Mark Debrock*, Symbolae, Facultatis Litterarum Lovaniensis, Series A, vol. 28. 383-415. Louvain, Belgium : Leuven Universitaire Pers.

Silberztein, Max. (2006). NooJ's Linguistic Annotation Engine. In Koeva, S.; Maurel, D. and Silberztein, M. (ed.), *INTEX/NooJ pour le Traitement Automatique des Langues*. Cahiers de la MSH Ledoux. Presses Universitaires de Franche-Comté, pp. 9-26.

Tutin, Agnès; Grossmann, Francis; Falaise, Achille and Kraif, Olivier (2009). Autour du projet Scientext : étude des marques linguistiques du positionnement de l'auteur dans les écrits scientifiques . In *Journées Linguistique de Corpus*. 10-12 septembre 2009, Lorient, France.

# An In-Context and Collaborative Software Localisation Model: Demonstration

Amel FRAISSE Christian BOITET Valérie BELLYNCK
LABORATOIRE LIG, Université Joseph Fourier, 41 rue des Mathématiques, 38041 Grenoble, France
Amel.fraisse@gmail.com, christian.Boitet@imag.fr,
Valerie.Bellynck@imag.fr

ABSTRACT

We propose a demonstration of our in context and collaborative software localisation model. It involves volunteer localisers and end users in the localisation process via an efficient and dynamic workflow: while using an application (in context), users knowing the source language of the application (often but not always English) can modify strings of the user interface presented by the application in their current context. The implementation of that approach to localisation requires the integration of a collaborative platform. That leads to a new tripartite localisation workflow. We have experimented with our approach on Notepad++. A demonstration video is proposed as a supplementary material.

---

KEYWORDS: Software localisation, machine translation, translation memories, incremental and collaborative translation, in context localisation, collaborative localisation

---

# Un modèle en-contexte et coopératif pour la localisation de logiciels : Démonstration

RESUME

Nous proposons une nouvelle approche qui permet la localisation en contexte et collaborative de la plupart des logiciels à source ouvert. Notre approche fait participer des bénévoles et les utilisateurs finals au processus de localisation via une organisation du travail efficace et dynamique: en même temps qu'ils utilisent une application ("en contexte"), les utilisateurs connaissant la langue source du logiciel (souvent mais pas toujours l'anglais) peuvent modifier des chaînes de l'interface utilisateur présentées par l'application dans leur contexte courant. L'implémentation de cette approche de la localisation requiert l'intégration d'une plate-forme collaborative. Cela mène à une nouvelle organisation du travail tripartite. Nous avons expérimenté et validé notre approche sur Notepad++. Une démonstration sera présenté.

---

MOTS-CLES: localisation de logiciels, traduction automatique, mémoire de traductions, traduction incrémentale et collaborative, localisation en contexte, localisation collaborative.

---

*Proceedings of COLING 2012: Demonstration Papers*, pages 141–146,
COLING 2012, Mumbai, December 2012.

# 1 Introduction

Currently, the translation of technical documents as well as user interface strings is entrusted only to professional translators. In practice, localisation project managers[1] send original versions of the files to be localised to several professional translators. Each translator translates and sends the translated versions to the localisation project manager. It seems impossible to continue in this way for most under-resourced languages, for reasons of cost, and quite often because of the scarcity or even lack of professional translators (costs increase while quality and market size decrease).

On the other hand, free software such as that produced by Mozilla (Mozilla, 2009) is translated by volunteer co-developers into many (more than 70) languages, in some cases more languages than commercial software. The localisation process is based on the contribution of volunteers (Vo-Trung, 2004), (Tong, 1987), (Lafourcade, 1991, 1996). Another situation (different from the translation of technical documentation) is that of occasional volunteer translators, who contribute without an organic connection to the project (Linux, 2005). Hence, it is possible to obtain high quality translations of documents that may be over a hundred pages long (such as articles of Wikipedia, or texts of Amnesty International and Pax Humana).

Another problem of the classical localisation process is that strings of the interface are often translated out of context. Hence, the choice of the appropriate translation is not always possible due to lack of context, and in such cases even a professional translator cannot produce a perfect translation.

As proposed in (Boitet, 2001), one solution to this problem is to involve end users with a knowledge of the source language (often but not always English) and who, during the use of software products, translate or improve "pretranslations" produced by machine translation (MT) or translation memory (TM) systems.

# 2 The new in context and collaborative localisation model

## 2.1 Basic principles

### 2.1.1 Involving volunteer translators and end users in the localisation process

As said above, localisation seems impossible for most under-resourced languages for reasons of cost, and scarcity or even lack of professional translators.

Our solution aims at involving non-professional translators such as volunteer localisers and above all end users. These groups have the capacity to participate effectively, since they have a better knowledge of the target language (generally their native language) and of the context of use of the application. In order to motivate this type of translators and to give them a better knowledge about the use context of UI (user interface) strings, localisation should be carried out while using the application.

[1] Localisation project managers: software publisher in the case of commercial software, and a community of volunteer localisers in the case of open source software.

### 2.1.2 From discontinuous, coordinated and out-of-context localisation to continuous, uncoordinated and in context localisation

The basic concept of our model is to renounce the idea of perfect translation, and to publish rough translations with a variable quality, which will be improved incrementally during the use of the application. Therefore, the translation process will be ongoing and improve continuously. This solves the problem of time and delays, since users do not have to wait for the final localised version in their language. They can download, at any time, a partially localised or non-localised version of the application.

Similarly, the localisation project manager may first publish a partially localised version that will be progressively localised through use, leading, eventually, to a completely localised version. Hence, the new process permits the incremental increase of both quality and quantity.

The same principle is already applied by many translation communities. The best known is the Wikipedia Community: content is added and translated continuously by contributors. Our guiding idea is to adapt this principle to the software localisation field.

## 2.2 Adaptation to software localisation

The localisation project manager should be allowed to ask professional translators and reviewers to translate the crucial parts of the software. Hence, our localisation model has to be applicable individually or collaboratively. The user has the choice to localise the application locally, without any exchange with other users, or to localise it collaboratively.

### 2.2.1 First Scenario: in context localisation through interaction with the collaborative platform

During the in context localisation, user can interact with the collaborative platform (SECTra_w), to get and submit translations. As shown in FIGURE 1, when the user right-clicks on any string within the interface, an edition pop-up related to the collaborative platform appears, and the user can enter a new translation, or choose one of the proposed translations. Clicking on the "localize" button sends the user translation to the collaborative platform, and the user interface is updated in real time.

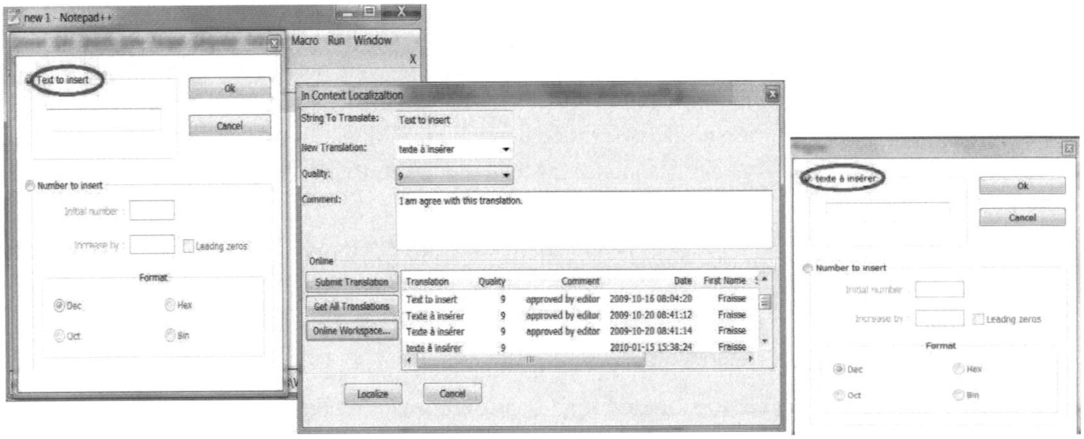

FIGURE 1 – In context localisation of the string "Text to insert" through interaction with the collaborative platform.

### 2.2.2 Second scenario: localising directly on the collaborative platform

This second scenario allows user to localize directly on SECTra_w (FIGURE 2). When the edition pop-up is displayed, the user clicks on the "Online workspace" button and is redirected to the page on the collaborative platform containing the string that has been chosen for translation. Then, the user enters a new translation, or chooses one of the proposed translations. When, s/he returns to the application (in the same context s/he left it), the interface has been updated.

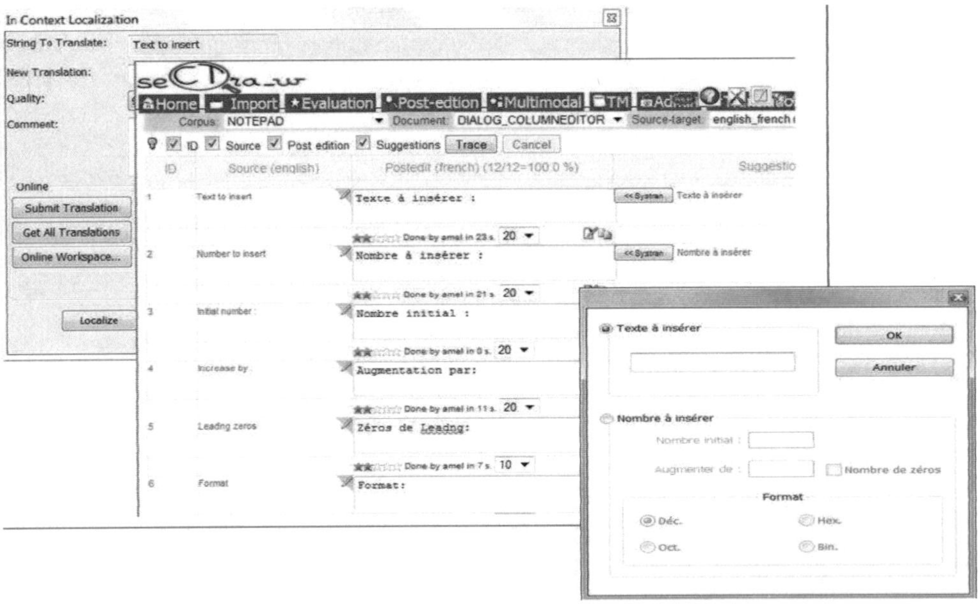

FIGURE 2 – Localising directly on the collaborative platform.

## References


Bey, Y., Kageura, K. and Boitet, C. (2008). BEYTrans: A Wiki-based Environment for Helping Online Volunteer Translators. Topics in Language Resources for Translation and Localisation, Yuste Rodrigo, 2008, 135–150.

Blanchon, H., Boitet, C. and Huynh, C. (2009). A Web Service Enabling Gradable Post-edition of Pre-translations Produced by Existing Translation Tools: Practical Use to Provide High-quality Translation of an Online Encyclopedia. MT Summit XII, Ottawa, Ontario, Canada, 26-30 August 2009, 8 p.

Boitet, C. (2001). Four technical and organizational keys for handling more languages and improving quality (on demand). In Proc. Machine Translation System, IAMT 8 p., Santiago de Compostela, September 2001.

Fraisse, A., Boitet, C., Blanchon, H. and Bellynck, V. (2009). Localisation interne et en contexte des logiciels commerciaux et libres. MajecSTIC Manifestation des jeunes chercheurs *en sciences et technologies de l'information et de la communication,* Avignon, France, 16-18 November 2009.

Huynh, C., Boitet, C., and Balnchon, H. (2008). SECTra_w.1: an online collaborative system for evaluating, post-editing and presenting MT translation corpora. LREC 2008: 6th Language Resources and Evaluation Conference, Marrakech, Morocco, 26-30 May 2008, 6 p.

Lafourcade, M. and Sérasset, G. (1996). Apple Technology Integration. A Web dictionary server as a practical example. In Mac Tech magazine, 12/7, 1996, pp. 25.

Lafourcade, M. (1991). ODILE-2, un outil pour traducteurs occasionnels sur Macintosh. In *Presses de l'univ*ersité de Québec, Université de Montréal, AUPELF-UREF ed., 1991, pp. 95-108.

Linux (2005). Linux documentation translation [online], available at: http://traduc.org/ [last accessed 12 May 2011].

Mozilla Localisation Project (2009), available at http://www-archive.mozilla.org/projects/l10n/ [last accessed 12 May 2011].

Tong, L.C. (1987). The Engineering of a translator workstation. In Computers and Translation, pp. 263-273.

Vo-Trung, H. (2004). Méthodes et outils pour utilisateurs, développeurs et traducteurs de logiciels en contexte multilingue, PhD thesis.

# Efficient Feedback-based Feature Learning for Blog Distillation as a Terabyte Challenge

*Dehong Gao, Wenjie Li, Renxian Zhang*

Department of Computing, the Hong Kong Polytechnic University. Hong Kong

{csdgao, cswjli, csrzhang}@comp.polyu.edu.hk

ABSTRACT

The paper is focused on blogosphere research based on the TREC blog distillation task, and aims to explore unbiased and significant features automatically and efficiently. Feedback from faceted feeds is introduced to harvest relevant features and information gain is used to select discriminative features, including the unigrams as well as the patterns of unigram associations. Meanwhile facing the terabyte blog dataset, some flexible processing is adopted in our approach. The evaluation result shows that the selected feedback features can greatly improve the performance and adapt well to the terabyte data.

KEYWORDS : Blog Distillation, Faceted Distillation, Feedback

## 1. Introduction

With the accelerated growth of social networks, both organizations and individuals have shown great interest in conveying or exchanging ideas and opinions. The blogosphere provides an ideal platform for communication. According to the statistics of Blogpulse(*blogpulse.com*) in Jan. 2011, more than 152 million blogs have been published. One interesting issue related to the massive blogs is to automatically explore authors' behaviours from their blog posts.

Research related to blog posts mainly focuses on opinion retrieval to identify topic-based opinion posts, which means retrieved posts should not only be relevant to the targets, but also contain subjective opinions about given topics. Generally, topic-based opinion retrieval can be divided into two parts using a separated relevance and opinion model or a unified relevance model. In separated models, posts are first ranked by topical relevance only, then, the opinion scores can be acquired by either classifiers, such as SVM (Wu Zhang and Clement Yu, 2007), or external toolkits like OpinionFinder(*www.cs.pitt.edu/mpqa/*) (David Hannah et al. 2007). The precision of the opinion retrieval is highly dependent on the precision of relevance retrieval. Huang et al propose a unified relevance model by integrating a query-dependent and a query-independent method, which achieved high performance in topic-based opinion retrieval (Huang et al., 2009).

Based on opinionated blogosphere identification, TREC introduces the faceted blog distillation track in 2009 with two subtasks: baseline distillation and faceted distillation. The former is to retrieve all the relevant feeds corresponding to given topics without any consideration of facets. The latter aims to re-rank the baseline feeds according to specific facets. For operational simplicity, TREC specifies three faceted inclination pairs (TREC Blog Wiki, 2009):

*Opinionated vs. Factual inclinations* aim to differentiate feeds expressing opinions from those describing factual information;

*Personal vs. Official inclinations* are to discriminate individual-authored feeds from organization-issued ones;

*Proceedings of COLING 2012: Demonstration Papers*, pages 147–154,
COLING 2012, Mumbai, December 2012.

*In-depth vs. shallow inclinations* have the purpose of separating feeds involving deep analysis from those conveying shallow thoughts.

So far, several methods have been attempted for faceted distillation. In (Richard mcCreadie et al, 2009), SVM and ME classifiers are introduced to predict the faceted inclinations of each feed according to pre-trained models. In (Mostafa Keikaha et al., 2009), feed faceted scores are heuristically given to re-rank feeds. For classification as well as re-ranking, the challenge is to select the features related to each inclination. Most work at present focuses on exploring heuristic features. For example, length of the posts is introduced for in-depth and shallow inclination ranking and occurrence of personal pronouns also serves as a feature for personal and factual inclination ranking (Mejova Yelena et al., 2009). Other heuristic features, like permalink number and comment number, are also commonly used in these inclination ranking (SeungHoon Na et al., 2009; Bouma Gerlof 2009; Kiyomi Chujo et al, 2010). However, we observe that for some facets these features are far from enough. For example, it is really hard to discover the indicative heuristic features for some facets like factual, personal and official inclinations. In view of this, we attempt to introduce some terms as common features from blog corpus. Cooperating with faceted feedback information, we first discover more (non-heuristic) feature candidates, including unigram features as well as some word collaborated patterns features, e.g., combination of unigrams "company" and "report", etc. These features are then selected by feature selection, in particular with point-wise mutual information. Furthermore, since the size of our experiment dataset is up to terabyte, we take some flexible processing to adapt to the massive dataset, which has been proved to be efficient in our experiments. In a word, we believe the benefits of this work can be twofold. (1) Rather than only using heuristic features, we can learn more faceted related features automatically, and this method can be directly applied in new defined facets. (2) By some flexible processing, our work is quite efficient for massive dataset.

## 2. Feedback Feature Learning

Our following work is based on the blog distillation, and as mentioned in the above section, baseline distillation subtask needs to be conducted before feature learning in faceted distillation. Thus, we first briefly introduce the baseline distillation. To enhance efficiency in the face of the huge and noisy raw data (2.3TB), we implement a distributed system and adopt the Indri tool(*www.lemurproject.org*) for our purpose, with its default language model and related toolkits. With the help of these tools, the top related feeds can be retrieved according to given topics in the baseline distillation.

Based on the ranking of the baseline distillation, we then focus on the **faceted blog distillation** and **feedback feature learning**. The key issue in faceted blog distillation is to discover the relevant and discriminative features for each faceted inclination, and determine the weight of each feature. To solve the issue above, our approach explores features from three orientations: *Heuristic Features* (*HF*), *available Lexicon Features* (*LF*), and *Corpora Learned Features* (*CF*).

*Heuristic Features* (*HF*), which have been used in some existing work, include Average Permalink/Sentence Length, Comment number, Organization Numbers, Opinion Rule, etc, which can be helpful for distinguishing some inclinations. In our approach, besides these heuristic features we also use the statistics of the presence of Cyber Words and Cyber Emoticons in feeds, which provides clues to personal and official feeds. Two public available cyberwords lists are used in our task, i.e., SmartDefine(*www.smartdefine.org*) including 465 words like "*IMNSHO* (which *means In My Not So Humble Opinion*)" and "*FAQ* (which means *Frequently Asked*

*Questions*)", and ChatOnline(*www.chatslang.com*), including 538 words like "*10x* (which means*Thanks*)" and "*Lemeno* (which means *Let me know*)". The integration these two acronyms lists is used as our acronyms lexicon to discover the acronyms in the tweets. Additionally, ChatOnline offers 273 commonly-used emoticons like "☺", "☹" and "^o^". These emoticons are used to detect the emoticon usage in blog posts, which is very practical in our experiments. Heuristic rules also defined to detect the word with repeating letters like *what'sssss up*", "*soooo guilty*" and "*Awesome!!!!*" etc. These repeating words usually show a strong emotion in the blog post. In case of *lexicon features*, we introduce the SentiWordNet(*sentiwordnet.isti.cnr.it*) and Wilson Lexicon (Wilson Theresa and Janyce Wiebe 2003), which are vital and commonly used in identifying opinionated inclination feeds. However, most of these features suit the opinionated inclination and may not work well in other inclinations, and may introduce noise to other inclinations, especially for the factual and shallow inclinations. Besides, because of employing two opinion lexicons, the feature structure is unbalanced for other facets. Thus, in order to overcome these defects and discover more faceted features, we take the effort to explore some useful features from corpora.

Here, we propose a feature expansion approach by **learning feature** candidates through feedback information of faceted feeds. The idea of learning feature is to introduce feature candidates from the first faceted ranking, and then learn some important feature candidates for new faceted ranking. Since TREC has released some annotated faceted feeds, it can be used as a criterion for feature learning. It is the advantage of this approach that it can learn useful features from feedback posts automatically. Different from inclination-dependent heuristic features, the learning process can be easily applied to any new inclination.

There are two steps to learn feedback features in feature expansion: feature candidate collections, and feature selection. In feature candidate collection, besides introducing the *unigram features* (*UF*), we consider the word associations, which we name as *pattern features* (*PF*). All high frequency unigrams are collected first as feedback feature candidates. However, for pattern features it is not feasible if we treat each pair of unigram as pattern candidates for the size of possible paired associations is nearly up to $4*10^8$ in our feature space. We need to measure the collaborative contribution of each pattern. Several information theoretic methods, such as Chi-square, log-likelihood ratio and mutual information, are applicable for this purpose. We choose Point-wise Mutual Information (PMI) for its easy implementation and relative performance, which are suitable for our massive dataset. The formula of PMI is as follows:

$$PMI(t_i, t_j) = log_2(P(t_i, t_j)/P(t_i)P(t_j))$$

where $P(t_i, t_j)$ is the joint probability that both unigrams appear in feeds, and $P(t_i)$ is the probability that a word $i$ appears in feeds.

By now, we have collected unigram and pattern feature candidates, which are mainly opinion-independent ones and unbiased for particular inclinations, resulting in more balanced feature structure. A byproduct of feature expansion is that the unprocessed feature candidates contain too much useless information, which not only wastes computing resources but also harms the performance especially for massive dataset. For example, if all unigrams (more than 20,000) and pattern features (5000 selected with PMI) are selected as features in our experiments, it will take unpredictable time to extract the features from all feeds. Therefore, we need to select the top discriminative features with feature selection methods. There are several commonly used feature selection approaches. According to (Hua Liu and Hiroshi Motoda, 2007), information gain (IG) is able to select both positive features and negative features. Thus, in our experiment IG is used to select features, and the formula is as follows:

$$IG(Ex, a) = H(Ex) - H(Ex|a)$$

where *Ex* is the set of all official annotated faceted feeds instances; *H*(*x*) represents the entropy; $a \in Attr$, *Attr* denotes all feature candidates including unigram and pattern features.

With lexicon-based features and feedback features, an unanswered question is how to determine the weight of both features. Though each opinion word has a polarity weight and a feature selection measure is assigned to each feedback features, these weights are not in the same scale. To unitize the weights of selected features, for each inclination we apply a SVM classifier with the default linear kernel and calculate the weight of a support vector from the trained model that corresponds to a feature. In linear kernel function, these weights stand for the coefficients of a linear function, and in certain degree they denote the importance of each support vector, which is the corresponding feature in our task. Eventually, the feeds are re-ranked with the sum of the products of the feature values and their weights.

## 3. Evaluation

The experiments are conducted on the blog08 collection(*ir.dcs.gla.ac.uk/test_collections*) crawled over 14 weeks. It contains permalinks, feeds, and related information. The size of the blog08 collection is up to 2.3TB. In order to efficiently handle the terabyte dataset and reduce noise, the raw dataset is first cleaned and filtered by several regular expression rules, e.g., removing unreadable text, filtering unnecessary HTML scripts, which reduce the size to 30% in total. Then, Indri is used to index the cleaned blog08 collection, and fetch the top 2000 related blog posts according to the 50 topics provided in TREC2009. Since the feeds are what the task is concerned with, we rank the feeds by summing the relevance scores of retrieved blog posts corresponding to the same feed number. The top 100 relevant feeds are obtained and evaluated in Table 1. TREC provides four measures: the mean average precision (MAP), R-Precision (rPrec), binary Preference (bPref) and Precision at 10 documents (P@10), among which MAP is the primary measure for evaluating the retrieval performance (TREC Blog Wiki, 2009).

| Baseline Distillation | MAP | R-Prec | P@10 | B-Pref |
|---|---|---|---|---|
| Language model | 0.2494 | 0.3047 | 0.3590 | 0.2611 |
| Official best | 0.2756 | 0.2767 | 0.3206 | 0.3821 |
| Official median | 0.1752 | 0.1986 | 0.2447 | 0.3282 |
| Official worst | 0.0624 | 0.0742 | 0.0980 | 0.1410 |

TABLE 1 – Evaluation of baseline distillation compared with official best, median and worst

As shown in Table 1, our Indri-based language model ranks competitively against official submissions. Based on our baseline feed ranking, we conduct the faceted distillation. We first investigate 1500 opinion words from Lexicons of SentiWordNet and Wilson, about 20 K high-frequency (presence more than 5 times) unigram features are first collected from the top ranking five feeds as feature candidates. Then, we calculate the PMI of every pair of unigrams as a criterion of selecting more contributable pattern features. The top 5000 pattern features are heuristically selected as another source of feature candidates.

With the above feature candidates, IG is employed to select the features that contribute more. Instead of using all instances in the official released answers, we calculate *H*(*Ex*|*a*) using the top five feeds in our experiments. This change can greatly reduce the complexity of computing and make our approach more adaptable for the massive data collection. The top five feeds are a good surrogate for the whole feed set as they are statistically found to contain an approximately equal number of faceted and non-faceted feeds. More importantly, this "shortcut approach" adapts very well to the large dataset. We select the top ranked features for each inclination (examples are illustrated in Table 2). From the table, we also find that selected words really have the trend to express the meaning of the inclination, like "*argument*", "*rather*", "*powerful*" for opinionated. More important is that we observe these selected features, especially for pattern features, are topic related. For example, unigrams in Personal inclination, "*Fish*", "*boat*", "*river*" usually are related with topic 1189 "*personal travel stories*"; the pattern feature in Opinionated inclination "[synthesis, membrane]" usually present in ophthalmology treatment articles like topic 1194 "*macular degeneration*"; the pattern feature in In-depth inclination "[genealogy, ancestor]" is frequently related with topic 1155 "*2012 catastrophe armageddon predictions*". A similar observation is also found in (Yi Hu and Wenjie Li, 2010), which points out that topical terms and its context can be quite useful in determining the polarity. Thus this may indicates that the topic words and patterns are important for faceted re-ranking as well. Then, these selected features are also used to train the faceted models, and then the weights of these features can be inferred by the trained models. In practice, we use the same strategy to randomly divide the top five feeds into training and testing datasets (ratio 4:1). Then, the weights of support vectors are calculated from trained models as the weights of these features for facet re-ranking. With selected features and their weights, feeds are re-ranked according to each inclination, and for comparison, ranking without feedback features (HF+LF) is evaluated as well.

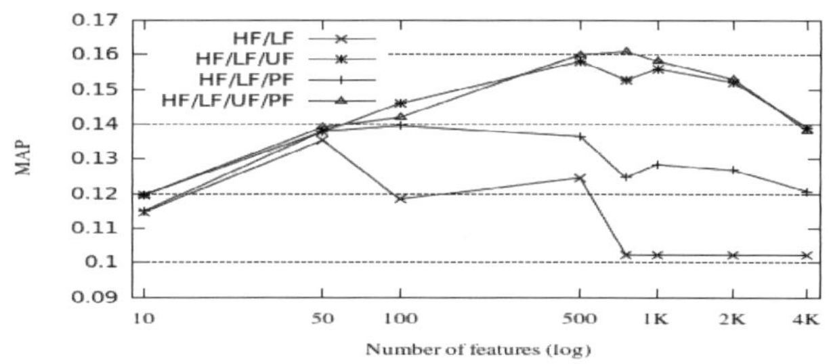


FIGURE 1 – Re-ranking with different number of features

Table 3 compares four rankings, re-ranking with heuristic and lexicon features [*HF+LF*]; re-ranking with heuristic, lexicon and unigram (top 500) features [*HF+LF+UF*]; re-ranking with heuristic, lexicon and pattern (top 500) features[*HF+LF+PF*] and re-ranking with heuristic, lexicon, unigram and pattern (top 750 features)[*HF+LF+UF+PF*]. The t-test is used to test whether a significant improvement can be achieved with feedback features. The T-values of [*HF+LF+UF*], [*HF+LF+PF*] and [*HF+LF+UF+PF*] are 4.78, 2.74 and 4.64, respectively, which are larger than $T_{0.05}$ = 1.76. This indicates that the re-rankings with feedback features achieve a significant improvement, and outperform the best of official runs. By using both unigram and pattern feedback features we obtain the best performance. From the evaluation of unigram features (*HF+LF+UF*) against without unigram features (*HF+LF*), we can find that great improvements are observed for factual, personal and official identification. It is thus plausible that those inclinations may be more amenable to the usage of words rather than some heuristic features. From the evaluation of pattern features (HF+LF+PF) against HF+LF, we can observe encouraging improvement on the shallow inclination, which may be the most difficult inclination for feature extraction, and this may also hint that the shallow inclination relies on word patterns more than single words, which coincides with our intuition that while a single word may be able to express opinionated or personal inclination, e.g., "rather", "better", "personally", it usually is hard to convey a shallow thought with only one word.

In the last experiment, comparisons are made to investigate the influence of different numbers of features selected. Figure 1 show four rankings mentioned above with different feature numbers. Obviously, the feedback feature is important for the faceted re-ranking. They peak at 750 features, 500 features and 100 features for re-ranking with the combination of unigram and pattern features, re-ranking with unigram features and re-ranking with pattern features, respectively. The flat tail of without-feedback approach (HF+LF) can be explained by the fact that only about 750 out of the 1500 features (shown by the points in the circle) are present in the features. We also notice that the pattern features have positive influence for faceted re-ranking, though there are only 0.83 percentage improvements in the point of 750. The bottom line shown in this figure is that re-ranking with feedback features outperforms that without feedback. This proves that feedback features are obviously effective in faceted blog distillation.

## 4. Conclusion

To sum up, feedback feature expansion coupled with feature selection is effective and efficient for faceted blog distillation and adapts well to the terabyte dataset. It helps to automatically discover relevant and discriminative features. Comparing with pattern features, unigram features play a more vital role in the tasks undertaken. In the future, we will investigate how to select more significant pattern features and use these pattern features to further improve the contribution.


## Acknowledgements

The work presented in this paper is supported by a Hong Kong RGC project (No. PolyU 5230/08E).


| | MAP | | | | | | |
|---|---|---|---|---|---|---|---|
| | **All** | **Opinionated** | **Factual** | **Personal** | **Official** | **In-depth** | **Shallow** |
| Best 09 | 0.1261 | 0.1259 | 0.1350 | 0.1855 | **0.1965** | 0.1489 | **0.1298** |
| HF+LF | 0.1022 | 0.1340 | 0.0222 | 0.1754 | 0.1143 | 0.1859 | 0.0701 |
| HF+LF+UF | 0.1581 | 0.1467 | 0.1322 | 0.2166 | **0.2333** | 0.2091 | 0.0748 |
| HF+LF+PF | 0.1365 | **0.1687** | 0.1546 | 0.2067 | 0.1043 | 0.1294 | 0.0906 |
| HF+LF+UF+PF | **0.1611** | 0.1472 | **0.1581** | **0.2351** | 0.1860 | **0.2210** | 0.0918 |

TABLE 3 – Evaluation against each inclination

| | **Opinionated** | **Factual** | **Personal** | **Official** | **In-depth** | **Shallow** |
|---|---|---|---|---|---|---|
| Unigram features | Political, national, Development, Maintain, Administration, Report, argument Powerful, chief | Election, target, agreement, status, Power, mission, Gravity, scientist, indicate | Fish, fly, catch, gear, Trout, boat, river, Lake, wait, sail | Breed, veterinarian , puppy, potty, groom, breed, purebred, bred | Ancestor, surgeon, surname, software, database, passenger, index, census | Learn, software, cosmetic, pocket, fine, surgeon, Procedure, religion, spiritual, tone |
| Pattern features | [Synthesis, membrane] [molecule, membrane] [metabolism, membrane] | [rocket, shuttle] [lunar, luna] [communist, missile] [thigh, underneath] [scalp, jaw] | [psychiatric , psychiatry] [marine, marina] [lunar, luna] [surgeon, surgery] | [veterinaria n, veterinary] [veterinaria n, rabbit] [dental, gum] [diarrhea, vomit] | [genealogy, ancestor] [genealogy, genealogist ] [census, genealogy] [census, ancestor] | [genealogy, genealogist] [genealogy, ancestor] [psychiatric, psychiatry] [census, genealogy] |

TABLE 2 – Examples of the selected Unigram and pattern features

## References


Bouma, Gerlof. (2009). *Normalized (Pointwise) Mutual Information in Collocation Extraction.* In proceedings of the Biennial GSCL Conference, P31–40, Tübingen, Gunter Narr Verlag.

David Hannah, Craig Macdonald, Jie Peng, Ben He and Iadh Ounis. (2007). *University of Glasgow at TREC2007: Experiments in Blog and Enterprise Tracks with Terrier.* In proceedings of the 15th Text Retrieval Conference.

Hua Liu and Hiroshi Motoda. (2007). *Computational Methods of Feature Selection.* Chapman&Hall/CRC, P257-268, London.

Kiyomi Chujo, Masao Utiyama, Takahiro Nakamura and Kathryn Oghigian. (2010). *Evaluating Statitically-extracted Domain-specific Word Lists.* Corpus, ICT, and Language Education. Glasgow, UK.

Mejova Yelena and Thuc Viet Ha. (2009). *TREC Blog and TREC Chem: A View from the Corn Fields*, In proceedings of TREC09, University of Iowa.

Mostafa Keikha, Mark Carman, et al. (2009). *University of Lugano at TREC2009 Blog Track.* In proceedings of TREC09. Lugano, Swiss.

Richard McCreadie, Craig Macdonald and Iadh Ounis. (2009). *University of Glasgow at TREC2009: Experiments with Terrier.* In proceedings of TREC2009. Glasgow, Scotland, UK.

Seung-Hoon Na, Yeha Lee, Sang-Hyob Nam, and Jong-Hyeok Lee. (2009). *Improving Opinion Retrieval Based on Query-Specific Sentiment Lexicon.* ECIR, Berlin Heidelberg.

TREC Blog Wiki. 2009. Http://ir.dcs.gla.ac.uk/wiki-/TREC-BLOG.

Wilson, Theresa, and Janyce Wiebe. (2003). *Identifying opinionated sentences.* In proceedings of NAACL03, P33–34.

Wu Zhang and Clement Y. (2007). *UIC at TREC 2007 Blog Track.* In proceedings of the 15th Text REtrieval Conference.

Xuanjing Huang, Bruce Croft, et al. (2009). *Fudan University: A Unified Relevance Model for Opinion Retrieval.* ACM of Conference on Information and Knowledge Management, Hong Kong.

Yi Hu and Wenjie Li. (2010). *Document Sentiment Classification by Exploring description model of topical terms.* Computer Speech and Language 25(Jul. 2010), P386-403.

# Beyond Twitter Text: A preliminary Study on Twitter Hyperlink and its Application

*Dehong Gao, Wenjie Li, Renxian Zhang*
Department of Computing, the Hong Kong Polytechnic University. Hong Kong
{csdgao, cswjli, csrzhang}@comp.polyu.edu.hk

ABSTRACT

While the popularity of Twitter brings a plethora of Twitter researches, short, plain and informal tweet texts limit the research progress. This paper aims to investigate whether hyperlinks in tweets and their linked pages can be used to discover rich information for Twitter applications. The statistical analysis on the analysed hyperlinks offers the evidence that tweets contain a large amount of hyperlinks and a high percentage of hyperlinks introduce substantial and informative information from external resources. The usage of hyperlinks is examined on a self-defined hyperlink recommendation task. The recommended hyperlinks can not only provide more descriptive or explanatory information for the corresponding trending topics, but also pave the way for further applications, such as Twitter summarization.

KEYWORDS : Twitter, Hyperlink Usage, Hyperlink Recommendation

## 1. Introduction

The shift of information center from the mainstream media to the general public drives a growth of social network sites among which Twitter is undoubtedly one of the popular applications now. In academia, Twitter researches have become a new hotspot (H. Kwak et al, 2010; D. Zhao and M. Rosson, 2009; M. Michael and N. Kouda, 2010). Existing researches mainly focus on tweet content and user communication, while ignoring external resources. However, the limitation is the plain and short tweet text, which contains 140 characters at most. Even worse, tweets are usually written with many informal expressions.

It has been reported in (TechInfo, 2010) that about 25% of tweets contain hyperlinks and the proportion is increasing. Recently, even Twitter itself also provides an interface to allow people pay close attention to the tweets with hyperlinks. This move probably implies that (1) tweets contain a large amount of hyperlinks; and (2) hyperlinks in tweets may provide useful information for understanding topics. For instance, at the time when we write this paper, "*William & Kate*" is a popular topic of conversation. When we follow some arbitrary hyperlinks in the tweets under this topic, we are often directed to the Web pages containing the detailed information about their royal honeymoon (http://styleite.com/gjhao), the video of royal wedding (http://bit.ly/ld72jW) and the comments on their expensive wedding (http://ow.ly/1cKi99). Without length limit, a Web page tends to use a longer text describing the topics. Especially some of these hyperlinked pages are written by professional editors, and are much more regular than ordinary tweets. "*William & Kate*" is just an example here. But it motivates us to seek for the answers for the following questions:

*Q1: How popular are hyperlinks in tweets?*
*Q2: Can these hyperlinks provide additional, useful and relevant information for understanding topics?*

*Proceedings of COLING 2012: Demonstration Papers*, pages 155–162,
COLING 2012, Mumbai, December 2012.

*Q3: What kinds of information can be explored from hyperlinked Web pages?*

To answer these questions, we download ten trending topics from Twitter.com and annotate 2018 hyperlinks in selected tweets to categorize the information presented in the hyperlinked pages. The statistical analysis of the annotation results indicates that 44% of tweets contain hyperlinks, among them 35% of examined hyperlinks are worth are worth further exploration, Actually, our study on hyperlink usage analysis indicates that about 70% of those valuable hyperlinked pages provide descriptive or explanatory information regarding the topics, which is much richer and more formal than that brought by tweets themselves. All these statistics suggests that hyperlinked pages can be used as external resources to assist understanding or interpretation of topics. They have many potential uses in Twitter applications. For example, *trending topics explanation and summarization*, can be generated from hyperlinked pages, rather than just from obscure and incoherent summary with informal tweets.

In this paper, the usage of hyperlinks is examined on a self-defined hyperlink recommendation task. Here, *hyperlink recommendation* is defined to recommend the high-quality hyperlinks (i.e., the hyperlinks that provide most relevant textual information beyond Twitter text) for trending topics. The task is cast as a typical binary classification problem. Considering the small size of available labelled dataset and unlimited unlabelled dataset, a semi-supervised learning technique, called co-training, is employed to Leveraging the huge amount of unlabelled data resource to enhance classification performance. The results are promising. We hope our study will shed some light on the researches of Twitter hyperlink and its applications.

## 2. Hyperlink Analysis

To collect enough tweets, the public Twitter APIs (dev.twitter.com) are used to download tweets from the Twitter websites in real-time. We manually select ten trending topics from Twitter.com and download 81,530 related tweets with Twitter APIs from March 2 to March 12, 2011. These trending topics cover the main categories of trending topics. To answer the question 1 in Introduction, analysis is carried out on these tweets to determine the ratio of tweets with hyperlinks. In overall, the tweets with hyperlinks account for 44% of all the tweets, which is much higher than the data (25%) reported in (TechInfo, 2010) in July, 2010. This statistics answers the first question raised in Section 1. Meanwhile, we can also observe that the tweets belonging to the technology and emergency categories are more likely to include hyperlinks.

With such a high proportion of tweets containing hyperlinks, the next issue concerned is to examine the percentage of the hyperlinks that can provide additional relevant information about the topic, or to say how many of the posted hyperlinks are useful for understanding or interpreting the topic (and the tweets about the topic`). This is to answer the question 2 in Introduction. To this end, we randomly selected 2018 hyperlinks for further analysis. These hyperlinks are annotated as *useful, off-topic, spam, error-links,* and *non-English* hyperlinks. The term *useful* here means that the Web pages can provide relevant information for trending topics while the *spam* hyperlinks refer to the Web pages with the evidential intention of advertising, e.g. advertisements, or some e-commercial pages. The *off-topic* hyperlinks are those pointing to the Web pages with no relevant information and the *error-link* hyperlinks are invalid ones. As exhibited in Figure 1.(a), among 2018 selected hyperlinks, the useful hyperlinks take up 35%. A much higher ratio is shown in the technology and emergency categories, while the ratio of meme category is much lower than the others. These observations indicate that the amount of hyperlinks in tweets can be used to provide related information for given trending topics. Meanwhile, the higher ratio in technology and emergency and the lower in meme category also indicate that the divergence of useful hyperlinks across the categories is striking. We also find that most non-useful hyperlinks are off-topic hyperlinks (42%), especially in Meme category. This indicates the necessity of useful hyperlinks identification.

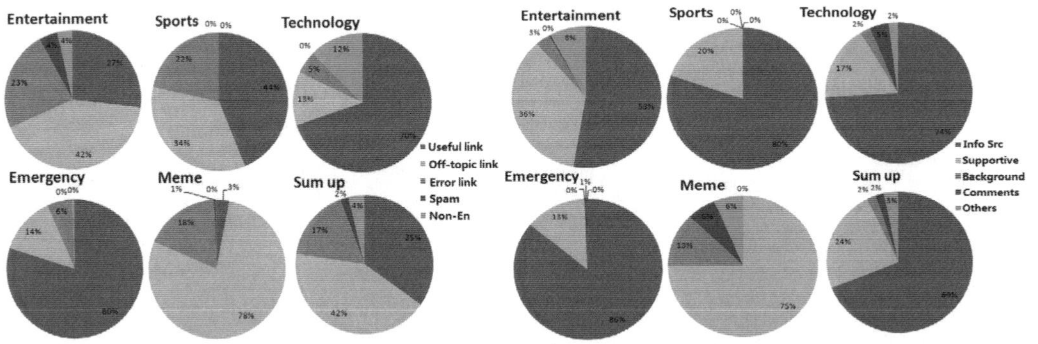


FIGURE 1 – (a) Proportion of useful hyperlinks; (b) Proportion of hyperlink purpose

To answer the question 3, the purpose of useful hyperlinked pages is investigated to evaluate what kind of information can be discovered from hyperlinked pages. We categorize the purpose of useful hyperlinked pages as *source information*, *background information*, *supportive information*, *comment* and *others*. These categories can direct researchers to explore different applications, e.g. information source Web pages is kind of help in trending topic explanations and summarization while the comment Web pages tends to be important in opinion mining. As Figure 1.(b) suggests 69% of the annotated useful hyperlinked pages convey information about the source of trending topics, which can be also regarded as explanations to the trending topics. Similarly, the higher ratios occur in the technology and emergency trending category and a lower ratio appears in the meme category.

Now we can conclude that tweets contain a large amount of hyperlinks and a high percentage of hyperlinks introduce substantial and informative information from external resources, though the quality of hyperlinks vary from category to category.

## 3. Hyperlink Recommendation

Since the statistics analysis on Twitter hyperlinks suggests that it is worth to explore the external information, we propose a new task, namely *hyperlink recommendation*, to recommend useful hyperlinks that provide most relevant information that beyond Twitter text for the corresponding trending topics. The significance of this hyperlink recommendation task is to pave the way for future researches that may need to identify the useful hyperlinks beforehand in order to enrich the text presentation of tweets or discover topic background information etc.

In this preliminary study, hyperlink recommendation is cast as a typical binary classification problem by separating the useful hyperlinks that provide the relevance information for a trending topic from the others. Useful hyperlinks are further ranked according to their relevance and credibility. The top ones are regards as the recommended hyperlinks. One problem is the insufficient labelled data for effective learning. Fortunately, compared with the limited annotated hyperlinks, a large amount of unlabelled Twitter hyperlinks are available from Twitter.com. Thus, we choose to adopt semi-supervised learning as a solution to incorporate the unlabelled data to enhance the classification performance.

We consider two sets of features for this classification task. They are the features related to tweets and topics of tweets, such as trending topics category and the average tweet length, and the features related to the hyperlinks and the linked target pages, such as PageRank (PR) value of the page and the domain of links (see Table 1). While a co-training technique is devised based on the assumptions that the given task can be described with two redundant feature sets and each set is sufficient enough for classification (M. Li and Z. Zhou, 2007), the design of these two independent sets of features is just coincident with the co-training assumption.

| **Features** | **Set** | **Examples** |
|---|---|---|
| Trending Topics Category | Twt | *Entertainment, Meme, etc.* |
| Trending Created Time | Twt | *ipad2"created_at":"2011-05-19T00:44:13", etc.* |
| Spelling Error | Twt | *"frinds-> friends", etc.* |
| Acronym / Emoticon | Twt | *FAQ, 10x, Lemeno, etc./ "☺", "☹", "^o^"* |
| Repeating letter word | Twt | *"soooo", "Awesome!!!!", etc.* |
| Average (tweet length)/(sentence number) | Twt | *(12, etc.)/(2, etc.)* |
| Similarity of tweet and trending | Twt | *0.17817, etc.* |
| PR value | Hyl | *"www.apple.com" (PR value:9)* |
| Domain feature | Hyl | *cnn or yahoo* |
| HF-ITF | Hyl | *0.4037, etc.* |
| Similarity of webpage and trending/tweets | Hyl | *0.1085, etc.* |

TABLE 1 – Hyperlink features and examples, where Twt/Hyl denote tweet/hyperlink feature set

As mentioned in Section 2, the quality of hyperlinks in different trending topic categories varies distinctly. Thus, the trending topic category is selected as one of the features. The created time of a trending topic is introduced as well. These two topic features can be extracted via the public APIs of "What the Trend" (www.whatthetrend.com). Regarding the tweet feature extraction, two perspectives are considered: text writing style and statistic information. The text writing style features focus on text expressions, including spelling error, acronym usage, emoticon usage, repeating letter word usage. The toolkits of Jazzy API are used to detect the spelling error. However, identifying the real spelling error in tweet is a challenging task when Twitter frequently broadcasts the messages that contains a large number of nouns not presents in a common dictionary (M. Kaufmann, 2010). The spelling checker will fail to recognize the correct nouns. Hence, we calculate the edit distance of the erroneous word and the suggested spelling by Jazzy. Only those pairs with distance less than 3 letters are corrected, like "*frinds-> friends*", "*Niether-> Neither*". For the acronym feature, we uses two publicly available acronyms word lists from SmartDefine (www.smartdefine.org) (e.g., "*FAQ: Frequently Asked Questions*") and ChatOnline (www.chatslang.com) (e.g., "*10x: Thanks*"). Meanwhile, ChatOnline offers 273 commonly-used emoticons like "☺", "☹" and "^o^". These emoticons are used to detect the emoticon usage in tweets text. The last feature about tweet writing style is the use of words with repeating letter or punctuation, like "*what'sssss up*", "*soooo guilty*" and "*Awesome!!!!*" etc. As for the tweet statistics features, average tweet length, average sentence words in tweets are concerned, and these features in certain degree reflect how much attention the tweet poster pay to the trending topic. Intuitively more attention implies that the tweet is more likely to contain a useful hyperlink. In case of hyperlink per se features, the domain information and Google Page-rank value are extracted, which indicate the global importance of hyperlinks. *hf-itf* of a hyperlink is also introduced, where *hf* denotes the frequency of hyperlinks present in one topic, and *itf* denotes the frequency of hyperlinks across all the topics. We also calculate the cosine similarity between a hyperlinked page text and the collective text of the tweets containing that hyperlink, and between a hyperlinked pages and the trending topic it resides to indicate the content similarity.

Typical co-training paradigm works as follows. Given a set of labelled instances $L$ and a set of unlabelled instances $U$, co-training will first define two features views ($V_1$ and $V_2$, corresponding to the feature sets related to tweets/topics and related to hyperlinks in this study) on each instance in $L$ and $U$, and specialize two classifiers ($C_1$ and $C_2$) on each view. In each iterative procedure, classifier $C_1$ and $C_2$ will be trained with labelled instance $L$ on feature set $V_1$ and $V_2$ respectively and label all instance in $U$. Then, the $n$ most confident new labelled instances $L'$ are allowed to update labelled dataset of $L$ for the next iteration. The iteration terminates when all unlabelled instance $U$ are labelled or nothing is changed. Normally, when parameter $n$ increases, the quality of new labelled instances will decline and lead the unstable of co-training. To avoid this problem, we define the most confident instances as the ones with the same predicted labels by both classifiers. The advantage of co-training is that with sufficient feature sets, classifier $C_1$ and classifier $C_2$ can learn information from the unlabelled dataset and exchange it with the other one.

Given the identified useful links for a given topic, we further rank them in terms of relevance and credibility and recommend the top ones to users. The ranking strategy is simple. We first rank the useful hyperlinks by their PR values which represent the global importance of hyperlinks. When several links receive the equal PR value, they are ordered according to the similarity between the hyperlinked page and the trending topic.

## 4. Experiments and Discussion

The experiments are conducted on the whole hyperlinks extracted from tweets, including both labeled and unlabeled hyperlinks. We come up with 230 labeled hyperlinks. We are randomly split into the training and test datasets (with ratio 4:1). Similarly, unlabeled hyperlinks are generated from the unlabeled hyperlinks. The evaluations of supervised learning on different feature sets are provided in Table 2 as the baseline of comparison. Figure 2 shows the co-training evaluations using different number of new labeled instances updated in each iteration ($n$). Comparing Table 2 and Figure 2, the significant improvement is observed in the precision of co-training, which indicates the co-training can utilize two feature sets information to predict higher accuracy labels. The higher precision and lower recall of NB classifier reflect that co-training can help NB learn some accurate rules to precisely predict the label, but cannot balance with the coverage. In contrast, SVM is able to learn some complex "rules", which can cover more instances, while the precision declines a bit.

| | NB P | NB R | NB F | SVM P | SVM R | SVM F |
|---|---|---|---|---|---|---|
| Integration | 0.35 | 0.91 | 0.51 | 0.78 | 0.91 | 0.84 |
| Tweet | 0.64 | 0.95 | **0.76** | 0.85 | 0.85 | **0.85** |
| Hyperlink | 0.35 | 0.91 | 0.51 | 0.35 | 0.91 | 0.51 |

TABLE 2 – Evaluation of supervised learning

Additionally, compared with the performance of supervised learning with hyperlink features, a remarkable increase can be achieved by introducing tweet features, which indicates tweet features play an important role in useful hyperlink classification. To certain degree, these tweet features can be regarded as features of tweet relevance, which means tweet relevance can be a good indicator of usefulness hyperlink. When taking a closer look at the wrongly predicted instances, we found two main sources of errors. The precision error mainly results from the non-text context type of the hyperlinked pages. For example, a video page can be regarded as useful by manual annotation, but with little text information it is hard for classifiers to predict correctly.

The recall error is mainly caused by the Web page that simply has word overlaps with a trending topic but not really related to it. For example, the Web page of selling ipad2 is prone to be regarded as related to the trending topic of the launch of apple's ipad2 by classifiers, but actually the page is not what the users care about.

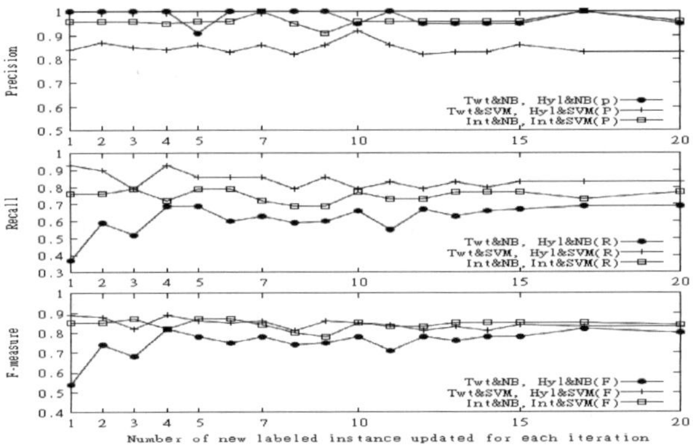


FIGURE 2 – Co-training evaluation

Eventually, useful hyperlinks are ranked by their PR value and their similarities with trending topics. The top two hyperlinks that are recommended for some example topics are illustrated in Table 3. These recommended hyperlinks provide the information about the trending topics, and help to understand the trending topics especially for technology and emergency category. For example, one of the recommended hyperlinks for "*#ipad2*" is the homepage of the Apple official website, and the other one presents the new properties of ipad2. The recommended hyperlinks for "Frankfurt Airport" are also linked to some predominate websites, e.g. jiHadwatch.com, webpartner.com, etc. However, the quality of recommended hyperlinks for meme trending topics is lower than the others. The reasons are: (1) the proportion of useful hyperlinks in meme is lower than that in the others and (2) there is too much unrelated information in this category. This also echoes the annotation findings.

In the future, we will continue to improve the performance of useful hyperlink classification by reducing the precision errors and recall errors. We would also like to further explore the usage of hyperlinks, and apply useful hyperlinks for potential applications.

## Acknowledgements

The work presented in this paper is supported by a Hong Kong RGC project (No. PolyU 5230/08E).

| Trending | Recommended Hyperlink |
|---|---|
| Frankfurt Airport | 1. http://bit.ly/g9hcTN (jiHadwatch.com)<br>2. http://bit.ly/hymUEl (webpartner.com) |
| #ipad2 | 1. http://www.apple.com/ (apple.com)<br>2. http://on.mash.to/dYhMHa (mashable.com) |
| #ilovemyfans | 1. http://bit.ly/iPTTon (twitpic.com)<br>2. http://mysp.ac/dH6vla (myspace.com) |
| Jon Diebler | 1. http://bit.ly/lZ64qe (Yahoo.com)<br>2. http://bit.ly/gZrLa2 (buzztap.com) |
| Adonis DNA | 1. http://bit.ly/e7TgOv (personalinjuryattorneyz.us)<br>2. http://aol.it/ghsgND (popeater.com) |

TABLE 3 – Examples of recommended hyperlinks and their domains

## References


H. Kwak and C. Lee et al, 2010. *What is Twitter, a social Network or a news Media*? ACM WWW10. Raleigh, North Carolina, USA.

D. Zhao and M. Rosson. (2009). *How and Why People Twitter: The Role that micro-blogging plays in informal communication at work*. ACM, GROUP09. Sanibel Island, Florida, USA.

M. Michael and N. Koudas. (2010). *TwitterMonitor: Trend Detection over the twitter stream*. ACM SIGMOD10. Indiana, USA.

TechInfo, 2010. http://bit.ly/muk2Uu.

M. Li and Z. Zhou. (2007). *Improve computer-aided diagnosis with machine learning techniques using undiagnosed samples*. IEEE Transactions on Systems, Man and Cybernetics.

M. Kaufmann. (2010). *Syntactic Normalization of Twitter Message*. ICON10, IIT Kharagpur, India.

# Rule Based Hindi Part of Speech Tagger

*Navneet Garg*[1,1], *Vishal Goyal*[2,1], *Suman Preet*[3,2]
(1) Department of Computer Science, Punjabi University, Patiala
(2) Department of Linguistics and Punjabi Lexicography, Punjabi University, Patiala.
navneetgarg123@rediffmail.com, vishal.pup@gmail.com,
virksumanpreet@yahoo.co.in

ABSTRACT

Part of Speech Tagger is an important tool that is used to develop language translator and information extraction. The problem of tagging in natural language processing is to find a way to tag every word in a sentence. In this paper, we present a Rule Based Part of Speech Tagger for Hindi. Our System is evaluated over a corpus of 26,149 words with 30 different standard part of speech tags for Hindi. The evaluation of the system is done on the different domains of Hindi Corpus. These domains include news, essay, and short stories. Our system achieved the accuracy of 87.55%.

KEYWORDS: POS, Tagging, Rules, Hindi.

*Proceedings of COLING 2012: Demonstration Papers*, pages 163–174,
COLING 2012, Mumbai, December 2012.

## 1. Introduction

Natural language processing is a field of computer science, artificial intelligence (also called machine learning) and linguistics concerned with the interactions between computers and human (natural) languages. Specifically, it is the process of a computer extracting meaningful information from natural language input and/or producing natural language output. Part of Speech tagger is an important application of natural language processing. Part of speech tagging is the process of assigning a part of speech like noun, verb, preposition, pronoun, adverb, adjective or other lexical class marker to each word in a sentence. There are a number of approaches to implement part of speech tagger, i.e. Rule Based approach, Statistical approach and Hybrid approach. Rule-based tagger use linguistic rules to assign the correct tags to the words in the sentence or file. Statistical Part of Speech tagger is based on the probabilities of occurrences of words for a particular tag. Hybrid based Part of Speech tagger is combination of Rule based approach and Statistical approach. Part of Speech tagging is an important application of natural language processing. It is used in several Natural Languages processing based software implementation. Accuracy of all NLP tasks like grammar checker, phrase chunker, machine translation etc. depends upon the accuracy of the Part of Speech tagger. Tagger plays an important role in speech recognition, natural language parsing and information retrieval.

## 2. Related Work

There have been many implementation of part of speech tagger using statistical approach, mainly for morphological rich languages like Hindi. Statistical techniques are easy to implement and require very less knowledge about the language.

Aniket Dalal et al., 2006 developed a system using Maximum Entropy Markov Model for Hindi. System required a feature function capturing the lexical and morphological feature of language and feature set was arrived after an in-depth analysis of an annotated corpus. The system was evaluated over a corpus of 15562 words with 27 different POS tags and system achieved the accuracy of 94.81%.

Smriti Singh et al., 2006 developed a part of speech tagger using decision tree base learning. This methodology uses locally annotated modestly sized corpora, exhaustive morphological analysis backed by high coverage lexicon. The heart of the system is detailed linguistic analysis of morph syntactic, handling of suffixes, accurate verb group identification and learning of disambiguation rules. The evaluation of the system was done with 4-fold cross validation of the corpora in the news domain and accuracy of the system is 93.45%.

Himanshu Aggarwal et al., 2006 developed a system using Conditional Random Fields for Hindi. A morph analyzer is used to provide information like root words and possible POS tags for training. The system was evaluated over a corpus of 21000 words with 27 different POS tags and system achieved the accuracy of 82.67%.

Manish Shrivastava et al., 2008 developed a system using Hidden Markov Model for Hindi. The System uses stemmer as a preprocessor to find the root of the words. The system was developed using 18 different pos tags and system achieved the accuracy of 93.12%.

Sanjeev Kumar Sharma et al., 2011 developed a system using Hidden Markov Model to improve the accuracy of Punjabi Part of Speech tagger. A module has been developed that takes output of the existing POS tagger as input and assign the correct tag to the words having more than one tag. The system was evaluated over a corpus of 26,479 words and system achieved the accuracy of 90.11%.

Pranjal Awasthi et al., 2006 developed a system using a combination of Hidden Markov Model and error driven learning. Tagging process consists of two stages, an initial statistical tagging using the TnT tagger, which is a second order Hidden Markov Model (HMM) and apply a set of transformation rules to correct the errors introduced by the TnT tagger. The system was developed using 26 different POS tags and accuracy of system is 79.66% using the TnT tagger and transformations in post processing improves the accuracy to 80.74%.

Shachi Mall et al., 2011 developed a system using a Rule based approach. The module reads the Hindi corpus and split the sentence into words according to the delimiter. The system finds the words in the database and assigns the appropriate tag to the words.

We can see that most of the taggers are developed using statistical techniques because these techniques are easy to implement and require very less knowledge about the language. In this paper, we presented a rule based approach to design part of speech tagger. Rule based approach required less amount of data and vast knowledge about the language. Rule based system is usually difficult to develop.

## 3. System Description

This system is developed using rule based approach and 30 different standard part of speech tags are [shown in Appendix A] used that are given by Department of Information Technology Ministry of Communications & Information Technology and some other tags that is time, date and number tag. Adverb tag is further classified into following categories i.e. adverb of manner (RB_AMN), adverb of location (RB_ALC), adverb of time (RB_TIME) and adverb of quantity (RB_Q). Collection of 18,249 words for different tags has been done. The system mainly works in two steps-firstly the input words are found in the database; if it is present then it is tagged. Secondly if it is not present then various rules are applied.

### 3.1 Algorithm

1. Input the text using file upload button or manually enter by user.
2. Tokenize the input text word by word.
3. Normalized the tokenized words. i.e. Separate out the punctuation marks and the symbols from the text.

4. Search the number tag by using Regular Expression.
For Example: - 2012, 1-2, 1.2, 12वें, २३, ६.७, ६-७ etc.

5. Search the date tag by using regular expression.
For Example: - 17/10/1985, 17-10-1985, etc.

6. Search the time tag by using regular expression.
For Example: - 12:10, 12:23:45 etc.

7. Search for the abbreviation using regular expression.
For Example: - ए.पी, आर.के. etc.

ē.pī, ār.kē

8. Search in database for different input words and tag the word according to corresponding tag.

9. Then different rules are applied to tag the unknown words.

10. Display the tagged data to the user.

## 3.2 Following Rules are applied to identify different Tags

### 1. Noun Identification Rules

**Rule 1**: If word is adjective then there is high probability that next word will be noun.

For Example:-

वह एक सच्चा देशभक्त है।

vah ēk saccā dēshbhakt hai.

In above example सच्चा (saccā) is adjective and देशभक्त (dēshbhakt) is noun.

**Rule 2**: If word is relative pronoun then there is high probability that next word will be noun.

For Example:-

ये वो घर है जिसे राजा ने बनवाया था।

yē vō ghar hai jisē rājā nē banvāyā thā.

In above example वो (vō) and जिसे (jisē) is relative pronoun and घर (ghar) and राजा (rājā) is noun.

**Rule 3:** If word is reflexive pronoun then there is high probability that next word will be noun.

For Example:-

वह अपने घर चला गया।

vah apnē ghar calā gayā .

In above example अपने (apnē) is reflexive pronoun and घर (ghar) is noun.

**Rule 4:** If word is personal pronoun then there is high probability that next word will be noun.

For Example:-

यह हमारा घर है।

yah hamārā ghar hai .

In above example हमारा (hamārā) is personal pronoun and घर (ghar) is noun.

**Rule 5:** If current word is post position then there is high probability that previous word will be noun.

For Example:-

उसने पानी में पत्थर फेंका।

usnē pānī mēṃ patthar phēṅkā .

In above example पानी (pānī) is noun and में (mēṃ) is post position.

**Rule 6:** If current word is verb then there is probability that previous word will be noun.

For Example:-

वह <u>भोजन खा</u> रहा है।

vah <u>bhōjan khā</u> rahā hai.

In above example भोजन (bhōjan) is noun and खा (khā) is verb.

**Rule 7:** If word is noun then there is probability that next or previous word will be noun.

For Example:-

वह <u>फ़ाइनल मुकाबले</u> में हार गए ।

vah <u>phaāinal mukāblē</u> mēṃ hār gaē.

In above example फ़ाइनल (phaāinal) and मुकाबले (mukāblē) both are noun.

There are more rules are applied to find the noun tags.

**2. Demonstrative Identification Rules**

**Rule 1:** If word is pronoun in database and next word is also pronoun, then first word will be demonstrative.

For Example:-

<u>वह कौन</u> है।

<u>vah kaun</u> hai.

In above example वह (vah) and कौन (kaun) both are pronoun.

**Rule 2:** If current word is pronoun in database and next word is noun, then curremt word will be demonstrative.

For Example: -

<u>वह मुंबई</u> नहीं जाएंगे।

<u>vah mumbī</u> nahīṃ jāēṅgē.

In above example वह (vah) is pronoun and मुंबई (mumbī) is noun.

**3. Proper Noun Identification Rules:-**

**Rule 1:** If current word is not tagged and next word is tagged as proper noun, then there is high probability that current word will be proper noun.

For Example: - आर.के. गोयल, राम गोयल

ār.kē. gōyal, rām gōyal

In above example आर.के.(ār.kē.), गोयल (gōyal) and राम (rām) are proper noun.

**Rule 2:** If current word is name and next word is surname then we tagged them as single proper name.

For Example: - सुरेश कुमार <N_NNP>

suresh kumār

In above example सुरेश (surēsh) is name and कुमार (kumār) is surname.

**4. Adjective Identification Rules:-**

**Rule 1:** If word ends with तर (tar), तम (tam), िक (ik) postfix then word is tagged as adjective.

For Example: - लघुतर, विशालतम, प्रामाणिक

laghutar, vishāltam, prāmāṇik

**5. Verb Identification Rules:-**

**Rule 1:** If current word is not tagged and next word tagged as a auxiliary verb, then there is high probability that current word will be main verb.

For Example:-

वह खाना खा रहा है।

vah khānā khā rahā hai.

In above example खा (khā) is main verb and रहा (rahā) is auxiliary verb.

The system can be understood by following example:-

**Input Hindi Sentence**

श्रीनगर में एक 200 साल पुरानी दरगाह में आग लगने के बाद प्रदर्शनकारियों ने पुलिस पर पथराव किया है और इलाके में तनाव है।

shrīngar mēṃ ēk 200 sāl purānī dargāh mēṃ āg lagnē kē bād pradrshankāriyōṃ nē pulis par pathrāv kiyā hai aur ilākē mēṃ tanāv hai.

**Output**

shrīngar <N_NNP> mēṃ <PSP> ēk <QT_QTC>200<NUMBER> sāl <N_NN> purānī <JJ> dargāh <N_NN> mēṃ <PSP> āg <N_NN> lagnē <V_VM> kē <PSP> bād <PSP> pradrshankāriyōṃ <N_NN> nē <PSP> pulis <N_NN> par <PSP> pathrāv <N_NN> kiyā <V_VM> hai <V_VAUX> aur <CC_CCD> ilākē <N_NN> mēṃ <PSP> tanāv <N_NN> hai <V_VAUX> .<RD_PUNC>

## 4. Evaluation and Result

Evaluation is done to enhance the performance of system on different domains of news. These domains include news, essay, and short stories. The system was evaluated on 26,149 words. The overall accuracy achieved by system is 87.55%. We have constructed three test data sets for testing. These test data sets are collected from different websites [15][16] of Hindi. Following table shows the different test cases for testing.

| Test No. | Domain | No. of words |
|---|---|---|
| Test Case 1 | News | 17233 |
| Test Case 2 | Essay | 5039 |
| Test Case 3 | Short Stories | 3877 |

**Table 5.1 Test Cases**

The evaluation metrics for the data set is precision, recall and F-Measure. These are defined as following:-

**Recall = Number of correct answer given by system / Total number of words.**

**Precision = Number of Correct answer / Total number of words.**

**F-Measure = $(\beta^2 + 1)$ PR / $\beta^2$R + P**

$\beta$ is the weighting between precision and recall and typically $\beta = 1$.

| | Recall | Precision | F-Meaure |
|---|---|---|---|
| Set-1 | 92.84% | 89.94% | 91.37% |
| Set-2 | 87.32% | 81.36% | 84.23% |
| Set-3 | 88.99% | 85.11% | 87.06% |

**Table 5.2 Accuracy of System on different Test Cases**

## Conclusion and Future Work

In this paper Part of Speech tagger using rule based technique has been discussed. Tokenized words are search in the database and if not found then appropriate rules are applied. Sometimes when we apply rules then system may tag the words with wrong POS tags.

If a sentence consists of 12 words out of which 8 words are unknown, then system fails to tag them. The reason behind it is hard to decide which rules should be handled first because word tagging resolution is based on neighbour's words.

By increasing the size of database accuracy of part of speech tagger can be increased. Hybrid based system can be developed to increase the accuracy of system. There is problem in handling the words that can act as both common noun and proper noun. So it becomes difficult for the system to tag the word correctly. When such a situation occur system tag the word as a common noun, there is high probability that word will be a common noun but in few cases it can act as proper noun. This limitation can be handled by using Hindi Named Entity Recognition system in future.

## References

[1] Aniket Dalal, Kumar Nagaraj, Uma Sawant and Sandeep Shelke. (2006). *Hindi Part-of-Speech Tagging and Chunking: A Maximum Entropy Approach*, In Proceeding of the NLPAI Machine Learning Competition, 2006.

[2] Manish Shrivastava and Pushpak Bhattacharyya. (2008). *Hindi POS Tagger Using Naive Stemming: Harnessing Morphological Information without Extensive Linguistic Knowledge*, International Conference on NLP (ICON08), Pune, India, and December, 2008.

[3] Agarwal Himashu, Amni Anirudh. (2006). *Part of Speech Tagging and Chunking with Conditional Random Fields,* In the proceedings of NLPAI Contest, 2006.

[4] Smriti Singh, Kuhoo Gupta, Manish Shrivastava, and Pushpak Bhattacharyya. (2006). *Morphological Richness Offsets Resource Demand-Experiences in Constructing a POS Tagger for Hindi*, In Proceedings of Coling/ACL 2006, Sydney, Australia, July, pp.779-786.

[5] Nidhi Mishra and Amit Mishra. (2011). *Part of Speech Tagging for Hindi Corpus*, In the proceedings of 2011 International Conference on Communication systems and Network Technologies, pp.554-558.

[6] Eric Brill. (1992). *A Simple Rule Based Part of Speech Tagger*, In Proceeding of the Third Conference on Applied Computational Linguistics (ACL), Trento, Italy, 1992, pp.112–116.

[7] Sanjeev Kumar Sharma and Gurpreet Singh Lehal. (2011). *Using Hidden Markov Model to Improve the Accuracy of Punjabi POS Tagger*, Computer Science and Automation Engineering (CSAE), 2011 IEEE International Conference on June 2011, pp. 697-701.

[8] Shachi Mall and Umesh Chandra Jaiswal. (2011). *Hindi Part of Speech Tagging and Translation*, In the proceedings of Int. J. Tech. 2011, Vol. 1: Issue 1, pp. 29-32.

[9] Pranjal Awasthi, Delip Rao and Balaraman Ravindran. (2006). *Part Of Speech Tagging and Chunking with HMM and CRF*, In the proceedings of NLPAI Contest, 2006.

[10] Dinesh Kumar and Gurpreet Singh Josan. (2010). *Part of Speech Taggers for Morphologically Rich Indian Languages: A Survey*, International Journal of Computer Applications (0975 – 8887) Volume 6– No.5, September 2010, pp.1-9.

[11] Sankaran Baskaran. *Hindi POS Tagging and Chunking,* Microsoft Research India, Banglore.

[12] Antony P J and Dr. Soman K P. (2011). *Part of Speech Tagging for Indian Languages: A Literature Survey*, International Journal of Computer Applications (0975 – 8887) Volume 34– No.8, pp.22-29.

[13] Mandeep Singh, Lehal Gurpreet, and Sharma Shiv. (2008). *A Part-of-Speech Tagset for Grammar Checking of Punjabi*, published in The Linguistic Journal, Vol 4, Issue 1, pp 6-22.

[14] http://en.wikipedia.org/wiki/Part-of-speech_tagging

[15] http://www.bbc.co.uk/hindi/

[16] http://www.bhaskar.com/

[17] http://en.wikipedia.org/wiki/Natural_language_processing

[18] http://en.wikipedia.org/wiki/Support_vector_ machine

[19] http://en.wikipedia.org/wiki/Hidden_Markov _model

[20] http://en.wikipedia.org/wiki/Maximum_entropy

## Appendix A

**Standard POS Tags**

| Sr. No | Category | | Label | Annotation Convention | Examples |
|---|---|---|---|---|---|
| | Top Level | Subtype | | | |
| 1. | Noun | | N | N | ladakaa, raajaa, kitaaba |
| 1.1 | | Common | NN | N_NN | kitaaba, kalama, cashmaa |
| 1.2 | | Proper | NNP | N_NNP | Mohan, ravi, rashmi |
| 1.3 | | Nloc | NST | N_NST | Uupara, niice, aage, piiche |
| 2 | Pronoun | | PR | PR | Yaha, vaha, jo |
| 2.1 | | Personal | PRP | PR__PRP | Vaha, main, tuma, ve |
| 2.2 | | Reflexive | PRF | PR_PRF | Apanaa, swayam, khuda |
| 2.3 | | Relative | PRL | PR_PRL | Jo, jis, jab, jahaaM, |
| 2.4 | | Reciprocal | PRC | PR_PRC | Paraspara, aapasa |

| | | | | | |
|---|---|---|---|---|---|
| 2.5 | Pronoun | Wh-word | PRQ | PR_PRQ | Kauna, kab, kahaaM |
| 2.6 | | Indefinite | PRI | PR_PRI | Koii, kis |
| 3 | Demonstrative | | DM | DM | Vaha, jo, yaha, |
| 3.1 | | Deictic | DMD | DM_DMD | Vaha, yaha |
| 3.2 | | Relative | DMR | DM_DMR | jo, jis |
| 3.3 | | Wh-word | DMQ | DM_DMQ | kis, kaun |
| 3.4 | | Indefinite | DMI | DM_DMI | KoI, kis |
| 4 | Verb | | V | V | giraa, gayaa, sonaa, haMstaa, hai, rahaa |
| 4.1 | | Main | VM | V_VM | giraa, gayaa, sonaa, haMstaa, |
| 4.2 | | Auxiliary | VAUX | V_VAUX | hai, rahaa, huaa, |
| 5 | Adjective | | JJ | JJ | sundara, acchaa, baRaa |
| 6 | Adverb | | RB | RB | jaldii, teza |
| 7 | Postposition | | PSP | PSP | ne, ko, se, mein |

| | | | | | |
|---|---|---|---|---|---|
| 8 | Conjunction | | CC | CC | aur, agar, tathaa, kyonki |
| 8.1 | | Co-ordinator | CCD | CC_CCD | aur, balki, parantu |
| 8.2 | | Subordinator | CCS | CC_CCS | Agar, kyonki, to, ki |
| 9 | Particles | | RP | RP | to, bhii, hii |
| 9.1 | | Default | RPD | RP_RPD | to,bhii, hii |
| 9.2 | | Interjection | INJ | RP_INJ | are, he, o |
| 9.3 | | Intensifier | INTF | RP_INTF | bahuta, behada |
| 9.4 | | Negation | NEG | RP_NEG | nahiin, mata, binaa |
| 10 | Quantifiers | | QT | QT | thoRaa, bahuta, kucha, eka, pahalaa |
| 10.1 | | General | QTF | QT_QTF | thoRaa, bahuta, kucha |
| 10.2 | | Cardinals | QTC | QT_QTC | eka, do, tiina, |
| 10.3 | | Ordinals | QTO | QT_QTO | pahalaa, duusaraa |
| 11 | Residuals | | RD | RD | |
| 11.1 | | Foreign word | RDF | RD_RDF | |

| | | | | | |
|---|---|---|---|---|---|
| | | | | | |
| 11.2 | Residuals | Symbol | SYM | RD_SYM | $, &, *, (, ) |
| 11.3 | | Punctuation | PUNC | RD_PUNC | ., : ; ? \| ! |
| 11.4 | | Unknown | UNK | RD_UNK | |

# *Fangorn*: A system for querying very large treebanks

*Sumukh GHODKE*[1] *Steven BIRD*[1,2]
(1) Department of Computing and Information Systems, University of Melbourne
(2) Linguistic Data Consortium, University of Pennsylvania
`sumukh.ghodke@gmail.com, sbird@unimelb.edu.au`

ABSTRACT
The efficiency and robustness of statistical parsers has made it possible to create very large treebanks. These serve as the starting point for further work including enrichment, extraction, and curation: semantic annotations are added, syntactic features are mined, erroneous analyses are corrected. In many such cases manual processing is required, and this must operate efficiently on the largest scale. We report on an efficient web-based system for querying very large treebanks called Fangorn. It implements an XPath-like query language which is extended with a linguistic operator to capture proximity in the terminal sequence. Query results are displayed using scalable vector graphics and decorated with the original query, making it easy for queries to be modified and resubmitted. Fangorn is built on the Apache Lucene text search engine and is available under the Apache License.

KEYWORDS: language resources, database query, annotation, syntax, parsing.

*Proceedings of COLING 2012: Demonstration Papers*, pages 175–182,
COLING 2012, Mumbai, December 2012.

# 1 Introduction

Treebanks play a central role in the analysis of language structures in a diverse range of areas including language modelling, machine translation, information extraction, and syntactic description. Manual annotation requires painstaking work by specialists, and this is too expensive to do on a large scale. Instead, it is standard to use a state-of-the-art parser on massive quantities of text and then manually post-edit the output. At the point of discovering and correcting a parse error, it is desirable to quickly locate other instances of the same error, regardless of where they appear in the corpus. Syntactic research depends on manual exploration of conditioning factors that allow us to identify constructions of interest, and these constructions will usually be rare. Such activities require efficient query over very large treebanks.

The last decade has seen the development of several corpus query tools, including TGrep2, TIGERSearch, Emu, Nite NXT Search, Netgraph, fsq, and Emdros (Rohde, 2001; Brants et al., 2002; Cassidy and Harrington, 2001; Heid et al., 2004; Mírovský, 2006; Kepser, 2003; Petersen, 2004). These tools are effective when the corpus fits in main memory, or when work can be done in batch mode (requiring a linear pass through the entire corpus on disk, typically taking tens of seconds). When the corpus is large, and when fast query processing is required, an entirely different approach is needed. *Fangorn* is designed to fill this gap. It is the outcome of an interdisciplinary research project combining the scaling properties of general purpose semi-structured databases and information retrieval engines with the features commonly found in corpus query tools (Ghodke and Bird, 2008, 2010).

In this paper we present the features of *Fangorn*, including its query language, its user interface, and its architecture. Finally, we describe areas for further research.

# 2 Background

Treebank query tools are often designed for specific annotation structures. Some tools are designed for phrase structure trees (e.g. TGrep2, TIGERSearch), while others are designed for dependency trees (e.g. Netgraph). Some are intended for corpora with multiple annotation types (e.g. Nite NXT Search, Emu). Some permit phrase structure trees with crossing branches (e.g. TIGERSearch) while others require strict trees (e.g. TGrep2). Some support query of extra properties on tree nodes or edges. Despite this diversity, there are still some abstract requirements that are common across all corpus query tools.

All tools support expressive query languages, although the great variety of syntax obscures the expressive similarity of the languages. Lai and Bird (2004) compare several corpus query languages and present a few generic requirements for treebank query languages. They state that the query language should include more than just simple navigational operators and include features such as: subtree matching, non-tree navigation (e.g. the "immediate following" operator explained later), secondary edges, and closure operators. They should also handle Boolean operators: conjunction, disjunction, and negation. The language should be able to specify the granularity of results. While query language operators depend largely on the structure of the data, some features such as finding secondary edges in a tree are specific to annotation style. Query languages usually support regular expressions over node labels, allowing search for label prefixes and suffixes (e.g. `N.*` for any noun-like syntactic category). Support for popular file formats is another requirement. Most corpus query tools accept one or more of the following annotation formats as inputs: Penn Treebank (Marcus et al., 1993), NEGRA (Skut et al., 1997), TIGER corpus (Brants et al., 2002), or custom XML formats.

Most tree query tools are not designed for very large data since they perform a linear pass over the entire collection, e.g. TGrep. More advanced tools store and index tree data using relational databases. However, relational databases are not efficient for storing and accessing trees (Zhang et al., 2001). On the other hand, semistructured databases have indexes that are specialised for efficient operations on large tree collections. Unfortunately, their query languages lack the required expressiveness. An ideal system for large scale treebank data should inherit the query language and annotation awareness from corpus query tools while borrowing the scaling features from semi-structured databases.

## 3 Query Language

*Fangorn* queries involve "path expressions", a series of navigations around the tree, e.g. from a node to its sibling, descendent, or ancestor. At each step, the type of navigation is specified by an operator and the type of node or terminal is specified with a string. For instance, `/NP` navigates to an NP child, `=>PP` navigates to a PP following sibling, and `/NP=>PP` combines both of these steps. Paths always begin at the root, and so a path expression that starts with `/S` can only navigate to the S node at the root of the tree. The descendent operator allows a path to skip to any descendent of the current node, so a path expression beginning with `//NP` navigates from the root to any NP node in the whole tree, in a single step. Paths can be arbitrarily long, e.g. `//NP=>S//VP->NN/table`; each time we add a step, we further restrict the number of possible matching trees. Paths can branch, and we use "filter expressions" (sub-paths contained in square brackets) to specify restrictions on the branches. Furthermore, these filter expressions can be combined using Boolean operators. The language used by *Fangorn* is defined in BNF as follows, where the axis operators and logical operators are given in Tables 1 and 2.

```
<expr> ::= <term> [<term>]*
<term> ::= <axis-operator><node-label> [<filter-expr>]
<filter-expr> ::= "[" <filter-element> [(AND|OR) <filter-element>]* "]"
<filter-element> ::= [NOT] <expr>
<node-label> ::= annotation_label | word | punctuation
```

| Operator | Symbol | Y |
|---|---|---|
| Descendant | $X//Y$ | $C_*, D_*$ |
| Child | $X/Y$ | $C_*$ |
| Ancestor | $X\backslash\backslash Y$ | $P, A$ |
| Parent | $X\backslash Y$ | $P$ |
| Following sibling | $X{==}{>}Y$ | |
| Immediately following sibling | $X{=}{>}Y$ | |
| Preceding sibling | $X{<}{==}Y$ | $S_*$ |
| Immediately preceding sibling | $X{<}{=}Y$ | $S_2$ |
| Following | $X{-}{-}{>}Y$ | $F_*$ |
| Immediately following | $X{-}{>}Y$ | $F_1$ |
| Preceding | $X{<}{-}{-}Y$ | $S_*$ |
| Immediately preceding | $X{<}{-}Y$ | $S_2$ |

Table 1: Navigation operators

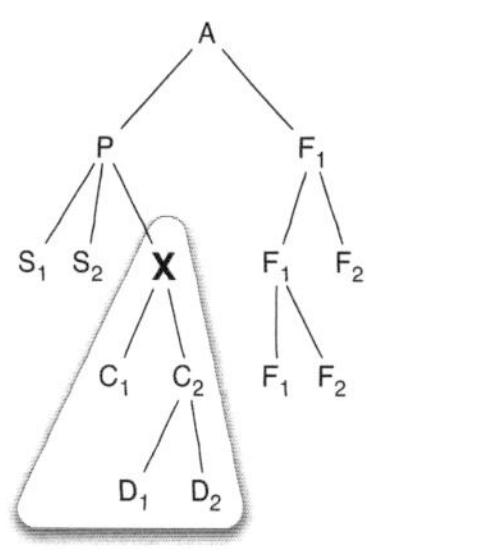


| Operator | Symbols |
|---|---|
| Conjunction | AND, and, & |
| Disjunction | OR, or, \| |
| Negation | NOT, not, ! |

Table 2: Logical operators

Filter expressions are responsible for the great expressiveness of path queries. Consider the query: `//VBG[<-is AND =>S AND -->PRP]`. Here, we are searching for any gerund VBG such

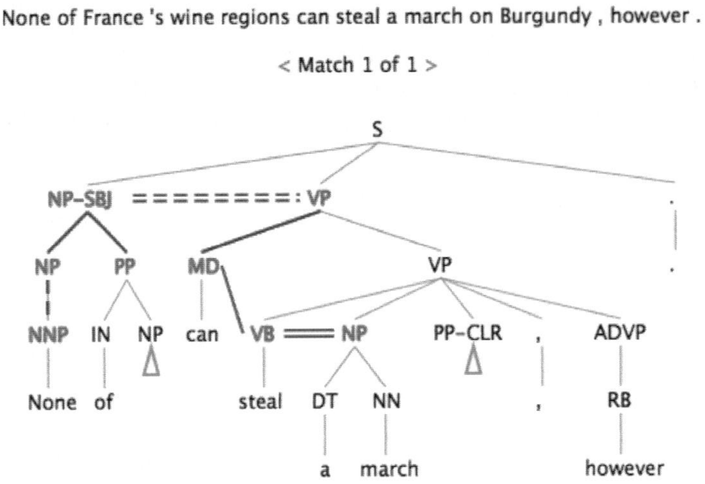


Figure 1: A result sentence from a page listing all results for a path query

that three conditions hold: it is immediately preceded by the word 'is', it has an immediately following sibling S, and it is followed somewhere later in the tree by a personal pronoun PRP.

The square brackets in the above query delimit the filter expression. Note that the contents of the filter expression can be arbitrarily complex. The above query could be extended by adding another step to one of the conjuncts as follows: `//VBG[<-is AND =>S AND -->PRP->TO]`.

The NOT operator may appear before any path expression inside a filter expression. For example, we can negate the earlier requirement concerning S as follows: `//VBG[<-is AND NOT =>S AND -->PRP]`. Similarly, the query to search for all occurrences of gerunds not preceded by the word 'is' is written as: `//VBG[NOT <-is]`.

Finally, filter expressions can be nested. For example, we can limit the S, requiring that it does not contain a PP, as follows: `//VBG[<-is AND =>S[NOT //PP] AND -->PRP]`.

## 4 User interface

*Fangorn* runs in a web browser. The entry point contains a simple search box where the query can be entered, along with a drop-down menu listing available corpora.[1] The page also displays the total number of sentences in the corpus that match the query and the time for executing the search.

Each matched sentence is rendered as an interactive scalable vector graphics (SVG) image. Figure 1 shows one annotated result sentence for the query `//NP-SBJ[/NP//NNP AND /PP]==>VP/MD->VB=>NP`. The NP-SBJ node has two child nodes NP and PP, whose edges are annotated using solid blue lines and a following sibling VP edge annotated using a double dashed red line. Blue lines are used for vertical operators (ancestor, descendant, parent, or child operators), while red lines are used for horizontal navigations. Double lines signify a sibling relationship, solid lines an immediate relationship, and dashed lines are used for closure operators. The trees are rendered in a minimally expanded form that ensures that the annotated result is always visible and cannot be accidentally collapsed.

[1] A demonstration system permits searches over Penn Treebank and the English Wikipedia (see `http://nltk.ldc.upenn.edu:9090`).

The other nodes in the sentence may be expanded or collapsed by clicking on the nodes or the triangle below collapsed nodes. Buttons are provided to expand/collapse all nodes in a tree, and to export each sentence as an SVG image or as text in Penn Treebank format. Displayed above each result tree is the corresponding sentence without annotations. When the mouse is positioned over a tree node, the corresponding span of words in the sentence is highlighted. When a sentence matches a query more than once, only the first match is displayed on screen while other matches can be viewed by clicking on the arrows on either side of the result.

Result trees are annotated with the path expression that was used to find them, so that users can immediately see why the tree was matched. This annotation can itself be edited, in order to modify and resubmit the query. The edit mode can be activated by clicking the "Build query from tree" button at the top right of each matched result in the result display screen. This window does not allow nodes in the tree to be collapsed on a mouse click, however, collapsed nodes can be expanded by clicking on the triangle below such nodes. The following operations can be performed in the edit query screen: (1) extend a query starting at a node, (2) edit label or delete query terms, and (3) change or negate operators joining two query terms.

## 5 Architecture

*Fangorn* uses a web client-server architecture. An embedded Jetty web server hosts the search engine software. The search engine is built using Apache Lucene, a popular and versatile open source text search engine toolkit. A corpus reader loads text corpora and converts the annotated sentences into a format easily digestible by the search engine. This step is called the analysis step and is explained later in this section. An embedded database is used to store corpora metadata, but this database is not used to answer tree queries. Searches can be performed from a browser once the web server is started.

The client browser receives results as Javascript objects from the server and renders them as SVG images. The SVG format was chosen because it is a compact vector format, and because event handlers can be easily attached to SVG elements to make them interactive. Not all browsers have adequate support for dynamically embedded SVG images, and so we designed the user interface specifically for the Mozilla Firefox browser.

The analysis step converts a treebank tree into tokens for indexing. Each node is assigned a 4-tuple of position numbers (left, right, depth, parent) that uniquely identify its location in the tree following the scheme used by LPath (Bird et al., 2006). This position information is enough to test whether two nodes satisfy an operator condition, avoiding the need to store the trees explicitly. The output of the analysis step is a sequence of tokens – essentially node labels in the treebank together with their position numbers – that are then indexed in the text search engine.

Lucene is configured to use two sets of inverted lists for the index. The first is the frequency index, which is a list of frequency postings lists. Each token's postings list maintains a sequence of document ids that contain the token together with the term-frequency in each document. (Note that each sentence is treated as its own document.) The second is the position index. This index typically stores an integer that identifies the sequential location of a token, and is used in phrase and proximity queries. However, in *Fangorn* the tree analysis step transforms a tree structure into a depth-first ordered sequence of tokens, and the integer position of a tree token is its depth-first position. The position index provides extra storage at each position (byte-array payloads), and we use these to store the tree position information.

Tree queries are processed using the frequency and position indexes. First, the frequency index identifies the sentences that contain the required terms in the query. Then, using the position index, the position lists of the query terms are joined pairwise, based on the structural relation between the two terms in a pair. This method of performing pairwise joins is called a path join. *Fangorn* implements a join algorithm similar to a path join, called the staircase join algorithm (Grust et al., 2003). It uses both the depth-first position and the tree position information to reduce the number of comparisons while executing the join. This join algorithm is faster in part because it does not find all matches in every sentence. Instead, it checks if a sentence has any match at all. When a match is spotted, the sentence id is registered and the search continues with a new sentence. Later, all matches within each sentence are found, but only for the limited number of sentences that are displayed in one page of results.

*Fangorn* can be installed on commodity hardware with at least about 2 GB of RAM. The server software is written in Java and can be installed on POSIX systems with little or no modifications. Microsoft Windows users may require tools that provide a POSIX-like environment to run maintenance scripts. A Java runtime version 5 or higher is required to be installed on the machine. Corpora can be added or removed from the search engine by running shell scripts distributed with the software. Currently, the Penn Treebank format is the only input format supported by the system.

## 6 Conclusion

Treebanks play a central role in the modelling of natural language grammar. The cyclic process of curating treebanks and retraining parsers on the improved annotations is set to continue for some time, and will continue to generate ever better treebanks. The bottleneck in this process is manual curation, and a major part of curation involves discovery of complex tree patterns that need to be edited in some way.

We have implemented an efficient system for querying very large treebanks, and it is available for download under the terms of the Apache License 2.0 from `http://code.google.com/p/fangorn`. A demonstration version is available at `http://nltk.ldc.upenn.edu:9090`. The system is built on top of Lucene, and its scaling performance can be expected to mimic that of text retrieval engines in general. The system has already been used for curating an ERG-style treebank (Bender et al., 2012).

The system inherits some limitations of the underlying query language concerning matching of node labels. For example `NP`, `NP-SBJ`, and `NP-SBJ-1` are all distinct labels. Yet we would expect a query containing `NP` to match any of these. Possible solutions are to extend the language to support regular expressions over node labels, or to encode grammatical relations (such as SBJ) as node attributes and refer to them using filter expressions. The system is also limited in the sense that it only works with phrase structure trees. It cannot be applied to dependency trees in its current form, since the descendent and ancestor relations cannot be checked using a single span-inclusion test. In spite of these expressive limitations, *Fangorn* sets a new standard for efficiency and ease of use for tree query systems.

## References

Bender, E. M., Ghodke, S., Baldwin, T., and Dridan, R. (2012). From database to treebank: On enhancing hypertext grammars with grammar engineering and treebank search. *Electronic Grammaticography*. To appear.

Bird, S., Chen, Y., Davidson, S. B., Lee, H., and Zheng, Y. (2006). Designing and evaluating an XPath dialect for linguistic queries. In *Proceedings of the 22nd International Conference on Data Engineering*, pages 52–61. IEEE Computer Society.

Brants, S., Dipper, S., Hansen, S., Lezius, W., and Smith, G. (2002). The TIGER Treebank. In *Proceedings of the workshop on Treebanks and Linguistic Theories*, pages 24–41.

Cassidy, S. and Harrington, J. (2001). Multi-level annotation of speech: an overview of the Emu Speech Database Management System. *Speech Communication*, 33:61–77.

Ghodke, S. and Bird, S. (2008). Querying linguistic annotations. In McArthur, R., Thomas, P., Turpin, A., and Wu, M., editors, *Proceedings of the Thirteenth Australasian Document Computing Symposium*, pages 69–72, Hobart, Tasmania.

Ghodke, S. and Bird, S. (2010). Fast query for large treebanks. In *Human Language Technologies: The 2010 Annual Conference of the North American Chapter of the Association for Computational Linguistics*, pages 267–275, Los Angeles, California. Association for Computational Linguistics.

Grust, T., Keulen, M., and Teubner, J. (2003). Staircase join: Teach a relational dbms to watch its (axis) steps. In *Proceedings of the 29th International Conference on Very Large Databases (VLDB)*, pages 524–535.

Heid, U., Voormann, H., Milde, J.-T., Gut, U., Erk, K., and Pado, S. (2004). Querying both time-aligned and hierarchical corpora with NXT search. In *Proceedings of the 4th International Conference on Language Resources and Evaluation*.

Kepser, S. (2003). Finite Structure Query: A tool for querying syntactically annotated corpora. In *Proceedings of the tenth Conference of the European Chapter of the Association for Computational Linguistics*, pages 179–186.

Lai, C. and Bird, S. (2004). Querying and updating treebanks: A critical survey and requirements analysis. In *Proceedings of Australasian Language Technology Workshop*, pages 139–146.

Marcus, M. P., Santorini, B., and Marcinkiewicz, M. A. (1993). Building a large annotated corpus of English: The Penn Treebank. *Computational Linguistics*, 19:313–30.

Mírovský, J. (2006). Netgraph: a tool for searching in Prague Dependency Treebank 2.0. In *Proceedings of 5th International Conference on Treebanks and Linguistic Theories*, pages 211–222.

Petersen, U. (2004). Emdros: a text database engine for analyzed or annotated text. In *Proceedings of the 20th International Conference on Computational Linguistics*, pages 1190–1193.

Rohde, D. (2001). Tgrep2 user manual. http://citeseer.ist.psu.edu/569487.html.

Skut, W., Krenn, B., Brants, T., and Uszkoreit, H. (1997). An annotation scheme for free word order languages. In *Proceedings of the Fifth Conference on Applied Natural Language Processing (ANLP)*, pages 88–95, Stroudsburg, PA, USA. Association for Computational Linguistics.

Zhang, C., Naughton, J., DeWitt, D., Luo, Q., and Lohman, G. (2001). On supporting containment queries in relational database management systems. In *Proceedings of the 2001 ACM SIGMOD International Conference on Management of Data*, pages 425–436, New York. ACM.

# CRAB Reader: A Tool for Analysis and Visualization of Argumentative Zones in Scientific Literature

*Yufan Guo*[1] *Ilona Silins*[2] *Roi Reichart*[1] *Anna Korhonen*[1]
(1) Computer Laboratory, University of Cambridge, UK
(2) Institute of Environmental Medicine, Karolinska Institute, Sweden
yg244@cam.ac.uk, ilona.silins@ki.se, Roi.Reichart@cl.cam.ac.uk, alk23@cam.ac.uk

ABSTRACT
Given the rapid publication rate in many fields of science, it is important to develop technology that can help researchers locate different types of information in scientific literature. A number of approaches have been developed for automatic identification of information structure of scientific papers. Such approaches can be useful for down-stream NLP tasks (e.g. summarization) and practical research tasks (e.g. scientific literature review), and can be realistically applied across domains when they involve light supervision. However, even light supervision requires some data annotation for new tasks. We introduce the CRAB Reader – a tool for the analysis and visualization of information structure (according to the Argumentative Zoning (AZ) scheme) in scientific literature which can facilitate efficient and user-friendly expert-annotation. We investigate and demonstrate the use of our tool for this purpose and also discuss the benefits of using the same tool to support practical tasks such as scientific literature review.

TITLE AND ABSTRACT IN CHINESE

# CRAB Reader: 分析和查看科技文献论证结构的工具

随着各个学科领域出版量的迅速增长，新的文本挖掘技术的开发对研究人员从海量科技文献中寻找有用信息至为重要。许多自动识别科技文献信息结构的技术的开发，对于自然语言处理领域的下游工作（例如文本摘要）以及实际的研究工作（例如科技文献的阅读）有很大帮助，尤其是基于弱监督学习的技术更能够实际应用于不同的学科领域。然而即使弱监督的学习依然需要一定量的人工标注数据以适应一项新任务。本文介绍了CRAB Reader：一款分析和查看科技文献论证结构的工具。该工具有助于高效便捷地对文献进行标注。本文研究并证实了该工具对于文献信息结构的自动分析和识别有重要作用，同时讨论了该工具为实际科研工作例如科技文献的阅读带来的便利。

KEYWORDS: Information Structure, Argumentative Zoning (AZ), Interactive Annotation, Active Learning.

KEYWORDS IN CHINESE: 信息结构，论证结构分析，交互式标注，主动学习.

*Proceedings of COLING 2012: Demonstration Papers*, pages 183–190,
COLING 2012, Mumbai, December 2012.

## 1 Introduction

There is a need to develop techniques that can help scientists locate and organize relevant information in rapidly growing scientific literature. Scientists have diverse information needs and are often interested in specific types of information in a paper. Although section headings (e.g. Methods, Results) can be an indicator of information categories of interest, many sections tend to include different types of information (e.g. the Discussion section may include information about methods and results and also provide a comparison against other peoples' work). An automatic analysis of the information category of each sentence is therefore important and can be useful for both natural language processing tasks as well as for scientists e.g. conducting literature review.

Different approaches have been developed for determining the information structure (aka. discourse, rhetorical, argumentative or conceptual structure) of scientific publications (Teufel and Moens, 2002; Mizuta et al., 2006; Shatkay et al., 2008; Teufel et al., 2009; Liakata et al., 2010; Guo et al., 2010). Some of this work has proved helpful for tasks such as information retrieval, information extraction, and summarization (Teufel and Moens, 2002; Mizuta et al., 2006; Tbahriti et al., 2006; Ruch et al., 2007). Most existing approaches are based on supervised learning and require large amounts of annotated data which limits their applicability to different domains . Recently (Guo et al., 2011b) has shown that weakly supervised learning (especially active learning) works well for determining the information structure of biomedical abstracts. This work is interesting since it can facilitate easier porting of the techniques to new tasks.

However, also approaches based on weak supervision require data annotation in real-world applications. Moreover, simulation of active learning (such as that conducted by (Guo et al., 2011b) who used a fully annotated corpus from which they restored the labels of selected sentences in each iteration) is not practical but real-time interactive annotation is needed.

This requires a development of an efficient and user-friendly annotation tool which can facilitate rapid expert-annotation of data according to categories of information structure in real-life scientific tasks. We introduce such a tool: the CRAB Reader - a tool that is capable of supporting not only off-line AZ annotation but also interactive AZ annotation through weakly supervised learning, along with visualization of information structure in scientific literature. The latter functionality can also be applied to support scientists in literature review.

The CRAB[1] reader enables analyzing biomedical articles according to the Argumentative Zoning (AZ) scheme – a scheme of information structure that describes the rhetorical progression in scientific papers (Teufel and Moens, 2002). However, since the AZ scheme has been shown to apply across different scientific domains (Teufel et al., 2009), the technology presented here can be widely applicable.

## 2 CRAB Reader

The CRAB Reader allows users to define a new scheme or to modify an existing scheme for information structure analysis. Currently, we use the Argumentative Zoning (AZ) scheme which was originally introduced by Teufel and Moens (2002) and which was first used to describe the rhetorical progression of scientific argument in computational linguistics papers. This scheme was subsequently adapted to other domains such as chemistry (Teufel et al., 2009) and biology (Mizuta et al., 2006). We adopt the latter version in our work, and use eight zone

[1] CRAB refers to the CRAB project which has developed text mining technology for the needs of cancer risk assessment (Korhonen et al., 2012).

categories, including Background, Problem (the research question), Method, Result, Conclusion, Connection (consistent studies), Difference (inconsistent studies) and Future-work.

Using the CRAB Reader, AZ annotation can be performed on each word, sentence, paragraph, or the entire document, depending on the requirement. Annotated papers are saved in the HTML format. Users can visualize zones in different colors in an annotated paper. CRAB Reader also supports interactive annotation which is useful for weakly supervised learning when used in conjunction with a classifier such as Support Vector Machines (SVM). More specifically, a classifier makes a request for the labels of particular sentences; in response to such a request, CRAB Reader presents the relevant sentences to the annotators, collects their annotations, and returns the labeled sentences to the classifier for further learning.

## 2.1 Importing articles

Users can import any paper in HTML format into CRAB Reader. Since the format of articles varies from journal to journal, an HTML paper needs to be transformed into XML and then formatted using XSLT (Extensible Stylesheet Language Transformations). Users need to define different style sheets for different journals. For example, the code in Figure 1 shows how to separate an abstract from the body of an article (see the <xsl:if> element), and how to format a section/subsection/paragraph (see the <xsl:for-each> element) given an article from *The Journal of Biological Chemistry*, where an <h2> tag refers to a section, an <h3/4/5> tag refers to a subsection, and a <p> tag refers to a paragraph. Currently, CRAB Reader provides style sheets for main journals on chemical risk assessment, but it can handle papers from other domains by integrating more templates. Potentially, PDF papers can also be imported into CRAB Reader after converted into HTML files, and there are various (free) tools available for converting PDF to HTML.

```
<xsl:for-each select="//div[@id='content-block']//div[@class='article fulltext-view']/div">
      <xsl:if test="contains(@class, 'section')-contains(@class, 'abstract')">
            <section>
                  <heading>
                        <xsl:value-of select="h2"/>
                  </heading>
                  <xsl:for-each select="p|h3|h4|h5">
                        <xsl:copy-of select="."/>
                  </xsl:for-each>
            </section>
      </xsl:if>
</xsl:for-each>
```

Figure 1: A fragment of the style sheet for *The Journal of Biological Chemistry*

## 2.2 Off-line annotation

Off-line annotation differs from interactive annotation in that users need to annotate an entire article instead of a small number of sentences selected by the machine. The off-line annotation tool in CRAB Reader is a Firefox plug-in written in XUL (XML User Interface Language). XUL is based on existing Web technologies such as CSS (Cascading Style Sheets) and JavaScript. Figure 2 shows how to use the tool in Firefox: users can select any amount of text by clicking where they want to begin, holding down the left mouse button, and then dragging the pointer over the text. Right-clicking the selected text opens a menu of zone categories such as Result, Conclusion, and so on. Users can then choose the appropriate category for annotation. The annotations are

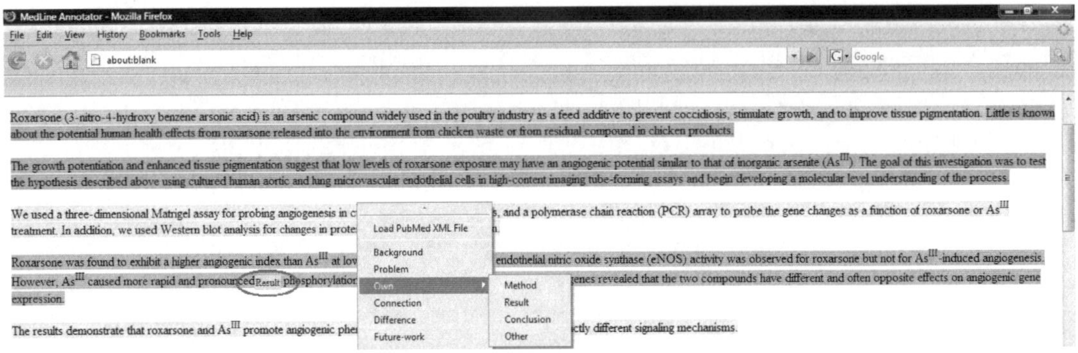


Figure 2: Off-line annotation

saved as an attribute for each word element e.g. <w Conclusion="1">indicate</w>.

## 2.3 Interactive annotation via active learning

Interactive annotation is based on a client/server model, where a client (annotator) makes a request for a new assignment (unlabeled sentences); the server then trains classifiers on existing labeled data, and compares their performance on each unlabeled data, from which it selects the most informative sentences as a new assignment for the annotator. After completing the assignment the annotator submits the annotations to the server. The server then updates the training data by incorporating the fresh labels for further learning. This process can be repeated many times that is called active learning. The idea of active learning is to create a high-performance classifier but to minimize the cost of annotation.

On the server side we tested the most popular classifiers including Naive Bayes classifier, Support Vector Machines (SVM), Maximum Entropy Model, Conditional Random Fields, among many others, and SVM is so far the best classifier for this task. The features listed below were used for classification. Most of them have been successfully used in recent related work (Teufel and Moens, 2002; Mullen et al., 2005; Merity et al., 2009; Guo et al., 2011b). The C&C POS tagger and parser (Curran et al., 2007) was used for extracting syntactic features such as grammatical relations (GR) from each sentence.

**Section**. Normalized section names (Introduction, Methods, Results, Discussion).

**Location in article/section/paragraph**. Each article/section/paragraph was divided into ten equal parts. Location was defined by the parts where the sentence begins and ends.

**Citation**. The number of citations in a sentence (0, 1 or more).

**Table and Figure**. The number of referred tables and figures in a sentence (0, 1 or more).

**N-gram**. Any unigrams and bigrams in the corpus (an n-gram feature equals 1 if it is observed in the sentence and 0 if not; the rest of the features are defined in a similar way).

**Verb**. Any verbs in the corpus.

**Verb Class**. Verbs are grouped into 60 categories by spectral clustering (Sun and Korhonen, 2009). Each category corresponds to a feature.

**Tense and Voice**. Tense and voice indicated by the POS tag of main verbs and auxiliary verbs. e.g. *have|VBZ be|VBN __|VBN* indicates present perfect tense, passive voice.

**Grammatical Relation**. Subject (*ncsubj*), direct object (*dobj*), indirect object (*iobj*) and second object (*obj2*) relations for verbs. e.g. *(ncsubj observed difference obj)*.

**Subj/Obj**. The subjects/objects appearing with any verbs in the corpus.

We implemented a number of query strategies for SVM-based active learning, including least confident sampling (Lewis and Gale, 1994), margin sampling (Scheffer et al., 2001), query-by-committee (Seung et al., 1992), etc. The interactive annotation interface is a dynamic web page (HTML form) that presents a list of sentences selected by the server for human to annotate, as shown in Figure 3. It also presents the context (in gray color) of each selected sentence (in blue color) to facilitate the annotation process. After a user completes the form and clicks on the submit button, the annotations are sent to a PHP (Hypertext Preprocessor) file and then written to the server as the training data for further learning. The web page also records the annotation time for each sentence, which is a more appropriate measure of annotation effort compared to training set size. As an example, Figure 4 shows the results for real-time active learning on 50 biomedical articles. Although the curves on the left and right panels look very similar, CRAB Reader does offer an opportunity to evaluate the performance of active learning in a more natural way.

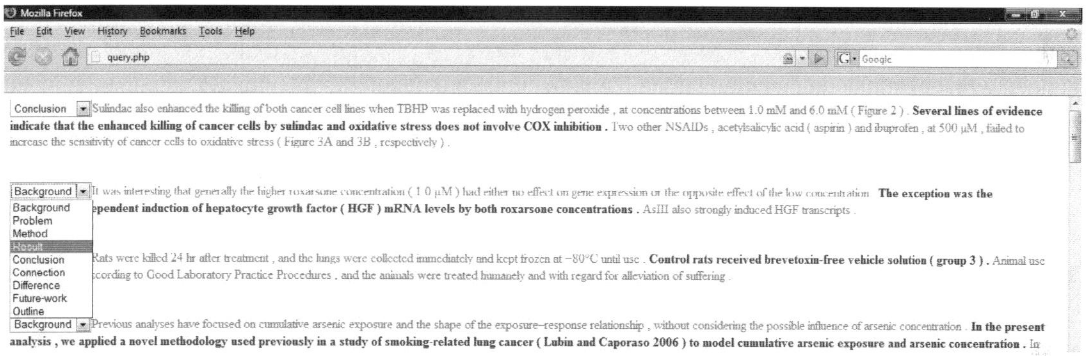


Figure 3: Interactive annotation

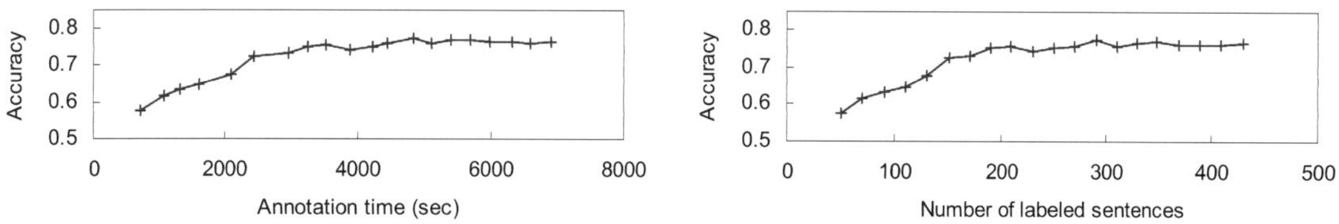


Figure 4: Performance of interactive annotation and active learning

## 2.4 Visualizing argumentative zones

We use CSS to specify the look and format of an annotated paper. Zones have different colors as shown in Figure 5. The zone label of any particular word will come up when you mouse over it, as shown in Figure 2. The advantage of using CSS is that it provides more flexibility for the visualization of zones and allows the same annotated paper to be presented in different styles for different users (see Figure 6). Also, since CSS separates the format from the content of a document, it makes it easier to insert automatic annotations into plain text so that we can visualize the information structure of any paper on demand.

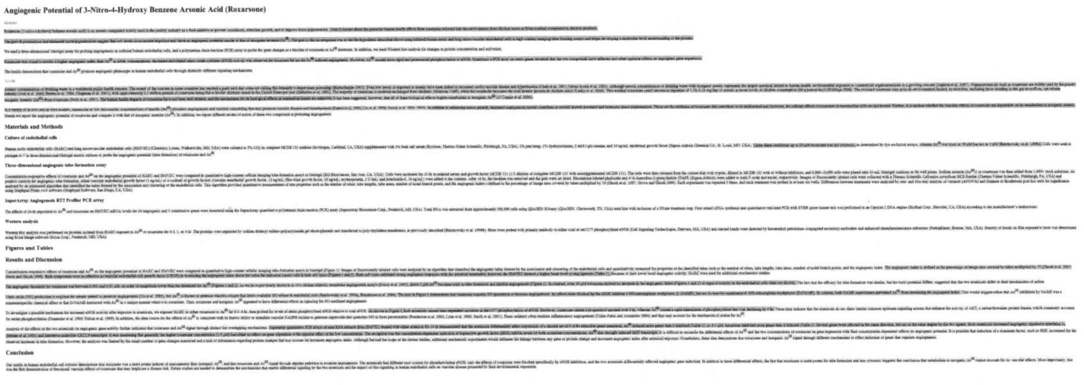


Figure 5: Visualization of all zones

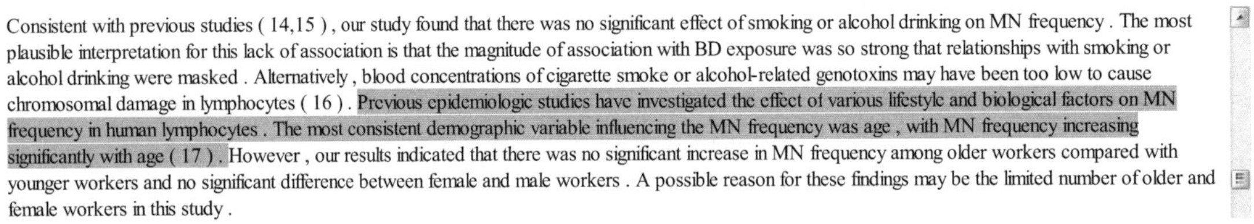

Consistent with previous studies ( 14,15 ) , our study found that there was no significant effect of smoking or alcohol drinking on MN frequency . The most plausible interpretation for this lack of association is that the magnitude of association with BD exposure was so strong that relationships with smoking or alcohol drinking were masked . Alternatively , blood concentrations of cigarette smoke or alcohol-related genotoxins may have been too low to cause chromosomal damage in lymphocytes ( 16 ) . Previous epidemiologic studies have investigated the effect of various lifestyle and biological factors on MN frequency in human lymphocytes . The most consistent demographic variable influencing the MN frequency was age , with MN frequency increasing significantly with age ( 17 ) . However , our results indicated that there was no significant increase in MN frequency among older workers compared with younger workers and no significant difference between female and male workers . A possible reason for these findings may be the limited number of older and female workers in this study .

Figure 6: Visualization of the "Difference" zone

## Conclusions and Future work

We have introduced CRAB Reader, a convenient tool for analysis and visualization of AZ for scientific literature review. Particularly, CRAB Reader supports real-time interactive annotation which makes it possible to apply weakly supervised learning to AZ for different tasks and domains. The tool has been used for creating a corpus of 50 AZ-annotated articles (8171 sentences), and has proved successful for active learning-based AZ on that corpus with 82% accuracy after labeling 500 sentences, which is just 2% lower than the accuracy of fully supervised learning.

In the future, we plan to use CRAB Reader for real-world applications of AZ such as question answering or customized summarization to speed up the literature review process. (Guo et al., 2011a) and (Guo et al., 2011c) have shown that users find the information in question from AZ-annotated abstracts significantly faster than from unannotated abstracts. However, is it realistic for full-text articles, given their high linguistic and informational complexity? We plan to conduct a similar question answering experiment to evaluate the usefulness of AZ-annotated articles in the context of a practical biomedical research task. We also plan to investigate whether AZ annotations are more informative than section headings for creating customized summaries for different research purposes.

## Acknowledgments

The work reported in this paper was funded by the Royal Society (UK) and EPSRC (UK) grant EP/G051070/1. YG was funded by the Cambridge International Scholarship. IS was funded by the Swedish Governmental Agency for Innovation System.

## References


Curran, J. R., Clark, S., and Bos, J. (2007). Linguistically motivated large-scale nlp with c&c and boxer. In *Proceedings of the ACL 2007 Demonstrations Session*, pages 33–36.

Guo, Y., Korhonen, A., Liakata, M., Karolinska, I. S., Sun, L., and Stenius, U. (2010). Identifying the information structure of scientific abstracts: an investigation of three different schemes. In *Proceedings of BioNLP*, pages 99–107.

Guo, Y., Korhonen, A., Liakata, M., Silins, I., Hogberg, J., and Stenius, U. (2011a). A comparison and user-based evaluation of models of textual information structure in the context of cancer risk assessment. *BMC Bioinformatics*, 69(12).

Guo, Y., Korhonen, A., and Poibeau, T. (2011b). A weakly-supervised approach to argumentative zoning of scientific documents. In *Proceedings of the 2011 Conference on Empirical Methods in Natural Language Processing*, pages 273–283.

Guo, Y., Korhonen, A., Silins, I., and Stenius, U. (2011c). Weakly supervised learning of information structure of scientific abstracts–is it accurate enough to benefit real-world tasks in biomedicine? *Bioinformatics*, 27:3179–85.

Korhonen, A., Séaghdha, D. O., Silins, I., Sun, L., Högberg, J., and Stenius., U. (2012). Text mining for literature review and knowledge discovery in cancer risk assessment and research. *PLoS ONE*, 7:e33427.

Lewis, D. D. and Gale, W. A. (1994). A sequential algorithm for training text classifiers. In *Proceedings of the 17th annual international ACM SIGIR conference on Research and development in information retrieval*, pages 3–12.

Liakata, M., Teufel, S., Siddharthan, A., and Batchelor, C. (2010). Corpora for the conceptualisation and zoning of scientific papers. In *Proceedings of LREC'10*.

Merity, S., Murphy, T., and Curran, J. R. (2009). Accurate argumentative zoning with maximum entropy models. In *Proceedings of the 2009 Workshop on Text and Citation Analysis for Scholarly Digital Libraries*, pages 19–26.

Mizuta, Y., Korhonen, A., Mullen, T., and Collier, N. (2006). Zone analysis in biology articles as a basis for information extraction. *International Journal of Medical Informatics on Natural Language Processing in Biomedicine and Its Applications*, 75(6):468–487.

Mullen, T., Mizuta, Y., and Collier, N. (2005). A baseline feature set for learning rhetorical zones using full articles in the biomedical domain. *SIGKDD Explor. Newsl.*, 7:52–58.

Ruch, P., Boyer, C., Chichester, C., Tbahriti, I., Geissbuhler, A., Fabry, P., Gobeill, J., Pillet, V., Rebholz-Schuhmann, D., Lovis, C., and Veuthey, A. L. (2007). Using argumentation to extract key sentences from biomedical abstracts. *Int J Med Inform*, 76(2-3):195–200.

Scheffer, T., Decomain, C., and Wrobel, S. (2001). Active hidden markov models for information extraction. In *Proceedings of the 4th International Conference on Advances in Intelligent Data Analysis*, pages 309–318.

Seung, H. S., Opper, M., and Sompolinsky, H. (1992). Query by committee. In *Proceedings of the fifth annual workshop on Computational learning theory*, pages 287–294.

Shatkay, H., Pan, F., Rzhetsky, A., and Wilbur, W. J. (2008). Multi-dimensional classification of biomedical text: Toward automated, practical provision of high-utility text to diverse users. *Bioinformatics*, 24(18):2086–2093.

Sun, L. and Korhonen, A. (2009). Improving verb clustering with automatically acquired selectional preference. In *Proceedings of EMNLP*, pages 638–647.

Tbahriti, I., Chichester, C., Lisacek, F., and Ruch, P. (2006). Using argumentation to retrieve articles with similar citations. *Int J Med Inform*, 75(6):488–495.

Teufel, S. and Moens, M. (2002). Summarizing scientific articles: Experiments with relevance and rhetorical status. *Computational Linguistics*, 28:409–445.

Teufel, S., Siddharthan, A., and Batchelor, C. (2009). Towards domain-independent argumentative zoning: Evidence from chemistry and computational linguistics. In *Proceedings of EMNLP*, pages 1493–1502.

# Automatic Punjabi Text Extractive Summarization System

*Vishal GUPTA*[1] *Gurpreet Singh LEHAL*[2]
(1) UIET, Panjab University Chandigarh, India
(2) Department of Computer Science, Punjabi University Patiala, Punjab, India
vishal@pu.ac.in, gslehal@gmail.com

ABSTRACT

Text Summarization is condensing the source text into shorter form and retaining its information content and overall meaning. Punjabi text Summarization system is text extraction based summarization system which is used to summarize the Punjabi text by retaining relevant sentences based on statistical and linguistic features of text. Punjabi text summarization system is available online at website: http://pts.learnpunjabi.org/default.aspx It comprises of two main phases: 1) Pre Processing 2) Processing. Pre Processing is structured representation of original Punjabi text. Pre processing phase includes Punjabi words boundary identification, Punjabi sentences boundary identification, Punjabi stop words elimination, Punjabi language stemmer for nouns and proper names, applying input restrictions and elimination of duplicate sentences. In processing phase, sentence features are calculated and final score of each sentence is determined using feature-weight equation. Top ranked sentences in proper order are selected for final summary. This demo paper concentrates on Automatic Punjabi Text Extractive Summarization System.

KEYWORDS : Punjabi Text Summarization System, Pre Processing Phase, Processing Phase, Punjabi stemmer for nouns and proper nouns, Punjabi Named Entity Recognition, Punjabi Keywords Identification

*Proceedings of COLING 2012: Demonstration Papers*, pages 191–198,
COLING 2012, Mumbai, December 2012.

## 1 Introduction

Automatic text summarization (Kyoomarsi et al., 2008; Gupta & Lehal, 2010) is reducing the source text into a shorter form retaining its information content and overall meaning. Text Summarization (Lin, 2009) Process can be divided into two phases: 1) Pre Processing phase (Gupta & Lehal, 2011a) is structured representation of the original text. 2) Processing (Fattah & Ren, 2008; Kaikhah, 2004; Neto et al., 2000) phase determines the final score of each sentence using feature-weight equation and top ranked sentences in proper order are selected for final summary. This paper concentrates automatic Punjabi text summarization system. Punjabi text Summarization system is text extraction based summarization system which is used to summarize the Punjabi text by retaining the relevant sentences based on statistical and linguistic features of text. Punjab is one of Indian states and Punjabi is its official language. For Punjabi language, Punjabi text summarization system is the only text summarizer and is available online: http://pts.learnpunjabi.org/default.aspx . Pre processing phase includes Punjabi words boundary identification, Punjabi sentences boundary identification, Punjabi stop words elimination, Punjabi language stemmer for nouns and proper names, allowing input restrictions to input text, elimination of duplicate sentences and normalization of Punjabi noun words in noun morph. In processing phase, various features influencing the relevance of sentences are decided and calculated. Some of statistical features are sentence length feature, keywords selection feature (TF-ISF approach) and number feature etc. Some of linguistic features that often increase the candidacy of a sentence for inclusion in summary are: sentence headline feature, next line feature, noun feature, proper noun feature, cue phrase feature and presence of headline keywords in a sentence etc. Final score of each sentence is determined using feature-weight equation. Weights of each feature are calculated using weight learning methods. Top ranked sentences in proper order are selected for final summary at selective compression ratios.

## 2 Pre Processing Phase of Punjabi Text Summarization System

Various sub phases of complete pre processing of Punjabi text summarization system are given below:

### 2.1 Punjabi language stop words elimination

Punjabi language stop words (Gupta & Lehal, 2011a) are most frequently occurring words in Punjabi text like: ਦੇ dē, ਹੈ hai, ਨੂੰ nūṃ and ਨਾਲ nāl etc. We have to eliminate these words from the original text otherwise, sentences containing them can get influence unnecessarily. We have made a list of Punjabi language stop words by creating a frequency list from a Punjabi corpus. Analysis of Punjabi corpus taken from popular Punjabi newspaper Ajit has been done. This corpus contains around 11.29 million words and 2.03 lakh unique words. We manually analyzed these unique words and identified 615 stop words. In the corpus, the frequency count of these stop words is 5.267 million, which covers 46.64% of the corpus.

### 2.2 Punjabi language stemmer for nouns and proper names

The purpose of stemming (Islam et al., 2007; Kumar et al., 2005; Ramanathan & Rao, 2003) is to obtain the stem or radix of those words which are not found in dictionary. If stemmed word is present in dictionary (Singh et al., 1999) then that is a genuine word, otherwise it may be proper name or some invalid word. In Punjabi language stemming (Gupta & Lehal, 2011b; Gill et al., 2007; Gill et al., 2009) for nouns and proper names, an attempt is made to obtain stem or radix of a Punjabi word and then stem or radix is checked against Punjabi noun morph and Proper names list. An in depth analysis of corpus was made and the possible eighteen noun and proper name suffixes were identified like ੀਆਂ īāṃ, ਿਆਂ iāṃ, ੂਆਂ ūāṃ and ਾਂ āṃ etc. and various rules for Punjabi noun stemming have been generated. The algorithm of Punjabi language stemmer for nouns and proper names has been published in (Gupta & Lehal, 2011b). The efficiency of this stemmer is 87.37%, which is tested over 50 Punjabi news documents of corpus and is ratio of actual correct results to total produced results by stemmer. Some results of Punjabi language stemmer for nouns and Proper names for various possible suffixes are ਫੁੱਲਾਂ phullāṃ "flowers" → ਫੁੱਲ phull "flower" with suffix ਾਂ āṃ, ਮੁੰਡੇ muṇḍē "boys"→ ਮੁੰਡਾ muṇḍā "boy" with suffix ੇ ē and ਫਿਰੋਜ਼ਪੁਰੋਂ phirōzpurōṃ → ਫਿਰੋਜ਼ਪੁਰ phirōzpur with suffix ੋਂ ōṃ etc.

## 2.3 Allowing input restrictions to input text

Punjabi Text Summarization system allows Unicode based Gurmukhi text as input. Gurmukhi is the most common script used for writing the Punjabi language. Majority of input characters should be of Gurmukhi, otherwise error will be printed. From the input text, calculate length of Gurmukhi characters, punctuation mark characters, numeric characters, English characters and other characters. If number of Gurmukhi characters are less than equal to number of punctuation characters or number of numeric characters or number of English characters or number of other characters then error message is produced, otherwise if number of English characters or number of other characters are greater than equal to 10% of total input characters length, then error is produced "Can not accept the input!!!".

## 2.4 Elimination of duplicate sentences from Punjabi input text

Punjabi Text Summarization system eliminates the duplicate sentences from the input Punjabi text. Duplicate sentences are deleted from input by searching the current sentence in to the sentence list which is initially empty. If current sentence is found in sentence list then that sentence is set to null otherwise it is added to the sentence list being the unique sentence. This elimination prevents duplicate sentences from appearing in final summary.

## 2.5 Normalization of Punjabi nouns in noun morph and input text

Problem with Punjabi is the non-standardization of Punjabi spellings. Many of the popular Punjabi noun words are written in multiple ways. For example, the Punjabi noun words ਤਿੱਬਤੀ tibbtī "tibbati", ਥਾਂ thāṃ "place" and ਦਸ਼ਾ dasaā "condition", ਬ੍ਰਿਗੇਡ brigēḍ "brigade" can also be written as ਤਿਬਤੀ tibtī "tibbati", ਥਾ thā "place" and ਦਸਾ dasā "condition", ਬਰਿਗੇਡ barigēḍ "brigade" respectively. To overcome this problem, input Punjabi text and Punjabi noun morph has been normalized for the various characters like ੱ aadak, ਂ bindi at top, Punjabi foot character ੍ for ਰ ra, ਵ v and ਹ ha and ਼ bindi at foot for ਸ਼, ਖ਼, ਗ਼, ਜ਼, ਫ਼, and ਲ਼. For doing normalization of Punjabi noun morph and Punjabi input text, replace all the occurences of ੱ aadak , ਂ bindi at top, ਼ bindi at foot with null character and replace all the occurences of Punjabi foot character ੍ with suitable ਰ ra or ਵ v or ਹ ha characters.

## 3 Processing Phase of Punjabi Text Summarization System

Various sub phases for processing phase of Punjabi text summarization system are given below:

### 3.1 Punjabi sentence relative length feature

This feature is calculated as published in (Fattah & Ren, 2008). Very short sentences are avoided for including in final summary as often they contain less information. On the other hand lengthy Punjabi sentences might contain lot of information. This feature is calculated by dividing number of words in a sentence with word count of largest sentence. Its value will be always less than or equal to 1.

### 3.2 Punjabi Keywords/ Title Keywords identification

Punjabi keywords identification system is first of its kind system available and is implemented by us as published in (Gupta & Lehal, 2011c). Prior to it no other Punjabi keywords identification system was available. Keywords are thematic words containing important information. Punjabi keywords are identified by calculating TF-ISF (Term Frequency-Inverse Sentence Frequency) (Neto et al., 2000) score. The TF-ISF measure of a noun word w in a sentence s, denoted TF-ISF(w,s), is computed by: TF-ISF(w,s)= TF(w,s)* ISF(w) where the term frequency TF(w,s) is the number of times that noun word w occurs in sentence s, and the inverse sentence frequency ISF(w) is given by the formula: ISF(w) = log(|S|/ SF(w)) , where the sentence frequency SF(w) is the number of sentences in which the noun word w occurs. Top scored Punjabi noun words (Top 20%) with high value of TF-ISF scores are treated as Punjabi keywords.

### 3.3 Numeric data identification

Numerical data (Fattah & Ren, 2008) is important and it is most probably included in the document summary. The sentence that contains numerical data (Digits, Roman and Gurmukhi numerals) is important and it is most probably included in the document summary. The score for this feature is calculated as the ratio of the number of numerical data in sentence over the sentence length.

### 3.4 Punjabi named entity recognition

Rules based Punjabi named entity recognition system is first of its kind system available and is implemented by us for identifying proper nouns as published in (Gupta & Lehal, 2011d). Prior to it, no other rule based Punjabi named entity system was available. It uses various gazetteer lists like prefix list, suffix list, middle name list, last name list and proper name lists for checking whether the given word is proper name or not. After doing aanalysis of Punjabi corpus, various gazetteer lists have been developed. The Precision, Recall and F-Score for condition based NER approach are 89.32%, 83.4% and 86.25% respectively.

### 3.5 Punjabi sentence headlines and next lines identification

In single/multi news documents, headlines are most important and are always included in the final summary. Line just next to headline might contain very important information related to summary and is usually included in summary. In Punjabi news corpus with 957553 sentences, the frequency count of these headlines/next lines is 65722 lines which covers 6.863% of the corpus.

In Punjabi headlines detection system, if current sentence does not ends with punctuation marks like '|' vertical bar etc. but ends with enter key or new line character then set the headline flag for that line to true. If the next subsequent line of this headline ends with punctuation marks like '|' vertical bar etc. but does not ends with enter key or new line character then set the next line flag to true for that line. Those Punjabi sentences which belong to headlines are always given highest score equal to 10 and their headline flags are set to true. The accuracy of Punjabi headline identification system and next line identification is 97.43% and 98.57% respectively which is tested over fifty Punjabi single/multi news documents. Next lines are always given very high weight equal to 9 and their next line flags are set to true.

### 3.6 Punjabi nouns and Proper names identification

Those Punjabi sentences containing nouns (Neto et al., 2002) and proper names are important. Input words are checked in Punjabi noun morph for possibility of nouns. Punjabi noun morph is having 37297 noun words. Proper nouns are the names of person, place and concept etc. not occurring in Punjabi Dictionary. From the Punjabi news corpus, 17598 words have been identified as proper nouns. Punjabi nouns and proper noun feature score is calculated by dividing number of Punjabi nouns/ proper names in a sentence with length of that sentence.

### 3.7 Punjabi Cue Phrase identification

Cue Phrases are certain keywords like in conclusion, summary and finally etc. These are very much helpful in deciding sentence importance. Those sentences which are beginning with cue phrases or which contain these cue phrases are generally more important than others. Firstly a list of Punjabi Cue phrases has been developed and then those sentences containing these Cue phrases are given more importance.

### 3.8 Calculation of scores of sentences and producing final summary

Final scores of sentences are determined from sentence-feature-weight equation. $w_1f_1+w_2f_2+w_3f_3+\ldots\ldots w_nf_n$ where $f_1, f_2, f_3\ldots\ldots f_n$ are different features of sentences calculated in the different subphases of Punjabi text summarization system and $w_1, w_2, w_3\ldots\ldots w_n$ are the corresponding feature weights of sentences. Mathematical regression (Gupta & Lehal, 2011e ; Fattah & Ren, 2008) has been used as model to estimate the text features weights for Punjabi text summarization. Three most important features of Punjabi text summarization system are Punjabi headline identification feature, Punjabi next line identification feature and number identification feature. Top ranked sentences in proper order are selected for final summary. In final summary, sentence coherence is maintained by properly ordering the sentences in the same order as they appear in the input text at the selective compression ratios.

## 4 Results and Discussions

Punjabi text summarization has been tested over fifty Punjabi news documents (with 6185 sentences and 72689 words) randomly taken from Punjabi Ajit news corpus having 11.29 million words and fifty Punjabi stories (with 17538 sentences and 178400 words) randomly taken from www.likhari.org website. We have applied four intrinsic measures of summary evaluation 1) F-Score 2) Cosine Similarity 3) Jaccard Coefficient and 4) Euclidean distance for Punjabi news documents and stories. Gold summaries (reference summaries) are produced by including most common sentences of manually produced summaries by three human experts at 10%, 30% and 50% compression ratios. For Punjabi news documents, value of average F-Score is 97.87%, 95.32% and 94.63% at 10%, 30% and 50% compression ratios respectively and value of average Cosine similarity is 0.9814, 0.9629 and 0.9522 at 10%, 30% and 50% compression ratios respectively. For Punjabi stories, value of average F-Score is 81.78%, 89.32% and 94.21% at 10%, 30% and 50% compression ratios respectively and value of average Cosine similarity is 0.8226, 0.8838 and 0.9432 at 10%, 30% and 50% compression ratios respectively. The results of intrinsic summary evaluation show that for Punjabi news documents, Punjabi text summarization system performs very well at 10% compression ratio, because at 10% compression ratio usually headlines and next lines are extracted which are enough to describe the whole text but for Punjabi stories, performance of Punjabi text summarization system is not good at 10% compression ratio, because headlines are not present in stories and only few lines are extracted in summary which are not enough to describe the sense of complete story. We have performed question answering task and keywords association task as extrinsic measures of summary evaluation at compression ratios 10%, 30% and 50% respectively for Punjabi news documents and Punjabi stories. For Punjabi news documents, the accuracy of question answering task is 78.95%, 81.38% and 88.75% at 10%, 30% and 50% compression ratios respectively. The results of question answering task show that for Punjabi news documents, performance of Punjabi text summarization system is low at 10% compression ratio because news documents are usually short and at 10% compression ratio, mainly headlines and next lines are extracted which are not sufficient to give all answers of question-answering task. For Punjabi stories, the accuracy of question answering task is 80.65%, 84.26% and 90.72% at 10%, 30% and 50% compression ratios respectively. For Punjabi news documents, the accuracy of keywords association task is 80.13%, 92.37% and 96.32% at 10%, 30% and 50% compression ratios respectively. For Punjabi stories, the accuracy of keywords association task is 84.29%, 90.68% and 95.16% at 10%, 30% and 50% compression ratios respectively. For Punjabi news documents and stories, the accuracy percentage for the task of keywords association is very well at 50% compression ratio because at 50% compression ratio, summary produced is enough to cover majority of gold keywords. Both intrinsic and extrinsic summary evaluation methods show that at 50% compression ratio, Performance of Punjabi text summarization system is good for both Punjabi news documents and Punjabi stories because summary produced is enough to describe the whole text.

## Conclusion

Punjabi Text Summarization system is first of its kind Punjabi summarizer and is available online at http://pts.learnpunjabi.org/default.aspx . Most of the lexical resources used in pre processing and processing such as Punjabi stemmer, Punjabi nouns normalizer, Punjabi proper names list, common English-Punjabi nouns list, Punjabi stop words list, Punjabi suffix and prefix list etc. had to be developed from scratch as no work was done previously in that direction. For developing these resources an in-depth analysis of Punjabi corpus, Punjabi dictionary and Punjabi morph had to be carried out using manual and automatic tools. This is first time that these resources have been developed for Punjabi and these can be beneficial for developing other Natural language processing applications for Punjabi.

## References


Ananthakrishnan Ramanathan and Durgesh Rao, (2003). A Light Weight Stemmer for Hindi. *In Workshop on Computational Linguistics for South-Asian Languages, EACL'03.*

Farshad Kyoomarsi, Hamid Khosravi, Esfandiar Eslami and Pooya Khosravyan Dehkordy. (2008). Optimizing Text Summarization Based on Fuzzy Logic. *In: proceedings of Seventh IEEE/ACIS International Conference on Computer and Information Science*, pages 347-352, University of Shahid Bahonar Kerman, UK.

Gurmukh Singh, Mukhtiar S. Gill and S.S. Joshi, (1999). Punjabi to English Bilingual Dictionary. *Punjabi University Patiala*, India.

Jimmy Lin (2009). Summarization. *Encyclopedia of Database Systems, Springer-Verlag* Heidelberg, Germany.

Joel larocca Neto, Alex A. Freitas and Celso A.A.Kaestner,(2002). Automatic Text Summarization using a Machine Learning Approach. *In Book: Advances in Artificial Intelligence: Lecture Notes in computer science*, Springer Berlin / Heidelberg, volume 2507, pages 205-215.

Joel Larocca Neto, Alexandre D. Santos, Celso A.A. Kaestner and Alex A. Freitas, (2000). Document Clustering and Text Summarization. *In Proceedings of 4th International Conference on Practical Applications of Knowledge Discovery and Data Mining*, pages 41-55, London.

Khosrow Kaikhah, (2004). Automatic Text Summarization with Neural Networks. *In Proceedings of IEEE international Conference on intelligent systems*, pages 40-44, Texas, USA.

Mandeep Singh Gill, Gurpreet Singh Lehal and S. S. Gill, (2007). A full form lexicon based Morphological Analysis and generation tool for Punjabi. *International Journal of Cybernatics and Informatics,* pages 38-47, Hyderabad, India.
http://www.advancedcentrepunjabi.org/punjabi_mor_ana.asp

Mandeep Singh Gill, Gurpreet Singh Lehal and S.S. Joshi, (2009). Part of Speech Tagging for Grammar Checking of Punjabi, *Linguistic Journal*, 4(1): 6-21, Road Town, Tortola British Virgin Islands.

Md. Zahurul Islam, Md. Nizam Uddin and Mumit Khan, (2007). A light weight stemmer for Bengali and its Use in spelling Checker. *In: Proceedings of 1st International Conference on Digital Comm. and Computer Applications (DCCA 2007)*, pages 19-23, Irbid, Jordan.

Mohamed Abdel Fattah and Fuji Ren (2008). Automatic Text Summarization. *In: Proceedings of World Academy of Science Engineering and Technology*, volume 27, pages 192-195.

Praveen Kumar, S. Kashyap, Ankush Mittal and Sumit Gupta, (2005). : A Hindi question answering system for E-learning documents. *In Proceedings of International Conference on Intelligent sensing and Information processing*, pages 80-85, Banglore, India

Vishal Gupta and Gurpreet Singh Lehal, (2010). A Survey of Text Summarization Extractive Techniques. *In International Journal of Emerging Technologies in Web Intelligence*, 2(3): 258-268.

Vishal Gupta and Gurpreet Singh Lehal, (2011a). Preprocessing Phase of Punjabi Language

Text Summarization. *In Proceedings of International conference on Information Systems for Indian Languages Communications in Computer and Information Science ICISIL2011*, pages 250–253, Springer-Verlag Berlin Heidelberg.

Vishal Gupta and Gurpreet Singh Lehal, (2011b). Punjabi language stemmer for nouns and proper nouns. *In proceedings of the 2nd Workshop on South and Southeast Asian Natural Language Processing (WSSANLP) IJCNLP*, pages 35-39, Chiang Mai, Thailand.

Vishal Gupta and Gurpreet Singh Lehal (2011c). Automatic Keywords Extraction for Punjabi Language. *International Journal of Computer Science Issues*, 8(5) : 327-331.

Vishal Gupta and Gurpreet Singh Lehal (2011d). Named Entity Recognition for Punjabi Language Text Summarization. *In International Journal of Computer Applications,* 33(3): 28-32.

Vishal Gupta and Gurpreet Singh Lehal (2011e). Feature Selection and Weight Learning for Punjabi Text Summarization. *In International Journal of Engineering Trends and Technology,* 2(2): 45-48.

# Complete Pre Processing phase of Punjabi Text Extractive Summarization System

Vishal GUPTA[1] Gurpreet Singh LEHAL[2]
(1) UIET, Panjab University Chandigarh, India
(2) Department of Computer Science, Punjabi University Patiala, Punjab, India
vishal@pu.ac.in, gslehal@gmail.com

ABSTRACT

Text Summarization is condensing the source text into shorter form and retaining its information content and overall meaning. Punjabi text Summarization system is text extraction based summarization system which is used to summarize the Punjabi text by retaining the relevant sentences based on statistical and linguistic features of text. It comprises of two main phases: 1) Pre Processing 2) Processing. Pre Processing is structured representation of the original Punjabi text. In Processing, final score of each sentence is determined using feature-weight equation. Top ranked sentences in proper order are selected for final summary. This paper concentrates on complete pre processing phase of Punjabi text summarization system. Pre processing phase includes Punjabi words boundary identification, Punjabi sentences boundary identification, Punjabi stop words elimination, Punjabi language stemmer for nouns and proper names, allowing input in proper format and elimination of duplicate sentences.

KEYWORDS : Punjabi Text Summarization System, Pre Processing Phase, Punjabi stemmer for nouns and proper nouns, Natural Language Processing

*Proceedings of COLING 2012: Demonstration Papers*, pages 199–206,
COLING 2012, Mumbai, December 2012.

## 1 Introduction

Automatic text summarization (Kyoomarsi et al., 2008) is reducing the source text into a shorter form retaining its information content and overall meaning. The goal of automatic text summarization is to present most important contents from information source to the user in a shorter version. Text Summarization (Gupta & Lehal, 2010) methods can be classified into abstractive and extractive summarization. An abstractive summarization method consists of understanding the original text and re-telling it in fewer words. Extractive summary deals with selection of important sentences from the original text. The importance of sentences is decided based on statistical and linguistic features of sentences. Text Summarization Process can be divided into two phases: 1) Pre Processing phase (Gupta & Lehal, 2011a) is structured representation of the original text. 2) In Processing (Fattah & Ren, 2008; Kaikhah, 2004; Neto, 2000) phase, final score of each sentence is determined using feature-weight equation. Top ranked sentences in proper order are selected for final summary. This paper concentrates on complete pre processing of Punjabi text extractive summarization system. Punjabi text Summarization system is text extraction based summarization system which is used to summarize the Punjabi text by retaining the relevant sentences based on statistical and linguistic features of text. Punjab is one of Indian states and Punjabi is its official language. Punjabi is spoken in India, Pakistan, USA, Canada, England, and other countries with Punjabi immigrants. Punjabi is written in 'Gurmukhi' script in eastern Punjab (India), and in 'Shahmukhi' script in western Punjab (Pakistan). For some of Indian languages like Hindi, Bengali etc. a number of automatic text summarization systems are available. For Punjabi, the only text summarization system available is online:http://pts.learnpunjabi.org/default.aspx and no other Punjabi summarizer is available in the world. Pre processing phase includes Punjabi words boundary identification, Punjabi sentences boundary identification, Punjabi stop words elimination, Punjabi language stemmer for nouns and proper names, allowing input in proper format, elimination of duplicate sentences and normalization of Punjabi noun words in noun morph.

## 2 Complete Pre Processing Phase of Punjabi Text Summarization System

Various Sub phases for complete pre processing of Punjabi text summarization system are given below:

### 2.1 Punjabi language stop words elimination

Punjabi language stop words (Gupta & Lehal, 2011a) are most frequently occurring words in Punjabi text like: ਦੇ dē, ਹੈ hai, ਨੂੰ nūṃ and ਨਾਲ nāl etc. We have to eliminate these words from the original text otherwise, sentences containing them can get influence unnecessarily. We have made a list of Punjabi language stop words by creating a frequency list from a Punjabi corpus. Analysis of Punjabi corpus taken from popular Punjabi newspaper Ajit has been done. This corpus contains around 11.29 million words and 2.03 lakh unique words. We manually analyzed these unique words and identified 615 stop words. In the corpus of 11.29 million words, the frequency count of these stop words is 5.267 million, which covers 46.64% of the corpus.

Sample input sentence:-

ਘਰੇਲੂ ਗੈਸ ਦੀ ਸਮੱਸਿਆ ਪਹਿਲ ਦੇ ਆਧਾਰ ਤੇ ਹੱਲ ਹੋਵੇਗੀ-ਥਿੰਦ

gharēlū gais dī samssiā pahil dē ādhār tē hall hōvēgī-thind

Sample output sentence:-

ਘਰੇਲੂ ਗੈਸ ਸਮੱਸਿਆ ਪਹਿਲ ਆਧਾਰ ਹੱਲ-ਥਿੰਦ

gharēlū gais samssiā pahil ādhār hall –thind

As we can see from the sample input and output of Punjabi stop words elimination sub phase that four stop words (ਦੀ dī, ਦੇ dē, ਤੇ tē, ਹੋਵੇਗੀ hōvēgī) have been eliminated from the sample output sentence.

## 2.2 Punjabi language stemmer for nouns and proper nouns

The purpose of stemming (Islam et al., 2007; Kumar et al., 2005; Ramanathan & Rao, 2003) is to obtain the stem or radix of those words which are not found in dictionary. If stemmed word is present in dictionary (Singh et al., 1999) , then that is a genuine word, otherwise it may be proper name or some invalid word. In Punjabi language stemming (Gupta & Lehal, 2011b; Gill et al., 2007; Gill et al., 2009) for nouns and proper names, an attempt is made to obtain stem or radix of a Punjabi word and then stem or radix is checked against Punjabi noun morph and proper names list. An in depth analysis of corpus was made and the eighteen possible noun and proper name suffixes were identified like ◌ੀਆਂ īāṃ, ਿ◌ਆਂ Iāṃ, ◌ੂਆਂ ūāṃ, ◌ਾਂ āṃ, ◌ੀਏ Īē, ◌ੇ Ē and ◌ੀਓ Īō etc.

Proper names are the names of person, place and concept etc. not occurring in Punjabi dictionary. Proper names play an important role in deciding a sentence's importance. From the Punjabi corpus, 17598 words have been identified as proper names. The percentage of these proper names words in the Punjabi corpus is about 13.84 %. Some of Punjabi language proper names are ਅਕਾਲੀ akālī, ਲੁਧਿਆਣਾ ludhiāṇā, ਬਾਦਲ bādal and ਪਟਿਆਲਾ paṭiālā etc.

Algorithm of Punjabi language stemmer for nouns and proper names is as below:

The algorithm of Punjabi language stemmer (Gupta & Lehal, 2011b) for nouns and proper names proceeds by segmenting the source Punjabi text into sentences and words. For each word of every sentence follow following steps:

Step 1: If current Punjabi word ends with ◌ੀਆਂ īāṃ, ਿ◌ਆਂ iāṃ, ◌ੂਆਂ ūāṃ then remove ਆਂ āṃ from end.

Step 2: Else If current Punjabi word ends with ◌ੀਏ īē then remove ਏ ē from end.

Step 3: Else If current Punjabi word ends with ◌ੀਓ Īō then remove ਓ ō from end.

Step 4: Else If current Punjabi word ends with ◌ੀਆ ā, ਈਆ īā then remove ਆ ā from end.

Step 5: Else If current Punjabi word ends with ਈ ī, ਵਾਂ vāṃ, ◌ਾਂ āṃ, ◌ੋਂ ōṃ, ◌ੀਂ īṃ and ਜ/ਜ਼/ਸ ja/z/s then remove the corresponding suffix from end.

Step 6: Else If current Punjabi word ends with ◌ੇ ē, ਿ◌ਓ iō, ◌ੋ ō, ਿ◌ਉਂ iuṃ and ਿ◌ਆ iā then remove the corresponding suffix and add kunna at the end.

Step 7: Current Punjabi Stemmed word is checked against Punjabi noun morph or Proper names list. If found, It is Punjabi noun or Punjabi Proper name.

Algorithm Input: ਫੁੱਲਾਂ phullāṃ (Flowers) and ਲੜਕੀਆਂ laṛkīāṃ (Girls)

Algorithm Output: ਫੁੱਲ phull (Flower) and ਲੜਕੀ laṛkī (Girl)

An in depth analysis of output of Punjabi language stemmer for nouns and proper names has been done over 50 Punjabi documents of Punjabi news corpus of 11.29 million words. The efficiency of Punjabi language noun and Proper name stemmer is 87.37%, which is tested over 50 Punjabi news documents of corpus and is ratio of actual correct results to total produced results by stemmer.

## 2.3 Normalization of Punjabi nouns in noun morph

Problem with Punjabi is the non-standardization of Punjabi spellings. Many of the popular Punjabi noun words are written in multiple ways. For example, the Punjabi noun words **ਤਿੱਬਤੀ** tibbtī, **ਥਾਂ** thāṃ and **ਦਸ਼ਾ** dasaā can also be written as **ਤਿਬਤੀ** tibtī, **ਥਾ** thā and **ਦਸਾ** dasā respectively. To overcome this problem Punjabi noun morph has been normalized for different spelling variations of same Punjabi noun words.

The algorithm for normalization of Punjabi nouns proceeds by copying noun_morph into another table noun_morph_normalized. For each noun word in table noun_morph_normalized follow the following steps:

Step 1 : Replace all the occurrences of ੱ aadak with null character.

Step 2 : Replace all the occurrences of ਂ Bindi at top with null character.

Step 3 :Replace all the occurences of ੍ Punjabi foot characters with any of suitable

ਰ (ra) or ਵ (v) or ਹ (ha)characters.

Step 4 :Replace all the occurrences of ਼ bindi at foot with null character.

Step 5 : noun_morph_normalized is now normalized.

Step 6: End of algorithm

Algorithm Input: ਟੱਬ ṭabb , ਰਕਮੀਂ rakmīṃ, ਆਕ੍ਰਿਤੀ ākritī and ਖ਼ਿਆਲ khaiāl

Algorithm Output: ਟਬ ṭab, ਰਕਮੀ rkamī, ਆਕਰਿਤੀ ākritī and ਖਿਆਲ khiāl

An exhaustive analysis has been done on fifty Punjabi news documents for normalization of Punjabi nouns and it is discovered that very less spelling variations are found. Only 1.562% noun words show the variations in their spellings. TABLE 1 shows that out of these 1.562% words, percentage of words having one, two or three variations:

| Number of Variants | Words Frequency (%) | Example |
|---|---|---|
| 1 | 99.95 | ਪੰਜਾਲ਼ੀ pañjālī, ਪੰਜਾਲੀ pañjālī |
| 2 | 0.046 | ਉੱਖਲ਼ੀ ukkhlaī, ਉਖਲ਼ੀ ukhlaī , ਉੱਖਲੀ ukkhlī |
| 3 | 0.004 | ਅੰਗਰੇਜੀ aṅgrējī, ਅੰਗਰੇਜ਼ੀ aṅgrēzī, ਅੰਗ੍ਰੇਜੀ aṅgrējī, ਅੰਗ੍ਰੇਜ਼ੀ aṅgrēzī |

TABLE 1 – Percentage Word Occurrence with Spelling Variations Count

Thus, above table represents that, the variations found for majority of the words is just 1 and in worst case, it can go up to 3. And no case has been found with more than three spelling variants.

## 2.4 Allowing input restrictions to input text

Punjabi Text Summarization system allows Unicode based Gurmukhi text as input. Gurmukhi is the most common script used for writing the Punjabi language. Punjabi Text Summarization system can accept maximum upto 1,00000 characters as input otherwise it will give error message. Majority of input characters should be of Gurmukhi otherwise error will be printed.

Algorithm:

Step 1 : If Uploaded input file is in Unicode based .txt format then calculate input character length and go to step 2, otherwise display the error message "Can not accept input of this type!!!"

Step 2 : If input character length> 1,00000 characters then display error message "Input length exeeds the limit" otherwise go to step 3.

Step 3 : From the input text, calculate length of Gurmukhi characters, Punctuation mark characters, numeric characters, English characters and other characters.

If Gurmukhi characters length is less than equal to Punctuation character length or numeric characters length or English Characters length or other characters length then display error message "Can not accept the input!!!"

Else If English characters length or other characters length is greater than equal to 10% of total input characters length then display error message "Can not accept the input!!!"

Else Go to Stop words elimination phase.

## 2.5 Elimination of duplicate sentences from Punjabi input text

Duplicate sentences are the redundant sentences which need to be deleted otherwise these can get the influence unnecessarily and due to which, certain other important sentences will not be displayed in the summary. Some summarization systems delete the duplicate sentences in the output summary and other systems delete them in the input itself. It is desirable to delete the duplicate sentences from input because numbers of input sentences are reduced and processing phase takes less time. Punjabi text summarization system eliminates the duplicate sentences from the input Punjabi text. An exhaustive analysis has been done on fifty Punjabi news documents for determining the frequency of duplicate sentences and it is discovered 9.60% sentences are duplicate. Minimum frequency of a duplicate sentence in a single Punjabi news document is two, maximum frequency is four and average frequency is three. Out of 9.6% duplicate sentences from fifty Punjabi news documents, there are 5.4% sentences with minimum frequency two, 2.29% sentences with average frequency three and 1.91% sentences with maximum frequency four. Duplicate sentences are deleted from input by searching the current sentence in to the sentence list which is initially empty. If current sentence is found in sentence list then that sentence is set to null otherwise it is added to the sentence list being the unique sentence. This elimination prevents duplicate sentences from appearing in final summary.

## 3 Pre processing algorithm for Punjabi text summarization system

The algorithm for complete Pre Processing Phase (Gupta & Lehal 2011a) proceeds by checking input Punjabi text into proper format and segmenting it into sentences and words. Set the scores of each sentence as 0. Normalize the Punjabi noun morph for different spelling variations of nouns. For each word of every sentence follow step 1 and step 2:

Step 1 : If current Punjabi word is stop word then delete all the occurrences of it from current sentence.

Step 2 :If current Punjabi word is not present in Punjabi dictionary, Punjabi noun morph, common English-Punjabi nouns list, Punjabi proper nouns list then apply Punjabi Noun and proper noun Stemmer for the possibility of Punjabi noun or proper noun.

Step 3: Delete redundant (duplicate) sentences from input text, to prevent them occurring in final summary and produce output of preprocessing phase.

TABLE 2 shows sample input and output sentences, for pre processing algorithm.

| Input Punjabi sentence | Output Punjabi sentence |
|---|---|
| ਮੁੱਖ ਮੰਤਰੀ ਨੇ ਕਿਹਾ ਕਿ ਉਹ ਅੱਜ ਕਾਂਗਰਸ ਉਮੀਦਵਾਰ ਭਰਤ ਸਿੰਘ ਬੈਲੀਵਾਲ ਲਈ ਵੋਟਾਂ ਦੀ ਅਪੀਲ ਕਰਨ ਲਈ ਆਏ ਹਨ ਪਰ ਵੋਟ ਪਾਉਣ ਤੋਂ ਪਹਿਲਾਂ ਪਾਰਟੀ ਦੀ ਨੀਤੀ, ਨਿਯਤ ਤੇ ਨੇਤਾ ਬਾਰੇ ਜਰੂਰ ਵਿਚਾਰ ਦੀ ਲੋੜ ਹੈ।<br>mukkh mantrī nē kihā ki uh ajj kāṅgras umīdvār bharat siṅgh bailīvāl laī vōṭāṃ dī apīl karan laī āē han par vōṭ pāuṇ tōṃ pahilāṃ pāraṭī dī nītī, niyat tē nētā bārē jarūr vicār dī lōṛ hai. | ਮੁੱਖ ਮੰਤਰੀ ਅੱਜ ਕਾਂਗਰਸ ਉਮੀਦਵਾਰ ਭਰਤ ਸਿੰਘ ਬੈਲੀਵਾਲ ਵੋਟ ਅਪੀਲ ਵੋਟ ਪਹਿਲ ਪਾਰਟੀ ਨੀਤੀ ਨਿਯਤ ਨੇਤਾ ਜਰੂਰ ਵਿਚਾਰ ਲੋੜ<br>mukkh mantrī ajj kāṅgras umīdvār bharat siṅgh bailīvāl vōṭ apīl vōṭ pahil pārāṭī nītī niyat nētā jarūr vicār lōṛ |

TABLE 2 – Pre processing algorithm sample input and output sentences

A through analysis of result of pre processing phase has been done on fifty Punjabi news documents and stories and it is discovered, that with pre processing phase there is gain in 32% efficiency of Punjabi Text Summarization system at 50% compression ratio.

## Conclusion

Punjabi text summarization system is first of its kind Punjabi summarizer and is available online at http://pts.learnpunjabi.org/default.aspx. In this paper, we have discussed the complete pre processing phase for Punjabi text summarization system. Most of the lexical resources used in pre processing such as Punjabi stemmer, Punjabi nouns normalizer, Punjabi proper names list, common English-Punjabi nouns list, Punjabi stop words list etc. had to be developed from scratch as no work was done previously in that direction. For developing these resources an in-depth analysis of Punjabi corpus, Punjabi dictionary and Punjabi morph had to be carried out using manual and automatic tools. This is first time that these resources have been developed for Punjabi and these can be beneficial for developing other NLP applications for Punjabi.

## References


Ananthakrishnan Ramanathan and Durgesh Rao, (2003). A Light Weight Stemmer for Hindi. In Workshop on Computational Linguistics for South-*Asian Languages, EACL '03.*

Farshad Kyoomarsi, Hamid Khosravi, Esfandiar Eslami and Pooya Khosravyan Dehkordy. (2008). Optimizing Text Summarization Based on Fuzzy Logic. In: proceedings of Seventh IEEE/ACIS International Conference on Computer and Information Science, pages 347-352, University of Shahid Bahonar Kerman, UK.

Gurmukh Singh, Mukhtiar S. Gill and S.S. Joshi, (1999). Punjabi to English Bilingual Dictionary. Punjabi University Patiala, India.

Khosrow Kaikhah, (2004). Automatic Text Summarization with Neural Networks. In Proceedings of IEEE international Conference on intelligent systems, pages 40-44, Texas, USA.

Mandeep Singh Gill, Gurpreet Singh Lehal and S. S. Gill, (2007). A full form lexicon based Morphological Analysis and generation tool for Punjabi. International Journal of Cybernatics and Informatics, pages 38-47, Hyderabad, India.
http://www.advancedcentrepunjabi.org/punjabi_mor_ana.asp

Mandeep Singh Gill, Gurpreet Singh Lehal and S.S. Joshi, (2009). Part of Speech Tagging for Grammar Checking of Punjabi, Linguistic Journal, 4(1): 6-21, Road Town, Tortola British Virgin Islands.

Md. Zahurul Islam, Md. Nizam Uddin and Mumit Khan, (2007). A light weight stemmer for Bengali and its Use in spelling Checker. In: Proceedings of 1st International Conference on Digital Comm. and Computer Applications (DCCA 2007), pages 19-23, Irbid, Jordan.

Mohamed Abdel Fattah and Fuji Ren (2008). Automatic Text Summarization. In: Proceedings of World Academy of Science Engineering and Technology, volume 27, pages 192-195.

Joel L. Neto, (2000). Document Clustering and Text Summarization. In: Proceedings of 4th Int. Conf. Practical Applications of Knowledge Discovery and Data Mining, pages 41-55, London.

Praveen Kumar, S. Kashyap, Ankush Mittal and Sumit Gupta, (2005). : A Hindi question answering system for E-learning documents. In Proceedings of International Conference on Intelligent sensing and Information processing, pages 80-85, Banglore, India

Vishal Gupta and Gurpreet Singh Lehal, (2010). A Survey of Text Summarization Extractive Techniques. In International Journal of Emerging Technologies in Web Intelligence, 2(3): 258-268.

Vishal Gupta and Gurpreet Singh Lehal, (2011a). Preprocessing Phase of Punjabi Language Text Summarization. In Proceedings of International conference on Information Systems for Indian Languages Communications in Computer and Information Science ICISIL2011, pages 250–253, Springer-Verlag Berlin Heidelberg.

Vishal Gupta and Gurpreet Singh Lehal, (2011b). Punjabi language stemmer for nouns and proper nouns. In proceedings of the 2nd Workshop on South and Southeast Asian Natural Language Processing (WSSANLP) IJCNLP, pages 35-39, Chiang Mai, Thailand.

# Revisiting Arabic Semantic Role Labeling using SVM Kernel Methods

*Laurel Hart, Hassan Alam, Aman Kumar*
*BCL Technologies, San Jose, California, USA*
{lhart, hassana, amank}@bcltechnologies.com

ABSTRACT

As a critical language, there is huge potential for the usefulness of an Arabic Semantic Role Labeling (SRL) system. This task involves two subtasks: predicate argument boundary detection and argument classification. Based on the innovations of Diab, Moschitti, and Pighin (2007) in the field of Arabic Natural Language Processing (NLP), SRL in particular, we are currently developing a system for automatic SRL in Arabic.

KEYWORDS: Arabic, semantic role labeling, SRL, predicate argument, boundary detection, argument classification.

*Proceedings of COLING 2012: Demonstration Papers*, pages 207–214,
COLING 2012, Mumbai, December 2012.

## 1 Introduction

The automatic detection and identification of semantic roles in a sentence—a process known as Semantic Role Labeling (SRL)—has many potential applications within computational linguistics. Imagine the uses for improving machine translation, information extraction, and document analysis, among other innovations. As the computational linguistics field has expanded, so has the amount of research into SRL. However, as with much language technology research, the main focus has been on English. Because of this, Arabic-language [1] technologies and methods are often adapted from tools that have succeeded for English, rather than developed on their own. Recent years have produced powerful development resources, such as an Arabic Treebank and Propbank, in both pilot and revised forms. The number of resources available for automatic parsing, POS -tagging, chunking, of Arabic still lags behind that of English, but has grown noticeably. As a critical language, there is huge potential for an Arabic SRL system to revolutionize Arabic-language tools.

Based on the innovations of Diab, Moschitti, and Pighin (2007) in Arabic SRL, we are currently developing a system for automatic SRL in Arabic. We are looking for feedback from the conference before fully implementing and reporting the performance of this system.

## 2 Arabic NLP

Arabic has a number of challenges which aren't present for other languages. It is unlike English in many ways, which suggests that directly applying English- language technology many not be the absolute optimal approach for an effective system. On the other hand, there is no reason not to utilize the work that has been done on SRL if it can be used in a cross- linguistic way. The best approach will be to build upon previous work and customize it to Arabic linguistic features, thus using the differences between English and Arabic to advantage.

One such feature is Arabic's rich morphology. In Arabic, nouns and adjectives encode information about number, gender, case, and definiteness. Verbs are even richer, encoding tense, voice, mood, gender, number, and person. These features are often expressed via diacritics, short vowels marked above or below letters [2].

A word in Arabic is typically formed by selecting one of approximately 5,000, 3-to-5-consonant roots, and adding affixes. [3] Diacritics are sometimes the only thing that specifies semantic differences between words, and for certain genres, especially online communication, they are often left out. In this case, it is a special challenge for an automated system to determine the difference.

Another feature is word order. While not completely free, Arabic allows for subject-verb- object (SVO, as in English), verb- subject-object (VSO), and more occasionally OSV and OVS. In the Arabic Treebank, SVO and VSO each equally account for 35% of the sentences [4].

[1] In this paper, the term "Arabic" is used to refer to Modern Standard Arabic. Other dialects will be specifically noted as such.
[2] Diab et al., 2007.
[3] Abbasi and Chen, 2005.
[4] Palmer et al., 2008.

Arabic allows for noun phrases which are more complex than those in English, particularly the possessive construction called *idafa*, which relies on the definiteness of the nouns to convey precise meaning.

Another feature worth mentioning, but not currently handled by this system, is pro-drop. Because nouns, adjectives, and verbs encode so much information, it is fairly common to completely drop the subject of a sentence because it is implied. An example of this given in (Palmer et al., 2008) is: *Akl AlbrtqAl* 'ate-[he] the-oranges.' In this context, the verb *Akl,* 'ate,' expresses the subject 'he,' which is not directly said. (Palmer et al., 2008) notes that 30% of the sentences in the Arabic Treebank are pro-dropped.

## 3 Related Work

One of the things that challenges Arabic NLP is that much progress in computational linguistics is focused on English. As a result, many Arabic language technologies are based on research done on English, and then revised to better fit the characteristics of Arabic. This is not necessarily detrimental, but it does affect the development process. This is the route taken in (Diab et al., 2007) : adapting techniques which have proven successful for English SRL for use in an Arabic system. Specifically, Moschitti's SVM-light-TK is trained and tested on Arabic data, using features which have proven effective for English and some other languages, which are referred to as the "standard set". The features were grouped into:

a) Phrase Type, Predicate Word, Head Word, Position and Voice, based on (Gildea and Jurafsky 2002);
b) Partial Path, No Direction Path, Head Word POS, First and Last Word/POS in Constituent and SubCategorization based on (Pradhan et al., 2003);
c) Syntactic Frame, based on (Xue and Palmer, 2004)

(Diab et al., 2008) extends the first, rudimentary system by tailoring it to Arabic- specific features. This tailoring manifests in the form of feature selection for the SVM. The new, Arabic-specific features consist of inflectional morphology, including number, gender, definiteness, mood, case, person; derivational morphology including lemma form of the words with explicitly-marked diacritics; the English gloss; vocalized form with full diacritics (much like lemma but including inflections); and unvowelized word as it appears in the sentence. Tree kernels were specifically chosen for the initial set of experiments in order to be able to deal with the immense set of possible features. Adding the Arabic-specific features was shown to significantly improve performance.

## 4 Experiment Design

### 4.1 Machine Learning Algorithm

As in (Diab et al., 2007) and (Diab et al., 2008), this system will be using SVM-light-TK. The SVM algorithm has been shown in numerous studies to handle noisy data and large feature sets well. Using Moschitti's Tree Kernel SVM will allow for an extensible system, better suited to the addition of Arabic features. For the present, however, mostly the standard SVM-light capability will be utilized with a polynomial kernel.

## 4.2 Data

The SVM will be trained on annotated data collected from news-oriented, Arabic-language blogs. For initial testing, the corpus is relatively small, with just over 100 sentences. These were run through Benajiba and Diab's AMIRA 2.0 POS tagger and BP chunk parser. They were then annotated with ARG0 and ARG1 in PropBank-like style, with adverbial and prepositional (ARGM) phrases annotated for later use. For this implementation, only ARG0 and ARG1 will be labeled. All of the sentences in this corpus included explicit subjects rather than pro-drop. Additionally, most of the sentences were of SVO form, with very little variation.

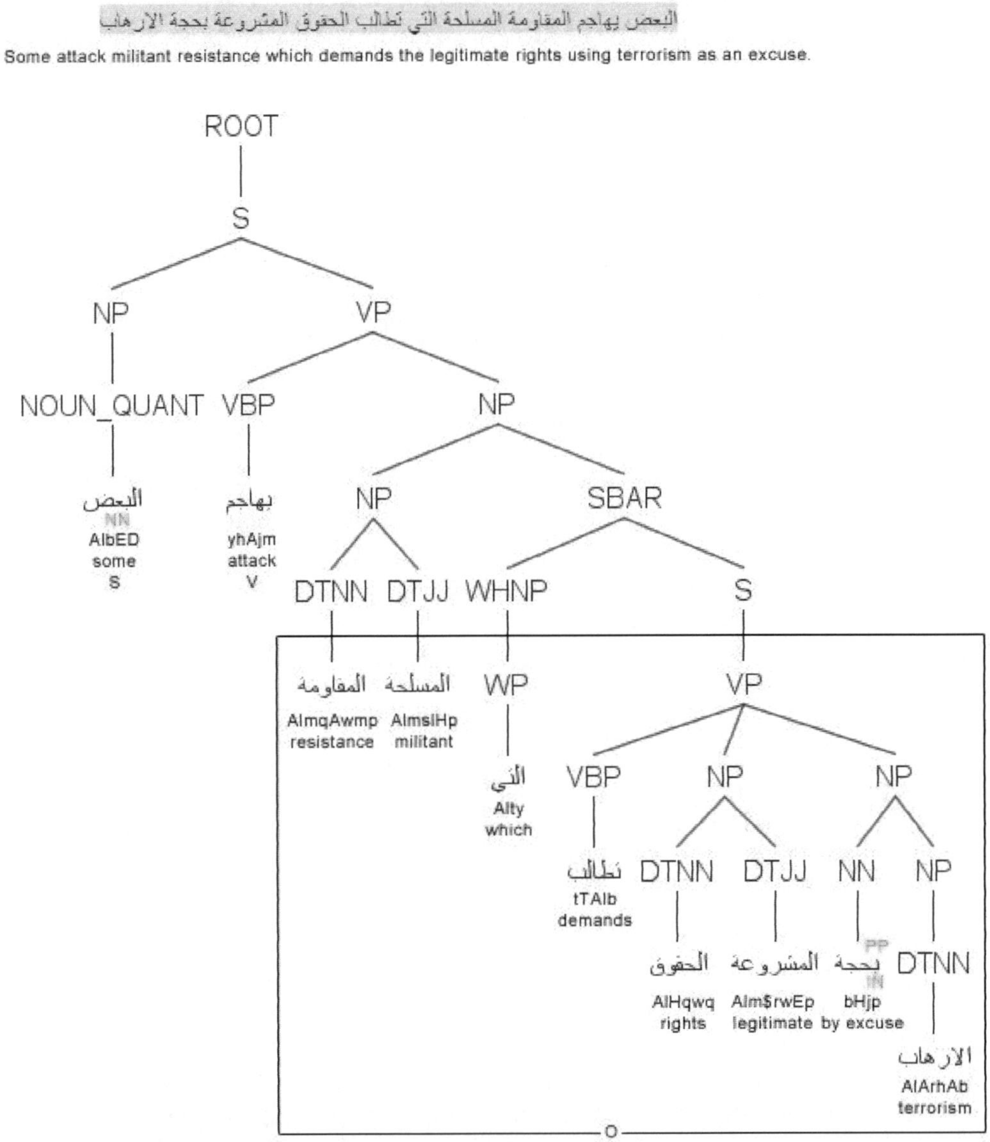


FIGURE 1 – A syntactic parse tree created using the Stanford Parser (factored Arabic grammar), then marked up to show semantic roles. "S" denotes the subject (ARG0), "V" denotes the predicate, "O" denotes the object (ARG1).

## 4.3 Predicate Argument Extraction and Argument Classification

Any SRL system involves extracting and labeling predicate structures. At the sentence level, this is constituted of two tasks: detecting the word span of arguments within the sentence, and classifying the arguments found by type (ARG0, ARG1, ARGM). (Diab, 2007 et al.) describes the general algorithm for doing so by the steps:

1. given a sentence from the *training-set*, generate a full syntactic parse-tree;
2. let *P* and *A* be the set of predicates and the set of parse-tree nodes (i.e. the potential arguments), respectively;
3. for each pair <*p, a*> ∈ *P* × *A*:

- Extract the feature representation set,;
- If the subtree rooted in *a* covers exactly the words of one argument of *p*, put $F_{p,a}$ in $T^+$ (positive examples), otherwise put it in $T^-$ (negative examples).

The $T^+$ and $T^-$ sets then serve to train the boundary classifier. With some restructuring, $T^+$ and $T^-$can also be used to train the argument classifier.

## 4.4 Features

The aspect that most distinguishes a system built for Arabic from one built for English is the selection of features. As mentioned above, (Diab et al., 2007)'s SRL system initially used the set of standard features before later adding Arabic-specific ones. Similarly, this system will first be developed using the standard set before experimenting with Arabic features. Following are brief descriptions of the feature types to be included.

- *Phrase Type*: The syntactic category of the phrase expressing the semantic roles. (Gildea and Jurafsky 2002)
- *Predicate Word*: Lemma form of the predicate word.
- *Head Word*: Syntactic head of phrase. (Pradhan et al., 2003)
- *Position*: Position of constituent relative to predicate (before or after).
- *Voice* : Active or passive classification of a sentence. This is included due to correspondence between active voice and subject, passive voice and object.
- *Path*: Syntactic path linking the argument and its predicate. For example, the path of ARG0 in Figure 1 is NQ↑NP↑S↓VP↓VBP.
- *Partial Path*: Section of the path that connects argument to the common parent of the predicate.
- *No Direction Path*: Path without directions.
- *Head Word POS*: Syntactic part of speech of the head word.
- *First and Last Word/POS in Constituent*: First and last words and part of speech of phrase.
- *SubCategorization*: Production rule expanding the predicate parent node. (Diab et al., 2008)
- *Syntactic Frame*: Noun phrase positions relative to the predicate.

# 5 Expected Results

Using the official CoNLL evaluator, (Diab et al., 2007)'s initial system was able to achieve overall F1 scores of 77.85 and 81.43 on classifying the arguments of the development and testing sets, respectively. Boundary detection results were also quite impressive, with F1 scores of 93.68 and 94.06. These results were yielded by use of only the standard features listed above. By adding in Arabic-specific features, utilizing tree kernels, and testing across a variety of models, (Diab,

2008 et al.) were able to increase the F1 score for automated boundary detection and argument classification to 82.17.

By drawing on previous work such as that of (Diab et al., 2007; Diab et al., 2008), we hope to achieve similar measures, possibly even improving upon them by applying research performed after the publication of (Diab et al., 2008).

## Conclusion and future work

Many of the next steps for expanding the system are quite clear, as the system has not been fully implemented yet.

In the future, more types of arguments will be labeled. This will be done by comparing the results of multiple 1-vs-ALL passes through the SVM trained for different argument types and selecting the highest score.

The system will also be tested on a larger, more representative corpus that possesses sentences exhibiting pro-dropping and more word-order variation. For our purposes, the SRL system should be able to detect these patterns.

During the development of the Arabic SRL system, we will continue to tailor it specifically to Arabic, and make more use of its unique linguistic features.

Constructive feedback on the design of this SRL system is welcomed.

## References


Abbasi, Ahmed, and Hsinchun Chen. "Applying Authorship Analysis to Extremist Group Web Forum Messages." *IEEE Intelligent Systems, Special Issue on Artificial Intelligence for National and Homeland Security* Sept. (2005): 67-75.

Benajiba, Yassine, and Mona Diab. *AMIRA 2.0*. Columbia University. Web. 2012. <http://nlp.ldeo.columbia.edu/amira/>.

Diab, Mona, Alessandro Moschitti, and Daniele Pighin. "CUNIT: A Semantic Role Labeling System for Modern Standard Arabic." *Proceedings of the 4th International Workshop on Semantic Evaluations (SemEval-2007)* June (2007): 133-36. Web.

Diab, Mona, Alessandro Moschitti, and Daniele Pighin. "Semantic Role Labeling Systems for Arabic using Kernel Methods."*Proceedings of ACL-08: HLT* June (2008): 798-806.

Gildea, Daniel, and Daniel Jurafsky. "Automatic Labeling of Semantic Roles." *Computational Linguistics* 28.3 (2002).

Green, Spence, and Christopher D. Manning. "Better Arabic Parsing: Baselines, Evaluations, and Analysis." *COLING 2010* (2010).

Joachims, Thorsten. "SVM$^{light}$." Cornell University, 14 Aug. 2008. Web. 2012.

Moschitti, Alessandro. "Tree Kernels in SVM-Light." University of Trento, Italy. Web. 2012. <http://disi.unitn.it/moschitti/Tree-Kernel.htm>.

Moschitti, Alessandro. "Making Tree Kernels practical for Natural Language Learning." *Proceedings of the Eleventh International Conference on European Association for Computational Linguistics* (2006). Print.

Palmer, Martha, Olga Babko-Malaya, Ann Bies, Mona Diab, Mohammed Maamouri, Aous Mansouri, and Wajdi Zaghouani. "A Pilot Arabic Propbank." (2008).

Pradhan, Sameer, Kadri Hacioglu, Wayne Ward, James H. Martin, and Daniel Jurafsky. "Semantic Role Parsing: Adding Semantic Structure to Unstructured Text." *Proceedings of ICDM-2003* (2003).

Xue, Nianwen, and Martha Palmer. "Calibrating Features for Semantic Role Labeling." (2004).

W. Zaghouani , M. Diab , A. Mansouri , S. Pradhan , M. Palmer, "The Revised Arabic PropBank," in: *Proceedings of the Fourth Linguistic Annotation Workshop, ACL 2010*, Uppsala, Sweden, 15-16 July 2010, pp. 222–226.

Zaghouani, Wajdi, Mona Diab, Aous Mansouri, Sameer Pradhan, and Martha Palmer. "The Revised Arabic PropBank." *Proceedings of the Fourth Linguistic Annotation Workshop, ACL 2010* 15 July (2012): 222-26.

# *fokas: Formerly Known As* A Search Engine Incorporating Named Entity Evolution*

*Helge HOLZMANN Gerhard GOSSEN Nina TAHMASEBI*
L3S Research Center, Appelstr. 9a, 30167 Hannover, Germany
{ holzmann, gossen, tahmasebi }@L3S.de

ABSTRACT
High impact events, political changes and new technologies are reflected in our language and lead to constant evolution of terms, expressions and names. This makes search using standard search engines harder, as users need to know all different names used over time to formulate an appropriate query. The *fokas* search engine demonstrates the impact of enriching search results with results for all temporal variants of the query. It uses NEER, a method for named entity evolution recognition. For each query term, NEER detects temporal variants and presents these to the user. A chart with term frequencies helps users choose among the proposed names to extend the query. This extended query captures relevant documents using temporal variants of the original query and improves overall quality. We use the New York Times corpus which, with its 20 year timespan and many name changes, constitutes a good collection to demonstrate NEER and *fokas*.

TITLE AND ABSTRACT IN GERMAN

## *fokas: Früher bekannt als* Eine Suchmaschine mit Einbindung von Namensevolution

Wichtige Ereignisse, politische Veränderungen und neue Technologien spiegeln sich in unserer Sprache wieder und führen zu einer ständigen Evolution von Begriffen, Ausdrücken und Namen. Dies erschwert die Suche mit herkömmlichen Suchmaschinen, da Nutzer zur Formulierung einer Anfrage sämtliche Namen kennen müssen, die im Laufe der Zeit verwendet wurden. Die Suchmaschine *fokas* zeigt den Einfluss des Anreicherns der Suchergebnisse mit den Ergebnissen für allen zeitlichen Varianten des Suchbegriffs. Sie verwendet NEER, eine Methode zur Erkennung von Namensevolution. NEER erkennt für jeden Suchbegriff alle zeitlichen Varianten und präsentiert diese dem Nutzer. Ein Termfrequenz-Diagramm ergänzt die Ergebnisse, um Nutzern bei der Wahl zwischen den vorgeschlagenen Namen zur Erweiterung der Anfrage zu unterstützen. Diese erweiterte Anfrage findet relevante Dokumente, die nur eine zeitliche Variante der ursprünglichen Anfrage verwenden, und verbessert dadurch die Gesamtqualität. Wir verwenden den Korpus der New York Times, der mit seiner Zeitspanne von 20 Jahren und vielen Namensänderungen eine gute Kollektion zur Demonstration von NEER und *fokas* ist.

KEYWORDS: Named Entity Revolution Recognition, unsupervised, NEER, search engine.

GERMAN KEYWORDS: Namensevolutionserkennung, nichtüberwacht, NEER, Suchmaschine.

*This work is partly funded by the European Commission under ARCOMEM (ICT 270239)

# 1 Introduction

Do you remember the bright yellow Walkman, Joseph Ratzinger or Andersen Consulting? Chances are you do not, because as the world around us changes, new terms are created and old ones are forgotten. High impact events, political changes and new technologies are reflected in our language and lead to constant evolution of terms, expressions and names. Most everyday tasks, like web search, have so far relied on the good memory of users or been restricted only to the current names of entities. As the web and its content grow older than some of its users, new challenges arise for natural language tasks like information retrieval to automatically determine relevant information, even when it is expressed using forgotten terms.

Language evolution is reflected in documents available on the web or in document archives but is not sufficiently considered by current applications. Therefore, if the users do not know different names referencing the same entity, information retrieval effectiveness becomes severely compromised. In this demonstration we present *fokas*, a search engine that knows about names used at different points in time to refer to the same named entity (called *temporal co-references*) and uses them to help users find all relevant documents. *fokas* is based on the NEER method (Tahmasebi et al., 2012b). NEER is an unsupervised method for named entity evolution recognition independent of external knowledge sources. It finds time periods with high likelihood of named entity evolution. By analyzing only these time periods using a sliding window co-occurrence method it captures evolving terms in the same context and thus avoids comparing terms from widely different periods in time. This method overcomes limitations of existing methods for named entity evolution and has a high recall of 90% on the New York Times corpus. Furthermore, using machine learning with minimal supervision leads to a precision to 94%.

In this demonstration we use the outcome of NEER to improve search on the New York Times corpus (NYTimes) by identifying temporal co-references and suggesting these to the user as possible query expansions. NYTimes serves as a good corpus because of its long time span (1986–2007), the wide range of topics and the high quality of the texts.

# 2 The NEER Method

**Identifying Change Periods** We use the Kleinberg algorithm (Kleinberg, 2003) to find bursts related to an entity. We retrieve all documents in the corpus containing the query term, group them into monthly bins and run the burst detection on the relative frequency of the documents in each bin. Each resulting burst corresponds to a significant event involving the entity. However, these bursts do not necessarily correspond to a name change. By choosing the `topB` strongest bursts we expect to find a subset of bursts which also captures change periods. We denote each **change period** $p_i$ for $i = 1, \ldots, \texttt{topB}$.

**Creating Contexts** After identifying change periods $p_i$ for an entity $w$ we use all documents $\mathbf{D}_{w_i}$ that mention the entity or any part of it and are published in the year corresponding to $p_i$. We extract nouns, noun phrases and named entities. All extracted terms are added to a **dictionary** and used for creating a co-occurrence graph (see Figure 1a). The co-occurrence graph is an undirected weighted graph which links two dictionary terms if and only if they are present in $\mathbf{D}_{w_i}$ within $k$ terms of each other. The weight of each link is the frequency with which the two terms co-occur in $\mathbf{D}_{w_i}$. The **context** of an entity $w$ are all terms co-occurring with $w$.

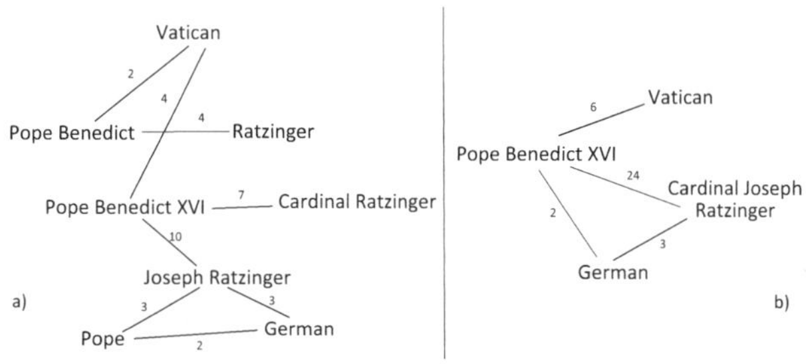


FIGURE 1: a) Example graph after creating contexts. b) After merging all direct co-references.

**Finding Temporal Co-references Classes** To find direct co-references (i.e., with lexical overlap) we make use of the contexts and the dictionaries. We consolidate the extracted terms by recognizing all variants of each term. The procedure for consolidation terms and groups of co-references is described in detail in (Tahmasebi et al., 2012b). During consolidation terms like *Pope*, *Pope Benedict* and *Pope Benedict XVI*, as well as *Ratzinger*, *Joseph Ratzinger* and *Cardinal Joseph Ratzinger* are considered **direct co-references** and merged. The result is displayed in Figure 1b.

**Indirect Co-references** Indirect co-references (i.e. without lexical overlap) are found implicitly by means of the direct co-references. After consolidation, all terms in the context are considered candidate indirect co-references. These are a mix between true indirect co-references, highly related co-occurrence phrases as well as noise. The quality of the indirect co-references is dependent on the named entity extraction, co-occurrence graph creation and filtering of the co-occurrence graph. In Figure 1b the terms *Vatican*, *German* and *Cardinal Joseph Ratzinger* are candidate co-references for *Pope Benedict XVI*. If NEER does not find any co-references for a term, all direct co-occurrences from the co-occurrence graphs (derived from the union of the change periods) are returned instead.

**Filtering Temporal Co-references** To remove noise and identify the true direct and indirect co-references we need to measure the temporal relatedness of terms. Unlike previous works that take temporal features into account it is not sufficient to consider relatedness over the entire time span of a collection. In Radinsky et al. (2011) the frequency of terms over times is used to capture the relatedness of terms like *war* and *peace* or *stock* and *oil*. These terms are considered related because they have similar frequencies over time. To fully capture temporal co-references we need global relatedness measures as well as a relatedness measure that captures how related terms are during the time periods where they can be related at all. To this end we allow a relatedness measure to consider only periods where both terms occur. In all cases we use the normalized frequencies. Details can be found in (Tahmasebi et al., 2012b).

We consider four relatedness measures: (1) Pearson's Correlation ($corr$) (Weisstein, 2012a), (2) Covariance ($cov$) (Weisstein, 2012b), (3) Rank correlation ($rc$) and (4) Normalized rank correlation ($nrc$).

The two first measures are standard relatedness measures where $corr$ measures linear dependence between random variables while $cov$ measures correlation between two random variables. The two last measures are rank correlation measures and inspired by the Kendall's tau coefficient that considers the number of pairwise disagreements between two lists. Our rank correlation coefficient counts an agreement between the frequencies of two terms for each time

FIGURE 2: *fokas* search page.

period where both terms experience an increase or decrease in frequency without taking into consideration the absolute values. The rank correlation is normalized by the total number of time periods. The normalized rank correlation considers the same agreements but is normalized with the total number of time periods where both terms have a non-zero term frequency.

Our filtering is based on machine learning. We use a random forest classifier (Breiman, 2001) consisting of a combination of decision trees where features are randomly extracted to build each decision tree. In total ten trees with three features each are constructed. We choose features from the similarity measures presented above. This means that for each term–co-reference pair $(w\ , w_c)$ found by NEER we calculate the $corr$, $cov$, $rc$ and $nrc$ measures. We also use the average of all four measures as a fifth feature. Finally we classify the pair as either 1 for $w_c$ being a correct co-reference of $w$ or 0 otherwise to train the classifier. We use the test set presented in (Tahmasebi et al., 2012a) for training.

## 3 Implementation

### 3.1 General Functionality

*fokas* stands for *formerly known as* which refers to the fact that named entities change their names over time. In *fokas*, the changed names (*temporal co-references*) will be used to expand the query posed to the system. The homepage of *fokas* mimics that of a common search engine (see Figure 2) and a typical workflow consists of the following steps:

1. enter a query string into the search field.
2. start searching by clicking the search button or selecting one of the suggested terms.
3. analyze search results, including found direct and indirect temporal co-references of the query term as well as a frequency chart of the different names.
4. select one or more relevant co-references (if any are available).
5. analyze the extended search results. Results containing only the added co-references are marked with an icon. The frequencies of the new co-references are added to the frequency chart.

While entering a query string in the search field the user will get a list of suggested terms (see Figure 3). The suggested terms are the names starting with the entered query string as well as

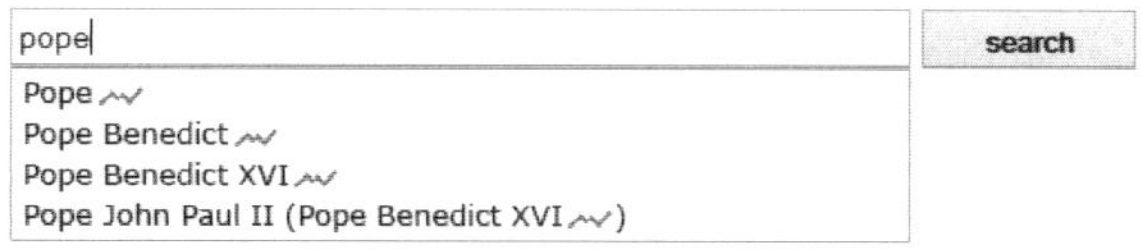


FIGURE 3: Additional query terms are suggested while typing a query.

the direct co-references found by applying NEER on the collection[1]. As shown in Figure 3, for the term *Benedict* the best matching co-references are presented (*Pope Benedict*, *Pope Benedict XVI*, *Pope John Paul II*). The first two are direct co-references for the term *Benedict*, while the last one is highly related as it refers to the previous pope. Clicking on one of the suggestions or the search button will start the search.

Next to each co-references in the suggestion box is a small graph symbol. Clicking on it will open a sidebar containing a term frequency chart and co-reference lists with all direct and indirect co-references found by NEER (see Figure 4). By clicking on one co-reference, the frequency of that term is added to the chart to help users decide the appropriateness and correctness of the chosen term.

The results of the search are presented as shown in Figure 4. The search result page has two columns. On the right hand side is the sidebar described above. The left hand side shows the search results from the articles of the New York Times corpus. These results are presented in a format similar to standard search engines, with a headline, a link to the full article and a short excerpt containing the query terms from the text of the article. The query terms (the entered query string or the selected co-references) are highlighted within the excerpt. Additionally, each result contains the publishing date of the appropriate article, which is specially relevant in the context of *fokas* and named entity evolution analysis.

*fokas* gives the user the ability to improve the search results by extending the query with co-references of the original query term. This can be done by selecting one or more co-references from the lists of direct or indirect co-references in the sidebar. This will immediately show the extended search results. Here all search results found through the selected co-references are marked with an icon. This lets the user directly conceive the advantage of a search augmented with the co-references of the term based on NEER, instead of only searching for the query term. The interface gives the user full control over the terms added to the query, supported by the displayed frequencies of each term.

## 3.2 Frequency Analysis Over Time

In addition to the search results, which are the main part of *fokas*, the frequency chart of the query is shown in the sidebar (see Figure 4, right hand side). This chart contains a graph for the query term as well as for each of the selected co-references showing the number of documents containing each term. This supports the user in selecting the co-references relevant to their query. The chart also helps to understand how NEER inferred the co-references for the query term and how the names of the appropriate entities changed over time. The blue graph shows the frequency of the query term. Each selected direct co-reference is illustrated by a green graph while the graphs for the indirect co-references are drawn in red.

[1]For efficiency reasons we currently compute co-references for a predefined set of names offline and only present these names.

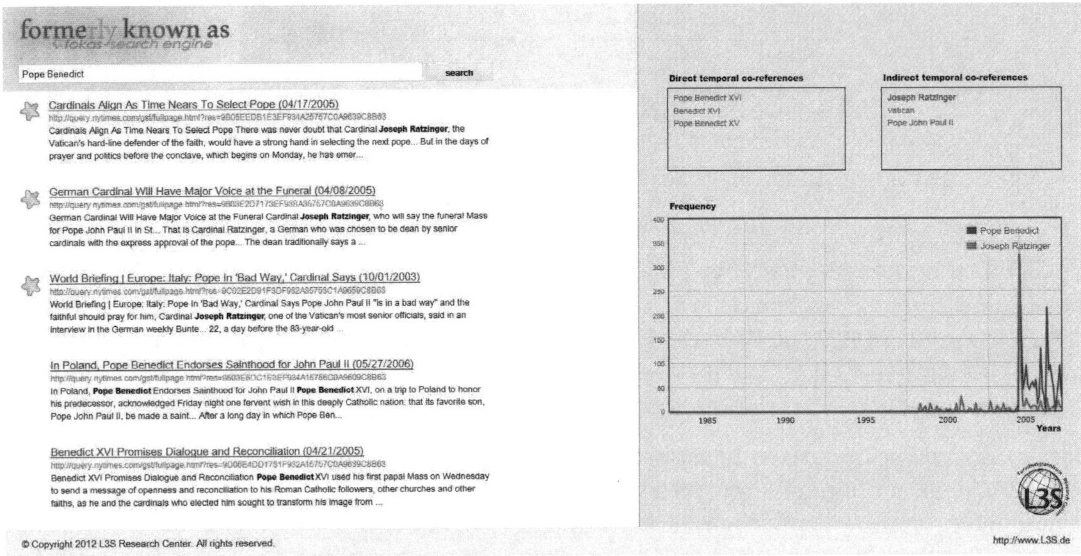


FIGURE 4: Search results enriched with results for co-references of the original query term.

As an example, the chart in Figure 4 shows the graph of the query for *Pope Benedict* after selecting the indirect co-reference *Joseph Ratzinger* to augment the results. This co-reference is a very valuable enrichment of the original query as the name *Pope Benedict* was not used before year 2005 at all. Thus, the users of *fokas* who are interested in all articles about Pope Benedict would not be able to find articles from the time before Joseph Ratzinger became Pope. Users of *fokas* will be alerted to this fact immediately and are able to take action. For example, by adding the term *Joseph Ratzinger* to the query *Pope Benedict* the user finds 34 documents (published in 2005 in the New York Times) containing only the term *Joseph Ratzinger* that would not have been found using plain keyword search.

## 4 Conclusion

*fokas* demonstrates a search engine that takes named entity evolution into account and allows users to query a document collection using temporal co-references. NEER allows us to find co-references for a wide range of terms in the New York Times corpus used by *fokas* for demonstration purposes. The lists of direct and indirect co-references and the frequency chart shown next to the search give users efficient tools for enriching their queries with their temporal variations. The highlighted search results give users a direct feedback about the improved results gained by including co-references. While *fokas* provides a well selected and filtered set of co-references based on NEER, it is not able to select the best queries for augmenting the search results automatically. *fokas* still requires interaction by the users but provides deeper insight and control, as well as transparency on how *fokas* and NEER work.

## References


Breiman, L. (2001). Random forests. In *Machine Learning*, pages 5–32.

Kleinberg, J. (2003). Bursty and hierarchical structure in streams. *Data Mining and Knowledge Discovery*, 7(4):373–397.

Radinsky, K., Agichtein, E., Gabrilovich, E., and Markovitch, S. (2011). A word at a time: computing word relatedness using temporal semantic analysis. In *WWW*, pages 337–346.

Tahmasebi, N., Gossen, G., Kanhabua, N., Holzmann, H., and Risse, T. (2012a). Named entitiy evolution dataset. Available online at `http://l3s.de/neer-dataset/`.

Tahmasebi, N., Gossen, G., Kanhabua, N., Holzmann, H., and Risse, T. (2012b). NEER: An unsupervised method for named entity evolution recognition. In *Proceedings of the 24th International Conference on Computational Linguistics (Coling 2012)*, Mumbai, India.

Weisstein, E. W. (2012a). Correlation coefficient. Retrieved 2012-11-05, from `http://mathworld.wolfram.com/CorrelationCoefficient.html`.

Weisstein, E. W. (2012b). Covariance. Retrieved 2012-11-05, from `http://mathworld.wolfram.com/Covariance.html`.

# An Annotation System for Development of Chinese Discourse Corpus

*Hen-Hsen Huang, Hsin-Hsi Chen*
Department of Computer Science and Information Engineering,
National Taiwan University, Taipei, Taiwan
hhhuang@nlg.csie.ntu.edu.tw, hhchen@csie.ntu.edu.tw

ABSTRACT

Well-annotated discourse corpora facilitate the discourse researches. Unlike English, the Chinese discourse corpus is not widely available yet. In this paper, we present a web-based annotation system to develop a Chinese discourse corpus with much finer annotation. We first review our previous corpora from the practical point of view, then propose a flexible annotation framework, and finally demonstrate the web-based annotation system. Under the proposed annotation scheme, both the explicit and the implicit discourse relations occurring on various linguistic levels will be captured and labelled with three-level PDTB tags. Besides, the sentiment information of each instance is also annotated for advanced study.

## 輔助中文語篇語料庫開發的標記系統

標記詳細語篇資訊的語料庫，對於語篇研究有很大的幫助。在英文語言處理，目前已有公眾可以取得的質量良好語篇語料庫。相較之下，中文領域尚未有這樣的公開資源。語篇標記的工作需要投入相當的人力和時間，爲了提高工作效率，我們開發了一套系統，透過網頁介面，可以對中文語料標記詳細的語篇資訊。在本文中，我們首先回顧過去標記的成果，指出根據中文的語言特性，需要特別考量的要點。針對這些要點，提出了一套高度彈性的框架。在這套框架下，標記者將圈選出外顯或內隱、句內或跨句等各式各樣的語篇關係，並且標上PDTB的三階語篇關係標籤。此外，每一個語篇實例的情緒資訊也一併標記，作爲將來進階研究之用。

KEYWORDS: Chinese Discourse Analysis, Corpus Annotation, Corpus Linguistics, Sentiment Analysis
KEYWORDS IN CHINESE: 中文語篇分析, 語料標記, 語料庫語言學, 情緒分析

*Proceedings of COLING 2012: Demonstration Papers*, pages 223–230,
COLING 2012, Mumbai, December 2012.

## 1 Introduction

The study of discourse analysis attracts a lot of attention in recent years. The release of the well-annotated datasets such as the Rhetorical Structure Theory Discourse Treebank (RST-DT) (Carlson et al., 2002) and the Penn Discourse TreeBank (PDTB) (Prasad et al., 2008) facilitate the discourse researches. Many related subtopics such as discourse segmentation and discourse relation recognition grow rapidly. Discourse corpus becomes the essential component for the researches.

Both the RST-DT and the PDTB are annotated on Wall Street Journal articles from the Penn Discourse Treebank that are written in English. In Chinese, no discourse corpus is widely available yet. To investigate the Chinese discourse analysis, research groups independently developed the discourse corpora for their needs. We annotated two corpora based on the Sinica Treebank for Chinese discourse relation recognition (Huang and Chen, 2011; 2012). At present, Zhou and Xue (2012) are annotating the Penn Chinese Treebank with the PDTB-style scheme.

English and Chinese natives have their own written styles. Chen (1994) showed that the number of sentence terminators (period, question and exclamation marks) is a little larger than segment separators (comma and semicolon) in English. In contrast, the segment separators outnumber the sentence terminators in Chinese with the ratio 7:2 (Chen, 1994). It results in many segments in Chinese sentences. Analyses of documents randomly sampling from Sinica Chinese Treebank (Huang et al., 2000) show the distribution of the number of segments in Chinese sentences is 1 segment (12.18%), 2 segments (18.35%), 3 segments (20.15%), 4 segments (15.72%), 5 segments (12.91%), 6-10 segments (17.72%), and more than 10 segments (2.97%). Long sentences tend to have more complex structural relationships and thus make Chinese discourse annotation challenging.

For our previous two discourse annotation work (Huang and Chen, 2011; 2012), different annotation schemes were used. One corpus was annotated on the sentence level with the PDTB four-class tags. Another corpus was annotated on the clause level with the Contingency and the Comparison relations from the PDTB four-class tags. In this paper, we consider the specific written style of Chinese sentences and propose a flexible annotation scheme to develop a new Chinese discourse corpus.

In this corpus, the three level discourse relation tags from the PDTB 2.0 are fully used (Prasad et al., 2007). The discourse units can be on various levels. An argument of a discourse pair can be as short as a clause and as long as several sentences. In addition, the nested discourse pairs are annotated in our scheme. For example, the sentence (S1) is a Chinese sentence that consists of three clauses. As illustrated in Figure 1, (S1) forms a Comparison discourse pair on the top level, and it contains a nested Contingency discourse pair. We annotate not only the discourse relations, but also the sentiment information of each discourse pair and its two arguments. As shown in Figure 1, the polarity of the first clause is positive, the polarity of the fragments that consist of the last two clauses is negative, and finally the whole statement (S1) constitute a polarity of negative. Such information is valuable for the study of the correlations between discourse relation and sentiment analysis.

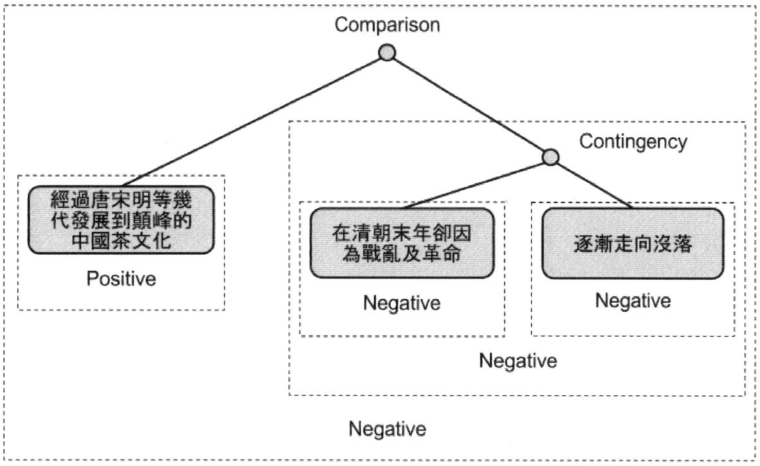


FIGURE 1 - Discourse structure and sentiment polarities of (S1).

(S1) 經過唐宋明等幾代發展到顛峰的中國茶文化 ('After several dynasties such as Tang, Song, and Ming, the Chinese tea culture developed to the peak')，在清朝末年卻因爲戰亂及革命 ('however, because of war and revolution at the end of the Qing Dynasty')，逐漸走向沒落 ('gradually declined')。

Constructing a well-annotated corpus with adequate amounts of data is not a trivial task. Various considerations and design processes should be involved. In this paper, we aim to share our experience of developing Chinese discourse corpora and introduce the approaches to facilitate the annotation work with a web-based system.

The rest of this paper is organized as follows. In Section 2, our previous two Chinese discourse corpora, which are annotated on the inter-sentential level and the intra-sentential level, respectively, are analyzed. Consideration and the annotation plan of the Chinese discourse corpus are described in Section 3. The design and its current status are given in Section 4. Finally, we conclude this paper in the last section.

## 2 Two Pilot Chinese Discourse Corpora

Two pilot Chinese discourse corpora were developed on the Sinica Treebank 3.1 (Huang et al., 2000), which is a traditional Chinese Treebank based on the Academic Sinica Balanced Corpus (Huang and Chen, 1992). To tackle the issue of Chinese discourse recognition, a moderate-sized corpus with the fundamental discourse relation was tagged as our first Chinese discourse corpus (Huang and Chen, 2011). For each article, annotators tag the discourse relation between every two successive sentences with one of the PDTB top four classes: *Temporal*, *Contingency*, *Comparison*, and *Expansion*. These four classes are the top level tags in the PDTB tagging system.

The downside of this corpus is that only a few Comparison and Contingency relations are labelled. After analysis, we find the Contingency and the Comparison relations tend to occur within a sentence, especially the Contingency relation. Since we annotate the relations on the inter-sentence level only, such instances are missing. Besides, the nested relations shown in Figure 1 are also completely missing in this corpus because only the relations between every two successive sentences are labelled.

To study the Contingency and the Comparison relations occurring in sentences and their nested structure, an intra-sentential corpus was constructed as our second corpus (Huang and Chen, 2012). The discourse unit in this corpus is clause, which is defined as a sequence of words in a sentence that are delimited by commas ('，'). Annotators decide the structure of a sentence and tag the relations between every successive clause in the sentence. To simplify the annotation work, only the sentences that consist of two, three, and four clauses are selected.

## 3 More Practical Considerations

To annotate a Chinese discourse corpus, we should tackle some practical issues. Firstly, the unit of a discourse argument is not regular. As mentioned in Section 1, an argument of a discourse pair may be as short as a clause, and may also be as long as several sentences. The more vexing case is the nested discourse relations illustrated in Figure 1. Annotators have to determine the correct boundary of arguments. That is important for training and testing discourse parsers.

Secondly, discourse markers are important clues for labelling discourse relations. In English, the explicit discourse markers are defined as three grammatical classes of connectives, including subordinating conjunctions, coordinating conjunctions, and adverbial connectives (Prasad et al., 2008). These words can be automatically extracted using a syntactic parser or a POS tagger. However, it is not clear what the Chinese discourse markers are. Cheng and Tian (1989) suggested a dictionary of Chinese discourse markers, which consist of many words including connectives and various parts of speech such as adverbs, verbs, prepositions, and time nouns.

Detecting the Chinese discourse markers automatically is not trivial. Wrong segmentation is prone to result in the less accurate marker detection. Besides, some words in a discourse marker dictionary are general function words that can be used in other purposes rather than discourse relation marking only. For example, the word 或 ("or") can be used as a discourse marker of the Expansion relation and a correlative conjunction. Thus, to disambiguate if a word is used as a discourse marker is necessary. Furthermore, the vocabulary of Chinese discourse markers is not a closed set. The explicit discourse markers are labelled by annotators on the character level.

Thirdly, veridicality is a property of a discourse relation that specifies whether both arguments of a discourse pair are truth or not (Hutchinson, 2004). In the three-level PTDB tagging scheme, the veridicality will be distinguished in different tags. For example, the tag CONTINGENCY:Condition:unreal-past indicates a discourse pair where the second argument of the pair did not occur in the past and the first argument denotes what the effect would have been if the second argument had occurred. By labelling the data with the full PDTB tagging scheme, the veridical information of the discourse pairs are naturally labelled at the same time.

Fourthly, sentiment polarity is another property of a discourse relation that indicates the sentiment transition between the two arguments of a discourse pair (Hutchinson, 2004).

Such information will help us realize the correlations between discourse relations and sentiment polarities.

## 4 An Annotation Framework

A flexible interface that allows annotators to label a variety of discourse relations with detailed information is proposed. An annotator first signs in to the online annotation system, and a list of articles that are assigned to the annotator are given. The annotator labels the articles one by one. As shown in Figure 2, the annotator selects the clauses that form a discourse pair in the text if it is found. The selected clauses will be denoted in the bold and red font. The annotator clicks the button "Create" when all the clauses belonging to this discourse pair are selected, and then the advanced annotation window will be popped up.

As shown in Figure 3, the discourse relation, the discourse marker, the boundaries of arguments, and the sentiment polarities of the two arguments and the entire discourse pairs are labelled in the pop-up window. The entire selected discourse pair is present in the top of the pop-up window. The following is the drop-down selection lists that correspond to the three levels of hierarchical discourse relation tags used in the PDTB. The next part is about to highlight the discourse markers from the text. As mentioned in Section 3, the annotator highlights the discourse marker on the character level. The annotator can select multiple characters for the phrase or the pairwise discourse marker such as "因為 …, 所以…" ("Because ..., so ..."). The implicit discourse relation is distinguished if no discourse marker is highlighted. And then, the annotator splits the first argument and the second argument by selecting the clauses belonging to the first argument. The rest clauses are regarded as the second argument. The last part of annotation is labeling the sentiment information. There are three types of sentiment polarity, i.e., positive, neutral, and negative. The polarities of the whole discourse pair and both of its two arguments will be labelled. The annotator is asked to judge the sentiment polarities on the pragmatic level. That is, the sentiment polarity of the text is not determined by the surface semantics, but by its real meaning. The annotator submits the annotation by clicking the button 'Save' and continues to look up another discourse pair in the article. The nested relations can be annotated in this interface by choosing the repeated clauses in different rounds.

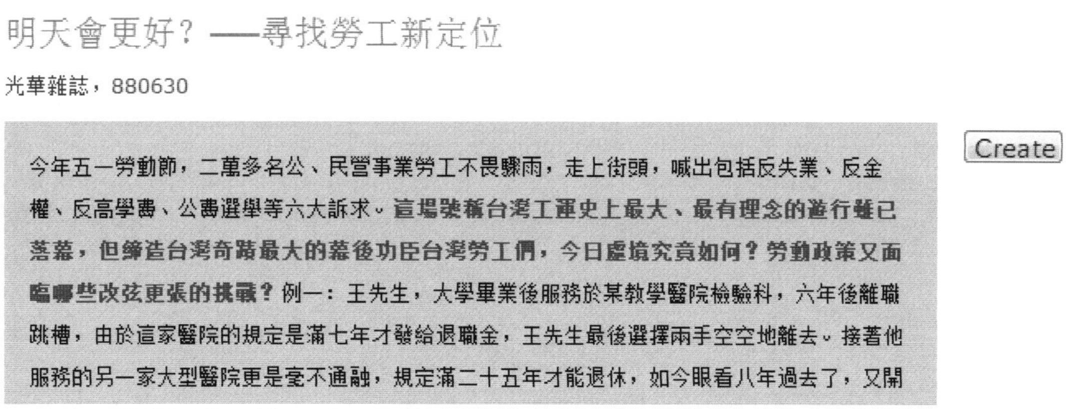

FIGURE 2 – Choosing a discourse pair on the web-based online system

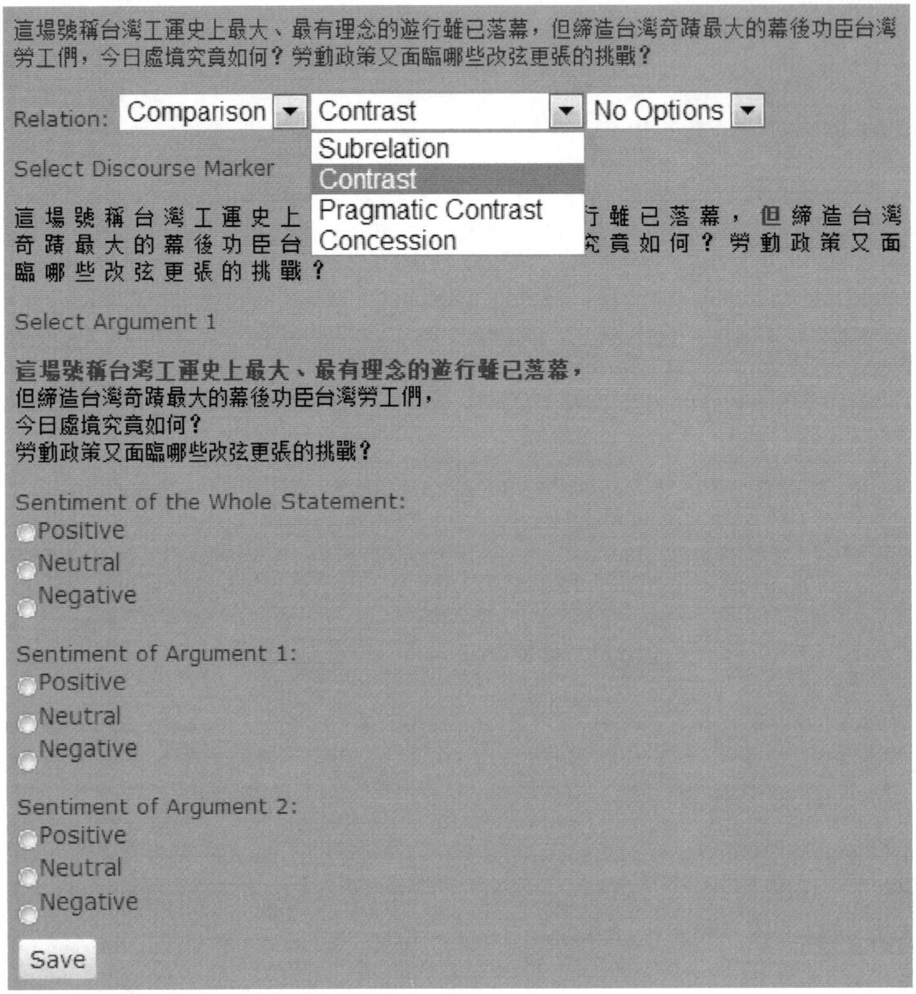


FIGURE 3 – Labeling the information for the chosen discourse pair with the web-based online system

## Conclusion

Discourse corpus is indispensable for the study of discourse analysis. In this paper, we address some considerations specific to Chinese language. A flexible annotation framework is proposed to cover a variety of discourse relations and determine the argument boundary of a relation. Furthermore, the sentiment polarities are also annotated on the discourse pairs and their arguments. Such a corpus is helpful for the exploration of the areas of Chinese discourse processing and sentiment analysis. The cost of the detailed annotation is much higher and the annotation task is time-consuming. In order to facilitate the complicated annotation work, we demonstrate a web-based system that supports annotators to do the work fast and accurately.

## Acknowledgments

This research was partially supported by Excellent Research Projects of National Taiwan University under contract 101R890858 and 2012 Google Research Award.

## References

Carlson, L., Marcu, D., and Okurowski, M.E. (2002). *RST Discourse Treebank*. Linguistic Data Consortium, Philadelphia.

Chen, H.H. (1994). The Contextual Analysis of Chinese Sentences with Punctuation Marks. *Literal and Linguistic Computing*, Oxford University Press, 9(4): 281-289.

Cheng, X. and Tian, X. (1989). Xian dai Han yu (現代漢語), San lian shu dian (三聯書店), Hong Kong.

Huang, C. R., Chen, F. Y., Chen, K. J., Gao, Z. M., and Chen, K. Y. (2000). Sinica Treebank: design, criteria, annotation guidelines, and on-line interface. In *the 2nd Chinese Language Processing Workshop*, pages 29-37, Hong Kong, China.

Huang, C.R. and Chen, K.J., (1992). A Chinese corpus for linguistics research. In *the 14th International Conference on Computational Linguistics* (*COLING-92*), pages 1214-1217, Nantes, France.

Huang, H.H. and Chen, H.H. (2011). Chinese discourse relation recognition. In *the 5th International Joint Conference on Natural Language Processing* (*IJCNLP 2011*). pages 1442-1446, Chiang Mai, Thailand.

Huang, H.H. and Chen, H.H. (2012). Contingency and comparison relation labeling and structure prediction in Chinese sentences. In *the 13th Annual Meeting of the Special Interest Group on Discourse and Dialogue* (*SIGDIAL 2012*), pages 261-269, Seoul, South Korea.

Hutchinson, B. (2004). Acquiring the meaning of discourse markers. In *the 42nd Annual Meeting of the Association for Computational Linguistics* (*ACL 2004*), pages 684-691, Barcelona, Spain.

Prasad, R., Miltsakaki, E., Dinesh, N., Lee, A., Joshi, A., Robaldo, L., and Webber, B. (2007). *The Penn Discourse Treebank 2.0 Annotation Manual*. The PDTB Research Group.

Prasad, R., Dinesh, N., Lee, A., Miltsakaki, E., Robaldo, L., Joshi, A., and Webber, B. (2008). The Penn Discourse TreeBank 2.0. In *the 6th Language Resources and Evaluation Conference* (*LREC 2008*), pages 2961-2968, Marrakech, Morocco.

Zhou, Y. & Xue, N. (2012). PDTB-style discourse annotation of Chinese text. In *the 50th Annual Meeting of the Association for Computational Linguistics* (*ACL 2012*), pages 69-77, Jeju, South Korea.

# Modeling Pollyanna Phenomena in Chinese Sentiment Analysis

Ting-Hao (Kenneth) Huang[1] Ho-Cheng Yu[2] Hsin-Hsi Chen[2]
(1) Carnegie Mellon University, 5000 Forbes Ave., Pittsburgh, PA 15213, U.S.
(2) National Taiwan University, No. 1, Sec. 4, Roosevelt Road, Taipei, 10617 Taiwan (R.O.C)
tinghaoh@cs.cmu.edu, p98922004@csie.ntu.edu.tw, hhchen@ntu.edu.tw

ABSTRACT

This paper proposes a method to enhance sentiment classification by utilizing the Pollyanna phenomena. The Pollyanna phenomena describe the human tendency to use positive words more frequently than negative words. This word-level linguistic bias can be demonstrated to be strong and universal in many languages. We perform detailed analyses of the Pollyanna phenomena in four Chinese corpora. Quantitative analyses show that for documents with few positive words, the word usages in documents from either the positive or the negative polarities become similar. Qualitative analyses indicate that this increase of similarity of word usage could be caused by the concentration of topics. By taking advantage of these results, we propose a partitioning strategy for sentiment classification and significantly improve the F1-score.

# 應用於中文情緒分析之波莉安娜效應研究

摘要

本研究提出一以波莉安娜效應改善情緒分類之方法。波莉安娜效應指於人類語用中，正面詞詞頻高於負面詞詞頻之語言現象。此一詞彙層次偏斜現象非僅存在許多語言中，且強度更十分顯著。本研究首先於四個中文語料庫中分析波莉安娜效應。定量分析顯示，含有較少正面詞彙的特定情緒傾向文件間，相較於正負面詞比例正常的文件間，具有較高的文字相似度；定性分析則指出，該現象乃由於主題集中化所造成。基於上述分析結果，本研究繼而提出一切分資料之策略以改進情緒分類效能，並於實驗中有效提升F1-score。

KEYWORDS : Sentiment Classification, Pollyanna Phenomena
KEYWORDS IN MANDARIN : 情緒分析, 情緒分類, 波莉安娜效應

*Proceedings of COLING 2012: Demonstration Papers*, pages 231–238,
COLING 2012, Mumbai, December 2012.

## 1 Introduction

The human tendency to use positive words more frequently than negative words was originally called "the Pollyanna Hypothesis," named after a fictional young girl with infectious optimism (Porter, 1913), by Boucher and Osgood (1969). This word-level linguistic positivity bias had been not only discussed by early studies, e.g., (Johnson et al., 1960) and (Zajonc 1968), but also explored by contemporary scholars. Zou (2004) analyzed the frequencies of the positive and negative Chinese words based on the Modern Chinese Frequency Dictionary (Wang 1986), and concluded their ratio as 7:3. Similar supporting evidences were also found in various other languages, e.g., English (Augustine et al., 2011; Garcia et al, 2012; Kloumann et al, 2012), Italian (Suitner and Maass, 2008), German and Spanish (Garcia et al, 2012), and even across 20 different languages (Rozin et al., 2010). In contrast, only a few works addressed this particular issue in opinion mining and sentiment analysis. These papers (Bolasco and della Ratta-Rinaldi, 2004; Brooke, 2009; Mohammad et al., 2009) demonstrated supporting evidences of the Pollyanna Hypothesis. Taboada et al. (2009) and Brooke et al. (2009) claimed the positivity bias could affect lexicon-based sentiment analysis systems like those of Kennedy and Diana (2006), and proposed an adjusting strategy (Taboada et al., 2011).

The contribution of this paper is three-fold: (1) To the best of our knowledge, we conduct the first detailed survey of the Pollyanna phenomena in various modern Chinese corpora. (2) Through quantitative and qualitative analyses, we discover that for the documents with relatively fewer positive words, the intra-polarity document similarity, of either positive or negative opinion polarity, significantly increases. (3) Based on our findings, we propose a strategy for sentiment classification and improve performance significantly.

## 2 Word-Level Linguistic Positivity Bias

In this section, we aim to explore details of the Pollyanna phenomena in Chinese. Our work focuses on the word-level linguistic bias, i.e., the unbalanced distributions of positive/negative words' occurrences.

| | | CTB | RECI | iPeen | MOAT |
|---|---|---|---|---|---|
| Basic Information | Data Type | Generic Corpus | News Opinion Summary | Restaurant Review | Evaluation Data |
| | Data Instance Type | Document | | | Sentence |
| | #Instance (Inst.) | 892 | 2,389 | 19,986 | 4,652 |
| | Avg. Inst. Length (#Word) | 532.25 | 60.36 | 331.84 | 16.06 |
| Sentimental Information | Opinion Polarity Label | Untagged | POS, NEG | POS, NEG, NEU | POS, NEG, NEU |
| | % Pos. Instance | - | 59.36% | 44.16% | 8.88% |
| | % Neg. Instance | - | 40.64% | 7.88% | 11.11% |
| | Avg. Pos. WF | 0.10 | 0.11 | 0.08 | 0.11 |
| | Avg. Neg. WF | 0.02 | 0.03 | 0.03 | 0.06 |
| | Avg. Bias | 0.66 | 0.47 | 0.48 | 0.15 |

TABLE 1: Statistics of the four corpora

## 2.1 Experimental Datasets

To realize the Pollyanna phenomena in Chinese, we analyze four modern corpora of different genres: opinionative real estate news (RECI), users' comments on restaurants (iPeen), a dataset for a multilingual opinion analysis task (MOAT), and a generic corpus (Chinese Treebank).

The Quarterly Report of Taiwan Real Estate Cycle Indicators (RECI) (Chin, 2010) has been collecting and analyzing Taiwan's opinionative real estate news, and releasing reports to the public every three months since 2002. Each RECI report contains 50 to 70 opinionative news excerpts labeled with opinion polarities. In this study, we select excerpts with "Positive" and "Negative" labels from 2002 to 2010 to set up a RECI corpus; iPeen (http://www.ipeen.com.tw/) is a restaurant review website. Each registered user can post his/her comments and rating points from 0, 5, ..., 55, to 60 toward any restaurants. We randomly collect about 20,000 non-empty posts from iPeen and tri-polarize the opinion polarities of posts. The posts with rating points lower than 20 are labeled as "Negative", those higher than 40 are labeled as "Positive", and the remaining posts are labeled as "Neutral"; The NTCIR Multilingual Opinion Analysis Task (MOAT) (Seki et al., 2008) provided a dataset for evaluating opinion mining technologies. We use the Traditional Chinese test set with the "strict" annotating standard. Each sentence in the set is annotated with opinion polarity by three assessors. All three assessors must provide the same label for a sentence, otherwise its label will be "Neutral"; Finally, the Chinese Treebank 5.1 (CTB) (Palmer et al., 2005) is also adopted for comparison. The statistics of these corpora are summarized in TABLE 1.

## 2.2 Deep Analysis

In document/sentence level, TABLE 1 demonstrates that the linguistic bias is not always positive. RECI and iPeen have different degrees of preference for positive document, while MOAT corpus has a slight higher percentage for negative sentences.

In word level, we tag all four corpora by an extended version of the NTU Sentiment Dictionary© (NTUSD) (Ku and Chen, 2007), which contains 9,365 positive words and 11,230 negative words. Every word in NTUSD is annotated by multiple human annotators and is examined by one or more experts. We then define positive word frequency (WF) in a document/sentence to be the total number of occurrences of positive words divided by the length of the document/sentence. (The negative word frequency is defined in the same way.) TABLE 1 shows that the average positive word frequencies in these four corpora are 1.83 to 5 times of those of negative words. The ratio Zou (2004) concluded between positive and negative words, i.e., 7:3, also fell within this range. We further propose an indicator Bias(d) in Equation (1) to measure the degree of word-level linguistic bias in a given document/sentence d.

$$\boldsymbol{Bias(d)} = \frac{C_p(d) - C_n(d)}{C_p(d) + C_n(d)}, \begin{cases} C_p(d) = (Number\ of\ positive\ words\ in\ d) + 1 \\ C_n(d) = (Number\ of\ negative\ words\ in\ d) + 1 \end{cases} \quad (1)$$

Bias(d) is a smoothed and normalized version of the positive-negative word count ratio. The absolute value of Bias(d) denotes the magnitude of bias, and the sign shows the direction of bias. The last row of TABLE 1 shows that the average biases in the document-based corpora (i.e., CTB, RECI and iPeen) are 0.66, 0.47, and 0.48, respectively; and 0.15 in the sentence-based corpus (i.e., MOAT). These values reflect that the word-level positivity bias is not only strong, but also universal. These four corpora all have different characteristics in many aspects, but all of them show strong agreements with the Pollyanna Hypothesis.

## 3 Intra- and Inter-Polarity Similarity Analysis

The above analyses raise an interesting question: What happens in those outlier documents whose positive-negative word ratios are "not that positive"? One intuitive guess is that those documents mostly represent negative opinions. However, when we look at the lower positively biased set, the number of negative documents is not always the largest; Another guess is that people tend to use fewer positive words only in some specific occasions or to describe some certain content, i.e., the use of words in those less positively biased documents could be possibly similar to each other. Our preliminary study suggests that this rise of similarity does not happen uniformly in all documents with lower bias values, but only in certain opinion polarity. In this section, we aim to quantitatively examine this observation. If this guess turns out to be true, it could be potentially beneficial for sentiment classification.

### 3.1 Methodology

Our goal is to measure the average degree of similarity of word use between documents of the same and different opinion polarities. The analyses are setup in the following way: First, we explore a bias value threshold $\beta$ from -1 to 1 in steps of 0.1. For each $\beta$, those documents with bias values smaller than $\beta$ form a lower set of $\beta$, and the remainder is called an upper set. In a lower set, we would then put documents of the same "target polarity" (positive or negative) together in a set $P_T$ and place all remaining documents -- including all neutral documents if any -- into a "non-target polarity" set $P_{NT}$. Note that RECI only has two sentiment polarities (see TABLE 1), so its target and non-target polarities are interchangeable. Second, we use the TF-IDF vectors to represent documents, and calculate four different average cosine similarities S of all document pairs (x, y) in a lower set as follows.

- $S_T : x, y \in P_T,\ x \neq y$
- $S_{NT} : x, y \in P_{NT},\ x \neq y$
- $S_{Inter} : x \in P_T,\ y \in P_{NT}$
- $S_{All} : x, y \in \text{lower set},\ x \neq y$

$S_T$, $S_{NT}$ and $S_{Inter}$ are then normalized by $S_{All}$. In this paper, we use the asterisk ($^*$) to indicate the normalized similarity. Finally, for every lower set with different $\beta$, we have three normalized similarities, i.e., $S_T^*$, $S_{NT}^*$ and $S_{Inter}^*$. The former two respectively represent the intra-polarity similarity of documents with target and non-target polarities, and the latter one represents the inter-polarity similarity of documents from different opinion polarities.

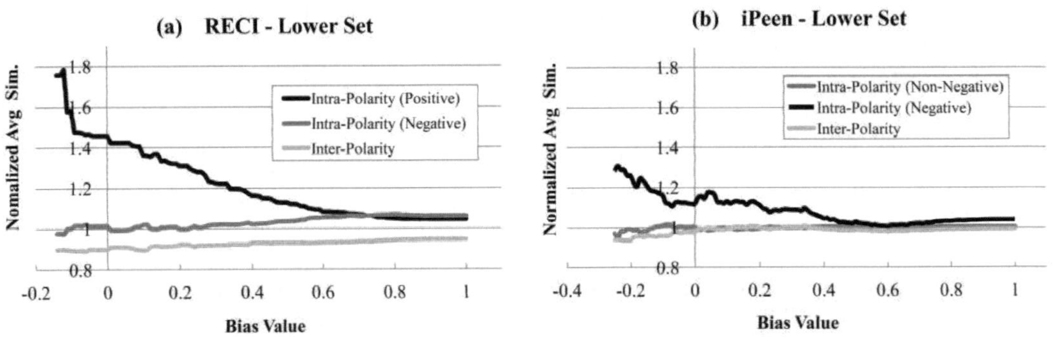


FIGURE 1: The curves of $S_T^*$, $S_{NT}^*$ and $S_{Inter}^*$ of the lower sets in (a) RECI ($P_T$ = Positive) and (b) iPeen ($P_T$ = Negative). The $S_T^*$ obviously rise up when bias value decreases.

### 3.2 Results and Discussion

In each of RECI, iPeen and MOAT, the $S_T^*$, $S_{NT}^*$ and $S_{Inter}^*$ are drawn with respect to the different bias values. FIGURE 1(a) and 1(b) are the resulting curves of RECI and iPeen, where positive and negative polarities are respectively explored as targets. These two figures confirm our guess: Within the target opinion polarity, the average cosine similarity among documents ($S_T^*$) obviously rises up in the portion of data which has less positivity bias, while the $S_{NT}^*$ and $S_{Inter}^*$ still remain stable. In other words, when we look at those outlier documents with lower bias values, for certain target opinion polarity, people actually tend to use more similar words with each other. Incidentally, we also analyze the same target polarities of the upper sets respectively in RECI and iPeen. But the curves do not display any obvious consistent trends. Another issue is the choice of the target polarity. We run the analysis in iPeen corpus when targeting at the other opinion polarity, i.e., positive. However, neither in the lower set nor in the upper set of iPeen corpus the similarities demonstrate any obvious trends. Meanwhile, we find that the $S_T^*$ in MOAT is always apparently higher than both $S_{NT}^*$ and $S_{Inter}^*$, regardless of bias values, lower/upper sets, and target polarity. It could be caused by its strict annotating standard which only accepts the labels with perfect inter-annotator agreement.

## 4 Qualitative Analysis

In the less positively biased portion of data, we have quantitatively observed the increase of cosine similarity among documents. Then the next question should naturally be, when using less positive words, what do people actually talk about? In this section, we adopt quantitative analyses and try to give an insightful interpretation.

In iPeen, we compare the negative documents in the upper set and the lower set (with partitioning bias value 0.1). In general, negative comments toward restaurants cover a wide range of topics. As expected, both the number of documents and the diversity of topics are much higher in the upper set. However, interestingly, we find that the negative comments mainly focus only on the "poor service" in the lower set. As a result, the topics of negative comments in the lower set become more focused than those in the upper set. This observation reasonably explains the increase of intra-class similarity of negative polarity in iPeen's lower set; In RECI, while the positive news in the upper set of RECI (with partitioning bias value 0.1) covers a wide range of topics, the positive news in the lower set of RECI mostly focus on the indicators and rates which would be better if reduced, e.g., unemployment rate, land value increment tax rate, lending rate, overdue loans ratio, inheritance tax, etc. As a result, the narrow focus of topics raises the intra-class similarity of positive polarity in RECI's lower set.

To conclude, the phenomena we find in Section 3 actually reflect the shrinkage of topics in the less positively biased portion of data. Most topics have strong preferences for positive words. However, few specific topics still relatively prefer negative words, e.g., the "poor service" of restaurant. These topics are emphasized when we isolate the lower positively biased data, and thus decide in which opinion polarity we can observed the rise of intra-polarity similarity.

## 5 Partitioning Strategy for Sentiment Classification

Our analyses above reveal the increase of intra-polarity similarity in certain part of data, and thus shed light on sentiment classification. In this section, we propose a strategy to partition the data sets by bias value, and train another model for the data portion which has lower positivity bias. A set of experiments are run to determine how much better this strategy can achieve.

The goal of our sentiment classifier is to predict the opinion polarity of documents respectively in RECI and iPeen. The TF-IDF vector of each document is adopted as features, and the libSVM (Chang and Lin, 2011) with linear kernel is selected as our model. One fifth of data are randomly selected as the testing set, and the rest are the training set. Without loss of generality, we select a bias value $\beta$ for each corpus based on the document distributions and the trend of $S_T^*$ mentioned in Section 2. Both training and testing data are partitioned by this bias value. Two different models are trained on the upper and lower sets of training data, and then are evaluated on the corresponding subsets of testing data, respectively. For comparison, we also train a classifier with the whole training data. In the experiments, we explore all possible target polarities mentioned in the previous sections. The results are shown in TABLE 3(a) and 3(b). Note that besides evaluating our partition strategy in the upper and lower sets separately, we also merge the results of the two classifiers together (refer to the "Whole" column). The outputs of the original approach are also evaluated in the upper set, the lower set, and the whole sets, respectively. As a result, when classifying the target polarities which we found in FIGURE 1, our partition strategy significantly increases the F1-scores both of target and non-target polarities in the whole testing set of iPeen ($p < 0.01$) and RECI ($p < 0.01$). Note that each of our Partition classifier actually beats the Original classifier by using less training data. On the other hand, as expected, our Partition strategy does not outperform the Original approach when predicting the positive polarity in iPeen, which is not the opinion polarity we observed in Section 3.

| (a) RECI | Polarity | Strategy | Lower | Upper | Whole |
|---|---|---|---|---|---|
| | **Pos.** | Original | .646 | .846 | **.833** |
| | | Partition | .692 | .874 | **.858**$^{**}$ |
| | **Neg.** | Original | .789 | .692 | **.726** |
| | | Partition | .869 | .704 | **.761**$^{**}$ |
| | #Positive Docs. | | 191 | 1,227 | 1,418 |
| | #Negative Docs. | | 348 | 623 | 971 |

| (b) iPeen | Polarity | Strategy | Lower | Upper | Whole |
|---|---|---|---|---|---|
| | **Neg.** | Original | .333 | .342 | **.341** |
| | | Partition | .342 | .342 | **.342**$^{**}$ |
| | **non-Neg.** | Original | .811 | .927 | **.921** |
| | | Partition | .870 | .929 | **.926**$^{**}$ |
| | #Negative Docs. | | 260 | 1,314 | 1,574 |
| | #Non-negative Docs. | | 932 | 17,480 | 18,412 |

TABLE 3: The F1-Score of Sentiment Classification in
(a) RECI, $\beta = 0.25$ (b) iPeen, $\beta = 0.15$, $P_T$ = Negative (**: $p < 0.01$).

## Conclusion and perspectives

In this paper, we first provide a detailed study of the Pollyanna phenomena in various genres of Chinese. Then we focus on those documents which have less positivity bias. Through quantitative analysis, we reveal the obvious increase of average similarity in certain opinion polarity among these outlier documents; and through qualitative analyses, we draw insights to indicate that the increase could be caused by the concentration of topics. Finally, by taking advantage of the rise of intra-polarity similarity, we propose a partitioning strategy for sentiment classification and significantly improve the F1-score. Our goal is to build a robust automatic mechanism for sentiment modeling, and Pollyanna gives us a good clue about it.

## Acknowledgments

We would like to thank Carolyn P. Rosé, Brian MacWhinney, Shoou-I Yu, Kuen-Bang Hou (Favonia), and the anonymous reviewers for their valuable comments.

## References


Augustine, A. A., Mehl, M. R., and Larsen, R. J.. (2011). A Positivity Bias in Written and Spoken English and Its Moderation by Personality and Gender. Social Psychological and Personality Science, 2(5): 508-515.

Bolasco, S. and della Ratta-Rinaldi, F.. (2004). Experiments on Semantic Categorisation of Texts: Analysis of Positive and Negative Dimension. In the 7es Journées internationales *d'Analyse statistique des Données Textuelles*, pages 202-210, Louvain La Neuve, Belgium.

Boucher, J. and Osgood, C. E.. (1969). The Pollyanna Hypothesis. Journal of Verbal Learning and Behavior, 8(1): 1-8.

Brooke, J.. (2009). A Semantic Approach to Automated Text Sentiment Analysis (Master's thesis). Simon Fraser University, British Columbia, Canada.

Brooke, J., Tofiloski, M., and Taboada M.. (2009). Cross-Linguistic Sentiment Analysis: From English to Spanish. In The International Conference of Recent Advances in Natural Language Processing (RANLP 2009), pages 50-54, Borovets, Bulgaria.

Chang, C.-C. and Lin, C.-J.. (2011). LIBSVM: A Library for Support Vector Machines. ACM Transactions on Intelligent Systems and Technology, 2(27): 1-27. Software available at http://www.csie.ntu.edu.tw/~cjlin/libsvm

Chin, Y.-L.. (2010). A Review and Discussion of Real Estate Cycle Indicators Analysis and Publication Method. Research Project Report. Architecture and Building Research Institute, Ministry of the Interior, Taiwan.

Garcia, D., Garas, A., and Schweitzer, F.. (2012). Positive Words Carry Less Information than Negative Words. EPJ Data Science 2012, 1(3).

Johnson, R. C., Thomson, C. W., and Frincke, G.. (1960). Word Values, Word Frequency, and Visual Duration Thresholds. Psychological Review, Vol. 67(5): 332-342.

Kennedy, A. and Inkpen, D.. (2006). Sentiment Classification of Movie and Product Reviews Using Contextual Valence Shifters. Computational Intelligence, 22(2): 110-125.

Kloumann, I. M., Danforth, C. M., Harris, K. D., Bliss, C. A., and Dodds, P. S.. (2012). Positivity of the English Language. PLoS ONE, 7(1): e29484.

Ku, L.-W. and Chen, H.-H.. (2007). Mining Opinions from the Web: Beyond Relevance Retrieval. Journal of American Society for Information Science and Technology, 58(12): 1838-1850.

Mohammad, S., Dunne, C., and Dorr, B.. (2009). Generating High-Coverage Semantic Orientation Lexicons from Overtly Marked Words and a Thesaurus. In The 2009 Conference on Empirical Methods in Natural Language Processing (EMNLP 2009), pages 599-608, Singapore.

Palmer, M., Chiou, F.-D., Xue, N., and Lee, T.-K.. (2005). Chinese Treebank 5.1. The LDC Corpus Catalog LDC2005T01U01.

Porter, E. H. (1913). Pollyanna. Boston, MA: L. C. Page.

Rozin, P., Berman, L., and Royzman, E.. (2010). Biases in Use of Positive and Negative Words Across Twenty Natural Languages. Cognition and Emotion, 24(3): 536-548.

Seki, Y., Evans, D. K., Ku, L.-W., Sun, L., Chen, H.-H., and Kando, N.. (2008). Overview of Multilingual Opinion Analysis Task at NTCIR-7. In The 7th NTCIR Workshop, pages 185-203, Tokyo, Japan.

Suitner, C. and Maass, A.. (2008). The Role of Valence in the Perception of Agency and Communion. European Journal of Social Psychology, 38(7): 1073-1082.

Taboada, M., Brooke, J., and Stede M.. (2009). Genre-Based Paragraph Classification for Sentiment Analysis. In The 10th Annual Meeting of the Special Interest Group in Discourse and Dialogue (SIGDIAL 2009), page 62-70, Queen Mary University of London, UK.

Taboada, M., Brooke, J., Tofiloski, M., Voll, K., and Stede, M.. (2011). Lexicon-Based Methods for Sentiment Analysis. Computational Linguistics, 37(2): 267-307.

Wang, H.. (1986). Modern Chinese Frequency Dictionary. Beijing, China: Beijing Language Institute Press.

Zajonc, R. B.. (1968). Attitudinal Effects of Mere Exposure. Journal of Personality and Social Psychology Monograph Supplement, 9(2): 1-27.

Zou, S.. (2004). On Positive and Negative Senses / 积极意义和消极意义二题. Chasing the Truth: Some Thoughts on Chinese Grammar Issues / 求真集:对汉语语法问题的一些思索. Beijing, Joint Publishing: 82-93.

# *Eating your own cooking:* automatically linking wordnet synsets of two languages

*Salil Joshi   Arindam Chatterjee   Arun Karthikeyan Karra*
*Pushpak Bhattacharyya*
(1) IBM Research India, Bangalore, India
(2) Symantec Labs, Pune, India
(3) Oracle Labs, Hyderabad, India
(4) CSE Department, IIT Bombay, Mumbai, India
saljoshi@in.ibm.com, arindam.chatterjee23@gmail.com,
arun.karthikeyan.arun@gmail.com, pb@cse.iitb.ac.in

## ABSTRACT
Linked wordnets are invaluable linked lexical resources. Wordnet linking involves matching a particular synset (concept) in one wordnet to a synset in another wordnet. We have developed an automatic wordnet linking system that is divided into a number of stages. Starting with a synset in the first language (also referred to as the source language), our algorithm generates a list of candidate synsets in the second language (also referred to as the target language). In consecutive stages, a heuristic is used to prune and rank this list. The winner synset is then chosen as the linkage for the source synset. The candidate synsets are generated using a bilingual dictionary (BiDict). Further, the earlier heuristics which we developed used BiDict to rank these candidate synsets. However, development of a BiDict is cumbersome and requires human labor. Furthermore, in several cases sparsity of the BiDict handicaps the ranking algorithm to a great extent. We have thus devised heuristics to eliminate the requirement of BiDict during the ranking process by using the already linked synsets. Once sufficient number of linked synsets are available, these heuristics outperform our heuristics which use a BiDict. These heuristics are based on observations made from linking techniques applied by lexicographers. Our wordnet linking system can be used for any pair of languages, given either a BiDict or sufficient number of already linked synsets. The interface of the system is easy to comprehend and use. In this paper, we present this interface along with the developed heuristics.

KEYWORDS: Wordnet Linking, Bilingual Dictionary, Resource reuse for linking.

# 1 Introduction

Wordnet Linking, as the name suggests, is the process of linking wordnet of one language to another. Efforts towards mapping synsets across wordnets have been going on for a while in various parts of the world. EuroWordNet (Vossen and Letteren, 1997) is one of the projects which is attempting to link wordnets across various European languages. Another effort towards wordnet linking can be found in the MultiWordNet (Pianta et al., 2002), aligning the Italian and the English language wordnets. Our linking process can be used for any pair of languages. Currently, we support linking for *Hindi to English*. Our wordnet linking system is automatic and involves deployment of heuristics to find the correct linkage. We initially developed BiDict (Bilingual Dictionary) based heuristics for ranking. The BiDict is a dictionary, mapping words from the source language to the target language. The usage of the such a dictionary has certain bottlenecks as follows:

1. **Human effort:** The development of the BiDict is cumbersome and requires considerable human efforts.
2. **Sparsity:** The BiDict is typically sparse in nature and hence in several cases the ranking results are error prone.
3. **Morphological issues:** The bilingual dictionary entries are categorized by their respective parts of speech. Hence in quite a few cases, the word forms differ in their morphology, which affects the performance of the system as the word form given in the synset and that in the dictionary do not match.

Due to the issues mentioned above, we had to find an alternative way of ranking the candidate synsets without using the BiDict. We decided to *eat our own cooking*. We devised a strategy to use the already linked synsets for this purpose. The heuristics based on this strategy perform better than the BiDict based heuristics. In our wordnet linking system, the user can select a source language (Hindi) synset which goes as input into the system, along with the desired heuristic (both with and without the usage of the BiDict), which is again opted by the user. The system outputs the top-5 candidate target language synsets, ranked by the chosen heuristic, which can be used for linking purposes.

The key features of the system are as follows:

1. **Minimized dependency on dictionary:** The system uses heuristics which use the information from already linked synsets, to generate candidate synsets of the target language. Since the bilingual dictionary has numerous bottlenecks in the process of pruning the candidate synsets, the tool provides an option of ranking the candidate synsets without such a knowledge source. This is beneficial for language pairs, where an efficient bilingual dictionary is not available that maps synsets, and a reasonable number of linked synsets are available.
2. **User friendliness:** Our system interface provides a nice visual experience. The design of the interface makes the operation of the interface completely clear to the end user.
3. **System independence:** The system is independent of the web browser and the operating system it is used on. Since the business logic is written in Java, the system can be easily ported on another machine.
4. **Ease of configuration:** The wordnets, BiDict and already linked synsets can be provided to the system through a simple change in the configuration. This is particularly useful in porting the system for wordnet linking for a different pair of languages.
5. **Easily interpretable output:** Our interface is designed in such a way that the user can easily understand the linking data being displayed. When the candidate synsets of the target language are exhibited, the user can click on each candidate, to view the details of the synsets

*i.e.,* each portion of the candidate synset (*viz.* synset id, gloss, example, *etc.*), is displayed separately, making the output easily comprehensible.

This paper is organized as follows. Section 2 lays down the system architecture of our wordnet linking system, followed by section 3 describing the heuristics employed for ranking candidate synsets. In section 4 we describe the operation of the tool, followed by section 5 comparing the results of the heuristics against the baseline. We conclude the paper with section 6.

## 2 System Architecture

Figure 1 shows the basic architecture of the model adopted to achieve linking of a Hindi synset with an English synset. Given a Hindi synset, the gloss, examples and synonymous words are parsed depending on the parts-of-speech (POS) and a bag of words are obtained. This bag of Hindi words are then translated to English using a Hindi-English bilingual dictionary. Using these translated bag of words and the English WordNet, candidate English synsets are selected. Now on each of these candidate synsets, the heuristics are applied and the synset to be linked in the target language is generated.

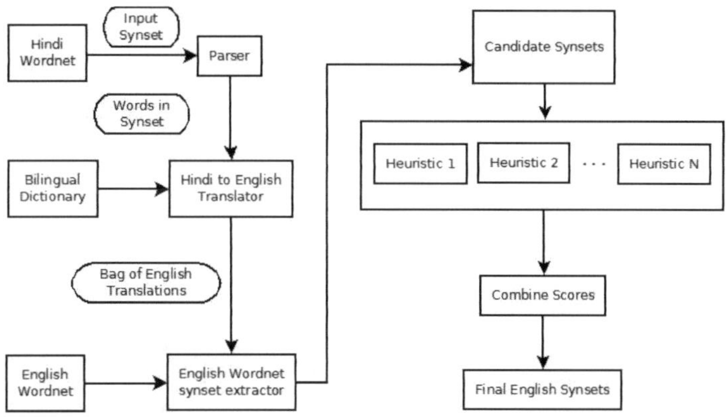


Figure 1: Hindi-English wordnet linking system architecture

## 3 Heuristics

As mentioned earlier, we have a set of heuristics for performing wordnet linking. Our initial heuristics made use of a bilingual dictionary, but due to the problems mentioned earlier, the results were error prone. We later developed heuristics which do not require any such dictionary for ranking purposes and yet provide comparable results in presence of already linked synsets. We present both types of heuristics in this section, each can be used under certain scenarios. Throughout this description, we follow the standard definitions for hypernym, hyponym, gloss, concept and synset (Fellbaum, 1998)

### 3.1 Heuristics based on Bilingual Dictionary

The heuristics that use the BiDict for ranking candidate synsets are as follows. These heuristics are particularly helpful in presence of a good quality BiDict:

1. **Monosemous Word Heuristic**- In this heuristic, the monosemous words in the source synset are only considered for obtaining the candidate synsets. First the translations of the monosemous words are obtained using the bilingual dictionary, then synsets containing these translations are chosen as candidate synsets.

2. **Single Translation Heuristic**- This heuristic is similar to the monosemous word heuristic. Here only those words which have single translations according to the bilingual dictionary are considered in obtaining the candidate synsets.
3. **Hyponymy/Hypernymy Word-bag Heuristics**- These heuristics rank candidates by finding the similarity of synset words of the hyponym/hypernym respectively, of the source synset with the candidate target synsets.
4. **Gloss/Synset/Concept Word-bag Heuristic**- These heuristics score the candidates based on the similarity between the words in the gloss or synset or concept respectively, on source and target sides.
5. **Synset/Concept Back Translation Heuristic**- These heuristics make use of synset or concept word translations respectively, from source to target language and vice versa. The candidates are ranked based on the combined score.

## 3.2 Heuristics based on already Linked Synsets

The primary aim of our work was to build a comprehensive, accurate and user friendly tool for wordnet linking. Since a low quality BiDict lowers the ranking performance of the system, we resorted to a strategy that avoids the usage of such a knowledge source for ranking, and makes use of the already linked synsets. The chief design strategy here was to find the closest synset from the existing set of linked synsets, to the synset in source language to be linked. The metric of *closeness* has been defined differently in different heuristics. These heuristics are particularly helpful in presence of sufficient number of already linked synsets.

### 3.2.1 Closest Common Synset Word-bag Heuristic

This heuristic uses the maximum intersection of the synset word-bags of the source synset to be linked and already linked synsets. Once this synset is found, its corresponding link on the target side is found. The candidate synsets are ranked based on the degree of intersection of synset words, with this synset in the target language. The heuristic score for each target language candidate synset is calculated follows:

$Score = |Target_{candidateSynsetWords} \cap Target_{closestSynsetWords}|$

### 3.2.2 Closest Common Concept Word-bag Heuristic

This heuristic uses the maximum intersection of the concept word-bags of the source synset to be linked and already linked synsets. It is similar to the Closest Common Synset Word-bag Heuristic, in operation. It uses the intersection of the concept word-bags instead of synset word-bags. Hence the heuristic score for each target language candidate synset is as follows:

$Score = |Target_{candidateConceptWords} \cap Target_{closestConceptWords}|$

### 3.2.3 Closest Hypernym Synset Heuristic

The total number of linked synsets from Hindi to English available is 24,124[1], which are manually inspected by our lexicographers. Among these 24,124 synsets, 18,441 (76.443%) are *nouns*. Hence a heuristic which performs well on nouns was desirable, as it would boost the accuracy of the entire system. More importantly, a strategy for finding similarity between the source language synset to be linked and the linked set of synsets was semantic relations available within the wordnet framework.

[1]as of June, 2012

Theoretically, the wordnet linking process should follow the hypernymy hierarchy of the source and target wordnets *i.e.,* if a synset *A* on source side is linked to synset *B* on target side, correspondingly synset *C* which is a hyponym of *A* in the source language wordnet should be linked to a hyponym of *B* on the target side. The heuristic score for each target language candidate synset can be calculated as follows:

$$Score = Distance_{hypernymy}(Target_{candidateSynset}, Target_{closestHypernym})$$

# 4 Interface Design

To support various web browsers on different operating systems, we have designed the web interface using standard open technologies. The interface runs using PHP5[2] on the server side, and for the GUI, we have used a javascript framework *viz.*, ExtJS v4.0[3] which provides a neat and aesthetic display to the user. Figure 2 shows the system interface. The main screen is divided into

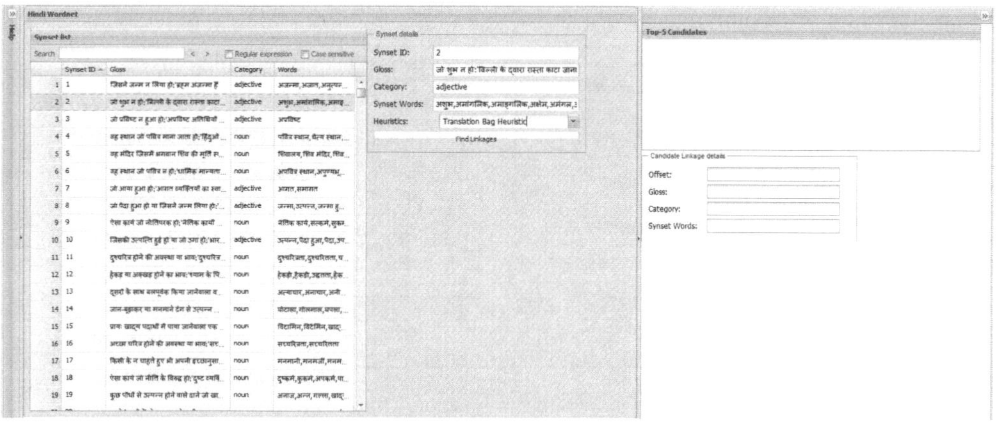

Figure 2: Screen-shot showing the main interface of the system

neatly arranged panels, which can be collapsed, in case if the monitor resolution can not display the complete interface. The screen-shot shows that currently the *Help* panel on the left is in collapsed form. Each synset in the list displays the Synset ID, gloss, POS category and the constituent words fetched from Hindi Wordnet. Selecting a row in this list automatically populates the synset details in the form adjacent to the grid. The list of synsets can be searched for a particular synset.

Once a source (Hindi) synset is chosen, the user simply needs to select a heuristic and submit the form. Based on the input synset and the heuristic, the system computes the candidate synsets, ranks them and returns top-5 candidates to the user. The outcome of this process is shown in figure 3.

# 5 Empirical evaluation

The system was tested on a total of 24,124 linked synsets manually inspected by our lexicographers. The results are shown in Table 1. We present the results for all the heuristics developed by us. Rows 1 to 9 summarize the performance of BiDict based heuristics, and rows 10 to 12 show the results obtained with heuristics which make use of already linked synsets. Row 13 compares the performance of all the heuristics against the random baseline, in which a random candidate synset is assigned as the linked synset. Clearly, the performance of heuristics is improved when they make use of already linked synsets for linking new synsets.

[2]`http://php.net/downloads.php`

[3]`http://www.sencha.com/products/extjs/`

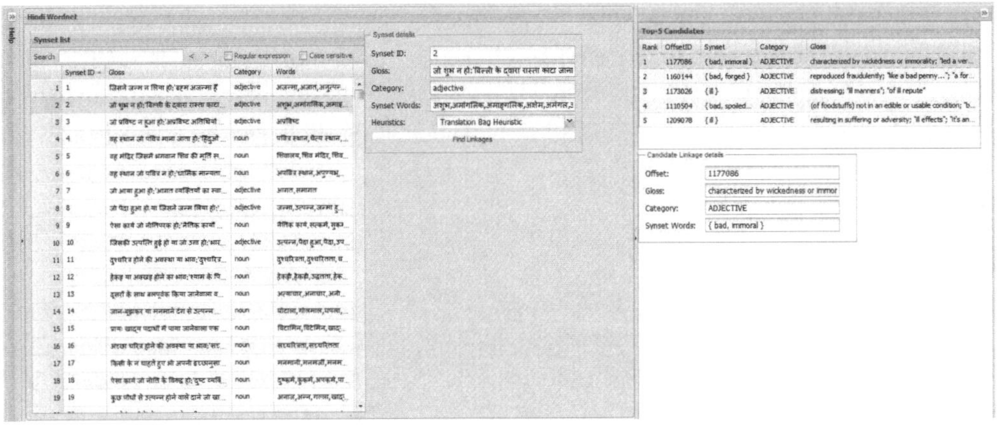

Figure 3: System interface showing the outcome of the linking process

| Heuristic | Coverage | Accuracy |
|---|---|---|
| Monosemous Word | 6644 (27.541 %) | 4194 (63.131 %) |
| Single Translation | 6100 (25.282 %) | 3458 (56.692 %) |
| Gloss Word-bag | 11298 (46.833 %) | 5241 (46.393 %) |
| Hypernymy Word-bag | 12127 (50.269 %) | 5041 (41.570 %) |
| Hyponymy Word-bag | 12127 (50.269 %) | 5712 (47.108 %) |
| Synset Word-bag | 12127 (50.269 %) | 6068 (50.044 %) |
| Concept Word-bag | 11298 (46.833 %) | 5731 (50.737 %) |
| Synset Back Translation | 12127 (50.269 %) | 6133 (50.574 %) |
| Concept Back Translation | 12127 (50.269 %) | 6312 (52.052 %) |
| Closest Hypernym Synset | 12127 (50.269 %) | 9671 (79.758 %) |
| Closest Common Synset Word-bag | 12127 (50.269 %) | 9032 (74.482 %) |
| Closest Common Concept Word-bag | 12127 (50.269 %) | 6694 (55.203 %) |
| Random Baseline | 12127 (54.071 %) | 3024 (24.936 %) |
| *Total number of synsets being mapped is 24,124* | | |
| *Average cardinality of candidate English synsets per Hindi synset is* ***25*** | | |

Table 1: System Performance for different heuristics and random baseline

# 6 Conclusion

In this work, we presented a tool for wordnet linking which uses heuristic based approach. The necessity of a BiDict for ranking process was circumvented by designing new heuristics which made use of the already linked set of synsets from source to target languages. These heuristics perform at par with the heuristics based on the BiDict. Once quality linked data between two languages is available, tasks like WSD, Machine Translation, Cross-lingual Information Retrieval, *etc.*, can benefit from it. Our on-line system interface is simple yet user-friendly and allows the user to make use of several linking heuristics which we have developed. The system can be easily adapted for a new pair of languages by simply supplying the language wordnets along with either a bilingual dictionary or already linked synsets across the two languages.

In the future, we would like to support more languages. We would also like to provide the users a facility of adding new heuristics to our system for better comparison.

## References


Fellbaum, C. (1998). *WordNet: An Electronic Lexical Database.*

Pianta, E., Bentivogli, L., and Girardi, C. (2002). Multiwordnet: developing an aligned multilingual database. In *Proceedings of the First International Conference on Global WordNet.*

Vossen, P. and Letteren, C. C. (1997). Eurowordnet: a multilingual database for information retrieval. In *In: Proceedings of the DELOS workshop on Cross-language Information Retrieval*, pages 5–7.

# *I Can Sense It:* a comprehensive online system for WSD

*Salil Joshi Mitesh M. Khapra Pushpak Bhattacharyya*
(1) IBM Research India, Bangalore, India
(2) IBM Research India, Bangalore, India
(3) CSE Department, IIT Bombay, Mumbai, India
`saljoshi@in.ibm.com, mikhapra@in.ibm.com, pb@cse.iitb.ac.in`

## Abstract
We have developed an online interface for running all the current state-of-the-art algorithms for WSD. This is motivated by the fact that exhaustive comparison of a new Word Sense Disambiguation (WSD) algorithm with existing state-of-the-art algorithms is a tedious task. This impediment is due to one of the following reasons: (1) the source code of the earlier approach is not available and there is a considerable overhead in implementing it or (2) the source code/binary is available but there is some overhead in using it due to system requirements, portability issues, customization issues and software dependencies. A simple tool which has no overhead for the user and has minimal system requirements would greatly benefit the researchers. Our system currently supports 3 languages, *viz.*, English, Hindi and Marathi, and requires only a web-browser to run. To demonstrate the usability of our system, we compare the performance of current state-of-the-art algorithms on 3 publicly available datasets.

Keywords: WSD System.

*Proceedings of COLING 2012: Demonstration Papers*, pages 247–254,
COLING 2012, Mumbai, December 2012.

## 1 Introduction

Several WSD algorithms have been proposed in the past ranging from knowledge based to unsupervised to supervised methods. These algorithms have their own merits and demerits, and hence it is desirable to compare a new algorithm with all of these to put the results in the right perspective. Even when the implementations of these algorithms are publicly available, running them can be cumbersome as it involves the following tedious steps:

1. Resolving portability issues of operating systems (*e.g.*, linux/windows)
2. Adhering to specific input/output formats
3. Installation issues involving software dependencies
4. Run-time issues pertaining to system requirements

The above process needs to be repeated for every algorithm that the user wants to compare her/his system with. Further, in many cases, there is no publicly available implementation of the algorithm, in which case the user has to bear significant overhead of re-implementing these algorithms.

To circumvent the above problems and to ensure ease of use, we have developed an online system, which allows the user to run several state-of-the-art algorithms. There is no overhead for the user, all (s)he needs is a web browser and the input file which may be sense tagged. Further, we also make provision for the developers of the new algorithms to integrate their algorithm in our system. This can be done by implementing a java interface exposed by us and upload the class file on our web-page.

Some of the important aspects of our system are as follows:

1. **Collection of several approaches** - Users can obtain results for state-of-the-art approaches like IMS (Zhong and Ng, 2010), PPR (Agirre et al., 2009), knowledge based approaches (Patwardhan et al., 2005) etc, for an easy comparison of all approaches on a single dataset.
2. **Parallel execution of several algorithms** - The user can choose to run multiple algorithms in parallel, over the same dataset. The associated overhead of scheduling jobs and managing system resources is handled by the server and the user is exempted of these hassles.
3. **Minimum supervision** - After submitting his/her request, the end user can continue with their work without having to constantly monitor the task. Our interface notifies the user when the results are available. Once the users is notified, (s)he needs to download a single zip file which contains all the output files.
4. **User Friendly** - Currently available systems are mostly without a Graphical User Interface (GUI). Our interface is visually aesthetic, can be viewed on different screen resolutions, and is very easy to use.
5. **Easy interpretability of the output** - Our interface provides an option of viewing the output files online where the disambiguated words are shown along with the gloss of the sense present in the wordnets. Most of the available tools only generate the results with the sense offsets, which are machine readable, but make the manual analysis difficult.
6. **Evaluation using standard metrics** - Our system evaluates all the algorithms selected by the user using standard evaluation metrics (precision, recall and F-score). This allows the user to easily compare the performance of the selected algorithms.
7. **Unifies the input/output formats** - Existing systems use non-standard input/output formats, which results in an additional burden of converting the dataset in the required formats. Our system supports different types of input file formats so that less conversions are required while providing the inputs. Further, the outputs are provided in a format compatible with UKB format, which can be easily parsed.

8. **Plug-and-play design** - If an implementation of a new approach is provided, it can be easily plugged into the system. Apart from exposing his/her algorithm to the public, and thereby increasing its visibility/use, this also allows the user to outsource her/his own computational load.

In this system demonstration, we explain the system which powers our interface. The paper is organized as follows: We describe the existing, publicly available systems in section 2. In section 3 we provide technical details about our system. Section 4 summarizes the evaluation results on 3 standard datasets. Section 5 concludes the paper presenting the salient points of our system and some future enhancements for our system.

## 2 Related Work

There are a few algorithms for which the implementation is publicly available. These include UKB (Agirre et al., 2009), IMS (Zhong and Ng, 2010), SenseLearner (Mihalcea and Csomai, 2005) and SenseRelate (Patwardhan et al., 2005). However, most of these have one or more of the overheads listed above. For example, UKB is currently available only for linux platforms. Further, the user needs to download and install these systems separately and run them on her/his machine which increases the computational cost. SenseLearner has an online interface, but in contrast to our system, it provides only a single algorithm and does not enable the user to compare the performance of different algorithms.

Our system is a one-stop-shop for comparing several algorithms (including UKB, IMS and SenseRelate) with minimum computational and manual overhead for the user. We would like to mention that internally our system uses the implementations provided by UKB, IMS and SenseRelate and hence it would provide the same results as obtained by independently downloading and using these systems. Apart from UKB, IMS and SenseRelate, our system also provides an implementation for McCarthy's approach (Koeling and McCarthy, 2007) and IWSD (Khapra et al., 2010).

## 3 System Details

Figure 1 shows the main interface of our system. We first provide an overview of the system introducing the inputs which it expects followed by explaining the online output viewer, which is an interesting feature of our system. We also provide details about the mechanism with which new algorithms can be easily added to the system. Kindly refer to the figure while reading this section.

### 3.1 Interface Design

To support various web browsers on different operating systems, we have designed the web interface using standard open technologies. The interface runs using PHP5[1] on the server side, and for the GUI, we have used a javascript framework *viz.*, ExtJS v4.0[2] which provides a neat and aesthetic display to the user.

### 3.2 User input

In order to use the system interface, the user needs to provide the following inputs:

1. **Language**: The language of the corpus file(s) for which the WSD algorithm needs to run. As

[1]http://php.net/downloads.php
[2]http://www.sencha.com/products/extjs/

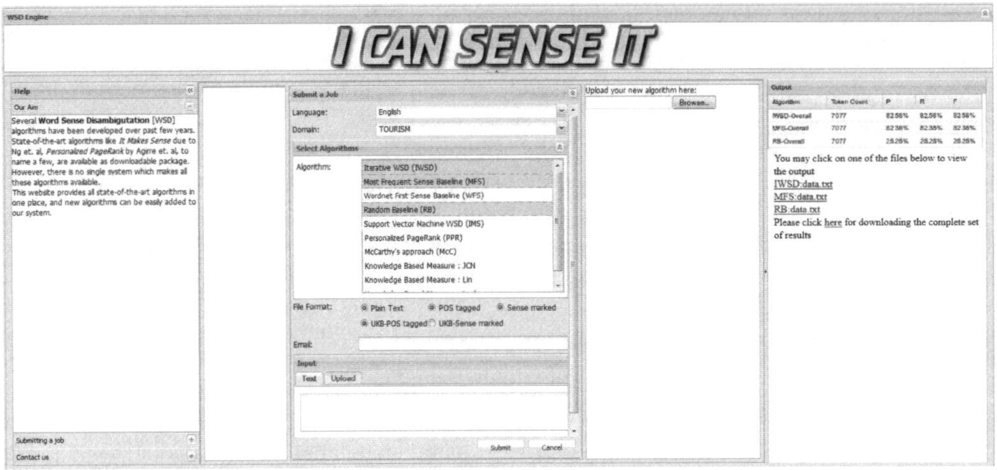


Figure 1: screen-shot of the online interface showing the results of a job along with the links to view the output files in our online output viewer

of now, we provide the user an option of selecting between *English*, *Hindi* and *Marathi* since we have the training datasets and morphological analyzers available for these languages.

2. **Domain**: Some of the state-of-the-art algorithms are domain specific, and in general, the WSD systems show better performance when the domain of the experiment is known in advance. Apart from an option of *Tourism* and *Health* domains for the languages mentioned above, we also support *News* domain for *Hindi*, and *SemCor* domain for *English*.
3. **Algorithms to be run**: The user can select one or more from the following:
   - IWSD (Iterative WSD) - A supervised WSD algorithm by (Khapra et al., 2010)
   - IMS (It Makes Sense) - An SVM based approach by (Zhong and Ng, 2010)
   - PPR (Personalized Page Rank) - A knowledge based approach by (Agirre et al., 2009)
   - McCarthy's approach - An unsupervised state-of-the-art algorithm by (Koeling and McCarthy, 2007)
   - Knowledge based measures - SenseRelate (Patwardhan et al., 2005) supports several knowledge based measures for WSD. We support 3 measures, *viz.*, Lesk, Lin and JCN out of these.
   - RB (Random Baseline)
   - WFS (Wordnet First Sense Baseline)
   - MFS (Most Frequent Sense Baseline)
4. **Input file format**: In the most basic form, the user can simply upload a plain text file containing one sentence per line. However, most algorithms perform better if the data is POS tagged. Our system does not perform POS tagging. Hence, we allow the user to upload POS tagged data in which each sentence is represented in the following format:
   $word_1\_<pos_1>\ word_2\_<pos_2> \cdots\ word_n\_<pos_n>$
   where $<pos_1>$, $<pos_2>$, *etc.*, are the POS tags of the respective words, and can take one of the 4 values, 1: Noun:, 2: Verb, 3: Adverb, 4: Adjective (since currently available wordnets support only these POS tags). If the user has sense marked gold data and wants to evaluate the performance of different algorithms on this data, then he/she can submit the input in the following format:
   $word_1\_<pos_1><offset_1>\ word_2\_<pos_2><offset_2> \cdots\ word_n\_<pos_n><offset_n>$
   where $<offset_1>$, $<offset_2>$, *etc.*, are the wordnet sense offsets of the respective words.

For processing these formats, our system requires a morphological analyzer or stemmer from the respective language. The gold data sense offsets will be compared against the outcome of the algorithm. Our algorithms use Princeton WordNet v2.1 for English. In addition to these simple formats, we also provide support to the following file format which is compatible with UKB:
$word_1$#<$roots_1$>#<$pos_1$>#<index>#<$offset_1$> $word_2$#<$roots_2$>#<$pos_2$>#<index># <$offset_2$> $\cdots$ $word_n$#<$roots_n$>#<$pos_n$>#<index>#<$offset_n$>
where <$roots_1$>, <$roots_2$>, *etc.*, represent morphological roots of the respective words. <index> represents the position of the word in the sentence and is stored as $w_1$, $w_2$ and so on. Please note that this format requires the input data to be at least POS tagged and optionally sense annotated. In case if the data is not sense annotated, the <$offset$> field will be represented with '1' for the words which are to be disambiguated and 0 otherwise. The output files generated by our system follow this format.

5. **E-mail address**: Depending on the size of the input and the number/type of algorithms chosen, the system will take some time to compute the results. For ease of use, an e-mail is sent to the user, once the computation is done. This email specifies a link from where (s)he will be able to download all the results.
6. **Input (Data)**: The user can either type the text to be disambiguated in the text box provided on the submission form, or (s)he can choose to upload a file containing the text. The uploaded file can be a zipped directory, in which case, it will be extracted on the server side, and all the constituent files will be used as the input dataset for running the algorithm.

## 3.3 Online output viewer

Our system generates the output files in UKB format as stated earlier. This output can be easily parsed, however, it is not suitable for manual analysis. Our interface provides the users with a facility of viewing the output online, where the sense tags are accompanied with the sense gloss and examples as available in the wordnet. This enables the user to easily comprehend the output. Figure 2 shows a screen-shot of the online output viewer. The interface also provides an *output* pane, where the results of the job are summarized, and a link to the results is provided, so that the user can download them. The same link is also sent to the user to the specified e-mail address.

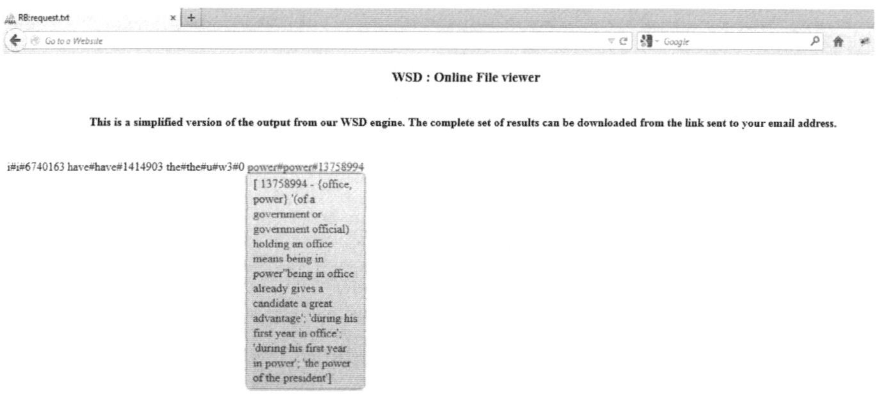


Figure 2: screen-shot of the online interface showing the online output viewer

### 3.4 Integration of new algorithms

As mentioned earlier, our system can integrate new algorithms on-the-fly. The developers who have a new algorithm, and wish to make it a part of our system, can submit their algorithms online, and such algorithms automatically get added to our system when uploaded.

Currently, our system can not automatically handle the software dependencies exhibited by the new algorithms, if any. In such cases, the new algorithm will not be useful to end users. To prevent this, the developers of the new algorithm can contact us and get the dependencies fixed. Our system runs on a linux based server, and the dependencies must be in the form of publicly available software packages compatible with linux systems.

The interaction between our system and the new algorithm will be in form a shell script, the details of which are provided on our web interface[3]. This shell script can, in turn, call its own resources, binaries and other shell scripts to read the input text files provided in specific format, and produce the output text files in specific format. The detailed instructions for integration, along with the sample text files, can also be accessed from our web interface.

## 4 Empirical evaluation

To demonstrate the use of our system, we have evaluated the performance of all the algorithms on 3 standard datasets[4]. The results are summarized in table 1. There are several knowledge based measures which SenseRelate supports. We show the results for a representative measure, *viz.*, Lesk (KB-Lesk).

| Algorithm | Tourism | | | Health | | | SemCor | | |
|---|---|---|---|---|---|---|---|---|---|
| | P% | R% | F% | P% | R% | F% | P% | R% | F% |
| **IWSD** | 77.00 | 76.66 | 76.83 | 78.78 | 78.42 | 78.60 | 67.42 | 66.27 | 66.82 |
| **PPR** | 53.10 | 53.10 | 53.10 | 51.10 | 51.10 | 51.10 | 50.42 | 50.42 | 50.42 |
| **IMS** | 78.82 | 78.76 | 78.79 | 79.64 | 79.59 | 79.61 | 68.38 | 67.82 | 68.02 |
| **McCarthy's approach** | 51.85 | 49.32 | 50.55 | N/A | N/A | N/A | N/A | N/A | N/A |
| **RB** | 25.50 | 25.50 | 25.50 | 24.61 | 24.61 | 24.61 | 21.08 | 21.08 | 21.08 |
| **WFS** | 62.15 | 62.15 | 62.15 | 64.67 | 64.67 | 64.67 | 63.49 | 63.49 | 63.49 |
| **MFS** | 77.60 | 75.2 | 76.38 | 79.43 | 76.98 | 78.19 | 67.75 | 65.87 | 66.57 |
| **KB-Lesk** | 50.86 | 50.84 | 50.85 | 51.80 | 51.78 | 51.79 | 39.59 | 39.24 | 39.41 |

Table 1: Precision, Recall and F-scores for various algorithms supported by our system

## 5 Conclusion

In this paper, we have described a system which allows for easy comparison of several state-of-the-art WSD systems. Since our system is an online system, it minimizes the overhead on the end user by eliminating the installation issues. Our system only depends on a morphological analyzer for the input data. Further, since all the computation takes place on our server, it drastically reduces the system requirements and computational efforts for the end user. The interface to the system is extremely user friendly, aesthetic and supports multiple input file formats. New algorithms can be integrated easily with our system with minimal additional efforts on part of the developer. The system also provides an online results viewer which is useful for manual analysis as it provides the sense gloss and examples for each disambiguated word.

In the future, we would like our system to support more and more languages.

[3] http://www.cfilt.iitb.ac.in/wsd-demo

[4] http://www.cfilt.iitb.ac.in/wsd/annotated_corpus

## References


Agirre, E., Lacalle, O. L. D., and Soroa, A. (2009). Knowledge-based wsd on specific domains: Performing better than generic supervised wsd. In *In Proceedings of IJCAI*.

Khapra, M., Shah, S., Kedia, P., and Bhattacharyya, P. (2010). Domain-specific word sense disambiguation combining corpus basedand wordnet based parameters. In *Proc. of GWC*, volume 10.

Koeling, R. and McCarthy, D. (2007). Sussx: Wsd using automatically acquired predominant senses. In *Proceedings of ACL/SIGLEX SemEval*, pages 314–317.

Mihalcea, R. and Csomai, A. (2005). Senselearner: Word sense disambiguation for all words in unrestricted text. In *Proceedings of the ACL 2005 on Interactive poster and demonstration sessions*, pages 53–56. Association for Computational Linguistics.

Patwardhan, S., Banerjee, S., and Pedersen, T. (2005). Senserelate:: Targetword: a generalized framework for word sense disambiguation. In *Proceedings of the ACL 2005 on Interactive poster and demonstration sessions*, pages 73–76. Association for Computational Linguistics.

Zhong, Z. and Ng, H. (2010). It makes sense: A wide-coverage word sense disambiguation system for free text. In *Proceedings of the ACL 2010 System Demonstrations*, pages 78–83. Association for Computational Linguistics.

# Collaborative computer-assisted translation applied to pedagogical documents and literary works

*Ruslan KALITVIANSKI, Christian BOITET, Valérie BELLYNCK*
GETALP-LIG, 41, rue des Mathématiques,
38400 St Martin d'Hères, FRANCE
ruslan.kalitvianski@imag.fr, christian.boitet@imag.fr,
valerie.bellynck@imag.fr

ABSTRACT

This paper showcases three applications of GETALP's iMAG (Interactive Multilingual Access Gateway) technology. IMAGs allow internet users to navigate a selected website in the language of their choice (using machine translation), as well as to collaboratively and incrementally improve the translation through a web-based interface. One of GETALP's ongoing projects is MACAU (Multilingual Access and Contributive Appropriation for Universities), a platform that allows users to reuse existing pedagogical material to generate adaptive content. We demonstrate how student- and teacher-produced lecture notes can be translated into different languages in the context of MACAU, and show the same approach applied to textbooks and to literary works.

# Применение коллективного автоматизированого перевода к учебным материалам и литературным работам

РЕЗЮМЕ

Эта статья демонстрирует три применения технологии iMAG (Interactive Multilingual Access Gateway) лаборатории GETALP-LIG. IMAG-и позволяют Интернет-пользователям посещать избранный веб-сайт на желаемом языке благодаря машинному переводу, а так же постепенно коллективно улучшать перевод через веб-интерфейс. Один из текущих проектов GETALP - MACAU (Multilingual Access and Contributive Appropriation for Universities), платформа, позволяющая пользователям использовать существующие педагогические материалы, чтобы генерировать персонализированные уроки. Мы показываем, как конспекты студентов и учителей могут быть переведены на различные языки в контексте MACAU, и демонстрируем применение данного подхода к учебникам и литературным работам.

KEYWORDS : MACHINE TRANSLATION, COMPUTER-ASSISTED TRANSLATION, PEDAGOGICAL DOCUMENTS, INTERACTIVE MULTILINGUAL ACCESS GATEWAY, IMAG, COLLABORATIVE TRANSLATION, POST-EDITING.

КЛЮЧЕВЫЕ СЛОВА: МАШИННЫЙ ПЕРЕВОД, АВТОМАТИЗИРОВАНЫЙ ПЕРЕВОД, УЧЕБНЫИЕ МАТЕРИАЛЫ, IMAG, КОЛЛЕКТИВНЫЙ ПЕРЕВОД, ПОСТРЕДАКТИРОВАНИЕ..

# 1 Interactive Multilingual Access Gateways

An iMAG (interactive Multilingual Access Gateway) to a website is a web service that allows users to access the site in a language of their choice (by translating it with one or several machine translation engines) and to improve the translation by post-editing (Boitet et al, 2008).

When the user chooses to display the page in a new language, the textual segments of the page are substituted either by a new translation or, if the page has been translated before, by their best translation retrieved from the translation memory. The translation of a segment can be edited by hovering the cursor above the segment. This brings up a bubble containing the segment in the source language, an editing zone and a choice of a score to be assigned to the post-edited translation. Figures 1 and 2 show the interface of iMAG-COLING.

Figure 1: COLING 2012 website accessed in Japanese through iMAG-COLING

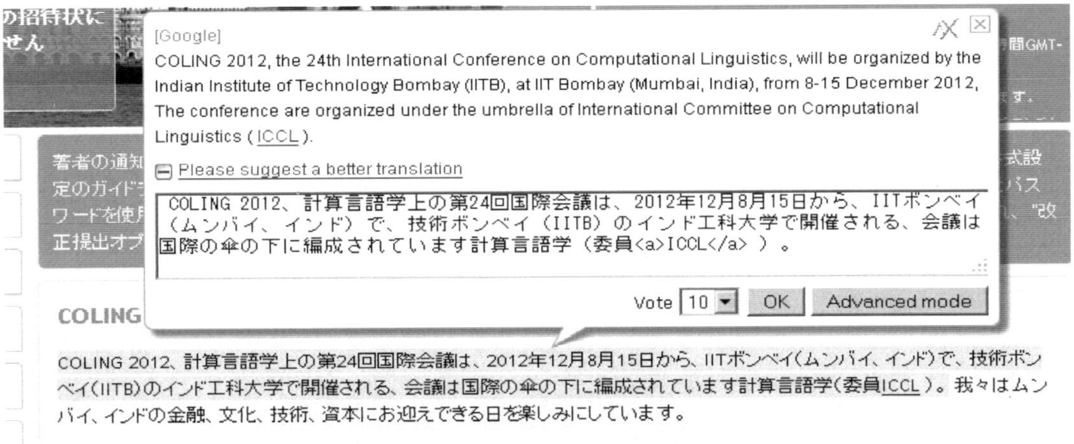


Figure 2: post-edition of the translation of a segment.

## 2 Translation of pedagogical content

One of our ongoing projects is MACAU (Multilingual Access and Contributive Appropriation for Universities), a platform that would allow its users to reuse existing pedagogical materials to improve them and generate pedagogical content that best fits their needs, given their preferences and their level of domain knowledge. This includes multilingualism, as well as choices of presentation, including topics, types of material and levels of abstraction.

IMAGs can be used by foreign students to access course content in their language and to collectively improve the translations when needed. A simple scenario within the context of MACAU would the following.

First, a set of documents is received. We can, for instance, consider a teacher-produced LaTeX file containing a course on computational complexity theory, and two MS Word documents, containing student-produced lecture notes.

These documents are converted to an iMAG-compatible format, which for the moment is html. In this example, we use HeVeA for the LaTeX → html conversion, and MS Word's built-in export tool. The resulting html documents can now be annotated with semantic information, allowing for later selective access and extraction. Annotations can indicate the level of abstraction of a section, its difficulty, pre-requisites, etc. Here, we use simple "span" tags to indicate the type of a section of the document (e.g. definition, example, illustration).

```
<P STYLE="margin-bottom: 0in">        = n² - 2 p (p+1) + n</P>
<P STYLE="margin-bottom: 0in"><BR>
</P>
<span class="macau" type="theorem">
<P STYLE="margin-bottom: 0in">   <U>Théorème</U> : Soit une MT
Z<SUB>k</SUB> à k bandes. Il existe une MT simple Z simulant <I>n</I>
pas de calcul de Z<SUB>k</SUB> par au plus <I>2n × (n + 2k + 1)</I>
pas de calcul de Z</P>
</span>
<P STYLE="margin-bottom: 0in"><BR>
</P>
```

Figure 3: semantic annotation of document sections.

The documents are then placed in a repository accessible to iMAG-MACAU that can be visited at http://service.aximag.fr//xwiki/bin/view/imag/macau-fr. Users can now navigate and post-edit the documents in different languages. Since iMAGs preserve the underlying html code of a page, the annotations are never lost and whatever content generated from these files using the semantic annotations, has its segments translated. We are currently developing tools that would allow reversible conversion in order to generate translations of documents in their initial formats.

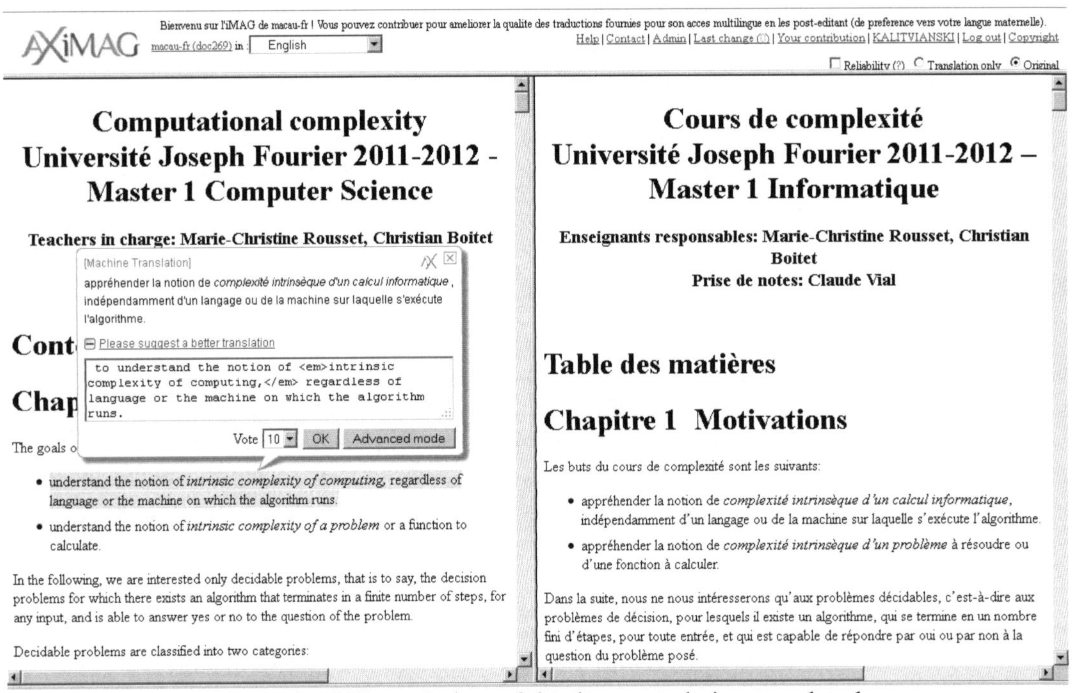


Figure 4: a bilingual view of the document being translated.

## 3 Translation of books

Many universities now release their educational materials free of charge, however they are usually unavailable in more than one or two languages, or available for a fee. IMAGs provide a rapid, convenient and cost-effective alternative for obtaining multilingual versions of educational materials such as textbooks that are converted into an iMAG-compatible format. As an example, readers are invited to visit the demonstration iMAG for the book "Bioelectromagnetism" by Jaakko Malmivuo and Robert Plonsey at http://service.aximag.fr//xwiki/bin/view/imag/BEMBOOK.

The use of volunteer workforce for the translation of literary works is a novel approach. Fig. 5 demonstrates a chapter of Rohit Manchanda's "Monastery, Sanctuary, Laboratory" being translated from English to Hindi.

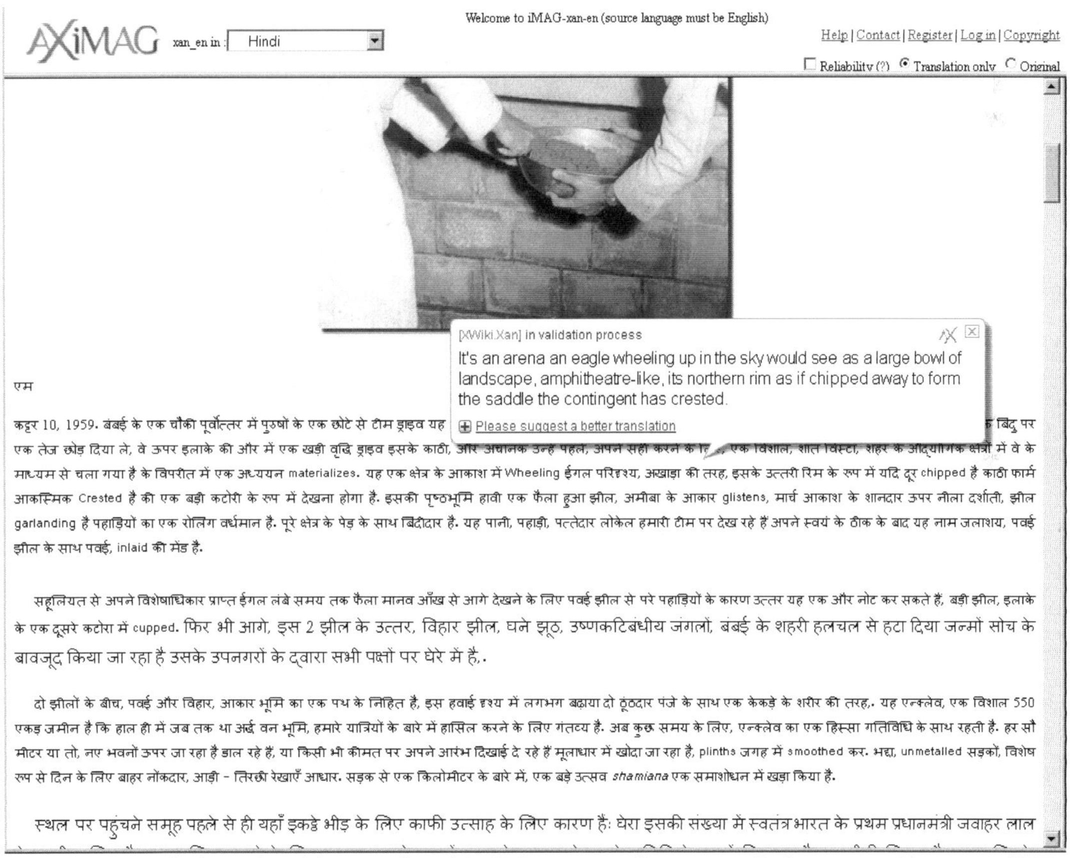


Figure 5: translation of Rohit Manchanda's "Monastery, Sanctuary, Laboratory: 50 years of IIT-Bombay"

Readers are invited to contribute at http://service.aximag.fr/xwiki/bin/view/imag/xan-en?u=http://www-clips.imag.fr/geta/User/christian.boitet/iMAGs-tests/en/ManchandaArticles/IITB-Monastery-Sanctuary-Laboratory

## References


Boitet, C., Bellynck, V., Mangeot, M., and Ramisch, C., (2008). *Towards Higher Quality Internal and Outside Multilingualization of Web Sites.* In Proceedings of ONII-08 (Summer Workshop on Ontology, NLP, Personalization and IE/IR), Mumbai, CFILT, IITB.

Maranget. L., $H^{E}V^{E}A$, *version 2.00.* Sources and documentation available at http://hevea.inria.fr/

Maranget. L., $H^{E}V^{E}A$, *un traducteur de* $L^{A}T_{E}X$ *vers HTML en Caml.* Available at http://pauillac.inria.fr/~maranget/papers/hevea/

Malmivuo, J., and Plonsey, R., (1995). *Bioelectromagnetism - Principles and Applications of Bioelectric and Biomagnetic Fields*, Oxford University Press, New York http://www.bem.fi/book/index.htm

Manchanda, R., (2008). *Monastery, Sanctuary, Laboratory: 50 Years of IIT-Bombay*, Macmillan India.

# Discrimination-net for Hindi

*Diptesh Kanojia   Arindam Chatterjee   Salil Joshi*
*Pushpak Bhattacharyya*
(1) Gautam Budh Technical University, Lucknow, India
(2) Symantec Labs, Pune, India
(3) IBM Research India, Bangalore, India
(4) CSE Department, IIT Bombay, Mumbai, India
dipteshkanojia@gmail.com, arindam.chatterjee23@gmail.com,
saljoshi@in.ibm.com, pb@cse.iitb.ac.in

## ABSTRACT
Current state-of-the-art Word Sense Disambiguation (WSD) algorithms are mostly supervised and use the $P(Sense|Word)$ statistic for annotation. This $P(Sense|Word)$ statistic is obtained after training the model on an annotated corpus. The performance of WSD algorithms do not match the efficiency and quality of human annotation. It is therefore important to know the role of the contextual clues in WSD. Human beings in turn, actuate the task of disambiguating the sense of a word, by gathering hints from the context words in the neighbourhood of the word. Contextual clues thus form the basic building block for the human sense disambiguation task. The need was thus felt for a tool, which could help us get a deeper insight into the human mind, while disambiguating polysemous words. As mentioned earlier, in the human mind, sense disambiguation highly depends on finding clues in corpus text, which finally lead to a winner sense. In order to make WSD algorithms more efficient, it is highly desirable to assimilate knowledge regarding contextual clues of words. In order to make WSD algorithms more efficient, it is highly desirable to assimilate knowledge regarding contextual clues of words, which aid in finding correct senses of words in that context. Hence, we developed a tool which could help a lexicographer mark the clues for disambiguating a word in a context. In the current phase, this tool lets the lexicographer select the clues from the gloss and example fields in the synset, and adds them to a database.

KEYWORDS: Sense discrimination, tool for generating discrimination-net.

*Proceedings of COLING 2012: Demonstration Papers*, pages 261–266,
COLING 2012, Mumbai, December 2012.

## 1 Introduction

Human annotators form a hypothesis as soon as they start reading the text. When they reach the target word sufficient information is gathered and they gain enough evidence to disambiguate it. Although in some cases, even reading the whole textmight not give sufficient clues to disambiguate a word. Machines have no such facility. The paragraph that the annotator is reading always gives him a vague idea of the word sense. In fact, the domain of the text being annotated gives away the most appropriate sense's idea (Khapra et al., 2010). Also, being familiar with the text beforehand stimulates the idea of a winner sense in the mind.Hence, to assure genuineness of our experiment we separated lines from different documents of the corpus and altered their order, such that, each sentence of text is taken from a separate sort of contextual scenario.

The cognitive load on the human brain while annotating the text is much more than one can imagine. As our expert lexicographers narrate, the hypothesis formation and rejection, work hand in hand as the senses are first narrowed down to a few most probable senses and then the winner sense is selected on the basis of matching the word with the gloss provided along with the sense.

One of the more important factors is the replaceability of synonyms provided along with in the sense window, if somehow narrowing down to a few senses and gloss matching tests are not enough, replaceability of the synonyms give the annotator a better understanding of the sense, which also works as verification in many cases.

The above mentioned factors along with the rich knowledge background form firm sense identification basis in one's mind and decides on an appropriate winner sense. Humans have a more powerful very imaginative visual sense of thinking, hence reading text stimulates visual background in a mind and this is again a very helpful factor in disambiguating a word written within a piece of text.

Hence the process of human annotation differs from machine completely. To study this process deeply, the clues which influence the decision of winner sense in a lexicographers mind need to be known to us. Hence, we went forth with the development of this tool, which lets us collect these clues, which would form base for a solid rule based framework in the future.

The key features of the system are as follows:

1. **Minimized human interaction:** The system requires the user to provide very less amount of input. All the user has to do, is to select on the contextual clues once a synset is displayed.
2. **User friendliness:** Our system interface provides a nice visual experience. The design of the interface makes the operation of the interface completely clear to the end user.
3. **System independence:** The system is independent of the web browser and the operating system it is used on. Since the business logic is written in Java, the system can be easily ported on another machine.
4. **Ease of configuration:** Our system currently uses the Hindi wordnet as the back-end knowledge source. However, it can be easily ported to support any language wordnet.
5. **Easily interpretable output:** Our interface is designed in such a way that the user can easily understand the ongoing process and the clues entered so far.

This paper is organized as follows. Section 2 lays down the system architecture of our wordnet linking system. In section 3 we describe the operation of the tool. We conclude the paper with section 4.

## 2 System Architecture

The tool starts by displaying a login page where a user must enter his credentials to enter the tool. Unregistered users are required to click on the create login button to go create a login user id and password for them, and their login must be approved by an administrator or by any of the registered Super Users on the website.

Once the login id is created and approved, a user can log in to the tool and start using it from the home page itself. The user gets to start clue marking from here itself. Synset words and Synset ID is displayed on the top along with a text box displaying the username of the user who last edited the current clue words, if ever edited. If there is no text field labeled clue words present on the page, there are no entries for the clues of this synset in the database.

User now has to identify the clue words in the gloss and example fields of the page displayed. Clues can be words or word phrases depending on the users interpretation of the synset word along with the lexical category it belongs to. Once the user selects clues with mouse selection on the screen, He clicks the add button to put them down in the Clues Text Box given below. User adds as many clues as possible and when the clues are finally complete, He should click Submit button to submit the clues in the database. The clues are added to the database and changes are reflected immediately in most cases. Due to some problems in specific browsers, if the clue changes are not being reflected immediately, The user should click refresh to check the clue changes made in the database. Clicking on refresh will fetch entries of clues from the database immediately.

If there are some clues already added to the database, and user wants to edit them, the clues text box it editable and user can edit the clues present there, when done with the editing, clicking on the submit button is again required to update the clues entry in the database.

It is advised that user only edits the clues if he has a complete idea about the synset word he is presently editing.

## 3 Interface Design

To support various web browsers on different operating systems, we have designed the web interface using standard open technologies. The interface runs using PHP5[1] on the server side, and the back-end database is maintained using MySQL[2]

Figure 1 shows the system interface. The Sense Discrimination Tool home page is shown above and it is described below:

1. **Administration Center:** For administrative users, Operations such as Approve, Reject, Ban and Super User and Delete user are present for an Administrator.
2. **Go To Synset ID:** Navigates to a particular Synset ID.
3. **Go To Synset Word:** Navigates to a particular Synset word, based on choice of user.
4. **Refresh:** Refreshes the page for showing updated clue words.
5. **About:** Opens a page explaining the tool
6. **Help:** Opens a page on how to use the tool, and who should use the tool.
7. **Logout:** Logs a user out.

Once the user has a login approved, (s)he needs to follow the steps mentioned below to use the tool:

[1] `http://php.net/downloads.php`

[2] `http://mysql.net/`

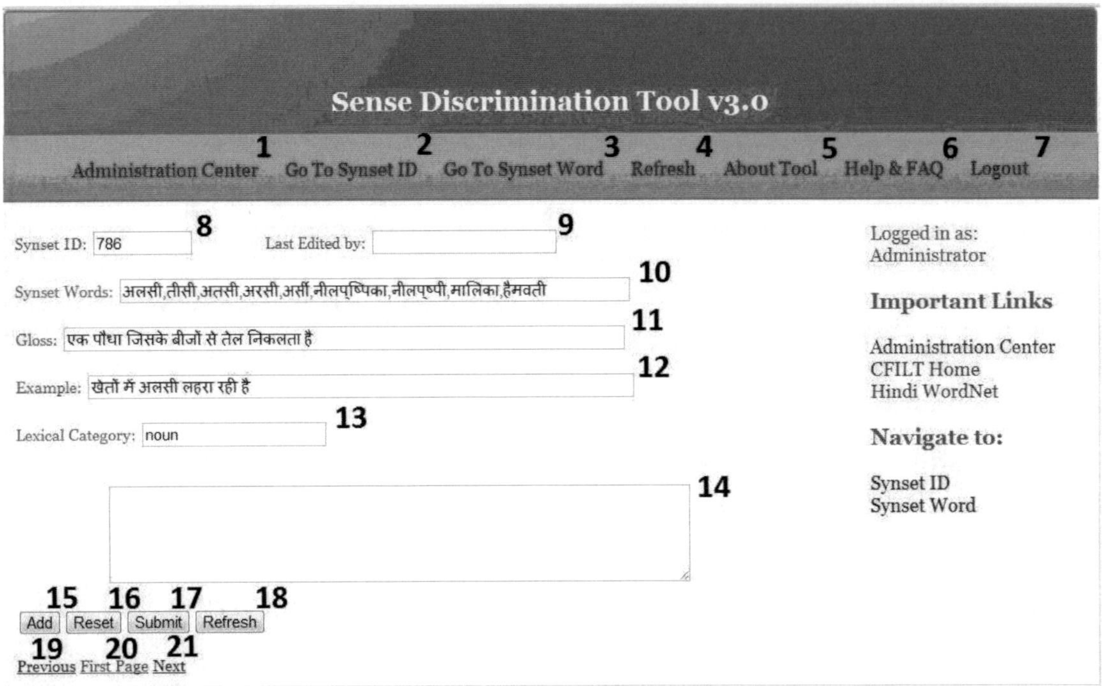


Figure 1: Screen-shot showing the main interface of the system

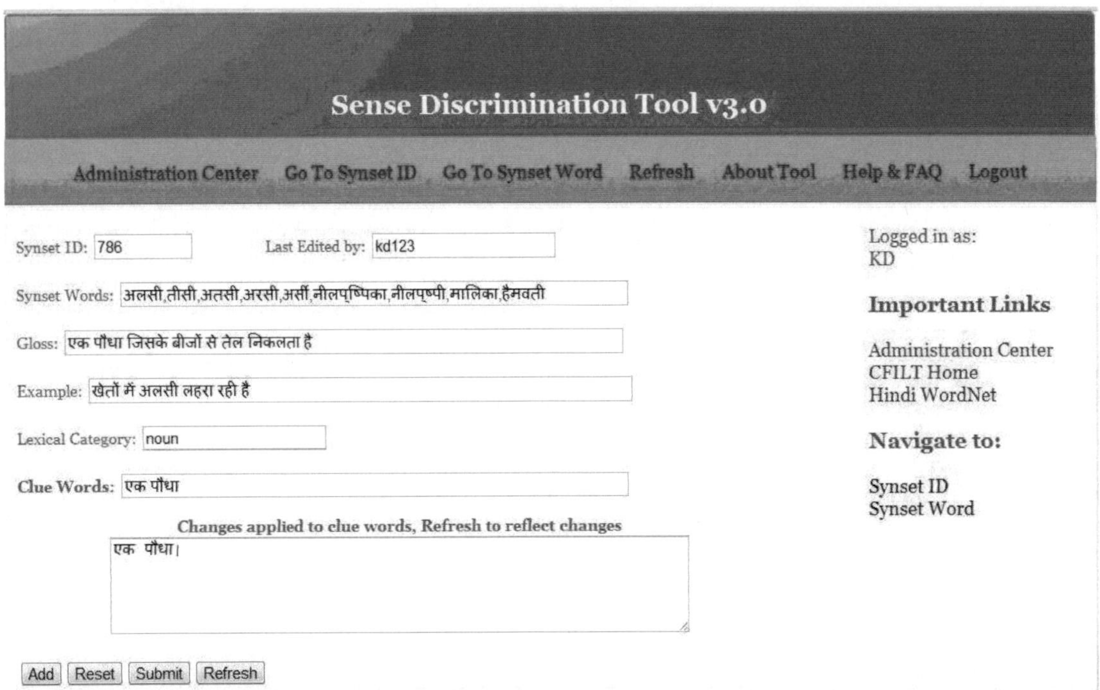


Figure 2: Screen-shot showing the working of the system

1. **Identify the synset word :** user has to identify the synset word in Synset Words and select

the word/phrase which you think helps disambiguate the word meaning and leads to the winner sense. Selection can be made by highlighting that word/phrase using mouse or using SHIFT key on the keyboard. The clues will be available in gloss and example.

2. **Gather the clues:** User needs to click on add to add them to the Clues Text Box14 and edit them for any changes, if needed. This makes the clues set final for addition to database.
3. **Submit the clues:** The user can then simply click on Submit to add the phrases to the database.
4. **Navigation across synsets:** Once the synset is done with, the user can move to the next or previous synset. This working is shown in figure 2.

The tool also provides several other facilities for searching a particular word, carrying out administrative tasks, searching for a particular synset, *etc.* Figure 3 shows the operation of searching a word. After entering the word in the text box, the user needs to click OK or press Enter. The navigation will take the user to a page where all the resulting instances of the input word in the Hindi WN database are present.

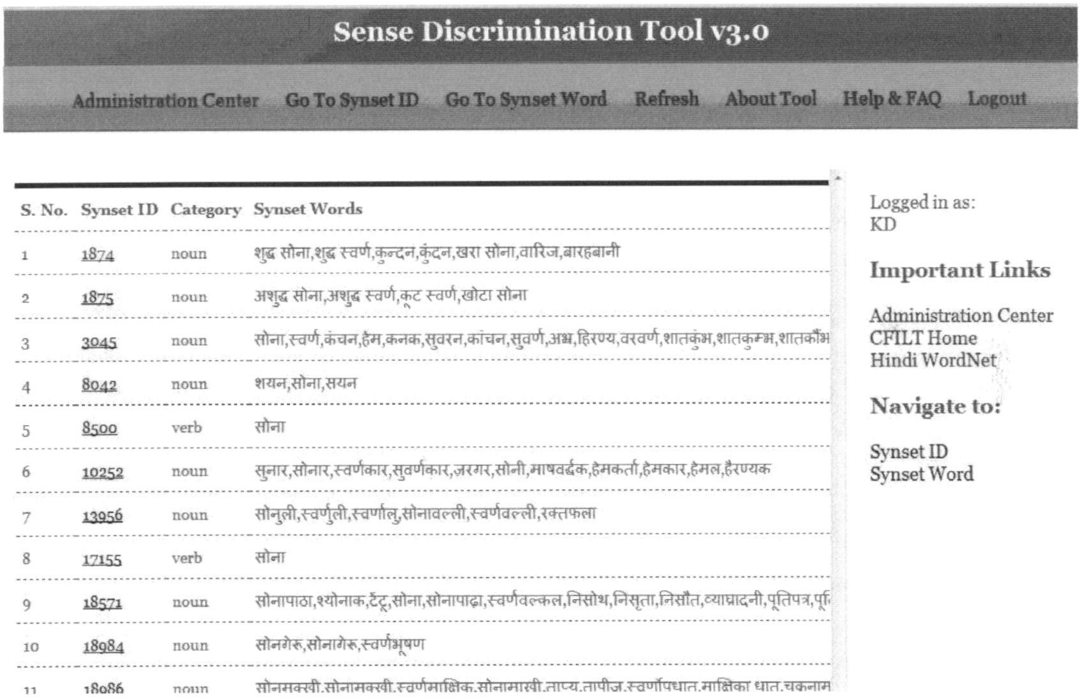


Figure 3: Screen-shot showing the navigational facility of the system

## 4 Conclusion

The aim of this paper was to illustrate a tool which allows annotators to conveniently specify the clues that they use for distinguishing between the various senses of a word is quite crucial in the task of word sense disambiguation. It is further important to utilize these clues so as to build a structure or a framework which allows for reducing the uncertainty of the sense of a particular word. We imagine that constructing a discrimination net in the form of a weighted graph will assist in calculating a score which will say something about this uncertainty. The underlying idea is that there are words with multiple senses as well as ones with unique senses, and by traversing this graph, we will eventually reach these unique senses and then determine the score.

In the future, we would like to help the users in generating the clues using the clues which are accumulated in the system so far.

## References

Khapra, M., Shah, S., Kedia, P., and Bhattacharyya, P. (2010). Domain-specific word sense disambiguation combining corpus based and wordnet based parameters. In *5th International Conference on Global Wordnet (GWC2010)*.

# Rule Based Urdu Stemmer

*Rohit Kansal Vishal Goyal G. S. Lehal*
Department of Computer Science Punjabi University, Patiala
Assistant Professor, Department of Computer Science, Punjabi University Patiala
Professor, Department of Computer Science, Punjabi University Patiala

rohitkansal87@yahoo.co.in vishal.pup@gmail.com gslehal@yahoo.com

***Abstract***

This paper presents Rule based Urdu Stemmer. In this technique rules are applied to remove suffix and prefix from the inflected words. Urdu is well spoken language all over the world but less work has been done on Urdu stemming. Stemmer helps us to find the root of the inflected word. Various possibilities of inflected words like وں (vao+noon-gunna), ے (badi-ye), یاں (choti-ye+alif+noon-gunna) etc. have been identified and appropriate rules have been developed for them.

Keywords-Urdu Stemmer, Stemmer, Urdu,Rules

*Proceedings of COLING 2012: Demonstration Papers*, pages 267–276,
COLING 2012, Mumbai, December 2012.

## 1 Introduction

Stemming is the process in which inflected words are reduced to find stem or root. There are various inflected words that can be reduced to stem.

e.g. In English language :

1) Act can have inflected words like actor, acted, acting etc.

2) Words like fishing, fished and fisher can be reduced to root word fish.

Similarly in Urdu various possibilities have been identified and rules have been developed appropriate

| | Inflected Word | Root Word |
|---|---|---|
| 1. | لڑکیاں<br>(laṛkīāṃ) | لڑکی<br>(laṛkī) |
| 2. | بستیاں<br>(bastīāṃ) | بستی<br>(bastī) |
| 3. | گاڑیاں<br>(gāṛīāṃ) | گاڑی<br>(gāṛī |
| 4. | کتابیں<br>(kitābēṃ) | کتاب<br>(kitāb) |
| 5. | میلے<br>(mēlē) | میلا<br>(mēlā) |

**Table 1 Examples of Urdu Stemmer**

### 1.1 Approaches

Stemming algorithms are classified under three categories- Rule Based, Statistical and Hybrid.

1) Rule Based approach - This approach applies a set of transformation rules to inflected words in order to cut prefixes or suffixes.

E.g. if the word ends in 'ed', remove the 'ed'.

2) Statistical approach - The major drawback of Rule Based approach is that it is dependent on database. Statistical algorithms overcome this problem by finding distributions of root elements in a database. There is no need to maintain the database.

3) Hybrid approach - It is combination of both Affix removal and Statistical approach.

Stemming is useful in Natural Language Processing problems like search engine, word processing problems and information retrieval. In this stemmer we have applied Rule Based Approach in which we apply rules on various possibilities of inflected words to remove suffixes or prefixes. In Urdu, the only stemmer available to us is Assas-Band developed by NUCES, Pakistan which maintains an Affix Exception List and works according to the algorithm to remove inflections.

## 2 Background and Related Work

The only Stemmer available to us in Urdu is Assas-Band developed by NUCES, Pakistan which maintains an Affix Exception List and works according to the algorithm to remove inflections. It has been developed by Qurat-ul-Ain-Akram et al. (2009) using Rule based approach. Urdu word is composed of sequence of prefix, stem and postfix. A word can be divided into prefix-stem-postfix. First the prefix is removed from the word which returns stem-postfix sequence. Then postfix is removed and stem is extracted. This system gives an accuracy of 91.2 %.This system worked as a base paper for our system. It gave an idea that how Urdu words should be handled and what are the challenges faced in handling them. We have also used Rule Based Approach but it is different from Assas-Band.

In 1968 Julie Beth Lovins developed the first English Stemmer. Then Martin Porter developed Porter Stemming Algorithm which is most widely used technique for stemming in English. Other work related to Indian Languages are like Pratik kumar popat et al.2010 developed Stemmer for Gujarati using Hybrid Approach. In this system optimal split position is obtained by taking all the possible splits of the word and selecting the split position which occur maximum. It gives an accuracy of 67.8 %. Dinesh Kumar et al.2011 developed a Stemmer for Punjabi using Brute Force Technique. It employs a look up table which contains relation between root forms and inflected forms. To stem a word, table is queried to find a matching inflection. If a matching inflection is found associated root word is returned. It achieves accuracy of 81.27 %.Sandeep Sarkar et al.2008 developed Rule Based Stemmer for Bengali which achieve an accuracy of 89 %. Ananthakrishnan Ramanathan et al. developed a lightweight stemmer for Hindi using suffix removal method. Suffix removal does not require a look up table. It achieves an accuracy of 88 %.Vishal Gupta et al.2011 developed stemmer for nouns and proper names for Punjabi language using Rule based approach. Various possibilities of suffixes have been identified and various rules have been generated. The efficiency of this system is 87.37 %.

## 3 Urdu Stemmer

An attempt has been made to develop Urdu Stemmer using Rule Based Approach in which we have developed rules to remove various prefixes and suffixes. We have designed Rule Based Approach Urdu Stemmer which helps us to find stem of various inflected words. For this we have developed a graphical user interface in which we can enter the input directly or we can also browse files. Database has been maintained of root words along with their frequencies. The collection of 101,483 unique words has been done. The flowchart of Urdu Stemmer is given below which explains the system step by step in detail.

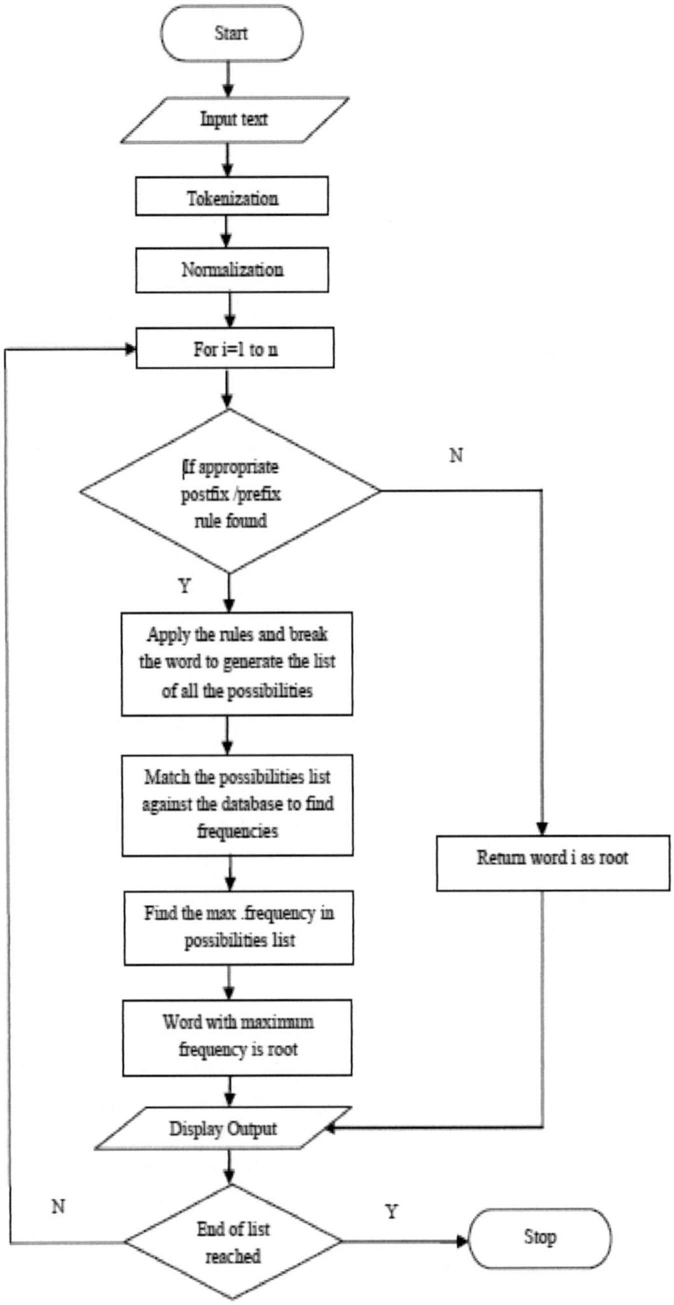


**Figure 1 Flowchart of Urdu Stemmer**

### 3.1 Algorithm

The algorithm of Urdu stemmer is explained in detail below:-

**i) Tokenization and Normalization-** In tokenization process the input text is tokenized word by word by using delimiter as space. In normalization special characters like ?,',",@ etc are eliminated.

**ii) Postfix/Prefix Rules-** After the normalization process postfix/prefix rules are applied on the word. If appropriate rules are found that can be applied then break the word and generate the list of various possibilities of the word. In some cases if appropriate rules are not found then system returns the same word as root word. The possibilities list is matched against the database to find frequencies. Then the frequencies are compared and word corresponding to the greatest frequency is returned as root. The word corresponding to the greatest frequency is returned as root because the word that occurs most frequently has the highest probability of being the root.
A corpus of 11.56 million words is used and 1,01,483 words are extracted from the corpus as unique words. These words are stored in the database along with their frequencies. The frequency of a word means how many times it repeats in the corpus.

Some of the postfix rules applied are-:

Rule 1- If word ends with وں (vao+noon-gunna) then remove وں (vao+noon-gunna) from end.

For example- رنگوں - رنگ
(raṅgōṃ) (raṅg)

Rule 2- If word ends with ے (badi-ye) then remove ے (badi-ye) from end and replace with ا (alif) .

For example- میلے - میلا
(mēlē) (mēlā)

Rule 3- If word ends with یوں (choti-ye +vao+noon-gunna) then remove یوں (choti-ye+vao+noon-gunna) from end and replace with ی (choti-ye).

For example- کویوں - کوی
(kaviyōṃ) (kavī)

Rule 4- If word ends with ؤں (vao- hamza+noon-gunna) then remove ؤں (vao- hamza+noon-gunna) from end.

For example- چاچاؤں - چاچا
(cācāōṃ) (cācā)

Rule 5- If word ends with یاں (choti- ye+alif+noon-gunna) then remove یاں (choti-ye+alif+noon-gunna) from end and replace with ی (choti-ye).

For example- کوٹیاں - کوٹی
(kōṭīyāṃ) (kōṭī)

Rule 6- If word ends with یں (choti- ye+noon-gunna) then remove یں (choti-ye + noon-gunna) from end.

For example- ڈھالیں - ڈھال
(ḍhālēṃ) (ḍhāl)

Rule 7- If word ends with ئیں (hamza + choti-ye+noon-gunna) then remove ئیں (hamza+choti-ye+noon-gunna) from end.

For example- مالائیں - مالا
(mālāēṃ) (mālā)

The rules above are some of the rules that are used in the Urdu stemmer. Similarly there are other postfix rules that can be applied which helps to find root in the system.

**iii)Prefix Rules-** Some of the prefix rules are applied to find the root word are given below:-

Rule 1- If word starts with بد (bay+daal) then remove بد (bay+daal) from beginning.

For example- بدصورت - صورت
(badsūrat) (sūrat)

Rule 2- If word starts with بے (bay+badi- ye)then remove بے (bay+badi-ye) from beginning

For example- بکدر - کدر
(bēkdar) (kadar)

So there are 32 postfix and prefix rules in total that we have used to develop this system.

**4 Results and Discussion**

We have tested this system on different Urdu news documents of 20,583 words to evaluate the performance of this system. The accuracy of this system is 85.14%. The news document consists of sports, national, international news. We have tried to cover different domains in order to find different types of inflected words. Test set 1 covers sports and business news. Test set 2 covers articles, short stories etc. Test set 3 covers news relating to health and science.

| Test Set no. | Area covered | No. of Words |
|---|---|---|
| Test Set 1 | Sports, Business news | 7261 |
| Test Set 2 | Articles, Short stories | 6239 |
| Test Set 3 | Health, Scientific news | 7083 |

**Table 2 Different test cases**

Following evaluation metrics are used to calculate the accuracy.

**Recall (R) = Correct answers given by system / Total possible correct answers**

**Precision (P) = Correct answers / Answers produced**

**F-Measure= $(\beta^2 + 1)$ PR / $\beta^2$ R + P**

**β is the weighting between precision and recall typically β=1. F-measure is called F1-Measure.**

**F1Measure= 2PR / (P+R).**

| Test set no. | Recall | Precision | F1-Measure |
|---|---|---|---|
| 1. | 90.90% | 81.18% | 86.11% |
| 2. | 88.39% | 80.35% | 84.17% |
| 3. | 89.43% | 81.30% | 85.15% |

**Table 3 Accuracy of different test cases**

The overall accuracy of the system is 85.15%.The overall performance of the system is good. In test cases we have observed that some rules are more used than other rules. Rule 1 and Rule 2 cover most of the inflected words. So these rules are applied more than other rules. Errors are due to dictionary error or syntax error. Dictionary error means word is not present in the database. When we apply rules and find the various possibilities but these possibilities may not be present in the database. If appropriate rule is not found but the word is inflected it can also give rise to error. The probability of dictionary error is very less because we have extracted unique words from corpus of 11.53 million words. We assume that such a large corpus cover most of the inflected words. The error is mainly due to syntax error. There is no standardization in Urdu which means there is more than one way of writing a particular word. Although we have tried to cover all the possibilities of writing a word but error may occur. Absence of Airaabs in most of the Urdu text increases the error rate. When Airaabs are not present in Urdu text, it becomes difficult to understand the word. The different rules give different accuracy because some rules are more frequently used more than other rules.

The rules that are more frequently used are shown below and with their accuracy which helps to find which rule occur most. The rule that occur more frequently show that the inflection corresponding to that particular word occur most.

| Urdu Stemmer Rules | Accuracy percentage of correct words |
|---|---|
| Rule 1 وں (vao+noon-gunna) | 95.41% |
| Rule 2 ے (badi-ye) | 94.74% |
| Rule 3 یوں (choti-ye+vao+ noon-gunna) | 87.21% |
| Rule 4 ؤں (vao-hamza+ noon-gunna) | 86.39% |
| Rule 5 یاں (choti-ye+alif+ noon-gunna) | 84.11% |
| Rule 6 یں (choti-ye+ noon-gunna) | 87.53% |
| Rule 7 ئیں (hamza +choti-ye+ noon-gunna) | 85.41% |

**Table 4 Accuracy of mostly common applied rules**

## Conclusion and Future Work

In this paper Urdu stemmer has been discussed using Rule Based Approach which removes suffixes and prefixes from the inflected word. Various possibilities like وں (vao+noon-gunna), ے (badi-ye), یاں (choti-ye+alif+noon-gunna) etc. have been identified and appropriate rules have been developed to remove inflections and find the root. The data collection is the main problem because text data in Urdu available to us is rare. The limitation can be handled by increasing the database in future to achieve more accurate results. Error can also occur due to spelling variations because there is no particular way of writing a word. There can be more than one way of writing a particular word in Urdu. Although we have tried to put all the possibilities of writing a word but still error may occur. Statistical approach can be applied to Urdu Stemmer in future.

## References

[1] Qurat-ul-Ain-Akram, Asma Naseer, Sarmad Hussain.(2009). *Assas –Band, an Affix-Exception list based Urdu Stemmer* In the Proceedings of the 7th Workshop on Asian Language Resources, ACL-IJCNLP , Suntec, Singapore, pp. 40–47.

[2] Dinesh Kumar, Prince Rana.(2011).*Stemming of Punjabi Words by using Brute Force Technique* In International Journal of Engineering Science and Technology (IJEST) Vol. 3 No. 2 , pp. 1351-1357.
[3] Sandipan Sarkar, Sivaji Bandyopadhyay.(2008). *Design of a Rule-based Stemmer for Natural Language Text in Bengali*, In the Proceedings of the IJCNLP-08 Workshop on NLP for Less Privileged Languages, Hyderabad, India, Asian Federation of Natural Language Processing, pp. 65–72.
[4] Vishal Gupta, Gurpreet Singh Lehal.(2011). *Punjabi Language Stemmer for nouns and proper name*, In the Proceedings of the 2nd Workshop on South and Southeast Asian Natural Language Processing (WSSANLP), IJCNLP , Chiang Mai, Thailand, pp. 35–39.
[5] Katik Suba, Dipti Jiandani, Pushpak Bhattacharyya.(2011).*Hybrid inflectional Stemmer and Rule-based Derivational Stemmer for Gujarati*, In the Proceedings of the 2nd Workshop on South and Southeast Asian Natural Language Processing (WSSANLP), IJCNLP , Chiang Mai, Thailand, November 8, 2011, pp. 1–8.
[6] Pratikkumar Patel, Kashyap Popat.(2010). *Hybrid Stemmer for Gujarati"* In the Proceedings of the 1st Workshop on South and Southeast Asian Natural Language Processing (WSSANLP), the 23rd International Conference on Computational Linguistics (COLING), Beijing, pp. 51–55.
[7] Ananthakrishnan Ramanathan, Durgesh D Rao *A Lightweight Stemmer For Hindi*, National Centre for Software Technology, In the Workshop on Computational Linguistics for South-Asian Languages, EACL. pp. 42-48.
[8] M.F. Porter, (1980). *An algorithm for suffix stripping,* Program, 14(3) pp. 130-137.
[9]http://en.wikipedia.org/wiki/Stemming_algorithms Accessed on November 2011
[10] Kashif Riaz.(2007). *Challenges in Urdu Stemming* (A Progressive Report In BCS IRSG Symposium: Future Directions in Information Access (FDIA 2007). http://citeseerx.ist.psu.edu/viewdoc/download/10.1.1.102.3051.pdf

# JMaxAlign: A Maximum Entropy Parallel Sentence Alignment Tool

Joseph Max Kaufmann
max.kaufmann@dac.us

## Abstract

Parallel corpora are an extremely useful tool in many natural language processing tasks, particularly statistical machine translation. Parallel corpora for certain language pairs, such as Spanish or French, are widely available, but for many language pairs, such as Bengali and Chinese, it is impossible to find parallel corpora. Several tools have been developed to automatically extract parallel data from non–parallel corpora, but they use language-specific techniques or require large amounts of training data. This paper demonstrates that maximum entropy classifiers can be used to detect parallel sentences between any language pairs with small amounts of training data. This paper is accompanied by JMaxAlign, a Java maxent classifier which can detect parallel sentences.

Keywords: Parallel Corpora, Comparable Corpora, Maximum Entropy Classifiers, Statistical Machine Translation.

*Proceedings of COLING 2012: Demonstration Papers*, pages 277–288,
COLING 2012, Mumbai, December 2012.

# 1 Introduction

Parallel corpora, one text translated into multiple languages, are used in all types of multilingual research, especially in Machine Translation (MT) tasks. Statistical Machine Translation (SMT) systems analyze parallel corpora in two languages to learn the set of rules that govern translation between them. Since SMT systems use statistical methods, they require lots of training data to produce useful results Smith et al. [2010]. Unfortunately, parallel corpora are very difficult to produce. Creating parallel corpora requires humans who are proficient in both the source and target languages. These translators usually are compensated in some form, which means that generating parallel corpora is both expensive and time consuming. It is possible to buy corpora, but not for every language pair. The Linguistic Data Consortium, one the largest providers of parallel corpora, contains corpora for less than 20 languages pairs [1]. Because of the utility of parallel corpora, several tools have been created which allow the automatic extraction of parallel corpora from non–parallel corpora. However, these tools have been designed to extract parallel corpora from a specific language pair, such as English–Hungarian (Tóth et al. [2005]) or Arabic–English Munteanu and Marcu [2005]. This paper describes JMaxAlign, a Java Maximum Entropy Alignment tool. JMaxAlign builds upon previous state-of-the-art research by using maximum entropy classifiers to detect parallel sentences. By doing so, it avoids dependence on hard–coded linguistic features (such as lists of stop words or cognates). This independence makes it useful for generation of parallel-corpora for low-resource language pairs, such as Hindi-Bengali or Chinese-Tamil.

# 2 Finding Parallel Sentences

The bulk of previous research that aims to detect parallel sentences uses a combination of two techniques: length-based similarity and lexical similarity.Length based similarity was originally developed by Gale and Church [1993]. Length-based similarity is the idea that long sentences are likely to have long translations and short sentences are likely to have short translations. This method is very effective for discarding non-parallel sentences. This is useful because parallel corpora extraction is frequently performed on a large corpora which may only contain a small amount of parallel data. When Adafre and de Rijke [2006] attempted to extract a parallel Dutch–English corpora from Wikipedia, they were able to substantially decrease the number of candidate sentences by discarding sentence pairs that have drastically different length. But to actually detect parallel sentences, they used the second technique, lexical similarity.

Lexical similarity is the fraction of the words in one sentence of the source language that are semantically equivalent to words in the corresponding sentence of the target language. There are many different ways to compute lexical similarity, but all require a bilingual dictionary. Adafre and de Rijke [2006] compute it by using a bilingual dictionary, and looking at the words in the English sentence that have translations in the Dutch sentence. Tools such as Hunalign Tóth et al. [2005] and the Microsoft Bilingual Sentence aligner Moore [2002] automatically generate their bilingual dictionary from the corpora, using pruning heuristics to narrow possible word translations. Other tools, such as Ma [2006] actually create a weighted bilingual dictionary, which uses TF-IDF to make rare words more indicative then parallelism.

[1] http://www.ldc.upenn.edu/Membership/Agreements/memberannouncement.shtml

While there are many ways to combine these two similarity measurse, previous research has shown using them to generate features for a maximum entropy classifier is an effective method. While there are no publicly available sentence tools that use this approach, it has been researched in several papers (such as Smith et al. [2010] and Mohammadi and QasemAghaee [2010]) and been shown to be a powerful technique. Specifically, Smith et al. [2010] used maximum entropy classifiers to detect parallel sentences in English and Spanish, and Mohammadi and QasemAghaee [2010] used them in the context of an Arabic–English pair. While English and Spanish belong to similar language families, English and Arabic are unrelated.

### 2.1 Motivation

The fact that maximum entropy classifiers achieved reasonable success when classifying English–Spanish parallel sentences and English–Arabic parallel sentences was the main motivator for the creation of JMaxAlign. This fact suggested that maximum entropy classifiers could learn the appropriate weights of lexical and sentence–length similarity. This is important because not all tools assume that these features need to be learned for a language pair. Hunalign, one of the most well known sentence alignment tools, does not make this assumption. Tóth et al. [2005] claim that "The relative weight of the two components [lexical and sentence–length similarity] was set so as to maximize precision on the Hungarian—English training corpus, but seems a sensible choice for other languages as well." Unfortunately, this is not the case. This is because sentences in agglutinative languages with rich morphologies (such as Hungarian or Turkish) generally have fewer words than semantically equivalent sentences in isolating languages (such as Spanish and English). This means that Hunalign's sentence–length measurement is *not* applicable to every language pair. Hunalign's implementation of lexical similarity suffers from two flaws. First, Hunalign attempts to assign a lesser weight to stop words (function words that primarily serve a grammatical purpose) when computing lexical similarity. This is logical, as stop words are not nearly as indicative of parallelism as rarer words. However, Hunalign uses hard–coded lists of English and Hungarian stop words, and provides no way to substitute a new list for different language pairs. Secondly, it does not account for why a word in one sentence is not aligned to a word in another sentence. A word can be unaligned because the dictionary does not include that word, or it can be unaligned because it truly has no corresponding alignment. The first means that the aligner lacks the knowledge necessary to compute the alignment, while the second is really indicates that the words are unaligned.

## 3 JMaxAlign

### 3.1 Architecture

JMaxAlign takes two parallel corpora as input. From these corpora, JMaxAlign computes build a probabilistic bilingual dictionary between the two languages of the corpora, and uses that dictionary to compute feature sets for each pair of parallel sentences[2]. These feature sets are then used to train a maximum entropy classifier for that language pair. The test data is then passed into the classifier, which outputs a boolean value for each sentence pair, indicating whether they are aligned or not. Figure 1 represents this process.

[2]Thanks to Stanford, for making the Stanford Classifier which is used as the maximum entropy classifier http://nlp.stanford.edu/software/classifier.shtml

Figure 1: Architecture of JMaxAlign

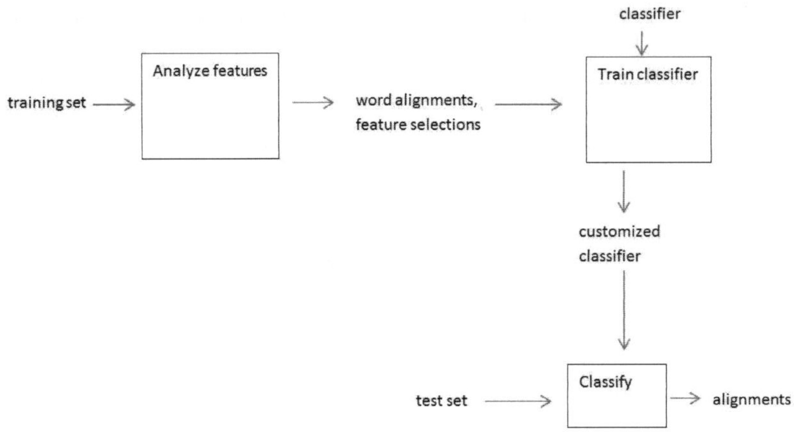


### 3.1.1 Lexical Alignments

After parallel corpora for training have been gathered, JMaxAlign computes the lexical alignments for each of the words in the parallel corpora. A lexical alignment is simply a set of possible translations (and optionally the probability of those translations) a word can have. Multiple words in one language can map to a single word in another. This is frequently due to differing uses of case. For example, German marks a noun and its modifier to indicate its case, while English does not. The English phrase *the dog* can be translated into German as der hund, den hund, dem hund, or des hundes.

These alignments are extremely important because they are the basis of the probabilistic bilingual dictionary that allows JMaxAlign to compute the lexical similarity of two sentences. JMaxAlign uses them to calculate the percentage of words in one sentence that have translations in the corresponding sentence. Turning parallel sentences into lexical alignments is a difficult task, but it has been extensively studied in the NLP community. JMaxAlign uses the Berkeley Aligner, an open–source tool written in Java that generates probabilistic word alignments from a set of parallel texts (the same texts that serves as the training data for the aligner). This aligner, described by Liang et al. [2006], works with either supervised or unsupervised training data (in this context, supervised means parallel sentences with hand–generated alignments, not just parallel sentences).

### 3.1.2 Feature Selection

Feature selection is the most important part of building a classifier. If a classifier is looking at the wrong features to decide whether sentences are parallel or not, it will not obtain accurate results.

**Length Ratio** The ratio of the length between the two sentences. Gale and Church [1993] showed that the length ratio between sentences that are in fact parallel is an effective way to determine parallelism.

**Percentage of Unaligned Words** This measures the lexical similarity of the two sentences. Having more words unaligned means that the two sentences have a lower lexical similarity. JMAxAlign computes lexical similarity by taking the number of unaligned words in both sentences, and dividing it by the total number of words in both sentences.

**Percentage of Unknown and Unaligned Words** One of the weaknesses of Hunalign was that it did not account for words that were not aligned because they had never been seen in training. This feature helps the classifier account for the fact that when there is a low amount of training data sentences may appear not to be aligned due to the large percentage of unknown words. It is computed by taking the number of unaligned and unknown words in both sentences, and dividing it by the total number of words in both sentences.

**Sum of Fertilities** Brown et al. [1993] defines the fertility of a word as the number of words it is connected to. One word can be aligned to multiple words in its corresponding translation. As Munteanu and Marcu [2005] writes, "The presence in an automatically computed alignment between a pair of sentences of words of high fertility is indicative of non–parallelism". A typical example of this is stop words. The appearance of words such as *a*, *the*, or *an* do not help us decide parallelism nearly as much as the appearance of words such as *carpet*, *burning*. or *elephant*. The latter set of words is much rarer, and therefore much more indicative of parallelism. In Hunalign, lists of hard–coded Hungarian and English stop words were used. Since it is time–consuming to create lists of stop words for each language pair, the sum fertilities measure is used.

**Longest Contiguous Span** Long contiguous spans of aligned words are highly indicative of parallelism, especially in short sentences. JMaxAlign compute longest contiguous span of aligned words in each sentence of the pair, and pick the longer of the two.

**Alignment Score** Following Munteanu and Marcu [2005] The alignment score is defined as as the normalized product of the translation probabilities of aligned word pairs. This is indicative of parallelism because non–parallel sentences will have less alignments and a lower score.

### 3.1.3 Classifier Training

After computing features from the training and testing data, the next step is to train a maximum entropy classifier. Even though JMaxAlign only requires the user to put in parallel sentences (positive training data), maximum entropy classifiers require negative training (non–parallel sentences). JMaxAlign simply randomly pairs sentences from the parallel corpus together to create negative training examples. When designing their Arabic–English maximum entropy classifier, Munteanu and Marcu [2005] assumed that randomly-generated nonparallel sentences were not sufficiently discriminatory. They created negative training examples by the same method that JMaxAlign did, but they filtered the sentences to only include the subset that had a length ratio less than 2.0, and over 50% of the words aligned. Munteanu and Marcu [2005] claimed that sentences that did not meet these characteristics could immediately be classified as non–parallel, and so there was no need to train the classifier on these sentences. This claim is problematic because it assumes that those numbers are appropriate choices, similar to the way that Tóth et al. [2005] assumed that their length–ratio was appropriate for all values. One of the main benefits of maximum entropy classifiers is that it does not force assumptions about how a certain set of linguistic properties will hold constant regardless of language pairs. Observe the following Turkish and English sentences

*Turkish*: ekoslovakyallatramadklarmzdan mydnz? *English*: Were you one of those who we failed to assimilate as a Czechoslovakian?

This is an extreme example, but it illustrates the dangers of assuming linguistic constants. These sentences are parallel, but would be immediately discarded by Munteanu and Marcu [2005]'s filter. Randomly generating negative sentences further benefits JMaxAlign by allowing it to learn the importance of the other features. While the features of the filter have been shown to be extremely useful discriminators, there is no need to include that bias in the classifier. There may be sentences that don't pass the filter but provide useful information about how fertilities or contiguous spans contribute to parallelism. Discarding them causes an unnecessary loss of information.

# 4 Results

## 4.1 Linguistic Similarity

Detecting similar sentence pairs is easier when the languages are more linguistically related. For example, when detecting English-Spanish language pairs, cognates could be used in the absence of a bilingual dictionary, but this is not the case for Arabic–Chinese. To evaluate JMaxAlign on its sensitivity to the language family of the languages, it was tested on two types of language pairs: language pairs from the same family ("similar language pairs"), and language pairs from different families ("dissimilar language pairs") In the first test, the training data used included 2000 parallel and 1000 non-parallel training examples, and the testing data included 5000 parallel examples and 5000 non-parallel examples. The parallel data was obtained from the Open Subtitles Corpora, a collection parallel sentences obtained from aligning movie subtitles Tiedemann et al. [2004]. The results are in Table 1 and Table 2.

Table 1: Similar Language Pairs

| Language 1 | L1 Family | Language 2 | L2 Family | Precision | Recall | F–Score |
|---|---|---|---|---|---|---|
| English | Germanic | German | Germanic | 86.75 | 87.62 | 87.81 |
| Spanish | Italic | Italian | Italic | 87.57 | 85.49 | 86.51 |
| Estonian | Uralic | Hungarian | Uralic | 54.99 | 99.75 | 70.89 |
| Polish | Slavic | Russian | Slavic | 90.08 | 92.51 | 91.28 |

Table 1 and 2 show that JMaxAlign is somewhat sensitive to the language families to which the languages belong. The F–Scores for the similar language pairs are, in general, higher than those for the dissimilar pairs. However, JMaxAlign is still able to produce useful results (F–Scores between 75% and 80%) for languages that are very dissimilar. The high recall scores that JMaxAlign achieves indicates that it is very good at classifying non-parallel

Table 2: Dissimilar Language Pairs

| Language 1 | L1 Family | Language 2 | L2 Family | Precision | Recall | F–Score |
|---|---|---|---|---|---|---|
| Arabic | Semitic | Spanish | Italic | 69.1 | 83.85 | 75.76 |
| German | Germanic | Italian | Italic | 83.89 | 80.3 | 82.04 |
| Spanish | Italic | Russian | Slavic | 79.84 | 79.17 | 79.50 |
| Hungarian | Uralic | Russian | Slavic | 87.05 | 74.09 | 83.09 |

sentences as non-parallel without the help of a filter, like the one Munteanu and Marcu [2005] proposes. Not using a filter is a non-trivial benefit for two reasons. First, it does not limit the amount of negative sentences that can be generated. If a training corpus only contains 5000 sentences, it may not be possible to find enough sentences that are not parallel and have a length ratio less than 2.0, and have over 50% of the words aligned.

## 4.2 Domain Sensitivity

No research has been done regarding the effect of domain on maximum entropy classifiers that generate parallel corpora, but the effect of domain is very important to any type of classifier. It is especially important for the use case of JMaxAlign, since it is very possible that the comparable corpora from which parallel corpora are being extracted may be in a different domain than the training data. For example, someone wishing to extract parallel corpora from Wikipedia might be forced to train JMaxAlign on a corpora constructed from government documents. JMaxAlign classifies the test sentences based on the similarity between their features and the features of the training data. If the corpora are from different domains, they will have different features. For this reason, training and testing on corpora from different domains can lower the quality of the results in many NLP tasks. This is particularly relevant to sentence alignment because extraction from a new data source may require training on out–of– domain parallel corpora.

To test the sensitivity of JMaxAlign to domain, two corpora were chosen from the Open Source Parallel Corpora[3], an online collection of many corpora. In both of these corpora, sentences were already segmented, so sentence-aligned gold standard data was available. The first is the KDE corpora, a collection of localization files for the K Desktop Environment. The second is the Open Subtitles corpora, which was generated aligning movie subtitles in different languages based on the time at which they appeared on the screen. Both corpora already marked sentence boundaries, so no sentence splitting tools were needed.

These corpora exhibit several differences. First, they are not equally parallel. Tiedemann et al. [2004] makes no observation about the accuracy of the Open Subtitles Corpora, but they note that “not all translations are completed and, therefore, the KDE corpus is not entirely parallel”. So there may be some noise in the training data. Second, they both capture a different type of language data. The Open Subtitles corpora are a collection of transcriptions of spoken sentences, while the KDE corpora are a collection of phrases used to internationalize the KDE.

The KDE corpora contain a very specific set of vocabulary. The data are also much more terse, and sentences are usually between one and five words. Conversely, the Open Subtitles

[3]http://opus.lingfil.uu.se/

corpora contain full grammatical sentences that are much longer. Since sentence-length similarity is a good indicator of non-parallelism, it was expected that cross-domain tests will show lower recall due to the different types of sentences in each of these corpora. This is because dictionaries generated by training on one set of corpora might not have large vocabulary overlap with a different corpora.

Tables 3 and 4 show the results of training and testing on all possible combinations of the KDE and Subtitles corpora. The "training" column indicates which corpora the training data came from and the "testing" column indicates which corpora the testing data came from. Each test was run with 5000 parallel and 3000 non-parallel training sentences, and tested on 5000 parallel and 5000 non-parallel sentences. In order to prevent the linguistic similarity of the language pairs could confound the effects of changing the testing and training domain, all domain combinations were tested on both similar and dissimilar language pairs. Table 3 shows the results of the domain tests for similar language pairs, and Table 4 shows the results for dissimilar language pairs.

Table 3: Similar Language Pairs

| Language Pair | Precision | Recall | F–Score | Training | Testing |
|---|---|---|---|---|---|
| Spanish–French | 96.26 | 49.04 | 64.93 | Subtitles | KDE |
| Spanish–French | 93.54 | 100.00 | 96.77 | Subtitles | Subtitles |
| Spanish–French | 99.9 | 49.97 | 66.62 | KDE | Subtitles |
| Spanish–French | 99.82 | 100.0 | 99.91 | KDE | KDE |
| Polish–Russian | 93.56 | 48.33 | 63.74 | Subtitles | KDE |
| Polish–Russian | 89.18 | 100 | 94.28 | Subtitles | Subtitles |
| Polish–Russian | 91.66 | 47.82 | 62.85 | KDE | Subtitles |
| Polish–Russian | 95.94 | 100.00 | 97.92 | KDE | KDE |

Table 4: Dissimilar Language Pairs

| Language Pair | Precision | Recall | F–Score | Training | Testing |
|---|---|---|---|---|---|
| English–Japanese | 94.84 | 48.67 | 64.33 | Subtitles | KDE |
| English–Japanese | 89.18 | 100.00 | 94.28 | Subtitles | Subtitles |
| English–Japanese | 87.4 | 46.63 | 60.82 | KDE | Subtitles |
| English–Japanese | 87.92 | 100.00 | 93.57 | KDE | KDE |
| Arabic–Spanish | 86.46 | 46.28 | 60.21 | Subtitles | KDE |
| Arabic–Spanish | 88.31 | 100 | 93.85 | Subtitles | Subtitles |
| Arabic–Spanish | 91.08 | 47.66 | 62.58 | KDE | Subtitles |
| Arabic–Spanish | 76.18 | 100.00 | 86.47 | KDE | KDE |

It is clear that altering testing and training domain has an effect on the quality of the results. Overall, the F–scores are higher for the similar language pairs when the testing and training domain are the same. This effect seems to be amplified on the dissimilar language pairs. The biggest effect of changing domain seems to e a significant drop in recall. This is probably due to the importance of the sentence-length feature. As stated earlier, sentence–length is extremely useful for determining which sentences are not parallel. By training on the Subtitles corpora, the classifier learns that the length of the sentences is an important discriminator. But that assumption does not hold true for the KDE corpora, since the sentences are frequently not complete grammatical sentences. If the two corpora were not such drastically different registers of language, this effect might not be so dramatic.

## 4.3 Training Data Size

Since parallel corpora are rarely available, the fact that JMaxAlign requires parallel training data is disadvantageous. To study the effects of training data, we varied the size of training data used to build a Dutch–Chinese parallel corpora. Dutch–Chinese was chosen because the two languages are very dissimilar. If the chosen language pair contained two similar languages, it would be possible to achieve high F-Scores with very little training data. The previous results have shown that dissimilar pairs generally have lower F–Scores, so there is more room for growth, which allows us to better see the effects of varying training data. The values in the Table 5 were generated by testing on 5000 sentences, 2500 parallel and 2500 non-parallel. All data in these tests were taken from the Open Subtitles Corpora. For this experiment, balanced training data sets were used (i.e., the same number of parallel and non-parallel sentences were used in testing). Table 5 shows that adding more training data

Table 5: Effects of increasing training data

| Training Data | Precision | Recall | F–Score |
|---|---|---|---|
| 1000 | 85.44 | 94.48 | 82.59 |
| 2000 | 73.41 | 94.49 | 82.62 |
| 3000 | 73.44 | 94.49 | 82.64 |
| 4000 | 73.44 | 94.49 | 82.64 |
| 5000 | 73.44 | 94.49 | 82.64 |
| 10000 | 73.44 | 94.49 | 82.64 |

has little effect on the functionality of the classifier. The high recall in Table 5 indicates that JMaxAlign is good at detecting non-parallel sentences. However, the low precision indicates that it does not always accurately classifying parallel sentences. However, the F–Score at 2000 sentences is almost the same as the F-Score at 1000 sentences. This seems to indicate that JMaxAlign is not able to take advantage of extra data. But this is not the case. JMaxAlign can take advantage of extra data in unbalanced training sets. Munteanu and Marcu [2005]'s Arabic–English classifier achieved the best results when training on corpora that contained 70% parallel sentences and 30% non–parallel sentences.Table 6 is the result of training JMaxAlign on the same Dutch-Chinese corpora with various unbalanced training sets.

Table 6 shows that the balance of parallel and non-parallel sentences can be altered to improve performance. When there are 3000 parallel sentences and 1000 non-parallel sentences, JMaxAlign is able to achieve a much higher precision than that 1000 parallel sentences and 3000 non-parallel sentences. This is impressive, because despite the high ratio of parallel to non-parallel sentences, JMaxAlign is still able to do a good job classifying non-parallel sentences. When the number of parallel sentences is increased to 5000, and the number of non-parallel sentences to 2500, recall increases by 20%. However, this

Table 6: Training on Unbalanced Corpora

| Parallel Sentences | Non-parallel Sentences | Precision | Recall | F–Score |
|---|---|---|---|---|
| 1000 | 3000 | 51.20 | 95.95 | 66.77 |
| 3000 | 1000 | 87.57 | 73.81 | 80.10 |
| 2500 | 5000 | 63.76 | 93.79 | 75.91 |
| 5000 | 2500 | 77.02 | 94.81 | 84.9 |
| 5000 | 10000 | 64.08 | 93.83 | 76.14 |
| 10000 | 5000 | 80.24 | 95.10 | 87.02 |
| 20000 | 10000 | 76.08 | 95.64 | 84.74 |

causes the precision to drop by 10%, because the lower ratio decreases JMaxAlign's bias towards finding parallel sentences. Doubling the data to 10000 paralle l sentences and 5000 non-parallel sentences cause the precision to rise by 3%, somewhat negating this effect. But again doubling the amount of data (to 20,000 parallel sentences and 10,000 parallel sentences) causes the precision to drop again, possibly due to overfitting. From Table 6, it seems that the best results for JMaxAlign are achieved with between 10,000-15,000 parallel sentences, and 2,500-5,000 non-parallel sentences.

## 5 Conclusion

This work has resulted in several contributions. First, is has advanced the state–of–the art for parallel sentence detection. It has shown that maximum entropy classifiers, while effected by linguistic similarity and domain, can produce useful results for almost any language pair. This will allow the creation of parallel corpora for many new languages. If seed corpora that are similar to the corpora from which you want to extract parallel sentences can be made, JMaxAlign should prove a very useful tool. Even if seed corpora cannot be created, the KDE corpora can be used. JMaxAlign can be tuned for precision or recall by altering the amount of negative and positive training examples, so researchers can decide what trade–off is most appropriate for their task. JMaxAlign is also open–source, meaning that other researchers can modify it by changing the underlying classifier, or adding language–specific features. The code can be found at https://code.google.com/p/jmaxalign/.

## References

S.F. Adafre and M. de Rijke. Finding similar sentences across multiple languages in Wikipedia. In *Proceedings of the workshop on new text: Wikis and blogs and other dynamic text sources*, pages 62–69, 2006.

Peter F. Brown, Vincent J. Della Pietra, Stephen A. Della Pietra, and Robert. L. Mercer. The mathematics of statistical machine translation: Parameter estimation. *Computational Linguistics*, 19:263–311, 1993.

W.A. Gale and K.W. Church. A program for aligning sentences in bilingual corpora. *Computational linguistics*, 19(1):75–102, 1993.

Percy Liang, Ben Taskar, and Dan Klein. Alignment by agreement. In *Proceedings of Human Language Technology Conference of the North American Chapter of the Association of Computational Linguistics*, HLT-NAACL '06, pages 104–111, Stroudsburg, PA, USA, 2006. Association for Computational Linguistics. doi: 10.3115/1220835.1220849. URL `http://dx.doi.org/10.3115/1220835.1220849`.

Xiaoyi Ma. Champollion: A robust parallel text sentence aligner. In *Proceedings of the fifth international conference on Language Resources and Evaluation (LREC)*, 2006.

M. Mohammadi and N. QasemAghaee. Building bilingual parallel corpora based on wikipedia. In *International Conference on Computer Engineering and Applications (ICCEA)*, volume 2, pages 264–268, 2010.

Robert C. Moore. Fast and accurate sentence alignment of bilingual corpora. In *Proceedings of the 5th Conference of the Association for Machine Translation in the Americas on Machine Translation: From Research to Real Users*, AMTA '02, pages 135–144, London, UK, 2002. Springer-Verlag. ISBN 3-540-44282-0. URL `http://dl.acm.org/citation.cfm?id=648181.749407`.

Dragos Stefan Munteanu and Daniel Marcu. Improving machine translation performance by exploiting non-parallel corpora. *Computational Linguistics*, 31:477–504, 2005.

J.R. Smith, C. Quirk, and K. Toutanova. Extracting parallel sentences from comparable corpora using document level alignment. In *NAACL-HLT*, pages 403–411, 2010.

Jörg Tiedemann, Lars Nygaard, and Tekstlaboratoriet Hf. The opus corpus – parallel and free. In *In Proceeding of the 4th International Conference on Language Resources and Evaluation (LREC*, pages 1183–1186, 2004.

Krisztina Toth, Richard Farkas, and Andras Kocsor. *Parallel corpora for medium density languages*, pages 590–596. Benjamins, 2005. URL `http://www.kornai.com/Papers/ranlp05parallel.pdf`.

# MIKE: An Interactive Microblogging Keyword Extractor using Contextual Semantic Smoothing

*Osama Ahmed Khan, Asim Karim*
Department of Computer Science, SBASSE
Lahore University of Management Sciences (LUMS)
Lahore, Pakistan
oakhan@lums.edu.pk, akarim@lums.edu.pk

ABSTRACT
Social media, such as tweets on Twitter and Short Message Service (SMS) messages on cellular networks, are short-length textual documents (short texts or microblog posts) exchanged among users on the Web and/or their mobile devices. Automatic keyword extraction from short texts can be applied in online applications such as tag recommendation and contextual advertising. In this paper we present MIKE, a robust interactive system for keyword extraction from single microblog posts, which uses contextual semantic smoothing; a novel technique that considers term usage patterns in similar texts to improve term relevance information. We incorporate Phi coefficient in our technique, which is based on corpus-based term-to-term relatedness information and successfully handles the short-length challenge of short texts. Our experiments, conducted on multi-lingual SMS messages and English Twitter tweets, show that MIKE significantly improves keyword extraction performance beyond that achieved by Term Frequency, Inverse Document Frequency (TFIDF). MIKE also integrates a rule-based vocabulary standardizer for multi-lingual short texts which independently improves keyword extraction performance by 14%.

KEYWORDS: Keyword Extraction, Microblogs, Short texts, Semantic Smoothing, SMS, Romanized Urdu, MIKE.

*Proceedings of COLING 2012: Demonstration Papers*, pages 289–296,
COLING 2012, Mumbai, December 2012.

| Type | Text |
|---|---|
| Message | *aj friday hay is jaldi chutti hogayi, aur wassey mein mob lekare jata hun, tm ne kal program dekha tha kya?* [It is Friday, therefore I got off early, otherwise I take mobile with me. Did you see the program yesterday?] |
| Tweet | *Tweet 3x Lens Cap Keeper Holder with Elastic Band Loop Strap: US$6.93 End Date: Sunday Sep-05-2010 11:15:10 PDTBuy it N...http://bit.ly/cZXiSP* |

Table 1: Examples of short texts

# 1 Introduction

Recently microblogs (e.g. Twitter) have become very popular for rapid information sharing and communication (Kwak et al., 2010). Typically, microblog posts and SMS messages are short-length documents written in an informal style. Two short-text examples are given in Table 1. The SMS message is a conversational text written primarily in Urdu (but in Latin script) mixed with some English words, while the tweet represents a short advertisement in English. Key challenges of short texts include noise (e.g. '$\beta$etter', ':)'), multiple languages (e.g. 'friday hay' [it is Friday]), varied vocabulary (e.g. abbreviations like 'Interpol', contractions like 'tc' [take care], acronyms like 'BBC' [British Broadcasting Corporation], proper nouns like 'Paris'), different styles (e.g. slangs like 'lol' [laughing out loud], colloquialism like 'wanna'), poor quality (e.g. typos like 'achieve'), and out-of-vocabulary words (e.g. 'gr8'). It is therefore necessary to propose and evaluate new text processing techniques for this varied document type.

Extensive preprocessing can address some of these challenges, but established resources and tools are not yet available for short texts. Furthermore, due to multi-varied nature of short texts (e.g. multi-linguality), external resources like Wikipedia and WordNet are not applicable. Therefore, in addition to adapting standard preprocessing procedures, we adopt a specialized standardizer (Khan and Karim, 2012) for transforming varied usage of terms in multiple languages to their standard forms.

Despite extensive preprocessing, individual short texts contain limited information for term relevance determination. This is because such documents are short in length (about 13 terms on average), while vocabulary size is large. Moreover, typically a specific term appears no more than once in a short text document, thus providing no information for its relevance rank in the document. However, we can exploit term-to-term semantic relatedness information harvested from similar short texts to reduce sparsity and improve relevance ranking of terms; a technique labeled as contextual semantic smoothing. Semantic smoothing of document models has been utilized previously for clustering and classification (Zhang et al., 2006; Nasir et al., 2011). To the best of our knowledge this is the first time that semantic smoothing has been applied to short-text processing in general and to keyword extraction in particular. Also, the incorporation of Phi coefficient in our technique validates its usefulness for improved term association in sparse datasets (Tan et al., 2002).

In this paper, we make the following key contributions. First, we develop a keyword extraction system for short texts, called MIKE that is based on contextual semantic smoothing of the TFIDF matrix using Phi coefficient. This methodology does not require an external knowledge source, is more efficient than iterative graph-based techniques, and caters for all of the above mentioned challenges of short texts. We also demonstrate robustness of MIKE, which is interactive in nature, for multi-varied and sparse short texts. Second, we evaluate the impact of various preprocessing procedures on keyword extraction performance.

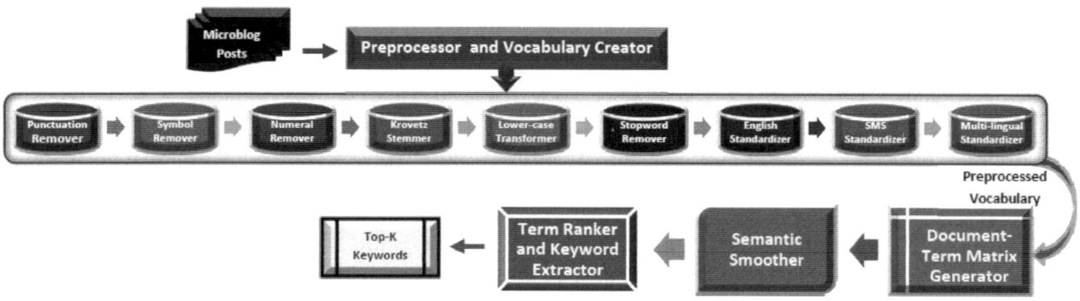


Figure 1: System Architecture of MIKE

In particular, we show that standardization of multi-lingual and multi-varied short texts through a rule-based standardizer can improve keyword extraction performance by 14%. Third, we perform our experiments on two short-text collections: a unique SMS collection from an SMS-based online social network (group messaging service) running in Pakistan, and a tweet collection from Twitter. The SMS collection contains significant proportions of messages typed in Romanized Urdu and other local languages, while the Twitter collection comprises English tweets only. This is the first time that an interactive keyword extraction system has been developed for short texts, and is evaluated on predominantly Romanized Urdu SMS messages.

The rest of the paper is organized as follows. We present the system architecture of MIKE in Section 2. Results from various experiments are provided in Sec 3. Our demonstration plan is laid out in Section 4.

## 2 System Architecture

In this section, we present the interactive system architecture of MIKE, which involves four processing modules: (1) preprocessor and vocabulary creator, (2) document-term matrix generator, (3) semantic smoother, and (4) term ranker and keyword extractor. These modules are discussed in detail ahead and in Figure 1. Given a collection of short texts or documents $\mathscr{D} = \{d_1, d_2, \ldots, d_N\}$ and domain-based information (stopword list and standardization lists), a keyword extraction technique outputs the top $K$ most descriptive terms from document $d_i$ as its keywords.

### 2.1 Preprocessor and Vocabulary Creator

The first module in MIKE preprocesses the collection of microblog posts and builds the vocabulary of terms out of it. Due to the presence of substantial variability and 'noise' in short-text documents when compared to conventional documents, several preprocessing procedures may be required. In this work, we implement the following procedures: (1) Punctuation removal; (2) Symbol removal; (3) Numeral removal; (4) Transformation to lower-case; (5) Stemming using Krovetz stemmer (Krovetz, 1995), which produces complete words as stems rather than truncated ones that can be produced by other stemmers. (6) Removal of stopwords using stopword list containing English articles and pronouns, obtained from AutoMap software[1]. (7) Application of English, SMS, and national/local language standardization lists.

[1]http://www.casos.cs.cmu.edu/projects/automap/

In order to tackle the issue of multi-varied composition of short texts, we apply three standardization lists. The English standardization list is obtained from AutoMap software[1]. This list maps British English and general English term variations to their respective American English forms. The SMS standardization list is built from two online sources[2 3]. This list transforms frequently used terms in English microblog texts to their standard forms.

For our SMS collection, which contain messages written in Urdu (national language) and local languages using Latin script, we apply the specialized standardizer that we have developed earlier (Khan and Karim, 2012). This standardizer is based on a rule-based model for multi-lingual texts, and maps varied usage of terms to their unique standard forms.

## 2.2 Document-Term Matrix Generator

Once the vocabulary is built, the second module represents the documents in vector space of size $M$, where $M$ is the vocabulary size. TFIDF is utilized here for weighting each term in a short text document since it is considered state-of-the-art among keyword extraction techniques (Wu et al., 2010). Now each document $d_i \in \mathcal{D}$ is mapped into the vector $\mathbf{x}_i = [x_{i1}, x_{i2}, \ldots, x_{iM}]$, where $x_{ij} \geq 0$ is the weight of term $t_j$ in document $d_i$. Notice that the computation of TFIDF requires the entire document collection; thus this method incorporates a corpus-based statistic of a term (its document frequency) alongwith local document information (its term frequency). After this transformation, the entire document collection $\mathcal{D}$ can be represented by the $N \times M$ matrix $\mathbf{X} = [\mathbf{x}_1, \mathbf{x}_2, \ldots, \mathbf{x}_N]^T$.

## 2.3 Semantic Smoother

A key contribution of this work is the evaluation of a contextual or corpus-based term-to-term semantic relatedness measure (Phi coefficient) on semantic smoothing and keyword extraction from short texts. The document-term matrix **X**, defined in the previous subsection, captures the relevance of each term in a document via its frequency in the document and the corpus (TFIDF); this matrix does not incorporate the semantic relatedness of terms in the collection $\mathcal{D}$. Therefore, we define an $M \times M$ term-term matrix **R** whose $(i, j)$ element, identified as $r_{ij}$, quantifies the semantic relatedness of terms $t_i$ and $t_j$. This matrix serves as a smoothing or scaling matrix for the original document-term matrix **X** to yield the modified document-term matrix (Nasir et al., 2011): $\bar{\mathbf{X}} = \mathbf{XR}$.

Matrix $\bar{\mathbf{X}}$ now incorporates local document information, global corpus information, as well as semantic relatedness between terms. For example, if a document contains three terms $(t_i, t_j, t_k)$ with equal frequency, and the semantic relatedness of $t_i$ is high with both $t_j$ and $t_k$ in the collection (while $t_j$ and $t_k$ are semantically related to $t_i$ only), then the smoothed weight of $t_i$ will become larger than that for both $t_j$ and $t_k$. We state our hypothesis as: "A term in a document should be ranked high for keywordness in the document, if the term possesses high local document structure value as well as high global (but contextually relevant since it is based on short texts from the same microblog collection) semantic relatedness value with the other terms present in the document". It is worth noting that this module generates the semantically smoothed document-term matrix via a single multiplication of the document-term and term-term matrices, as opposed to the multiple iterations required in graph-based techniques (Mihalcea and Tarau, 2004).

[2]http://www.sms-text-guide.com/sms-text-language.html
[3]http://www.smsdictionary.co.uk/abbreviations

### 2.3.1 Semantic Relatedness measure

We select Phi coefficient as the term-to-term semantic relatedness measure for constructing matrix **R**:

$$PhiCoefficient = \frac{ad - bc}{\sqrt{(a+b)(c+d)(b+d)(a+c)}} \quad (1)$$

The pairwise term co-occurrence distributions are formed by the term co-occurrence contingency table (Table 2). Each cell in this 2 × 2 table shows the number of documents exhibiting a particular term co-occurrence behavior (e.g. $b$ is the number of documents in the collection in which $t_i$ occurs and $t_j$ does not [identified with $\bar{t}_j$]). Due to the short length of microblog posts, we assume the co-occurrence window size to be the document length. This choice is supported by our preliminary results which demonstrated that this setting outperformed all other settings where window size was assigned a value less than the document length.

| | $t_j$ | $\bar{t}_j$ |
|---|---|---|
| $t_i$ | $a$ | $b$ |
| $\bar{t}_i$ | $c$ | $d$ |

Table 2: Term co-occurrence contingency table

The Phi coefficient is the Pearson's correlation coefficient for binary variables and its value lies in the interval $[-1, +1]$. It is a statistically sound measure of correlation which additionally possesses the following two significant characteristics (Tan et al., 2002). First, it is anti-symmetric under row and column permutations of the contingency table, i.e., it effectively distinguishes between positive and negative correlations between items. Second, it is a symmetric inversion invariant measure which does not get affected when the contingency table is inverted. Phi coefficient is the only measure among co-occurrence based measures that possesses these strong properties.

## 2.4 Term Ranker and Keyword Extractor

The final module outputs the top $K$ terms from each document as its keywords. Given the original or smoothed document-term matrix ($\mathbf{X}$ or $\bar{\mathbf{X}}$), the top $K$ keywords for document $d_i$ are the top $K$ terms in the document (in the $i$th row of the document-term matrix) with the highest term weights. In the next section we evaluate performances of two keyword extraction techniques: the original document-term matrix (TFIDF), and the smoothed document-term matrix (TFIDF × **R**) on multiple short-text collections.

# 3 Experimental Results

Tables 3, 4 and 5, alongwith Figure 2 highlight significant results generated by our experiments.

# 4 Demonstration Plan

In the demonstration we will show the system interfaces for user interaction during the process of feeding in real-time microblog posts and visualizing keywords automatically generated by MIKE in result. In addition we will present users option to explore different combinations of preprocessing procedures as desired for various types of microblog posts. Also, users can provide different values of $K$ as input; the desired number of top keywords

| | $K=1$ | | | $K=3$ | | | $K=5$ | | |
|---|---|---|---|---|---|---|---|---|---|
| | $PR$ | $RE$ | $FM$ | $PR$ | $RE$ | $FM$ | $PR$ | $RE$ | $FM$ |
| SMS TFIDF | **58.4** | **60.4** | **59.4** | 47.1 | 50.0 | 48.5 | 39.7 | 61.9 | 48.4 |
| SMS TFIDF+Phi | 57.2 | 59.1 | 58.1 | **48.9** | **52.0** | **50.4** | **41.7** | **65.0** | **50.8** |
| Twitter TFIDF | **49.4** | **50.0** | **49.7** | 42.7 | 45.0 | 43.8 | 39.5 | 67.1 | 49.8 |
| Twitter TFIDF+Phi | 46.5 | 47.1 | 46.8 | **44.0** | **46.3** | **45.1** | **40.9** | **69.5** | **51.5** |

Table 3: Keyword Extraction Results for SMS and Twitter collections ($PR$ = Precision, $RE$ = Recall, $FM$ = F-measure)

| Size | SMS | | Twitter | |
|---|---|---|---|---|
| | TFIDF | TFIDF+Phi | TFIDF | TFIDF+Phi |
| 2,000 | 55.8 | 57.4 | 45.5 | 46.5 |
| 5,000 | 50.7 | 53.2 | 44.1 | 45.9 |
| 10,000 | 50.7 | 52.9 | 44.2 | 45.8 |
| 20,000 | 48.5 | 50.4 | 43.8 | 45.1 |

Table 4: Robustness of MIKE for SMS and Twitter collections in F-measure for $K=3$

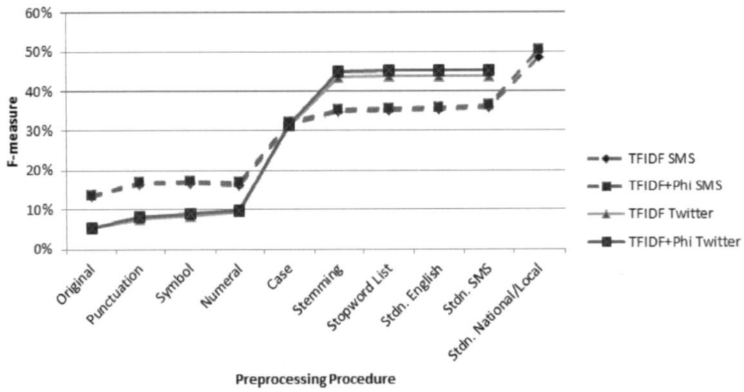


Figure 2: Significance of our rule-based multi-lingual standardizer among various preprocessing procedures in F-measure for $K=3$

| | $K=1$ | $K=3$ | $K=5$ |
|---|---|---|---|
| Message TFIDF | friday | friday jaldi [early] chhutti [holiday] | friday jaldi chhutti mobile program |
| Message TFIDF+Phi | friday | friday chhutti mobile | friday chhutti mobile program daikha [see] |
| Tweet TFIDF | lens | lens cap keeper | lens cap keeper band sunday |
| Tweet TFIDF+Phi | lens | lens cap holder | lens cap holder end sunday |

Table 5: Keywords generated from microblog posts (see Table 1) for TFIDF and TFIDF+Phi techniques

for a document. The keywords generated by MIKE can be considered as personalized tags or advertising keywords, which are recommended for users for their respective collection of microblog posts in their selected social networks.

We will describe the system components briefly, alongwith their requirements, functionality and inter-connectivity. We will demonstrate the working of multi-lingual standardizer that we have built up earlier, and now is incorporated in MIKE. We will summarize the implementation technique on which MIKE is based and outline our key contributions in the system development. We will also narrate the practical development lessons learned through this work, our original research findings, and our first-hand experiences with this research prototype system.

## References


Khan, O. A. and Karim, A. (2012). A rule-based model for normalization of SMS text. In *Proceedings of the 24th IEEE International Conference on Tools with Artificial Intelligence*, ICTAI '12. IEEE.

Krovetz, R. (1995). *Word sense disambiguation for large text databases*. Phd thesis, University of Massachusetts, Amherst, USA.

Kwak, H., Lee, C., Park, H., and Moon, S. (2010). What is Twitter, a social network or a news media? In *Proceedings of the 19th International Conference on World Wide Web*, WWW '10, pages 591–600, New York, NY, USA. ACM.

Mihalcea, R. and Tarau, P. (2004). TextRank: Bringing order into texts. In *Proceedings of the 2004 Conference on Empirical Methods in Natural Language Processing*, EMNLP'04, New York, NY, USA. ACL.

Nasir, J., Karim, A., Tsatsaronis, G., and Varlamis, I. (2011). A knowledge-based semantic kernel for text classification. In Grossi, R., Sebastiani, F., and Silvestri, F., editors, *String Processing and Information Retrieval*, volume 7024 of *Lecture Notes in Computer Science*, pages 261–266. Springer Berlin / Heidelberg.

Tan, P.-N., Kumar, V., and Srivastava, J. (2002). Selecting the right interestingness measure for association patterns. In *Proceedings of the 8th ACM SIGKDD International Conference on Knowledge Discovery and Data Mining*, KDD '02, pages 32–41, New York, NY, USA. ACM.

Wu, W., Zhang, B., and Ostendorf, M. (2010). Automatic generation of personalized annotation tags for Twitter users. In *Human Language Technologies: The 2010 Annual Conference of the North American Chapter of the Association for Computational Linguistics*, NAACL '10, pages 689–692, Stroudsburg, PA, USA. ACL.

Zhang, X., Zhou, X., and Hu, X. (2006). Semantic smoothing for model-based document clustering. In *Proceedings of the 6th International Conference on Data Mining*, ICDM '06, pages 1193–1198. IEEE.

# Domain Based Classification of Punjabi Text Documents

*Nidhi, Vishal Gupta*
University Institute of Engineering and Technology, Panjab University
naseeb.nidhi@gmail.com, vishal@pu.ac.in

ABSTRACT

With the dramatic increase in the amount of content available in digital forms gives rise to a problem to manage this online textual data. As a result, it has become a necessary to classify large texts (documents) into specific classes. And Text Classification is a text mining technique which is used to classify the text documents into predefined classes. Most text classification techniques work on the principle of probabilities or matching terms with class name, in order to classify the documents into classes. The objective of this work is to consider the relationship among terms. And for this, Sports Specific Ontology is manually created for the first time. Two new algorithms, Ontology Based Classification and Hybrid Approach are proposed for Punjabi Text Classification. The experimental results conclude that Ontology Based Classification (85%) and Hybrid Approach (85%) provide better results.

KEYWORDS: Punjabi Text Classification, Ontology Based Classification, Naive Bayes Classification, Centroid Based Classification.

*Proceedings of COLING 2012: Demonstration Papers*, pages 297–304,
COLING 2012, Mumbai, December 2012.

# 1. Introduction

A review of the literature shows that no prior work has been done to classify the Punjabi documents. Therefore the objective of the work is to develop a system that takes Punjabi text documents as input and classify them into its corresponding classes using classification algorithm selected by user. These classes are: ਕ੍ਰਿਕਟ (krikaṭ) (Cricket), ਹਾਕੀ (hākī) (Hockey), ਕਬੱਡੀ (kabḍḍī) (Kabaddi), ਫੁਟਬਾਲ (phuṭbāl) (Football), ਟੈਨਿਸ (ṭainis) (Tennis), ਬੈਡਮਿੰਟਨ (baiḍminṭan) (Badminton). These classes are defined by analyzing the Punjabi Corpus used for the classification task. And for classifying these documents, two new approaches are proposed for Punjabi language, Ontology Based Classification and Hybrid Approach. For Ontology Based Classification, Sports specific Ontology is manually created in Punjabi Language for the first time that consist of terms related to the class. E.g. Cricket class consists of following terms ਬੱਲੇਬਾਜ਼ੀ (batting), ਗੇਂਦਬਾਜ਼ੀ (bowling), ਫੀਲਡਿੰਗ (fielding), ਵਿਕਟ (wicket), Football class consist of ਗੋਲਕੀਪਰ (Goalkeeper), ਗੋਲ (Goal), ਫਾਰਵਰਡ (Forward), ਮਿਡਫੀਲਡਰ (Mid-fielder), ਡਿਫੈਂਡਰ (Defender) etc. An advantage of using Ontology is, there is no requirement of training set i.e. labeled documents and it can also be beneficial for developing other NLP applications in Punjabi. And to compare the efficiency of proposed algorithms, standard classification algorithms results, Naïve Bayes and Centroid Based Classification are compared using F-score and Fallout.

# 2. Proposed algorithm for Punjabi Text Classification

For Punjabi Text Classification, initials steps that need to do are following:

- Prepare Training Set for Naïve Bayes and Centroid Based Classifier. The documents in the training set are tokenized and preprocessed. Stopwords, punctuations, special symbols, name entities are extracted from the document.
- For each class, centroid vectors are created using training set.

After initial steps, Punjabi Text Classification is implemented into three main phases:

- Preprocessing Phase
- Feature Extraction Phase
- Processing Phase

## 2.1 Pre-processing Phase

Each Unlabelled Punjabi Text Documents are represented as "Bag of Words". Before classifying, stopwords, special symbols, punctuations (<,>, :,{,},[,],^,&,*,(,) etc.) are removed from the documents, as they are irrelevant to the classification task. Table 1 shows lists of some stopwords that are removed from the document.

| | | | | |
|---|---|---|---|---|
| ਲਈ (laī) | ਨੇ (nē) | ਆਪਣੇ (āpaṇē) | ਨਹੀਂ (nahīṃ) | ਤਾਂ (tāṃ) |
| ਇਹ (ih) | ਹੀ (hī) | ਜਾਂ (jāṃ) | ਦਿੱਤਾ (dittā) | ਹੋ (hō) |

TABLE 1- Stopwords List

## 2.2 Feature Extraction Phase

After pre-processing, input documents still contain redundant or non-relevant features that increase the computations. Therefore, to reduce the feature space, along with statistical approaches, language dependent rules and gazetteer lists are also used by analyzing the documents. TFXIDF weighting is the most common statistical method used for feature extraction [Han J. and Kamber M. 2006] using equation (1).

$$W(i) = tf(i)*\log(N/N_i) \quad (1)$$

### 2.2.1 Linguistic Features

And to extract the language dependent features, Hybrid Approach is used that include Rule Based Approach and List Lookup approach. A number of rules specific for Punjabi language is formed to extract the language dependent features are following:

1. Name Rule
   a. if word is found, its previous word is checked for middle name.
   b. if middle name is found, its previous word is extracted as first name from the document. Otherwise, word is extracted from the document.
2. Location Rules
   a. if word is found, it is extracted from the document.
   b. if Punjabi word ਵਿਖੇ (vikhē) or ਜ਼ਿਲ੍ਹੇ (zilhē) is found, its previous word is extracted as location name.
   c. if Punjabi word ਪਿੰਡ (piṇḍ) is found, its next word is extracted as location name.
3. Date/Time Rules
   a. if month or week day is found, it is extracted.
   b. if Punjabi words ਅੱਜ (ajj), ਕੱਲ (kall), ਸਵੇਰ (savēr), ਸ਼ਾਂਮ (shāmm), ਦੁਪਹਿਰ (duphir) etc. are found, they are extracted.
4. Numbers/Counting
   a. if any numeric character is found, it is extracted.
   b. if Punjabi words ਇੱਕ (ikk), ਦੂਜਾ (dūjā), ਦੋ (dō), ਪਹਿਲਾ (pahilā), ਛੇਵੀਂ (chēvīṃ) etc. are found, they are extracted.
5. Designation Rule
   a. if designation found e.g. ਕਪਤਾਨ (kaptān), ਕੋਚ (kōc), ਕੈਪਟਨ (kaipṭan), it is extracted.
6. Abbreviation
   a. if words like ਆਈ (āī), ਸੀ (sī), ਐਲ (ail), ਪੀ (pī), ਬੀ (bī) etc. are found, they are extracted.

### 2.2.2 Gazetteer Lists

Lists prepared for classifying Punjabi Text Documents are following:

- Middle Names

- Last names
- Location Names
- Month Names
- Day Names
- Designation names
- Number/Counting
- Abbreviations
- Stop words
- Sports Specific Ontology (e.g. preparing list for class ਹਾਕੀ (Hockey) that contain all of its related terms like ਸਟਰਾਈਕਰ (Striker), ਡਰਿਬਲਰ (Dribbler), ਪੈਨਲਟੀ (Penalty) etc.

## 2.3 Processing Phase

At this phase, classification algorithms are applied as following:

### 2.3.1 Naive Bayes Classification

Multinomial Event Model of Naive Bayes is used [McCallum and Nigam 1998; Chen et al. 2009] and for classification assign class Ci to the document if it has maximum posterior probability with that class.

### 2.3.2 Centroid Based Classification

Calculate the distance between each Centroid vector (c) and document vector (d); assign that class to the document that is having minimum Euclidean distance from the Centroid vector [Chen et al. 2008].

### 2.3.3 Ontology Based Classification

Traditional Classification methods ignore relationship between words. But, in fact, there exist a semantic relation between terms such as synonym, hyponymy etc. [Wu and Liu 2009]. The Ontology has different meaning for different users, in this classification task, Ontology stores words that are related to particular sport. Therefore, with the use of domain specific ontology, it becomes easy to classify the documents even if the document does not contain the class name in it. After feature extraction phase, for classification, calculate the frequency of extracted terms that are matched with terms in ontology. E.g. assign class cricket to the unlabelled document, if frequency of matching terms with class cricket ontology is maximum. If no match is found or a document shows same results for two or more classes then that document is not classified into any class, and left for manual classification.

### 2.3.4 Hybrid Approach

In hybrid approach, the two algorithms Naïve Bayes and Ontology based Classifier are combined for better results of classification. Using TF, TFXIDF or Information Gain (IG) as feature selection method sometimes results in features that are irrelevant. Therefore, Class Discriminating Measure (CDM), a feature evaluation metric for Naïve Bayes calculates the effectiveness of the feature using probabilities, is used for feature extraction. The results shown in [Chen et al. 2009], indicate that CDM is best feature selection approach than IG. The term having CDM value less than defined threshold value is ignored. And the remaining terms are used to represent the input unlabelled document. CDM for each term is calculated using (2)

$$CDM(w) = |\log P(w|Ci) - \log P(w|\overline{Ci})| \quad (2)$$

Where $P(w|Ci)$ = probability that word w occurs if class value is i

$P(w|\overline{Ci})$ = probability that word w occurs when class value is not i

$i=1,2,.....6$

Calculate the frequency of extracted terms that are matched with terms in ontology. Assign class Badminton to the unlabelled document, if the frequency of matching terms is maximum with class badminton. If no match is found or a document shows same results for two or more classes then that document is not classified into any class, and left for manual classification.

## 2.4 Classified Documents

After processing phase, unlabelled documents are classifies into classes.

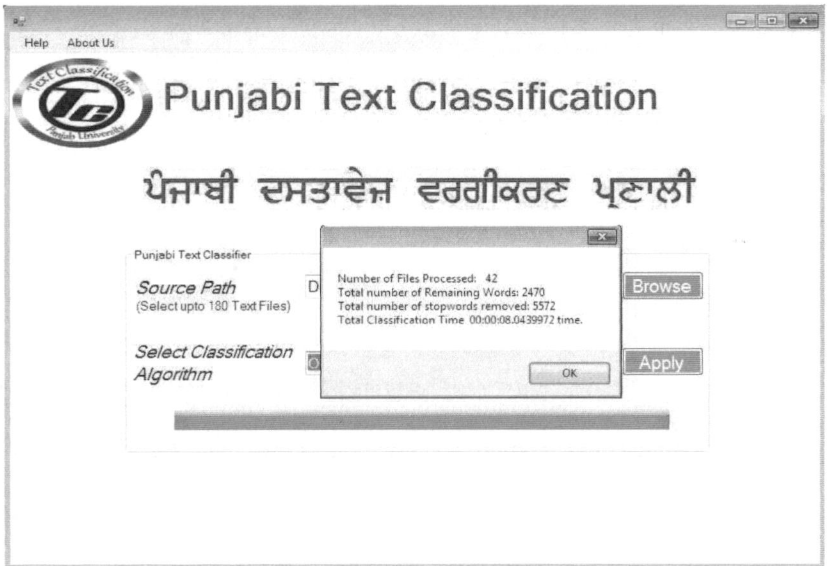


FIGURE 1- Punjabi Text Classifier System

Figure 1 shows the system takes 8 secs 04 ms to classify 42 Punjabi Text Documents. It also gives information about number of stopwords removed and number of words that are left after preprocessing phase.

# 3 Experimental Evaluations

## 3.1 Dataset

The corpus used for Punjabi Text Classification contains 180 Punjabi text documents, 45 files are used as Training Data. Training set contains total 3313 words. All the documents in the corpus are sports related and taken from the Punjabi News Web

Sources such as jagbani.com. The system has been implemented using C#.net platform. The stopword list is prepared manually contains 2319 words. The data structures used are files and arrays. Stopwords list, gazetteer lists and ontology are stored in text file. During the implementation, these files are stored into arrays to read the contents fast.

## 3.2 Experimental Results

F-score [Sun and Lim 2001] for each class is calculated for each classifier using equation (3)

F-Score = (2*Precision*Recall)/ (Precision + Recall) (3)

Precision = (docs correctly classified in class Ci)/ (total docs retrieved in class Ci)

Recall = (docs correctly classified in class Ci)/ (total relevant docs in test set that belong to class Ci)

| | Badminton | Cricket | Football | Hockey | Kabaddi | Tennis |
|---|---|---|---|---|---|---|
| Ontology Based Classification | 0.84 | 0.89 | 0.89 | 0.81 | 0.88 | 0.8 |
| Hybrid Classification | 0.83 | 0.91 | 0.88 | 0.84 | 0.8 | 0.88 |
| Centroid Based Classification | 0.64 | 0.85 | 0.8 | 0.64 | 0.67 | 0.81 |
| Naïve Bayes Classification | 0.87 | 0.77 | 0.46 | 0.63 | 0.42 | 0.75 |

TABLE 2- F-Score of each class using different classification techniques

From Table 2, it is concluded that on average Ontology (85%) and Hybrid Based Classification (85%) shows better results than standard algorithms, Naive Bayes (64%) and Centroid Based Classification (71%) for Punjabi Language. Even the fallout results shows that 2% of the documents retrieved by system are irrelevant in case of Ontology and Hybrid Based Classification where as 5% and 6% non-relevant documents are retrieved if Centroid and Naive Bayes Algorithm are chosen respectively.

## Conclusion

It is first time that two new algorithms Ontology and Hybrid Based Approach are proposed and implemented for classification of Punjabi documents as previously no other Punjabi document classifier is available in the world. The experimental results conclude that Ontology and Hybrid Classification provide better results in comparison to Naïve Bayes and Centroid Based for Punjabi documents.

## References

CHEN JINGNIAN, HUANG HOUKUAN, TIAN SHENGFENG AND QU YOULI (2009). Feature selection for text classification with Naïve Bayes. In: Expert Systems with Applications: An International Journal, Volume 36 Issue 3, Elsevier.

CHEN LIFEI, YE YANFANG AND JIANG QINGSHAN (2008). A New Centroid-Based Classifier for Text Categorization. In: Proceedings of IEEE 22nd International Conference on Advanced Information Networking and Applications, DOI= 10.1109/WAINA.2008.12.

HAN JIAWEI AND KAMBER MICHELIN (2006). Data Mining: Concepts and Techniques. Morgan Kaufmann Publishers, 2nd edition, USA, 70-181.

McCALLUM, A. AND NIGAM, K. (1998). A comparison of event models for naive Bayes text classification. In: AAAI98 workshop on learning for text categorization. 41-48. Technical Report WS-98-05. AAAI Press.

PUNJABI LANGUAGE (2012). In: http://en.wikipedia.org/wiki/Punjabi_language.

PUNJABI NEWS CORPUS

SUN AIXIN AND LIM Ee-PENG 2001. Hierarchical Text Classification and Evaluation. In: Proceedings of the 2001 IEEE International Conference on Data Mining(ICDM 2001), Pages 521-528, California, USA, November 2001.

WU GUOSHI AND LIU KAIPING (2009). Research on Text Classification Algorithm by Combining Statistical and Ontology Methods. In: International Conference on Computational Intelligence and Software Engineering, IEEE. DOI= 10.1109/CISE.2009.5363406.

# Open Information Extraction for SOV Language based on Entity-Predicate Pair Detection

*Woong−Ki Lee*[1] *Yeon−Su Lee*[1] *Hyoung−Gyu Lee*[1]
*Won−Ho Ryu*[2] *Hae−Chang Rim*[1]
(1) Department of Computer and Radio Communications Engineering
Korea University, Seoul, Korea
(2) Software R&D Center, Samsung Electronics Co., Ltd.
Suwon-si, Gyeonggi-do, Korea
`{wklee,yslee,hglee,rim}@nlp.korea.ac.kr`
`wonho.ryu@samsung.com`

ABSTRACT
Open IE usually has been studied for English which of one of subject-verb-object(SVO) languages where a relation between two entities tends to occur in order of entity-relational phrase-entity within a sentence. However, in SOV languages, two entities occur before the relational phrase so that the subject and the relation have a long distance. The conventional methods for Open IE mostly dealing with SVO languages have difficulties of extracting relations from SOV style sentences.
In this paper, we propose a new method of extracting relations from SOV languages. Our approach tries to solve long distance problems by identifying an entity-predicate pair and recognizing a relation within a predicate. Furthermore, we propose a post-processing approach using a language model, so that the system can detect more fluent and precise relations. Experimental results on Korean corpus show that the proposed approach is effective in improving the performance of relation extraction.

KEYWORDS: relation extraction, SOV language, predicate extraction.

*Proceedings of COLING 2012: Demonstration Papers*, pages 305–312,
COLING 2012, Mumbai, December 2012.

# 1 Introduction

Relation extraction detects the relationship between entities from natural language text and makes the information as a structured data. In the traditional relation extraction task, the relationship that needs to be extracted is pre-defined, according to the domain specific goal. Recently, the World Wide Web provides vast amounts of documents and internally accumulates a variety of valuable relational information. Therefore, extracting and utilizing the information from a large web corpus become a hot research issue.

Banko et al. (2007) announced the first proposed system as a new paradigm called Open IE. The goal of Open IE system is to extract all possible correct relationships between entities without pre-defining the relationships. Open IE has shown successful result in some degree. Hereafter, a lot of research has been carried out on Open IE like TextRunner (Yates et al., 2007), REVERB (Etzioni et al., 2011) and WOE (Wu and Weld, 2010). However, most previous approaches have been proposed for English corpus. Although they are language independent approaches, when applied to another kind of language such as Korean, an unexpected problem occurs. English is a SVO(Subject-Verb-Object) word order language. In most cases, a relational phrase appears between subject(an entity) and object(another entity). Therefore, they naturally assume that the phrase is associated with the subject entity.

However, in SOV language such as Korean, Japanese and Turkish, by default, the subject, object, and verb usually appear in that order. And the modifiers should always be placed before their modificands. Moreover, the word order is relatively free. Therefore, it is difficult to extract a relationship by using English like assumption. The following example is a sentence from a newspaper article.

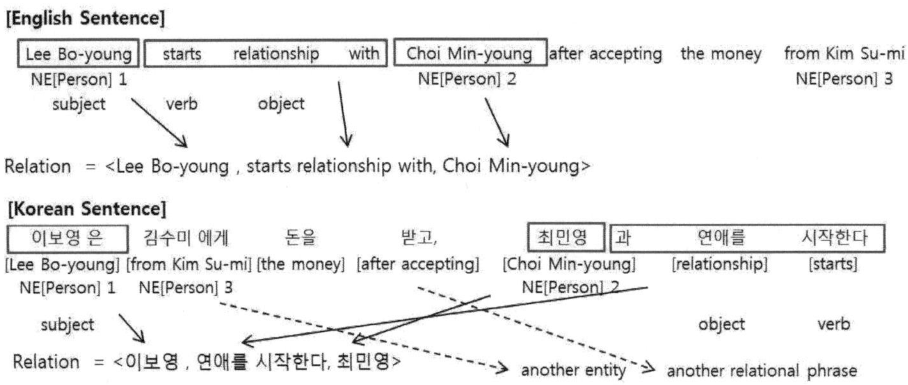


Figure 1: Word ordering and relation extraction: SVO vs. SOV

In Figure 1, the relational phrase of "이보영(Lee Bo-young[PERSON])" is "돈을 받고 (accepting the money from)" and "연애를 시작한다(starts relationship with)". The noticeable difference from the English sentence is that the entity, "이보영(Lee Bo-young[PERSON])", and the relational phrase, "연애를 시작한다(starts relationship with)", is far apart. Moreover, before appearing the phrase, another irrelevant entity, "김수미(Kim Su-mi[PERSON])", and the relational phrase, "돈을 받고(accepting money from)", appear. Because of these characteristics, it is impossible to apply the assumption of English (a relational phrase appears between two entities) to Korean sentences. In the strict sense, there exist two relational tuples in this sentence. Another is <Lee Bo-young, accepting the money from,

Kim Su-mi>. However, it is also impossible to extract this tuple by the assumption in English. To solve the problem, we consider the connectivity between entities and predicate in the first place. And then, we identify if there exist a relationship in the connected tuple. In addition, to extract a comprehensible phrase, we apply a language model to the relation tuple.

# 2 Open IE System for SOV Language

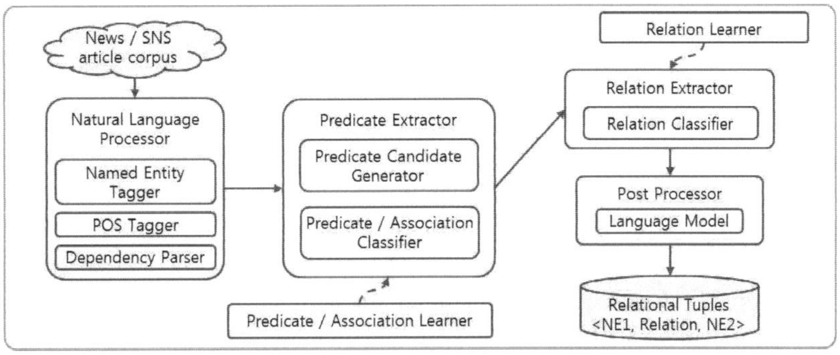


Figure 2: System architecture

Figure 2 shows the architecture of our proposed system. It takes a web corpus as an input and a set of relation tuples <NE1, Relation, NE2> as an output. First, the corpus is pre-processed. The named entities in a sentence are recognized and the sentence is POS-tagged and parsed to a dependency tree.

The relation extraction process comprises two key modules. The first module, *predicate extractor* generates <entity, predicate> pair candidates by using a simple POS constraint and classifies whether the predicate is a proper one of the entity by using the maximum entropy classifier. The second module, *relation extractor* finds another entity in an entity-predicate pairs that are classified into a correct one at the previous step. And then, it transforms two entities and the predicate into a candidate relation tuple form. Finally, the maximum entropy classifier decides if the candidate relation tuple represents a correct relationship between two entities.

## 2.1 Predicate Extraction

### 2.1.1 Predicate Candidates Generation

First, we generate predicate candidates that can be connected for one NE. We assume that the "predicate" is based on a verb phrase. We follow the Etzioni et al. (2011)' verb-based constraints to prevent the relational phrase from being incomprehensible. The predicate candidates are generated through the proposed algorithm, as shown in Figure 3. The start point of a predicate is a NP chunk and the end point is a verb or the end of a sentence. The reasons of extracting both the verb and the adjacent NP chunk are as follows. 1) In SOV language, the subject is far away from the verb. However, the other entity (an object or an adverb) is adjacent to the verb. 2) We restrict the predicate to the one including a relational meaning.

### 2.1.2 Entity-Predicate Pair Detection

The predicate classifier is the part of deciding whether the predicate in an entity-predicate pair extracted from the predicate generator describes about the entity or not. In Figure 1,

```
Define Set: StartSet, EndSet, CandidateSet
for( i=0; i< sentence.length; i++ )
        if( (POS(i),...) match "(adjective | noun)* (noun)" )
                put i to StartSet
for( j=0; j< sentence.length; j++ )
        if( POS(j) match "(verb | ending)" )
                put j to EndSet

for( i=0; i < StartSet.size; i++ )
        for( j=0; j < EndSet.size; j++ )
                if( StartSet[i] < EndSet[j] )
                        put < i, j > to CandidateSet
```

Figure 3: Predicate candidate generation algorithm

according to the predicate generation pattern, candidates are generated as follows. P1:<이보영(Lee Bo-young[PERSON]), 최민영과 연애를 시작한다(starts relationship with Choi Min-young[PERSON])>, P2:<김수미(Kim Su-mi[PERSON]), 최민영과 연애를 시작한다(starts relationship with Choi Min-young[PERSON])>, etc. In this case, the predicate of P1 is a correct description about the entity, Lee Bo-young. But the predicate of P2 is an inappropriate description about the entity, Kim Su-mi. The goal of the predicate classifier process is to detect a correct or incorrect connection between an entity and a predicate, to improve the performance of relation extraction.

For classifying correct entity-predicate pairs, we use Maximum Entropy classifier which is one of Machine Learning method. The classifier assigns probability that the predicate is correct and is connected to the entity. Classifier is learned by supervised learning and uses the following features in Table 1. The features are grouped into three major categories.

| Surface | Syntactic | Semantic |
|---|---|---|
| · Sentence length<br>· Predicate length<br>· Distance NE1 ~ predicate<br>· # of other entities in sentence<br>· Existence of verb between NE1 and predicate<br>· Position of NE1 and phrase | · Functional words next to NE1<br>· POS tags in predicate<br>· POS tags in left/right side of predicate<br>· POS tags at the boundary of predicate<br>· The length of dependency link between NE1 and predicate | · NE1 type<br>· Verb type<br>· Existance of matched verb frame |

Table 1: Surface, syntactic and semantic features used

In order to investigate the connection between an entity and a predicate, we use the distance between an entity and a predicate, whether there is a verb between an entity and a predicate, the postposition next to an entity etc. as a feature. And for the purpose of identifying the suitability of a predicate as description, we use the predicate length, POS tag of predicate and others. The dependency link is the number of links between the entity and predicate in dependency tree. The type of entity indicates the type that the entity belongs to, like "PERSON", "PROGRAM", "LOCATION" and so forth. We build a set of verb-arguments frames for each high-frequent verb by using the collocation of a verb and argument types. We decide the argument type by using the functional words attached. There are four argument types: S(Subject), O(Object), B(Adverbial) and C(Complement). We assign same type to the verbs which have the same frame. The feature presents both whether the predicate includes some important information and whether the argument and the predicate are connected semantically.

## 2.2 Relation Extraction

In this step, we extract relation tuples from the entity-predicate pairs. First, we separate the other entity, NE2, from the predicate and convert the NE1, NE2, and the rest phrases of predicate to a relation tuple form. And we classify whether the tuple is a correct relation tuple or not. For example, from an entity-predicate pair, <신세경(Sin Se-kyoung[PERSON]), 인기 프로그램 무한도전에 출연한다(make an appearance on the famous TV program Muhan-dojeon[TV PROGRAM])>, we can get two relation tuples, R1:<신세경(Sin Se-kyoung[PERSON]), 인기 프로그램(famous TV program), 무한도전(Muhan-dojeon[TV PROGRAM])>와 R2:<신세경(Sin Se-kyoung[PERSON]), 출연한다(make an appearance on), 무한도전(Muhan-dojeon[TV PROGRAM])>. Among the R1 and R2, only the R2 is a correct tuple. To determine that the candiate relation tuple is correct, we use the Maximum Entropy classifier learned by supervised learning. Like the predicate classifier, we use several surface, syntactic and semantic features. Additionally, to judge that the triple has a relationship, we uses the following features in Table 2.

| Surface | Syntactic | Semantic |
|---|---|---|
| · The precedency between the NE2 and the rest phrase<br>· Position of NE2 | · Functional words next to NE2<br>· POS tags in left/right side of two entities | · Type of NE2 |

Table 2: Additionally used features for relation extraction

## 2.3 Post-processing Using Language Model

We propose a new post-processing method using a language model, in addition to the relation extraction method based on the predicate extraction. The LM-based approach is motivated by the following common errors, which may be incorrect relations in spite of high probabilities given by our relation classifier. For example, the tuple <박명수 (Park Myoung-su[PERSON]), 평화가 찾아왔다 (the peace comes to), 무한도전(Muhan-dojeon[TV PROGRAM])> can be outputted by the system described in the previous section. These erroneous tuples cannot usually produce a fluent and comprehensible sentence when concatenating their entities and the relational phrase. Therefore, this problem can be solved by using a language model.
We measure the perplexity of the word sequence generated by concatenating two entities and the relational phrase in order of the occurrence in its original sentence. The relation tuples that have a higher perplexity than a threshold are removed from the final set of relation tuples. To construct the Korean 5-gram language model, we use the refined Sejong corpus (Kang and Kim, 2004) consisted of 6,334,826 sentences.

# 3 Experiments

## 3.1 Experimental Environment

We have experimented with our method on the Korean news corpus crawled in television program domain from August 13, 2011 to November 17, 2011. The corpus consists of 118K articles and 11.4M sentences. We have performed named entity recognition for pre-processing of this news corpus and have sampled 7,686 sentences containing one or more entities from the NE-recognized corpus. Among these annotated sentences, 4,893 sentences, 2,238 sentences, and 555 sentences are used as the training set for the entity-predicate pair detection, the training set for relation extraction, and the test set for relation extraction, respectively. We used the precision, the recall, and the f-measure as evaluation metrics. When matching between a gold relational phrase and a system output to measure these metrics, we adopted the relaxed matching in which the difference between two target phrases boundaries was permitted up to two words on both the left and the right of each phrase.

### 3.2 Evaluation of Relation Extraction

We first evaluated the effectiveness of the entity-predicate pair detection. We compared the performance of extracting the relation tuples after the proposed detection phase with the performance of the baselines that extract the tuples without the phase. We set two baseline systems. The first is the system that passes all possible entity-predicate pairs to the relation extraction phase after the predicate candidate generation (ALL). The second is the system that passes only the entity-predicate pairs including the nearest entity for each predicate candidate to the relation extraction phase (NEAR). Table 3 shows the performance of relation extraction of the baseline systems and the proposed system. In this experiment, the classification threshold was optimized on the development set by using the f-measure as the objective function. As shown in Table 3, the proposed approach outperformed both the baseline systems. These results show that our additional phase is effective in finding the relation between two entities in SOV language such as Korean. This also shows that it is helpful to consider first the relationship between an entity and its predicate, prior to recognizing the relationship between two entities.

| System | Precision | Recall | F-measure |
|---|---|---|---|
| ALL | 0.4540 | 0.4726 | 0.4631 |
| NEAR | 0.5177 | 0.5000 | 0.5087 |
| Proposed | 0.5223 | 0.5616 | 0.5413 |

Table 3: Effectiveness of the entity-predicate pair detection phase

## 4 Demo

Our Open IE system's two key modules, the predicate extractor and the relation extractor were implemented in C++. In addition, to provide users with searching service, we developed extra modules, a ranker and a viewer. The predicate extractor and the relation extractor work periodically as a batch job. However the ranker and the viewer work on demand. Optionally, users can enter the duration, an entity name or a (part of) relation. Then the system looks up the relation DB and shows the following results.

· Relation tuple view
· Relation tuple view including a user-queried entity
· Entity view related to a user-queried relational phrase
· Entity view related to a user-queried entity

We implemented the searching service as a web application.

## 5 Conclusions

In this paper, we propose a new Open IE system for SOV language. In order to extract relation in SOV language, the system extracts entity-predicate pairs by considering the connectivity between an entity and a predicate, prior to identifying a relationship between two entities. We have shown that our system is effective in improving the performance of relation extraction. The paper's contributions are as follows. First, though the word order is relatively free or there is long distance between an entity and a predicate, the relation is extracted successfully. Second, our post-processing approach using a language model has an effect on finding more fluent and precise relations.

## Acknowledgments

This work was supported by Software R&D Center, SAMSUNG ELECTRONICS Co., Ltd.

## References

Banko, M., Cafarella, M., Soderland, S.and Broadhead, M., and Etzioni, O. (2007). Open information extraction from the web.

Etzioni, O., Fader, A., Christensen, J., Soderland, S., and Center, M. (2011). Open information extraction: The second generation. In *Twenty-Second International Joint Conference on Artificial Intelligence*.

Kang, B.-M. and Kim, H. (2004). Sejong korean corpora in the making. In *Proceedings of LREC 2004*, pages 1747–1750.

Wu, F. and Weld, D. (2010). Open information extraction using wikipedia. In *Proceedings of the 48th Annual Meeting of the Association for Computational Linguistics*, pages 118–127. Association for Computational Linguistics.

Yates, A., Cafarella, M., Banko, M., Etzioni, O., Broadhead, M., and Soderland, S. (2007). Textrunner: open information extraction on the web. In *Proceedings of Human Language Technologies: The Annual Conference of the North American Chapter of the Association for Computational Linguistics: Demonstrations*, pages 25–26. Association for Computational Linguistics.

# An Omni-font Gurmukhi to Shahmukhi Transliteration System

*Gurpreet Singh LEHAL*[1] *Tejinder Singh SAINI*[2] *Savleen Kaur CHOWDHARY*[3]
(1) DCS, Punjabi University, Patiala
(2) ACTDPL, Punjabi University, Patiala
(3) CEC, Chandigarh Group of Colleges, Landran, Mohali
gslehal@gmail.com, tej@pbi.ac.in, iridiumsavleen@gmail.com

ABSTRACT

This paper describes a font independent Gurmukhi-to-Shahmukhi transliteration system. Even though Unicode is gaining popularity, but still there is lot of material in Punjabi, which is available in ASCII based fonts. A problem with ASCII fonts for Punjabi is there is no standardisation of mapping of Punjabi characters and a Gurmukhi character may be internally mapped to different keys in different Punjabi fonts. In fact there are more than 40 mapping tables in use for the commonly used Punjabi fonts. Thus there is an urgent need to convert the ASCII fonts to standard mapping, such as Unicode without any loss of information. Already many such font converters have been developed and are available online. But one limitation is that, all these systems need manual intervention in which the user has to know the name of source font. In the first stage, we have proposed a statistical model for automatic font detection and conversion into Unicode. Our system supports around 225 popular Gurmukhi font encodings. The ASCII to Unicode conversion accuracy of the system is 99.73% at word level with TOP1 font detection. The second stage is conversion of Gurmukhi to Shahmukhi at high accuracy. The proposed Gurmukhi to Shahmukhi transliteration system can transliterate any Gurmukhi text to Shahmukhi at more than 98.6% accuracy at word level.

KEYWORDS: n-gram language model, Shahmukhi, Gurmukhi, Machine Transliteration, Punjabi, Font, Font detection, font Conversion, Unicode

*Proceedings of COLING 2012: Demonstration Papers*, pages 313–320,
COLING 2012, Mumbai, December 2012.

# 1 Introduction

There are thousands of fonts used for publishing text in Indian languages. Punjabi (Gurmukhi) alone has more than 225 popular fonts which are still in use along with Unicode. Though online web content has shown the sign of migration from legacy-font to Unicode but books, magazine, news paper and other publishing industry is still working with ASCII based fonts. They have not adopted Unicode due to following reasons:

- Lack of awareness of Unicode standard
- People resist to change, due to Unicode typing issues and little support of Unicode in publishing software they are working with
- Less availability of Unicode fonts has shown very less verity of text representation

A problem with ASCII fonts for Punjabi is there is no standardisation of mapping of Punjabi characters and a Gurmukhi character may be internally mapped to different keys in different Punjabi fonts. For example, the word ਪੰਜਾਬੀ is internally stored at different keys as shown in figure 1. Therefore, there is an urgent need to develop a converter to convert text in ASCII based fonts to Unicode without any loss of information. Already many such font converters have been developed and are available online. But one limitation with all these systems is that the user has to know the name of source font. This may not be a big issue but there are many occasions when a user may not be aware of the name of the ASCII font and in that case he cannot convert his text to Unicode. To overcome this hurdle, we have developed a font identification system, which automatically detects the font and then converts the text to Unicode.

0070+004D+006A+0077+0062+0049 in *Akhar*
0066+002E+0075+006A+0057+0067 in *Gold*
0070+00B5+006A+003B+0062+0049 in *AnandpurSahib*
0067+007A+0069+006B+0070+0068 in *Asees*
0050+005E+004A+0041+0042+0049 in *Sukhmani*
00EA+00B3+00DC+00C5+00EC+00C6 in *Satluj*

FIGURE 1– Internal representation of ਪੰਜਾਬੀ in different fonts

# 2 Omni-Font Detection and Conversion to Unicode

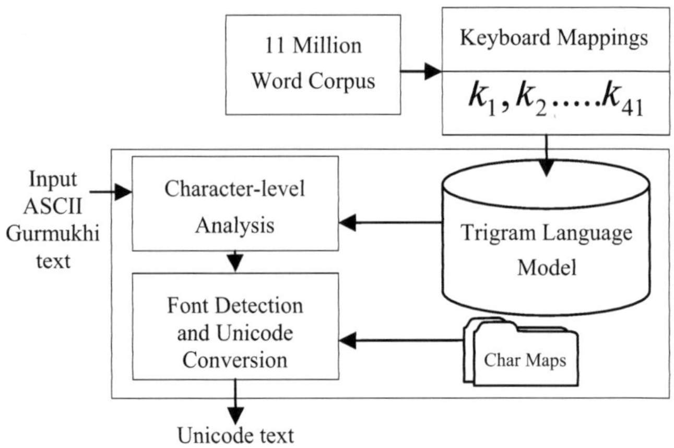


FIGURE 2– Model Components

Our system supports around 225 popular Gurmukhi font encodings. Some of the popular fonts supported are *Akhar, Anmol Lipi, Chatrik, Joy, Punjabi, Satluj* etc. In fact, these fonts correspond to 41 keyboard mappings. It means if $k_1, k_2 \ldots. k_{41}$ be the 41 keyboard mappings and $f_1, f_2 \ldots\ldots f_{225}$ be the Gurmukhi fonts, then each of fonts $f_i$ will belong to one of the keyboard mapping $k_i$. We could also have multiple fonts belonging to same keyboard map and fonts belonging to same keyboard map have same internal mappings for all the Gurmukhi characters. For example, *Akhar2010R* and *Joy* font belong to same keyboard map family. The problem is now reduced from 225 distinct fonts to just 41 group classes corresponding to each keyboard map. Therefore, our font detection problem is to classify the input text to one of these 41 keyboard mappings. It could be thought of as a 41 class pattern recognition problem. The proposed system is based on character-level trigram language model (see figure 2). We have trained the trigrams corresponding to each keyboard map. For training purpose a raw corpus of 11 million words has been used. To identify the font of a text, all the character trigrams are extracted and their probability is determined in each of the keyboard map. The keyboard map having maximum product of trigram probability is identified as the keyboard map corresponding to the input text.

## 2.1 Font Detection

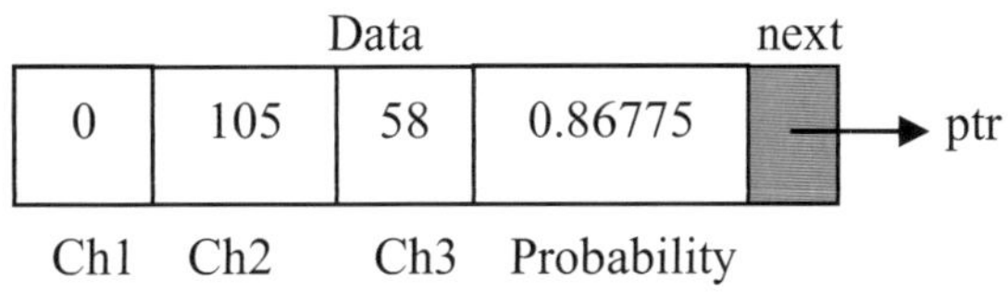

FIGURE 3– Tri-gram Character Node

The omni font detection problem is formulated as character level trigram language model. The single font has 255 character code points. Therefore, in a trigram model, we need to process 255x255x255=$255^3$ code points for a single keyboard map. But we are dealing with 41 distinct keyboard maps so the memory requirement will be further increased to process and hold 41x $255^3$ code points. After detailed analysis we found that the array representation of this task is sparse in nature i.e. the majority of code points in omni fonts have zero values. We observed that each keyboard map has around 26,000 non-zero code points which is 0.156% of the original code points. Hence, to avoid sparse array formation, we have created trigram link list representation (see figure 3) having on an average 26,000 trigram nodes for only valid code points with respect to each keyboard map. The structure of the node is expressed in figure 2. The trigram probability of a word $w^l$ having length $l$ is:

$$w^l = \prod_{i=1}^{l} P(c_i \mid c_{i-1}, c_{i-2}) \qquad (1)$$

The total probability of input text sentence is:

$$w_{1,n} = \sum_{1}^{n} w^l \text{ and the keyboard map is detected by K= arg max } \sum_{1}^{k} \sum_{1}^{n} w^l \qquad (2)$$

## 2.2 Font Conversion

After the identification of the keyboard map, the handcrafted mapping table of identified font is used by the system to transform input text into Unicode characters and finally produce the output Unicode text. Special care has been given for transforming long vowels ਉ[ʊ], ਊ[u], ਓ[o], ਅ[ə], ਆ[ɑ], ਇ[ɪ], ਈ[i], ਏ[e], ਐ[æ], ਔ[ɔ] and Gurmukhi short vowel sign ਿ[ɪ]. This is because in Unicode these nine independent vowels ਉ[ʊ], ਊ[u], ਓ[o], ਅ[ə], ਆ[ɑ], ਇ[ɪ], ਈ[i], ਏ[e], ਐ[æ], ਔ[ɔ] with three bearer characters Ura ੳ[ʊ], Aira ਅ [ə] and Iri ੲ[ɪ] have single code points and need to be mapped accordingly as shown in figure 4. There are no explicit code points for half characters in Unicode. They will be generated automatically by the Unicode rendering system when it finds special symbol called halant or Viram [੍]. Therefore, Gurmukhi transformation of subjoined consonants is performed by prefixing halant ੍ symbol along with the respective consonant.

| | | | |
|---|---|---|---|
| Long Vowels | ਅ[ə] + ਾ → ਆ[ɑ] | ੳ + ੁ → ਉ[ʊ] | ੲ + ਿ → ਇ[ɪ] |
| | ਅ[ə] + ੈ → ਐ[æ] | ੳ + ੂ → ਊ[u] | ੲ + ੀ → ਈ[i] |
| | ਅ[ə] + ੌ → ਔ[ɔ] | ੳ + ੋ → ਓ[o] | ੲ + ੇ → ਏ[e] |
| Short Vowel [ਿ] | ਕ[k] + ਿ → ਕਿ | | |
| Nukta Symbol | ਸ + ਼ = ਸ਼; ਖ + ਼ = ਖ਼ | ਗ + ਼ = ਗ਼; ਜ + ਼ = ਜ਼; | ਫ + ਼ = ਫ਼; ਲ + ਼ = ਲ਼; |
| Subjoined Consonants | ਨ+੍+ਹ = ਨ੍ਹ [nʰ] | ਪ+੍+ਰ = ਪ੍ਰ [pr] | ਸ+੍+ਵ = ਸ੍ਵ [sv] |

FIGURE 4– Unicode Transforming Rules

The Unicode transformation becomes complex when Gurmukhi short vowel *Sihari* [ਿ] and subjoined consonants comes together at a single word position. For example, consider the word ਪ੍ਰਿੰਸ. In omni font *Sihari* [ਿ] come as first character. But according to Unicode it must be after the bearing consonant. Therefore, it must go after the subjoined consonant ੍+ਰ as shown in figure 5.

ਪ੍ਰਿੰਸ (Omni-Font) → ਿ ਪ ੍ਰ ੰ ਸ

→ ਪ + ੍ + ਰ + ਿ + ੰ + ਸ → ਪ੍ਰਿੰਸ (Unicode)

FIGURE 5– Complex Unicode Transformation

## 3 Gurmukhi-to-Shahmukhi Transliteration System

The overall transliteration process is divided into three tasks as shown in figure 6.

### 3.1 Pre-Processing

The integration of omni font detection and conversion module enhances the scope, usefulness and utilization of this transliteration system. The Gurmukhi word is cleaned and prepared for transliteration by passing it through the Gurmukhi spell-checker and normalizing it according to the Shahmukhi spellings and pronunciation as shown in Table 1.

| Sr. | Gurmukhi Word | Spell-Checker | Normalized | Shahmukhi |
|---|---|---|---|---|
| 1 | ਖੁਦਗਰਜ /khudgaraj/ | ਖ਼ੁਦਗ਼ਰਜ਼ /k̲hudġaraz/ | ਖ਼ੂਦਗ਼ਰਜ਼ /k̲hūdġaraz/ | خودغرض |
| 2 | ਖੁਸ਼ੀ /khushī/ | ਖ਼ੁਸ਼ੀ /k̲hushī/ | ਖ਼ੂਸ਼ੀ /k̲hūshī/ | خوشی |
| 3 | ਫਰੰਗੀ /pharṅgī/ | ਫ਼ਰੰਗੀ /farṅgī/ | ਫ਼ਰੰਗੀ /farṅgī/ | فرنگی |

TABLE 1– Spell-Checking and Normalization of Gurmukhi Words

### 3.2 Transliteration Engine

The normalised form of Gurmukhi word is first transliterated to Shahmukhi by using dictionary lookup. Dictionary lookup is a limited but effective and fast method for handling the complex spelling words of Shahmukhi and transliteration of proper nouns. Therefore, a one-to-one

Gurmukhi-Shahmukhi dictionary resource has been created and used for directly transliterating frequently occurring Gurmukhi words and transliterating Gurmukhi words with typical Shahmukhi spellings.

**Gurmukhi Stemmer:** In our case, stemming is primarily a process of suffix removal. A list of common suffixes has been created. We have taken only the most common Gurmukhi suffixes such as ੋਂ, ਓਂ, ਿਓਂ, ੀਂ, ੋ etc. The Shahmukhi transliteration of these suffixes is stored in the suffix list. Thus if the word ਸਕੂਲੋਂ is not found, we search the suffix list and find suffix ੋਂ. This suffix ੋਂ is removed from ਸਕੂਲੋਂ and the resultant word ਸਕੂਲ is then searched again in the dictionary. If found then the transliterated word اسکول is then appended with وں, which is the Shahmukhi transliteration of the suffix ੋਂ. Thus, the correct transliteration i.e. اسکولوں is achieved.

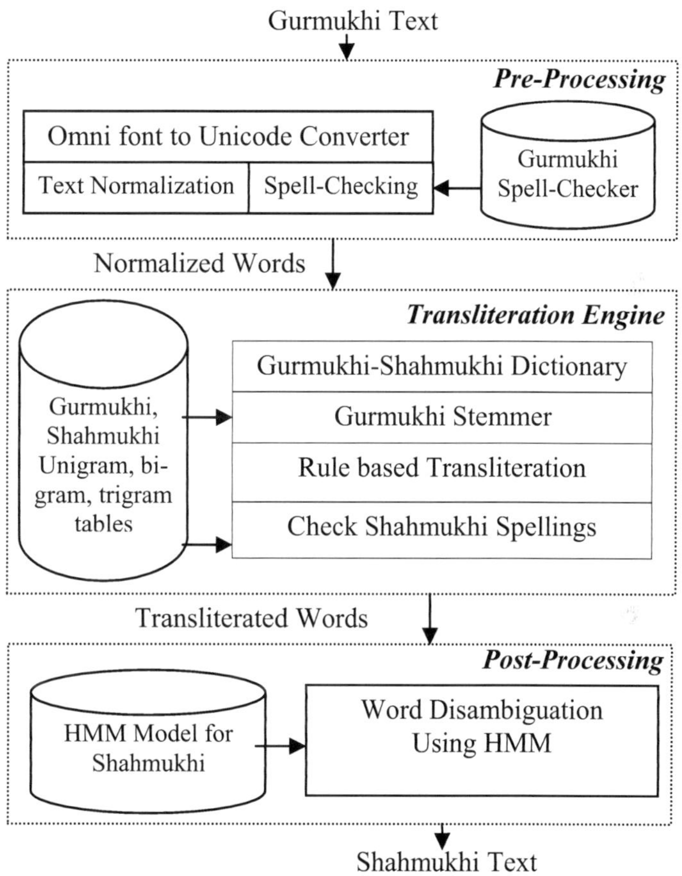

FIGURE 6– System Architecture

### 3.2.1 Rule-base Transliteration

The rule based transliteration is used when dictionary lookup and Gurmukhi stemmer failed to transliterate the input word. Using the direct grapheme based approach; Gurmukhi consonants and vowel are directly mapped to similar sounding Shahmukhi characters. In case of multiple equivalent Shahmukhi characters or one-to-many mappings, the most frequently occurring Shahmukhi character is selected. Thus, ਹ is mapped to ہ and ਜ਼ is mapped to ز. Besides, these simple mapping rules, some special pronunciation based rules have also been developed. For example, if two vowels in Gurmukhi come together, then Shahmukhi symbol Hamza is placed in between them. After simple character based mapping we resolve character ambiguity. That is, the Gurmukhi characters with multiple Shahmukhi mappings, all word forms using all possible mappings are generated and the word with the highest frequency of occurrence in the Shahmukhi word frequency list is selected. For example, consider the Gurmukhi word ਸਾਹਿਬ. It has two ambiguous character ਸ[s] and ਹ[h]. The system will generate all the possible forms and then choose the most frequent صاحب (6432) unigram as output as shown in the figure 7. Finally, the output word is inspected for correct spelling using Shahmukhi resources.

| | | | | | |
|---|---|---|---|---|---|
| *Char1* | ਸ | → س | ਸ → ص ਸ → ث | *All forms (with unigram frequency)* | |
| *Char2* | ਾ | → ا | | ساہب(0) | ساحب(0) |
| *Char3* | ਹ | → ہ | ਹ → ح | صاہب(0) | صاحب(6432) |
| *Char4* | ਿ | → nil | | ثاہب(0) | ثاحب(0) |
| *Char5* | ਬ | → ب | | *Selected →* *(most frequent)* | صاحب |

FIGURE 7– Steps for handling Multiple Character Mapping

### 3.3 Post-Processing

The transliteration of Gurmukhi word ਹਾਲ has two Shahmukhi spellings with different senses as حال (state, condition, circumstance) and ہال (Hall; big room). In post-processing we have modelled 2nd order HMM for Shahmukhi word disambiguation where the number of HMM states are corresponding to each word in the sentence and their possible interpretations or ambiguity. The transition probabilities and inter-state observation probabilities are calculated as proposed by Thede and Harper (1999) for POS system.

## 4 Evaluation and Results

There are two main stages of our system first is font detection and Conversion of detected font to Unicode and the second stage is conversion of Gurmukhi text to Shahmukhi. The evaluation results of both the stages are:

**Font Detection and Conversion Accuracy:** In order to test font detection module we have a set of 35 popular Gurmukhi fonts. A randomly selected test data of having 194 words and having 962 characters (with spaces) is converted into different Gurmukhi fonts and used for system testing. The font detection module has correctly predicted 32 fonts. Hence, they have 100% conversion rate into Unicode. The remaining 3 fonts were not correctly recognized and confused with other fonts with which the character mapping table is almost similar. The fonts varied by only 2-3 code maps and hence the confusion. But this confusion did not create much problem in the subsequent Unicode and then Shahmukhi conversion.

**Transliteration Accuracy:** We have tested our system on more that 100 pages of text compiled from newspapers, books and poetry. The overall transliteration accuracy of this system is 98.6% at word level, which is quite high. In the error analysis we found that this system fails to produce good transliteration when the input words have typical spellings. The accuracy of this system can be increased further by increasing the size of the training corpus and having plentiful of data covering maximum senses of all ambiguous words in the target script.

## Conclusion

For the first time a high accuracy Gurmukhi-Shahmukhi transliteration system has been developed, which can accept data in any of the popular Punjabi font encoding. This will fulfil the demand from the users to develop such a system, where the Gurmukhi text in any font could be converted to Shahmukhi.

## References


Lehal G.S. (2009), A Gurmukhi to Shahmukhi Transliteration System. In *Proceedings of ICON: 7th International Conference on Natural Language Procesing,* pages 167-173, Hyderabad, India.

Lehal, G. S. (2007). Design and Implementation of Punjabi Spell Checker, *International Journal of Systemics, Cybernetics and Informatics*, pages 70-75.

Malik, M.G.A. (2006). Punjabi Machine Transliteration. In *Proceedings of the 21st International Conference on Computational Linguistics and 44th Annual Meeting of the ACL*, pages 1137-1144.

Saini, T. S., Lehal, G. S. and Kalra, V. S. (2008). Shahmukhi to Gurmukhi Transliteration System. In *Proceedings of 22nd international Conference on Computational Linguistics (Coling)*, pages 177-180, Manchester, UK.

Saini, T. S. and Lehal, G. S. (2008). Shahmukhi to Gurmukhi Transliteration System: A Corpus based Approach. *Research in Computing Science*, 33:151-162, Mexico.

Thede, S.M., Harper, M.P. (1999). A Second-Order Hidden Markov Model for Part-of-speech Tagging, In *Proceedings of the 37th annual meeting of the ACL on Computational Linguistics,* pages 175-182.

Davis, M., Whistler, K. (Eds.) (2010). Unicode Normalization Forms, *Technical Reports*, Unicode Standard Annex #15, Revision 33. Retrieved February 22, 2011, from http://www.unicode.org/reports/tr15/tr15-33.html

# THUTR: A Translation Retrieval System

Chunyang Liu*, Qi Liu*, Yang Liu, and Maosong Sun
Department of Computer Science and Technology
State Key Lab on Intelligent Technology and Systems
National Lab for Information Science and Technology
Tsinghua University, Beijing 100084, China
{liuchunyang2012,flaminglq,liuyang.china,sunmaosong}@gmail.com

ABSTRACT
We introduce a translation retrieval system *THUTR*, which casts translation as a retrieval problem. Translation retrieval aims at retrieving a list of target-language translation candidates that may be helpful to human translators in translating a given source-language input. While conventional translation retrieval methods mainly rely on parallel corpus that is difficult and expensive to collect, we propose to retrieve translation candidates directly from target-language documents. Given a source-language query, we first translate it into target-language queries and then retrieve translation candidates from target language documents. Experiments on Chinese-English data show that the proposed translation retrieval system achieves 95.32% and 92.00% in terms of P@10 at sentence level and phrase level tasks, respectively. Our system also outperforms a retrieval system that uses parallel corpus significantly.

TITLE AND ABSTRACT IN CHINESE

## THUTR：一个译文检索系统

我们介绍一个译文检索系统THUTR。该系统将翻译视作为一个检索问题。译文检索旨在为输入的源语言文本搜索一组候选翻译，为翻译人员提供帮助。传统的译文检索方法主要基于双语语料库，其面临的主要问题是构建双语语料库代价高昂。为此，我们提出使用单语语料库实现译文检索。给定源语言查询，我们首先将其翻译成目标语言查询，然后再从单语语料库中检索候选译文。在汉英数据上的实验表明，我们提出的译文检索系统分别在句子级和短语级取得95.32%和92.00%的P@10值。我们的系统也显著超过了使用平行语料库的译文检索系统。

KEYWORDS: Translation retrieval, monolingual corpus, statistical machine translation.

KEYWORDS IN CHINESE: 译文检索；单语语料库；统计机器翻译.

*Chunyang Liu and Qi Liu have equal contribution to this work

*Proceedings of COLING 2012: Demonstration Papers*, pages 321–328,
COLING 2012, Mumbai, December 2012.

# 1 Introduction

This demonstration introduces a **translation retrieval** system *THUTR*, which combines machine translation and information retrieval to provide useful information to translation users. Unlike machine translation, our system casts translation as a retrieval problem: given a source-language string, returns a list of ranked target-language strings that contain its (partial) translations from a large set of target-language documents.

Figure 1: A screenshot of the translation retrieval system.

For example, as shown in Figure 1, given a Chinese query, our system searches for its translations in a large set of English documents and returns a list of ranked sentences. [1] Although the retrieved documents might not be exact translations of the query, they often contain useful partial translations to help human translators produce high-quality translations. As the fluency of target-language documents are usually guaranteed, the primary goal of translation retrieval is to find documents that are *relevant* to the source-language query. By relevant, we mean that retrieved documents contain (partial) translations of queries.

Our system is divided into two modules:

1. *machine translation module*: given a source-language query, translates it into a list of translation candidates;
2. *information retrieval module*: takes the translation candidates as target-language queries and retrieves relevant documents.

Generally, the MT module ensures the fidelity of retrieved documents and the IR module ensures the fluency. Therefore, the relevance can be measured based on the coupling of translation and retrieval models.

We evaluate our system on Chinese-English data. Experiments show that our translation retrieval system achieves 95.32% and 92.00% in terms of P@10 at sentence level and phrase level tasks, respectively. Our system also significantly outperforms a retrieval system that uses parallel corpus.

[1] In our system, each document is a single sentence.

## 2 Related Work

Translation retrieval is firstly introduced in translation memory (TM) systems (Baldwin and Tanaka, 2000; Baldwin, 2001). Translation equivalents of maximally similar source language strings are chosen as the translation candidates. This is similar with example-based machine translation (Nagao, 1984) that translates by analogy based on parallel corpus. Unfortunately, these systems suffer from a major drawback: the amount and domain of parallel corpus are relatively limited. Hong et al. (2010) propose a method for mining parallel data from the Web. They focus on parallel data mining and report significant improvements on MT experiments.

Many researchers have explored the application of MT techniques to information retrieval tasks. Berger and Lafferty (1999) introduce a probabilistic approach to IR based on statistical machine translation models. Federico and Bertoldi (2002) divide CLIR into two translation models: a query-translation model and a query-document model. They show that offering more query translations improves retrieval performance. Murdock and Croft (2005) propose a method for sentence retrieval but in a monolingual scenario. They incorporate a machine translation in two steps: estimation and ranking. Sanchez-Martinez and Carrasco (2011) investigate how to retrieve documents that are plausible translations of a given source language document using statistical machine translation techniques.

## 3 System Description

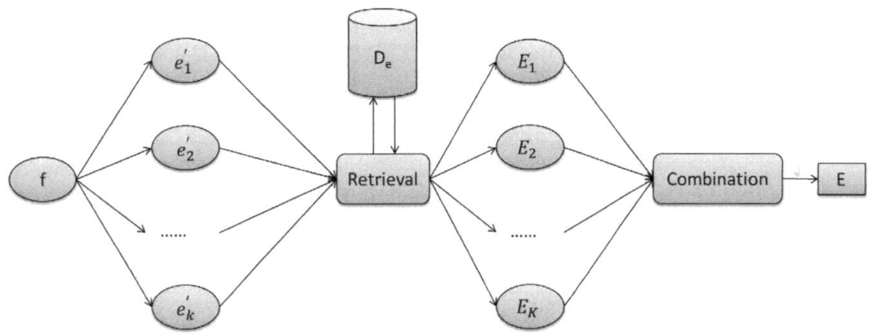


Figure 2: System architecture.

Given a source language query $f$, conventional translation retrieval systems (Baldwin and Tanaka, 2000; Baldwin, 2001) search for a source string $\hat{f}$ that has the maximal similarity with $f$ in a parallel corpus $D_{f,e} = \{(f_1, e_1), \ldots, (f_N, e_N)\}$:

$$\hat{f} = \arg\max_{f' \in D_{f,e}} \left\{ sim(f, f') \right\} \tag{1}$$

where $sim(f, f')$ calculates the similarity between two source language strings $f$ and $f'$. Then, retrieval systems return the target language string $\hat{e}$ corresponding to $\hat{f}$ in $D_{f,e}$. Therefore, conventional translation retrieval systems only rely on source language string matching and do not actually consider the translation probability between $f$ and $\hat{e}$.

Alternatively, given a source language query $f$, our translation retrieval system searches for a target string $\hat{e}$ that has the maximal translation probability with $f$ in a monolingual corpus $D_e = \{e_1, \ldots, e_M\}$ :

$$\hat{e} = \arg\max_{e \in D_e} \left\{ P(e|f) \right\} \tag{2}$$

where $P(e|f)$ is the probability that $e$ contains a translation of $f$.

This problem definition is similar with cross-lingual information retrieval (CLIR) (Ballesteros and Croft, 1997; Nie et al., 1999) except for the relevance judgement criterion. While CLIR requires the retrieved documents to be relevant to users' information need, translation retrieval expects to return documents containing the translations of queries. For example, given a Chinese query "奥运会" (i.e., "*Olympic Games*"), both "*Olympic Games*" and "*London*" are relevant in CLIR. However, in translation retrieval, only "*Olympic Games*" is relevant. Therefore, translation retrieval can be seen as a special case of CLIR.

The translation probability $P(e|f)$ can be further decomposed by introducing a target language query $e'$ as a hidden variable:

$$P(e|f) = \sum_{e'} P(e, e'|f) = \sum_{e'} P(e'|f) \times P(e|e') \tag{3}$$

where $P(e'|f)$ is a **translation model** and $P(e|e')$ is a **retrieval model.** [2]

In this work, we use a phrase-based model as the translation model. Phrase-based models (Och and Ney, 2002; Marcu and Wong, 2002; Koehn et al., 2003) treat phrase as the basic translation unit. Based on a log-linear framework (Och and Ney, 2002), the phrase-based model used in our system is defined as

$$P(e'|f) = \frac{score(e', f)}{\sum_{e'} score(e', f)} \tag{4}$$

$$score(e', f) = P_{\phi}(e'|f)^{\lambda_1} \times P_{\phi}(f|e')^{\lambda_2} \times P_{lex}(e'|f)^{\lambda_3} \times P_{lex}(f|e')^{\lambda_4} \times exp(1)^{\lambda_5} \times exp(|e'|)^{\lambda_6} \times P_{lm}(e')^{\lambda_7} \times P_d(f, e')^{\lambda_8} \tag{5}$$

The $\lambda$'s are feature weights that can be optimized using the minimum error rate training algorithm (Och, 2003).

We use the vector space model for calculating the cosine similarity of a target language query $e'$ and a target language document $e$.

Therefore, the decision rule for translation retrieval is [3]

$$\hat{e} = \arg\max_{e} \Big\{ \sum_{e'} P(e'|f) \times P(e|e') \Big\} \tag{6}$$

$$\approx \arg\max_{e,e'} \Big\{ score(e', f) \times sim(e', e) \Big\} \tag{7}$$

The pipeline of our translation retrieval system is shown in Figure 2. Given a source language query $f$, the system first obtains a $K$-best list of target language query candidates: $e'_1, e'_2, \ldots, e'_K$. For each target language query $e'_k$, the system returns a list of translation candidates $E_k$. These translation candidates are merged and sorted according to Eq. (7) to produce the final ranked list $E$.

[2] Such "query translation" framework has been widely used in CLIR (Nie et al., 1999; Federico and Bertoldi, 2002) In this work, $e'$ is a translation of $f$ produced by MT systems and $e$ is a target language document that probably contains a translation of $f$. While $e'$ is usually ungrammatical and erroneous, $e$ is often written by native speakers.

[3] In practice, we add a parameter $\lambda_9$ to Eq (12) to achieve a balance between translation model and retrieval model: $score(e', f) \times sim(e', e)^{\lambda_9}$. We set $\lambda_9 = 2$ in our experiments.

## 4 Experiments

We evaluated our translation retrieval system on Chinese-English data that contains $2.2M$ sentence pairs. They are divided into three parts:

1. Training set ($220K$): training phrase-based translation model and feature weights.
2. Query set ($5K$): source language queries paired with their translations.
3. Document set ($1.99M$): target language sentences paired with their corresponding source language sentences.

The statistical machine translation system we used is Moses (Koehn et al., 2007) with its default setting except that we set the maximal phrase length to 4. For language model, we used SRI Language Modeling Toolkit (Stolcke, 2002) to train a 4-gram model with modified Kneser-Ney smoothing (Chen and Goodman, 1998). Our retrieval module is based on Apache Lucene, the state-of-the-art open-source search software. [4]

### 4.1 Sentence Level

We first evaluated our system at sentence level: treating a source language sentence as query. Given the bilingual query set $\{(f_1^q, e_1^q), \ldots, (f_Q^q, e_Q^q)\}$ and the bilingual document set $\{(f_1^d, e_1^d), \ldots, (f_D^d, e_D^d)\}$, we treat $\{f_1^q, \ldots, f_Q^q\}$ as the query set and $\{e_1^q, \ldots, e_Q^q, e_1^d, \ldots, e_D^d\}$ as the document set. Therefore, relevance judgement can be done automatically because the gold standard documents (i.e., $\{e_1^q, \ldots, e_Q^q\}$) are included in the document set. The evaluation metric is $P@n$, $n = 1, 10, 20, 50$.

| phrase length | BLEU | P@1 | P@10 | P@20 | P@50 |
|---|---|---|---|---|---|
| 1 | 11.75 | 83.12 | 89.38 | 90.80 | 92.52 |
| 2 | 24.15 | 89.54 | 93.66 | 94.36 | 95.08 |
| 3 | 27.48 | 90.46 | 94.26 | 94.98 | 95.52 |
| 4 | 28.37 | 90.62 | 94.44 | 95.28 | 95.86 |
| 5 | 30.12 | 90.50 | 94.14 | 94.98 | 95.66 |
| 6 | 29.52 | 90.40 | 94.42 | 94.96 | 95.56 |
| 7 | 29.96 | 90.62 | 94.40 | 95.10 | 95.74 |

Table 1: Effect of maximal phrase length.

Table 1 shows the effect of maximal phrase length on retrieval performance. Beside retrieval precisions, Table 2 also lists the BLEU scores of query translation. Retrieval performance generally rises with the increase of translation accuracy. Surprisingly, our system achieves over 90% in terms of $P@1$ when the maximal phrase length is greater than 2. This happens because it is much easier for translation retrieval to judge relevance of retrieved documents than conventional IR systems. We find that the performance hardly increase when the maximal phrase length is greater than 3. This is because long phrases are less likely to be used to translate unseen text. As a result, extracting phrase pairs within 4 words is good enough to achieve reasonable retrieval performance.

Table 2 shows the effect of the $K$-best list translations output by the MT system. It can be treated as "query expansion" for translation retrieval, which proves to be effective in other IR

[4]http://lucene.apache.org/

| | P@1 | P@10 | P@20 | P@50 |
|---|---|---|---|---|
| 1-best | 90.62 | 94.44 | 95.28 | 95.86 |
| 10-best | 91.88 | 95.32 | 96.16 | 96.84 |

Table 2: Effect of $K$-best list translations.

systems. We find that providing more query translations to the retrieval module does improve translation quality significantly.

| system | P@1 | P@10 | P@20 | P@50 |
|---|---|---|---|---|
| parallel | 34.48 | 58.62 | 63.98 | 70.88 |
| monolingual | 69.04 | 81.17 | 83.68 | 87.45 |

Table 3: Comparison to translation retrieval with parallel corpus.

We also compared our system with a retrieval system that relies on parallel corpus. Table 3 shows the results for retrieval systems using parallel and monolingual corpora, respectively. Surprisingly, our system significantly outperforms retrieval system using parallel corpus. We notice that Baldwin (2001) carefully chose data sets in which the language is controlled or highly constrained. In other words, a given word often has only one translation across all usages and syntactic constructions are limited. This is not the case for our datasets. Therefore, it might be problematic for conventional retrieval systems to calculate source language string similarities. This problem is probably alleviated in our system by providing multiple query translations.

## 4.2 Phrase Level

| | P@1 | P@10 |
|---|---|---|
| 1-best | 64.00 | 88.00 |
| 10-best | 72.00 | 92.00 |

Table 4: Results of phrase level retrieval.

Finally, we evaluated our system at phrase level: a source language phrase as query. We selected 50 phrases from the source language query set. The average length of a phrasal query is 2.76 words. On average, a query occurs in the source language query set for 3 times. Given a source query, our system returns a list of ranked target language documents. Relevance judgement was performed manually. Table 5 shows the results of phrase level evaluation. We compared between using 1-best translations and 10-best translations produced by MT systems. The $P@10$ for using 10-best translations reaches 92%.

## Conclusion

We have presented a system *THUTR* that retrieves translations directly from monolingual corpus. Experiments on Chinese-English data show that our retrieval system achieves 95.32% and 92.00% in terms of $P@10$ for sentence level and phrase level queries, respectively. In the future, we would like to extend our approach to the web that provides enormous monolingual data. In addition, we plan to investigate more accurate retrieval models for translation retrieval.

## Acknowledgments

This work is supported by NSFC project No. 60903138, 863 project No. 2012AA011102, and a Research Fund No. 20123000007 from Microsoft Research Asia.

## References


Baldwin, T. (2001). Low-cost, high-performance translation retrieval: Dumber is better. In *ACL 2001*.

Baldwin, T. and Tanaka, H. (2000). The effects of word order and segmentation on translation retrieval performance. In *COLING 2000*.

Ballesteros, L. and Croft, B. (1997). Phrasal translation and query expansion techniques for cross-language information retrieval. In *SIGIR 1997*.

Berger, A. and Lafferty, J. (1999). Information retrieval as statistical translation. In *SIGIR 1999*.

Chen, S. F. and Goodman, J. (1998). An empirical study of smoothing techniques for language modeling. Technical report, Harvard University Center for Research in Computing Technology.

Federico, M. and Bertoldi, N. (2002). Statistical cross-language information retrieval using n-best query translations. In *SIGIR 2002*.

Hong, G., Li, C.-H., Zhou, M., and Rim, H.-C. (2010). An empirical study on web mining of parallel data. In *COLING 2010*.

Koehn, P., Hoang, H., Birch, A., Callison-Burch, C., Federico, M., Bertoldi, N., Cowan, B., Shen, W., Moran, C., Zens, R., Dyer, C., Bojar, O., Constantin, A., and Herbst, E. (2007). Moses: Open source toolkit for statistical machine translation. In *ACL 2007 (the Demo and Poster Sessions)*.

Koehn, P., Och, F., and Marcu, D. (2003). Statistical phrase-based translation. In *NAACL 2003*.

Marcu, D. and Wong, D. (2002). A phrase-based, joint probability model for statistical machine translation. In *EMNLP 2002*.

Murdock, V. and Croft, B. (2005). A translation model for sentence retrieval. In *EMNLP 2005*.

Nagao, M. (1984). A framework of a mechanical translation between japanese and english by analogy principle. In Elithorn, A. and Banerji, R., editors, *Artificial and Human Intelligence*. North-Holland.

Nie, J.-Y., Simard, M., Isabelle, P., and Durand, R. (1999). Cross-language information retrieval based on parallel texts and automatic mining of parallel texts from the web. In *SIGIR 1999*.

Och, F. (2003). Minimum error rate training in statistical machine translation. In *ACL 2003*.

Och, F. and Ney, H. (2002). Discriminative training and maximum entropy models for statistical machine translation. In *ACL 2002*.

Sanchez-Martinez, F. and Carrasco, R. (2011). Document translation retrieval based on statistical machine translation techniques. *Applied Artificial Intelligence*, 25(5).

Stolcke, A. (2002). Srilm - an extensible language modeling toolkit. In *ICSLP 2002*.

# Recognition of Named-Event Passages in News Articles

*Luis Marujo*[1,2] *Wang Ling*[1,2] *Anatole Gershman*[1]
*Jaime Carbonell*[1] *João P. Neto*[2] *David Matos*[2]
(1)Language Technologies Institute, Carnegie Mellon University, Pittsburgh, PA, USA
(2)L²F Spoken Systems Lab, INESC-ID, Lisboa, Portugal
{lmarujo,lingwang,anatoleg,jgc}@cs.cmu.edu,
{Joao.Neto,David.Matos}@inesc-id.pt

ABSTRACT

We extend the concept of *Named Entities* to *Named Events* – commonly occurring events such as battles and earthquakes. We propose a method for finding specific passages in news articles that contain information about such events and report our preliminary evaluation results. Collecting "Gold Standard" data presents many problems, both practical and conceptual. We present a method for obtaining such data using the Amazon Mechanical Turk service.

TITLE AND ABSTRACT IN PORTUGUESE

## Reconhecimento de Passagens de Eventos Mencionados em Notícias

Estendemos o conceito de *Entidades Mencionadas* para *Eventos Mencionados* – eventos que ocorrem frequentemente como batalhas e terramotos. Propomos uma forma de encontrar passagens especificas em artigos que contenham informação sobre tais eventos e reportamos os nossos resultados preliminares. Colecionar um "Gold Standard" releva muitos problemas, tanto práticos como conceptuais. Apresentamos um método para obter tais dados usando o Amazon Mechanical Turk.

---

KEYWORDS : Named Events, Named Entities, Crowdsourcing, Multi-class Classification
KEYWORDS IN PORTUGUESE : Eventos Mencionados, Entidades Mencionadas, Crowdsourcing, Classificacao Multi-classe

---

*Proceedings of COLING 2012: Demonstration Papers*, pages 329–336,
COLING 2012, Mumbai, December 2012.

## 1 Introduction

*Modern Newspapers* have been organized into news articles since their invention in the early 17th century (Stephens 1950). These articles are usually organized in an "inverted pyramid" structure, placing the most essential, novel and interesting elements of a story in the beginning and the supporting materials and secondary details afterwards. This structure was designed for a world where most readers would read one newspaper per day and one article on a particular subject. This model is less suited for today's world of online news where readers have access to thousands of news sources. While the same high-level facts of a story may be covered by all sources in the first few paragraphs, there are often many important differences in the details "buried" further down. Readers who are interested in these details have to read through the same materials multiple times. Automated personalization services decide if an article has enough new content of interest to the reader, given the previously read articles. Rejection of an article simply because it covers topics already presented to the user misses important new information.

To solve this problem, automated systems have to be able to identify passages dealing with specific events and extract specific details such as: *who*, *what*, and *where*. For example, an article about a particular war may describe several battles in different geographical locations, but only some of which previously covered in other articles. The same article may also contain information about other events not directly related to the battles, such as food shortages and international reaction.

In this work, we focus on the problem of identifying passages dealing with *Named Events* – commonly occurring events such as battles, bankruptcy, earthquakes, etc. Such events typically have generic names such as "battle" and sometimes have specific names such as "Battle of Waterloo." More importantly, they have recognizable high-level structures and components as well as specific vocabularies. These structures were explored in the 1970s (Schank and Abelson 1977), but the early methods did not scale-up and were abandoned.

In the late 1990s, the problem was addressed under the *Topic Detection and Tracking* (TDT) trend (Yang, Pierce, and Carbonell 1998)(Yang et al. 1999)(Allan, Papka, and Lavrenko 1998). This work assumed that each news article had one and only one topic. The goal was to track articles by their topics. More recent work (Feng & Allan, 2007)(Nallapati et al. 2004) on *Event Threading* tried to organize news articles about armed clashes into a sequence of events, but still assumed that each article described a single event. *Passage Threading* (Feng and Allan 2009) extends the event threading by relaxing the one event per news article assumption and using a binary classifier to identify "violent" passages or paragraphs.

In this paper, we investigate methods for automatically identifying multi-sentence passages in a news article that describe named events. Specifically, we focus on 10 event types. Five are in the violent behavior domain: terrorism, suicide bombing, sex abuse, armed clashes, and street protests. The other five are in the business domain: management changes, mergers and acquisitions, strikes, legal troubles, and bankruptcy. We deliberately picked the event categories where language often overlaps: business events are often described using military metaphors.

Our approach was to train a classifier on a training set of sentences labeled with event categories. We used this classifier to label all sentences in new documents. We then apply different approaches to cluster sequences of sentences that are likely to describe the same event.

For our experiments, we needed a set of documents where the pertinent passages and sentences are labeled with the appropriate event categories. We used Amazon's Mechanical Turk[1] (AMT) service to obtain such a set.

The main contributions of this paper are the following:

- Using sentence-level features to assign event-types to sentences.
- Aggregating sequences of sentences in passages that are likely to contain information about specific events.
- Mechanical Turk service to obtain a usable set of labeled passages and sentences.

The rest of this paper is organized as follows. Section 2 outlines our named event recognition process. The creation of a "Gold Standard" dataset is described in section 3 as well as a new technique to improve the quality of AMT data. Section 4 explains how the experiments were performed and their results. Section 5 presents the conclusions and future work.

## 2 Technical Approach

We used a two-step approach to find named event passages (NEP) in a document. First, we used a previously trained classifier to label each sentence in the document. Second, we used both a rule-based model and HMM based statistical model to find contiguous sequences of sentences covering the same event. For the classifier part, we adopted a supervised learning framework, based on Weka (Hall et al. 2009).

## 2.1 Features and feature extraction

As features, we used key-phrases identified by an automatic key-phrase extraction algorithm described in (Marujo et al. 2012). Key phrases consist of one or more words that represent the main concepts of the document.

Marujo (2012) enhanced a state-of-the-art Supervised Key Phrase Extractor based on bagging over C4.5 decision tree classifier (Breiman, 1996; Quinlan, 1994) with several types of features, such as shallow semantic, rhetorical signals, and sub-categories from Freebase. The authors also included 2 forms of document pre-processing that were called light filtering and co-reference normalization. Light filtering removes sentences from the document, which are judged peripheral to its main content. Co-reference normalization unifies several written forms of the same named entity into a unique form.

Furthermore, we removed key-phrases containing names of people or places to avoid over-fitting. This was done using Stanford Named Entities Recognizer NER (Finkel, Grenager, and Manning 2005). We kept the phrases containing names of organizations because they often indicate an event type, e.g., FBI for crime, US Army for warfare, etc.

Due to the relatively small size of our training set, some of the important words and phrases were missing. We augmented the set with the action verbs occurring in the training set.

[1] https://www.mturk.com

## 2.2 Ensemble Multiclass Sentence Classification

The first problem we faced is the selection and training of a classifier to label each sentence. We used 11 labels – 10 categories plus "none-of-the-above". We trained three classifiers: SVM (Platt 1998), C4.5 Decision Tree with bagging (Quinlan 1994, Breiman 1996) and Multinomial Naïve Bayes (McCallum and Nigam 1998). The final sentence classification is obtained by combining the output of 3 classifiers using a Vote meta-algorithm with combination rule named majority voting (Kuncheva 2004, Kittler et al. 1998).

## 2.3 Selection of Passages

Once each sentence is labeled, we need to identify passages that most likely contain the descriptions of named events. The simples approach is to aggregate contiguous sequences of identical labels, which we consider as baseline. The problem with this method is that it is very sensible to sentence classification errors. Because a single classification error within a passage means that passage will not be correctly identified. To illustrate this problem, suppose that the true sequence of classifications in a small example document is: "A A A A B B", where A and B are some possible labels of events. The correct passages would be "A A A A" and "B B". However, a single classification error can make the sequence "A B A A B B". In this case, we would form 4 passages, which is very far from the correct sequences of passages. Thus, a smarter approach to extract passages from classifications is developed where we take into account possible classification errors from the sentence classifier when forming blocks. For this purpose, we propose an HMM-based passage-aggregation algorithm which maximizes the probability $P(B_n|C_{n-L},\dots,C_n)$ of a passage spanning positions $n\text{-}L$ through $n$, given the previous $L$ classifications $C_{n-L},\dots,C_n$. We estimate this probability using a maximum likelihood estimator as:

$$P(B_n|C_{n-L},\dots,C_n) = \frac{N(B_n,C_{n-L},\dots,C_n)}{N(C_{n-L},\dots,C_n)}$$

Where $N(B_n,C_{n-L},\dots,C_n)$ is the number of occurrences of the sequence of classifications $C_{n-L},\dots,C_n$ where the passage ends at position $n$ normalized by$N(C_{n-L},\dots,C_n)$- the number of occurrences of the same sequence. We also perform Backoff smoothing, i.e.: when the sequence with length $L$ is not observed, we find the sequence with length $L\text{-}1$, then $L\text{-}2$ if necessary. Given a document with the sequence of classifications $C_1,\dots,C_N$, we want to find the sequence of blocks $B_a,\dots,B_N$, so that we optimize the objective function:

$$P(B_a,\dots B_N) = \prod_{B_a,\dots B_N} P(B_n|C_{n-L})$$

This optimization problem is performed in polynomial time using a Viterbi approach for HMM.

# 3 Crowdsourcing

## 3.1 General information

For training and evaluation, we needed a set of news stories with passages annotated with the corresponding event categories. Obtaining such a dataset presents both conceptual and practical difficulties. Designations of named events are subjective decisions of each reader with only moderate agreement between them (see Table 2, column 1). We used Amazon Mechanical Turk (AMT) service to recruit and manage several annotators for each story. Each assignment (called

HIT) asked to label 10 sentences and paid $0.05 if accepted by us. We selected 50 news articles for each of the 10 named events and we created 5 HITS for each of sequence of 10 sentences from 500 news articles in our set. We also suspect that the sequence of sentences would influence labelling. For example, even a neutral sentence might be labelled "bankruptcy" if the neighbouring sentences were clearly about bankruptcy. To verify this hypothesis, we created a condition with randomized order of sentences from different stories. Our data supported this hypothesis (see Table 1), which has an important implication for feature selection. In the future, we plan to include contextual features from the neighbouring sentences.

| **Ann. Mode** | **Bank.** | **M&A** | **M. Chang.** |
|---|---|---|---|
| Sequential | 35% | 47% | 39% |
| Random | 24% | 33% | 34% |

Table 1: Proportion of sentence labels matching the topic of the article

Our first practical problem was to weed out bad performers who took short cuts generating meaningless results. We used several heuristics such as incomplete work, fast submission, randomness, etc. to weed out bad HITs.

Even after eliminating bad performers, we still have a problem of disagreements among the remaining performers. We give each label a score equal to the sum of all votes it received. We also explored an alternative scoring formula using a weighted sum of the votes. The weight reflects the performer's reputation from previous HITs (the proportion of accepted HITs) and the discrepancy in the amount of time it normally takes to do a HIT (assuming a Gaussian distribution of the time it takes to perform a HIT). To evaluate these alternatives, we used Fleiss kappa metric (Fleiss 1971) to measure the agreement between expert labeling and the top-scoring labels (weighted and un-weighted) produced by the AMT performers.

In Table 2, K(C) is the agreement among all performers. $K(L_C,L_E)$ is the agreement between the expert and the top-scoring labels using un-weighted votes. $K(L_W,L_E)$ is the agreement between expert and the top-scoring labels using weighted votes. Using weighted votes, on average, produces a small improvement in the agreement with expert opinion.

| **CAT** | **K(C)** | **$K(L_C,L_E)$** | **$K(L_W,L_E)$** |
|---|---|---|---|
| Terrorism | 0.401 | 0.738 | **0.788** |
| S. Bombing | 0.484 | 0.454 | **0.553** |
| Sex abuse | 0.455 | 0.354 | **0.420** |
| M. Changes | 0.465 | **0.509** | 0.491 |
| M&A | 0.408 | 0.509 | **0.509** |
| Arm. Clashes | 0.429 | **0.655** | 0.630 |
| Street Protest | 0.453 | **0.603** | 0.587 |
| Strike | 0.471 | **0.714** | 0.709 |
| L. Trouble | 0.457 | **0,698** | 0,694 |
| Bankruptcy | 0.519 | **0.638** | **0.638** |
| **AVG.** | **0.454** | **0.575** | **0.592** |

Table 2: Inter-annotator agreements (p-value $< 0.05$)

## 4 Experiments and Evaluation

First, we trained our sentence-labeling classifier on the training set of 50 news stories from the "Gold Standard" set labeled by the Amazon Mechanical Turk performers. We then applied this classifier to the remaining 450 stories in the Gold Standard set. We used two metrics to compare the algorithm's performance to the Gold Standard: F1 and nDCG (Jarvelin et al., 2000). For the first metric, for each sentence, we used the best-scoring label from the Gold Standard using the weighted sum of the votes and the best label produced by our classifier. For the second, we used lists of labels ordered by their scores Table 3.

| CAT | P | R | F1 | nDCG |
|---|---|---|---|---|
| Terrorism | 0.758 | 0.650 | 0.700 | 0.853 |
| S. Bombing | 0.865 | 0.724 | 0.788 | 0.934 |
| Sex abuse | 0.904 | 0.705 | 0.792 | **0.951** |
| M. Changes | 0.780 | 0.599 | 0.678 | 0.873 |
| M&A | 0.805 | 0.569 | 0.667 | 0.899 |
| Arm. Clashes | 0.712 | 0.594 | 0.789 | 0.816 |
| Street Protest | 0.833 | 0.697 | **0.845** | 0.921 |
| Strike | 0.758 | 0.650 | 0.700 | 0.842 |
| L. Trouble | 0.626 | 0.569 | 0.667 | 0.735 |
| Bankruptcy | **0.907** | 0.786 | 0.842 | 0.940 |
| None of ab. | 0.727 | **0.907** | 0.807 | 0.834 |
| **Weight. AVG.** | **0.752** | **0.750** | **0.737** | **0.880** |

Table 3: Named-event classification results using 10 fold cross-validation (p-value < 0.01).

For comparison, we calculated the average scores for the individual human labellers measured against the rest of the labellers. We obtained F1 = 0.633 and nDCG = 0.738, which is lower than the performance obtained by our classifier. To compare the results of the HMM-based passage aggregator to the baseline we used the standard B-cube metrics (Bagga, 1998) applied to the sentence rather than word boundaries. For the "Gold Standard" of passage boundaries, we used contiguous blocks of best-scoring labels produced by the human performers (in Table 4).

| CAT | P | R | F1 |
|---|---|---|---|
| Baseline | 0.554 | 0.626 | 0.588 |
| HMM based | 0.489 | **0.903** | **0.634** |

Table 4: Passage evaluation

## Conclusions and Future work

We introduced a new supervised information extraction method to identify named-event passages. On a sentence-by-sentence basis, our method outperformed human labellers (nDCG = 0.880 vs 0.738, F1 = 0.737 vs 0.633). Our HMM-based aggregation algorithm outperformed the baseline (F1 = 0.634 vs. 0.588). While our results show promise, they should be viewed as a preliminary step towards extraction of named-event information, the main goal of this research. Another contribution of this work is the use of the AMT to obtain useable data from a diverse set of performers. We report several procedures to weed out bad performers from data.

## Acknowledgments

This work was supported by Carnegie Mellon Portugal Program.

## References

Allan, James, Sridhar Mahadevan, and Ramesh Nallapati. 2004. "Extraction of Key Words from News Stories." CIIR Technical Report.

Allan, James, Ron Papka, and V. Lavrenko. 1998. "On-line new event detection and tracking." Pp. 37–45 in *Proceedings of the 21st annual international ACM SIGIR conference on Research and development in information retrieval*. ACM.

Breiman, Leo. 1996. "Bagging predictors." *Machine Learning* 24(2):123-140.

Bagga, Amit; Baldwin, Breck . 1998. "Algorithms for Scoring coreference chains." Pp.563–566 in *the First International Conference on Language Resources and Evaluation Workshop in Linguistics Coreference*

Feng, Ao, and James Allan. 2007. "Finding and linking incidents in news." *Proceedings of the sixteenth ACM conference on Conference on information and knowledge management - CIKM '07.*

Feng, Ao, and James Allan. 2009. "Incident threading for news passages." Pp. 1307–1316 in *Proceeding of the 18th ACM conference on Information and knowledge management*. New York, New York, USA.

Finkel, Jenny Rose, Trond Grenager, and Christopher Manning. 2005. "Incorporating Non-local Information into Information Extraction Systems by Gibbs Sampling." Pp. 363-370 in *Proceedings of the 43nd Annual Meeting of the Association for Computational Linguistics (ACL 2005)*.

Fleiss, J.L. 1971. "Measuring nominal scale agreement among many raters." *Psychological Bulletin* 76(5):378.

Hall, Mark et al. 2009. "The WEKA data mining software: an update." *ACM SIGKDD Explorations Newsletter* 11(1):10–18.

Hastie, T., and Robert Tibshirani. 1998. "Classification by pairwise coupling." *The annals of statistics* 26(2):451–471.

Jarvelin, K., and Jaana. Kekalainen. 1996. "IR evaluation methods for retrieving highly relevant documents." *Proceedings of the 23rd annual international ACM SIGIR 96.*

Kittler, J., Mohamad Hatef, Robert P.W. Duin, Jiri Matas. 1998. "On Combining Classifiers" *IEEE Transactions on Pattern Analysis and Machine Intelligence*. 20(3):226–239

Kucheva, L. 2004. "Combining Pattern Classifiers: Methods and Algorithms". John Wiley and Sons.

Marujo, Luís, Anatole Gershman, Jaime Carbonell, Robert Frederking, and João P Neto. 2012. "Supervised Topical Key Phrase Extraction of News Stories using Crowdsourcing , Light Filtering and Co-reference Normalization Pre-Processing." in *Proceedings of 8th International Conference on Language Resources and Evaluation (LREC)*.

McCallum, A., and Kamal Nigam. 1998. "A comparison of event models for naive bayes text classification." Pp. 41–48 in *AAAI-98 workshop on learning for text categorization*.

Medelyan, Olena, Vye Perrone, and Ian H. Witten. 2010. "Subject metadata support powered by Maui." P. 407 in *Proceedings of the 10th annual joint conference on Digital libraries - JCDL '10*. New York, New York, USA.

Nallapati, Ramesh, Ao Feng, Fuchun Peng, and James Allan. 2004. "Event threading within news topics." P. 446 in *Proceedings of the Thirteenth ACM conference on Information and knowledge management - CIKM '04*. New York, New York.

Platt, J.C. 1998. "Fast Training of Support Vector Machines using Sequential Minimal Optimization." Pp. 637-649 in *Advances in Kernel Methods - Support Vector Learning*.

Quinlan, JR. 1994. "C4.5: programs for machine learning." *Machine Learning* 16:235-240.

Ribeiro, Ricardo, and D.M. Matos. 2011. "Revisiting Centrality-as-Relevance□: Support Sets and Similarity as Geometric Proximity." *Journal of Artificial Intelligence Research*.

Schank, Roger C., and Robert P. Abelson. 1977. "Scripts, Plans, Goals, And Understanding: An Inquiry into Human Knowledge Structures". Lawrence Erlbaum Associates, Hillsdale, New Jersey, USA

Stephens, Mitchell. 1950. "History of Newspapers." *Collier's Encyclopedia*.

Yang, Yiming et al. 1999. "Learning approaches for detecting and tracking news events." *Intelligent Systems and their Applications, IEEE* 14(4):32–43.

Yang, Yiming, Tom Pierce, and Carbonell. 1998. "A Study of Retrospective and On-line Event Detection." *Proceedings of the 21st annual international ACM SIGIR 98*

# Nonparametric Model for Inupiaq Morphology Tokenization

*ThuyLinh Nguyen*[1] *Stephan Vogel*[2]
(1) Carnegie Mellon University.
(2) Qatar Foundation, Qatar.
thuylinh@cs.cmu.edu, svogel@qf.org.qa

**Abstract**

We present how to use English translation for unsupervised word segmentation of low resource languages. The inference uses a dynamic programming algorithm for efficient blocked Gibbs sampling. We apply the model to Inupiaq morphology analysis and get better results than monolingual model as well as Morfessor output.

Keywords: Nonparametric model, Gibbs sampling, morphology tokenization.

*Proceedings of COLING 2012: Demonstration Papers*, pages 337–344,
COLING 2012, Mumbai, December 2012.

## 1 Introduction

The tasks of morphological analysis or word segmentation have relied on word-formation rules or on available pretokenized corpora such as a Chinese word list, the Arabic or Korean treebanks, or the Czech dependancy treebank. However, these resources are expensive to obtain and for small or endangered languages, these resources are even not available. In recent years, unsupervised methods have been developed to infer the segmentation from unlabeled data such using minimal description length (Creutz and Lagus, 2007), log-linear model (Poon et al., 2009), nonparametric Bayesian model (Goldwater et al., 2009).

| | | |
|---|---|---|
| 1. | Aŋun maqpiġaaliuġaa Aiviq . | *the man is writing the book for Aiviq* . |
| | Aŋun(*man*) maqpiġaa(*book*) liuġ(*writing*) aa Aiviq(*Aiviq*) . | |
| 2. | Aŋun maqpiġaaliuŋitkaa Aiviq . | *the man is not writing the book for Aiviq* . |
| | Aŋun(*man*) maqpiġaa(*book*) liu(*writing*) ŋit(*not*) kaa Aiviq(*Aiviq*) . | |

Table 1: Two examples of Inupiaq text, their English translations and their morphology tokenizations and English alignments.

A different promising approach is using information from a second language to learn the morphology analysis of the low resource language. Look at the example of Inupiaq[1] and its English translation in Table 1. Without knowing the language, let alone its morphology, we can conjecture that Inupiaq morpheme equivalent to English's "not" must be a substring of "maqpiġaaliuŋitkaa" and be overlaping with"ŋitk". This derivation is not possible without English translation.

This paper presents a nonparametric model and blocked Gibbs sampling inference to automatically derive morphology analysis of a text through its English translation. [2](Snyder and Barzilay, 2008) also applied a Bayesian model with Dirichlet Process priors to multilingual word segmentation task. Their prior distribution of souce word and target word alignment is defined based on the phonetic matching between two words. The bilingual word segmentation therefore benefits only when the source language and the target language belongs to the same family but does not achieve the same benefit when two languages are unrelated, such as using English translation to segment Arabic or Hebrew. We model the base distribution of target-source word alignment depends on the cooccurance of the two words in parallel corpora, independent of the language pair, the experiment results show the benefit of using English translation for Inupiaq morphology analysis.

Our model inherits (Nguyen et al., 2010)'s model of joint distribution of tokenized source text and its alignment to the target language. The alignment consists of at most one-to-one mappings between the source and target words with null alignments possible on both sides. To get samples of the posterior distribution, we use blocked Gibbs sampling algorithm and sample the whole source sentence and its alignment at the same time. The inference uses the dynamic programming method to avoid explicitly considering all possible segmentations of the source sentence and their alignments with the target sentence. Our inference technique is an extension of the forward sampling-backward filtering presented by (Mochihashi et al., 2009) for monolingual word segmentation. Dynamic programming algorithm has been also employed to sample PCFG parse trees (Johnson et al., 2007) and grammar-based word segmentation (Johnson and Goldwater, 2009).

[1] Inupiaq is a language spoken in Northern Alaska

[2] We use the term *bilingual word segmentation* for the problem we are working on to differentiate with *monolingual word segmentation* problem of learning to segment the text without translation reference.

In the next section we will discuss the model. Section 3 will describe the inference in detail. Experiments and results will be presented in section 4.

# 2 Model

A source sentence $\bar{\mathbf{s}}$ is a sequence of $|\bar{\mathbf{s}}|$ characters $\left(c_1, c_2 \ldots c_{|\bar{\mathbf{s}}|}\right)$. A segmentation of $\bar{\mathbf{s}}$ is a sentence $\mathbf{s}$ of $|\mathbf{s}|$ words $s_i$:$\left(s_1, \ldots, s_{|\mathbf{s}|}\right)$. We use the notation with bar on top $\bar{\mathbf{s}}$ to denote a sequence of characters to distinguish with a sequence of segmented words $\mathbf{s}$. In sentence $\mathbf{s}$, the set of aligned words is $\mathbf{s}_{\text{al}}$ the set of nonaligned words is $\mathbf{s}_{\text{nal}}$, each word in $\mathbf{s}_{\text{al}}$ aligns to a word in the set of aligned target words $\mathbf{t}_{\text{al}}$, the set of nonaligned target words is $\mathbf{t}_{\text{nal}}$.

In the first example Inupiaq segmentation in Table 1, the segmented $\mathbf{s} =$ "Aŋun maqpiġaa liuġ aa Aiviq ." the set $\mathbf{s}_{\text{al}} = \{$Aŋun, maqpiġaa liuġ, Aviq$\}$, $\mathbf{s}_{\text{nal}} = \{$aa$\}$, the mapping of $\mathbf{s}_{\text{al}}$ and $\mathbf{t}_{\text{al}}$ is $\{$ Aŋun(*man*), maqpiġaa(*book*), liuġ(*writing*), Aiviq(*Aiviq*)$\}$, the set of unaligned target is $\mathbf{t}_{\text{nal}} = \{$the, the, for $\}$.

The generative process of a sentence $\mathbf{s}$ and its alignment $\mathbf{a}$ consists of two steps. In the first step, $\mathbf{s}$ and the alignments of each word in $\mathbf{s}$ are generated, each source word is either null aligned or aligned to a target word. In the second step, the model generates null aligned target words. More specifically, the two steps generative process of $(\mathbf{s}, \mathbf{a})$ as follows:

1. Repeatedly generate word $s_i$ and its alignment:
   - Generate the word $s_i$ with probability $\mathsf{p}\left(s_i\right)$.
   - Mark $s_i$ as not aligned with probability $\mathsf{p}\left(\mathsf{null} \mid s_i\right)$ or aligned with probability $\left(1 - \mathsf{p}\left(\mathsf{null} \mid s_i\right)\right)$.
     - If $s_i$ is aligned, $s \in \mathbf{s}_{\text{al}}$, generate its aligned target word $t_{a_i} \in \mathbf{t}_{\text{al}}$ with probability $\mathsf{p}\left(t_{a_i} | s_i\right)$.
2. Generate the set of non-aligned target words $\mathbf{t}_{\text{nal}}$ given aligned target words $\mathbf{t}_{\text{al}}$ with probability $\mathsf{p}\left(\mathbf{t}_{\text{nal}} | \mathbf{t}_{\text{al}}\right)$.

We model the source word distibution $\mathsf{p}(s)$, null aligned source word $\mathsf{p}(\mathsf{null} \mid s)$ and null aligned target words $\mathsf{p}\left(\mathbf{t}_{\text{nal}} | \mathbf{t}_{\text{al}}\right)$ similar to the same model described in (Nguyen et al., 2010). The main difference is in how we define the base distribution of a target word given a source word $\mathsf{p}(t | s)$.

## 2.1 Source-Target Alignment Model

The probability $\mathsf{p}(t|s)$ that a target word $t$ aligns to a source word $s$ is drawn from a Pitman-yor process $t \mid s \sim \text{PY}\left(d, \alpha, \mathsf{p}_0(t|s)\right)$ here $d$ and $\alpha$ are the input parameters, and $\mathsf{p}_0(t|s)$ is the base distribution.

In word alignment model, highly co-occuring word pairs are likely to be the translation of each other, this is the intuition behind all the statistical word alignment model. However, the standard IBM word alignment models are not applicable to define conditional distribution of a pair of sequence of characters as the source side and a target word. We propose source-target alignment base distribution that captures the cooccurence of a sequence of source characters $\bar{c} = \left(c_1, \ldots c_{|\bar{c}|}\right)$ and a target word $t$ as follows.

Given the sentence pair $(\mathbf{s}, \mathbf{t})$, let $\mathsf{count}(\bar{c}, t)_{(\mathbf{s},\mathbf{t})}$ be the number of times the pair $(\bar{c}, t)$ cooccur. In Table 1, the example 1 has $\mathsf{count}(\text{aa}, \textit{the})_{(\mathbf{s},\mathbf{t})} = 2$; $\mathsf{count}(\text{maqpiga}, \textit{book})_{(\mathbf{s},\mathbf{t})} = 1$.

$$
\alpha\left(l,k,\mathbf{t}_1,t\right) = \begin{cases} \mathrm{p}\left(\text{null} \mid c_{l-k+1}^{l}\right)\mathrm{p}\left(c_{l-k+1}^{l}\right)\sum\limits_{u=1}^{l-k}\sum\limits_{\substack{t'\in\mathbf{t}_1\\ \text{or } t'=\text{null}}}\alpha\left(l-k,u,\mathbf{t}_1\setminus t',t'\right) & \text{if } t=\text{null} \\ \left(1-\mathrm{p}\left(\text{null} \mid c_{l-k+1}^{l}\right)\right)\mathrm{p}\left(c_{l-k+1}^{l}\right)\mathrm{p}\left(t \mid c_{l-k+1}^{l}\right) & \text{if } t \text{ is not null} \\ \sum\limits_{u=1}^{l-k}\sum\limits_{\substack{t'\in\mathbf{t}_1\setminus t\\ \text{or } t'=\text{null}}}\alpha\left(l-k,u,\mathbf{t}_1\setminus t',t'\right) & \end{cases}
$$

Figure 1: Forward function $\alpha\left(l,k,\mathbf{t}_1,t\right)$.

Given the training parallel corpora $\mathcal{T}$ number of times $(\bar{c},t)$ cooccur in $\mathcal{T}$ is $\mathsf{count}(\bar{c},t)_{\mathcal{T}} = \sum_{(\mathbf{s},\mathbf{t})\in\mathcal{T}}\mathsf{count}(\bar{c},t)_{(\mathbf{s},\mathbf{t})}$.

Note that if "maqpiga" is the translation of "book" by cooccuring in sentence pairs, any substring of the word such as "m", "ap" also coocur with "*book*", but *book* is not their translation candidate. We therefore remove these counts from corpora coocurence count. Let $\bar{c'}$ be a substring of $\bar{c}$, if $\mathsf{count}(\bar{c'},t)_{\mathcal{T}} = \mathsf{count}(\bar{c},t)_{\mathcal{T}}$, $\mathsf{count}(\bar{c'},t)_{\mathcal{T}} > \theta_1$ and $\mathsf{length}\left(\bar{c'}\right) < \theta_2$, we remove $\mathsf{count}(\bar{c'},t)_{\mathcal{T}}$ from the count, $\mathsf{count}(\bar{c'},t) = 0$. Here $\theta_1$ and $\theta_2$ are the input thresholds to avoid removal of low frequency words or long words. We define the base distribution for any sequence of character $\bar{c}$ and a target word $t$ as: $\mathrm{p}_0\left(t \mid \bar{c}\right) = \frac{\mathsf{count}(\bar{c},t)}{\sum_t \mathsf{count}(\bar{c},t)}$.

## 3 Inference

We use blocked Gibbs sampling algorithm to generate samples from the posterior distribution of the model. In our experiment, the variables are potential word boundaries and sentence alignments. We first initialize the training data with an initial segmentation and alignment. Then the sampler iteratively removes a sentence from the data and samples the segmentation and alignment of the sentence given the rest of training set. The new sentence is then added to the corpus. This process continues until the samples are mixed up and represent the posterior of interest.

We apply the dynamic programming Forward filtering - Backward sampling algorithm. The Forward filtering step calculates the marginalized probabilities of variables and the Backward sampling step uses these probabilities to sample the variables.

### 3.1 Forward Filtering

We define the forward function $\alpha\left(l,k,\mathbf{t}_1,t\right)$ to iteratively calculate the marginalized probabilities in step 1 of generation process. That is the probability of the substring $c_1^l$ with the final $k$ characters being a word aligned to $t$ and $c_1^{l-k}$ aligns to the subset target words $\mathbf{t}_1$.

Figure 1 shows how to calculate $\alpha\left(l,k,\mathbf{t}_1,t\right)$, the mathematic derivation of the function is similar to forward function of HMM model. We will give the detail in a technical report.

### 3.2 Backward Sampling

The forward filtering step calculates function $\alpha\left(l,k,\mathbf{t}_1,t\right)$ in the order of increasing $l$. At the end of the source sentence, the forward filtering step calculates the forward variables $\alpha\left(|\mathbf{s}|,k,\mathbf{t}_1,t\right)$ for any $k \le |\mathbf{s}|$, $\mathbf{t}_1 \subset \mathbf{t}$ and $t \in \mathbf{t}$, $t \notin \mathbf{t}_1$. That is the probability that the sentence $\mathbf{s}$ has the last word with length $k$ and the word aligns to $t$, the rest of the sentence aligns to the set $\mathbf{t_1}$. The set of corresponding aligned target words is $\mathbf{t_1} \cup \{t\}$.

So the marginalized probability in step 1 of the generation process is

$$\mathsf{p}\left(\cancel{\mathbf{s}}, \mathbf{t}_{\text{al}}\right) = \sum_{k} \sum_{\substack{t' \in \mathbf{t_1} \setminus t \\ \text{or } t' = \text{null}}} \alpha\left(\cancel{|\mathbf{s}|}, k, \mathbf{t_1} \setminus t', t'\right)$$

We have the marginalized probability that any $\mathbf{t}_{\text{nal}} \subset \mathbf{t}$ is the set of nonaligned target word: $\mathsf{p}\left(\cancel{\mathbf{s}}, \mathbf{t}_{\text{al}}, \mathbf{t}_{\text{nal}}\right) = \mathsf{p}\left(\cancel{\mathbf{s}}, \mathbf{t}_{\text{al}}\right) \times \mathsf{p}\left(\mathbf{t}_{\text{nal}} \mid \mathbf{t}_{\text{al}}\right)$.

In backward sampling, we first sample the set of nonaligned target words $\mathbf{t}_{\text{nal}}$ proportional to the marginalized probability $\mathsf{p}\left(\cancel{\mathbf{s}}, \mathbf{t}_{\text{al}}, \mathbf{t}_{\text{nal}}\right)$.

Once we got the set of aligned target words $\mathbf{t}_{\text{nal}}$ for string $\mathbf{s}$, we sample the length $k$ of the last word of the sentence according to its marginalized probability:

$$\sum_{\substack{t \in \mathbf{t}_{\text{al}} \\ \text{or } t = \text{null}}} \alpha\left(\cancel{|\mathbf{s}|}, k, \mathbf{t}_{\text{al}} \setminus t, t\right).$$

then sample the alignment $t$ of the last word $c_{\cancel{|\mathbf{s}|}-k+1}^{\cancel{|\mathbf{s}|}}$ proportional to $\alpha\left(\cancel{|\mathbf{s}|}, k, \mathbf{t}_{\text{al}} \setminus t, t\right)$. The process continues backward until we reach the beginning of the sentence.

# 4 Empirical Results

The Inupiaq-English data is from an ellicit parallel corpora which consists of 2933 parallel sentences of average 4.34 words per Inupiaq sentence, 6 words per English sentences. On average, each Inupiaq word has 11.35 characters. Our task is to segment Inupiaq into morphemes with average 2.31 morphemes per word. The number of morphemes per word has high variance, Inupiaq usually has subject and oblique as separate words and the rest of the sentence as one long word. It is a rich morphology language with relatively free reordering. For example, both sentences "Maqpiaaliuġniaġaa Aiviq Paniattaam" and "Aiviq maqpiaaliuġniaġaa Paniattaam" have the same translation *"Paniattaaq will write a book for Aiviq"*.

## 4.1 Experiment Setup

We report the best result of experiments with different values hyperparameter $p_0$ (from $0.5 \ldots 0.9$ and 0.95, 0.99) which model the source word null alignment and the parameter represent word length distribution. All other hyperparameters are fixed before the experiment. The MCMC inference algorithm starts with an initial segmentation as full word form and initial monotone alignment. The inference samples 100 iterations through the whole training set. The inference adopts simulated annealing to speed convergence of the sampler and approximates the samples around the MAP solution. In the last 10 iterations, the inference uses a temperature parameter $\tau$ and starts cooling down from 1, $\frac{9}{10}$ to $\frac{1}{10}$. The last iteration represents the MAP solution and is the segmentation output. We leave the analysis of inference convergence to the future work. We report the segmentation accuracy on F-score of:[3] **BF**: word boundries score; **F**: word token score: both boundaries of a word must be correctly identified to be counted as correct; **LF**: instead of reporting the word-token accuracy as F, LF represents word-type score.

[3] the evaluation script is on http://homepages.inf.ed.ac.uk/sgwater/resources.html

One word in rich morphology language is often equivalent to several English words. But English has morphology in the language too, an English past tense verb or plural noun are equivalent to two morphemes. We also experiment our bilingual model with the target side is tokenized English. The tokenized English is the result pf manually convert English past tense verbs into "verb PAST", plural nouns into "lematize_noun PL", all other words are lemmatized. For example, the sentence *The men sang* is converted to *The man PL sing PAST*.

## 4.2 Empirical Results

| | F | BF | LF |
|---|---|---|---|
| HDP-Monolingual | 35.02 | 62.62 | **30.51** |
| Morfessor | 35.53 | 63.98 | 29.72 |
| Bilingual | 35.83 | 65.68 | 29.80 |
| Bilingual-tokenized Eng | **39.15** | **66.71** | 30.15 |

Table 2: Inupiaq morphology analysis results: comparing the baseline scores (upper row) and our scores (lower row).

Table 2 presents our segmentation results. The top rows are monolingual baselines, the bottom rows are our bilingual results using either English or tokenized English as the target language. The best score belongs to bilingual model using tokenized English for unsupervised segmentation.

For monolingual baselines, we use (Goldwater et al., 2009)'s monolingual nonparametric word segmentation. The HDP-Monolingual result in Table 2 is the best score from nearly 100 experiments of their model with different hyperparameters. Unlike (Snyder and Barzilay, 2008) report that bilingual word segmentation do not benefit when two languages are different. Our bilingual model still has better performance than the nonparametric monolingual word segmentation on F, BF and average scores. The informative source-target base distribution contribute to this better result.

We also use Morfessor (Creutz and Lagus, 2007), an unsupervised morphology analysis as another monolingual baseline. Morfessor is the state-of-the-art unsupervised segmentation for complex morphology languages such as Finish, Czech. The bilingual model using tokenized English significantly outperforms Morfessor result. Our experiment on small Inupiaq-English data is typical for low resource language scenario. The morphology analysis of the parallel data then can be used as supervised data for monolingual segmentation task without given English translation.

# 5 Conclusion

We have presented a bilingual nonparametric word segmentation model for low resource languages. The inference uses a dynamic programming algorithm for an efficient blocked Gibbs sampling. The experiment shows the benefit of using translation in word segmentation task.

# References

Creutz, M. and Lagus, K. (2007). Unsupervised models for morpheme segmentation and morphology learning. *ACM Trans. Speech Lang. Process.*, 4(1):1–34.

Goldwater, S., Griffiths, T. L., and Johnson, M. (2009). A Bayesian Framework for Word Segmentation: Exploring the Effects of Context. *Cognition*, 112(1):21–54.

Johnson, M. and Goldwater, S. (2009). Improving Nonparameteric Bayesian Inference: Experiments on Unsupervised Word Segmentation with Adaptor Grammars. In *Proceedings of*

*NAACL-HLT '09*, pages 317–325, Stroudsburg, PA, USA. Association for Computational Linguistics.

Johnson, M., Griffiths, T., and Goldwater, S. (2007). Bayesian inference for PCFGs via Markov chain Monte Carlo. In *Proceedings of NAACL-HLT '07*, pages 139–146, Rochester, New York. Association for Computational Linguistics.

Mochihashi, D., Yamada, T., and Ueda, N. (2009). Bayesian Unsupervised Word Segmentation with Nested Pitman-Yor Language Modeling. In *Proceedings of ACL:09*, pages 100–108, Suntec, Singapore. Association for Computational Linguistics.

Nguyen, T., Vogel, S., and Smith, N. A. (2010). Nonparametric Word Segmentation for Machine Translation. In *Proceedings of Coling-10*, pages 815–823, Beijing, China.

Poon, H., Cherry, C., and Toutanova, K. (2009). Unsupervised Morphological Segmentation with Log-Linear Models. In *Proceedings NAACL'09*, pages 209–217.

Snyder, B. and Barzilay, R. (2008). Unsupervised multilingual learning for morphological segmentation. In *Proceedings of ACL-08: HLT*, pages 737–745, Columbus, Ohio. Association for Computational Linguistics.

# Stemming Tigrinya Words for Information Retrieval

*Omer Osman Ibrahim*[1] *Yoshiki Mikami*[1]
(1) Nagaoka University of Technology, Nagaoka, Japan
sangor@gmail.com,mikami@kjs.nagaokaut.ac.jp

ABSTRACT

The increasing penetration of internet into less developed countries has resulted in the increase in the number of digital documents written in many minor languages. However, many of these languages have limited resources in terms of data, language resources and computational tools. Stemming is the reduction of inflected word forms into common basic form. It is an important analysis process in information retrieval and many natural language processing applications. In highly inflected languages such as Tigrinya, stemming is not always straightforward task. In this paper we present the development of stemmer for Tigrinya words to facilitate the information retrieval. We used a hybrid approach for stemming that combines rule based stemming which removes affixes in successively applied steps and dictionary based stemming which reduces stemming errors by verifying the resulting stem based on word distance measures. The stemmer was evaluated using two sets of Tigrinya words. The results show that it achieved an average accuracy of 89.3%.

KEYWORDS : Tigrinya, Stemming, Information Retrieval, Stop Word , Search Engine

*Proceedings of COLING 2012: Demonstration Papers*, pages 345–352,
COLING 2012, Mumbai, December 2012.

# 1 Introduction

Most Information Retrieval (IR) systems use inverted indexes for indexing and searching purposes. An inverted index contains a collection of terms and their corresponding occurrences in documents. However, a single word may occur in a number of morphological variants in the index, thus, increasing the size of the index and decreasing retrieval performance. Therefore, it is important to reduce different variants of words to their corresponding single form before indexing.

Stemming is a normalization step that reduces the morphological variants of words to a common form usually called a stem by the removal of affixes. Among the many normalization steps that are usually performed before indexing, stemming has significant effect in both the efficiency and the effectiveness of IR for many languages (Pirkola, A. & Järvelin, K. 2001). In addition to Information retrieval, stemming is also important in many other natural language processing application such as machine translation, morphological analysis and part of speech tagging. The complexity of stemming process varies with the morphological complexity of a natural language. Tigrinya belongs to the Semitic language family that includes languages like Arabic, Hebrew and Amharic. Those languages are highly inflected and derived. Thus, a hybrid approach would be a good choice to get correct stems so as to increase search precision. Dictionary verification applied after suffix stripping can further enhance the accuracy of the stemmer and it can also give meaningful stems. In this paper we report the development of stemming procedure for Tigrinya that combines rule based suffix stripping and dictionary based verification.

The rest of the paper is organized as follows. In section 2, we briefly review background information on the Tigrinya language and stemming approaches. In Section 3, we briefly present the Corpus used in this research. The stemming approach used is detailed in Section 4. The evaluation of the stemmer is discussed in Section 5. Finally, the conclusion of the research is given in Section 6.

# 2 Background

## 2.1 The Tigrinya Language

Tigrinya is a language spoken in the east African countries of Eritrea and Ethiopia. It is one of the two official languages of the State of Eritrea. It is also a working language of the Tigray region of Ethiopia. It is estimated to be spoken by over six million people both countries (http://www.ethnologue.com). Tigrinya is a Semitic language of the afro-Asiatic family originated from the ancient Geez language. It is closely related to Amharic and Tigre.Tigrinya is written in Geez script also called Ethiopic. Ethiopic Script is syllabic, each symbol represents 'consonant + vowel' characteristics. Each Tigrinya base character also known as "Fidel" has seven vowel combinations. Tigrinya is written from left to right. Tigrinya is a 'low resource' language having very limited resources: data, linguistic materials and tools.

## 2.2 Tigrinya Morphology

Tigrinya is a highly inflected language and has a complex morphology. It exhibits the root and pattern morphological system. The Tigrinya root is a sequence of consonants and it represents the basic form for word formation. Tigrinya makes use of prefixing, suffixing and internal changes to form inflectional and derivational word forms. Tigrinya Nouns are inflected for gender, number, case and definiteness. For example,ሃገራት(hagerat) - countries, ተማሃራይ (temaharay) - male student, ተማሃሪት (temaharit) - female student.Tigrinya adjectives are inflected for gender and number. For example, ጸሊም(Selim), ጸለምቲ (Selemti) meaning 'black' (masculine), 'blacks' respectively. Like other Semitic languages Tigrinya has rich verb morphology.Tigrinya verbs show different morphosyntactic features based on the arrangement of consonant (C) -vowel (V) patterns. For example, the root 'sbr' /to break/ of pattern (CCC) has forms such as 'sebere' (CVCVCV) in Active, 'te-sebre'(te-CVCCV) in Passive.

### 2.3 Related Work

Anjali Ganesh Jivani (Anjali Ganesh Jivani, 2011) classifies stemmers in to three broad categories: truncating, statistical and mixed. Truncating stemmers are related with removal of the affix of a word. They apply a set of rules to each word to strip the known set of affixes. The first stemmer following such algorithm was developed by Julie Beth Lovins in 1968 (Lovins,1968). A latter such stemmer was proposed by Martin Porter in 1980 (Porter, 1980). The major disadvantage of such stemmers is that they need large set of affixes and prior knowledge of the language morphology.

Yassir et. al. (Yassir, 2011) reported an enhanced stemmer for Arabic that combines light stemming and dictionary based stemming. In their research they included handling of multi-word expression and named entity recognition. They reported that the average accuracy of their enhanced stemmer was 96.29%. Sandip and Sajip (Sandip et. al. 2009) reported a rule based stemmer for Bengali that also uses stem dictionary for further validation . They used a part of speech(POS) tagger to tag the text and apply POS specific rules to output the stem. Not much work has been reported for Tigrinya language stemming compared to other languages. Tigrinya is a an under-resource language with very few computational work done on it. However, there is a pioneering work done on Tigrinya language morphological analysis and generation by Michael Gasser (Michael Gasser, 2009 ). Yonas Fissaha reported a rule based Tigrinya stemmer on his locally published thesis and reported an accuracy of 86% (Yonas Fissaha, 2011). We could not find any other publication on Tigrinya Stemmer following Hybrid approach.

## 3 The Corpus used

This work is part of an ongoing research to design a Tigrinya language Search Engine. As part of the research, we have crawled significant number of documents from the web using a language specific crawler that was specifically designed for Tigrinya web content. Our corpus includes a number of Tigrinya pages from different domains including news, religious, political, sport and so on. After cleaning the data, we generated a Tigrinya word lexicon of size 690,000 unique words. Finally, it was used to generate list of prefixes, suffixes and list of stop words for Tigrinya. The corpus is freely available for researchers in Tigrinya language and can be downloaded from the Eritrean NLP website (Eri-NLP: http://www.eri-nlp.com).

## 4 The Tigrinya Stemmer

The stemmer was developed to conflate different inflected forms of words into a common term so as to increase retrieval recall and decrease the size of the index. In addition to that, since different inflections of the same base word can have different stems, we as much as possible wanted to put such forms in to a common stem so as to increase the precision of retrieval.

The stemmer follows a step by step transformation of a word until it finally outputs the possible stem. Firstly, the word is checked for apostrophe suffixes attached. Next, any other punctuations or accents concatenated to the word are removed. The resulting string is then normalized for letter inconsistencies. It is then checked against stop word list. If not in the list, it is transliterated and passed to the prefix removal routine. The result is then forwarded to the suffix removal routine. The result is then further checked for single and double letter duplicates. Finally the resulting stem is verified in the stem dictionary. If an exact match is found it is taken as the final stem. If no exact match is found, possible candidates stems are selected from the dictionary based on the inclusion of the stems in the stripped string. If more than one stems are selected, the one closest to the stripped string is selected based on the string distance metric. If two or more of the candidate stems selected from the dictionary have the same distance from the stripped word, the stem with high frequency on the corpus is selected as a final result. Finally, the final selected stem is transliterated back to Ethiopic and displayed as an output.

## 4.1 Suffix Removal

In many Tigrinya web documents an apostrophe or other similar mark is placed at the end of words to add suffix or to show that a letter has been omitted. In most of these words the character represents the letter in the 'እ' series. For example, ይኹን'ምበር is meant to be read as ይኹን እምበር, ኣመሓላለፉ'ሎ are meant to be read ኣመሓላለፉ ኣሎ. In most cases, the character used is the apostrophe, the right single quotation mark or the left single quotation mark. Thus, a routine that handles such suffixes is added. It removes such suffixes in addition to any other punctuations concatenated to the word. Tigrinya uses Ethiopic punctuation which lies in the Unicode range of \u1360-\u1368. This makes sure that no non-letter characters remain in the string.

## 4.2 Normalization

The Ethiopic Script includes different letters that have the same sound in a language. The letters 'ሰ' (se) and 'ሠ' (se), letters 'ጸ' (Tse) and ፀ (Tse) are some examples. Although most Tigrinya writings have one of these forms, some writers use them interchangeably. In Eritrea the 'ጸ' series is used while in Ethiopia the ፀ series is used. Thus, a single Tigrinya word may exist in two different variations on many web documents. For example, መጽሄት(meShEt) and መፅሄት (me'ShEt) are two variants of the same word meaning 'pamphlet'. Such variant forms have negative effect on precision of retrieval. Thus, a routine is added to convert such variants in to a single form.

## 4.3 Transliteration

After the string is normalized, it is first checked against the stop word list. Stemming a stop word is a useless process because stop words are not indexed. Hence, only those words that are not on the list are further processed by the stemmer. The transliteration step converts the Ethiopic string to Latin. We need this because the Ethiopic Script is Syllabic where both consonants and vowels are joined together in a Symbol. Thus, without transliteration it is very difficult to make word analysis such as affix removal or string comparison. By transliterating we convert the Tigrinya Symbols to their corresponding consonant + vowel combinations which makes it suitable for affix removal. For example, the word ሃገራት /hagerat/ meaning 'Countries' is composed of the stem ሃገር /hager/ and the number marker suffix ኣት/at/. In this case, the letter ኣ'a' which is part of the suffix is fused in the letter ራ/ra/.If the suffix removal is done before Romanization, either the ት/t/ or ራት/rat/ can be removed which leads to wrong stem. Romanizing the word to /hagerat/ makes it convenient to delete the suffix /at/ and retrieve the stem /hager/.We used the transliteration conventions of SERA - 'System for Ethiopic representation in ASCII' with few exceptions (Firdyiwek and Yacob, 1997).

## 4.4 The Affix Removal

This is the step where most of the inflections are removed. Tigrinya affixes include prefixes which are placed before a word and suffixes placed after the stem of a word. A Tigrinya word contains zero or more prefixes and zero or more suffixes. Our affix removal algorithm depends on a list of prefixes and suffixes. For this purpose, we have manually compiled a 153 set of prefixes and 204 set of Suffixes from our corpora mentioned in Section 3. The main disadvantage of affix removal strategies is that they require the knowledge of the language's morphology beforehand. Given the complex morphology of Tigrinya words, it is not easy to come up with a general set of context sensitive rules that govern the affix removal process. However, we have constructed a basic set of affix removal rules by studying various Tigrinya words with different parts of speech. The affix removal algorithm is similar to the one used by (Alemayehu and Willet ,2002) on Amharic. It iteratively removes the longest matched affix from a word by considering the minimum stem length. It also considers the length of the word to be stemmed so that to decrease over-stemming. The shortest Tigrinya word consists of two consonants. Hence, for a word to be further processed, it should at least have three consonants.

## 4.5 Duplicate Consonant Handling

Some Tigrinya verbs are derived by doubling of a consonant form. This words are of two types: those words containing consecutive consonants of the same form and those words containing one consonant form followed by the same consonant of different form. For example, consider the word ተሰሓሓቢ /teseHaHabi/. The Romanized form of the word shows that the consonant 'H' occurs consecutively. In the consonant-vowel fused form, forth form ሓ (Ha) is doubled in the word. In this specific case, after the prefix step removes the prefix 'te', the remaining word ሰሓሓቢ /seHaHabi/ is handled by removing the double consonant and changing it to the sixth form to give ሰሕብ. For the second types consider a word of the form $XYC_6C_4WZ$ where each of the letters represent a consonant-vowel Ethiopic form. The sixth order($C_6$) is followed by the fourth order($C_4$). In such forms, $C_4$ is deleted. For example, the word ምንግጋር /mnggar/. The affix removal step gives us the word ንግጋር /nggar/ and it is reduced to ንግር /ngr/. By studying the patters in many such words, we have constructed a set of rules for changing such forms.

## 4.6 Dictionary Verification

This step is introduced to further increase the accuracy of the stemmer. It helps put different stems of the same word into a single form. The Tigrinya stem dictionary employed was constructed manually from the corpus and it contains a stem, its Romanized form and its frequency in the corpus. Firstly, the resulting string is searched in the stem lexicon for an exact match. If found, it is returned as a final stem and the process is terminated. This is done as a means of validation of the correctness of the stem. If an exact match is not found, verification is done as follows: all the stems that are contained in the stripped string are selected as candidate stems. To select the most likely stem, we introduce string distance metric between the string and the potential stem candidates. The candidate with minimum distance from the word is given highest priority. We use the Levenshtein Edit distance (Levenshtein, 1966). The Levenshtein distance (commonly known as Edit Distance) between two strings is the minimum number of operations needed to change one string into another. The edit distance between each candidate stem and the string is calculated. Those candidates that are above a certain edit distance are removed from the candidates list. This is important because sometimes stems which are unrelated to the word may be selected as candidates stems. In order to avoid the wrong matching of such stems, the candidates which are very far from the word are removed from the selection. This ensures that only the stems which are related to the word get considered and thus avoids inconsistent matching which would lead to a wrong stem. The remaining candidates are ranked on the basis of their edit distances. Finally, the stem with minimum distance from the string is selected as a final result of the stemmer. If two or more of the candidates have equal edit distance, their frequency on the corpus is used and the more frequent stem is selected as final result.

## 5 Evaluation and Discussion

To evaluate the design of the stemmer, it was implemented in C# programming language. The stemmer was then tested using two sets of words. The purpose of the evaluation was to calculate the accuracy of the stemmer. The set of words used for evaluation were selected from different domains. The first sample was extracted from an Eritrean news paper (Hadas Eritra) and the first 1200 unique words were selected. The second sample was extracted from an online Tigrinya Bible. Similarly the first 1300 unique words were selected. The test samples were supplied to the stemmer and the results were manually checked. On the first sample the stemmer achieved an accuracy of 89.92% while the accuracy on the second sample was 88.6%.

The stemmer produces some over-stemmed and under-stemmed words. However, the accuracy rate was acceptable for the purpose of our work which is to develop a Lucerne Analyzer for Tigrinya. The use of the dictionary checking method was the core reason for enhancement. The stemming errors during the affix removal step were fixed by the dictionary based stemmer. However, the dictionary based stemming is not be applied to words that are not in the stem lexicon. The repetitive consonant handling and the apostrophe suffixes steps contribute much less than the other steps because the number of such Tigrinya words is small. We can easily get the root of a Tigrinya word from its stem by deleting all vowels from the stem to get a sequence of consonants.

## 6 Conclusion and Future Work

In this paper we presented a stemmer for the highly inflected Tigrinya language. The stemmer was designed for the purpose of representing different forms of a Tigrinya word with single form to enhance the effectiveness of Tigrinya Information Retrieval applications. Although the overall accuracy was satisfactory, it can further be enhanced for higher accuracy and meaningful stems.

Tigrinya inflections vary with part of speech (POS) of the words. Currently there is no POS tagger for Tigrinya. Introducing a POS tagger would help apply different affix removal rules on the basis of POS of a word. Adoption of more context sensitive rules would also give better results. The distance metric used gives the same priority to both consonants and vowels. However, the root of Tigrinya words consists of only consonants. Thus, adopting a distance metric that considers this would also increase the matching rate of the dictionary based stemmer. Further study on the above points will be done in the future to improve the accuracy of the stemmer. The stemmer will be used to study the effectiveness of stemming in Tigrinya information retrieval and to develop a Tigrinya language Search Engine.

## References


Pirkola, A. & Järvelin, K. (2001) :*Morphological typology of languages for IR*. Journal of Documentation, 57 (3): 330-348.

*Ethnologue, Languages of the World* (2011) : http://www.ethnologue.com.

Michael Gasser. (2009). *Semitic morphological analysis and generation using finite state transducers with feature structures*. In Proceedings of the 12th Conference of the European Chapter of the ACL, pages 309–317, Athens, Greece.

Anjali Ganesh Jivani et al, (2011). *A Comparative Study of* Stemming *Algorithms* , Int. J. Comp. Tech. Appl., Vol 2 (6), 1930-1938.

J. B. Lovins,(1968). *Development of a stemming algorithm*, Mechanical Translation and Computer Linguistic., vol.11, no.1/2, pp. 22-31.

Porter M.F (1980). "*An algorithm for suffix stripping*". Program:14, 130-137.

Krovetz Robert(1993). "*Viewing morphology as an inference process*". Proceedings of the 16th annual international ACM SIGIR conference on Research and development in information retrieval: 191-202.

Yasir Alhanini, Mohd Juzaiddin Ab Aziz, (2011).*The Enhancement of Arabic Stemming by Using Light Stemming and Dictionary-Based Stemming*, Journal of Software Engineering and Applications, 4: 522-526, ISI Wos, DBLP.

Sandipan Sarkar and Sivaji Bandyopadhyay,(2009). *Study on Rule-Based Stemming Patterns and Issues in a Bengali Short Story-Based Corpus*. In ICON.

Yonnas Fissiha (2011):*Developement of Stemming algorithm for Tigrinya,* URL: http://etd.aau.edu.et

Alemayehu, N., Willett, P. (2002). *Stemming of Amharic words for information retrieval. Literary and Linguistic Computing* 17(1), 1-17

Firdyiwek, Yitna and Daniel Yaqob. (1997). *The system for Ethiopic representation in ASCII* URL: citeseer.ist.psu.edu/56365.html.

V. Levenshtein (1966). *Binary codes capable of correcting deletions, insertions and reversals.* Soviet Physics Doklady, 10(8):707–710.

Eri-NLP (2012): *Eritrean Language Research Website*, URL: http://www.eri-nlp.com/resources

# OpenWordNet-PT: An Open Brazilian Wordnet for Reasoning

Valeria de Paiva[1] Alexandre Rademaker[2] Gerard de Melo[3]
(1) School of Computer Science, University of Birmingham, England
(2) Escola de Matemática Aplicada, FGV, Brazil
(3) ICSI, Berkeley, USA
valeria.depaiva@gmail.com, alexandre.rademaker@fgv.br, demelo@icsi.berkeley.edu

ABSTRACT
Brazilian Portuguese needs a Wordnet that is open access, downloadable and changeable, so that it can be improved by the community interested in using it for knowledge representation and automated deduction. This kind of resource is also very valuable to linguists and computer scientists interested in extracting and representing knowledge obtained from texts. We discuss briefly the reasons for a Brazilian Portuguese Wordnet and the process we used to get a preliminary version of such a resource. Then we discuss possible steps to improving our preliminary version.[1]

KEYWORDS: Wordnet, Portuguese, lexical resources, SUMO Ontology.

KEYWORDS IN $L_2$: Wordnet, Português, recursos léxicos, SUMO.

[1]Acknowledgments: We would like to thank Francis Bond for help in getting OpenWordNet-PT online and for general discussions. We also thank Adam Pease for introducing us and helping to start this project.

*Proceedings of COLING 2012: Demonstration Papers*, pages 353–360,
COLING 2012, Mumbai, December 2012.

## 1 Motivation

WordNet (Fellbaum, 1998) is an extremely valuable resource for research in Computational Linguistics and Natural Language Processing in general. WordNet has been used for a number of different purposes in information systems, including word sense disambiguation, information retrieval, automatic text classification, automatic text summarization, and dozens of other knowledge intensive projects.

We started a project at Fundação Getulio Vargas (FGV) in Brazil, whose goal, in the long run, is to use formal logical tools to reason about knowledge obtained from texts in Portuguese. Originally we had expected to be able to use some existing Brazilian Wordnet, out of the box, but it turns out that these are not available in the form that we need it. There are some attempts.

There is the project WordNet.PT (Portuguese WordNet) from the "Centro de Linguistica da Universidade de Lisboa" headed by Prof. Palmira Marrafa. But this is available online only, no download available and, as far as we can see on their webpages, little development has happened recently to this project. The WordNet.PT version available online has about 19000 lexical expressions, from different semantic fields. The fragment made available online includes expressions from subdomains such as art, clothing, geography, health, institutions, living entities and transportation, but no description of other domains and/or future releases of the database are discussed. The group has also a newer version of WordNet.PT called `WordNet.PT`$_{\texttt{global}}$ (Marrafa et al., 2011) which pays attention to different varieties of Portuguese, like African variations of the language. But while this is very interesting for linguistic comparative research and useful for online queries (`http://www.clul.ul.pt/wnglobal/`), this smaller version of WordNet.PT is not available for download and hence cannot be the target of modifications and improvements.

There is also the MultiWordNet project and its Portuguese version MWN.PT, developed by Antônio Branco and colleagues at the NLX-Natural Language and Speech Group, of the University of Lisbon, Department of Informatics. According to their description (`http://mwnpt.di.fc.ul.pt/`), MWN.PT, the MultiWordnet of Portuguese (version 1), spans over 17,200 manually validated concepts/synsets, linked under the semantic relations of hyponymy and hypernymy. These concepts are made of over 21,000 word senses/word forms and 16,000 lemmas from both European and American variants of Portuguese. It includes the sub-ontologies under the concepts of Person, Organization, Event, Location, and Artworks, which are covered by the top ontology made of the Portuguese equivalents to all concepts in the 4 top layers of the English Princeton WordNet and to the 98 Base Concepts suggested by the Global Wordnet Association, and the 164 Core Base Concepts indicated by the EuroWordNet project. But again this wordnet is available online only and with a restrictive license that requires payment.

Finally, there is a first version of a Brazilian Portuguese version of Wordnet developed by Bento Dias da Silva and collaborators (Dias-Da-Silva et al., 2000; Scarton and Aluisio, 2009). But this also cannot be downloaded, is not available online and is not being maintained on an open access basis, which is one of the strongest points of Princeton WordNet.

Open access availability is one of the main reasons we would like to create a new Portuguese Wordnet, which we are calling OpenWordNet-PT (or OpenWN-PT for short). This is because we believe that resources like Wikipedia and WordNet need to be open and modifiable by others in order to improve over time.

With a similar philosophy of open access to ours, there is also the work of Hugo Oliveira and Paulo Gomes on Onto.PT ((Gonçalo Oliveira et al., 2011)), another lexical ontology for the Portuguese language, structured similarly to Princeton's WordNet, in the process of development at the University of Coimbra, Portugal. Unlike our own OpenWordNet-PT, Onto.PT is not connected to the synsets in the Princeton WordNet. Due to this, existing Princeton WordNet-focused resources like inter-lingual links in EuroWordNet, mappings to the SUMO ontology and DBpedia/YAGO cannot be used in conjunction with this resource.

## 2 OpenWordNet-PT

OpenWordNet-PT is being created by drawing on a two-tiered methodology so as to offer high precision for the more salient and frequent words of the language, but also high recall in order to cover a wide range of words in the long tail. We thus combine manual base concept annotation with statistical cross-lingual projection techniques.

### 2.1 Cross-Lingual Projection

As a starting point, we applied the UWN/MENTA methodology (de Melo and Weikum, 2009, 2010), developed by one of the authors of this paper in conjunction with Gerhard Weikum, to the Portuguese language.

In a first step, the information in the English Princeton WordNet is projected to Portuguese by using translation dictionaries to map the English members of a synset to possible Portuguese translation candidates. In order to disambiguate and choose the correct translations, feature vectors for possible translations are created by computing graph-based statistics in the graph of words, translations, and synsets. Additional monolingual wordnets and parallel corpora are used to enrich this graph. Finally, statistical learning techniques are then used to iteratively refine this information and build an output graph connecting Portuguese words to synsets.

In a second step, Wikipedia pages are linked to relevant WordNet synsets by learning from similar graph-based features as well as gloss similarity scores. Such mappings allow us to attach the article titles of the Portuguese Wikipedia with WordNet synsets, thus further increasing the coverage.

### 2.2 Base Concept Annotation

Using cross-lingual projection, we obtain a resource with good coverage. In order to have high precision for the most important concepts of a language, we rely on human annotators.

In particular, we decided to rely on a set of Base Concepts. The Global WordNet Association aims at the development of wordnets for all languages of the world and to extend the existing wordnets to full coverage and many parts-of-speech. In 2006, the association launched a project to start building a completely free worldwide wordnet "grid". This grid would be built around a shared set of concepts, which would be expressed in terms of the original Wordnet synsets and SUMO (Niles and Pease, 2001) terms.

The vision of a global grid of wordnets in many languages that draw on a common set of concepts is very appealing, as it enables many cross-lingual applications. The suggestion of the Global WordNet Association is to build a first version of the grid around the set of 4689 "Common Base Concepts" and to make the grid free, following the example of the Princeton WordNet. The Base Concepts are supposed to be the most important concepts in the various wordnets of different languages. The importance of the concepts was measured in terms of two main criteria: (1) A high position in the semantic hierarchy; (2) Having many relationships to other concepts. The procedure described as the EuroWordNet "expand approach" seemed sensible: First translate the synsets in the Princeton WordNet to Portuguese, then take over the relations from Princeton and revise, adding the Portuguese terms that satisfy different relations. Then we hope to revise thoroughly to guarantee the consistency of the taxonomy and to make sure that all lexical items with a heavy use in Portuguese were described. This process is under development at the moment. Currently, Portuguese annotators are revising the base concepts by manually choosing appropriate Portuguese words and by manually writing appropriate Portuguese gloss descriptions.

## 2.3 Project Status

OpenWordNet-PT is freely available as an open-source project[2]. The data is also available for online browsing[3] via the online interface developed by Francis Bond (Bond and Paik, 2012). This interface, depicted in Fig. 1, is particularly insightful, as it displays Portuguese entries in conjunction with entries in several other languages given by other open-source wordnet projects.

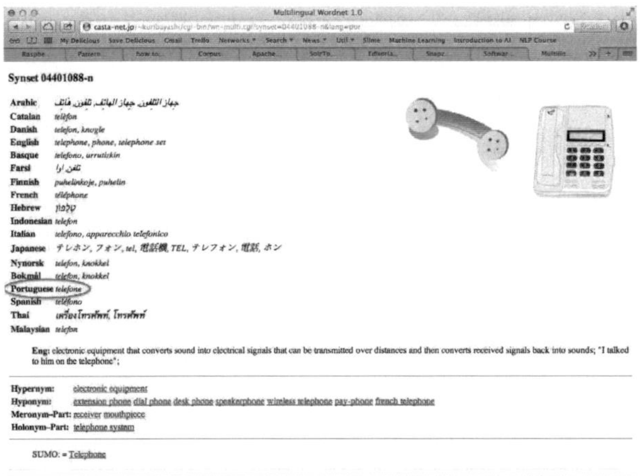


Figure 1: Francis Bond's Open Multilingual Wordnet website

In total, our resource has 62,034 sense-word pairs, and 45,421 unique words. These include 2,498 manually entered sense-word pairs as well as an additional 1,299 manually written Portuguese synset glosses. Additional statistics regarding the lexical coverage are provided in the appendix.

The raw coverage seems reasonable in number of terms in the ontology, but we need to make sure that the quality of the items is comparable and in particular that the level of detail is approximately the right one for our intended application.

[2] https://github.com/arademaker/wordnet-br/

[3] http://casta-net.jp/~kuribayashi/cgi-bin/wn-multi.cgi

# 3 Perspectives

## 3.1 OpenWordNet-PT and SUMO

We started from an informal project discussing how logic and automated reasoning could have a bigger impact, if coupled with natural language processing. We also wanted to make sure that we could obtain some (ideally most) of the advances already made for English text understanding to Portuguese text understanding and reasoning.

Building on previously developed technology, like the Xerox PARC XLE (Xerox Language Engine) system and trying to adapt that system to Brazilian Portuguese seemed a good idea. However, the AI and logic components of the system come at the end of a long pipeline of modules which require expertise on processing of natural language. In particular we felt that a Brazilian Portuguese version of WordNet that could be freely distributed to others was an essential part of it.

Wordnet is an important component of the XLE Unified Lexicon (UL (Crouch and King, 2005)), as the logical formulae created by the Abstract Knowledge Representation (AKR) component of the system are given meaning, in terms of Wordnet synsets. A previous version of the system used, instead of the Unified Lexicon, the proprietary Cyc (Lenat, 1995) concepts as semantics. As discussed in (De Paiva et al., 2007) the sparseness of Cyc concepts was the main reason to move away from Cyc onto a version of the Bridge system based on the unified lexicon and WordNet.

Having a Brazilian version of WordNet and a mapping from Portuguese words to that would allow us to use a knowledge representation system very similar to the AKR (Abstract Knowledge Representation) used in the PARC Bridge system. Having our version of the Portuguese WordNet based on basic concepts we hope to leverage the huge manual construction effort which constitutes the mapping from WordNet to SUMO (Niles and Pease, 2003).

Through a partnership with Adam Pease, (the technical editor of SUMO), we additionally intend to use the SUMO hierarchy to check the consistency between the Portuguese version of WordNet and the English one.

## 3.2 Intended Application

The main application we envisage for our work in OpenWordNet-PT is related to the entries in the Brazilian Dictionary of Historical Biographies (in Portuguese DHBB), one of the main knowledge resources implemented as a result of the archival efforts of the Fundação Getulio Vargas. The DHBB consists of 7,553 dictionary entries, out of which 6,584 are biographies of important politicians in Brazil's recent history. There are also 969 topical entries, concerning institutions, events and descriptions relating to the history and economy of Brazil after 1930. The dictionary is available online, but since the project was started in the 1970s the information is not properly linked, which makes querying its data somewhat unwieldy.

We intend to process all of the DHBB entries and we plan to extract from them the main SUMO concepts referenced. Using these main SUMO concepts we want to bootstrap a fledgeling Ontology of Historical Biographies, already started and documented in the Development section of SUMO. From the analysis of the SUMO concepts uncovered in the biographical entries, we want to discover new relationships between the historical characters described in the DHBB.

Here are some examples of the kinds of questions that this association of text of biography entry with collections of SUMO concepts will allow us to answer: (1) Amongst Brazilian first rank politicians how many are from São Paulo? (2) Has the proportion of Paulistas increased of decreased since the 1930s? Since 1965 when Brasilia became the Capital of Brazil has the proportion changed? (3) What are the important Brazilian political families, corresponding to the Kennedys, the Bushs, etc? (4) What are the prevalent occupations among Brazilian historical figures? Are they mostly lawyers by training?

## 4 Conclusion

OpenWordNet-PT combines high recall with high precision for the more salient words in the language. The work in this project is only starting, but we have many plans to measure and increase the quality of the Portuguese lexical resource, as well as many plans to use the resource in its current form. The data is freely available for download as well as for online browsing.

## References


Bond, F. and Paik, K. (2012). A survey of wordnets and their licenses. In *Proceedings of the 6th Global WordNet Conference (GWC 2012)*, Matsue.

Crouch, D. and King, T. (2005). Unifying lexical resources. In *Proceedings of the Interdisciplinary Workshop on the Identification and Representation of Verb Features and Verb Classes*, Saarbruecken, Germany.

de Melo, G. and Weikum, G. (2009). Towards a universal wordnet by learning from combined evidence. In *Proceedings of the 18th ACM Conference on Information and Knowledge Management (CIKM 2009)*, pages 513–522, New York, NY, USA. ACM.

de Melo, G. and Weikum, G. (2010). Menta: inducing multilingual taxonomies from wikipedia. In *Proceedings of the 19th ACM international conference on Information and knowledge management*, pages 1099–1108. ACM.

De Paiva, V., Bobrow, D., Condoravdi, C., Crouch, R., Karttunen, L., King, T., Nairn, R., and Zaenen, A. (2007). Textual inference logic: Take two. *Proceedings of the Workshop on Contexts and Ontologies, Representation and Reasoning*, page 27.

Dias-Da-Silva, B. C., Moraes, H. R., Oliveira, M. F., Hasegawa, R., Amorim, D. A., Paschoalino, C., and Nascimento, A. C. (2000). Construção de um thesaurus eletrônico para o português do brasil. In *Processamento Computacional do Português escrito e falado (Propor)*, pages 1–10.

Fellbaum, C. (1998). *WordNet: An electronic lexical database*. The MIT press.

Gonçalo Oliveira, H., Pérez, L. A., Costa, H., and Gomes, P. (2011). Uma rede léxico-semântica de grandes dimensões para o português, extraída a partir de dicionários electrónicos. *Linguamática*, 3(2):23–38.

Lenat, D. (1995). Cyc: A large-scale investment in knowledge infrastructure. *Communications of the ACM*, 38(11):33–38.

Marrafa, P., Amaro, R., and Mendes, S. (2011). Wordnet.pt global – extending wordnet.pt to portuguese varieties. In *Proceedings of the First Workshop on Algorithms and Resources for Modelling of Dialects and Language Varieties*, pages 70–74, Edinburgh, Scotland. Association for Computational Linguistics.

Niles, I. and Pease, A. (2001). Towards a standard upper ontology. In *Proceedings of the international conference on Formal Ontology in Information Systems-Volume 2001*, pages 2–9. ACM.

Niles, I. and Pease, A. (2003). Linking lexicons and ontologies: Mapping wordnet to the suggested upper merged ontology. In *Proceedings of the 2003 International Conference on Information and Knowledge Engineering*, Las Vegas, Nevada.

Scarton, C. and Aluisio, S. (2009). Herança automática das relações de hiperônimia para a wordnet.br. Technical Report NILC-TR-09-10, USP, Sao Carlos, SP, Brazil.

## A Some OpenWordNet-PT Statistics

In Table 1, columns 1-3 numbers by POS are: (1) word-sense-pairs; (2) unique words/terms; and (3) synsets with portuguese words. Columns 4-6 apresent averages of polysemy and senses by POS: (4) the average polysemy (number of senses per word, tot avg. 1.3658); (5) the average polysemy excluding monosemous, (number of senses per word excluding words with only one sense, tot. avg. 3.0100); and (6) the average number of sense lexicalizations excluding unlexicalized (number of words per synset for those synsets that have at least one Portuguese word, tot. avg. 1.4836).

| | (1) | (2) | (3) | (4) | (5) | (6) |
|---|---|---|---|---|---|---|
| Nouns | 45,751 | 31,438 | 35,869 | 1.2755 | 2.9681 | 1.4553 |
| Verbs | 7,155 | 4,265 | 3,724 | 1.9213 | 3.9200 | 1.6776 |
| Adjectives | 7,402 | 5,193 | 4,996 | 1.4816 | 2.8145 | 1.4254 |
| Adverbs | 1,726 | 917 | 1,305 | 1.3226 | 2.3849 | 1.8822 |
| Total | 62,034 | 41,813 | 45,421 | | | |

Table 1: The size of OpenWN-BR and averages about polysemy and senses

In Table 2, column (1) shows the number of relations from Princeton WordNet where either source or target synset have a Portuguese lexicalization. Column (2) shows the number of relations from Princeton WordNet where both source and target synset have a Portuguese lexicalization.

| | (1) Source or Target | (2) Source and Target |
|---|---|---|
| hypernymy | 68,002 | 22,002 |
| instance-of/has-instance | 7,899 | 4,540 |
| part meronymy | 7,964 | 4,247 |
| member meronymy | 8,591 | 2,802 |
| substance meronymy | 637 | 332 |
| has-category | 6,494 | 2,213 |
| cause | 163 | 76 |
| entailment | 370 | 162 |
| similar | 13,998 | 3,524 |
| closely-related | 2,595 | 1,117 |
| attribute | 1,068 | 516 |
| antonym | 4,907 | 1,863 |

Table 2: Relations from Princeton WordNet

# WordNet Website Development And Deployment Using Content Management Approach

*Neha R Prabhugaonkar*[1] *Apurva S Nagvenkar*[1] *Venkatesh P Prabhu*[2]
*Ramdas N Karmali*[1]
(1) GOA UNIVERSITY, Taleigao - Goa
(2) THYWAY CREATIONS, Mapusa - Goa
`nehapgaonkar.1920@gmail.com`, `apurv.nagvenkar@gmail.com`,
`venkateshprabhu@thywayindia.com`, `rnk@unigoa.ac.in`

ABSTRACT
The WordNets for many official Indian languages are being developed by the members of the IndoWordNet Consortium in India. It was decided that all these WordNets be made open for public use and feedback to further improve their quality and usage. Hence each member of the IndoWordNet Consortium had to develop their own website and deploy their WordNets online. In this paper, the Content Management System (CMS) based approach used to speed up the WordNet website development and deployment activity is presented. The CMS approach is database driven and dynamically creates the websites with minimum input and effort from the website creator. This approach has been successfully used for the deployment of WordNet websites with friendly user interface and all desired functionalities in very short time for many Indian languages.

KEYWORDS: WordNet, Content Management System, CMS, WordNet CMS, IndoWordNet, Application Programming Interface, API, WordNet Templates, IndoWordNet Database, Website.

*Proceedings of COLING 2012: Demonstration Papers*, pages 361–368,
COLING 2012, Mumbai, December 2012.

# 1 Introduction

WordNet is an important lexical resource for a language which helps in Natural Language Processing (NLP) tasks such as machine translation, information retrieval, word sense disambiguation, multi-lingual dictionary creation etc. WordNet is designed to capture the vocabulary of a language and can be considered as a dictionary cum thesaurus and much more (Miller, 1993), (Miller, 1995), (Fellbaum, 1998). The IndoWordNet is a linked structure of WordNets of major Indian languages from IndoAryan, Dravidian and Sino-Tibetan families. These WordNets have been created by following the expansion approach from Hindi WordNet which was made available free for research in 2006 (Bhattacharyya, 2010).

Most of these language WordNets have reached the necessary critical mass required to open them for public and research use. Feedback from users was the next step to further improve the quality of these resources and increase their usability. Hence, the Consortium decided to make all these WordNets available for public feedback and validation of synsets through online deployment. It was also desirable to have standardisation across all WordNet websites with respect to the user interface, functionality, storage, security, etc. After considering schemes such as Wiki, Blog, Forum and Content Management System we realised that Content Management System was the best option available to publish WordNet content. We also evaluated freely available CMS's like Jhoomla, Seagull, PHP-Nuke, etc. and concluded that these CMS's were bulky for the task that we set to achieve. From maintenanace point of view it was desirable that non-technical person should be able to create and maintain the website with minimal effort and time. So a decision was taken to develop a new CMS for website creation.

The rest of the paper is organised as follows – section 2 introduces the general concept and functionalities of a CMS, section 3 presents the framework and design of our WordNet CMS. The implementation and deployment details of WordNet CMS are presented in section 4. Section 5 presents the results and the conclusions.

# 2 Content Management System (CMS)

CMS allows you to deploy and manage the content within your website with little technical knowledge.

## 2.1 Advantages of CMS

The common advantages of CMS are:

- ***Designed with non-technical authors in mind:*** You can manage the dynamic content of your site with great ease by adding new content, editing existing content or publishing new content.
- ***Ease of Maintenance:*** In case of traditional websites there is no proper separation of roles when it comes to website developer and content creator. Any changes to the content, menus or links have to be made through an HTML editor. This can at times be difficult for non technical content creator. Absence of "back end" or "admin" feature requires someone with necessary technical skills to make the changes. Without a CMS, the content quality is not properly monitored and becomes inconsistent. CMS gives direct control over the content on the website to the content creator. The back end database stores the content appearing on the website and other important information.
- ***Consistent Presentation:*** CMS offers well-defined templates for content presentation on the site to maintain a consistent look and feel. Normally, these can be changed and

customised so that the site will have a unique look. It also means that a site redesign can take around ten minutes for the simple changes.

- ***Integration of new modules/components:*** New features and functionality can be easily integrated as source code for modules which are responsible for all the functionality provided by the website are also maintained in the back end database.
- ***Role based permissions:*** This helps in content management. Role based access can be provided to create/edit/publish (Author/Editor/Administrator) content.
- ***User-friendly interface:*** Basic Computer knowledge is required to operate a CMS and therefore no need of specialized technical manpower to manage the website.
- ***Control over Meta data in Web page:*** You can control the Meta data with appropriate keywords that reflect the content on each page and expected search engine behaviour.
- ***Decentralised maintenance:*** You do not need specialized software or any specific kind of technological environment to access and update the website. Any browser device connected to the Internet would be sufficient for the job.
- ***Automatic adjustments for navigation:*** When you create a new navigation item, a new item in a menu, or a new page of any kind, the CMS automatically reconfigures the front end navigation to accommodate it.
- ***Security:*** The CMS stores information in a database system where access control mechanisms can more easily restrict access to your content. The information is only accessible via the CMS thereby providing better protection for site's content from many common and standard web site attacks.

## 2.2 Databases used

We have also implemented a relational database to store the WordNet data. This database design (IndoWordNet database) supports storage for multiple WordNets in different languages. The design has been optimised to reduce redundancy. The data common across all languages is stored in a separate database and its size is 1.8 MB. The data specific to a language is stored in the database of respective language. The database size may differ from language to language depending on the synset information. For Konkani the size of this database is 7 MB for thirty thousand synsets. An object-oriented API (IndoWordNet API) has also been implemented to allow access of WordNet data independent of the underlying storage design. The IndoWordNet API allows simultaneous access and updates to single or multiple language WordNets. The heart of the WordNet CMS is a database (CMS database) that stores all the CMS data which is necessary to deploy all the implemented modules. The size of the CMS database is 1 MB for Konkani and should be the same for others.

# 3 Framework and Design of WordNet CMS

The block diagram of WordNet CMS is shown below in figure 1. An important feature of WordNet CMS is a customizable template, to customize the overall look and layout of a site. A template is used to manipulate the way content is delivered to a web browser. Additionally using CSS within the template design, one can change the colours of backgrounds, text, and links or just about anything that one could within an ordinary XHTML code. The designs for these are all set within the template's CSS file(s) to create a uniform look across entire site, which makes it easy to change the whole look just by altering one or two files rather than every single page (Brinkkemper, 2008).

Template also provides the framework that brings together default functionality and features

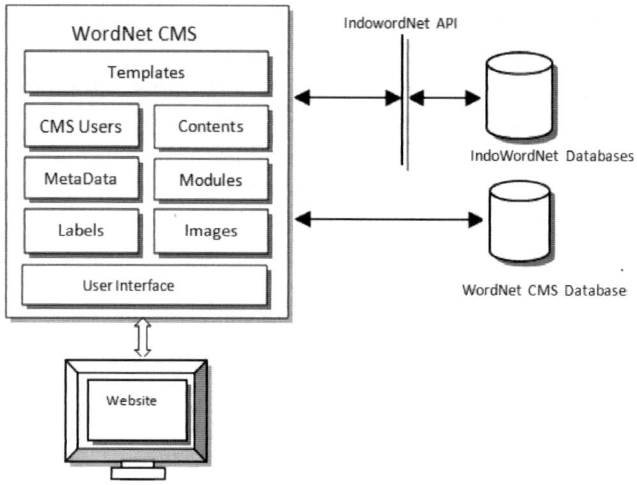


Figure 1: Block diagram of WordNet CMS.

implemented through modules. Functionality and features can be customized or added by the user by customizing the default modules or adding new modules. This offers advantage over traditional websites where such change needs redesign of the entire website. The navigation menus and links are also auto generated to reflect these changes.

## 3.1 WordNet CMS Modules

A module is an independent component of WordNet CMS which offers a specific functionality. These modules depend on CMS database. While the addition of new modules does not require any changes to the CMS database, new tables may need to be added to store data specific to module functionality. Presently there are six default modules, namely Web Content module, FAQ module, WordNet module, Word Collection module, Terminology module, and Feedback module.

1. ***WordNet module:*** Provides online access to the WordNet data. The basic functionality supported are search for synsets containing a word, access synsets related through semantic and lexical relationships and compare two or more synsets.
2. ***Web content module:*** Textual or visual content that is encountered as part of the user experience on websites. A wide range of content can be published using the CMS. This can be characterised as: simple pages, complex pages, with specific layout and presentation and dynamic information sourced from databases, etc. The examples of Web Content are Introduction, About WordNet, About Us, Credits, Contact Us, etc.
3. ***Frequently asked questions (FAQ) module:*** Listed questions and answers, all supposed to be commonly asked in some context, and pertaining to a particular topic.
4. ***Terminology module:*** The technical or special terms used in a business, science or special subject domain. For WordNet CMS, it is a vocabulary of technical terms used in Natural Language Processing.
5. ***Words Collection module:*** The list of all words available in synsets of a particular language. Selecting a word opens its synsets WordNet module.
6. ***Feedback module:*** Valuable feedback from visitors and users of the website that helps

to improve the overall experience of the site, and its contents. Feedback can range from general visitor's views, comments, and suggestions to discrepancies in synset data and complaints.

The CMS also supports creation of multilingual user interface for the website and customizable on-screen keyboard for all languages. The multilingual user interface is supported through suitably implemented Content and Label components of the CMS. Role based access mechanism is available to restrict access to certain parts and features of the CMS to different users. The WordNet CMS also allows control of Meta data embedded in the generated web page so as to reflect the content on each page as well as provide search engines clues to how the web page should be handled. The WordNet CMS supports both left-to-right and right-to-left text rendition and allows adjustment of the layout as per direction in which content language in written through a simple setting of a flag.

## 3.2 Architecture of WordNet CMS

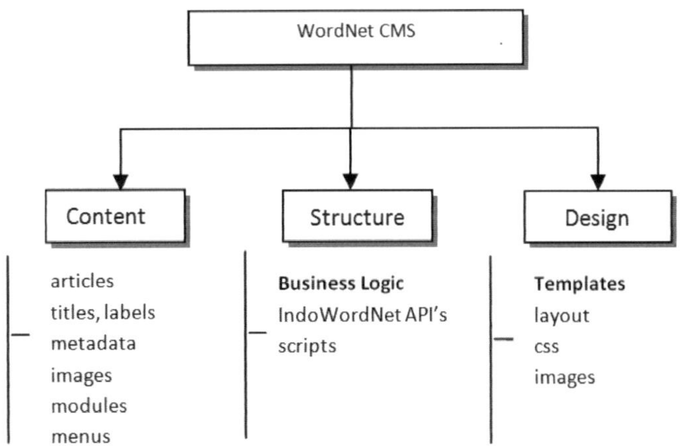


Figure 2: Architecture of WordNet CMS.

As seen in figure 2 above the WordNet CMS is implemented in three layers: Design, Structure, and Content (not to be confused with Content module). The functional division among these three layers allows many advantages throughout the life cycle of the website deployed using CMS. Each layer of the CMS can be recreated and adjusted independent of the other layers. The Design layer can be completely reworked for a new user interface without the need for any adjustments to Structure or Content. The Structure layer can be enhanced for additional functionality with no changes required to Design and Content. Content layer can be changed with no need to adjust the front-end design or functional structure. This three layer architecture makes CMS highly flexible and customizable as per user requirement.

# 4 Implementation and Deployment Details

The WordNet CMS is developed using PHP scripting language and can be hosted on any Web Server which supports PHP version 5.3.15 and above. Currently MySQL version 5.5.21 is used as database. The CMS development was done using XAMPP on 32 bit Microsoft Windows platform. These softwares can be downloaded from their respective sites. The Konkani WordNet website created using WordNet CMS has been deployed on Fedora 16 Linux Platform using Apache version 2.2.22 and MySQL version 5.5.21 which come bundled with Fedora 16 Linux Platform.

## Conclusion and perspectives

The graph in figure 3 below shows the average number of days required to build and deploy the website using the traditional method and using WordNet CMS. The total time taken to develop WordNet website using traditional method was around 47 days. It took 7 days to design the layout and template of the website, 30 days to implement the website and 10 days for the deployment phase. In case of websites which were deployed using the WordNet CMS, the number of days taken was comparatively very less. For the design phase, it took 2 days to design the layout and template, the structure remains the same and therefore hardly any time was spent on coding and debugging. It took another 2 days for the deployment phase. Therefore the total number of days to create and deploy the website using the WordNet CMS was around 5 days.

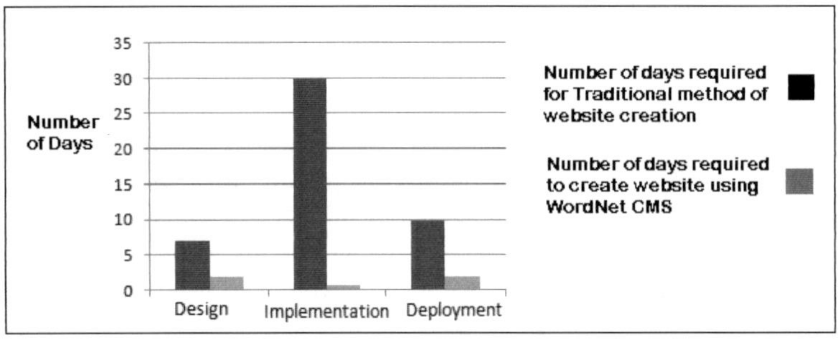


Figure 3: Deployment time requirement analysis.

From the above analysis, we conclude that the WordNet CMS can be used for the speedy deployment of WordNet websites with minimal effort, with good user interface and features by a non technical content creator in a very short time for any language. The enhancements planned for the WordNet CMS are as follows:

1. To develop an installation wizard so that the installation of the CMS is automated.
2. Implementation of Reports module. This will help to keep track of the users visiting the website, provide statistics related to validation of synsets, feedback tracking, etc.
3. Allow further customization of website user interfaces by the website user depending upon the user category such as students, teachers, researchers, linguists, etc. for better user experience.

The WordNet CMS has been successfully used by many IndoWordNet members to design their own language WordNet website.

## Acknowledgements

This work has been carried out as a part of the Indradhanush WordNet Project jointly carried out by nine institutions. We wish to express our gratitude to the funding agency Department of Information Technology, Ministry of Communication and Information Technology, Govt. of India and our sincere gratitude to Dr. Jyoti Pawar, Goa University for her guidance.

## References

George A. Miller, Richard Beckwith, Christiane Fellbaum, Derek Gross, and Katherine Miller (Revised August 1993). *Introduction to WordNet: An On-line Lexical Database.*

George A. Miller 1995. *WordNet: A Lexical Database for English.*

Fellbaum, C. (ed.). 1998. *WordNet: An Electronic Lexical Database, MIT Press.*

Jurriaan Souer, Paul Honders, Johan Versendaal, Sjaak Brinkkemper 2008. *A Framework for Web Content Management System Operations and Maintenance.*

Pushpak Bhattacharyya, Christiane Fellbaum, Piek Vossen 2010. *Principles, Construction and Application of Multilingual WordNets, Proceedings of the 5th Global WordNet Conference (Mumbai-India), 2010.*

# A Demo for Constructing Domain Ontology from Academic Papers

*Feiliang REN*
Northeastern University, Shenyang, 110819, P.R.China

renfeiliang@ise.neu.edu.cn

ABSTRACT

Traditional construction methods of domain ontology usually have following two limits. First, these methods usually depend on some high cost resources. Second, these methods are easily to result in error propagation because of the errors introduced in the concept identification step. In this paper we present a demo that constructs domain ontology with an easy method. And three main features distinguish our method from traditional methods. First, the proposed method uses academic papers to construct domain ontology. Second, the proposed method carefully selects some keywords in these academic papers as domain concepts. Thus error propagation is reduced accordingly. Third, the proposed method mines hierarchical relations among concepts with a graph generation and conversion method. The effects of our proposed method are evaluated from two perspectives in an IT domain ontology which is constructed with the proposed method: the quality of domain concepts and the quality of concept's relations. And evaluation results show that both of them achieve high qualities.

KEYWORDS : Domain Ontology; Graph Generation; Graph Conversion; Ontology Concept; Hierarchical Relation

*Proceedings of COLING 2012: Demonstration Papers*, pages 369–376,
COLING 2012, Mumbai, December 2012.

## 1 Introduction

Domain ontology is a kind of domain related ontology knowledge which usually contains three basic items: domain concepts, concept relations and concept interpretations. Because it is well known that domain ontology can reduce or eliminate conceptual and terminological confusion for many hot research areas such as semantic web, informational retrieval, question and answering, machine translation, and so on, a lot of researchers have been devoting to constructing various domain ontologies for decades. Compared with general purpose ontology like WordNet, domain ontology has following two features.

First, all of the ontology items must be related to the same domain. It is easily to understand that the domain concept is crucial to domain ontology because the other two ontology items will center around it. To achieve high quality domain ontology, the domain concepts must be accurately identified.

Second, domain concepts are dynamic: new concepts are constantly emerging.

Because of these features, two barriers are put up for the construction of domain ontology. One is how to identify domain concepts accurately. And the other is how to update domain ontology timely when new concepts emerge? To construct a practical and useful domain ontology, these barriers must be overcome effectively.

Traditional construction methods of domain ontology cannot overcome these barriers effectively. First, because of the technology limits, many errors are introduced during the process of identifying domain concepts. Second, traditional method usually cannot respond to concept's change timely. Even more serious, these methods usually depend on some high cost resources like other general purpose ontology, right concept tagged corpus, right relation tagged corpus and so on. However, these resources are not always acquired easily, especially for those resource-lack languages.

In this paper, we present a demo that construct domain ontology with an easy way, and it can overcome above barriers effectively. The proposed method takes academic papers as data source and selects some keywords in these academic papers as domain concepts. And the hierarchical relations among concepts are mined with a graph generation and conversion method. When new concepts emerge, domain ontology can be completely reconstructed easily.

## 2 Our Basic Idea and System Architecture

Usually academic papers are easily acquired even for those resource-lack languages. Among these papers there are three implicit but widely acknowledged facts which are useful for domain ontology construction. First, it is certain that authors will submit their paper to those journals that are related to their research fields. Thus we can say that academic papers have been classified into appropriate domains before submitted as these research fields are nature classification of domains. So it is easily to collect some papers in a specific domain according to journals' research scopes. Second, keywords are usually used to discover paper theme in a concise way and they usually contain rich information that is related to a specific domain. Thus keywords are born concepts in the domain where they belong to. Third, there are usually two kinds of keywords in an academic paper. One is more related to paper's domain, while the other is more related to paper theme. So if we use a directed graph to describe a domain ontology, keyword frequency can be used to reveal a kind of hierarchical relation among keywords: high frequency keywords are usually more related to domain and should be placed in the higher levels of the ontology graph; while low frequency keywords are usually more related to paper themes and should be placed in the lower levels of the ontology graph.

These facts indicate that domain ontology can be constructed in such an easy way: using academic papers as data source, selecting some keywords as domain concepts, and mining hierarchical relations among concepts based on their frequencies.

Based on these analyses, we design our domain ontology construction method whose system architecture is shown in Figure 1.

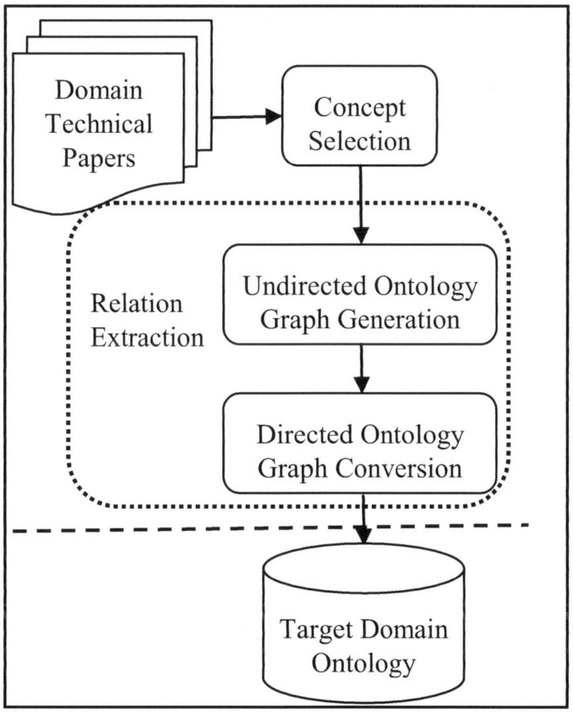


FIGURE 1. SYSTEM ARCHITECTURE

There are three main components in our domain ontology construction method: concept selection, undirected ontology graph generation and directed ontology graph conversion. And the latter two components can been viewed as a relation extraction model.

## 3 Our Method

Concept Selection

We have pointed out that keywords are born concepts in the domain where they belong to. But we should also notice that some keywords are so common that will appear in several completely different domains. Obviously these keywords are not appropriate for taking as concepts in a specific domain. Here we use two methods to select some keywords as appropriate concepts.

The first one is the *tf*idf* method. We think a keyword will be appropriate for taking as domain concept if it has a high frequency in a target domain but a low frequency in other domains. Based on this idea, using *tf*idf* value to select concept from keywords is a natural choice.

The second one is to remove all of the abbreviation keywords that are made up of capital letters because it is hard to understand the real meaning of an abbreviation keyword. For example, there is such keyword like "*TMT*", none can understand its real meaning is "*Trustable Machine Translation*" if there are not any contexts provided. Thus these abbreviations are more likely to introduce confusions than to eliminate confusions in some applications that need domain ontology. So we remove all of those abbreviation keywords from the concept list that is generated by the *tf*idf* method.

## 3.1 Relation Extraction

In an ontology graph, we take those selected concepts as vertexes and use directed edges to represent the hierarchical relations among concepts. After concept selection, two steps are taken to mine this kind of hierarchical relation. The first step is to construct an undirected graph based on co-occurrence information among concepts. The second step is to convert this undirected graph into a directed graph.

### Step 1: Undirected Ontology Graph Construction

In this step, our basic idea is that if two concepts appear in the same paper's keyword list, there will be a potential hierarchical relation among them. And we use undirected edges to describe these potential relations among concepts. Thus the aim of this undirected ontology graph construction step is to find all of these potential relations. Specifically, if two concepts appear in the same paper's keyword list, an undirected weighted edge will be added between them. In the final undirected ontology graph, the weight of an edge is the co-occurrence frequency of this edge's two adjacent concepts. The detail of this construction algorithm is shown in FIGURE 2.

---

**Input**: Concept set *CSet* and keyword list set $C=\{S_1,S_2,...,S_n\}$

**Output**: Undirected Ontology Graph G=(V(G),E(G))

---

**Algorithm**:

1. **Initialize** G, set V=*CSet*, E(G)= Φ
2. **For** $i=1$ to $n$ **Do**

   **For each** two keywords $k_{im},k_{in} \in S_i \cap V$

   **If** edge $(k_{im},k_{in}) \in$ E(G) **then** Set $W(k_{im},k_{in})=W(k_{im},k_{in})+1$;

   **Else** Add edge $(k_{im},k_{in})$ in $E(G)$ and Set $W(k_{im},k_{in})= 1$;

3. **Remove** all edges whose weights less than a given threshold θ
4. **Return** *G*

---

FIGURE 2. Undirected Ontology Graph Construction

In FIGURE 2, $W(k_{im},k_{in})$ is the weight of undirected edge $(k_{im},k_{in})$, V(G) and E(G) are vertex set and edge set of the ontology graph respectively.

**Step 2: Directed Ontology Graph Conversion**

This step aims to make those potential hierarchical relations explicit. That is to say we need to convert those undirected edges into directed edges so as to reveal the farther-child relations among concepts. As we have pointed our previously, in an undirected edge, the high frequency concept is usually more related to the target domain and thus should be taken as a farther vertex; while the low frequency keyword is usually more related to paper theme and thus should be taken as a child vertex. Based on this idea, we design a conversion algorithm to make those potential hierarchical relations explicit. And the detail of this algorithm is shown in FIGURE 3.

**Input**: Undirected Ontology Graph G

**Output**: Directed Ontology Graph G'

**Algorithm**:

1. **For each** undirected edge $(c_i, c_j) \in E(G)$

    **If** $deg(c_i)\text{-}deg(c_j) > \theta$ **Change** $(c_i, c_j)$ to $<c_i, c_j>$;

    **Else If** $deg(c_j)\text{-}deg(c_i) > \theta$ **Change** $(c_i, c_j)$ to $<c_j, c_i>$;

    **Else Change** $(c_i, c_j)$ to $<c_j, c_i>$ and $<c_i, c_j>$;

2. **Return** *G'*

FIGURE 3. Directed Graph Conversion

In FIGURE 3, $<c_i, c_j>$ denotes a directed edge from concept $c_i$ to concept $c_j$. And $deg(c_i)$ denotes the degree of concept $c_i$.

After this step, we construct a directed ontology graph. In this graph, every vertex denotes a concept, and every directed edge denotes a hierarchical relation in which its starting concept denotes an upper father vertex and its ending concept denotes a lower child vertex.

After this step, the remaining directed edges and their adjacent concepts together constitute the final domain ontology graph.

# 4 Approach Evaluation

## 4.1 Data Preparation

For Chinese, almost all published academic papers can be downloaded from a Website (http://www.cnki.net/) and all of these papers have been classified into proper domains on the Web. From this Website, we downloaded more than four hundred thousand of academic papers in *Information Technology* (IT for short) domain that span almost the past thirty years.

With these data, we constructed an IT domain ontology with the proposed method and used it to evaluate the proposed approach. Specifically, we set the thresholds of *tf* and *idf* to 2 during the process of concept selection. That is to say, only those keywords whose *tf* values are greater than 2 and *idf* values are less than 2 will be selected as domain concepts. Finally, we constructed the target IT domain ontology that contains 383176 concepts and 239720 hierarchical relations.

## 4.2 Evaluation Strategy

In this paper, we use accuracy, recall and F1 value to evaluation method. All of these evaluations are performed by five experienced human experts who come from our research group. And we randomly select 500 concepts from our domain ontology. And we also randomly select 500 relations from our domain ontology as test relation set. And the evaluation results are shown in Table 1 and Table 2 respectively.

| | Our Method |
|---|---|
| Accuracy | *93.6%* |
| Recall | 84.2% |
| F1 | *88.7%* |

TABLE 1 – Concept Evaluation Results

| | Our Method |
|---|---|
| Accuracy | 88.4% |
| Recall | 80.2% |
| F1 | 84.1% |

TABLE 2 –Relation Evaluation Results

From our experimental results we can see that the domain ontology constructed with our methods achieves far higher quality. We think following reasons play major roles for this result. First, our method takes keywords as domain concepts. It is well known that most of the keywords are domain terms, so they are nature domain concepts. Thus our method effectively avoids the error propagation which will often trouble traditional domain ontology construction methods. Second, our concept relation discovery method is mainly based on the co-occurrence of two concepts and the frequency of each adjacent concept. From the experimental results it can be seen that our method well captures the writing habits of most researchers when they writing technical papers. From the experimental results we can also see that our method is very effective. It can construct a domain ontology with rich concepts and hierarchical relations.

## 5 Conclusions

In this paper, we propose a simple but effective domain ontology construction method. Our method uses academic papers as data source and selects some keywords in these academic papers as domain concepts. The hierarchical relations among concepts are mined based on a graph generation and conversion method.

Compared with other domain ontology construction methods, our method has following novel aspects. First, the proposed method can be used to construct domain ontology for many languages. In our method, the used data source is a kind of very common resource that can be acquired easily for many languages. Thus the proposed method has a large scope and can be easily transplanted to any languages even for those resource-lack languages. Second, the proposed method can construct some domain ontologies with high qualities in both concept quality and relation quality. Third, the proposed method is easily implemented. It doesn't use any complex technologies or high-cost resource. Any researchers can implement our work easily. Fourth, the proposed method is suitable to construct some large-scale domain ontologies.

## Acknowledgements

This paper is supported by the National Natural Science Foundation of China (Grand No. is 61003159, 61100089, 61073140, and 61272376).

## References


R. Navigli, P.Velardi, A.Gangemi, "Ontology Learning and Its Application to Automated Terminology Translation", IEEE Intelligent Systems, 2003, pp.22-31.

Navigli, Roberto, and Paola Velardi. 2004. "Learning Domain Ontologies from Document Warehouses and Dedicated Web Sites". Journal of Computational Linguistics, volume 30: 151-179.

P.Cimiano and J.Volker. "Text2Onto-A Framework for Ontology Learning and Data-driven Change Discovery", Proceedings of NLDB 2005.pp227-238.

Buitelaar, Paul, Daniel Olejnik, and Michael Sintek. 2004. A Protégé Plug-In for Ontology Extraction from Text Based on Linguistic Analysis. In the Proceedings of the 1st European Semantic Web Symposium:31-44

H.Poon and P.Domingos. "Unsupervised Ontology Induction from Text", Proceedings of the 48th Annual Meeting of the Association for Computational Linguistics, July 2010, pp.296–305.

H.Tan and P.Lambrix. "Selecting an Ontology for Biomedical Text Mining", Proceedings of the Workshop on BioNLP, June 2009, pp.55–62.

D.Estival, C.Nowak and A.Zschorn. "Towards Ontology-Based Natural Language Processing". Proceeedings of the Workshop on NLP and XML, 2004, pp59-66.

J.Uwe Kietz and R.Volz. "Extracting a Domain-Specific Ontology from a Corporate Intranet". Proceedings of CoNLL-2000 and LLL-2000, pp.167-175.

A.Maedche and S.Staab, "Ontology Learning for the Semantic Web", IEEE Intelligent Systems, Vol.16, no.2, 2001, pp.72-79.

Shih-Hung Wu and Wen-Lian HSU, "SOAT: a semi-automatic domain ontology accuisition tool from Chinese corpus", Proceedings of the 19th international conference on Computation linguistics (COLING 2002), pp1-5.

Sara Salem and Samir AbdeRahman, "A Multiple-Domain Ontology Builder", Proceedings of the 23rd International Conference on Computation Linguistics (COLING 2010), pp967-975.

Pinar Wennerberg, "Aligning Medical Domain Ontologies for Clinical Query Extraction", Proceedings of the EACL 2009 Student Research Workshop, pp79–87.

Jantine Trapman and Paola Monachesi, "Ontology engineering and knowledge extraction for crosslingual retrieval", International Conference RANLP 2009, pp455–459.

Mihaela Vela and Thierry Declerck, "Concept and Relation Extraction in the Finance Domain", Proceedings of the 8th International Conference on Computational Semantics, 2009, pp346–350.

Tingting He, Xiaopeng Zhang, Xinghuo Ye, "An Approach to Automatically Constructing Domain Ontology", PACLIC 2006, pp150-157.

Chu-Ren Huang, Ya-Jun Yang and Sheng-Yi Chen, "An Ontology of Chinese Radicals: Concept Derivation and Knowledge Representation based on the Semantic Symbols of Four Hoofed-Mammals", 22nd Pacific Asia Conference on Language, Information and Computation (PACLIC 2008), pp189–196.

Chu-Ren Huang, "Text-based construction and comparison of domain ontology: A study based on classical poetry", PACLIC 2004, pp17-20.

He Tan, Rajaram Kaliyaperumal, Nirupama Benis, "Building frame-based corpus on the basis of ontological domain kwowledge", Proceedings of the 2011 Workshop on Biomedical Natural Language Processing, ACL-HLT 2011, pp74–82.

# A Practical Chinese-English ON Translation Method Based on ON's Distribution Characteristics on the Web

*Feiliang REN*
Northeastern University, Shenyang, 110819, P.R.China

renfeiliang@ise.neu.edu.cn

ABSTRACT

In this paper, we present a demo that translate Chinese-English organization name based on the input organization name's distribution characteristics on the web. Specifically, we first experimentally validate two assumptions that are often used in organization name translation using web resources. From experimental results, we find out several distribution characteristics of Chinese organization name on the web. Then, we propose a web mining method based on these distribution characteristics. Experimental results show that our method is effective. It can improve the inclusion rate of correct translations for those Chinese organization names whose correct translations often occur on the web, and it can also improve the BLEU score and accuracy for those Chinese organization names whose correct translations rarely occur on the web.

KEYWORDS : organization name translation, distribution characteristics, web resource, machine translation

*Proceedings of COLING 2012: Demonstration Papers*, pages 377–384,
COLING 2012, Mumbai, December 2012.

# 1 Introduction

Named entity (NE) translation is very important to many Natural Language Processing (NLP) tasks, such as cross-language information retrieval and data-driven machine translation. Generally NE translation has three main sub-tasks which are person name (PER) translation, location name (LOC) translation, and organization name (ON) translation. And ON translation is attracting more and more research attention.

There are a large amount of resources on the web, thus researchers usually assume that for every NE to be translated, its correct translation exists somewhere on the web. Based on this assumption, recent researchers (Y.Al-Onaizan et al., 2002, Huang et al., 2005, Jiang et al., 2007, Yang et al., 2008, Yang et al., 2009, Ren et al., 2009, and so on) have focused on translating ON with the assistance of web resources. And the performance of ON translation using web resources depends greatly on the solution of the following problem: how can we find the web pages that contain the correct translations effectively? Solving this problem usually involves some query construction methods. Some researchers (Huang et al., 2005, Yang et al., 2009, Ren et al., 2009, and so on) prefer to constructing bilingual queries to find the web pages that contain the correct translations. They further propose another assumption that both the input NE and its correct translation exist somewhere in some mix-language web pages. Based on this assumption, they think bilingual queries are the most useful clues that can be used to find these web pages.

These two assumptions are essential for those ON translation methods using web resources. Their validity will determine the validity of those ON translation methods using web resources. So we think it is very necessary to validate these two assumptions experimentally. However, to our best knowledge, there are no related works on the research of validating these two assumptions.

In this paper, we focus on the following two issues. The first issue is to experimentally validate these two assumptions. The second issue is to propose an effective web mining method for Chinese ON translation.

# 2 Our Basic Idea

In this section, we carried out some experiments to validate these two assumptions. We use some bilingual ON translation pairs as test data to validate whether these ON translation pairs and their monolingual ON parts can be easily found on the web. The test data are extracted from LDC2005T34. In order to analyze the validity of these two assumptions thoroughly, we divide these ON translation pairs into different groups according to the keyword types of their Chinese parts. And 20 groups that have the maximal amount of ON translation pairs are selected as final test data. In our experiments, following three kinds of queries are constructed for every ON translation pair in the test data:

Q1: only the Chinese ON.

Q2: only the English ON.

Q3: the ON translation pair.

We obtain at most 10 web pages from Bing (http://www.bing.com/) for every query, and compare the inclusion rates of different test groups respectively. For Q1 and Q2, the inclusion rate is defined as the percentage of ON translation pairs whose queries are completely contained in the returned web pages. And for Q3, the inclusion rate is defined as the percentage of ON translation pairs whose Chinese parts and English parts are both contained in the returned web pages. And the experimental results are shown in table 1.

| Keyword types | Num | inclusion rate(%) | | | |
|---|---|---|---|---|---|
| | | Q1 | Q2 | Q3 | Q3' |
| committee | 3444 | 77.09 | 72.97 | 13.30 | 20.76 |
| company | 2315 | 65.49 | 61.17 | 7.17 | 12.53 |
| factory | 971 | 67.35 | 47.79 | 11.23 | 13.80 |
| college | 572 | 95.80 | 86.19 | 29.20 | 34.97 |
| institute | 531 | 85.31 | 71.37 | 18.27 | 26.55 |
| center | 467 | 75.16 | 51.61 | 8.99 | 12.21 |
| bureau | 409 | 83.86 | 81.42 | 16.38 | 24.21 |
| agency | 349 | 75.93 | 73.07 | 17.48 | 21.49 |
| university | 294 | 97.28 | 94.22 | 47.28 | 62.93 |
| ministry | 258 | 82.56 | 83.33 | 16.67 | 26.74 |
| bank | 180 | 81.67 | 88.33 | 28.89 | 33.89 |
| party | 137 | 85.40 | 89.05 | 18.25 | 26.28 |
| organization | 131 | 67.94 | 83.97 | 12.98 | 21.37 |
| restaurant | 126 | 81.75 | 92.86 | 30.95 | 48.41 |
| union | 125 | 72.00 | 87.20 | 16.00 | 22.40 |
| group | 123 | 51.22 | 70.73 | 4.07 | 6.50 |
| school | 98 | 82.65 | 45.92 | 6.12 | 8.16 |
| area | 76 | 67.11 | 85.53 | 23.68 | 27.63 |
| team | 73 | 83.56 | 89.04 | 12.33 | 16.44 |
| hospital | 56 | 92.86 | 71.43 | 28.57 | 39.29 |
| Total | 10735 | 75.81 | 69.91 | 14.49 | 20.75 |

TABLE 1. INCLUSION RATE COMPARISONS

From table 1 we can draw following conclusions.

The first one is that the correct translations for most of Chinese ONs do exist on the web, but more effective clues are needed to find them. Besides, experimental results also tell us that only bilingual query is not enough to find the web pages that contain the correct translations. This conclusion can be further confirmed by another experiment whose results are denoted as Q3' in table 1. The query construction method for Q3' is the same as the method for Q3, but the definition of inclusion rate between them is different. And the inclusion rate for Q3' is defined as the percentage of ON translation pairs whose English parts are contained in the returned web pages. In fact, the experimental results of Q3' are the upper bound of the correct translation inclusion rate that can be obtained by using bilingual queries. But they are still far lower than the results of Q2, which is the true inclusion rate of the correct translations.

The second conclusion is that the inclusion rates for different types of Chinese ON are different greatly. To further investigate this conclusion, we pick out some ON translation pairs that have the highest inclusion rate for Q2 and Q3'. We find out that most of the ONs in these ON translation pairs are multinational companies, government agencies, research institutes, university names and so on. The ONs in these ON translation pairs often occur on the web and the available web resources for them are huge. For such kind of an ON translation pair, it is easier to find both some monolingual web pages that contain one of its monolingual ONs and some mix-language web pages that contain the source ON part and the target ON part. On the other hand, we also pick out some ON translation pairs that have the lowest inclusion rate for Q2 and Q3'. We find out that the ONs in these ON translation pairs rarely occur on the web directly, and most of the ONs in these ON translation pairs have following two characteristics. Firstly they usually have a lot of modifiers, and the lengths of them are long too. Secondly, there are usually some nested sub-ONs in them. Based on these characteristics, we think if the ON translation pairs that rarely occur on the web were segmented into several small translation pairs (such as chunk translation pairs), the inclusion rate of these small translation pairs would improve. And further experiments confirm our idea. These experimental results are shown in table 2. In table 2, the test data are extracted from the ON translation pairs whose English parts cannot be found on the web. Three types of chunks in the Chinese ON parts are defined as [Chen and Zong, 2008] did, and these chunks are Regionally Restrictive Chunk (RC), Keyword Chunk (KC), and Middle Specification Chunk (MC). The test ON translation pairs are chunked and aligned manually and every chunk translation pair is viewed as a new ON translation pair. From table 2 we find that both the monolingual chunk parts and the chunk translation pairs are easier to be found on the web. We take our above idea as the third conclusion. Moreover, from the inclusion rates for Q1 and Q2 in table 2 we can see that smaller text units are easier to be found on the web, so this conclusion is also suitable to those ON translation pairs that often occur on the web.

| Keyword types | Chunk num | Inclusion rate (%) | | | |
|---|---|---|---|---|---|
| | | Q1 | Q2 | Q3 | Q3' |
| committee | 2514 | 100 | 100 | 38.46 | 55.33 |
| company | 2248 | 100 | 100 | 26.25 | 34.48 |
| factory | 1065 | 100 | 100 | 41.22 | 46.2 |
| college | 182 | 100 | 100 | 59.34 | 75.82 |
| institute | 441 | 100 | 100 | 63.72 | 79.59 |
| center | 588 | 100 | 100 | 59.35 | 65.99 |
| bureau | 175 | 100 | 100 | 70.86 | 86.86 |
| agency | 263 | 100 | 100 | 65.02 | 79.85 |
| university | 37 | 100 | 100 | 75.68 | 94.59 |
| ministry | 108 | 100 | 100 | 83.33 | 92.59 |
| bank | 44 | 100 | 100 | 61.36 | 65.91 |
| party | 30 | 100 | 100 | 60 | 66.67 |
| organization | 27 | 100 | 100 | 88.89 | 88.89 |
| restaurant | 42 | 100 | 100 | 80.95 | 88.1 |
| union | 44 | 100 | 100 | 77.27 | 77.27 |
| group | 94 | 100 | 100 | 46.81 | 55.32 |
| school | 154 | 100 | 100 | 77.27 | 81.17 |
| area | 25 | 100 | 100 | 64 | 72 |

| | | | | | |
|---|---|---|---|---|---|
| team | 23 | 100 | 100 | 60.87 | 60.87 |
| hospital | 40 | 100 | 100 | 57.5 | 62.5 |
| Total | 8144 | 100 | 100 | 42.98 | 54.15 |

TABLE 2. INCLUSION RATE OF CHUNK TRANSLATION PAIRS

# 3 Our Web Mining Method for Chinese ON Translation

## 3.1 Motivations of Our Method

Based on above analysis, we design a web mining method for Chinese-English ON translation as shown in Fig 1.

**Input**: a Chinese ON $O_c$ to be translated
**Output**: a Query set $QS$ and a recommended translation result

Algorithm:

1. Segment $O_c$ into $RC_c$, $MC_c$, and $KC_c$,.
2. Generate translation candidates for $O_c$ and the segmented chunks, denote these translation candidates as $O_e$, $RC_e$, $MC_e$, and $KC_e$. Add "$O_c + O_e$", "$O_c + RC_e$", "$O_c + KC_e$", and "$O_c + MC_e$" into $QS$. Take $RC_e$, $MC_e$, and $KC_e$ as queries respectively and goto step 3.
3. Submit input query to search engine and revise this query according to some rules. Repeat this procedure until the input query cannot be revised any more.
4. Take "$RC_e + MC_e$", "$KC_e + RC_e$" and "$KC_e + MC_e$" as queries respectively and goto step 3.
5. Take "$RC_e + MC_e + KC_e$", "$KC_e + RC_e + MC_e$" and "$KC_e + MC_e + RC_e$" as queries respectively and goto step 3.
6. If there is a query that has been revised in step 5, take it as the recommended translation result. Otherwise, "$RC_e$ $MC_e$ $KC_e$" is selected as the recommended translation result. Add this recommended result into $QS$.
7. Return $QS$ and the recommended translation result.

FIGURE 1. OUR WEB MINING METHOD

In Fig 1, we use NEUTrans [Xiao et al., 2009] system to generate translation candidates for the input. The training corpus for NEUTrans consists of about 370K bilingual sentences that are extracted from the corpora of LDC2005T10, LDC2003E07, LDC2003E14 and LDC2005T06.

In the third step of Fig 1, for a given query $q$ (its original Chinese source text is denoted as $q_c$) and the returned web pages, one of following rules is used to revise $q$, and we denote the revised result as $q'$.

**Rule 1:** If $q$ is completely contained in the web pages, take $q$ as $q'$.

**Rule 2:** If $q$ cannot be completely contained in the web pages, and if we can find such a continuous English text $s$ in a web page that is subjected to following three conditions, take $s$ as $q'$.

(1) Submit $s$ to search engine and it can be completely contained in the returned web pages.

(2) $s$ has the largest similarity with $q$. And the similarity is computed with following formula 1.

$$Sim(q,s) = \frac{SameWord(q,s)}{Len(q) + Len(s)} \quad (1)$$

This condition is required to solve the reordering problem in ON translation.

(3) If there is a word $w_i$ in s that does not appear in $q$, we require that $w_i$ must have at least one dictionary translation item that appears in $q_c$ or $w_i$ must not have any dictionary translation items. This condition is required to solve the out-of-vocabulary (OOV) translation problem and the translation item selection problem in ON translation.

**Rule 3**: If $q$ cannot be revised by rule 1 and rule 2, take $q$ as $q'$ directly.

## 4 Experiments

In this section, we evaluate the obtained recommended translation results with the metrics of BLEU score and accuracy. In this experiment, test data consists of 500 Chinese ONs that are randomly selected from those Chinese ONs whose correct translations don't exist on the web. The entire test ONs are chunked manually. Experimental results are shown in table 3.

| Num | Average Length | BLEU Score | | Top1 Accuracy | |
|---|---|---|---|---|---|
| | | NEUTrans | Our | NEUTrans | Our |
| 500 | 3.7 words | 0.1811 | 0.2326 | 11.6% | 19.4% |

TABLE 3. RESULTS OF THE SECOND EXPERIMENT

From these results we can see that our method can improve the efficiency of web mining greatly for Chinese ON translation. Compared with the baseline systems, our method obtains higher inclusion rate and higher translation performance.

## Conclusions

The main contribution of this paper is that we validate the two assumptions that are often used in ON translation using web resources. Another contribution of this paper is that we find out some distribution characteristics of Chinese ON on the web. These distribution characteristics are very useful for designing appropriate web mining method for Chinese ON translation using web resources. Besides, we propose a novel web mining method based on these distribution characteristic for Chinese ON translation. And experimental results show that our method is effective.

## Acknowledgements

This paper is supported by the National Natural Science Foundation of China (Grand No. is 61003159, 61100089, 61073140, and 61272376).

## References

[1] Chen Hsin-Hsi, Changhua Yang, and Ying Lin. 2003. Learning formulation and transformation rules for multilingual named entities. Proceedings of the ACL 2003 Workshop on Multilingual and Mixed-language Named Entity Recognition. pp1-8.

[2] Fan Yang, Jun Zhao, Bo Zou, Kang Liu, Feifan Liu. 2008. Chinese-English Backward

Transliteration Assisted with Mining Monolingual Web Pages. ACL2008. pp541-549.

[3] Fan Yang, Jun Zhao, Kang Liu. A Chinese-English Organization Name Translation System Using Heuristic Web Mining and Asymmetric Alignment. Proceedings of the 47th Annual Meeting of ACL and the 4th IJCNLP of the AFNLP. 2009. pp387-395

[4] Fei Huang, Ying Zhang, Stephan Vogel. 2005. Mining Key Phrase Translations from Web Corpora. HLT-EMNLP2005, pp483-490.

[5] Fei Huang, Stephan Vogel and Alex Waibel. 2003. Automatic Extraction of Named Entity Translingual Equivalence Based on Multi-feature Cost Minimization. Proceedings of the 2003 Annual Conference of the Association for Computational Linguistics, Workshop on Multilingual and Mixed-language Named Entity Recognition.

[6] Fei Huang, Stephan vogel and Alex Waibel. 2004. Improving Named Entity Translation Combining Phonetic and Semantic Similarities. Proceedings of the HLT/NAACL. pp281-288.

[7] Feiliang Ren, Muhua Zhu, Huizhen Wang, Jingbo Zho, Chinese-English Organization Name Translation Based on Correlative Expansion. Proceedings of the 2009 Named Entities Workshop, ACL-IJCNLP 2009. pp143-151

[8] Feng, Donghui, Yajuan LV, and Ming Zhou. 2004. A new approach for English-Chinese named entity alignment. Proceedings of the Conference on Empirical Methods in Natural Language Processing (EMNLP 2004), pp372-379.

[9] Hany Hassan and Jeffrey Sorensen. 2005. An Integrated Approach for Arabic-English Named Entity Translation. Proceedings of ACL Workshop on Computational Approaches to Semitic Languages. pp87-93.

[10] Hsin-Hsi Chen and Yi-Lin Chu. 2004. Pattern discovery in named organization corpus. Proceedings of 4th International Conference on Language, Resource and Evaluation. pp301-303.

[11] Lee, Chun-Jen and Jason S.Chang and Jyh-Shing Roger Jang. 2004a. Bilingual named-entity pairs extraction from parallel corpora. Proceedings of IJCNLP-04 Workshop on Named Entity Recognition for Natural Language Processing Application. pp9-16.

[12] Lee, Chun-Jen, Jason S.Chang and Thomas C. Chuang. 2004b. Alignment of bilingual named entities in parallel corpora using statistical model. Lecture Notes in Artificial Intelligence. 3265:144-153.

[13] Long Jiang, Ming Zhou, Lee-Feng Chien, Cheng Niu. 2007. Named Entity Translation with Web Mining and Transliteration. IJCAI-2007.

[14] Moore, Robert C. 2003. Learning translations of named-entity phrases form parallel corpora. ACL-2003. pp259-266.

[15] Peter F. Brown, Vincent J. Della Pietra, Stephen A. Della Pietra, and Robert L. Mercer. 1993. The Mathematics of Statistical Machine Translation: Parameter Estimation. Computational Linguistics, 19(2):263-311.

[16] Tong Xiao, Rushan Chen, Tianning Li, Muhua Zhu, Jingbo Zhu, Huizhen Wang and Feiliang Ren. 2009. NEUTrans: a Phrase-Based SMT System for CWMT2009. Proceedings of 5th China Workshop on Machine Translation.

[17] Y.Al-Onaizan and K. Knight. 2002. Translating named entities using monolingual and bilingual resources. In Proceedings of the 40th Annual Meeting of the Association for Computational Linguistics, pp400-408.

[18] Yufeng Chen, Chengqing Zong. A Structure-based Model for Chinese Organization Name Translation. ACM Transactions on Asian Language Information Processing, 2008, 7(1), pp1-30.

# Elissa: A Dialectal to Standard Arabic Machine Translation System

Wael Salloum and Nizar Habash
Center for Computational Learning Systems
Columbia University
{wael,habash}@ccls.columbia.edu

## Abstract

Modern Standard Arabic (MSA) has a wealth of natural language processing (NLP) tools and resources. In comparison, resources for dialectal Arabic (DA), the unstandardized spoken varieties of Arabic, are still lacking. We present Elissa , a machine translation (MT) system from DA to MSA. Elissa (version 1.0) employs a rule-based approach that relies on morphological analysis, morphological transfer rules and dictionaries in addition to language models to produce MSA paraphrases of dialectal sentences. Elissa can be employed as a general preprocessor for dialectal Arabic when using MSA NLP tools.

## إِليسَّا: نظَامٌ حَاسوبيٌّ لـلتَّرجمةِ الآليَّةِ من العَامِّيَّاتِ العربيَّةِ إِلَى العربيَّةِ الفُصحَى

توجدُ أدَوَاتٌ ومَوَاردُ كثيرةٌ لمعَالجةِ اللّغةِ العربيَّةِ الفُصحَى حَاسوبيّاً بينَمَا لَا تـتوفَّرُ أدوَاتٌ ومَوارِدُ مُمَاثلةٌ لمُعَالجة العَاميَّاتِ العربيَّة، وهي النُّسخُ المحكيَّةُ غيرُ القيَاسيَّةِ من اللُّغة العربيَّة. سنقدمُ في بحثنَا هذَا إِليسَّا، وهي نظَامٌ حَاسوبيٌّ يقومُ بِالتَّرجمةِ الآليَّةِ من العَاميَّاتِ العربيَّة إِلَى العربيَّة الفُصحَى. تعتمدُ إِليسَّا حـلَّاً مبنيَّاً علَى القوَاعدِ، تستخدِمُ فيه التَّحليلَ الصَّرفيَّ لـلكلمةِ ومجموعـةً من قوَاعدِ التَّرجمـةِ ومعَاجمَ عَامِّيَّةً لإنشَـاءِ مرَادفَاتٍ وترجمَاتٍ لـلكلمَاتِ العَامِّيَّةِ، إِضَافةً إِلَى نمَاذِجَ لُغويَّـةٍ لاختيَارِ الجملـةِ الفُصحَى الأَفضل طلَاقةً بينَ جميعِ الجُمَلِ المـُمكنة. يمكنُ استخدَامُ إِليسَّا لمُعَالجة العَاميَّاتِ العربيَّةِ قبلَ استخدَامِ أدوَاتٍ مُعَدَّةٍ للّغةِ العربيَّةِ الفُصحَى عليهَا.

---

Keywords: Dialectal Arabic, Arabic Natural Language Processing, Machine Translation, Rule-Based Machine Translation, Morphology.

Keywords in $L_2$:

العَاميَّات العربيَّـة، مُعَالجة الـلغة العربية حَاسوبيَّاً، الترجمة الآلية، الترجمة الآلية المعتمدة عَلَى القوَاعد، عِلمُ الصَّرف.

---

*Proceedings of COLING 2012: Demonstration Papers*, pages 385–392,
COLING 2012, Mumbai, December 2012.

# 1 Introduction

Much work has been done on Modern Standard Arabic (MSA) natural language processing (NLP) and machine translation (MT). MSA has a wealth of resources in terms of morphological analyzers, disambiguation systems, annotated data, and parallel corpora. In comparison, research on dialectal Arabic (DA), the unstandardized spoken varieties of Arabic, is still lacking in NLP in general and MT in particular. In this paper we present Elissa, our DA-to-MSA MT system.[1] To process Arabic dialects with available MSA tools, researchers have used different techniques to map DA words to their MSA equivalents (Chiang et al., 2006; Sawaf, 2010; Salloum and Habash, 2011). Having a publicly available tool that translates DAs to MSA can help researchers extend their MSA resources and tools to cover different Arabic dialects. Elissa currently handles Levantine, Egyptian, Iraqi, and to a lesser degree Gulf Arabic.

The Elissa approach can be summarized as follows. First, Elissa uses different techniques to identify dialectal words in a source sentence. Then, Elissa produces MSA paraphrases for the selected words using a rule-based component that depends on the existence of a dialectal morphological analyzer, a list of morphological transfer rules, and DA-MSA dictionaries. The resulting MSA is in a lattice form that we pass to a language model for n-best decoding which selects the best MSA translations.

# 2 Challenges for Processing Arabic and its Dialects

Contemporary Arabic is in fact a collection of varieties: MSA, the official language of the Arab World, which has a standard orthography and is used in formal settings; and DAs, the commonly used informal native varieties, which have no standard orthographies but have an increasing presence on the web. Arabic, in general, is a morphologically complex language which has rich inflectional morphology, expressed both templatically and affixationally, and several classes of attachable clitics. For example, the Arabic word وسيكتبونها *w+s+y-ktb-wn+hA*[2] 'and they will write it' has two proclitics (+و *w+* 'and' and +س *s+* 'will'), one prefix -ي *y-* '3rd person', one suffix ون- *-wn* 'masculine plural' and one pronominal enclitic ها+ *+hA* 'it/her'. DAs differ from MSA phonologically, morphologically and to some lesser degree syntactically. The morphological differences are most noticeably expressed in the use of clitics and affixes that do not exist in MSA. For instance, the Levantine Arabic equivalent of the MSA example above is وحيكتبوها *w+H+y-ktb-w+hA* 'and they will write it'. The optionality of vocalic diacritics helps hide some of the differences resulting from vowel changes; compare the diacritized forms: Levantine *wHayikitbuwhA* and MSA *wasayaktubuwnahA*.

All of the NLP challenges of MSA (e.g., optional diacritics and spelling inconsistency) are shared by DA. However, the lack of standard orthographies for the dialects and their numerous varieties pose new challenges. Additionally, DAs are rather impoverished in terms of available tools and resources compared to MSA, e.g., there is very little parallel DA-English corpora and almost no MSA-DA parallel corpora. The number and sophistication of morphological analysis and disambiguation tools in DA is very limited in comparison to MSA (Duh and Kirchhoff, 2005; Habash and Rambow, 2006; Abo Bakr et al., 2008; Salloum and Habash, 2011; Habash et al., 2012). MSA tools cannot be effectively used to handle DA, e.g., Habash and Rambow (2006) report that over one-third of Levantine verbs cannot be analyzed using an MSA morphological analyzer.

[1] Elissa's home page can be found at http://nlp.ldeo.columbia.edu/elissa/.

[2] Arabic transliteration is presented in the Habash-Soudi-Buckwalter scheme (Habash et al., 2007): (in alphabetical order) *AbtθjHxdðrzsšSDTĎςγfqklmnhwy* and the additional symbols: ' ء, Â أ, Ǎ إ, Ā آ, ŵ ؤ, ŷ ئ, ħ ة, ý ى.

## 3 Related Work

Much work has been done in the context of MSA NLP (Habash, 2010). In contrast, research on DA NLP is still in its early stages: (Kilany et al., 2002; Kirchhoff et al., 2003; Duh and Kirchhoff, 2005; Habash and Rambow, 2006; Chiang et al., 2006; Habash et al., 2012; Elfardy and Diab, 2012). Several researchers have explored the idea of exploiting existing MSA rich resources to build tools for DA NLP (Chiang et al., 2006). Such approaches typically expect the presence of tools/resources to relate DA words to their MSA variants or translations. Given that DA and MSA do not have much in terms of parallel corpora, rule-based methods to translate DA-to-MSA or other methods to collect word-pair lists have been explored (Abo Bakr et al., 2008; Sawaf, 2010; Salloum and Habash, 2011). Using closely related languages has been shown to improve MT quality when resources are limited (Hajič et al., 2000; Zhang, 1998). This use of "resource-rich" related languages is a specific variant of the more general approach of using pivot/bridge languages (Utiyama and Isahara, 2007; Kumar et al., 2007). Sawaf (2010) built a hybrid DA-English MT system that uses an MSA pivoting approach. In his approach, DA is normalized into MSA using character-based DA normalization rules, a DA morphological analyzer, a DA normalization decoder that relies on language models, and a lexicon. Similarly, we use some character normalization rules, a DA morphological analyzer, and DA-MSA dictionaries. In contrast, we use hand-written morphological transfer rules that focuses on translating DA morphemes and lemmas to their MSA equivalents. We also provide our system to be used by other researchers. In previous work, we built a rule-based DA-MSA system to improve DA-to-English MT (Salloum and Habash, 2011). We applied our approach to ATB-tokenized Arabic. Our DA-MSA transfer component used feature transfer rules only. We did not use a language model to pick the best path; instead we kept the ambiguity in the lattice and passed it to our SMT system. In this work, we run Elissa on untokenized Arabic, we use feature, lemma, and surface form transfer rules, and we pick the best path of the generated MSA lattice through a language model. In this paper, we do not evaluate Elissa. We reserve the evaluation to a future publication.

## 4 Elissa

Elissa is a Dialectal Arabic to Modern Standard Arabic Translation System. It is available for use by other researchers. In Elissa 1.0 (the version we present in this paper), we use a rule-based approach (with some statistical components) that relies on the existence of a dialectal morphological analyzer, a list of hand-written transfer rules, and DA-MSA dictionaries to create a mapping of DA to MSA words and construct a lattice of possible sentences. Elissa uses a language model to rank and select the generated sentences.

### 4.1 Elissa Input/Output

Elissa supports input encoding in Unicode (UTF-8) or Buckwalter transliteration (Buckwalter, 2004). Elissa supports untokenized (i.e., raw) input only. The output of Elissa can be encoded also in Unicode or Buckwalter transliteration. Elissa supports the following types of output:

1. **Top-1 sentence.** Elissa uses an untokenized MSA language model to rank the paths in the MSA translation output lattice. In this output format, Elissa selects the top-1 choice (the best path) from the ranked lattice.

2. **N-Best sentences.** Using the untokenized MSA language model, Elissa selects the top 'n' sentences from the ranked lattice. The integer 'n' is configurable.

3. **Map file.** Elissa outputs a file that contains a list of entries of the format: source-word, weight, target-phrase. The weight is calculated in the transfer component not by the language model.

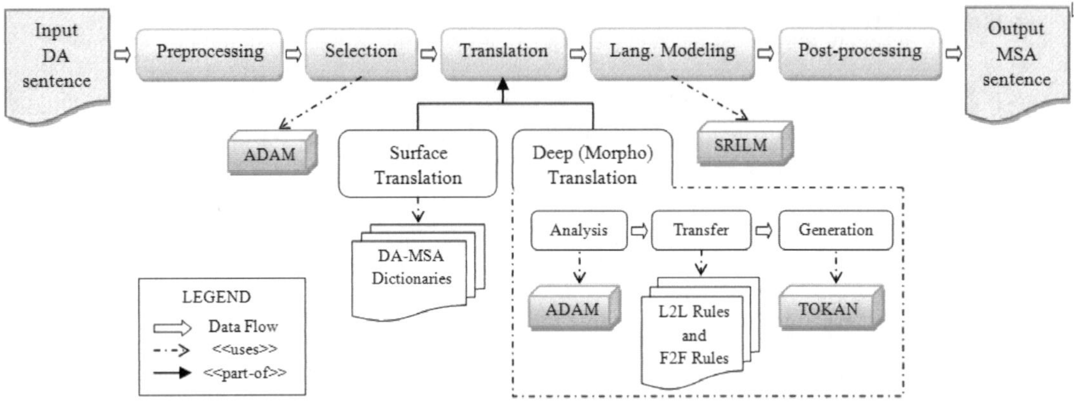


Figure 1: This diagram highlights the different steps inside Elissa and some of its third-party dependencies. ADAM is an Analyzer for Dialectal Arabic Morphology (Salloum and Habash, 2011). TOKAN is a general tokenizer for Arabic (Habash, 2007). SRILM is SRI Language Modeling Toolkit (Stolcke, 2002). ADAM and TOKAN are packaged with Elissa.

This variety of output types makes it easy to plug Elissa with other systems and to use it as a dialectal Arabic preprocessing tool for other MSA systems, e.g., MADA (Habash and Rambow, 2005) or AMIRA (Diab et al., 2007).

## 4.2 Approach

Our approach, illustrated in Figure 1, consists of three major steps proceeded by a *preprocessing* step, that prepares the input text to be handled (e.g., UTF-8 cleaning), and succeeded by a *post-processing* step, that produces the output in the desired form (e.g., top-1 choice in Buckwalter transliteration). The three major steps are:

1. **Selection.** Identify the words to handle, e.g., dialectal or OOV words.

2. **Translation.** Provide MSA paraphrases of the selected words to form an MSA lattice.

3. **Language Modeling.** Pick the n-best fluent sentences from the generated MSA lattice according to a language model.

### 4.2.1 Selection

In the first step, Elissa decides which words to paraphrase and which words to leave as is. It provides different alternative settings for selection, and can be configured to use different subsets of them:

1. **User Token-based Selection.** The user can mark specific words for selection using the tag '/DIA' after the word. This allows dialect identification tools, such as AIDA (Elfardy and Diab, 2012), to be integrated with Elissa.

2. **User Type-based Selection.** The user can specify a list of words to select what is listed in it (OOV) or what is not listed in it (INVs – in-vocabulary).

3. **Dialectal Morphology Word Selection.** Elissa uses ADAM (Salloum and Habash, 2011) to select two types of dialectal words: words that have DA analyses only or DA/MSA analyses.

4. **Dictionary-based Selection.** Elissa selects words that exist in our DA-MSA dictionaries.

5. **All.** Elissa selects every word in an input sentence.

#### 4.2.2 Translation

In this step, Elissa translates the selected words to their MSA equivalent paraphrases. These paraphrases are then used to form an MSA lattice. The translation step has two types: *surface translation* and *deep (morphological) translation*. The surface translation depends on DA-to-MSA dictionaries to map a selected DA word directly to its MSA paraphrases. We use the Tharwa dictionary (Diab et al., 2013) and other dictionaries that we created. The morphological translation uses the classic rule-based machine translation flow: analysis, transfer and generation.

1. **Morphological Analysis** produces a set of alternative analyses for each word.
2. **Morphological Transfer** maps each analysis into one or more target analyses.
3. **Morphological Generation** generates the surface forms of the target analyses.

**Morphological Analysis.** In this step, we use a dialectal morphological analyzer, ADAM, (Salloum and Habash, 2011). ADAM provides Elissa with a set of analyses for each dialectal word in the form of lemma and features. These analyses will be processed in the next step, Transfer.

**Morphological Transfer.** In the transfer step, we map ADAM's dialectal analyses to MSA analyses. This step is implemented using a set of transfer rules (TRs) that operate on the lemma and feature representation produced by ADAM. These TRs can change clitics, features or lemma, and even split up the dialectal word into multiple MSA word analyses. Crucially the input and output of this step are both in the lemma and feature representation. A particular analysis may trigger more than one rule resulting in multiple paraphrases. This only adds to the fan-out which started with the original dialectal word having multiple analyses.

Elissa uses two types of TRs: lemma-to-lemma (L2L) TRs and features-to-features (F2F) TRs. L2L TRs simply change the dialectal lemma to an MSA lemma. The mapping is provided in the DA-MSA dictionaries we use. On the other hand, F2F TRs are more complicated and were written by experts. These rules work together to handle complex transformations such as mapping the DA circumfix negation to a separate word in MSA and adjusting for verb aspect difference. The following is an example illustrating the various rules working together: Elissa creates the MSA analysis for ولم يذهبوا إليها *wlm yðhbwA ǍlyhA* 'And they did not go to it – lit. and+did+not they+go to+it' starting with the DA analysis for وماراحولا *wmArAHwlA* 'lit. and+not+went+they+to+it'.

**Morphological Generation.** In this step, we generate Arabic words from all analyses produced by the previous steps. The generation is done using the general tokenizer/generator TOKAN (Habash, 2007) to produce the surface form words. Although TOKAN can accommodate generation in specific tokenizations, in the work we report here we generate only in untokenized form. Any subsequent tokenization is done in a post-processing step (see Section 4.1). The various generated forms are used to construct the map files and word lattices. The lattices are then input to the language modeling step presented next.

#### 4.2.3 Language Modeling

The language model (LM) component uses SRILM (Stolcke, 2002) lattice-tool for weight assignment and n-best decoding. Elissa comes with a default 5-gram LM file (trained on ~200M untokenized

Arabic words) and default configurations; however, users can change the default configurations and even specify their own LM file.

## 5 Example

| | |
|---|---|
| **DA source** | بهالحالة ماحيكتبولو شي عحيط صفحتو لأنو ماخبرهن يوم اللي وصل عالبلد.<br>*bhAlHAlħ mAHyktbwlw šy EHyT SfHtw lÂnw mAxbrhn ywm Ally wSl EAlbld.* |
| **Human Reference** | In this case, they will not write on his page wall because he did not tell them the day he arrived to the country. |
| **Google Translate** | Bhalhalh Mahiketbolo Shi Ahat Cefhto to Anu Mabrhen day who arrived Aalbuld. |
| **Human DA-to-MSA** | في هذه الحالة لن يكتبوا له شيئا على حائط صفحته لأنه لم يخبرهم يوم وصل إلى البلد.<br>*fy hðh AlHAlħ ln yktbwA lh šyŷA ElY HAŷT SfHth lÂnh lm yxbrhm ywm wSl ĂlY Albld.* |
| **Google Translate** | In this case it would not write him something on the wall yet because he did not tell them day arrived in the country. |
| **Elissa DA-to-MSA** | في هذه الحالة لن يكتبوا شيء علي حائط صفحته لانه لم يخبرهم يوم الذي وصل الي البلد.<br>*fy hðh AlHAlħ ln yktbwA šy' Ely HAŷT SfHth lAnh lm yxbrhm ywm Alðy wSl Aly Albld.* |
| **Google Translate** | In this case it would not write something on the wall yet because he did not tell them the day arrived in the country. |

Table 1: An illustrative example for DA-to-English MT by pivoting (bridging) on MSA. Elissa's Arabic output is Alif/Ya normalized (Habash, 2010).

Table 1 shows a illustrative example of how pivoting on MSA can dramatically improve the translation quality of a statistical MT system that is trained on mostly MSA-to-English parallel corpora. In this example, we use Google Translate Arabic-English SMT system. The table is divided into three parts. The first part shows a dialectal (Levantine) sentence, its reference translation to English, and its Google Translate translation. The Google Translate translation clearly struggles with most of the dialectal words, which were probably unseen in the training data (i.e., out-of-vocabulary – OOV) and were considered proper nouns (transliterated and capitalized). The lack of DA-English parallel corpora suggests pivoting on MSA can improve the translation quality. In the second part of the table, we show a human MSA translation of the DA sentence above and its Google Translate translation. We see that the results are quite promising. The goal of Elissa is to model this DA-MSA translation automatically. In the third part of the table, we present Elissa's output on the dialectal sentence and its Google Translate translation. The produced MSA is not perfect, but is clearly an improvement over doing nothing as far as usability for MT into English.

## Future Work

In the future, we plan to extend Elissa's coverage of phenomena in the handled dialects and to new dialects. We also plan to automatically learn additional rules from limited available data (DA-MSA or DA-English). We are interested in studying how our approach can be combined with solutions that simply add more dialectal training data (Zbib et al., 2012) since the two directions are complementary in how they address linguistic normalization and domain coverage.

## Acknowledgment

This paper is based upon work supported by the Defense Advanced Research Projects Agency (DARPA) under Contract No. HR0011-12-C-0014. Any opinions, findings and conclusions or recommendations expressed in this paper are those of the authors and do not necessarily reflect the views of DARPA.

## References

Abo Bakr, H., Shaalan, K., and Ziedan, I. (2008). A Hybrid Approach for Converting Written Egyptian Colloquial Dialect into Diacritized Arabic. In *The 6th International Conference on Informatics and Systems, INFOS2008*. Cairo University.

Buckwalter, T. (2004). Buckwalter arabic morphological analyzer version 2.0. LDC catalog number LDC2004L02, ISBN 1-58563-324-0.

Chiang, D., Diab, M., Habash, N., Rambow, O., and Shareef, S. (2006). Parsing Arabic Dialects. In *Proceedings of the European Chapter of ACL (EACL)*.

Diab, M., Hacioglu, K., and Jurafsky, D. (2007). *Arabic Computational Morphology: Knowledge-based and Empirical Methods*, chapter Automated Methods for Processing Arabic Text: From Tokenization to Base Phrase Chunking. Springer.

Diab, M., Hawwari, A., Elfardy, H., Dasigi, P., Al-Badrashiny, M., Eskander, R., and Habash, N. (Forthcoming – 2013). Tharwa: A multi-dialectal multi-lingual machine readable dictionary.

Duh, K. and Kirchhoff, K. (2005). POS tagging of dialectal Arabic: a minimally supervised approach. In *Proceedings of the ACL Workshop on Computational Approaches to Semitic Languages*, Semitic '05, pages 55–62, Ann Arbor, Michigan.

Elfardy, H. and Diab, M. (2012). Token level identification of linguistic code switching. In *Proceedings of the 24th International Conference on Computational Linguistics (COLING), IIT Mumbai, India.*

Habash, N. (2007). Arabic Morphological Representations for Machine Translation. In van den Bosch, A. and Soudi, A., editors, *Arabic Computational Morphology: Knowledge-based and Empirical Methods*. Springer.

Habash, N. (2010). *Introduction to Arabic Natural Language Processing*. Morgan & Claypool Publishers.

Habash, N., Eskander, R., and Hawwari, A. (2012). A morphological analyzer for egyptian arabic. In *Proceedings of the Twelfth Meeting of the Special Interest Group on Computational Morphology and Phonology*, pages 1–9, Montréal, Canada.

Habash, N. and Rambow, O. (2005). Arabic Tokenization, Part-of-Speech Tagging and Morphological Disambiguation in One Fell Swoop. In *Proceedings of the 43rd Annual Meeting of the Association for Computational Linguistics (ACL'05)*, pages 573–580, Ann Arbor, Michigan.

Habash, N. and Rambow, O. (2006). MAGEAD: A Morphological Analyzer and Generator for the Arabic Dialects. In *Proceedings of the 21st International Conference on Computational Linguistics and 44th Annual Meeting of the Association for Computational Linguistics*, pages 681–688, Sydney, Australia.

Habash, N., Soudi, A., and Buckwalter, T. (2007). On Arabic Transliteration. In van den Bosch, A. and Soudi, A., editors, *Arabic Computational Morphology: Knowledge-based and Empirical Methods*. Springer.

Hajič, J., Hric, J., and Kubon, V. (2000). Machine Translation of Very Close Languages. In *Proceedings of the 6th Applied Natural Language Processing Conference (ANLP'2000)*, pages 7–12, Seattle.

Kilany, H., Gadalla, H., Arram, H., Yacoub, A., El-Habashi, A., and McLemore, C. (2002). Egyptian Colloquial Arabic Lexicon. LDC catalog number LDC99L22.

Kirchhoff, K., Bilmes, J., Das, S., Duta, N., Egan, M., Ji, G., He, F., Henderson, J., Liu, D., Noamany, M., Schone, P., Schwartz, R., and Vergyri, D. (2003). Novel Approaches to Arabic Speech Recognition: Report from the 2002 Johns Hopkins Summer Workshop. In *IEEE International Conference on Acoustics, Speech, and Signal Processing*, Hong Kong, China.

Kumar, S., Och, F. J., and Macherey, W. (2007). Improving word alignment with bridge languages. In *Proceedings of the 2007 Joint Conference on Empirical Methods in Natural Language Processing and Computational Natural Language Learning (EMNLP-CoNLL)*, pages 42–50, Prague, Czech Republic.

Salloum, W. and Habash, N. (2011). Dialectal to Standard Arabic Paraphrasing to Improve Arabic-English Statistical Machine Translation. In *Proceedings of the First Workshop on Algorithms and Resources for Modelling of Dialects and Language Varieties*, pages 10–21, Edinburgh, Scotland.

Sawaf, H. (2010). Arabic dialect handling in hybrid machine translation. In *Proceedings of the Conference of the Association for Machine Translation in the Americas (AMTA)*, Denver, Colorado.

Stolcke, S. (2002). Tokenization, morphological analysis, and part-of-speech tagging for arabic in one fell swoop. In *In Proceedings of ICSLP 2002*, volume 2, pages 901–904.

Utiyama, M. and Isahara, H. (2007). A comparison of pivot methods for phrase-based statistical machine translation. In *HLT-NAACL*, pages 484–491.

Zbib, R., Malchiodi, E., Devlin, J., Stallard, D., Matsoukas, S., Schwartz, R. M., Makhoul, J., Zaidan, O., and Callison-Burch, C. (2012). Machine translation of arabic dialects. In *HLT-NAACL*, pages 49–59.

Zhang, X. (1998). Dialect MT: a case study between Cantonese and Mandarin. In *Proceedings of the 36th Annual Meeting of the Association for Computational Linguistics and 17th International Conference on Computational Linguistics*, ACL '98, pages 1460–1464, Montreal, Canada.

# Domain Based Punjabi Text Document Clustering

*Saurabh Sharma, Vishal Gupta*
University Institute of Engineering & Technology, Panjab University, Chandigarh
saurabhsharma381@gmail.com, vishal@pu.ac.in

ABSTRACT

Text Clustering is a text mining technique which is used to group similar documents into single cluster by using some sort of similarity measure & separating the dissimilar documents. Popular clustering algorithms available for text clustering treats document as conglomeration of words. The syntactic or semantic relations between words are not given any consideration. Many different algorithms were propagated to study and find connection among different words in a sentence by using different concepts. In this paper, a hybrid algorithm for clustering of Punjabi text document that uses semantic relations among words in a sentence for extracting phrases has been developed. Phrases extracted create a feature vector of the document which is used for finding similarity among all documents. Experimental results reveal that hybrid algorithm performs better with real time data sets.

KEYWORDS: Natural Language Processing, Text Mining, Text Document Clustering, Punjabi Language, Karaka Theory.

*Proceedings of COLING 2012: Demonstration Papers*, pages 393–400,
COLING 2012, Mumbai, December 2012.

## 1. Introduction

The current study was undertaken specifically for clustering of text documents in Punjabi Language as no prior work has been done in this language as per review of literature done to carry out this study. It is an attempt in this direction to provide a solution for text clustering in Punjabi Language, by developing a new hybrid approach of text clustering, which will be immensely useful to the researchers who wish to undertake study and research in vernacular languages. The study proposed and implemented a new algorithm for clustering of Punjabi text documents by combining best features of the text clustering algorithms i.e. Clustering with frequent Item Sets, Clustering with Frequent Word Sequences, keeping in view the semantics of Punjabi language. Efficiency of the three algorithms for Punjabi Text Document Clustering was compared using Precision, Recall & F-Measure.

## 2. Proposed approach for Punjabi text clustering

Positional languages, which come in the category of Context Free Grammars (CFGs) have used popular approaches for text clustering. A context-free grammar is a formal system that describes a language by specifying how any legal text can be derived from a distinguished symbol called the axiom, or sentence symbol. It consists of a set of productions, each of which states that a given symbol can be replaced by a given sequence of symbols. The sentence structure of Punjabi is different as it belongs to the category of Free order language, unlike in English. Hence, features of free order languages were to be taken into consideration for clustering of Punjabi text.

Paninian framework, a technique for formalism, has been used for extraction of phrases for Indian languages. Karaka relation between verbs and nouns in a sentence is used to analyse the sentence. Sudhir K Mishra [2007] whose work focused on the theory of Karaka, (Panini : Adhikara sutra [Bharati, A. and Sangal, R. 1990]), for analyzing the structure of a sentence in Sanskrit Language, did the prominent work in this category.

Any factor that contributes to the accomplishment of any action is defined as karaka. Punjabi language identifies eight sub types like Hindi and Sanskrit [Bharti, A. and Sangal, R. 1993]. The karaka relations are syntactico-semantic (or semantico-syntactic) relations between the verbal and other related constituents in a sentence. They by themselves do not give the semantics. Instead they specify relations which mediate between vibhakti of nominals and verb forms on one hand and semantic relations on the other [Kiparsky 1982; Cardona 1976; Cardona 1988].

### 2.1 Pre-processing Phase

In text clustering, some techniques used in pre-processing are removal of punctuation marks, removal of stop words, stemming of words, normalization (where the same word exists in different spellings in case of multilingual words).

For pre-processing, the Algorithm takes Punjabi text documents as input. The first step in pre-processing comprises of removal of punctuation marks. Stop words are not removed, since Karaka theory [Bharati, A. and Sangal, R. 1990] is being used for generating phrases. Karaka theory works only on complete sentences, which necessarily includes, stop words. This does away with the requirement of removal of stop words.

Next step is normalization of those words which are used with different spellings. Purpose of normalization is to maintain uniformity of spelling in all documents which contain that word. This helps in better clustering results. Otherwise some documents may not be identified just because of the difference in spellings.

## 2.2 Algorithm Details

After the completion of pre-processing step, phrases are extracted from sentences with the help of karaka list. Karaka List is the collection of words which are used to specify role of words as nouns, verbs, objects and gives information about semantics of the sentence.

To overcome the drawback of Frequent Item Sets [Fung et. al. 2003] and Frequent Word Sequences [Li, Y. et. al. 2008] that generated long Sequences by trying all combinations of 2-word sequences using Apriori algorithm [Agrawal R. and Srikant, R. 1994], *Karaka* list is used in proposed approach.

Extraction of phrases from the document with the help of Karaka list generates a document vector containing phrases of various lengths in the same order in which they were originally in input document. This dissuades the computation of k-length sequences in number of steps by trying all possible combinations of (k-1)-length sequences.

### 2.2.1 Calculation of Term frequency of Phrases

Term Frequency is a numerical statistic which reflects how important a word is to a document in a collection. It is often used as a weighting factor in information retrieval and text mining. The value of Term Frequency increases proportionally to the number of times a word appears in the document which helps to control the fact that some words are generally more common than others. For each phrase, we calculate the Term Frequency, by counting the total number of occurrence in the document.

### 2.2.2 Finding top k Frequent Phrases

Sort all phrases by Term Frequency in descending order. Then declare top k phrases as Key phrases. These key phrases will be used for finding similarity among all other documents. The value of k is a very important factor for better clustering results. The valid value of k ranges from 1 to n, where n is number of phrases in a document. For experimental results, 20% of phrases are used as value of k.

### 2.2.3 Finding Similar Documents and Creating Initial Clusters

In this step, initial clusters are created by matching key phrases of documents with each other. If a phrase is found common between two documents, then it is assumed that these documents may belong to the same cluster. All matched documents will be searched for common Cluster Title by using Cluster Titles list.

The main idea of using Cluster Title List is to avoid overlapping clusters, meaningless or ambiguous titles of Clusters. To avoid this major drawback, manually created list of Cluster Titles for specific domain have been used. Text data has been taken for Sports domain. List of Cluster Titles specific to sports have been created manually as no such list is available in Punjabi language.

Documents with same Cluster Title are placed into same cluster. If two documents contain matching phrase but do not contain same Cluster Title, then it is assumed that both documents do not belong to same cluster.

### 2.2.4 Calculate term frequency of each term for each document and sort them to find top k frequent terms

After creating initial clusters, all those documents which are not placed in any cluster, are placed in a cluster named "Unrecognized". Since, some documents may contain cluster titles but did not appear in top k Frequent Phrases, for those unrecognized documents, VSM model is used [Salton et. al. 1975] i.e. now document is represented as a collection of single word terms obtained by splitting all phrases. The difference between Term and Phrase is that by splitting a single phrase of N word length, N different terms have been obtained. For each unrecognized document, Term Frequency for each term in the document is calculated. Then, all terms are sorted based on their Term Frequency in document, to find top k frequent terms of the document. The value of k can be varied as per the users' discretion from 5%, 10%, 20% and so on. Higher the value of k, more terms will be considered for finding cluster for unrecognized document.

### 2.2.5 Find cluster frequent terms for new clusters

After calculating top k frequent terms for each unrecognized document. Now, top k Cluster Frequent Terms for each cluster will be identified. Term Frequency of each term of the conceptual document is calculated.

### 2.2.6 For each unrecognized document assign a cluster

Cluster for unrecognized document, by matching top k Frequent Terms of document with top k Cluster Frequent Terms of each document, is identified.

### 2.2.7 Final Clusters

After processing of unrecognized documents, final clusters containing documents from initial cluster and documents from unrecognized documents are created.

## 3. Experimental Evaluation

| Natural Classes | F-Measure |
|---|---|
| ਹਾਕੀ (Hockey) | 0.99 |
| ਕ੍ਰਿਕਟ (Cricket) | 0.93 |
| ਟੈਨਿਸ (Tennis) | 0.87 |
| ਫੁਟਬਾਲ (Football) | 0.93 |
| ਬੈਡਮਿੰਟਨ (Badminton) | 1.00 |
| ਮੁੱਕੇਬਾਜ਼ੀ (Boxing) | 0.89 |

Table 1. Natural Classes for Hybrid Approach

## 3.1 Data Set

The text documents are denoted as unstructured data. It is very complex to group text documents. The document clustering requires a pre-processing task to convert the unstructured data values into a structured one. The documents are data elements with large dimensions. The system was tested for 221 text documents collected from various Punjabi News websites which comprised of news articles on sports. This dataset was categorized into 7 Natural classes (see table 1), which were used for the evaluation of all three algorithms.

## 3.2 Experimental Results and Discussion

To evaluate the accuracy of the clustering results generated by clustering algorithms, F-measure is employed. Let us assume that each cluster is treated as if it were the result of a query and each natural class is treated as if it were the relevant set of documents for a query. The recall, precision, and F-measure for natural class $K_i$ and cluster $C_j$ are calculated as follows:

$$\text{Precision}(K_i, C_j) = n_{ij} / |C_j| \quad (2)$$

$$\text{Recall}(K_i, C_j) = n_{ij} / |K_j| \quad (3)$$

$$\text{F-Measure}(K_i, C_j) = \frac{2 * [\text{Precision}(K_i, C_j) * \text{Recall}(K_i, C_j)]}{[\text{Precision}(K_i, C_j) + \text{Recall}(K_i, C_j)]} \quad (4)$$

where $n_{ij}$ is the number of members of natural class $K_i$ in cluster $C_j$ . Intuitively, $F(K_i;C_j)$ measures the quality of cluster $C_j$ in describing the natural class $K_i$, by the harmonic mean of Recall and Precision for the "query results" $C_j$ with respect to the "relevant documents" $K_i$.

In fig.1 the graph plotted for Precision, Recall and F-Measure for all the three algorithms that were studied for clustering of Punjabi text documents, the two algorithms namely, Frequent Itemset and Frequent word sequence, shows a good precision but a very poor recall value. This leads to a very low value of F-Measure which is indicative of its overall poor performance. On the other hand, Hybrid algorithm that shows good Precision, Recall and F-Measure, outperform other two algorithms and hence generate best clustering results.

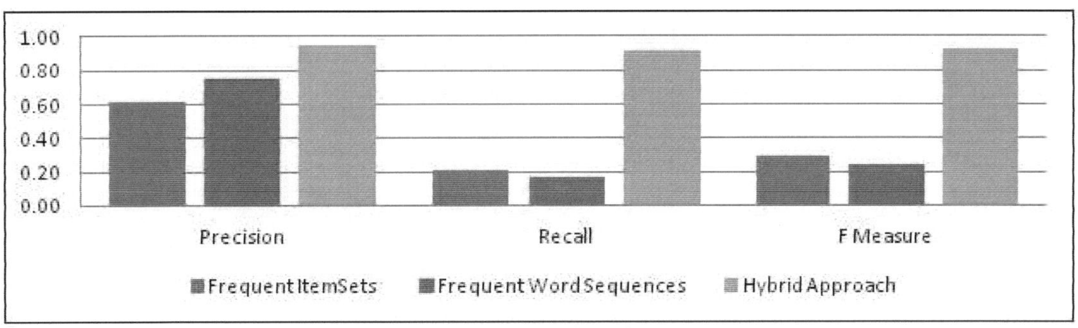


Fig 1 Precision, Recall and F-Measure

## 3.3 Error Analysis

During the development of this algorithm, several problems for improving clustering results were encountered. These problems and reason for errors in clustering result are discussed below.

**Different Spellings in Different Documents results in True Negative.** In case of words, which are originally from other languages than the one under purview, e.g. English word 'football' can be written as ਫੁਟਬਾਲ or ਫੁੱਟਬਾਲ. Now, during clustering phase, efforts are made to find similarity between two documents about football, but having different spellings, that do not match. To overcome this problem, we have used normalization of Cluster Titles in pre-processing step.

**Phrases containing Important Terms but not coming in Top k Frequent Phrases, results in True Negatives.** For example, a document contains news about football. But word 'football' is appearing only one or two times in whole document, then it is very hard to capture this desired information in top k Frequent phrases. To overcome this problem, VSM approach is utilized after creating Initial clusters. In this step, top k Frequent Terms are identified. Advantage of applying this step is utilizing those meaningful terms which are not captured in top k Frequent phrases, but very vital for efficient, effective & correct clustering of documents.

**Multiple Key Phrases matches with Multiple Cluster Titles results in False Positive and True Negative.** For example, a document contains an article on football, but uses some terms common with other sports e.g. team, goal, match referee etc. then it becomes difficult to identify the exact cluster for the document. To overcome this problem, the number of matching Cluster frequent Terms are counted for each matching cluster. Document is, then, placed in that cluster which has maximum number of matching Cluster frequent Terms.

## 4. Conclusion

Domain based Punjabi Text clustering software is logically feasible, efficient and practical for Punjabi text documents. It is more feasible and has a better performance than Frequent Itemsets and Frequent Word Sequences with reference to Punjabi Text Documents. The results are validated and drawn from the experimental data. This approach focuses on the semantics of a sentence. Proposed work shows better results as it uses a list of Cluster Title candidates, which does not allow the construction of huge number of clusters with meaningless names. This algorithm was not tested with benchmark data set, because all available data sets are for English language only. Dataset for Punjabi language is created manually because no such benchmark dataset is available for Punjabi language.

## References

AGRAWAL R. AND SRIKANT, R. (1994)). *Fast Algorithms for Mining Association Rules*. In Proceedings of the 20th International Conference on Very Large Data Bases. Morgan Kaufmann Publishers Inc. San Francisco, CA, USA. , 487 - 499. ISBN:1-55860-153-8.

BHARATI, A. AND SANGAL, R. (1990). *A karaka based approach to parsing of Indian languages*. In Proceedings of the 13th conference on Computational linguistics. Association for Computational Linguistics Stroudsburg, PA, USA. 3, 25-29. ISBN:952-90-2028-7 doi>10.3115/991146.991151

BHARATI, A. AND SANGAL, R. (1993). *Parsing free word order languages in the Paninian framework*. In Proceedings of the 31st annual meeting on Association for Computational Linguistics. Association for Computational Linguistics Stroudsburg, PA, USA. 105-111. doi>10.3115/981574.981589

CARDONA, G. (1976). *Panini: A Survey of Research*, Mouton, Hague-Paris.

CARDONA, G. (1988). *Panini: His Work and Its Tradition* (Vol. 1: Background and Introduction), Motilal Banarsidas, Delhi.

FUNG, B.C.M., WANG, K. AND ESTER, M. (2003). *Hierarchical Document Clustering Using Frequent Itemsets*. In Proceedings of SIAM International Conference on Data Mining.

KIPARSKY, P. (1982). *Some Theoretical Problems in Panini's Grammar*. Bhandarkar Oriental Research Institute, Poona, India.

LI, Y., SOON M. CHUNG, S. M. AND HOLT, J. D. (2008). *Text document clustering based on frequent word meaning sequences*. Data & Knowledge Engineering, 64, 1, 381-404.

MISHRA, S. K. (2007). *Sanskrit Karaka Analyzer for Machine Translation*. M.Phil dissertation. Jawaharlal Nehru University, New Delhi.

SALTON, G., WONG, A. AND YANG, C. S. (1975). *A vector space model for automatic indexing*. Communications of the ACM. ACM New York, NY, USA. 18, 11, 613 - 620. doi>10.1145/361219.361220

# Open source multi-platform NooJ for NLP

*Max* SILBERZTEIN[1] *Tamás* VÁRADI[2] *Marko* TADIĆ[3]
(1) UNIVERSITÉ DE FRANCHE-COMTÉ, Besançon, France
(2) RESEARCH INSTITUTE FOR LINGUISTICS MTA, Budapest, Hungary
(3) FACULTY OF HUMANITIES AND SOCIAL SCIENCES ZAGREB UNIVERSITY, Zagreb, Croatia
max.silberztein@univ-fcomte.fr, varadi.tamas@nytud.mta.hu,
marko.tadic@ffzg.hr

ABSTRACT

The purpose of this demo is to introduce the linguistic development tool NooJ. The tool has been in development for a number of years and it has a solid community of computational linguists developing grammars in two dozen languages ranging from Arabic to Vietnamese[1]. Despite its manifest capabilities and reputation, its appeal within the wider HLT community was limited by the fact that it was confined to the .NET framework and it was not open source. However, under the auspices of the CESAR project it has recently been turned open source and a JAVA and a MONO version have been produced. In our view this significant development justifies a concise but thorough description of the system, demonstrating its potential for deployment in a wide variety of settings and purposes. The paper describes the history, the architecture, main functionalities and potential of the system for teaching, research and application development.

KEYWORDS : NooJ, Finite-State NLP, Local Grammars, Linguistic Development Tools, INTEX, Information extraction, text mining

[1] See http://nooj4nlp.net/pages/resources

*Proceedings of COLING 2012: Demonstration Papers*, pages 401–408,
COLING 2012, Mumbai, December 2012.

## 1 Introduction

The purpose of the paper and the demonstration is to introduce the NLP system NooJ in its new incarnation as an open-source, cross-platform system. The porting into JAVA, recently created under the supervision of Max Silberztein, the developer of the system, within the CESAR project, as well as the recent steep development path of the core system, justifies a brief overview and demonstration of the potential of the system for a wide variety of computational linguistic applications. For lack of space we will concentrate on two issues: how NooJ is capable of supporting development of a wide variety of grammars of different strength and formalism and how efficiently it can do so. Accordingly, ***Section two*** gives a brief general overview, ***section three*** discusses the architecture, ***section four*** describes the expressive power and suitability of NooJ to develop grammars of various formalisms, ***section five*** will contain a brief discussion of the processing efficiency of the system.

## 2 General description of NooJ

NooJ is a self-contained corpus analysis and comprehensive linguistic development tool, employing an efficient uniform formalism that enables the system to be deployed for a range of NLP tasks. A more flexible and powerful successor to INTEX (Silberztein, 1993), which was created at the LADL to develop sophisticated yet robust computational linguistic analyses, NooJ has far surpassed its predecessor both in terms of implementation and linguistic and computational power and efficiency (see sections 4 and 5 for details).

## 3 Architecture

The system consists of three modules, corpus handling, lexicon and grammar development that are integrated into a single intuitive graphical user interface (command line operation is also available). An essential feature of NooJ is that these modules are seamlessly integrated and are internally implemented in finite state technology (with optional important enhancements, see below).

### 3.1 Corpus handling

NooJ is geared towards developing grammars processing large amounts of texts and therefore contains a full-fledged ***corpus processing module***, indexing, annotation and querying of corpora is a basic functionality. Corpora's size are typically up to 200MB+ (e.g. one year of the newspaper Le Monde), and we have experimented with the MEDLINE corpus (1GB+) successfully. Text can be imported in a wide variety of formats and a lexical analysis is immediately applied on the basis of a robust dictionary module that has a built-in morphological analyser. The result of the lexical analysis becomes the initial tier in a set of stand-off annotation levels containing at first POS and morphological codes as well as the result of any morphological grammars that carried out typical pre-processing normalisations of the text. This basic annotation, amounting to indexing of the corpus, can be enhanced with an arbitrary number of further tiers as subsequent syntactic grammars are applied in a cascaded manner. The corpus handling facility provides instant feedback for the coverage of grammars in the form of concordances, the annotation of which can be manually filtered before applying to the text. NooJ can handle pre-annotated corpora, providing that the XML annotations that represent lexical information follow a few requirements.

## 3.2 Lexical module

NooJ contains a robust dictionary module, which, together with its integrated morphological grammars, is designed to handle simple words, affixes and multi-word units. The lexical module is capable of handling full-fledged dictionaries, for example, the Hungarian system consists of cc. 72000 lemmas representing over120 million word forms, which the system can efficiently analyse and generate. Dictionary entries consist of POS and any number of typed features describing the morphological, syntactic, semantic etc. characteristics of the lemma, including, for example, foreign language equivalents.

Morphology is implemented by specifying paradigms that define all possible affix sequences, employing morphological operators to take care of assimilation, stem changes etc. Morphological grammars can be written in a graphical interface to segment and analyse compound word forms, to treat spelling variants as well as to implement guessers to handle unknown words.

## 3.3 Syntactic module

One of the most attractive features of the system that immediately appeals to users is the ease with which sophisticated grammars (of various levels of computing power) can be built in graph form and applied to corpora as a query (Beesley & Karttunen, 2003)(see, Figure 1, for an example). This feature alone makes NooJ ideal for teaching and rapid application development tool alike. The graphs have alternative textual notation in case that mode of definition proves more applicable.

The original philosophy behind developing NooJ was to employ fast finite state technology to exploit its potential in describing local dependencies in language in all their complex details. This led to the development of local grammars capturing sophisticated distributional distinctions, which are applied in a cascaded manner to yield, hopefully, a comprehensive parsing of text. (Gross, 1997)

Recently, a number of enhancements have been introduced that significantly increased the expressive power and the elegance of grammars that can be devised in NooJ. Such advanced features include use of variables, lexical constraints, agreement over long distance dependencies and the generation of word forms required by the grammar. As a result, in its current stage of development NooJ allows implementation of grammars that represent various levels of computing power. This will be the focus of attention in Section 4.

## 3.4 Implementation

Originally available only on the .NET and Mono platforms, the system has recently been ported to JAVA. NooJ's engine and its user interface are decoupled and the corresponding API has been defined to ease the task of porting both to Java. The Java version of NooJ has been implemented using the Swing GUI components. The resulting JAVA system, currently in final integration testing phase, will be published soon together with source code and documentation. NooJ is capable of processing texts in over 150 file formats (including HTML, MSWORD, PDF, RTF, all version of ASCII and Unicode, etc.), NooJ internal engine processes texts in UTF8.

## 4 The expressive power of NooJ grammars

Beside being a corpus processor (that can process large texts in real time) as well as a linguistic development tool (used to implement large number of linguistic resources), NooJ offers a unified formalism that can be used to enter grammars of the four type of the Chomsky-Schützenberger hierarchy (Chomsky & Schützenberger, 1963):

- NooJ's Regular Expressions and finite-state graphs are compiled into finite-state automata and transducers. For instance, the graph in Figure 1 recognizes the set of correct sequences of preverbal particles in French.

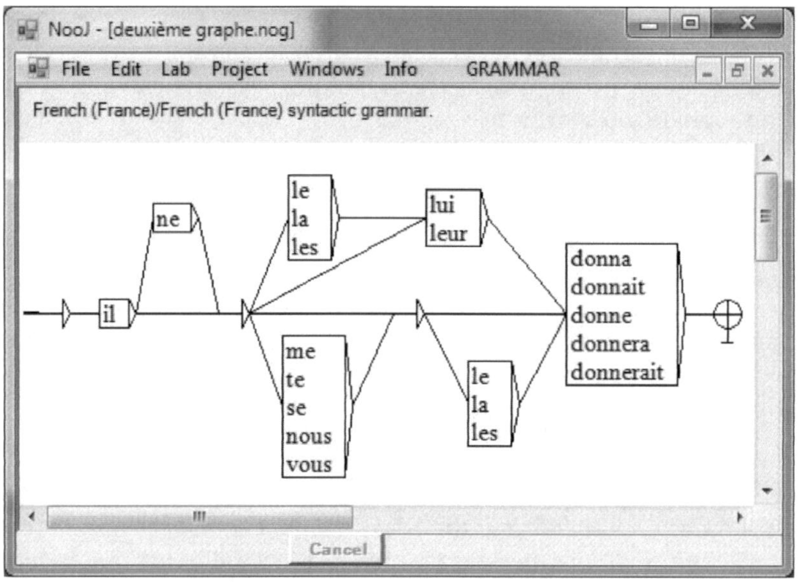


**Figure 1 Implementing Type3 grammars**

- NooJ's Context-Free Grammars and recursive graphs are compiled into finite-state machines or push-down automata[2]. For instance, the grammar in Figure 2 contains two graphs that recognize transitive sentences in French GN (NounPhrase). <V> (Verb) GN (NounPhrase).
- NooJ's Context-Sensitive grammars have two components: a FS or CFG finite-state component, and a constraint-resolution component. For instance, the graph in

[2] Note that most real world CFGs have either left or right recursions, which can be removed automatically. Left-recursive and right-recursive Context-Free Grammars are turned into equivalent non-recursive grammars and subsequently compiled into finite-state machines.

Figure 3 recognizes the language $a^nb^nc^n$ in two steps: The finite-state graph recognizes the language a*b*c*, then, for all sequences recognized by the finite-state graph, the constraints: (here: <$B$LENGTH=$A$LENGTH> and <$C$LENGTH=$A$LENGTH>) are checked.

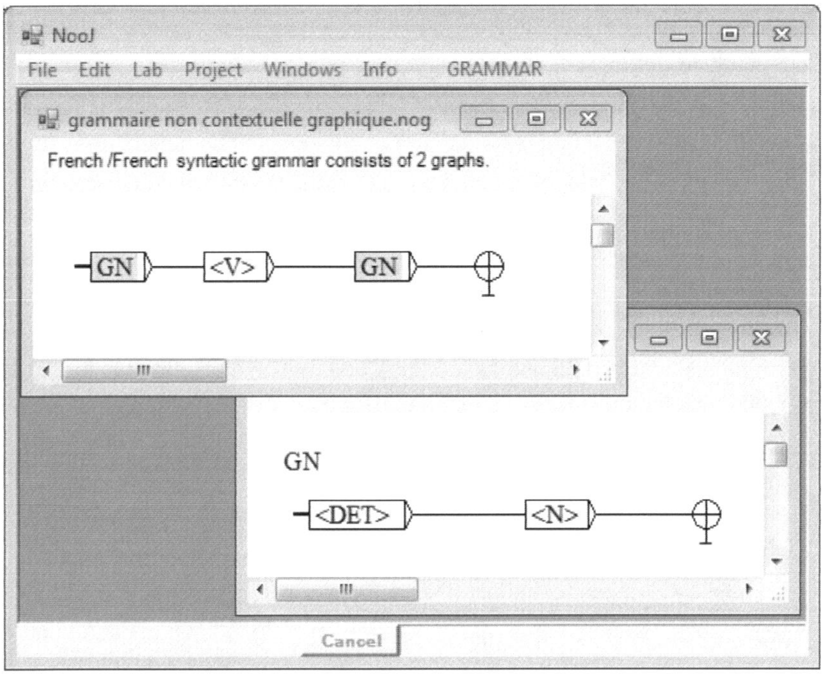


**Figure 2 Implementing Context-Free Grammars**

- NooJ's transformational grammars also have two components: one finite-state or context-free grammar component, and a component that produces and parses outputs based on variables' values. For instance, the three grammars in Figure 4 compute the Passive form, the negation form and the pronominalized form of a given sentence.

The fact that NooJ's enhanced transducers can produce sequences that can in turn be parsed by the same, or other transducers gives NooJ the power of a Turing-Machine.

In effect, these different types of grammars and machines make NooJ the equivalent to a large gamut of formalisms used in Computational Linguistics, including XFST (Beesley & Karttunen, 2003), GPSG (Gazdar, Klein, Pullum, & Sag, 1985), CCG (Steedman & Baldridge, 2011) and TAG (Joshi & Schabes, 1997), LFG (Kaplan & Bresnan, 1994) and HPSG (Pollard & Sag, 1994). The fact that the same exact notation is used in all four of grammars/machines makes NooJ an ideal tool to parse complex phenomena that involve phenomena across all levels of linguistic phenomena.

## 5 Efficiency

NooJ's parsers are extremely efficient compared with other NLP parsers. Compared with INTEX, GATE (Hamish Cunningham, 2002) or XFST (which have very efficient finite-state parsers). NooJ's finite-state graphs are compiled dynamically *during* parsing, instead of being compiled (determinized and minimized) *before* parsing. NooJ often needs to optimize only a fraction of large grammars (typically, 100,000+ states), and ends the parsing of large corpora much faster than it would have been necessary to just fully compile them.

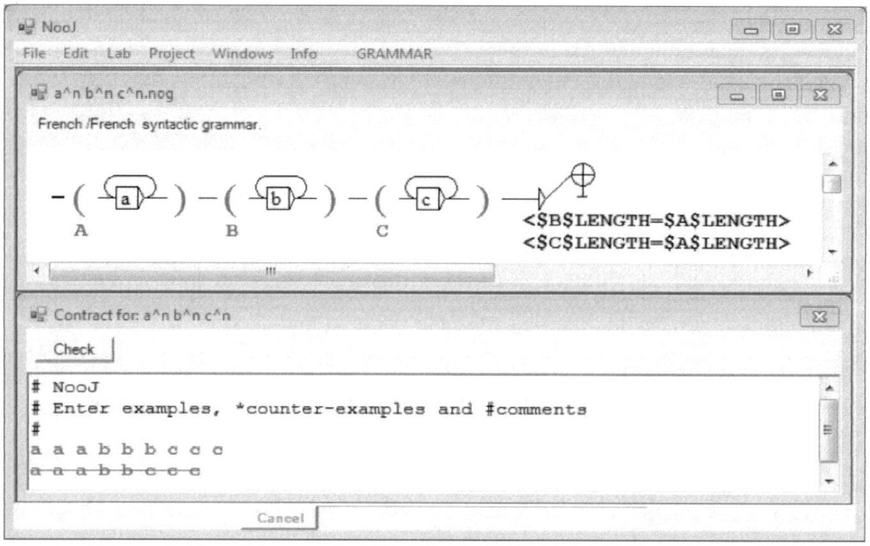


**Figure 3 Implementing Context-Sensitive Grammars**

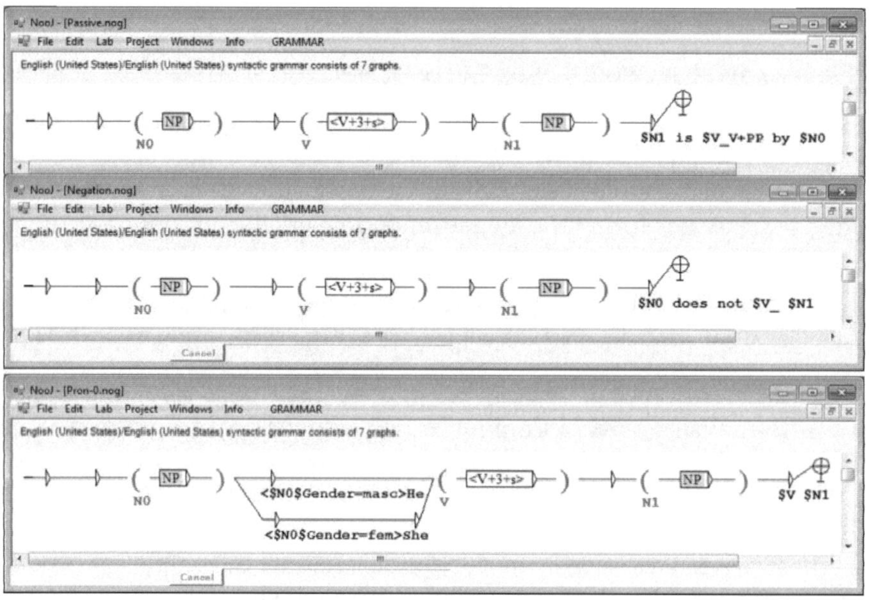


**Figure 4 Implementing Unrestricted Grammars**

NooJ's parsers are also much more efficient than the parsers that process context-sensitive formalisms such as TAG, CCG or LFG, because when parsing a context-sensitive language, NooJ actually starts by parsing their finite-state superset, and then applies a series of constraints to filter out the result. See for instance how the context-sensitive language a^n b^n c^n is processed in Figure 3: in a first step, a finite-state automaton recognizes the language a* b* c* in O(n); in the second step, NooJ checks each of the two constraints in constant time. In other words, when applying this context-sensitive grammar (as well as many "classical" grammars used to describe realistic linguistic phenomena), NooJ's parser performs in O(n), as opposed to O(n^6) which is the typical efficiency for parsers available for mildly context-sensitive formalisms such as TAG.

## 6 Resources

There are over 20 language modules already available for download from NooJ's WEB site www.nooj4nlp.net, including 5 that have open source dictionaries and morphology. When the open source of NooJ is published, the goal of the METANET CESAR consortium is to release open source modules for the languages covered by the CESAR project.

NooJ provides half a dozen tools to help linguists develop new language modules rapidly. The first versions of the latest NooJ modules (Turkish and Serbian) have been developed in less than a year.

## 7 Conclusions

The recent porting to JAVA, the publication of its source code and, more importantly, its enhanced features developed in recent years suggest that the NooJ system has reached a major milestone in its development. We hope that this paper and the live demonstration will serve to argue the case that these major developments open up new perspectives for a wider range of application within the computational linguistic community.

## References


Beesley, R. K., & Karttunen, L. (2003). *Finite State Morphology.* Stanford: CSLI Studies in Computational Linguistics.

Bresnan, J. (Ed.). (1982). *The Mental Representation of Grammatical Relations.* Cambrdige, MA: MIT Press.

Chomsky, N., & Schützenberger, M. P. (1963). The algebraic theory of context free languages. In P. Braffort, & D. Hirchberg (Eds.), *Computer Programming and Formal Languages* (pp. 118-161).

Gazdar, G., Klein, E. H., Pullum, G. K., & Sag, I. A. (1985). *Generalized Phrase Structure Grammar.* Oxford: Blackwell.

Gross, M. Lexicon-Grammar. The Representation of Compound Words. *COLING 1986,* (pp. 1-6).

Gross, M. (1997). The Construction of Local Grammars. In E. Roche, & Y. Schabes (Eds.), *Finite State Language Processing* (pp. 329-352). Cambridge, Mass.: MIT Press.

Hamish Cunningham, D. M. (2002). GATE: an Architecture for Development of Robust HLT Applications. *Proceedings of the 40th Anniversarsary Meeting of the ACL* (pp. 168-175). Philadeplphia: ACL.

Joshi, A. K., & Schabes, I. (1997). Tree Adjoining Grammars. In G. Rozenberg, & A. Salomaa, *Handbook of Formal Languages* (Vol. 3, pp. 69-120). Berlin: Springer Verlag.

Kaplan, R. M., & Bresnan, J. (1994). Lexical-Functional Grammar: A Formal System for Grammatical Representation. In M. Dalrymple, R. M. Kaplan, J. T. Maxwell, & A. Zaenen (Eds.), *Formal Issues in Lexical-Functional Grammar* (Lecture Notes No. 47 ed., pp. 29-131). CSLI Publications.

Pollard, C., & Sag, I. A. (1994). *Head-driven phrase structure grammar.* Chicago: Unversity of Chicago Press.

Silberztein, M. (1993). *Dictionnaires électroniques et analyse automatique de textes : le système INTEX.* Paris: Masson Ed.

Silberztein, M. (1998). INTEX: An integrated FST toolbox. In D. Wood, & S. Yu, *Automata Implementation* (pp. 185-197). Berlin, Heidelberg: Springer.

Steedman, M., & Baldridge, J. (2011). Combinatory Categorial Grammar. In R. Borsley, & K. Borjars (Eds.), *Non-Transformational Syntax* Oxford: Blackwell pp. 181-224..

# Punjabi Text-To-Speech Synthesis System

*Parminder SINGH*[1] *Gurpreet Singh LEHAL*[2]
(1) GURU NANAK DEV ENGINEERING COLLEGE, Ludhiana, Punjab, India
(2) PUNJABI UNIVERSITY, Patiala, Punjab, India
parminder2u@gmail.com, gslehal@gmail.com

ABSTRACT

Speech based interface can play a vital role for the successful implementation of computerized systems for masses. As a tool for this purpose, effort has been made for the development of a Text-To-Speech (TTS) synthesis system for Punjabi language written in Gurmukhi script. Concatenative method has been used to develop this TTS system. Syllables have been reported as good choice of speech unit for speech databases of many languages. Since Punjabi is a syllabic language, so syllables has been selected as the basic speech unit for this TTS system, which preserves within unit co-articulation effects. System involves development of algorithms for pre-processing, schwa deletion and syllabification of the input Punjabi text, as well as speech database for Punjabi. A syllable based Punjabi speech database has been developed that stores articulations of syllable sounds at starting, middle and end positions of the word for producing natural sounding synthesized speech.

KEYWORDS : Speech synthesis, Punjabi speech database, Punjabi syllables.

*Proceedings of COLING 2012: Demonstration Papers*, pages 409–416,
COLING 2012, Mumbai, December 2012.

# 1 Introduction

Text-To-Speech (TTS) synthesis system has extensive range of applications in everyday life. In order to makê the computerized systems more interactive and helpful to the users, especially physically and visibly impaired and illiterate masses, the TTS synthesis systems are in great demand for the Indian languages. Concatenative speech synthesis technique has been used for the development of this system. Punjabi is a syllabic language (Singh, 2002), so syllables has been selected as the basic speech units and output waveform is generated by concatenating the syllable sounds, which preserves within unit co-articulation effects (Raghavendra, Desai, Yegnanarayana, Black, & Prahallad, 2008; Narayana & Ramakrishnan, 2007). Syllable sounds in different contexts have been marked in pre-recorded sound file and stored in the speech database to get natural sounding synthesized speech.

## 1.1 Research background

### 1.1.1 Punjabi language

Punjabi is an Indo-Aryan language spoken by more than hundred million people those are inhabitants of the historical Punjab region (in north western India and Pakistan) and in the Diasporas particularly Britain, Canada, North America, East Africa and Australia. It is written from left to right using Gurmukhi (an abugida derived from the *Laṇḍā* script and ultimately descended from Brahmi script) as well as Shahmukhi (a version of the Arabic script) scripts. This TTS system for Punjabi language has been developed for Gurmukhi script. In Gurmukhi script, which follows the *"one sound-one symbol"* principle, the Punjabi language has thirty eight consonants, ten non-nasal vowels and same numbers of nasal vowels (see Figure 1) (Singh & Lehal, 2010).

ਸ ਹ ਕ ਖ ਗ ਘ ਙ
ਚ ਛ ਜ ਝ ਞ ਟ ਠ ਡ ਢ ਣ
ਤ ਥ ਦ ਧ ਨ ਪ ਫ ਬ ਭ ਮ
ਯ ਰ ਲ ਵ ੜ ਸ਼ ਖ਼ ਗ਼ ਜ਼ ਫ਼ ਲ਼
} Consonants

ਇ ਈ ਏ ਐ ਅ ਆ ਔ ਉ ਊ ਓ Non-nasal Vowels
ਇੰ ਈਂ ਏਂ ਐਂ ਅੰ ਆਂ ਔਂ ਉਂ ਊਂ ਓਂ Nasal Vowels

FIGURE 1 – Punjabi consonants and vowels

### 1.1.2 Punjabi syllables

Defining syllable in a language is a complex task. There are many theories available in phonetics and phonology to define syllable. In phonetics, the syllables are defined based upon the articulation (Krakow, 1999). However in phonological approach, the syllables are defined by the different sequences of the phonemes. So, combination of phonemes gives rise to next higher unit called syllable. Further, combination of syllables produces larger units like morphemes and words. So, syllable is a unit of sound which is larger than phoneme and smaller than word. In every language, certain sequences of phonemes and hence syllables are recognized. Using these phonetic sequences and hence structures, all possible syllables can be formed those have been discovered so far in ancient and recent literary works. In addition, all theoretically possible syllables can be composed that may or may not yet be used in a language, but valid in the sense that these follow rendering rules for the language at present (Joshi, Shoff, & Mudur, 2003). A syllable must have a vowel, without vowel, syllable cannot exist. In Punjabi seven types of syllables are recognized (Singh, 2002) – V, VC, CV, VCC, CVC, CVCC and CCVC (where V and C represents vowel and consonant respectively), which combine in turn to produce words. The occurrence of syllables of last type CCVC is very rare, and has not been considered in the present work.

Punjabi language has thirty eight consonants, ten non-nasal vowels and same numbers of nasal vowels; so, the above said seven syllable types results 11,27,090 syllables in Punjabi with non-nasal vowels and the same number of syllables with nasal vowels and thus giving total of 22,54,180 syllables in Punjabi.

### 1.1.3 Schwa deletion in Punjabi language

Schwa is a mid-central vowel that occurs in unstressed syllables. Phonetically, it is a very short neutral vowel sound, and like all vowels, its precise quality varies depending on its adjacent consonants. Each consonant in Punjabi (written in Gurmukhi script) is associated with one of the vowels. Other vowels, except schwa ('ਅ' the third character of Punjabi alphabet and written as [ə] in International Phonetic Alphabet (IPA) transcription), are overtly written diacritically or non-diacritically around the consonant; however schwa vowel is not explicitly represented in orthography. The orthographical representation of any language does not provide any implicit information about its pronunciation and is mostly ambiguous and indeterminate with respect to its exact pronunciation. The problem in many of the languages is mainly due to the existence of schwa vowel that is sometimes pronounced and sometimes not, depending upon certain morphological factors. In order to determine the proper pronunciation of words, it is necessary to identify which schwas are to be deleted and which are to be retained. *Schwa deletion* is a phonological phenomenon where schwa is absent in the pronunciation of a particular word, although ideally it should have been pronounced (Choudhury, Basu, & Sarkar, 2004). The process of schwa deletion is one of the complex and important issue for grapheme-to-phoneme conversion, which in turn is required for the development of a high quality text-to-speech (TTS) synthesizer. In order to produce natural and intelligible speech, the orthographic representation of input has to be augmented with additional morphological and phonological information in order to correctly specify the contexts in which schwa vowel is to be deleted or retained (Narasimhan, Sproat, & Kiraz, 2004).

Mostly phonological schwa deletion rules have been proposed in literature for Indian languages. These rules take into account morpheme-internal as well as across morpheme-boundary information to explain this phenomenon (Narayana & Ramakrishnan, 2007). The morphological analysis can improve the accuracy of schwa deletion algorithm which is a diachronic and sociolinguistic phenomenon (Singh, 2002; Singh & Lehal, 2010). The syllable structure and stress assignment in conjunction with morphological analysis can also be used to predict the presence and absence of schwa (Tyson & Nagar, 2009).

Vowels, except schwa ([ਅ]), are represented diacritically when these come along with consonants (known as half vowels), otherwise as such. The consonant sound varies according to the vowel attached to consonant. For example, consonant [ਸ] conjoined with vowel [ਈ] (having diacritic ੀ) results a single orthographic unit "ਸੀ", having pronunciation of a consonant-vowel sequence /ਸ+ਈ/ (/si/) however when this consonant comes with vowel [ਆ] the resulting single unit [ਸਾ] will be pronounced as /ਸ+ਆ/ (/sā/).

Consonants represented in orthography without any attached diacritic, basically have the associated inherent schwa vowel that is not represented diacritically. While pronouncing any written word, the speaker retains the intervening schwa vowel associated with a consonant where required and eliminate it from pronunciation where it is not required. In Punjabi, inherent schwa following the last consonant of word is elided. For example, Punjabi word "ਸੜਕ" ([sədəkə] means road) pronounced as \ ਸ ਅ ੜ ਕ \ (\s ə d k\) is represented orthographically with only the consonant characters [ਸ], [ੜ] and [ਕ]. Schwa following the last consonant [ਕ] is deleted as per rule said above and deletion of schwa following the second consonant [ੜ] makes the word monosyllabic of type CVCC (Consonant-Schwa-Consonant-Consonant).

## 2 Implementation

The working of this Punjabi TTS system can be divided into two modules: Offline Process and Online Process. These two subparts are discussed in the following subsections.

### 2.1 Offline process

Offline process of this TTS system involved development of the Punjabi speech database. In order to minimize the size of speech database, effort has been made to select a minimal set of syllables covering almost whole Punjabi word set. To accomplish this all Punjabi syllables have been statistically analyzed on the Punjabi corpus having more than hundred million words. Interesting and very important results have been obtained from this analysis those helped to select a relatively smaller syllable set (about first ten thousand syllables (0.86% of total syllables)) of most frequently occurring syllables having cumulative frequency of occurrence less than 99.81%, out of 1156740 total available syllables (Singh & Lehal, 2010). An algorithm has been developed based on the set covering problem for selecting the minimum number of sentences containing above selected syllables for recording of sound file in which syllable positions are marked. The developed Punjabi speech database is having starting and end positions of the selected syllable-sounds labeled carefully in pre-recorded sound file. As the pronunciation of a syllable varies depending on its position (starting, middle or end) in the word, so separate entries for these three positions has been made in the database for each syllable. In order to increase the naturalness of the system a good number of most frequently occurring words of corpus have been stored in the database as such.

### 2.2 Online process

Online process is responsible for pre-processing of the input text, schwa deletion, syllabification and then searching the syllables in speech database. First module, *Pre-processing* involves expansion of abbreviations, numeric figures and special symbols etc. present in the input text to the full word form, so that these should be spoken correctly.

Second module, *Schwa Deletion* is an important step for the development of a high quality Text-To-Speech synthesis system. During utterance of words not every schwa following a consonant is pronounced. For proper pronunciation of word, schwas which are not to be uttered have to be identified in the orthographic form of word for deletion. A rule based schwa deletion algorithm has been developed for Punjabi. These rules are based on mainly three parameters: grammatical constraints, inflectional rules and morphotactics of Punjabi language, which play important role for identification of schwa to be deleted for correct pronunciation of input word. For example, the vowel-consonant pattern for Punjabi word "ਮਰਦ" ([mərədə] means man) is CCC. Grammatically, there must be schwa vowel following each consonant in Punjabi but the word's pronunciation specifies the existence of schwa [ə] /ਅ/ sound after the first consonant only. So, schwa following the first consonant [ਮ] will be retained, however schwa vowels following the second [ਰ] and third [ਦ] consonants will be deleted. The accuracy of developed schwa deletion algorithm is about 98.27% (Singh & Lehal, 2011).

Third module, *Syllabification* of the words of input text is a challenging task. A universal tendency for syllables to have onsets has long been claimed in phonological theory. This preference is built into rule based approaches to syllabification formulated, for example, as the onset first principle (Kahn) or the core syllabification principle (Clements) (Chiosain, Welby & Espesser, 2012). A rule based syllabification algorithm has been developed, which syllabifies the input word into the corresponding syllables. Syllabification rules are mostly language specific. For syllabification the phonotactic constraints of Punjabi have been followed. So, rules have been devised based on the position of vowels and consonants in a word, to segment input word into corresponding syllables. For example, table 1 below shows syllabification of some words; where C, V and n stands for consonant, vowel and nasal respectively.

| **Input word** | **CV pattern of input word (after Schwa deletion)** | **Output of Syllabification module** | **CV pattern of word syllables** |
|---|---|---|---|
| ਆਇਆ | VVV | ਆ ਇ ਆ | V V V |
| ਇੰਗਲੈਂਡ | VnCCvnC | ਇੰਗ ਲੈਂਡ | VnC CvnC |
| ਸਮਾਜਿਕ | CSCvCvC | ਸ ਮਾ ਜਿਕ | CS Cv CvC |
| ਕਰਵਾਉਣ | CSCCvVC | ਕਰ ਵਾ ਉਣ | CSC Cv VC |
| ਰਾਜਨੀਤਕ | CvCCvCC | ਰਾਜ ਨੀਤਕ | CvC CvCC |
| ਟੂਰਨਾਮੈਂਟ | CvCCvCvnC | ਟੂਰ ਨਾ ਮੈਂਟ | CvC Cv CvnC |
| ਪਾਕਿਸਤਾਨ | CvCvCCvC | ਪਾ ਕਿਸ ਤਾਨ | Cv CvC CvC |
| ਅਧਿਕਾਰੀਆਂ | VCvCvCvVn | ਅ ਧਿ ਕਾ ਰੀ ਆਂ | V Cv Cv Cv Vn |
| ਵਿਦਿਆਰਥੀਆਂ | CvCvVCCvVn | ਵਿ ਦਿ ਆਰ ਥੀ ਆਂ | Cv Cv VC Cv Vn |

TABLE 1 – Output of the syllabification module.

The developed syllabification module has been tested on about first 10,000 most frequently used words of Punjabi, selected from a Punjabi corpus having about 1,04,42,574 total words and 2,32,565 unique words. It has been found that accuracy of the syllabification module is about 97.89%.

Syllables of input text are first searched in the Punjabi speech database for corresponding syllable-sound positions in recorded sound file and then these syllable sounds are concatenated. Normalization of the synthesized Punjabi sound is done in order to remove discontinuities at the concatenation points and hence producing smooth and natural sound. Synchronous-OverLap-Add (SOLA) method is used to achieve a shorter or longer playback time than original waveform. A good quality sound is being produced by this TTS system for Punjabi language.

## Conclusions

A fairly good quality Punjabi Text-To-Speech synthesis system has been developed for Punjabi. During the development of this TTS system, it has been observed that for a concatenative speech synthesis system, the important features that must be taken care of are: selection of basic speech unit for concatenation, statistical analysis of selected speech units on corpus, corpus must be carefully selected and unbiased; and marking of the speech units in recorded sound file. The last one is most important and quality of the output speech depends, how carefully speech units are marked in recorded sound file. Correct schwa deletion is very important for natural pronunciation of the output synthesized speech. Schwa basically controls articulation of the sound wave and hence pronunciation. Syllabification process is language specific and involves grammatical rules of the language as well as knowledge of how local inhabitants syllabify a word during its utterance in a natural way. Syllabification with good accuracy is providing a strong base for high quality of the output synthesized speech.

## References


Chiosain, M.N., Welby, P. & Espesser, R. (2012). Is the syllabification of Irish a typological exception? An experimental study. *Journal of Speech Communication*, 54(1): 68–91.

Choudhury, M., Basu, A. & Sarkar, S. (2004). A Diachronic Approach for Schwa Deletion in Indo Aryan Languages. In *Workshop of the ACL Special Interest Group on Computational Phonology (SIGPHON), Association for Computations Linguistics*, pages 20–27, Barcelona.

Joshi, R.K., Shoff, K. & Mudur, S.P. (2003). A unified phonemic code based scheme for effective processing of Indian Languages. In *23rd Internationalization and Unicode Conference,* Prague.

Krakow, R.A. (1999). Physiological organization of syllables: a review. *Journal of Phonetics*, 27: 23–54.

Narasimhan, B., Sproat, R. & Kiraz, G. (2004). Schwa-Deletion in Hindi Text-to-Speech Synthesis. *International Journal of Speech Technology*, 7(4): 319–333.

Narayana, M.L., Ramakrishnan, A.G. (2007). Defining syllables and their stress in Tamil TTS corpus. In *Workshop on Image and Signal Processing (WISP-2007)*, pages 92–95, IIT Guwahati, India.

Raghavendra, E.V., Desai, S., Yegnanarayana, B., Black, A.W., & Prahallad K. (2008). Global syllable set for building speech synthesis in Indian languages. In *IEEE Workshop on Spoken Language Technologies (SLT-2008)*, pages 49–52, Goa, India.

Singh, P. (2002). *Sidhantik Bhasha Vigeyan*, 4th Edition, Madan Publications, India, pages 371–372.

Singh, P. & Lehal, G.S. (2010). Statistical Syllables Selection Approach for the Preparation of Punjabi Speech Database. In *5th International Conference for Internet Technology and Secured Transactions (ICITST-2010)*, pages 1–4, London, UK, IEEE.

Singh, P. & Lehal, G.S. (2011). A Rule Based Schwa Deletion Algorithm for Punjabi TTS System. In *International Conference on Information Systems for Indian Languages (ICISIL-2011),* vol. 139, pages 98–103, Patiala, India, Springer.

Tyson, N.R. & Nagar, I. (2009). Prosodic Rules for Schwa-Deletion in Hindi Text-to-Speech Synthesis. *International Journal of Speech Technology*, 12(1): 15–25.

# EXCOTATE: An Add-on to MMAX2 for Inspection and Exchange of Annotated Data

*Tobias STADTFELD* *Tibor KISS*
Sprachwissenschaftliches Institut
Ruhr-Universität Bochum
stadtfeld@linguistics.rub.de, kiss@linguistics.rub.de

ABSTRACT

In this paper, we present an add-on called EXCOTATE for the annotation tool MMAX2. The add-on interacts with annotated data stored in and spread over different MMAX2 projects. The data can be inspected, revised, and analyzed in a tabular format, and will be reintegrated into MMAX2 projects afterwards. It is based on Microsoft Excel with extensive usage of the script language Visual Basic for Applications.

KEYWORDS : ANNOTATION, INSTANCE-BASED REPRESENTATION, MMAX2, EXCEL, ADD-ON

*Proceedings of COLING 2012: Demonstration Papers*, pages 417–422,
COLING 2012, Mumbai, December 2012.

## 1 The Scenario

Annotation mining sometimes requires the manual annotation of large data sets, such as the annotation of preposition senses (cf. A. Müller et al., 2011). These annotations have been carried out with the annotation tool MMAX2 (C. Müller and Strube 2006). It allows the declaration of multiple layers and stores data in an xml-standoff format. As the annotation scheme for preposition senses is itself subject to evolutionary development, already annotated data require manual re-annotation or correction. It is thus necessary to inspect, and quite often also to re-annotate already processed sentences containing prepositions under investigation.

Due to the design of MMAX2, the search for particular annotations in the vast amount of data is cumbersome. In some applications, searching becomes practically impossible since the data has to be spread over various MMAX2 projects to allow efficient processing within MMAX2.

To overcome this inherent problem of MMAX2 and to allow inspection and analysis from a different – tabular – perspective, we have developed an annotation add-on to MMAX2 based on *Microsoft Excel* (Microsoft Corporation, 2010). It is used to search for and correct instances that require a do-over of their current annotation. The name of the add-on – EXCOTATE – reflects its basis as well as its purpose.

## 2 General Requirements and Advantages of Microsoft Excel

With MMAX2 at hand, we did not intend to create a new stand-alone annotation tool, and hence introduce an additional data format. Such a format would require the synchronization of existing MMAX2-project files, as well as the duplication of the scheme files that describe the encoding rules in an MMAX2 project. Due to the frequency by which changes in the annotation scheme are conducted, this would have resulted in high maintenance and was therefore considered unacceptable.

The choice of Microsoft Excel as a basis for an add-on was guided by several considerations. Using commercial spreadsheet software might be considered controversial, but it offers various advantages over a "from the scratch" approach. Many recent tools in computational linguistics have been implemented and maintained by (PhD) students. This has the major disadvantage that support, bug fixing and the development of extensions come to a rapid end when the students in question move on to different tasks. This disadvantage can be at least partially circumvented, if one chooses popular and widely common software as a foundation and reduces further custom modifications to a minimum.

Besides these rather general thoughts, Microsoft Excel offers several technical advantages making it almost ideal for annotating instance-based data:

*Data validation* is a core functionality of Excel, ensuring that an annotator can only set values for attributes that have been defined legitimate.

*Sorting* and *filtering* are also core functions and quite helpful if one wants to investigate the data in more detail; a task which in most annotation tools can only be fulfilled, if at all, when using a search query with its own syntax to be learned upfront.

Further, *exporting* data from a spreadsheet to a data-mining tool is almost trivial, as all popular tools provide CSV-support.

Finally, Microsoft Excel offers the possibility to encode hierarchical graphs using the script language *Visual Basic for Applications* (Microsoft Dynamics, 2006). With the help of dynamically created VBA code, changes to one attribute lead to automatic changes of dependent attributes.

## 3 Description of the Data and Scripts

In the following, we will offer descriptions of the input data, the scripts that are used to automatically build EXCOTATE instances from the data and the functionality of EXCOTATE itself.

### 3.1 MMAX2 Projects and Scheme Files

In light of performance limitations and experienced drawbacks in lucidity when opening too many sentences within the annotation tool, we decided to restrict individual MMAX2 projects to a maximum number of 50 sentences. All data are stored as MMAX2 projects after a completed processing step; all files created besides MMAX2 projects are mere temporary files.

The meaning of the preposition is the key-feature in the annotation task. Hence, it forms the basis for an instance-based representation of the data in a shallow spreadsheet. Every MMAX2 project contains an xml file that declares all tokens contained in this particular project along with an id. All additional layers of information are optional. We declared several layers, two of which are the sentence and the preposition-meaning layer. Each layer is stored in an individual xml file, in which the *ids* of the words spanned by this particular layer are being named along with attributes and their values. Figure 1 exemplifies this for the preposition-meaning layer.

```
<markable id="markable_1" span="word_298" mmax_level="prep-meaning" modal="+" local ="na" (...) />
<markable id="markable_2" span="word_1373" mmax_level="prep-meaning" modal="na" local ="na" (...) />
```

FIGURE 1 – Sample of two markables in a preposition-meaning-markable file.

The attributes for annotation in a MMAX2 project are declared within the correspondent scheme file of a layer. Here, the availability of specific attributes can be defined as being dependent on another attribute showing a particular value. This results in the provision of decision trees in which the annotator may choose the next steps for a precise interpretation of a preposition (cf. A. Müller et al., 2011). For example, *he is working at a school* would be a candidate to be classified as *local* (mother node) in general and also as (localized at an) *institution* (child node). We currently use sub-trees with a depth of one to a total depth of over seven chained attributes and their respective values in one tree (cf. A. Müller 2012).

### 3.2 Creation of an EXCOTATE Instance

The creation of an EXCOTATE instance containing the information of several MMAX2 projects should be automated. It therefore requires some sort of script, which acts as a transformation between both programs. To create Excel files from within a script, we decided to use the Perl module *Spreadsheet::WriteExcel*[1]. This module offers support for all necessary functions within Excel, as data validation, auto filtering and the automated insertion of VBA code into an Excel worksheet, and the ability to declare write-protected cells. We create *xls* as well as *xlsx* versions.[2]

[1] Available on www.cpan.org

[2] See module *Excel::Writer::XLSX* for xlsx support.

To create an EXCOTATE instance, the first step is to generate a list of all MMAX2 projects to be included in such. Successively, every project is processed by the following steps.

We decided to annotate exactly one preposition per sentence to allow for an instance-based representation of the data. Therefore, the first information to be written into every row into the first of two sheets is the string of the preposition and also a simple continuous number as an id. In addition, the path to the root directory of the MMAX2 project the data originated from is also stored. This step obviously differs in minor details depending on the data to be annotated but the remaining script is generic. If additional layers from a MMAX2 project shall be included into EXCOTATE, these layers have to be declared as parameters and the respective scheme files need to be parsed.

As the scheme files include the declaration of all possible attributes, it is a straightforward task to initialize each attribute as a column and read the respective value of this attribute in the affiliated MMAX2 file. If the attribute is not set, a default value (*na = not applicable*) is used. Figure 2 gives a simplified overview of the first rows of an EXCOTATE worksheet.

| *Basic information* | | | *meta-information layer* | | *preposition-meaning layer* | | |
|---|---|---|---|---|---|---|---|
| id | mmax_path | preposition | annotation status | comment | local | local_ extension | modal |
| 1 | über\match_1-50 | über | done | interesting | na | na | + |
| 2 | über\match_1-50 | über | problem | idiomatic | local_ext | institution | na |

FIGURE 2 – Sample of first worksheet. child of

In our annotation task the layer *meta-information* is used to mark the status of the annotation and to set a comment if needed. The comment attribute is declared as a free text attribute in the scheme file and as such does not possess a default value. The *preposition-meaning* layer lists all attributes one can use for the meaning of the preposition in a given context. We decided to output the context in which the preposition occurred as a string value in an additional attribute column named *context* in the basic information section (not included in Figure 2), while marking the pertinent preposition in the string by an unique symbol (**).

Annotators err during annotation, especially when annotating vast amounts of data. Therefore, we make use of the data validation functionality of Excel by setting a list of legitimate values for every column (attribute). The list can easily be obtained from the already parsed scheme file of the layer the attribute belongs to. Free text attributes, such as the comment attribute, are automatically recognized as such and therefore excluded from this functionality.

The data validation function adds a comfortable drop-down menu to all attributes with more than one value, allowing an easy and error resistant adjustment of the values by an annotator. The first row of the Excel sheet has to be write-protected, as the header should never be changed. In addition, we add the functionality of an *autofilter* to the header, allowing an annotator to only show rows that contain specifically chosen values for an attribute. The *annotation status* attribute is frequently used in this fashion to display only those cases in which the annotation is marked as problematic and therefore should be revised.

As we want to reintegrate all layers included in the sheet back into the original MMAX2 projects, we also need to store the position of the *markables* defined in the MMAX2 files. To do so, we store the information on every span of every *markable* in a second worksheet, but in the same cell the attribute of this *markable* is saved. An ongoing id in both sheets is needed due to the possibility of sorting the rows of the first sheet and is therefore used to keep both sheets synchronized. As the basic information is used for other purposes than storing annotations, we do not need to store any values on their position. The information on the position of a markable can contain only one token or span over multiple words. To maintain the functionality, the second worksheet is never to be changed and is declared write protected as a whole to hinder accidental changes.

Data validation, auto filtering etc. are functions directly amenable from the utilized Perl module. However, when it comes to coding dependencies between specific attributes and their values, these functions reach their limits. Dependencies between attributes occur frequently in our project, since some of our defined meanings show a hierarchical structure. If a most specific branch (which corresponds most closely to specific senses of a preposition) in a decision tree is changed, its mother(s) may change as well. Hence, we would like Excel to automatically adjust all influenced attributes to their corresponding values. So to speak, child nodes should rectify their parents' values if changed. Similarly, changes at a mother node will influence daughter nodes, and this should be reflected as well.

To fulfill these requirements, we analyzed the hierarchies encoded in the scheme files and stored for every attribute (and its values) its respective parent node. In addition, we internally stored which column position holds which attribute. The next step was to automatically create VBA code, which would capture these hierarchies and could be inserted into the Excel sheet to be used during annotation. A working sample of this code is exemplified in Figure 3.

```
Option Explicit
Private Sub Worksheet_Change(ByVal Target As Range)
  'error handler
  On Error GoTo ErrorHandler
  'disable events
  Application.EnableEvents = False
  'how big is the sheet?
  Dim number_of_rows
  number_of_rows = _
  ActiveSheet.Cells(Rows.Count,1).End(xlUp).Row
  'update the attributes
  'first row is header and therefore excluded
  If Target.Row > 1 And number_of_rows >= Target.Row Then
        hierarchy_update Target
  End If
  ErrorHandler:
      Application.EnableEvents = True  're-enable events
End Sub
```

```
Sub hierarchy_update(ByVal Target As Range)
    (...)
    If Target.Column = 7 Then
            update_col_7 Target
    End If
    (...)
End Sub

Sub update_col_7(ByVal Target As Range)
    Dim row As Long
    'only rows changed will be checked
    For row = Selection.Row To _
    Target(Target.Cells.Count).Row
      If Not Cells(row, Selection.Column)._
      EntireRow.Hidden Then
          Cells(row, 6).Value = "local_extension"
      End If
    Next row
End Sub
```

FIGURE 3 – Sample of VBA code to handle hierarchical dependencies between attributes.

While the first subroutine (*Worksheet_Change*) is static, the other routines are created dynamically, depending on the hierarchy coded in the scheme files and the overall number of attributes involved. When a change in the Excel sheet is detected, the subroutine of the changed column is called. For all rows, which have been involved in the change, all parent and child nodes of this particular attribute are set to the logical correct value.

## 3.3 EXCOTATE

After creating an Excel file using the aforementioned script, an annotator can directly use it to re-annotate the data. Annotators are allowed to hide columns they do not need during annotation, e.g. preposition meanings never being used with the preposition at hand, but should of course never delete columns. Also rearranging the columns and the use of copy and paste are problematic. If an annotator wishes to change the value of an attribute on multiple rows, he or she can use the mouse to drag-fill the focused cells.

Even with over 135 columns and several thousands instances, Excel does not show any mentionable performance issues.

### 3.4 Reintegration of EXCOTATE

After correction within EXCOTATE, the sheet needs to be reintegrated into the original MMAX2 projects. Fortunately, reintegration can simply be achieved by completely recreating the layers with the information at hand. Layers not included in the EXCOTATE file, but present in a MMAX2 project remain untouched and are in no need of alteration.

## Conclusion and perspectives

We have described the creation of Excel files from MMAX2 projects in generic terms. Over time extensions have been added to meet specific requirements unique to our project. However, we see EXCOTATE as a quite useful supplement to annotate data in general.

There are some types of annotations that are not as easily transformed from MMAX2 to EXCOTATE and vice versa. Complex annotations, such as syntactic or semantic structures cannot be stored in a flat data representation as it is the case within EXCOTATE. Only with some restrictions and therefore special treatment of these layers, information on layered structures can be processed. Since these are the type of annotations MMAX2 was developed for in the first place, information on these layers are only stored in an EXCOTATE instance when it is crucial input for a statistical analysis.[3]

## References


Kiss, T., Keßelmeier, K., Müller, A., Roch, C., Stadtfeld, T. and Strunk, J. (2010). A logistic regression model of determiner omission in PPs. Paper for *Proceedings of Coling 2010*. Beijing, China.

Microsoft Corporation. (2010). *Microsoft Excel 2010 Product Guide*.

Microsoft Dynamics. (2006). *VBA Developer's Guide. Release 9.0*.

Müller, C. and Strube, M. (2006). Multilevel annotation of linguistic data with MMAX2. In Sabine Braun, Kurt Kohn, and Joybrato Mukherjee, (eds.). *Corpus Technology and Language Pedagogy: New Resources, New Tools, New Methods.* Peter Lang, Frankfurt a.M., pages 197-214.

Müller, A., Roch, C., Stadtfeld, T. and Kiss, T. (2011). Annotating spatial interpretations of German prepositions. In: O'Conner, Lisa (ed.): *2011 Fifth IEEE International Conference on Semantic Computing,* pages 459 - 466. Stanford, CA.

Müller, A. (2012). Location and Path – Annotating Senses of the German Prepositions *auf* and *über*, submitted to Workshop on Semantic Annotation and the Integration and Interoperability of Multimodal Resources and Tools. LREC 2012.


[3] A detailed description of the statistical analysis of the data is to be found in (Kiss et al., 2010).

# Bulgarian Inflectional Morphology in Universal Networking Language

*Velislava STOYKOVA*
INSTITUTE FOR BULGARIAN LANGUAGE - BAS, 52, Shipchensky proh. str., bl. 17, 1113 Sofia, Bulgaria
vstoykova@yahoo.com

ABSTRACT
The paper presents a web-based application of semantic networks to model Bulgarian inflectional morphology. It demonstrates the general ideas, principles, and problems of inflectional grammar knowledge representation used for encoding Bulgarian inflectional morphology in Universal Networking Language (UNL). The analysis of UNL formalism is outlined in terms of its expressive power to present inflection, and the principles and related programming encodings are explained and demonstrated.

KEYWORDS: Morphology and POS tagging, Grammar and formalisms, Underresourced languages.

*Proceedings of COLING 2012: Demonstration Papers*, pages 423–430,
COLING 2012, Mumbai, December 2012.

# 1 Introduction

Modeling inflectional morphology is a key problem for any natural language processing application of Bulgarian language. It can result in a wide range of real applications however different formal models and theories offer different insights for encoding of almost all grammar features, and allow the use of related principles for encoding.

# 2 General problems with applications of word inflectional morphology

The problems with natural language processing applications for word inflectional morphology are generally of two types (i) the problems of language theory at the level of phonology, morphonology, and morphology, and (ii) the adequacy of existing methodologies and techniques to offer the applications capable to interpret the complexity of natural language phenomena. Thus, the context of natural language formal representations and interpretations of inflectional morphology is the logical framework which are capable to deal with regularity, irregularity, and subregularity and have to provide a logical basis for interpreting such language phenomena like suppletion, syncretism, declension, conjugation, and paradigm.

## 2.1 The traditional academic representation and computational morphology formal models of inflectional morphology

The traditional interpretation of inflectional morphology given at the academic descriptive grammar works (Popov and Penchev, 1983) is a presentation of tables. The tables consist of all possible inflected forms of a related word with respect to its subsequent grammar features. The artificial intelligence (AI) techniques offer a computationally tractable encoding preceded by a related semantic analysis, which suggest a subsequent architecture. Representing inflectional morphology in AI frameworks is, in fact, to represent a specific type of grammar knowledge.

The computational approach to both derivational and inflectional morphology is to represent words as a rule-based concatenation of morphemes, and the main task is to construct relevant rules for their combinations. The problem how to segment words into morphemes is central and there are two basic approaches of interpretation (Blevins, 2001). The first is Word and Paradigme (WP) approach wich uses paradigme to segment morphemes. The secound is Item and Agreement (IA) approach which uses sub-word units and morpho-syntactic units for word segmentation. With respect to number and types of morphemes, the different theories offer different approaches depending on variations of either stems or suffixes as follows:

(i) Conjugational solution offers invariant stem and variant suffixes, and

(ii) Variant stem solution offers variant stems and invariant suffix.

Both these approaches are suitable for languages, which use inflection rarely to express syntactic structures, whereas for those using rich inflection some cases where phonological alternations appear both in stem and in concatenating morpheme a "mixed" approach is used to account for the complexity. Also, some complicated cases where both prefixes and suffixes have to be processed require such approach.

We evaluate the "mixed" approach as a most appropriate for the task because it considers both stems and suffixes as variables and, also, can account for the specific phonetic alternations. The additional requirement is that during the process of the inflection all generated inflected rules (both using prefixes and suffixes) have to produce more than one type of inflected forms.

| | | | | | |
|---|---|---|---|---|---|
| **pref1** | **pref2** | **root** | **suff1** | **suff2** | **ending** |

Figure 1: The word structure according to the general linguistic morphological theory.

## 2.2 Interpreting sound alternations

The sound alternations influence the inflectional morphology of almost all part-of-speech of standard Bulgarian language and as a result they form irregular word forms. In fact, we have a rather unsystematically formed variety of regular and irregular sound alternations which is very difficult to be interpreted formally.

The phonetic alternations in Bulgarian are of various types and influence both derivational and inflectional morphology. The general morphological theory offers a segmentation of words (Fig. 1) which consists of root to which prefixes, suffixes or endings are attached. In Bulgarian, all three types of morphemes are used and additional difficulties come from the fact that sound alternations can be occurred both in stems, prefixes, suffixes, and also on their boundaries which suggest extremely complicated solutions.

# 3 The Universal Networking Language

In the UNL approach, information conveyed by natural language is represented as a hypergraph composed of a set of directed binary labelled links (referred to as "relations") between nodes or hypernodes (the "Universal Words"(WS)), which stand for concepts (Uchida and Della Senta, 2005). UWs can also be annotated with "attributes" representing context information (UNL, 2011).

*Universal Words* (UWs) represent universal concepts and correspond to the nodes to be interlinked by "relations" or modified by "attributes" in a UNL graph. They can be associated to natural language open lexical categories (noun, verb, adjective and adverb). Additionally, UWs are organized in a hierarchy (the UNL Ontology), and are defined in the UNL Knowledge Base and exemplified in the UNL Example Base, which are the lexical databases for UNL. As language-independent semantic units, UWs are equivalent to the sets of synonyms of a given language, approaching the concept of "synset" used by the WordNet.

*Attributes* are arcs linking a node to itself. In opposition to relations, they correspond to one-place predicates, i.e., function that take a single argument. In UNL, attributes have been normally used to represent information conveyed by natural language grammatical categories (such as tense, mood, aspect, number, etc). Attributes are annotations made to nodes or hypernodes of a UNL hypergraph. They denote the circumstances under which these nodes (or hypernodes) are used. Attributes may convey three different kinds of information: (i) The information on the role of the node in the UNL graph, (ii) The information conveyed by bound morphemes and closed classes, such as affixes (gender, number, tense, aspect, mood, voice, etc), determiners (articles and demonstratives), etc., (iii) The information on the (external) context of the utterance. Attributes represent information that cannot be conveyed by UWs and relations.

*Relations*, are labelled arcs connecting a node to another node in a UNL graph. They correspond to two-place semantic predicates holding between two UWs. In UNL, relations have

Bulgarian Dictionary

Lemma search

**Statistics**

| Class | UNL-NL Dictionary | | | NL Dictionary |
|---|---|---|---|---|
| | UWs | Lemmas | Polysemy | |
| Adjectives | 288 | 509 | 1.77 | 388 |
| Adverbs | 171 | 229 | 1.34 | 199 |
| Nouns | 694 | 881 | 1.27 | 735 |
| Verbs | 529 | 843 | 1.59 | 682 |
| Other | 0 | 0 | 0.00 | 0 |
| All | 1682 | 2462 | 1.46 | 2004 |

Figure 2: The statistical word distribution of part-of-speech for UNL interpretation of Bulgarian inflectional morphology.

been normally used to represent semantic cases or thematic roles (such as agent, object, instrument, etc.) between UWs.

*UNL-NL Grammars* are sets of rules for translating UNL expressions into natural language (NL) sentences and vice-versa. They are normally unidirectional, i.e., the enconversion grammar (NL-to-UNL) or deconversion grammar (UNL-to-NL), even though they share the same basic syntax.

In the UNL Grammar there are two basic types of rules: (i) Transformation rules - used to generate natural language sentences out of UNL graphs and vice-versa and (ii) Disambiguation rules - used to improve the performance of transformation rules by constraining their applicability.

The UNL offers an universal language-independent and open-source platform for multilingual web-based applications (Boitet and Cardenosa, 2007) available for many laguages (Martins, 2011) including Slavonic languages like Russian (Boguslavsky, 2005) as well.

## 3.1 Representing Bulgarian inflectional morphology in UNL

The UNL specifications offer types of grammar rules particularly designed to interpret inflectional morphology both with respect to prefixes, suffixes, infixes, and to sound alternations taking place during the process of the inflection. Thus, UNL allows two types of transformation inflectional rules: (i) A-rules (affixation rules) apply over isolated word forms (as to generate possible inflections) and (ii) L-rules (linear rules) apply over lists of word forms (as to provide transformations in the surface structure). Affixation rules are used for adding morphemes to a given base form, so to generate inflections or derivations. There are two types of A-rules: (i) simple A-rules involve a single action (such as prefixation, suffixation, infixation and replacement), and (ii) complex A-rules involve more than one action (such as circumfixation).

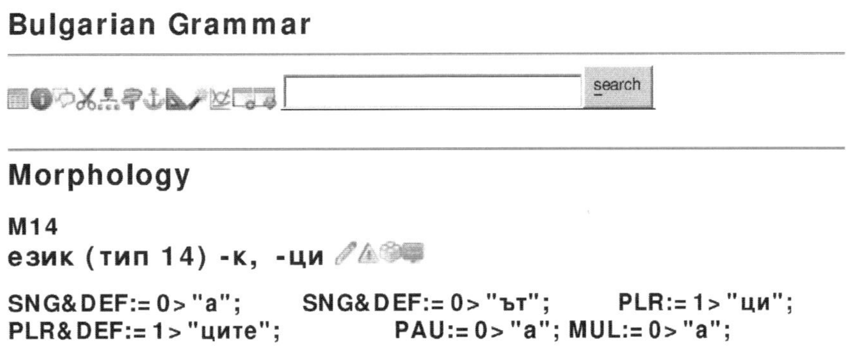


Figure 3: The inflectional rules definitions for the word "‘ezik'".

There are four types of simple A-rules: (i) prefixation, for adding morphemes at the beginning of the base form, (ii) suffixation, for adding morphemes at the end of the base form, (iii) infixation, for adding morphemes to the middle of the base form, (iv) replacement, for changing the base form.

The analysed application of Bulgarian inflectional morphology (Noncheva and Stoykova, 2011) was made within the framework of the project 'The Little Prince Project' of the UNDL Foundation aimed to develop UNL grammar and lexical resources for several european languages based on the book 'The Little Prince'. Hence, the lexicon is limitted to the text of the book. It offers the interpretation of inflectional morphology for the nouns, adjectives, numerals, pronouns (Stoykova, 2012) and verbs which uses A-rules (Fig. 2).

The UNL interpretation of nouns defines 74 word inflectional types. Every inflectional type uses its own rules to generate all possible inflected forms for the features of number and definiteness. Here we are analysing the inflectional rules of Bulgarian word for *language* "ezik"[1].

`base form = ezik` `SNG&DEF:=0>"a";`

`SNG&DEF:=0>"ut"; PLR:=1>"ci";`

`PLR&DEF:=1>"cite"; PAU:=0>"a"; MUL:=0>"a";`

The inflectional rules for generation of all inflected word forms are defined as separate rules (Fig. 3). The suffixation rules for adding: `SNG&DEF:=0>"a";`, `SNG&DEF:=0>"ut";`, `PAU:=0>"a";`, `MUL:=0>"a";` use the idea of introducing stems to which the inflectional morphemes are added. A-rules for replacement also reflect the idea of introducing inflectional stems consisting of root plus infix `PLR:=1>"ci";`, `PLR&DEF:=1>"cite";`.

The generated inflected word forms of the example Bulgarian word for *language* "‘ezik'" are given at the Fig.4. In general, the UNL lexical information presentation scheme underlie the idea of WordNet for semantic hierarchical representation and allows the presentation of synonyms and the translation of the word as well, which also is introduced in the application.

Adjectives are defined by using 14 word inflectional types and every inflectional type uses its own rules to generate all possible inflected forms for the features of gender, number and def-

[1] Here and elsewhere in the description we use Latin alphabet instead of Cyrillic. Because of mismatching between both some of Bulgarian phonological alternations are assigned by two letters instead of one in Cyrillic alphabet.

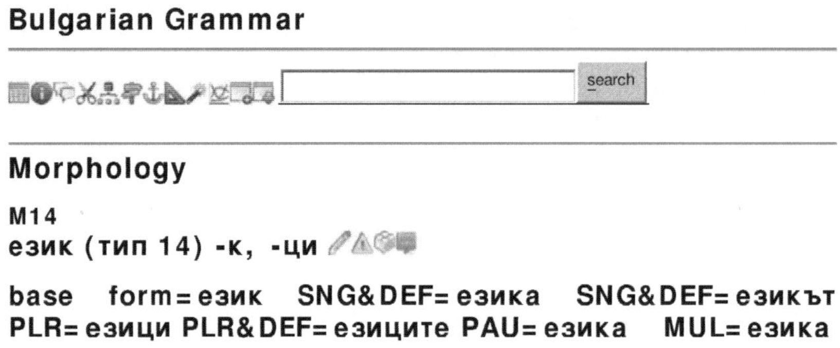


Figure 4: The word forms of the word "“ezik”" generated by the system.

initeness. The interpretation of numerals and pronouns consist of 5 and 6 word inflectional types, respectively. Alternatively, verbs are represented in 48 inflectional types. The UNL interpretation, also, offers syntactic and semantic account. The syntacitc account is represented by 21 syntactic rules for subcategorization frame and linearization, and rules to define the semantic relations.

In general, the UNL interpretation of Bulgarian inflectional morphology offers a sound alternations interpretation mostly by the use of A-rules. The inflectional rules are defined without the use of hierarchinal inflectional representation even they define the related inflectional types. The sound alternations and the irregularity are interpreted within the definition of the main inflectional rule.

The UNL application, also, represents a web-based intelligent information and knowledge management system which allows different types of semantic search with respect to the context like semantic co-occurrence relations search, keywords or key concepts search, etc.

## Conclusion

The demonstrated application of Bulgarian inflectional morphology uses the semantic networks formal representation schemes and the UNL as a formalism. However, it encodes the inflectional knowledge using both the expressive power and the limitations of the formalism used. The UNL knowledge representation scheme offers well defined types of inflectional rules and differentiates inflectional, semantic, and lexemic hierarchies. The treatment of inflectional classes as nodes in the inflectional hierarchy is used extensively, as well.

The application is open for further improvement and development by introducing additional grammar rules and by enlarging the database for the use in different projects.

## References

(2011). URL http://www.undl.org.

Blevins, J. (2001). Morphological paradigms. *Transactions of the Philosophical society*, 99:207–210.

Boguslavsky, I. (2005). Some lexical issues of unl. *In J. Cardenosa, A. Gelbukh, E. Tovar (eds.) Universal Network Language: Advances in Theory and Applications. Research on Computing Science*, 12:101–108.

Boitet, C., B. I. and Cardenosa, J. (2007). An evaluation of unl usability for high quality multi-lingualization and projections for a future unl++ language. *In A. Gelbukh, (ed.)* Proceedings of CICLing, Lecture Notes in Computer Sciences, 4394:361–376.

Martins, R. (2011). Le petit prince in unl. *In Proceedings from Language Resources Evaluation Conference 2011*, pages 3201–3204.

Noncheva, V., S. Y. and Stoykova, V. (2011). The little prince project – encoding of bulgarian grammar. http://www.undl.org(UNDL Foundation).

Popov, K., G. E. and Penchev, J. (1983). The Grammar of Contemporary Bulgarian Language *(in Bulgarian)*. Bulgarian Acdemy of Sciences Publishing house.

Stoykova, V. (2012). The inflectional morphology of bulgarian possessive and reflexive-possesive pronouns in universal networking language. *In A. Karahoca and S. Kanbul (eds.) Procedia Technology*, 1:400–406.

Uchida, H., Z. M. and Della Senta, T. (2005). *Universal Networking Language*. UNDL Foundation.

# Central and South-East European Resources in META-SHARE

*Tamás VÁRADI*[1] *Marko TADIĆ*[2]
(1) RESERCH INSTITUTE FOR LINGUISTICS, MTA, Budapest, Hungary
(2) FACULTY OF HUMANITIES AND SOCIAL SCIENCES, ZAGREB UNIVERSITY, Zagreb, Croatia
varadi.tamas@nytud.mta.hu, marko.tadic@ffzg.hr

ABSTRACT

The purpose of this demo is to introduce the Language Resources, Tools and Services (LRTS) that are being prepared within the *Central and South-East European Resources* (CESAR) project. To the computational linguistic community the languages covered by CESAR (Bulgarian, Croatian, Hungarian, Polish, Serbian and Slovakian) were so far considered under-resourced and their language resources and tools being insufficient or hard to obtain, with limited coverage and processing capabilities. The CESAR project, functioning as an integral part of META-NET initiative, aims to change this situation by coordinating all relevant national stakeholders, to enlarge and enhance the existing LRTSs, as well as connect them multi-lingually in various ways. The most important aim of the project is to make all LRTSs for respective languages accessible on-line through the common European LRTS distribution platform META-SHARE. This demo will present how this platform can be used in different scenarios and how researchers or industry partners can easily access CESAR Language Resources, Tools and Services.

KEYWORDS : language resources, language tools, language services, CESAR, META-NET, META-SHARE, Bulgarian, Croatian, Hungarian, Polish, Serbian, Slovakian

*Proceedings of COLING 2012: Demonstration Papers*, pages 431–438,
COLING 2012, Mumbai, December 2012.

## 1 Introduction

The purpose of the paper and the accompanying demonstration is to introduce the Language Resources, Tools and Services (LRTS) that are being prepared within the *Central and South-East European Resources* (CESAR) project. The CESAR project functions as an integral part of the larger, Europe-wide initiative META-NET[1], that tries to coordinate efforts for 30+ European languages in the field of LRTS. META-NET started as a network of excellence in 2010 and after a year it turned into a large META-NET initiative that encompasses and interlinks four EC-funded projects, resulting in a truly Europe-wide conglomerate of computational linguistic and NLP communities. CESAR is one of the projects involved. ***Section 2*** gives a brief description of the project within the META-NET context; ***section 3*** discusses its general aims and describes the META-SHARE [2] platform; ***section 4*** describes the CESAR results obtained so far and demonstrate their availability on-line; finally, the paper ends with a brief conclusion and suggestion for future development.

## 2 General CESAR description

CESAR stands for *Central and South-East European resources*, a CIP ICT-PSP-2010-4 *Theme 6: Multilingual Web* Pilot B type project, funded in 50:50% scheme by EC and national funding sources. The project started on 1$^{st}$ February 2011 and its duration is 24 months. The partners of the project are academic institutions coming from six Central and South-East European countries, namely, Bulgaria, Croatia, Hungary, Poland, Serbia and Slovakia, representing respective languages. Although some of these languages might be considered not to be completely under-resourced any more, still for most of them LRTSs have been developed mostly in a sporadic manner, in response to specific project needs, with relatively little regard to their long-term sustainability, IPR status, interoperability, reusability in different contexts as well as to their potential deployment in multilingual applications. In this respect, CESAR languages should be regarded as under-resourced languages and CESAR is aiming to change this situation.

## 3 Aims

High fragmentation and a lack of unified access to language resources are among key factors that hinder European innovation potential in language technology development and research. In that context the general aims of CESAR are coordinated with other projects in META-NET initiative.

### 3.1 Coordinating stakeholders

Even for languages with relatively well developed LRTSs, it is difficult or in many cases impossible to get access to resources that are scattered around different places, are not accessible online, reside within research institutions and companies and exist as "hidden language resources", similar to the existence of the "hidden web". CESAR wants to

[1] http://www.meta-net.eu.

[2] http://www.meta-share.eu

overcome this situation at the respective national levels by coordinating researchers, industrials and policy makers, and by putting them in their proper roles at the national LRTS landscape.

## 3.2 Actions with LRTSs in CESAR

In principle, the CESAR project doesn't produce new resources, but puts most of its efforts in their upgrading, extending and cross-lingual alignment.

The upgrade task mostly focuses on reaching META-SHARE compliance by upgrade for interoperability (changing annotation format, type, tagset), metadata-related work (creation, enhancement, conversion, standarization) and harmonization of documentation (conversion to open formats, reformatting, linking).

Existing resources are being extended or linked across different sources to improve their coverage and increase their suitability for both research and development work. This task took into account the specific goals of the project, identified gaps in the respective language community, and most relevant application domains. Probably the best example is merging of two pre-existing competitive Polish inflectional lexica (Morfeusz and Morfologik) with different coverage and encoding systems, into one large unified one (Polimorf Inflectional Dictionary).

Cross-lingual alignment of resources is the most demanding task and it will be applied only to a small number of resources close to the end of the project, mostly by producing collocational dictionaries and n-grams from national corpora using the common methodology.

## 3.3 META-SHARE

META-SHARE is a sustainable network of repositories of language data, tools and related web services documented with high-quality metadata, aggregated in central inventories allowing for uniform search and access to resources. Data and tools can be both open and with restricted access rights, free of charge or for-a-fee. META-SHARE targets existing but also new language data, tools and systems required for building and evaluating new technologies, products and services. In this respect, reuse, combination, repurposing and re-engineering of language data and tools play a crucial role.

META-SHARE is on its way to becoming an important component of a language technology marketplace for HLT researchers and developers, language professionals (translators, interpreters, localisation experts, etc.), as well as for industrial players that provide innovative HLT products and services to the markets.

META-SHARE users have a single sign-on account and are able to access everything within the repository. Each language resource has a permanent locator (PID). One of the key features of META-SHARE will be metadata harvesting, allowing for discovering and sharing resources across many repositories.

At the moment there are 1248 language resources, tools or services accessible through META-SHARE and they are distributed over 100+ languages, four main resource types (corpus, lexical/conceptual model, tool/service, language description) and four main media types (text, audio, image, video).

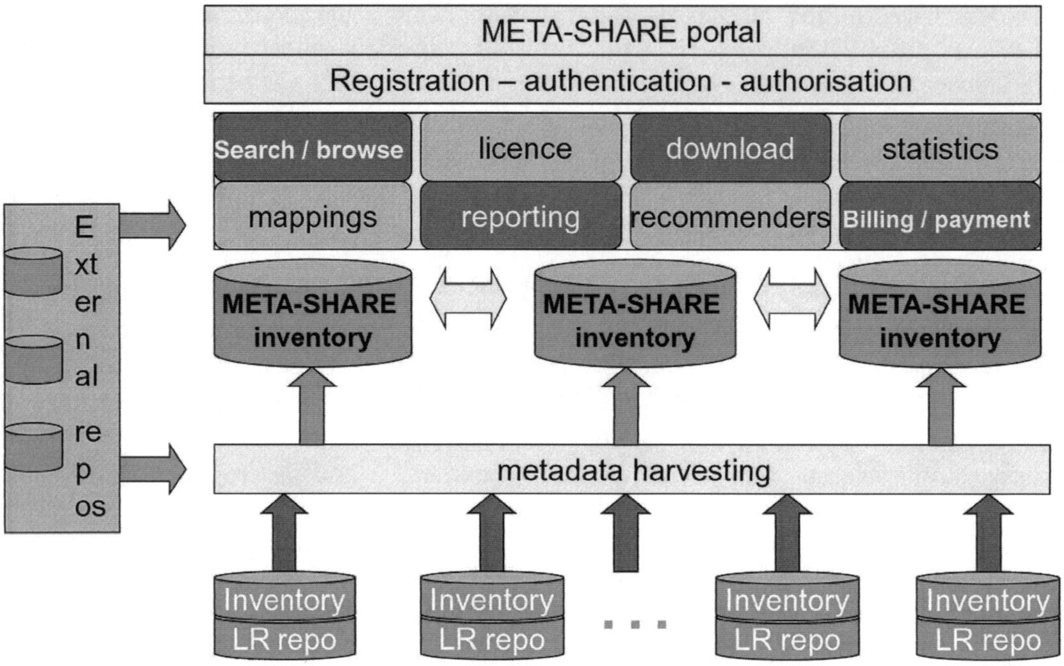


**Figure 1: General structure of META-SHARE (Piperidis 2012)**

Extensive usage of advanced metadata schemata for description enables automatic harvesting and discovery of resources within the network of repositories (Gavrilidou et al. 2012).

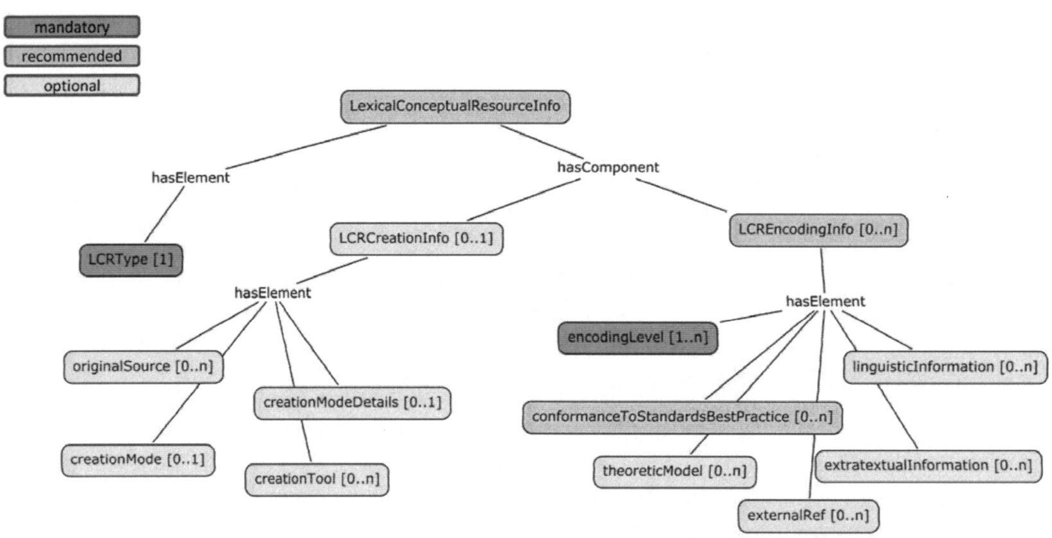


**Figure 2: Metadata schema for Lexical/Conceptual resource (Monachini, 2011)**

## 4 CESAR LRTSs in META-SHARE

The description of CESAR resources were prepared in compliance with the META-SHARE component-based metadata model. The taxonomy of LRTSs includes two-level hierarchy, with general main resource type and type-dependent subclassification. The metadata were prepared by CESAR partners with the intention of providing detailed informaton on each LRTS. It is planned that CESAR LRTSs will be submitted to META-SHARE in three separate batches. So far for the first two batches all relevant metadata have been uploaded in November 2011 and July 2012, with the third planned for January 2013.

Currently, after two batches in CESAR META-SHARE node 127 CESAR LRTSs are accessible, out of which there are 68 corpora, 16 dictionaries, 3 lexicons, 4 wordnets, 8 speech databases and 28 tools, but the number is changing with each new LRTS made accessible through this platform. To illustrate the size of LR in cumulative numbers over six CESAR languages, what is accessible now encompasses 1.7 billion tokens in monolingual corpora, 41.8 million tokens in parallel corpora, and 1.6 million lexical entries/records.

Within the META-SHARE platform a specialised editor for entering metadata about individual LRTS was developed. It enables finetuning the metadata about each resource.

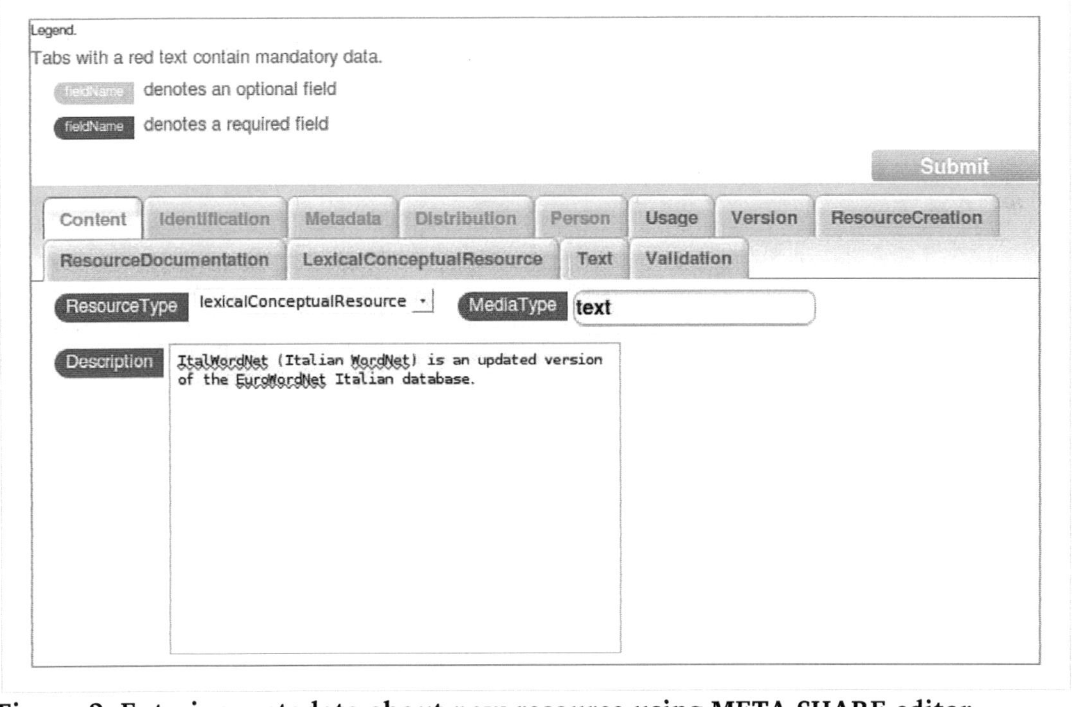


**Figure 3: Entering metadata about new resource using META-SHARE editor**

However, to speed up the development time, CESAR metadata descriptions were prepared in XML format off-line in accordance with the predefined schema and uploaded into the CESAR META-SHARE node, currently operated by IPIPAN, Warsaw for all CESAR partners. Referenced resources are stored by their respective owners.

Once the metadata about LRTS is stored, META-SHARE enables the user to use a search function, so that users can search and browse through the network of repositories in the most flexible way possible, using the panel with different filtering criteria available on the left hand side of the META-SHARE website window. An overall search engine is also available on the top.

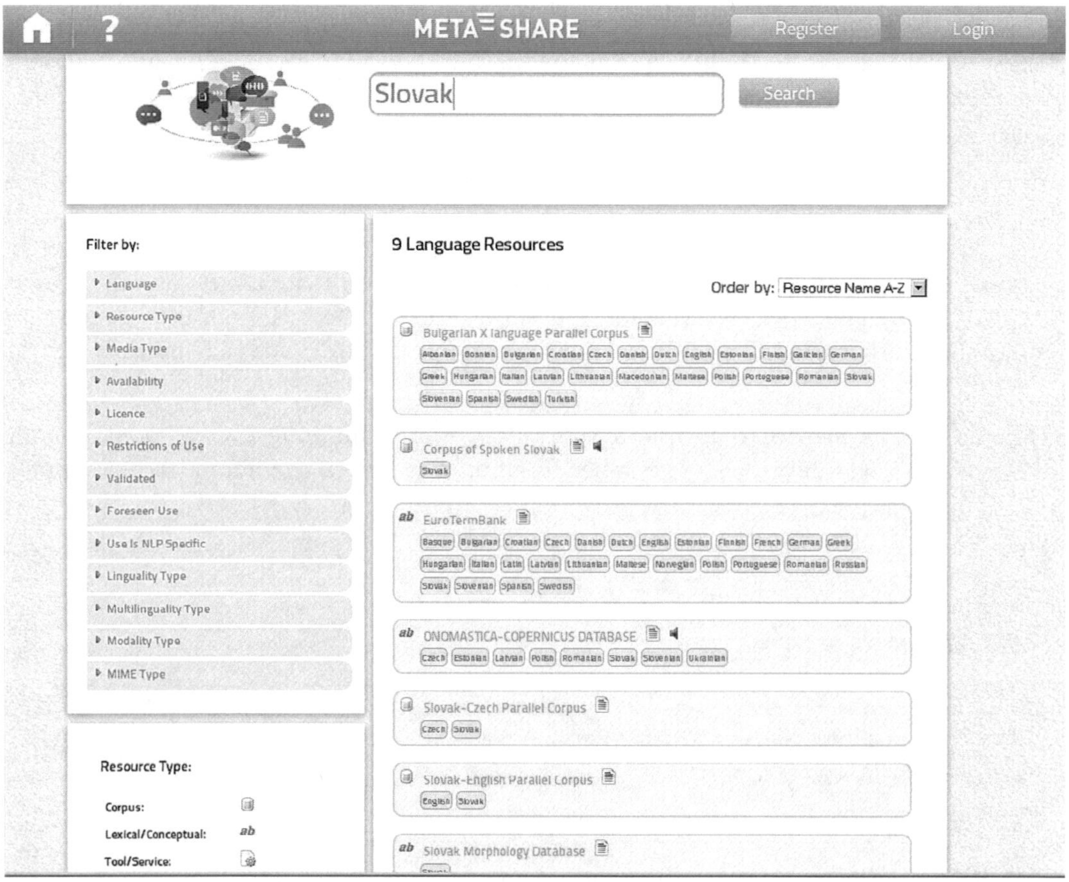


**Figure 4: Search results of a query in META-SHARE**

It is our intention to demonstrate to the research community in computational linguistics and NLP the features and possibilities of META-SHARE platform, particularly stressing the visibility and accessibility of LRTSs for six Central and South-East European under-resourced languages.

## Conclusions and future development

With this demo paper we intend to demonstrate to the computational linguistic community how simple it has become to find in the META-SHARE platform language resources, tools and services for languages covered by CESAR that are usually considered under-resourced or at least not easy to access. The future steps in the CESAR project will include the uploading of the final batch or LRTSs and particularly publishing of NooJ, the open source NLP development environment, newly ported into JAVA under the aegis of the CESAR project.

## Acknowledgment

This paper presents work done in the framework of the project CESAR, funded by DG INFSO of the European Commission through the ICT-PSP Program, Grant agreement no.: 271022.

## References

Federmann, C., Giannopoulou, I., Girardi, C., Hamon, O., Mavroeidis, D., Minutoli, S., Schröder, M. *META-SHARE v2: An Open Network of Repositories for Language Resources including Data and Tools*. LREC2012, (pp. 3300-3303).

Garabík, R., Koeva, S., Krstev, C., Ogrodniczuk, M., Przepiórkowski, A., Stanojević, M., Tadić, M., Váradi, T., Vicsi, K. Vitas, D. & Vraneš, S. (2011) CESAR resources in META-SHARE repository. LTC2011 (pp. 583).

Gavrilidou, M., Labropoulou, P., Desipri, E., Giannopoulou, I., Hamon, O. & Arranz, V. (2012) *The META-SHARE Metadata Schema: Principles, Features, Implementation and Conversion from other Schemas*. Workshop "Describing LRs with Metadata: Towards Flexibility and Interoperability in the Documentation of LR". LREC2012 (pp. 5-12).

Lyse, G. I., Desipri, E., Gavrilidou, M., Labropoulou, P., Piperidis, S. (2012) *META-SHARE overview*. Workshop on the Interoperability of Metadata, Oslo, 2012-06-05.

Monachini, M. (2011) *Metadata for Lexical and Conceptual Resources*. Athens Workshop IPR-Metadata, Athens, 2011-10-10/11.

*META-SHARE documentation & user manual* (2012) [http://www.meta-net.eu/meta-share/].

*META-SHARE knowledge base* (2012) [http://metashare.ilsp.gr/portal/knowledgebase].

Piperidis, S. (2012) The META-SHARE Language Resources Sharing Infrastructure: Principles, Challenges, Solutions. LREC2012, (pp. 36-42)

# Markov Chains for Robust Graph-based Commonsense Information Extraction

*Niket Tandon*[1,4] *Dheeraj Rajagopal*[2,4] *Gerard de Melo*[3]
(1) Max Planck Institute for Informatics, Germany
(2) NUS, Singapore
(3) ICSI, Berkeley
(4) PQRS Research, pqrs-research.org
ntandon@mpi-inf.mpg.de, tsldr@nus.edu.sg, demelo@icsi.berkeley.edu

**Abstract**

Commonsense knowledge is useful for making Web search, local search, and mobile assistance behave in a way that the user perceives as "smart". Most machine-readable knowledge bases, however, lack basic commonsense facts about the world, e.g. the property of ice cream being cold. This paper proposes a graph-based Markov chain approach to extract common-sense knowledge from Web-scale language models or other sources. Unlike previous work on information extraction where the graph representation of factual knowledge is rather sparse, our Markov chain approach is geared towards the challenging nature of commonsense knowledge when determining the accuracy of candidate facts. The experiments show that our method results in more accurate and robust extractions. Based on our method, we develop an online system that provides commonsense property lookup for an object in real time.

KEYWORDS: commonsense knowledge, knowledge-base construction.

*Proceedings of COLING 2012: Demonstration Papers*, pages 439–446,
COLING 2012, Mumbai, December 2012.

## 1 Introduction

For a search query like *"what is both edible and poisonous?"*, most search engines retrieve pages with the keywords *edible* and *poisonous*, but users increasingly expect direct answers like *pufferfish*. If a user wants *hot drinks*, a mobile assistant like Siri should search for cafés, not sleazy bars. Commonsense knowledge (CSK) has a wide range of applications, from high-level applications like mobile assistants and commonsense-aware search engines (Hsu et al., 2006) to NLP tasks like textual entailment and word sense disambiguation (Chen and Liu, 2011).

State-of-the-art sources like Cyc and ConceptNet have limited coverage, while automated information extraction (IE) typically suffers from low accuracy (Tandon et al., 2011), as IE patterns can be noisy and ambiguous. Large-scale high precision IE remains very challenging, and facts extracted by existing systems thus have rarely been put to practical use. Previously, Li et al. (Li et al., 2011) filtered facts extracted from a large corpus by propagating scores from human seed facts to related facts and contexts. However, their method does not handle the very ambiguous patterns typical of CSK. FactRank (Jain and Pantel, 2010) uses a simple graph of facts to find mistyped or out-of-domain arguments. However, they do not exploit the large number of seeds provided by databases like ConceptNet for robust pattern filtering.

In contrast, our work proposes a joint model of candidate facts, seed facts, patterns and relations geared towards Web-scale CSK extractions. Standard IE deals with fact patterns like *<X> is married to <Y>* that are fairly reliable, so the same tuple is rarely encountered for multiple relations simultaneously and the resulting graphs are sparse. Our approach instead deals with CSK IE. Owing to the much more generic nature of patterns, e.g. *<X> is/are/can be <Y>*, an extracted tuple frequently has more than one candidate relation, leading to much more challenging graphs. This paper addresses these challenges with a graph-based Markov chain model that leverages rich Web-scale statistics from one or more large-scale extraction sources in order to achieve high accuracy. We develop an online system that can lookup commonsense property knowledge in real time. We make use of anchored patterns for fast lookup. The system provides a ranked property tag cloud. These scores are obtained using our graph-based Markov chain model.

## 2 Approach

**Tuple Graph Representation.** We follow the standard bootstrapped IE methodology, where seed facts lead to patterns, which in turn induce newly discovered candidate facts (Pantel and Pennacchiotti, 2006). We apply it, however, to Web-scale N-Grams data. For a given candidate fact $T$, a directed *tuple graph* $G_{\mathrm{T}} = (V, E)$ is created. The node set includes nodes for the candidate tuple $T$, for the pattern set $P$ that extracted $T$, for the seed set $S$ that induced $P$, as well as all for the relations $R$ that $s \in S$ belong to, plus an additional artificial relation node `NO_RELATION` to account for noise. A weighted edge from the tuple node $v_t$ to one or more patterns $v_p$ corresponds (after normalization) to a tuple probability $Pr(p|t)$, which is estimated using the pattern frequency in an extraction source like the Google N-grams dataset. The outgoing edge weights of a node are normalized to sum to 1 in order to give us such probabilities. A weighted edge from a pattern node $v_p$ to one or more seed nodes $v_s$ corresponds to $Pr(s|p)$ probabilities, which are estimated as the seed confidence scores delivered by the source of the seeds (ConceptNet in our case). These, too, are normalized as above. A weighted edge from a seed node $v_s$ to a relation node $v_r$ corresponds to the conditional relation probability $Pr(r|s)$, and is estimated as 1 over the number of relations a seed belongs to. A weighted edge from every node to `NO_RELATION` with the edge weight proportional to the average

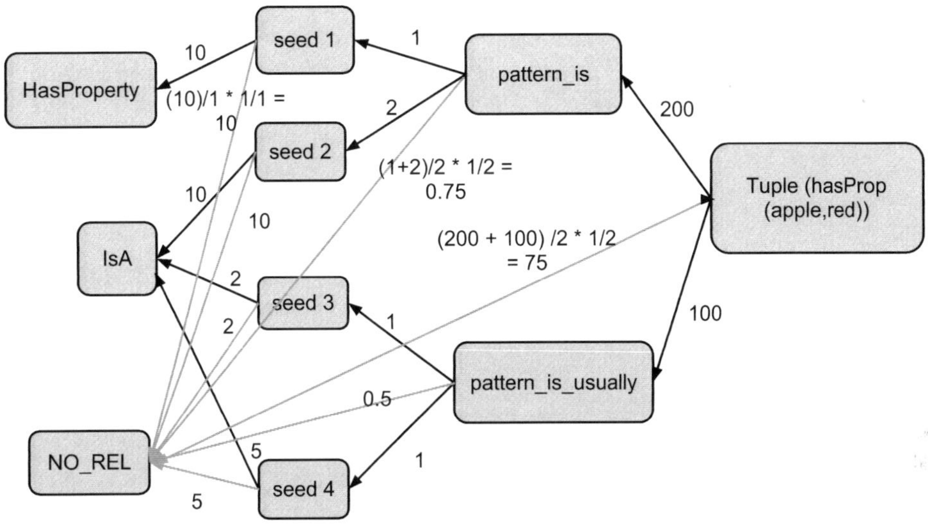


Figure 1: Sample tuple graph with k1=1, k2=1

of outgoing edges of the node and inversely proportional to the number of outgoing edges as $\sum_i out_i/num_{out}{}^{k1} num_{out}^{k2}$, where k1 and k2 are parameters. The first component provides scaling and the second component depicts lower chances of noise when the tuple matches several patterns or when a pattern is generated from several seeds. All other node pairs remain unconnected in the adjacency matrix. Figure 1 shows an example of a tuple graph. One of the desirable properties of this model is that it is localized, allowing us to consider the local graph $G_T$ for each tuple instead of a single graph with potentially millions of seeds, patterns and tuples. Our method can thus be parallelized very easily without additional communication overhead.

**Fact scoring and classification.** The Markov chain consists of states for every node and a transition matrix $Q$. The state transition probabilities in $Q$ are fixed by taking the edge weights and 1) incorporating random transitions to the `NO_RELATION` state in order to account for uncertainty and noise, and 2) additionally incorporating a random restart jump from any $v \in V$ to $v_t$ with probability $\alpha$ (instead of the unmodified transitions with probability $1-\alpha$), in order to satisfy ergodicity properties. One can then prove that a random walk using $Q$ has a well-defined and unique stationary distribution over the nodes. The stationary probability of being at a certain relation node can be leveraged to classify the relation that the tuple belongs to, along with the confidence of classification. When the tuple matches few patterns it is likely to be noisy. For such tuple graphs, `NO_RELATION` has a higher stationary probability because the other edges carry low weights. We use the standard power iteration method to compute the stationary distribution using $Q$. Upon convergence, we determine the relation node $v_r$ whose stationary distribution is the highest. If this is the `NO_RELATION` node, the fact is treated as noise and rejected.

## 3 System

The system takes as input a common noun like `car`, `flower` and provides a scored list of commonsense properties with visualization. The first step involves constructing semi-instatiated patterns(SIP) from the input, i.e. anchoring the input with patterns. For example, `car/NN is very */JJ`, `car/NN seems really */JJ` are some SIPs in the current example. These SIPs are looked up in three resources: Google N-grams corpus, Wikipedia full text and Microsoft N-grams.

For fast lookup, we construct a SIP online lookup system:

- An index lookup over Wikipedia: Wikipedia XML dump was converted to text format and indexed in Lucene with stop-words included. We developed a lookup service takes a SIP as input and fetches relevant text by looking up the index for fast retrieval required for our online system.

- An index lookup over Google N-grams corpus: Google has published a dataset of raw frequencies for n-grams ($n = 1, \ldots, 5$) computed from over 1,024G word tokens of English text, taken from Google's web page search index. In compressed form, the distributed data amounts to 24GB. We developed an index lookup service over Google n-grams such that given a SIP, all relevant Google 5-grams are fetched. 5-grams provide the largest context and are therefore preferred over 4-grams.

- Bing N-grams Web service caller: Microsoft's Web N-gram Corpus is based on the complete collection of documents indexed for the English US version of the Bing search engine. The dataset is not distributed as such but made accessible by means of a Web service described using the WSDL standard. The service provides smoothed n-gram language model based probability scores rather than raw frequencies (Wang et al., 2010). We enable SIP lookup over this service.

The results from these resources are then merged to generate tuple statistics of the form: `x,y,[pattern:score]`. These statistics form the input to our Markov chain method which provides a scored list of facts which are then displayed. Due to the locality of our approach, the system operates online. Figure 2 shows the flow of the system.

Figure 3,4 provides screenshot for the output of property lookup for `flower` and `fish` at pattern support 2.

## 4 Experiments

### 4.1 Experimental Setup

Using ConceptNet, we obtain patterns of the form `X_NN` is very `Y_JJ`, where the subscripts are part-of-speech tags, *X* is the subject, *Y* is the object and *is very* is the pattern predicate. We retrieve the top patterns for a relation extracted from ConceptNet, sorted by frequency (i.e., how often it is present in ConceptNet's OMCS sentences). Such patterns may sometimes be too generic (e.g. *<X> are <Y>*), and lead to noise during fact extraction, but the model accounts for this. For tuple extraction, our primary source of extraction (RW1) are the Google 5-grams data.

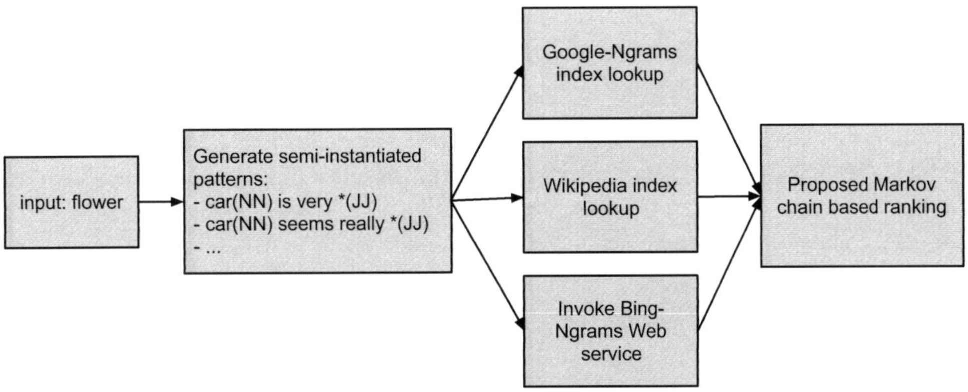


Figure 2: System flow diagram

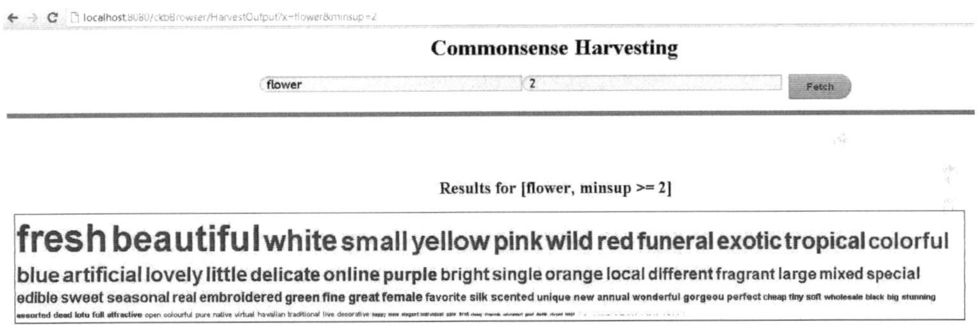


Figure 3: Screenshot for output of: flower

## 4.2 Experimental results

The gold set consists of 200 manually classified facts, 100 negative and 100 positive. The parameter selection for NO_RELATION edge weight is performed over F1 score. The best parameters are obtained at small k1 and large k2 values, see Figure 5. The minimum pattern support is 2, i.e. candidate assertions with less than 2 patterns matched are dropped because they have insufficient evidence.

As baseline, we consider the reliability of a tuple ($r_t$) using the state-of-the-art modified Pointwise Mutual Information (PMI) by (Pantel and Pennacchiotti, 2006). Table 1 reports the evaluation results. The markov chain approaches significantly gain accuracy over the baseline.

Figure 4: Screenshot for output of: fish

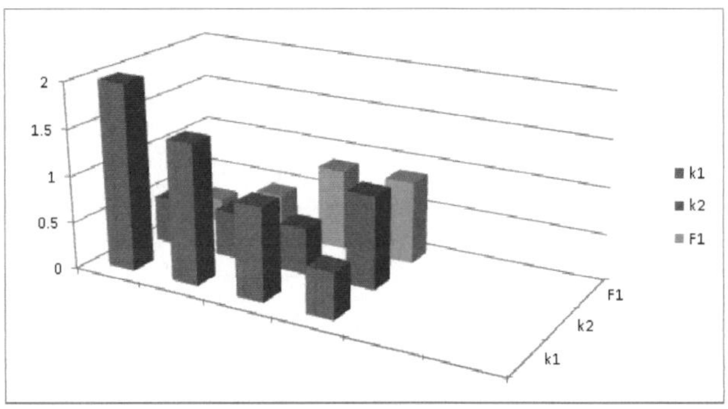


Figure 5: Parameter selection based on F1 measure, small k1 and large k2 performs best

| Method | Precision | Recall | F1 |
|---|---|---|---|
| PMI | 0.84 ± 0.1 | 0.83 | 0.84 |
| Proposed method | 0.88 ± 0.0901 | 0.854 | 0.8861 |

Table 1: Results

## 5 Conclusion

We have presented a novel approach for joint commonsense information extraction. Our method shows clear improvements over several commonly used baselines and can easily be integrated into existing information extraction systems. We have applied our algorithm within a larger setup that also incorporates Web-scale language models. Together, this framework allows us to extract large yet clean amounts of commonsense knowledge from the Web.

## References


Chen, J. and Liu, J. (2011). Combining conceptnet and wordnet for word sense disambiguation. In *Proceedings of 5th International Joint Conference on Natural Language Processing*, pages 686–694, Chiang Mai, Thailand. Asian Federation of Natural Language Processing.

Hsu, M.-H., Tsai, M.-F., and Chen, H.-H. (2006). Query expansion with ConceptNet and WordNet: An intrinsic comparison. In *Information Retrieval Technology*.

Jain, A. and Pantel, P. (2010). Factrank: Random walks on a web of facts. In *Proceedings of the 23rd International Conference on Computational Linguistics*, pages 501–509. Association for Computational Linguistics.

Li, H., Bollegala, D., Matsuo, Y., and Ishizuka, M. (2011). Using graph based method to improve bootstrapping relation extraction. *Computational Linguistics and Intelligent Text Processing*, pages 127–138.

Pantel, P. and Pennacchiotti, M. (2006). Espresso: Leveraging generic patterns for automatically harvesting semantic relations. In *Proceedings of the 21st International Conference on Computational Linguistics and the 44th annual meeting of the Association for Computational Linguistics*, pages 113–120. Association for Computational Linguistics.

Tandon, N., de Melo, G., and Weikum, G. (2011). Deriving a web-scale common sense fact database. In *Twenty-Fifth AAAI Conference on Artificial Intelligence*.

Wang, K., Thrasher, C., Viegas, E., Li, X., and Hsu, B.-j. P. (2010). An overview of microsoft web n-gram corpus and applications. In *Proceedings of the NAACL HLT 2010 Demonstration Session*, pages 45–48, Los Angeles, California. Association for Computational Linguistics.

# Visualization on Financial Terms via Risk Ranking from Financial Reports

Ming-Feng Tsai[1,2] Chuan-Ju Wang[3]
(1) Department of Computer Science, National Chengchi University, Taipei 116, Taiwan
(2) Program in Digital Content & Technologies, National Chengchi University, Taipei 116, Taiwan
(3) Department of Computer Science, Taipei Municipal University of Education, Taipei 100, Taiwan
mftsai@nccu.edu.tw, cjwang@tmue.edu.tw

ABSTRACT
This paper attempts to deal with a ranking problem with a collection of financial reports. By using the text information in the reports, we apply learning-to-rank techniques to rank a set of companies to keep them in line with their relative risk levels. The experimental results show that our ranking approach significantly outperforms the regression-based one. Furthermore, our ranking models not only identify some financially meaningful words but suggest interesting relations between the text information in financial reports and the risk levels among companies. Finally, we provide a visualization interface to demonstrate the relations between financial risk and text information in the reports. This demonstration enables users to easily obtain useful information from a number of financial reports.

KEYWORDS: Text Ranking, Stock Return Volatility, Financial Report, 10-K Corpus.

*Proceedings of COLING 2012: Demonstration Papers*, pages 447–452,
COLING 2012, Mumbai, December 2012.

## 1 Introduction

Financial risk is the chance that a chosen investment instruments (e.g., stock) will lead to a loss. In finance, volatility is an empirical measure of risk and will vary based on a number of factors. This paper attempts to use text information in financial reports as factors to rank the risk of stock returns.

Considering such a problem is a text ranking problem, we attempt to use learning-to-rank techniques to deal with the problem. Unlike the previous study (Kogan et al., 2009), in which a regression model is employed to predict stock return volatilities via text information, our work utilizes learning-to-rank methods to model the ranking of relative risk levels directly. The reason of this practice is that, via text information only, predicting ranks among real-world quantities should be more reasonable than predicting their real values. The difficulty of predicting the values is partially because of the huge amount of noise within texts (Kogan et al., 2009) and partially because of the weak connection between texts and the quantities. Regarding these issues, we turn to rank the relative risk levels of the companies (their stock returns).

By means of learning-to-ranking techniques, we attempt to identify some key factors behind the text ranking problem. Our experimental results show that in terms of two different ranking correlation metrics, our ranking approach significantly outperforms the regression-based method with a confidence level over 95%. In addition to the improvements, through the learned ranking models, we also discover meaningful words that are financially risk-related, some of which were not identified in (Kogan et al., 2009). These words enable us to get more insight and understanding into financial reports.

Finally, in this paper, a visualization interface is provided to demonstrate the learned relations between financial risk and text information in the reports. This demonstration not only enables users to easily obtain useful information from a number of financial reports but offer a novel way to understand these reports.

The remainder of this paper is organized as follows. In Section 2, we briefly review some previous work. Section 3 presents the proposed ranking approach to the financial risk ranking problem. Section 4 reports experimental results and provides some discussions and analyses on the results. We finally conclude our paper and provide several directions for future work.

## 2 Related Work

In the literature, most text ranking studies are related to information retrieval (Manning et al., 2008). Given a query, an information retrieval system ranks documents with respect to their relative relevances to the given query. Traditional models include Vector Space Model (Salton et al., 1975), Probabilistic Relevance Model (Robertson and Sparck Jones, 1988), and Language Model (Ponte and Croft, 1998). In addition to the conventional models, in recent years there have also been some attempts of using learning-based methods to solve the text ranking problem, such as (Freund et al., 2003; Burges et al., 2005; Joachims, 2006), which subsequently brings about a new area of learning to rank in the fields of information retrieval and machine learning. Considering the prevalence of learning-to-rank techniques, this paper attempts to use such techniques to deal with the ranking problem of financial risk.

In recent year, there have been some studies conducted on mining financial reports, such as (Lin et al., 2008; Kogan et al., 2009; Leidner and Schilder, 2010). (Lin et al., 2008) use a weighting scheme to combine both qualitative and quantitative features of financial reports together, and propose a method to predict short-term stock price movements. In the work, a Hierarchical Agglomerative Clustering (HAC) method with K-means updating is employed to improve the purity of the prototypes of financial reports, and then the generated prototypes are used to predict stock price movements. (Leidner and Schilder, 2010) use text mining techniques to detect whether there is a risk within a company, and classify the detected risk into several types. The above two studies both use a classification manner to mine financial reports. (Kogan et al., 2009) apply a regression approach to predict stock return volatilities of companies via their financial reports; in specific, the Support Vector Regression (SVR) model is applied to conduct mining on text information.

## 3 Our Ranking Approach

In finance, volatility is a common *risk* metric, which is measured by the standard deviation of a stock's returns over a period of time. Let $S_t$ be the price of a stock at time $t$. Holding the stock for one period from time $t-1$ to time $t$ would result in a simple net return: $R_t = S_t/S_{t-1}$ (Tsay, 2005). The volatility of returns for a stock from time $t-n$ to $t$ can be defined as

$$v_{[t-n,t]} = \sqrt{\frac{\sum_{i=t-n}^{t}(R_i - \bar{R})^2}{n}}, \tag{1}$$

where $\bar{R} = \sum_{i=t-n}^{t} R_i/(n+1)$.

We now proceed to classify the volatilities of $n$ stocks into $2\ell + 1$ risk levels, where $n, \ell \in \{1, 2, 3, \cdots\}$. Let $m$ be the sample mean and $s$ be the sample standard deviation of the logarithm of volatilities of $n$ stocks (denoted as $\ln(v)$). The distribution over $\ln(v)$ across companies tends to have a bell shape (Kogan et al., 2009). Therefore, given a volatility $v$, we derive the risk level $r$ via:

$$r = \begin{cases} \ell - k & \text{if } \ln(v) \in (a, m - sk], \\ \ell & \text{if } \ln(v) \in (m - s, m + s), \\ \ell + k & \text{if } \ln(v) \in [m + sk, b), \end{cases} \tag{2}$$

where $a = m - s(k+1)$ when $k \in \{1, \cdots, \ell - 1\}$, $a = -\infty$ when $k = \ell$, $b = m + s(k+1)$ when $k \in \{1, \cdots, \ell - 1\}$, and $b = \infty$ when $k = \ell$. Note that $r$ stands for the concept of *relative* risk among $n$ stocks; for instance, the stock with $r = 4$ is much more risky than that with $r = 0$.

After classifying the volatilities of stock returns (of companies) into different risk levels, we now proceed to formulate our text ranking problem. Given a collection of financial reports $D = \{\mathbf{d_1}, \mathbf{d_2}, \mathbf{d_3}, \cdots, \mathbf{d_n}\}$, in which each $\mathbf{d_i} \in \mathbb{R}^d$ and is associated with a company $c_i$, we aim to rank the companies via a ranking model $f : \mathbb{R}^d \to \mathbb{R}$ such that the rank order of the set of companies is specified by the real value that the model $f$ takes. In specific, $f(\mathbf{d_i}) > f(\mathbf{d_j})$ is taken to mean that the model asserts that $c_i \succ c_j$, where $c_i \succ c_j$ means that $c_i$ is ranked higher than $c_j$; that is, the company $c_i$ is more risky than $c_j$ in this work.

This paper adopts Ranking SVM (Joachims, 2006) for our text ranking problem. Within a year, if the ground truth (i.e., the relative risk level) asserts that the company $c_i$ is more risky than $c_j$, the constraint of Ranking SVM is $\langle \mathbf{w}, \mathbf{d_i} \rangle > \langle \mathbf{w}, \mathbf{d_j} \rangle$, where $\mathbf{w}, \mathbf{d_i}, \mathbf{d_j} \in \mathbb{R}^d$, and $\mathbf{d_i}$ and $\mathbf{d_j}$ are two word vectors. Then, the text ranking problem can be expressed as the following constrained

| Method | 2001 | 2002 | 2003 | 2004 | 2005 | 2006 | Average |
|---|---|---|---|---|---|---|---|
| **Feature: TFIDF** | **Kendall's Tau (Kendall, 1938)** | | | | | | |
| SVR (baseline) | 0.517 | 0.536 | 0.531 | 0.515 | 0.515 | 0.514 | 0.521 |
| Ranking SVM | **0.539** | **0.549** | **0.543** | **0.526** | **0.539** | **0.525** | **0.537* (6.57E-4)** |
| **Feature: TFIDF** | **Spearman's Rho (Myers and Well, 2003)** | | | | | | |
| SVR (baseline) | 0.549 | 0.567 | 0.562 | 0.545 | 0.544 | 0.540 | 0.551 |
| Ranking SVM | **0.571** | **0.580** | **0.575** | **0.556** | **0.568** | **0.551** | **0.567* (6.97E-4)** |

Numbers in brackets indicate the $p$-value from a paired $t$-test. Bold faced numbers denote improvements over the baseline, and * indicates that the entry is statistically significant from the baseline at 95% confidence level.

Table 1: Experimental Results of Different Methods.

optimization problem.

$$\min_{\mathbf{w}} V(\mathbf{w},\xi) = \frac{1}{2}\langle \mathbf{w},\mathbf{w}\rangle + C\sum \xi_{i,j,k}$$
$$\text{s.t.} \begin{cases} \forall(\mathbf{d_i},\mathbf{d_j}) \in Y_1 : \langle \mathbf{w},\mathbf{d_i}\rangle \geq \langle \mathbf{w},\mathbf{d_j}\rangle + 1 - \xi_{i,j,1} \\ \dots \\ \forall(\mathbf{d_i},\mathbf{d_j}) \in Y_n : \langle \mathbf{w},\mathbf{d_i}\rangle \geq \langle \mathbf{w},\mathbf{d_j}\rangle + 1 - \xi_{i,j,n} \\ \forall i \forall j \forall k : \xi_{i,j,k} \geq 0, \end{cases} \tag{3}$$

where $\mathbf{w}$ is a learned weight vector, $C$ is the trade-off parameter, $\xi_{i,j,k}$ is a slack variable, and $Y_k$ is a set of pairs of financial reports within a year.

## 4 Experiments and Analysis

In this paper, the 10-K Corpus (Kogan et al., 2009) is used to conduct the experiments; only Section 7 "management's discussion and analysis of financial conditions and results of operations" (MD&A) is included in the experiments since typically Section 7 contains the most important forward-looking statements. In the experiments, all documents were stemmed by the Porter stemmer, and the documents in each year are indexed separately. In addition to the reports, the twelve months after the report volatility for each company can be calculated by Equation (1), where the price return series can be obtained from the Center for Research in Security Prices (CRSP) US Stocks Database. The company in each year is then classified into 5 risk levels ($\ell = 2$) via Equation (2). For regression, linear kernel is adopted with $\epsilon = 0.1$ and the trade-off $C$ is set to the default choice of SVM$^{light}$, which are the similar settings of (Kogan et al., 2009). For ranking, linear kernel is adopted with $C = 1$, all other parameters are left for the default values of SVM$^{Rank}$.

Table 1 tabulates the experimental results, in which all reports from the five-year period preceding the test year are used as the training data (we denote the training data from the $n$-year period preceding the test year as $\mathbf{T}^n$ hereafter). For example, the reports from year 1996 to 2000 constitute a training data $\mathbf{T}^5$, and the resulting model is tested on the reports of year 2001. As shown in the table, with the feature of TF-IDF, our results are significantly better than those of the baseline in terms of both two measures. In addition to using $\mathbf{T}^5$ as the training data, we also conduct other 4 sets of experiments with $\mathbf{T}^1, \mathbf{T}^2, \mathbf{T}^3, \mathbf{T}^4$ to test the reports from

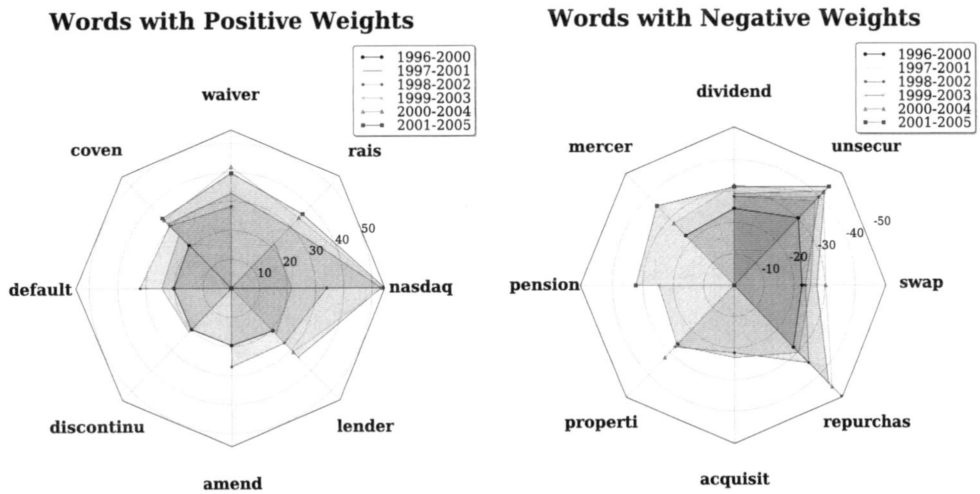


Figure 1: Positive and Negative Weighted Terms Across Different Models.

year 2001 to 2006; [1] there are in total 30 testing instances including the experiments with $\mathbf{T}^5$. The results show that in terms of both measures, our results with TF-IDF are significantly better than the baseline.[2]

Figure 1 illustrates the top positive and negative weighted terms appearing more than twice in the six $\mathbf{T}^5$ models trained on TF-IDF; these terms (8 positive and 8 negative) constitute the radar chart in Figure 1. Almost all the terms found by our ranking approach are financially meaningful; in addition, some of highly risk-correlated terms are not even reported in (Kogan et al., 2009).

We now take the term *defaut* (only identified by our ranking approach) as an example. In finance, a company "defaults" when it cannot meet its legal obligations according to the debt contract; as a result, the term "default" is intuitively associated with a relative high risk level. One piece of the paragraph quoted from the original report (from AFC Enterprises, Inc.) is listed as follows:

> *As of December 25, 2005, approximately $3.0 million was borrowed under this program, of which we were contingently liable for approximately $0.7 million in the event of* **default**.

## Conclusion

This paper adopts learning-to-rank techniques to rank the companies to keep them in line with their relative risk levels via the text information in their financial reports. The experimental results suggest interesting relations between the text information in financial reports and the risk levels among companies; these findings may be of great value for providing us more insight and understanding into financial reports. Finally, we provide a visualization interface to demonstrate the relations between financial risk and text information in the reports. This demonstration enables users to easily obtain useful information from a number of financial reports.

[1] Due to the page limits, some of the results are not listed in the paper, but they are available from the authors upon request.

[2] The $p$-value from a paired $t$-test for Spearman's Rho is 1.21E-4 and for Kendall's Tau is 7.27E-5.

Future directions include how to reduce the noise within texts, and how to incorporate Standard Industrial Classification (SIC) into our ranking approach. In addition, a hybrid model consisting of both financial and text information may be also one of our future directions.

## References


Burges, C., Shaked, T., Renshaw, E., Lazier, A., Deeds, M., Hamilton, N., and Hullender, G. (2005). Learning to rank using gradient descent. In *Proceedings of the 22nd international conference on Machine learning*, ICML '05, pages 89–96. ACM.

Freund, Y., Iyer, R., Schapire, R. E., and Singer, Y. (2003). An efficient boosting algorithm for combining preferences. *J. Mach. Learn. Res.*, 4:933–969.

Joachims, T. (2006). Training linear svms in linear time. In *Proceedings of the 12th ACM SIGKDD international conference on Knowledge discovery and data mining*, KDD '06, pages 217–226. ACM.

Kendall, M. (1938). A new measure of rank correlation. *Biometrika*, 30(1/2):81–93.

Kogan, S., Levin, D., Routledge, B., Sagi, J., and Smith, N. (2009). Predicting risk from financial reports with regression. In *Proceedings of Human Language Technologies: The 2009 Annual Conference of the North American Chapter of the Association for Computational Linguistics*, pages 272–280. ACL.

Leidner, J. L. and Schilder, F. (2010). Hunting for the black swan: risk mining from text. In *Proceedings of the ACL 2010 System Demonstrations*, ACLDemos '10, pages 54–59. ACL.

Lin, M.-C., Lee, A. J. T., Kao, R.-T., and Chen, K.-T. (2008). Stock price movement prediction using representative prototypes of financial reports. *ACM Trans. Manage. Inf. Syst.*, 2(3):19:1–19:18.

Manning, C., Raghavan, P., and Schutze, H. (2008). *Introduction to information retrieval*. Cambridge University Press.

Myers, J. and Well, A. (2003). *Research design and statistical analysis*, volume 1. Lawrence Erlbaum.

Ponte, J. M. and Croft, W. B. (1998). A language modeling approach to information retrieval. In *Proceedings of the 21st annual international ACM SIGIR conference on Research and development in information retrieval*, SIGIR '98, pages 275–281. ACM.

Robertson, S. E. and Sparck Jones, K. (1988). Relevance weighting of search terms. In *Document retrieval systems*, pages 143–160. Taylor Graham Publishing.

Salton, G., Wong, A., and Yang, C. S. (1975). A vector space model for automatic indexing. *Commun. ACM*, 18(11):613–620.

Tsay, R. (2005). *Analysis of financial time series*. Wiley-Interscience.

# UNL Explorer

Hiroshi Uchida[1] Meiying Zhu[1] Khan Md. Anwarus Salam[1,2]
(1) UNDL Foundation, Tokyo, Japan.
(2) The University of Electro-Communications, Tokyo, Japan.
uchida@undl.org, zhu@undl.org, khan@undltokyo.org

ABSTRACT

Universal Networking Language (UNL) is a language for computer to represent knowledge and information described in natural languages. Universal Words (UWs) constitute the vocabulary of UNL. The UNL Explorer is a web based application, which combines all the components of UNL system to be accessible online. The users of UNL Explorer are not only researchers and linguists who are interested to work with UNL technologies, but also general people who want to communicate free from language barriers. This paper describes the features of UNL Explorer. In brief, UNL Explorer provides many powerful features such as multilingual context search, multilingual communication such as UNL Talk and multilingual dictionary. Using multilingual context search users can retrieve documents in any language. Moreover, UNL Explorer shows the documents in various languages such as English, Japanese and more than 40 languages. Users can also access the UWs based multilingual dictionaries. UNL Society members can contribute online for updating their language dictionary entries.

KEYWORDS: Multilingual Context Search; Machine Translation; Multilingual Dictionary; Universal Networking Language (UNL); Ontology;

*Proceedings of COLING 2012: Demonstration Papers*, pages 453–458,
COLING 2012, Mumbai, December 2012.

## 1 Introduction

Universal Networking Language (UNL) is a language for computer to represent knowledge and information described in natural languages. Universal Words (UWs) constitute the vocabulary of UNL. UW is a word for constructing UNL expressions (UNL Graph). So keys to the information in UNL documents are UWs. UWs are stored in the UW dictionary.

UNL Explorer is a web based application, which combines all the components of UNL system to be accessible online. The users of UNL Explorer are not only researchers and linguists who are interested to work with UNL technologies, but also general people who want to communicate free from language barriers. This paper describes the features of UNL Explorer.

In brief, UNL Explorer provides many powerful features such as multilingual context search, multilingual communication such as UNL Talk, multilingual dictionary and UNL Ontology. Using multilingual context search users can retrieve documents in any language. UNL Explorer provides very promising solution for search. Moreover, UNL Explorer shows the documents in various languages such as English, Japanese and more than 40 languages. Users can also access the UWs based multilingual dictionaries. UNL Society members can contribute online for updating their language dictionary entries.

## 2 BACKGROUND

### 2.1 Universal Networking Language (UNL)

UNL initiative was originally launched in 1996 as a project of the Institute of Advanced Studies of the United Nations University (UNU/IAS)[1]. Describing the detail technical information UNL book was first published in 1999 (Uchida et. al. 1999). In 2001, the United Nation University set up the UNDL Foundation[2], to be responsible for the development and management of the UNL project. In 2005, a new technical manual of UNL was published (Uchida et. al. 2005), which defined UNL as an knowledge and information representation language for computer. UNL has all the components to represent knowledge described in natural languages. UWs constitute the vocabulary of UNL and each concept that natural languages have is represented as unique UW. A UW of UNL is defined in the following format:

<uw> =:: <headword>[<constraint list>]

Here, English words or phrases are used for headword, because of easy understanding for the people in the world. UW can be a word, a compound word, a phrase or a sentence. Universal Words (UWs) constitute the vocabulary of UNL. UW is a word for constructing UNL expressions (UNL Graph). So keys to the information in UNL documents are UWs. UWs are stored in the UW dictionary. UWs are inter-linked with other UWs using “relations” to form the UNL expressions of sentences. These relations specify the role of each word in a sentence. Using "attributes" it can express the subjectivity of author. Currently, UWs are available for many languages such as Arabic, Bengali, Chinese, English, French, Indonesian, Italian, Japanese, Mongolian, Russian, Spanish and so forth.

---

[1]http://www.ias.unu.edu/

[2]http://www.undl.org/

## 2.2 UNL Ontology

UNL Ontology is a semantic network with hyper nodes. It contains UW System which describes the hierarchy of the UWs in lattice structure, all possible semantic co-occurrence relations between each UWs and UWs definition in UNL. With the property inheritance based on UW System, possible relations between UWs can be deductively inferred from their upper UWs and this inference mechanism reduces the number of binary relation descriptions of the UNL Ontology. In the topmost level UWs are divided into four categories: adverbial concept, attributive concept, nominal concept and predicative concept.

# 3 UNL Explorer

UNL Explorer[3] is a web based application, which combines all the components of UNL system to be accessible online. In brief, UNL Explorer provides many powerful features such as multilingual context search, multilingual communication such as UNL Talk, multilingual dictionary and UNL Ontology.

Multilingual context search enable the people to retrieve desired documents by the natural language query of any language. Each document is provided in UNL by automatically analysing the original document, together with the original document. The queries are converted into UNL. Then the system try to match this UNL graph with the existing UNL documents with inference. Knowledge which is necessary to make inference are provided in UNL Ontology, especially in UWs definition.

Retrieved documents or any other documents can be shown in various languages such as English, Japanese and more than 40 languages, by automatically generating each language sentences from UNL expressions.

This function allows the users to translate any documents in different languages. This allows the users to communicate across language barriers by UNL Talk. This option can be very useful for communicating in cross-cultural communication. To realize this function the system need the UW dictionaries for many languages, which defines the correspondence between UWs and each languages words.

This data can be access as multilingual dictionary. UNL Society members can contribute online for updating their language dictionary entries. Figure1 shows the UNL Explorer screen shot with explanations of the options.

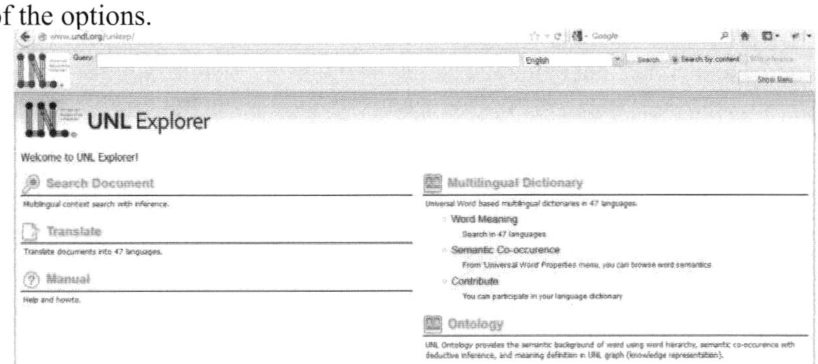


FIGURE 1 –UNL Explorer Homepage screen shot

[3]http://www.undl.org/unlexp/

## 3.1 Multilingual Context Search

Multilingual context search enable the people to retrieve desired documents by the natural language query of any language. UNL Explorer provides multilingual search facility for UNL documents. For this each document is provided in UNL by automatically analysing the original document, together with the original document. The queries are converted into UNL. Then the system try to match this UNL graph with the existing UNL documents with inference. Knowledge which is necessary to make inference is provided in UNL Ontology, especially in UWs definition. To perform multilingual context search user can write the search query in text box and click the Search button.

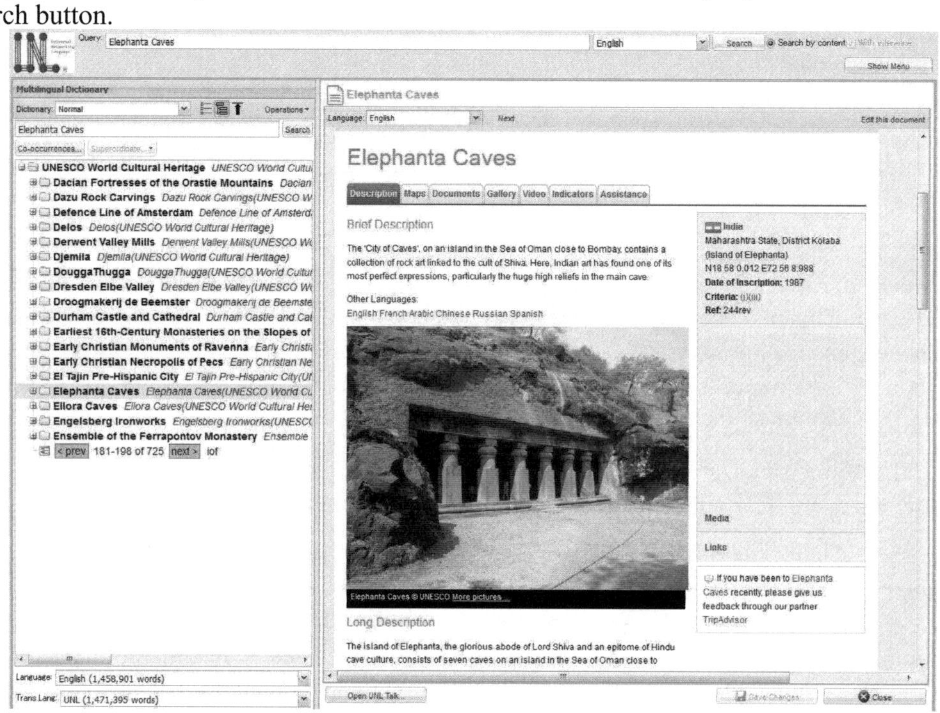


FIGURE 2 –UNL Explorer screen shot showing the UNESCO document on "Elephanta Caves"

Retrieved documents or any other documents can be shown in various languages such as English, Japanese and more than 40 languages, by automatically generating each language sentences from UNL expressions. Search Query: Write the Keyword or Content to search from UNL Information and Knowledge Management System. The UNL Explorer will show the results in UNL or in a desired natural language by Deconverting the UNL expressions of the information using the UNL Deconverter. In background UNL Explorer translates using UNL Enconverter and Deconverter. Both UNL EnConverter and Deconverter support different languages such as Chinese, English, Japanese and so forth.

## 3.2 UNL Talk

UNL Talk allows the users to communicate across language barriers by UNL Talk. This option can be very useful for communicating in cross-cultural communication. To realize this function the system need the UW dictionaries for many languages, which defines the correspondence between UWs and each languages words. Figure 3 shows the screen shot of UNL Talk where the authors are communicating using Bengali and English. Each users can see the messages in their mother language.

FIGURE 3 –Screen shot of UNL Talk where users communicating in Bengali and English

## 3.3 Multilingual Dictionary

One of the most unique features of UNL Explorer is the multilingual dictionary which is available for more than 40 languages. This multilingual dictionary is based on UWs dictionaries for many languages, which defines the correspondence between UWs and each languages words. Users can use the dictionary side by side for any of these language pair.

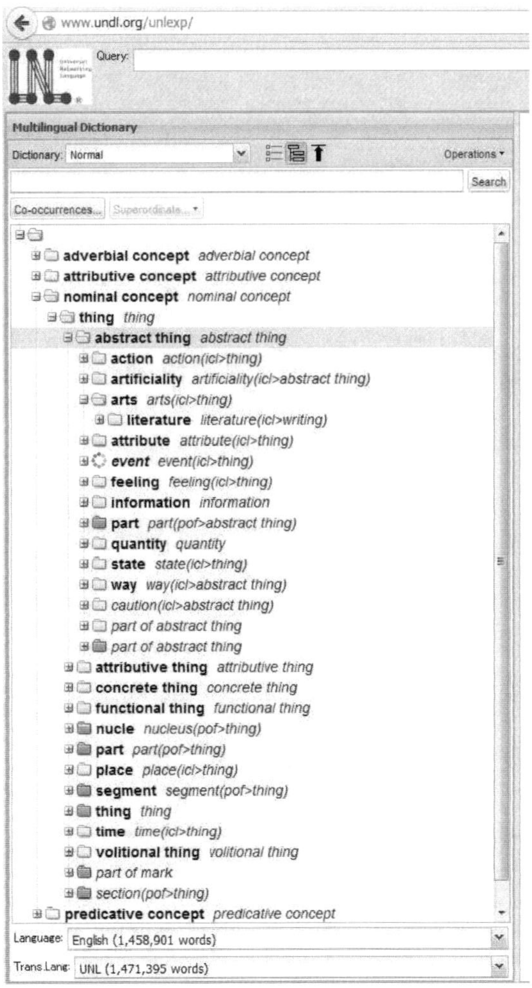


FIGURE 4– Multilingual dictionary frame showing English-UNL

UNL Explorer users can browse the multilingual dictionary which comes in the left side, which we refer as "multilingual dictionary frame" as shown in Figure 4. This tool also provides the search facility for UWs dictionary. Users can search the meaning of a word in any languages. Users can choose their desired language pairs from the options given in the downside of the multilingual dictionary frame. Figure 4 shows the screen shot of Universal Words frame. It displays the UWs system hierarchy (a lattice structure) in a plain tree form. Information can be navigated through the UWs system and users are also able to know the position of each concept of a UW in the conceptual hierarchy at the same time.

UNL Explorer also provides an advanced search facility for discovering UWs relations from UNL Ontology. This option allows user to get the semantic co-occurrence of any UWs. Users can also check incoming and outgoing relationships of each UWs using this facility. This UNL Ontology search mechanism is accessible for computer program using UNL Explorer API. However, to use this API, user need to be a UNL society member by signing an agreement with UNDL Foundation.

UNL Society members can contribute online for updating their language dictionary entries. From 'Universal Word' Properties menu, users can browse the word semantics. It is possible to edit the UWs dictionaries online. UNL society members can also download the UWs dictionaries.

To ensure every language speakers can create the correct UWs dictionary entry, UNL Explorer provide the explanation of UWs in different natural languages (Khan et. al., 2011). It is a novel contribution for auto generating the UWs explanations from the semantic background provided by UNL Ontology.

## Conclusion

In this paper, we described the features of online based UNL Explorer. For making the people freely communicate with each other in their mother language, UNL technology is very promising. UNL Explorer provides useful features such as multilingual context search, multilingual communication using UNL Talk and multilingual dictionary for general users. UNL Explorer also provides API for researchers and application developers to use UNL technologies such as UNL EnConverter, DeConverter, UWs Dictionary, UNL Ontology based on corpus.

## References

H. Uchida, M. Zhu, T. Della Senta. "A gift for a millenium". Tokyo: IAS/UNU. 1999.

H. Uchida, M. Zhu, and T. Della Senta. "The Universal Networking Language", 2nd ed. UNDL Foundation, 2005.

Khan Md. Anwarus Salam, Hiroshi Uchida and Tetsuro Nishino. "How to Develop Universal Vocabularies Using Automatic Generation of the Meaning of Each Word", 7th International Conference on Natural Language Processing and Knowledge Engineering (NLPKE'11), Tokushima, Japan. ISBN: 978-1-61284-729-0. Page 243 – 246. 2011.

# An SMT-driven Authoring Tool

*Sriram Venkatapathy*[1] *Shachar Mirkin*[1]
(1) Xerox Research Centre Europe
`sriram.venkatapathy@xrce.xerox.com,shachar.mirkin@xrce.xerox.com`

ABSTRACT
This paper presents a tool for assisting users in composing texts in a language they do not know. While Machine Translation (MT) is pretty useful for understanding texts in an unfamiliar language, current MT technology has yet to reach the stage where it can be used reliably without a post-editing step. This work attempts to make a step towards achieving this goal. We propose a tool that provides suggestions for the continuation of the text in the source language (that the user knows), creating texts that can be translated to the target language (that the user does not know). In terms of functionality, our tool resembles text prediction applications. However , the target language, through a Statistical Machine Translation (SMT) model, drives the composition and not only the source language. We present the user interface and describe the considerations that underline the suggestion process. A simulation of user interaction shows that composition speed can be substantially reduced and provides initial positive feedback as to the ability to generate better translations.

KEYWORDS: Statistical Machine Translation.

*Proceedings of COLING 2012: Demonstration Papers*, pages 459–466,
COLING 2012, Mumbai, December 2012.

## 1 Introduction

A common task in today's multilingual environments it to compose texts in a language that the author is not fluent in or not familiar with at all. This could be a prospective tourist sending an email to a hotel abroad or an employee of a multinational company replying to customers who speak another language than his own. A solution to such problems is to enable handling multilingual text-composition using Machine Translation technology. The user composes a text in his own (*source*) language and it is then automatically translated to the *target* language. Machine translation technology can be used rather effectively to interpret texts in an unfamiliar language. Automatic translations are often good enough for understanding the general meaning of the text, even if they do not constitute a perfect translation or are not perfectly written. On the other hand, the state-of-the-art MT technology is often not suitable for directly composing foreign-language texts. Erroneous or non-fluent texts may not be well-received by the readers. This is especially important in business environments, where the reputation of the company may be harmed if low-quality texts are used by it. The output of the MT system must therefore go through a *post-editing* process before the text can be used externally. That is, a person who is fluent in both the source and the target languages must review and correct the target text before it is sent or displayed. Obviously, such a post-editing step, which requires knowledge of both languages, makes the process slow, expensive and even irrelevant in many cases.

In this work we present an approach driven by Statistical Machine Translation for enabling users to compose texts that will be translated more accurately to a language unfamiliar to them. This is a step towards composition of texts in a foreign language that does not depend on knowledge of that language.

The composition of the text in the desired language is a two-step process:

1. Through an interactive interface the user is guided to **quickly** compose a text in his native language that *can be* more **accurately** translated to the target language. The composition guidance is powered by the SMT-system.
2. The text is translated by the SMT system.

Hence, the SMT system plays a dual role in this method, for interactive composition of source-language texts and for their translation into the target language. Its role in the composition of the source by the user is what enables improving the accuracy of the translation. The interface prompts the user to choose those phrases that can be translated more accurately by the SMT system. In contrast, a text composed directly by the user might contain terminology or sentence structure that the SMT system cannot successfully translate.

Apart from improving the accuracy of the translation, this method may also improve composition speed. This is made possible by the interface that allows the user to click on desired phrases to extend the current text, thereby saving typing. Composition speed is further improved by displaying complete sentences from the translation memory that are similar to the user's input at any given time and which the user can simply select to be translated.

## 2 Related work

To our knowledge, there has been no previous work where interactive authoring is driven by an SMT model.

Interactive tools for MT-targeted authoring were proposed in several works. (Dymetman et al., 2000) suggested a method for assisting monolingual writers in the production of multilingual documents based on a parallel grammar; (Carbonell et al., 2000) propose a tool to produce controlled texts in the source language; (Choumane et al., 2005) provide interactive assistance to authors based on manually defined rules, for tagging the source text in order to reduce its syntactic ambiguity. In contrast, our method does not depend on predefined templates or rules for a constrained language, but is tightly coupled with the SMT models which are learnt automatically from parallel corpora.

Tools for computer-assisted translation (CAT) are meant to increase the productivity of translators. A fundamental difference between these and our suggested tool is that CAT systems are designed for translators and operate on the **target** side of the text, assuming their users know both the source and target languages, or at least the target language. For example, (Koehn and Haddow, 2009) proposed a CAT system [1] which suggests words and phrases for target-side sentence completion based on the phrase table. (Koehn, 2010) and (Hu et al., 2011) propose translation by monolinguals, but also rely on users fluent in the target language.

Our tool bears resemblance to *text prediction* applications, such as smart-phone keyboards. In comparison to these, our tool suggests the next phrase(s) based both on the user's input and the translatability of these phrases, according to an SMT model. This naturally stems from the different purpose of our tool - to compose a text in **another** language.

## 3 Interactive interface

In this section, we present the interactive interface that enables users to compose texts in a language they do not know (see Figure 1). To compose a text, the user starts typing in his native language (English in this example) in the top text-box. The interface allows the user to perform the following primary operations at any point of time: (1) **Phrase selection:** Select one of the phrase suggestions to expand the sentence. The number of suggested phrases is controlled by the user through the interface, (2) **Sentence selection:** Select an entire sentence from a list of sentences similar to the partial input. Words that match the typed text are highlighted, and (3) **Word composition:** The user may go on typing if he does not want to use any of the provided suggestions. Any selected text is also editable.

Whenever the space button is hit, new phrase and sentence suggestions are instantly shown. A mouse click on a suggested sentence copies it to the top text box, replacing the already typed text; a selection of a phrase appends it to the typed text. Phrases are ordered by their estimated "appropriateness" to the typed text (see details in Section 4). Throughout the process, the partial translation (to French in our example) can be shown with the toggle show/hide translation button.

## 4 SMT-Driven authoring

The goal of our work is to enable users to compose a text in a language they know that can be translated accurately to a language which they do not know. We assume that when starting to type, the user typically has some intended message in mind, whose meaning is set, but not its exact wording. This enables us to suggest text continuations that will preserve the intended meaning, but phrased in a way that it will be better translated. This is achieved by a guidance method that is determined by three factors:

[1] www.caitra.org

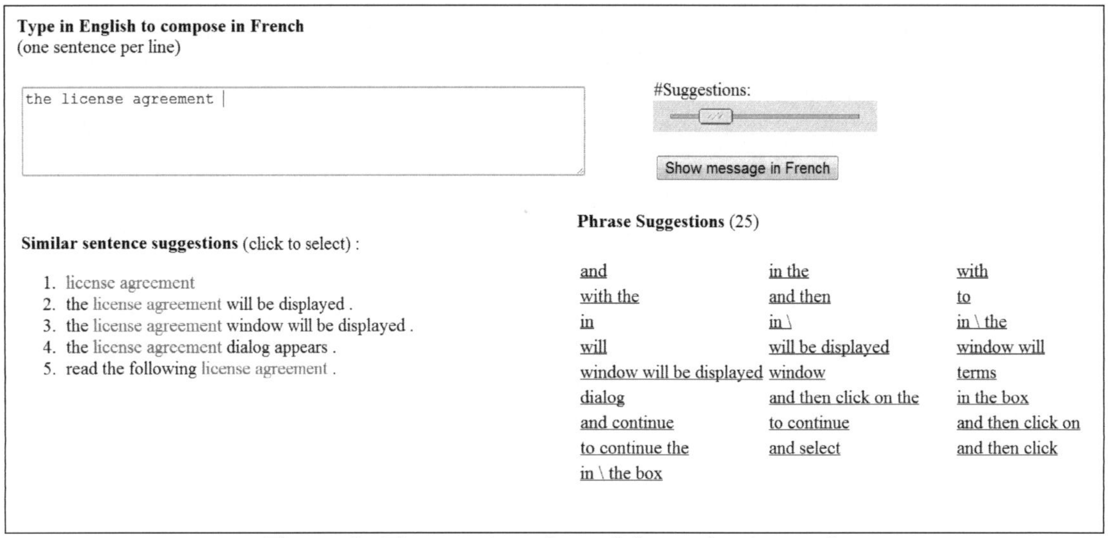

**Figure 1:** The user interface of the authoring tool.

1. **Fluency**: The phrase suggestions shown should be fluent with respect to the input already provided by the user. As our setting is interactive, the fluency of the source text must be maintained at any given time.
2. **Translatability**: The ability of the SMT system to translate a given source phrase. This is a factor controlled by the authoring tool by proposing phrases that can be translated more accurately, thereby moving towards a better translation of the intended text.
3. **Semantic distance**: The semantic distance between the composed source text and the suggestions. This criterion is required in order to ensure our suggestions are not simply those that are easy to translate, thus preventing a deviation from the meaning of the intended text (in contrast to deviating from the wording). A high distance corresponds to a different meaning of the composed message relative to the intended one. In such cases, the SMT system cannot be expected to generate a translation whose meaning is close to the desired one.

To rank proposed phrases we use a metric whose aim is to both minimize the semantic deviation of suggested phrases from the already typed text and to maximize the translatability of the text. That, while maintaining the fluency of the sentence. This metric is a weighted product of individual metrics for each of the three above factors. Briefly, to maintain source fluency we suggest only those phrases whose prefix overlaps with the suffix of the user's partial input. We use the SRILM toolkit (Stolcke, 2002) to obtain the per-word-perplexity of each suggested phrase, and normalize it by the maximal perplexity of the language model. This yields a normalized score over different phrase lengths. We assessed two metrics for estimating phrase translatability. The first is based on conditional entropy (*CE*), following (DeNero et al., 2006) and (Moore and Quirk, 2007). The idea is that a source phrase is more translatable if it occurs frequently in the training data and has more valid options for translation. The second is the maximum translation score (*MTS*), computed from the translation features in the SMT phrase table, maximized over all phrase-table entries for a given source phrase. To minimize meaning deviation, we compute the averaged DICE coefficient (Dice, 1945) between the suggested phrase and the already-typed input, which measures the tendency of their words to co-occur according to corpus statistics. We applied a sigmoid function to the translatability scores to bring them to [0-1] range, and used the square root of the DICE score in order to scale it to a more similar range of the other scores.

## 5 Implementation

The interactive nature of our proposal requires instant response from the authoring tool. This is a critical requirement, even if large translation models and corpora are employed, as users would find it useless if response to their actions is not instantaneous. To enable immediate suggestions of phrases, we create an inverted index of the phrase table, indexing all prefixes of the source phrases in the table. This enables instantly providing suggestion by retrieving from the index all phrase table entries which have the typed few words as prefix. Indexing and retrieval in our implementation are done using the Lucene search engine[2].

## 6 Evaluation

We empirically measured the utility of the interface for the task of composing texts in an unfamiliar language by computing the cost of the text composition and the accuracy of the translation of the composed text. Ideally, this needs to be done manually by human evaluators, yet at this stage we performed the evaluation through a simulator that emulates a human who is using the interface. The simulator's goal is to compose a text using the authoring tool while remaining semantically close to the intended text the user had in mind. For our purposes, the intended texts are existing corpus sentences which we try to reconstruct. The simulator attempts to reconstruct these texts by making the least possible 'effort'. If it is possible, an entire sentence is selected; otherwise the longest possible matching phrase is chosen. If no such match is found, words from the intended text are copied to the sentence being recomposed, which is equivalent to a composition by the user.

We applied the simulation of two datasets for our experiments: (1) Technical Manuals Dataset (TM), and (3) News commentary Dataset - WMT2007 (NC).

**Evaluating composition cost** To assess composition cost we used a simulator that tries to reconstruct the intended text exactly. That is, the simulator selects a phrase suggestion only if it is identical to the following word(s) of the intended text. Let us assume, for instance, that the intended text is *'the license agreement will be displayed next'* and the text *'the license agreement'* has already been composed. The simulator can either select a sentence identical to the entire intended text or to select the longest prefix of the phrase *'will be displayed next'* from among the suggested phrases. The results when applying this simulator are presented in Figure 2. As shown in the figure, word composition is reduced when the tool is being used, and unsurprisingly, more suggestions yield a greater save in composition cost. We further see that the *CE* metric is preferable over *MTS*, better ranking the suggestions which leads to their selection rather their composition.

**Evaluating translation accuracy** By design, the simulator mentioned above cannot assess potential gains in translation accuracy. To achieve that we must allow it to compose texts that are different from the original ones. For that purpose we created additional simulators, which can – to some extent – modify the intended text, generating simple paraphrases of it by allowing substitution of function words or content words by their synonyms. For instance,

[2] `http://lucene.apache.org`

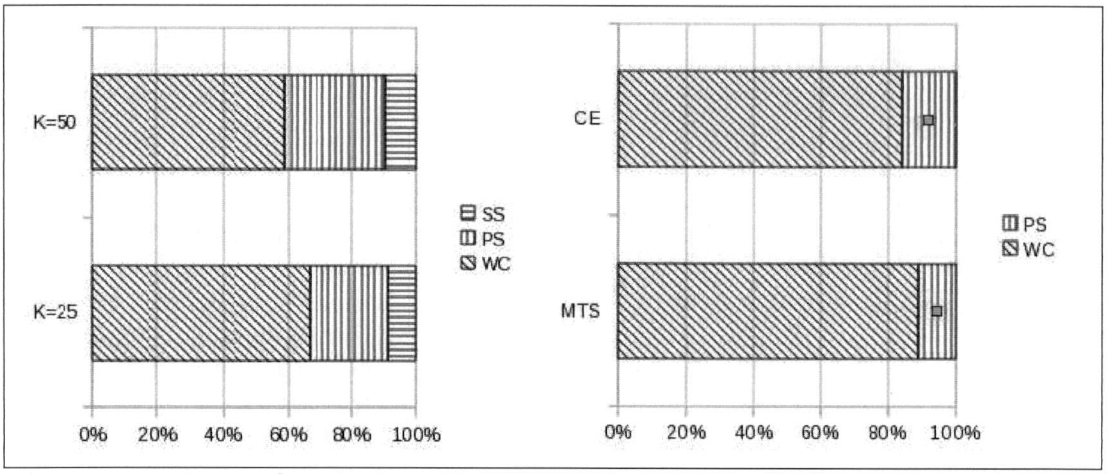

**Figure 2:** Percentage of word compositions (WC), phrase selections (PS) and Sentence Selection (SS) using different values of $k$ on a technical manuals dataset (left) and using different translatability metrics (*CE* and *MTS*) on the News Commentary dataset (right).

the words *'will be displayed next'* in the intended text may be replaced in this simulation by the phrase suggestion *'is shown next'*. We applied these simulators on the test sets, but very few replacements occurred. This result does not allow us to report translation performance scores at this stage and calls for rethinking the simulation methodology and for manual evaluation. Yet, in some cases changes were made by the simulator and resulted with improved translations, as measured by the BLEU score (Papineni et al., 2002). As an example, in the sentence *'The candidate* ***countries*** *want to experience quick economic growth . . . '*, the word *countries* was replaced by *states*, resulting in a better BLEU score (0.2776 vs. 0.2176).

## 7 Conclusions and future work

This work represents a step towards more accurate authoring of texts in a foreign language. While not constituting at this stage an alternative to post-editing, it may enable reducing the effort incurred by such a process. We proposed a tool for assisting the user during the composition of a text in his native language where next-words suggestions are driven by an SMT-model, such that the eventual translation would be better than if the user had written the text by himself. Through our evaluation we have demonstrated that composition speed can be increased and exemplified a better translation that is produced when using the tool.

Thus far, our approach and tool were evaluated using a simulation. This limited our ability to assess the full potential of the tool. A next step would be a field-test with human users, measuring the actual composition time, the translation results, and the post-editing effort required when using the tool in comparison to using "regular" MT technology.

In future research we plan to investigate further translatability and the semantic relatedness estimations and automatically tune the metric weights. We further wish to improve the user interface to enhance its utility. Specifically we wish to merge phrase suggestions that are substrings of other suggestions in order to present a more compact list thus making the selection faster and more efficient.

## References


Carbonell, J. G., Gallup, S. L., Harris, T. J., Higdon, J. W., Hill, D. A., Hudson, D. C., Nasjleti, D., Rennich, M. L., Andersen, P. M., Bauer, M. M., Busdiecker III, R. F., Hayes, P. J., Huettner, A. K., Mclaren, B. M., Nirenburg, I., Riebling, E. H., Schmandt, L. M., Sweet, J. F., Baker, K. L., Brownlow, N. D., Franz, A. M., Holm, S. E., Leavitt, J. R. R., Lonsdale, D. W., Mitamura, T., and Nyberg, r. E. H. (2000). Integrated authoring and translation system.

Choumane, A., Blanchon, H., and Roisin, C. (2005). Integrating translation services within a structured editor. In *Proceedings of the 2005 ACM symposium on Document engineering*, DocEng '05, pages 165–167, New York, NY, USA. ACM.

DeNero, J., Gillick, D., Zhang, J., and Klein, D. (2006). Why generative phrase models underperform surface heuristics. In *Proceedings of the Workshop on Statistical Machine Translation*, StatMT '06, pages 31–38, Stroudsburg, PA, USA.

Dice, L. R. (1945). Measures of the amount of ecologic association between species. *Ecology*, 26(3):297–302.

Dymetman, M., Lux, V., and Ranta, A. (2000). Xml and multilingual document authoring: Convergent trends. In *IN COLING*, pages 243–249. Morgan Kaufmann.

Hu, C., Resnik, P., Kronrod, Y., Eidelman, V., Buzek, O., and Bederson, B. B. (2011). The value of monolingual crowdsourcing in a real-world translation scenario: simulation using haitian creole emergency sms messages. In *Proceedings of the Sixth Workshop on Statistical Machine Translation*, WMT '11, pages 399–404, Stroudsburg, PA, USA.

Koehn, P. (2010). Enabling monolingual translators: Post-editing vs. options. In *Human Language Technologies: The 2010 Annual Conference of the North American Chapter of the Association for Computational Linguistics*, pages 537–545, Los Angeles, California. Association for Computational Linguistics.

Koehn, P. and Haddow, B. (2009). Interactive assistance to human translators using statistical machine translation methods. In *Proceedings of MT Summit XII*, Ottawa, Canada.

Moore, R. and Quirk, C. (2007). An iteratively-trained segmentation-free phrase translation model for statistical machine translation. In *Proceedings of the Second Workshop on Statistical Machine Translation*, pages 112–119, Prague, Czech Republic. Association for Computational Linguistics.

Papineni, K., Roukos, S., Ward, T., and Zhu, W.-J. (2002). BLEU: a Method for Automatic Evaluation of Machine Translation. In *Proceedings of ACL*, Philadelphia, Pennsylvania, USA.

Stolcke, A. (2002). Srilm-an extensible language modeling toolkit. In *Proceedings International Conference on Spoken Language Processing*, pages 257–286.

# Generating Questions from Web Community Contents

*Baoxun Wang*[1] *Bingquan Liu*[1]
*Chengjie Sun*[1] *Xiaolong Wang*[1] *Deyuan Zhang*[2]
(1) School of Computer Science and Technology, Harbin Institute of Technology, Harbin, China
(2) School of Computer, Shenyang Aerospace University, Shenyang, China
{bxwang, liubq, cjsun, wangxl, dyzhang}@insun.hit.edu.cn

ABSTRACT
Large amounts of knowledge exist in the user-generated contents of web communities. Generating questions from such community contents to form the question-answer pairs is an effective way to collect and manage the knowledge in the web. The parser or rule based question generation (QG) methods have been widely studied and applied. Statistical QG aims to provide a strategy to handle the rapidly growing web data by alleviating the manual work. This paper proposes a deep belief network (DBN) based approach to address the statistical QG problem. This problem is considered as a three-step task: *question type determination*, *concept selection* and *question construction*. The DBNs are introduced to generate the essential words for question type determination and concept selection. Finally, a simple rule based method is used to construct questions with the generated words. The experimental results show that our approach is promising for the web community oriented question generation.

KEYWORDS: statistical question generation, deep belief network, web community.

*Proceedings of COLING 2012: Demonstration Papers*, pages 467–474,
COLING 2012, Mumbai, December 2012.

# 1 Introduction

Automatic question generation (QG) is a challenging task in the NLP field, and its difficulties are being realized by the researchers gradually. Since 2008, the workshop on QG[1] has been offering the shared task and evaluation on this problem. At present, the QG technique tends to be mainly applied in the interaction oriented systems (Rus et al., 2007; Harabagiu et al., 2005) (e.g., computer aided education, help desk, dialog systems, etc.). In most systems, the original source texts are parsed and transformed into the questions with the rules. The parser and rule based methods always maintain considerable accuracy, and the generating results can be directly presented to the users.

In this paper, we aim to address the web-community oriented question generation in a statistical learning way. A deep belief network (DBN) is proposed to generate the essential elements of the questions according to the answers, based on the joint distributions of the questions and their answers learned by the network from a number of user-generated QA pairs in the web communities. The generated words are then reorganized to form the questions following some simple rules.

The rest of this paper is organized as follows: Section 2 surveys the related work. Section 3 details our approach to question generation. Experimental results are given and discussed in Section 4. Finally, conclusions and future directions are drawn.

# 2 Related Work

To our knowledge, there is no previous work that concentrates on statistically generating questions from the web content freely posted by users, as we do in this paper. Nevertheless, the basic work has been done on the definition and evaluation of automatic QG. Nielsen (2008) gives the definition of QG and considers this problem as a three-step process. A question taxonomy for QG is proposed in (Nielsen et al., 2008) with a detailed question branch offered. The overall description of the QG task is proposed in (Rus and Graesser, 2009; Rus et al., 2010). Rus et al. (2007) and Vanderwende (2008) have discussed the evaluation of the QG systems.

The technique of question generation is essential to some education related fields, such as educational assessment, intelligent tutoring, etc. Brown et al. (2005) have described an approach to automatically generating questions for vocabulary assessment. Hoshino and Nakagawa (2005) have developed a real-time system which generates questions on English grammar and vocabulary. A template based QG method is proposed in (Wang et al., 2008) to evaluate the learners' understanding after reading a medical material. In conclusion, the purpose of such QG systems is different from our goal in this paper. It should be noted that the nature of automatic question generation is different depending on the application within which it is embedded (Nielsen, 2008).

# 3 Generating Questions using the Deep Belief Network

Nielsen (2008) defines the question generation task as a 3-step process: *question type determination, concept selection* and *question construction*. Basically, the architecture of our work follows this definition. Figure 1 illustrates the framework of our QG research: the human-generated QA pairs crawled from the cQA portals are used to train two DBN models to generate the question words (5W1H[2]) and the content words independently for the input source

[1] http://www.questiongeneration.org

[2] 5W1H stands for the 6 common question words in English: what, when, where, who, why, and how.

knowledge text. The essential words automatically generated by the deep networks are then organized with the manually written patterns to form the final questions.

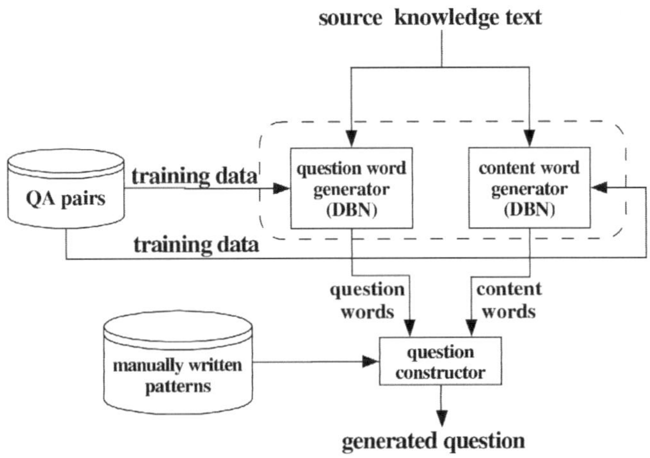


Figure 1: Framework of our statistical QG approach.

In this section, a deep network for the community content oriented QG is presented. Given the word occurrence information of an answer, the trained networks are expected to generate the words of the question. Our motivation of proposing the DBN to handle the QG problem is to build the semantic links between the questions and the answers. Intuitively, the words in the answers are helpful to provide the clues for predicting the essential words of the corresponding questions. Our DBN models are designed to learn the semantic relationships of the words in the QA pairs, and obtain the hidden clues in a statistical way. In detail, we utilize the ability of the deep network to map the QA pairs into a semantic feature space, where the joint distributions of the questions and their answers are modeled.

## 3.1 The Restricted Boltzmann Machine

A DBN is composed of several stacked "Restricted Boltzmann Machines". The Restricted Boltzmann Machine (RBM) can be used to model an ensemble of binary vectors (Hinton, 2002; Hinton and Salakhutdinov, 2006). Salakhutdinov and Hinton (2009) have proposed a deep graphical model composed of RBMs into the information retrieval field, which shows that this model is able to obtain semantic information hidden in the word-count vectors. The RBM is a two-layer network(Hinton, 2002), the bottom layer represents a visible vector $\mathbf{v}$ and the top layer represents a latent feature vector $\mathbf{h}$. The matrix W contains the symmetric interaction terms between the visible units and the hidden units. In the RBM, the visible feature vectors can be used to compute the "hidden features" in the hidden units. The RBM model can reconstruct the inputs using the hidden features.

## 3.2 Training a Deep Belief Network for QG

Our work is inspired by (Hinton et al., 2006), which proposes a DBN for image labeling. In their research, the trained deep net is able to give the labels based on the input images. The illustration of our DBN model is given by Figure 2. Basically, this model is composed of three layers, and here each layer stands for the RBM described in Subsection 3.1. In this network, the function of the bottom layer and the middle layer is to reduce the dimension of the visible answer vectors by mapping them into a low-dimensional semantic space. The top layer is essential to the QG task, since the question vectors and the mapped answer vectors are joined together and the joint distribution of QA pairs are modeled in this layer.

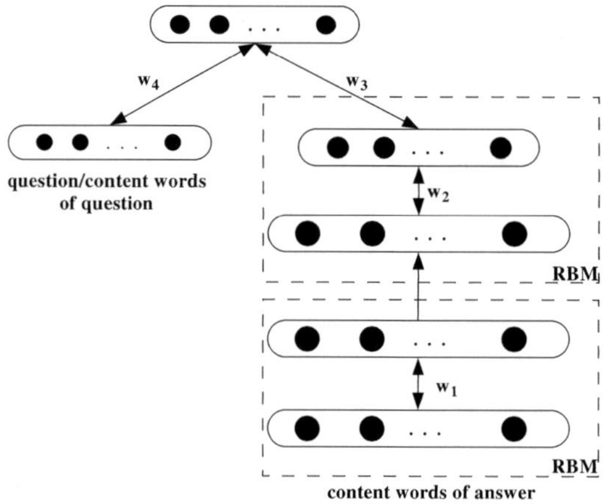


Figure 2: The DBN for Question Generation.

Here we take the bottom layer as an example to explain the pretraining procedure of the DBN, because the computing procedures of the three layers are indeed the same. Given the training set of binary answer vectors based on the statistics of the word occurrence, the bottom layer generates the corresponding hidden features. The hidden features are then used to reconstruct the Bernoulli rates for each word in the answer vectors after stochastically activating the hidden features. Then the hidden features are activated with the reconstructed input vectors. We use 1-step Contrastive Divergence (Hinton, 2002) to update the parameters by performing gradient ascent. After training one layer, the **h** vectors are then sent to the higher-level layer as its "training data". The training method of the rest two layers is the same with the bottom's. It should be noted is that in the top layer, the question vector and the mapped answer vector are joined together to form a new vector as the "input vector", and their weight matrixes are concatenated correspondingly.

During the pre-training procedure, a greedy strategy is taken to train each layer individually, so it is necessary to fine-tune the weights of the entire network. In order to tune the weights, the network is unrolled, taking the answers as the input data to generate the corresponding questions at the output units. Using the cross-entropy error function, the network can be tuned by performing back propagation through it and the objective is to reduce the generation error further. The procedure is the same with that described in (Hinton et al., 2006).

### 3.3 Generating the Questions

The word predicting work can be completed with the trained deep networks: we send the binary answer vectors to the right branch of the DBN to perform a level-by-level computation. In the top layer, the network gets the top feature vector using the mapped answer vector. With the top feature, the model performs a reverse computation to generate the real-value vector

| Question Word | Pattern |
|---|---|
| how | how+to+$< verb >$+$< adj^* >$+$< noun >$+? |
| what | what+to+$< verb >$+for+$< adj^* >$+$< noun >$+?<br>what+is+$< adj^* >$+$< noun >$+to+$< verb >$+$< noun >$+? |
| where | where+can+i+$< verb >$+$< adj^* >$+$< noun >$+? |
| how much | how much+for+$< verb >$+$< adj^* >$+$< noun >$+? |
| how many | how many +$< adj^* >$+$< noun >$+to+$< verb >$+? |

Table 1: Examples of the patterns for question construction.

at the output question units. To get the question word, we only have to find the one with the highest value. In order to obtain the content words, the generated values need to be sorted in descending order, then the top ranked $n$ words are selected.

A collection of patterns guided by the question words is used to accomplish the final step of QG. The question words influence not only the order of the generated content words, but also the selection and the positions of the additional function words (e.g., prepositions). Table 1 gives some examples of the patterns designed by us. The spirit of the patterns is to reorganize the content words generated by the DBN, and help to add necessary function words, based on the guiding question words.

# 4 Experiments

## 4.1 Experimental Setup

**Dataset:** In this paper, the datasets come from the "Travel" category of Yahoo! Answers. We have chosen 4 different topics: *trip plans*, *cutting down expense*, *necessary items*, and *VISA application*. Based on each topic, various queries are submitted to the cQA service and the "resolved questions" with their best answers are crawled. After filtering the questions whose answers are less than 10 words or containing the URLs only, from each topic we get 4,500 QA pairs for training and 100 randomly selected QA pairs for testing.

**Baseline:** Noticing that there are no previous studies focusing on the statistical QG, this paper introduces three popular statistical methods as the baselines to predict the essential words of questions for comparison: *Naive Bayesian*, *K-Nearest Neighbor*, and *Latent Semantic Indexing*.

**Evaluation:** The performance of the network generating the question words is evaluated by calculating the precision of the generated results; and the performance of the content word generation is evaluated by calculating the ratio of the number of the successful generations to the number of the total generations strictly. In this procedure, only if all the top 3 generated content words appear in the original question sentence, the generation is considered to be successful, otherwise, the generation is considered to be unsuccessful.

## 4.2 Results and Analysis

Table 2 lists the evaluating results for the question word generation (QWG) task and the content word generation (CWG) task on our datasets from Yahoo! Answers. From the tables, it can be observed that our DBN based model has outperformed the baseline methods as expected, which shows the considerable potential of our approach on the web content oriented question generation. From the user-generated QA pairs, the networks eventually learn the semantic knowledge for modeling the joint distributions of the questions and their answers. Due to the effective modeling work, the DBNs can predict the words in a question when given the corre-

| Method | Precision of essential word generation | | | | | | | |
|---|---|---|---|---|---|---|---|---|
| | trip plans | | cutting down expense | | necessary items | | VISA application | |
| | QWG | CWG | QWG | CWG | QWG | CWG | QWG | CWG |
| NB | 0.19 | 0.28 | 0.27 | 0.38 | 0.23 | 0.32 | 0.28 | 0.35 |
| KNN | 0.22 | 0.26 | 0.36 | 0.45 | 0.25 | 0.36 | 0.33 | 0.42 |
| LSI | 0.25 | 0.30 | 0.42 | 0.48 | 0.32 | 0.41 | 0.37 | 0.46 |
| DBN | 0.36 | 0.51 | 0.62 | 0.72 | 0.57 | 0.69 | 0.53 | 0.58 |

Table 2: Results of question / content word generation on the datasets from Yahoo! Answers.

sponding answer, although the lexical gaps exist between them and the feature sparsity is a common problem.

We can see that our method's precision of content word generation is higher than that of question word generation. This is reasonable because it tends to be easier to obtain the semantic links between the content words in the questions and those in the answers. For the question words, however, the clues hidden in the answers for prediction are less obvious. In this situation, the average precision of QWG has reached 52%, which indicates the deep network's ability to acquire the hidden semantic features.

| | |
|---|---|
| original | How do I go about planning my trip to Machu Picchu? |
| generated | How to plan a trip (travel) to Machu Picchu? |
| original | What should i pack for travel to Paris, and i'm a woman? |
| generated | What to take for the travel to Paris as a woman? |
| original | How much money will I need for the trip to Greece? |
| generated | How much money for taking the trip to Greece? |

Table 3: Question samples generated from the answers in the cQA corpora.

To show the performance of our generating approach directly, some generating samples are given in Table 3. In this table, the questions in the QA pairs from our testing data are taken as the original questions, and the corresponding answers are used to get the generated questions. As shown in Table 3, the generated questions are mostly shorter than the original ones. The reason is that our methodology focuses on the major contents of the object question sentences, and the less important contents are ignored.

## Conclusions

In this paper, we have proposed a deep belief network based statistical approach to generating questions according to the user-generated web community contents. The contributions of this paper can be summarized as follows: (1) this paper has presented a statistical method for web community oriented question generation. (2) by modeling the joint distributions of the QA pairs, the deep network is able to learn the semantic relationship between the words in the questions and their answers, so as to generate the essential words of the questions.

## Acknowledgement

The authors are grateful to the anonymous reviewers for their constructive comments. Special thanks to Dr. Rodney D. Nielsen. This work is supported by the National Natural Science Foundation of China (61100094 and 61272383), Research Fund for the Doctoral Program of Higher Education of China (20102302120053).

## References


Brown, J., Frishkoff, G., and Eskenazi, M. (2005). Automatic question generation for vocabulary assessment. In *Proceedings of EMNLP'05: HLT*, pages 819–826, Vancouver, British Columbia, Canada. ACL.

Harabagiu, S., Hickl, A., Lehmann, J., and Moldovan, D. (2005). Experiments with interactive question-answering. In *In Proceedings of ACL 05*, pages 60–69.

Hinton, G. E. (2002). Training products of experts by minimizing contrastive divergence. *Neural Computation*, 14.

Hinton, G. E., Osindero, S., and Teh, Y.-W. (2006). A fast learning algorithm for deep belief nets. *Neural Computation*, 18(7):1527–1554.

Hinton, G. E. and Salakhutdinov, R. R. (2006). Reducing the dimensionality of data with neural networks. *Science*, 313(5786):504–507.

Hoshino, A. and Nakagawa, H. (2005). A real-time multiple-choice question generation for language testing: a preliminary study. In *Proceedings of the second workshop on Building Educational Applications Using NLP*, EdAppsNLP 05, pages 17–20, Morristown, NJ, USA. ACL.

Nielsen, R., Buckingham, J., Knoll, G., Marsh, B., and Palen, L. (2008). A taxonomy of questions for question generation. In *Proceedings of Workshop on the Question Generation Shared Task and Evaluation Challenge*.

Nielsen, R. D. (2008). Question generation: Proposed challenge tasks and their evaluation. In *Proceedings of the Workshop on the Question Generation Shared Task and Evaluation Challenge*, Arlington, Virginia.

Rus, V., Cai, Z., and Graesser, A. C. (2007). Evaluation innatural language generation: The question genera-tion task. In *Proceedings of Workshop on Shared Tasks and Com-parative Evaluation in Natural Language Generation*.

Rus, V. and Graesser, A. (2009). The question generation task and evaluation challenge. Technical report, Institute for Intelligent Systems.

Rus, V., Wyse, B., Piwek, P., Lintean, M., Stoyanchev, S., and Moldovan, C. (2010). The first question generation shared task evaluation challenge. In *Proceedings of the Sixth International Natural Language Generation Conference (INLG 2010)*, Trim Castle, Ireland.

Salakhutdinov, R. and Hinton, G. (2009). Semantic hashing. *Int. J. Approx. Reasoning*, 50(7):969–978.

Vanderwende, L. (2008). The importance of beingimportant: Question generation. In *Proceedings of the Workshop on the Question Generation Shared Taskand Evaluation Challenge*.

Wang, W., Hao, T., and Liu, W. (2008). Automatic question generation for learning evaluation in medicine. In *Advances in Web Based Learning,ICWL 2007*, volume 4823 of *Lecture Notes in Computer Science*, pages 242–251. Springer Berlin / Heidelberg.

# Demo of iMAG possibilities: MT-postediting, translation quality evaluation, parallel corpus production

*WANG Ling Xiao, ZHANG Ying, Christian BOITET, Valerie BELLYNCK*
Lingxiao.Wang@imag.fr, Ying.Zhang@imag.fr,
Christian.Boitet@imag.fr, Valerie.Bellynck@imag.fr

ABSTRACT

An interactive Multilingual Access Gateway (iMAG) dedicated to a web site S (iMAG-S) is a good tool to make S accessible in many languages immediately and without editorial responsibility. Visitors of S as well as paid or unpaid post-editors and moderators contribute to the continuous and incremental improvement of the most important textual segments, and eventually of all. Pre-translations are produced by one or more free MT systems. Continuous use since 2008 on many web sites and for several access languages shows that a quality comparable to that of a first draft by junior professional translators is obtained in about 40% of the (human) time, sometimes less. There are two interesting side effects obtainable without any added cost: iMAGs can be used to produce high-quality parallel corpora and to set up a permanent task-based evaluation of multiple MT systems. We will demonstrate (1) the multilingual access to a web site, with online postediting of MT results "à la Google", (2) postediting in "advanced mode", using SECTra_w as a back-end, enabling online comparison of MT systems, (3) task-oriented built-in evaluation (postediting time), and (4) application to a large web site to get a trilingual parallel corpus where each segment has a reliability level and a quality score.

KEYWORDS: Online post-editing, interactive multilingual access gateway, free MT evaluation

TITLE AND ABSTRACT IN CHINESE

# iMAG功能展示：
# 机器翻译后编辑，翻译质量评估，平行语料生成

简述

一个iMAG (interactive Multilingual Access Gateway, 多语言交互式网关) 是很好的面向一个网站的工具，它可以提供对该网站的多语言访问，并且无需任何编辑。通过iMAG访问该网站的用户，可以作为有偿或无偿的后编辑人员或是管理者，来对该网站的文本段进行可持续的、增量的改进。该网站的预翻译是由一个或多个免费的MT系统提供的。自从2008年以来，通过iMAG对多个网站进行多语言的持续访问结果表明，对于相对翻译质量，首轮由初级翻译者提供的翻译，使用iMAG只占纯人工翻译40%的时间，或更少。iMAG有两个非常吸引人的方面并且无需额外成本：iMAG能用于产生高质量的平行语料，而且可以通过多个MT系统对其进行长久性的评估。我们将要展示：(1) 多语言访问目标网站，并对Google提供的预翻译进行在线后编辑，(2) 后编辑的高级模式，SECTra作为后台模块，可实现MT系统的在线比较，(3) 面向任务的评估（后编辑时间），和 (4) 应用到大型网站，可获得三种语言的平行语料，每个文字段都拥有可靠性和质量的评分。

关键词：在线后编辑，多语言交互网关，免费MT评估

*Proceedings of COLING 2012: Demonstration Papers*, pages 475–482,
COLING 2012, Mumbai, December 2012.

# 1 Introduction

An iMAG is a website used as a gateway allowing a multilingual access to one (in general) or several elected websites. The name "iMAG" stands for interactive Multilingual Access Gateway.

Apparently, an iMAG is similar to existing well-known translation gateways such as Google Translate, Systran, Reverso, etc. The first essential difference is that an iMAG is only used for elected websites. This allows the iMAG to manage the multilingualization of certain websites better than existing translation gateways. With an iMAG, we can enhance the quality of translated pages, starting from raw output of general-purpose and free MT servers, usually of low quality and often understandable unless one understands enough of the source language.

An iMAG is dedicated to an elected website, or rather to the elected sublanguage defined by one or more URLs and their textual content. It contains a translation memory (TM), both dedicated to the elected sublanguage. Segments are pre-translated not by a unique MT system, but by a (selectable) set of MT systems. Systran and Google are mainly used now, but specialized systems developed from the post-edit part of the TM, and based on Moses, will be also used in the future.

iMAG also contains a module SECTra (Système d'Exploitation de Corpus de Traductions sur le web), in English, "Contributive Operating System of Translation Corpora on the Web". SECTra is a Web-based system offering several services, such as supporting MT evaluation campaigns and online post-editing of MT results, to produce reference translations adapted to classical MT systems not built by machine learning from a parallel corpus.

# 2 Manipulation and pre-translation in the iMAG page

## 2.1 Access multilingual website by iMAG

Figure 1 shows the iMAG access interface to LIG (the Grenoble computer science laboratory) website. We choose target language (Chinese) in the pull-down menu. The page is now accessed in Chinese language. One or more free MT servers, in this case Google Translate and Systran, produce initial translations.

Figure 1: Access website of Grenoble computer science laboratory by iMAG

## 2.2 Post-edition and evaluation in web page context

In iMAG, user can also optimize the translation results. As shown in Figure 2, when the user moves the mouse on translation unit (for example: a word, a title), the system will automatically pop up a small dialog box. This dialog box display source language content in blue font, and user can post edit and evaluate the translation results.

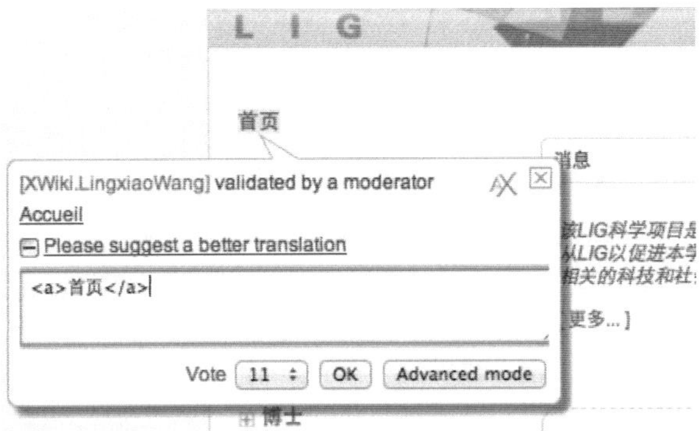


Figure 2. Optimize translation results in iMAG interface

If user is an anonymous, or non-privileged, this optimize translation and ratings only display to him, and he can't enter the advanced mode. If user has privilege, optimize translation and ratings will be stored in the system database, and also display to publics. If database contains multiple optimizes translations, system will select translation, which has the highest scores and time recently. For those users who have the appropriate permissions, they can come into "Advanced mode", and arrives into SECTra. This will be described in chapter 3.

## 2.3 Visualization of the translation quality

In the translated page, users can view quickly and clearly the translation quality of web pages by “reliability” mode. As shown in Figure 3, a color bracket encloses each translation unit. If user post-edit in this page, then his result will be displayed directly on the page, at the same time, bracket's color will be changed based on user permissions. Green brackets indicate that the translation results are edited and saved by privileged user. Orange means the translation results are edited and saved locally by anonymous users (only for anonymous users). Red indicate the translation results have never been edited. If the user clicks on the Original button, the left side of the browser will display the translation results; the right side displays the source language page.

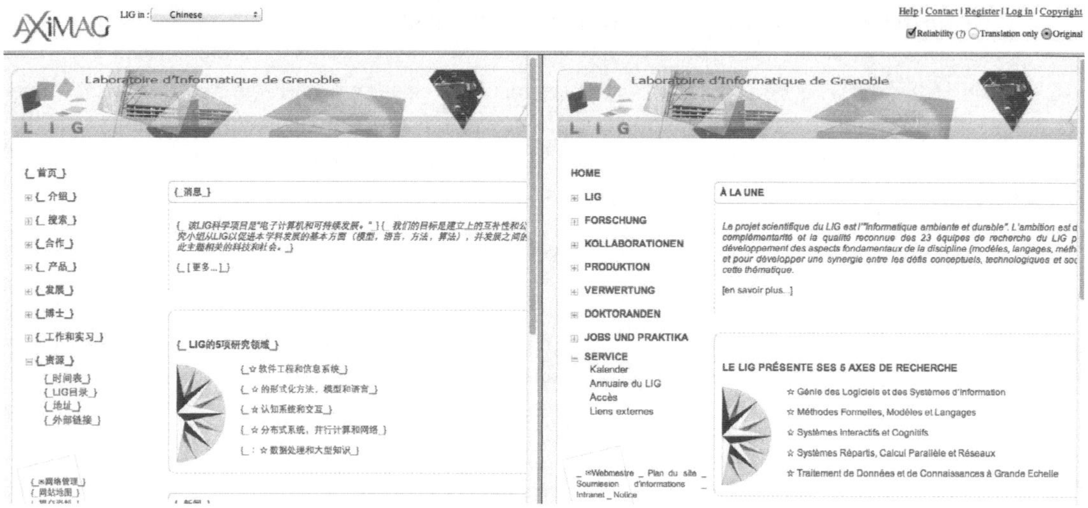


Figure 3. iMAG page display in "reliability", "original" mode

## 2.4 Interaction between iMAG and SECTra

Another possibility is to use the advanced mode (see the chapter 2.2), which consists in post-editing a pseudo-document that is in fact a part of the translation memory.

*Remark: content of chapter 2 will be on display in the video 1.*

## 3 Post-edition of TMs in "Advance Mode" (SECTra)

In order to obtain the translation results with the high quality, post-editing is a very important point, but also the most time-consuming work. In "Advance Mode" (SECTra), we can quickly get high quality translation results with minimum price. Figure 4 shows the interface of SECTra post-editing features.

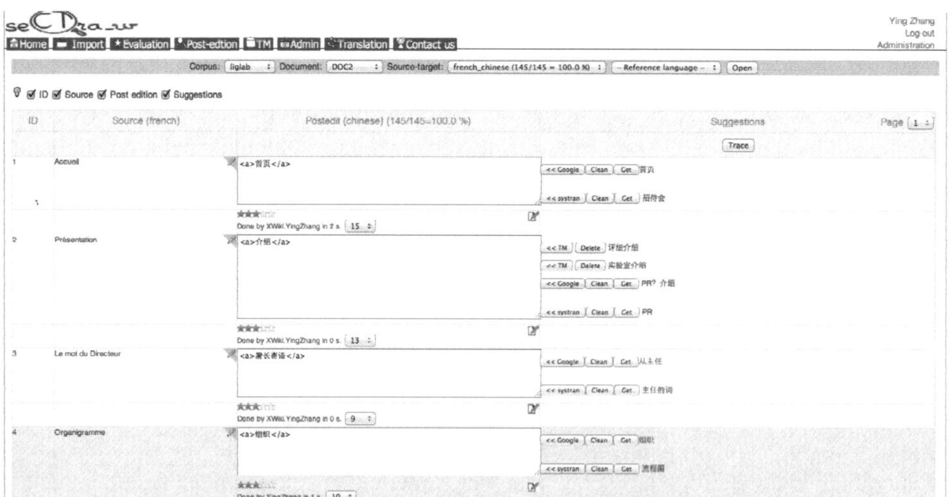


Figure 4: Advanced mode (SECTra screen).

## 3.1 Proposition of translation in SECTra

The first time user create an iMAG, he can select different machines translations systems for his website. Certainly he can also add new machine translation system later in SECTra. In interface of post edit, SECTra allows us to do operations for machine translation results (such as Google Translate, Systran translation), and translation memory database.

- For machine translation: clear translation result, re-call the machine translation system, and use the translation result.
- For translation memory: delete translation memory, use translation memory

## 3.2 Comparison between current translation and MT/TM results

As shown in Figure 5, users can compare distance between the current translation and translation memory, or between the current translation and machine translation.

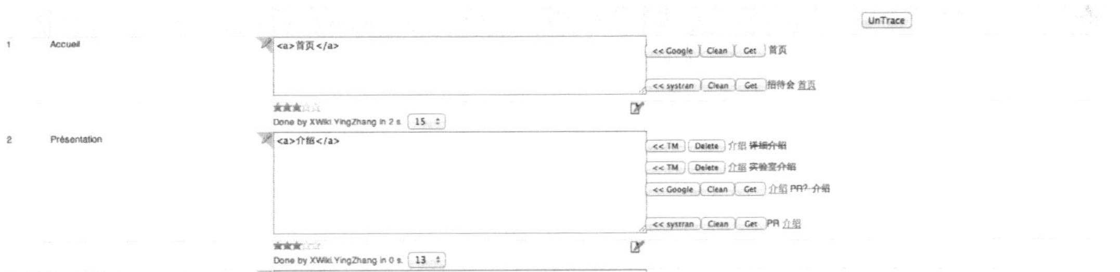

Figure 5: Comparison between current translation and MT/TM results

SECTra can also provide a reference language, which helps users to better post-edit, as shown in Figure 6.

Figure 6: Interface with reference language

## 3.3 Post-edition and evaluation

Users can also vote the number of stars and the value of rating for these post-editions. The number of stars is the control ability of the language pair (the source language and the target language) of the current post-edition. The value of rating is the satisfaction level of the current post-edition.

In the process of post-edition, the system will automatically record the time and segments number. As the first two authors are Chinese, they have experimented with French-Chinese (on a town web site) and with Chinese-English (on a Chinese web site dedicated to a famous Chinese NLP scientist). Here are the results.

| Language pair | Human PE time | Human first draft time | # segments | # source words (or characters) | # target words (or characters) |
|---|---|---|---|---|---|
| Fr->Zh | 17 mins | 72 mins | 76 | 303 (Fr) — 1.16 p. | 519 (Zh) — 1.3 p. |
| Zh->En | 16 mins | 75 mins | 32 | 495 (Zh) — 1.25 p. | 307 (En) — 1.16 p. |

### 3.4 Visualization of post-edition in iMAG Web pages

Post-edition results will be displayed directly on the iMAG Web page, and bracket's color will be changed based on user permissions (see the chapter 2.3).

*Remark: content of chapter 3 will be on display in the video 2.*

## 4. To obtain a high-quality parallel corpus

### 4.1 Filtering and selection of segments

On the platform of the SECTra, the user can export corpus of TM. At the time of export, we can filter segments by stars and scores. In Figure 7, for example the source language is French, the target language is Chinese, and we can select part of segments for export.

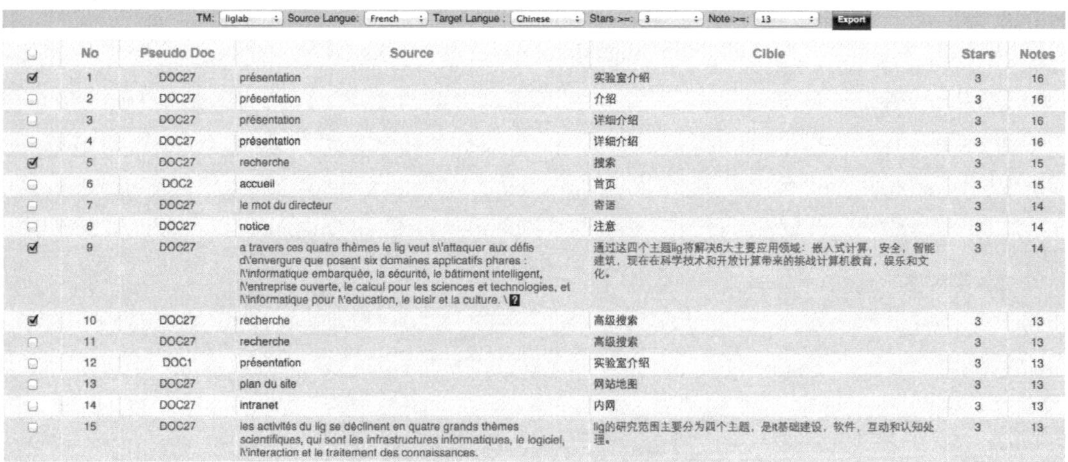
TM: liglab Source Langue: French Target Langue : Chinese Stars >=: 3 Note >=: 13 Export

| No | Pseudo Doc | Source | Cible | Stars | Notes |
|---|---|---|---|---|---|
| 1 | DOC27 | présentation | 实验室介绍 | 3 | 16 |
| 2 | DOC27 | présentation | 介绍 | 3 | 16 |
| 3 | DOC27 | présentation | 详细介绍 | 3 | 16 |
| 4 | DOC27 | présentation | 详细介绍 | 3 | 16 |
| 5 | DOC27 | recherche | 搜索 | 3 | 15 |
| 6 | DOC2 | accueil | 首页 | 3 | 15 |
| 7 | DOC27 | le mot du directeur | 寄语 | 3 | 14 |
| 8 | DOC27 | notice | 注意 | 3 | 14 |
| 9 | DOC27 | a travers ces quatre thèmes le lig veut s\'attaquer aux défis d\'envergure que posent six domaines applicatifs phares : l\'informatique embarquée, la sécurité, le bâtiment intelligent, l\'entreprise ouverte, le calcul pour les sciences et technologies, et l\'informatique pour l\'education, le loisir et la culture. \? | 通过这四个主题lig将解决6大主要应用领域：嵌入式计算，安全，智能建筑，现在在科学技术和开放计算带来的挑战计算机教育，娱乐和文化。 | 3 | 14 |
| 10 | DOC27 | recherche | 高级搜索 | 3 | 13 |
| 11 | DOC27 | recherche | 高级搜索 | 3 | 13 |
| 12 | DOC1 | présentation | 实验室介绍 | 3 | 13 |
| 13 | DOC27 | plan du site | 网站地图 | 3 | 13 |
| 14 | DOC27 | intranet | 内网 | 3 | 13 |
| 15 | DOC27 | les activités du lig se déclinent en quatre grands thèmes scientifiques, qui sont les infrastructures informatiques, le logiciel, l\'interaction et le traitement des connaissances. | lig的研究范围主要分为四个主题，是it基础建设，软件，互动和认知处理。 | 3 | 13 |

Figure 7. Interface of export corpus

### 4.2 Production of parallel corpus and download

For the selected parallel corpus, the system will generate two txt files, and users may download these files, the results shown in Figure 9.

Figure 8. Corpus files

Figure 9. Downloaded corpus files

*Remark: content of chapter 4 will be on display in the video 3.*

## 5. Conclusion and perspectives

Continuous use since 2008 on many web sites and for several access languages shows that a quality comparable to that of a first draft by junior professional translators is obtained in about 40% of the (human) time, sometimes less.

In the near future, the system will be integrated Moses, and based on Moses for provide more accurate TA results.

## References

(2009) *A Web-oriented System to Manage the Translation of an Online Encyclopedia Using Classical MT and Deconversion from UNL.* Proc. CCC 2009

(2010) *The iMAG concept: multilingual access gateway to an elected Web site with incremental quality increase through collaborative post-edition of MT pretranslations.*

(2008) *an Online Collaborative System for Evaluating, Post-editing and Presenting MT Translation Corpora.* Proc. LREC-08, Marrakech, 27-31/5/08, ELRA/ELDA, ed., 8 p.

Huynh C.-P., Blanchon H. & Nguyen H.-T. (2008) *A Web-oriented System to Manage the Translation of an Online Encyclopedia Using Classical MT and Deconversion from UNL.* Proc. CI-2008 (WS of ASWC-08), Bangkok, 9/12/08, ACL, ed., 8 p.

# Jane 2: Open Source Phrase-based and Hierarchical Statistical Machine Translation

*Joern Wuebker   Matthias Huck   Stephan Peitz   Malte Nuhn*
*Markus Freitag   Jan-Thorsten Peter   Saab Mansour   Hermann Ney*
Human Language Technology and Pattern Recognition Group
Computer Science Department
RWTH Aachen University
D-52056 Aachen, Germany
`<surname>@cs.rwth-aachen.de`

ABSTRACT
We present Jane 2, an open source toolkit supporting both the phrase-based and the hierarchical phrase-based paradigm for statistical machine translation. It is implemented in C++ and provides efficient decoding algorithms and data structures. This work focuses on the description of its phrase-based functionality. In addition to the standard pipeline, including phrase extraction and parameter optimization, Jane 2 contains several state-of-the-art extensions and tools. Forced alignment phrase training can considerably reduce rule table size while learning the translation scores in a more principled manner. Word class language models can be used to integrate longer context with a reduced vocabulary size. Rule table interpolation is applicable for different tasks, e.g. domain adaptation. The decoder distinguishes between lexical and coverage pruning and applies reordering constraints for efficiency.

KEYWORDS: statistical machine translation, open source toolkit, phrase-based translation, hierarchical translation.

*Proceedings of COLING 2012: Demonstration Papers*, pages 483–492,
COLING 2012, Mumbai, December 2012.

## 1 Introduction

This work describes version 2 of Jane, an open source statistical machine translation (SMT) toolkit. Jane 2 provides implementations for the standard pipeline for SMT, including rule table generation, parameter optimization, and decoding. The two dominating paradigms in current research, the phrase-based (Koehn et al., 2003) and the hierarchical (Chiang, 2007) approach to SMT, are fully supported. While there are other open source toolkits available which are capable of performing similar or even the same tasks, Jane 2 has some unique properties that make it an attractive alternative for research.

**Efficiency.** Jane 2 implements several different decoding algorithms which make use of state-of-the-art pruning techniques and efficient data structures in order to minimize memory usage and runtime. It is capable of on-demand loading of language and translation models, and its flexible parameterization allows for fine-grained configuration tradeoffs between efficiency and translation quality.

**Parallelization.** Most operations—including phrase extraction, optimization, and decoding—can be parallelized under an Oracle Grid Engine or Platform LSF batch system.

**Documentation.** The extensive manual (Vilar et al., 2012b) contains simple walkthroughs to get started as well as descriptions of the features and their parameters.

**Extensibility.** A modular design and flexible extension mechanisms allow for easy integration of novel features and translation approaches.

Jane is developed in C++ with special attention to clean code. It was originally released as a purely hierarchical machine translation toolkit. Version 1 is described in detail in (Vilar et al., 2010a), (Stein et al., 2011), and (Vilar et al., 2012a). Jane 2 is available under an open source non-commercial license and can be downloaded from `www.hltpr.rwth-aachen.de/jane`. Here we focus on presenting Jane's phrase-based translation mode, which has been added to the toolkit in version 2.*

## 2 Related Work

**Moses** (Koehn et al., 2007) is a widely used open source toolkit for statistical machine translation. It was originally designed for phrase-based decoding, but now also supports the hierarchical paradigm. Moses provides tools for the complete machine translation pipeline, contains implementations for a wide variety of different models and is well documented.

**Joshua** (Li et al., 2009) is written in Java and implements the full pipeline for hierarchical machine translation. In addition to standard hierarchical rule tables, it is capable of extracting syntax augmented machine translation (SAMT) grammars (Zollmann and Venugopal, 2006).

**cdec** (Dyer et al., 2010) is a flexible decoding framework with a unified representation for translation forests.

**Ncode** (Crego et al., 2011) implements the $n$-gram-based approach to machine translation (Mariño et al., 2006). Reordering is performed by creating a lattice in a preprocessing step, which is passed on to the monotone decoder.

**Phrasal** (Cer et al., 2010) is an open source machine translation package with a Java implementation of the phrase-based machine translation paradigm. Phrasal is capable of extracting and translating with discontinuous phrases (Galley and Manning, 2010).

**NiuTrans** (Xiao et al., 2012) is developed in C++ and supports phrase-based, hierarchical phrase-based and syntax-based models.

*See (Huck et al., 2012b) for a description of novel features for hierarchical translation in version 2 of Jane.

# 3 Overview of the Jane 2 Open Source SMT Toolkit

## 3.1 Rule extraction

Jane 2 provides a single-command framework for rule extraction of both hierarchical and phrase-based rule tables. Rule extraction is done using a two pass algorithm which allows extracting only the rules needed to translate a specific corpus. This is especially useful for cutting down the large amount of rules that arise during extraction of hierarchical rules. A binary rule table format allows on-demand loading of the necessary phrases to minimize memory consumption. Both hierarchical and phrase-based extraction implement heuristics to make sure that every word is extracted with a single-word phrase, even if they are are not consistent with the bilingual alignment. Besides calculating source-to-target and target-to-source phrase probabilities, Jane 2 features a customizable IBM1 scorer and binary count features. Further, Jane 2 includes multiple tools that allow pruning, filtering and modifying rule tables.

In the standard setting, each sentence pair in the training corpus is assigned a weight of 1. A new feature in Jane 2 is weighted phrase extraction for phrase-based rules, which allows assigning arbitrary weights for each sentence pair. This feature can be utilized for domain adaptation, where the weight represents the relatedness of the sentence pair to the domain.

## 3.2 Rule table interpolation

Jane 2 also includes a functionality for rule table interpolation which is especially interesting for combining in-domain and out-of-domain data. Having specified a set of rule tables $T_1, \ldots, T_i, \ldots, T_I$ to interpolate, Jane 2 can be configured to include all combinations of union and intersection for the entries contained in the input rule tables. Furthermore, the number and types of features to create from the input tables can be specified. Currently available options include *loglinear* ($\sum_{i=1}^{I} f_i \cdot c_i$), *linear* ($\log \sum_{i=1}^{I} \exp(f_i) \cdot c_i$), *copy* ($f_i$, $i$ fixed), *max* ($\max_{i=1}^{I} f_i$) and *ifelse* ($f_i$,lowest $i$ s.t. $T_i$ contains the rule). The algorithm to create the output table is efficient (linear time), given the input rule tables are sorted.

## 3.3 Decoders

**Hierarchical translation.** Jane implements three parsing-based search strategies for hierarchical translation: *cube pruning* (Chiang, 2007), *cube growing* (Huang and Chiang, 2007) with various heuristics for language model score computation (Vilar and Ney, 2009), and *source cardinality synchronous cube pruning* (Vilar and Ney, 2012). Pruning settings can be configured flexibly for all hierarchical search algorithms.

**Phrase-based translation.** The phrase-based decoding algorithm in Jane 2 is a *source cardinality synchronous search* (SCSS) procedure and applies separate pruning to lexical and coverage hypotheses similar to (Zens and Ney, 2008). The distinction between lexical and coverage hypotheses has been shown to have a significant positive effect on the scalability of the algorithm. For efficient decoding, language model look-ahead (Wuebker et al., 2012) can be applied. Jane 2 also provides an additional *FastSCSS* decoder, which can only produce single-best output, but is considerably faster by not maintaining separate model costs and by deleting recombined hypotheses.

## 3.4 Optimization

Log-linear feature weights (Och and Ney, 2002) can be optimized with either the Downhill Simplex algorithm (Nelder and Mead, 1965), Och's minimum error rate training (MERT) (Och, 2003), or the Margin Infused Relaxed Algorithm (MIRA) (Chiang et al., 2009).

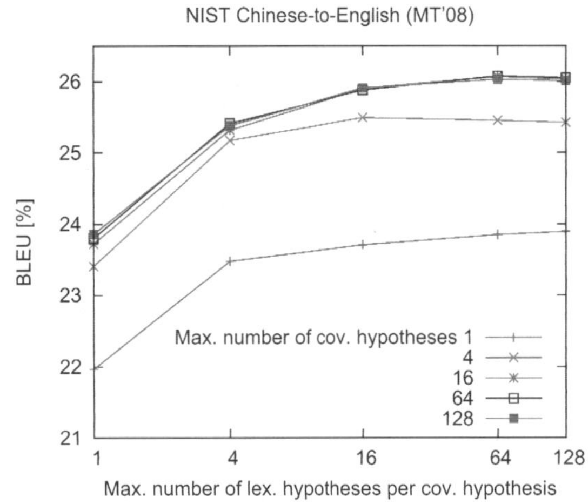


Figure 1: Effect of pruning parameters in the phrase-based decoder for the NIST Chinese→English translation task.

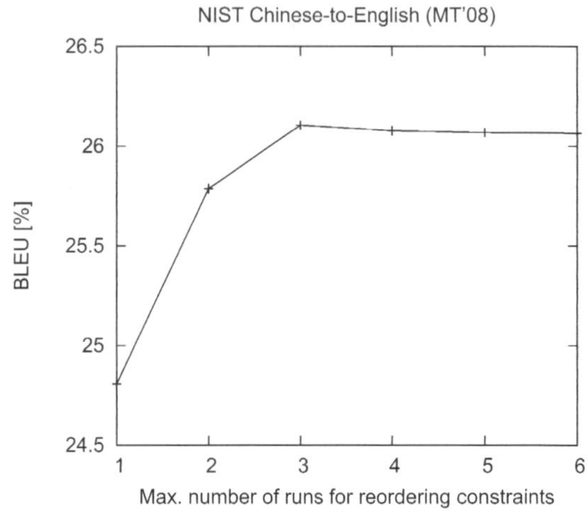


Figure 2: Effect of IBM phrase reordering constraints in the phrase-based decoder for the NIST Chinese→English translation task.

The challenge for optimization techniques is to find a good local optimum while avoiding bad local optima. Downhill Simplex and Och's method work well for a relatively small set of scaling factors. In experiments, Och's method yields better results and needs a lower number of iterations than Downhill Simplex. Both Downhill Simplex and Och's method have problems with large amounts of scaling factors (Chiang et al., 2008). (Watanabe et al., 2007) first used MIRA in SMT, which the authors claim to work well with a huge amount of features. (Chiang et al., 2009) get a significant improvement with an extremely large amount of features optimized by MIRA. Our implementation is very similar to the one presented in the above mentioned papers. MIRA is a good choice for a scaling factor set of more than 40 features.

### 3.5 Additional functionality

Jane additionally implements a number of advanced techniques. These range from discriminative word lexicon (DWL) models and triplet lexicon models (Mauser et al., 2009; Huck et al., 2010) over syntactic enhancements like parse matching (Vilar et al., 2008), preference grammars (Venugopal and Zollmann, 2009; Stein et al., 2010), soft string-to-dependency translation (Peter et al., 2011) and pseudo-syntactic enhancements like poor man's syntax (Vilar et al., 2010b) to discriminative lexicalized reordering extensions (Huck et al., 2012a).

## 4 Phrase-based Translation with Jane 2

### 4.1 Lexical and coverage pruning

In this section, we evaluate the effect of lexical pruning per coverage and coverage pruning per cardinality (Zens and Ney, 2008) in Jane's phrase-based decoder.

For a foreign input sentence $f_1^J$ of length $J$, the set of source positions that are already translated (*covered*) in one state of the search process of the phrase-based translation system is called a *coverage* $C \subseteq \{1, \ldots, J\}$. *Lexical hypotheses* may differ in their coverage, in the current source sentence position, as well as in their language model history. The term *coverage hypothesis* is used to refer to the set of all lexical hypotheses with the same coverage $C$. In *lexical pruning per coverage*, the scores of all lexical hypotheses that have the same coverage $C$ are compared. In *coverage pruning per cardinality*, the scores of all coverage hypotheses

| | English→French | | German→English | |
|---|---|---|---|---|
| | BLEU [%] | TER [%] | BLEU [%] | TER [%] |
| Baseline | 31.7 | 50.5 | 29.2 | 50.2 |
| + word class LM | 32.0 | 50.1 | 29.8 | 49.7 |

Table 1: Comparison of baseline systems and systems augmented with a 7-gram word class language model on different language pairs.

that share the same cardinality $c = |C|$ are compared. The score of a coverage hypothesis is for this purpose defined as the maximum score of any lexical hypothesis with coverage $C$. Histogram pruning is applied with parameters $N_C$ for coverage pruning per cardinality and $N_L$ for lexical pruning per coverage. Thus, if there are more than $N_C$ coverage hypotheses for a particular cardinality $c$, only the best $N_C$ candidates are kept, and if there are more than $N_L$ lexical hypotheses for a particular coverage $C$, only the best $N_L$ candidates are kept, respectively. Note that all lexical hypotheses with coverage $C$ are dismissed if a coverage hypothesis $C$ gets pruned.

We present empirical results on the NIST Chinese→English MT'08 translation task (NIST, 2008). We work with a parallel training corpus of 3.0 M Chinese–English sentences pairs (77.5 M Chinese / 81.0 M English running words). We evaluate all combinations of $N_C \in \{1, 4, 16, 64, 128\}$ and $N_L \in \{1, 4, 16, 64, 128\}$. The results are shown in Figure 1. Values beyond 16 of any of the two pruning parameters barely yield any additional improvement.

## 4.2 Reordering constraints

Restricting the possible reorderings is important in order to keep the search procedure tractable (Knight, 1999). Many decoders are limited to applying a jump distance limit. The search algorithm implemented in Jane 2 in addition is capable of discarding all source-side coverages with more than a maximum number of isolated contiguous runs. This restriction is known as *IBM phrase reordering constraints* (Zens et al., 2004). Configuring a maximum of one run is equivalent to monotone translation in this terminology. In the experiments from Section 4.1, we adopted the IBM phrase reordering constraints with a maximum of four runs and a jump distance limit of ten. We now evaluate the maximum runs parameter in the range from 1 to 6 with $N_C = 64$ and $N_L = 64$. The results are shown in Figure 2. Values beyond three do not improve translation quality any further, while monotone translation is considerably worse than translation with reorderings enabled.

## 4.3 Word class language models

In addition to the standard language model, a language model based on word classes can be used for phrase-based decoding in Jane 2. By clustering words into word classes, e.g. with the tool *mkcls* (Och, 2000), the vocabulary size is reduced and language models with higher $n$-gram order can be trained. By using a higher order in the translation process, the decoder is able to capture long-range dependencies.

In Table 1 the impact of the word class language model on different language pairs is shown. The experiments were carried out on the English→French and German→English MT tracks (TED task) of the IWSLT 2012 evaluation campaign (IWSLT, 2012). By applying a 7-gram word class language model, we achieve improvements of up to +0.6% BLEU and 0.5% TER.

| system | Bleu [%] | Ter [%] | memory | words/sec |
|---|---|---|---|---|
| Jane | 20.1 | 63.7 | 10G | 7.7 (18.1) |
| Moses | 19.0 | 65.1 | 22G | 1.8 |
| Moses with Jane rule table | 20.1 | 63.8 | 19G | 1.9 |

Table 2: Comparison of Moses with the phrase-based Jane 2 SCSS decoder, and its fast implementation optimized for single-best output (FastSCSS, in parentheses). All models are loaded into memory before decoding and loading time is eliminated for speed computation.

## 4.4 Forced alignment phrase training

Jane 2 features a framework to easily perform forced alignment phrase training, as described by (Wuebker et al., 2010). Phrase training is called with a single command for any number of iterations. Leave-one-out and cross-validation are automatically applied. It is made efficient by first performing bilingual phrase matching before search and by discarding the language model. To achieve good coverage of the training data, *backoff phrases* can be added to the translation model on-the-fly and *fallback runs* allow the decoder to retry with different parameterization, if aligning a sentence pair failed. This phrase training can considerably reduce rule table size, while providing a more statistcally sound way of estimating the translation probabilities.

## 4.5 Comparison with Moses

We compare the phrase-based decoder implemented in Jane 2 with Moses on the German→English task of the *EMNLP 2011 Sixth Workshop on Statistical Machine Translation* (WMT, 2011) on `newstest2009` in Table 2, keeping track of memory consumption and decoding speed. We use the same 4-gram LM for both Moses and Jane, and MERT is run separately for each setup. Jane's rule table is trained with three iterations of forced alignment (see Section 4.4). Moses is run in its standard setup (without lexicalized reordering models). For comparison we also ran Moses with our rule table. In this setup, Jane outperforms Moses by 1.1% Bleu. Moses can close the gap by using Jane's rule table. When the translation and language model are loaded into memory, Jane's memory consumption is about half that of Moses, and it is four times faster (ten times when using the FastSCSS decoder).

# 5 Conclusions

Jane is a flexible and efficient state-of-the-art SMT toolkit that is freely available to the scientific community. Jane's implementation of a source cardinality synchronous search algorithm for phrase-based translation has been released with version 2 of the toolkit. The algorithm applies separate pruning to lexical and coverage hypotheses and allows for restricting the possible reorderings via IBM phrase reordering constraints. A word class language model can be utilized during decoding. Phrase translation models can optionally be trained using forced alignment with leave-one-out.

## Acknowledgments

This work was partly achieved as part of the Quaero Programme, funded by OSEO, French State agency for innovation. The research leading to these results has also received funding from the European Union Seventh Framework Programme (FP7/2007-2013) under grant agreement n° 287658 and the FP7 project T4ME Net, Contract n° 249119.

## References


Cer, D., Galley, M., Jurafsky, D., and Manning, C. D. (2010). Phrasal: A Statistical Machine Translation Toolkit for Exploring New Model Features. In *Proceedings of the NAACL HLT 2010 Demonstration Session*, pages 9–12, Los Angeles, CA, USA.

Chiang, D. (2007). Hierarchical phrase-based translation. *Computational Linguistics*, 33(2):201–228.

Chiang, D., Knight, K., and Wang, W. (2009). 11,001 New Features for Statistical Machine Translation. In *Proc. of the Human Language Technology Conf. / North American Chapter of the Assoc. for Computational Linguistics (HLT-NAACL)*, pages 218–226, Boulder, CO, USA.

Chiang, D., Marton, Y., and Resnik, P. (2008). Online Large-Margin Training of Syntactic and Structural Translation Features. In *Proceedings of the 2008 Conference on Empirical Methods in Natural Language Processing*, pages 224–233, Honolulu, HI, USA.

Crego, J. M., Yvon, F., and Mariño, J. B. (2011). Ncode: an Open Source Bilingual N-gram SMT Toolkit. *The Prague Bulletin of Mathematical Linguistics*, 96:49–58.

Dyer, C., Lopez, A., Ganitkevitch, J., Weese, J., Ture, F., Blunsom, P., Setiawan, H., Eidelman, V., and Resnik, P. (2010). cdec: A Decoder, Alignment, and Learning framework for finite-state and context-free translation models. In *Proceedings of the ACL 2010 System Demonstrations*, ACLDemos '10, pages 7–12, Uppsala, Sweden.

Galley, M. and Manning, C. (2010). Accurate Non-Hierarchical Phrase-Based Translation. In *Proc. of the Human Language Technology Conf. / North American Chapter of the Assoc. for Computational Linguistics (HLT-NAACL)*, pages 966–974, Los Angeles, CA, USA.

Huang, L. and Chiang, D. (2007). Forest Rescoring: Faster Decoding with Integrated Language Models. In *Proceedings of the 45th Annual Meeting of the Association for Computational Linguistics*, pages 144–151, Prague, Czech Republic.

Huck, M., Peitz, S., Freitag, M., and Ney, H. (2012a). Discriminative Reordering Extensions for Hierarchical Phrase-Based Machine Translation. In *Proc. of the 16th Annual Conf. of the European Association for Machine Translation (EAMT)*, pages 313–320, Trento, Italy.

Huck, M., Peter, J.-T., Freitag, M., Peitz, S., and Ney, H. (2012b). Hierarchical Phrase-Based Translation with Jane 2. *The Prague Bulletin of Mathematical Linguistics*, (98):37–50.

Huck, M., Ratajczak, M., Lehnen, P., and Ney, H. (2010). A Comparison of Various Types of Extended Lexicon Models for Statistical Machine Translation. In *Proc. of the Conf. of the Assoc. for Machine Translation in the Americas (AMTA)*, Denver, CO, USA.

IWSLT (2012). TED task of the IWSLT 2012 evaluation campaign. `http://www.iwslt2012.org/index.php/evaluation-campaign/ted-task/`.

Knight, K. (1999). Decoding Complexity in Word-Replacement Translation Models. *Computational Linguistics*, 25(4):607–615.

Koehn, P., Hoang, H., Birch, A., Callison-Burch, C., Federico, M., Bertoldi, N., Cowan, B., Shen, W., Moran, C., Zens, R., Dyer, C., Bojar, O., Constantine, A., and Herbst, E. (2007). Moses: Open Source Toolkit for Statistical Machine Translation. In *Annual Meeting of the Association for Computational Linguistics (ACL), demonstration session*, pages 177–180, Prague, Czech Republic.

Koehn, P., Och, F. J., and Marcu, D. (2003). Statistical Phrase-Based Translation. In *Proceedings of the 2003 Meeting of the North American chapter of the Association for Computational Linguistics (NAACL-03)*, pages 127–133, Edmonton, Canada.

Li, Z., Callison-Burch, C., Dyer, C., Ganitkevitch, J., Khudanpur, S., Schwartz, L., Thornton, W., Weese, J., and Zaidan, O. (2009). Joshua: An Open Source Toolkit for Parsing-based Machine Translation. In *Proceedings of the 4th EACL Workshop on Statistical Machine Translation (WMT09)*, pages 135–139, Athens, Greece.

Mariño, J. B., Banchs, R. E., Crego, J. M., de Gispert, A., Lambert, P., Fonollosa, J. A. R., and Costa-Jussà, M. R. (2006). N-gram-based Machine Translation. *Computational Linguistics*, 32(4):527–549.

Mauser, A., Hasan, S., and Ney, H. (2009). Extending Statistical Machine Translation with Discriminative and Trigger-Based Lexicon Models. In *Proc. of the Conf. on Empirical Methods for Natural Language Processing (EMNLP)*, pages 210–217, Singapore.

Nelder, J. A. and Mead, R. (1965). A Simplex Method for Function Minimization. *The Computer Journal*, 7:308–313.

NIST (2008). Open machine translation 2008 evaluation (MT08). `http://www.itl.nist.gov/iad/mig/tests/mt/2008/`.

Och, F. J. (2000). mkcls: Training of word classes. `http://www.hltpr.rwth-aachen.de/web/Software/mkcls.html`.

Och, F. J. (2003). Minimum Error Rate Training in Statistical Machine Translation. In *Proc. of the 41th Annual Meeting of the Association for Computational Linguistics (ACL)*, pages 160–167, Sapporo, Japan.

Och, F. J. and Ney, H. (2002). Discriminative Training and Maximum Entropy Models for Statistical Machine Translation. In *Proceedings of the 40th Annual Meeting of the Association for Computational Linguistics*, pages 295–302, Philadelphia, PA, USA.

Peter, J.-T., Huck, M., Ney, H., and Stein, D. (2011). Soft String-to-Dependency Hierarchical Machine Translation. In *Proc. of the Int. Workshop on Spoken Language Translation (IWSLT)*, pages 246–253, San Francisco, CA, USA.

Stein, D., Peitz, S., Vilar, D., and Ney, H. (2010). A Cocktail of Deep Syntactic Features for Hierarchical Machine Translation. In *Proc. of the Conf. of the Assoc. for Machine Translation in the Americas (AMTA)*, Denver, CO, USA.

Stein, D., Vilar, D., Peitz, S., Freitag, M., Huck, M., and Ney, H. (2011). A Guide to Jane, an Open Source Hierarchical Translation Toolkit. *The Prague Bulletin of Mathematical Linguistics*, (95):5–18.

Venugopal, A. and Zollmann, A. (2009). Preference Grammars: Softening Syntactic Constraints to Improve Statistical Machine Translation. In *Proceedings of Human Language Technologies: The 2009 Annual Conference of the North American Chapter of the Association for Computational Linguistics*, pages 236–244, Boulder, Colorado, USA.

Vilar, D. and Ney, H. (2009). On LM Heuristics for the Cube Growing Algorithm. In *Proc. of the Annual Conf. of the European Assoc. for Machine Translation (EAMT)*, pages 242–249, Barcelona, Spain.

Vilar, D. and Ney, H. (2012). Cardinality pruning and language model heuristics for hierarchical phrase-based translation. *Machine Translation*, 26(3):217–254.

Vilar, D., Stein, D., Huck, M., and Ney, H. (2010a). Jane: Open Source Hierarchical Translation, Extended with Reordering and Lexicon Models. In *ACL 2010 Joint Fifth Workshop on Statistical Machine Translation and Metrics MATR*, pages 262–270, Uppsala, Sweden.

Vilar, D., Stein, D., Huck, M., and Ney, H. (2012a). Jane: an advanced freely available hierarchical machine translation toolkit. *Machine Translation*, 26(3):197–216.

Vilar, D., Stein, D., Huck, M., Wuebker, J., Freitag, M., Peitz, S., Nuhn, M., and Peter, J.-T. (2012b). Jane: User's Manual. `http://www.hltpr.rwth-aachen.de/jane/manual.pdf`.

Vilar, D., Stein, D., and Ney, H. (2008). Analysing Soft Syntax Features and Heuristics for Hierarchical Phrase Based Machine Translation. In *Proc. of the Int. Workshop on Spoken Language Translation (IWSLT)*, pages 190–197, Waikiki, HI, USA.

Vilar, D., Stein, D., Peitz, S., and Ney, H. (2010b). If I Only Had a Parser: Poor Man's Syntax for Hierarchical Machine Translation. In *Proc. of the Int. Workshop on Spoken Language Translation (IWSLT)*, pages 345–352, Paris, France.

Watanabe, T., Suzuki, J., Tsukada, H., and Isozaki, H. (2007). Online Large-Margin Training for Statistical Machine Translation. In *Proceedings of the 2007 Joint Conference on Empirical Methods in Natural Language Processing and Computational Natural Language Learning (EMNLP-CoNLL)*, pages 764–773, Prague, Czech Republic.

WMT (2011). EMNLP 2011 Sixth Workshop on Statistical Machine Translation. `http://www.statmt.org/wmt11/`.

Wuebker, J., Mauser, A., and Ney, H. (2010). Training Phrase Translation Models with Leaving-One-Out. In *Proc. of the 48th Annual Meeting of the Association for Computational Linguistics (ACL)*, pages 475–484, Uppsala, Sweden.

Wuebker, J., Ney, H., and Zens, R. (2012). Fast and Scalable Decoding with Language Model Look-Ahead for Phrase-based Statistical Machine Translation. In *Annual Meeting of the Assoc. for Computational Linguistics*, pages 28–32, Jeju, Republic of Korea.

Xiao, T., Zhu, J., Zhang, H., and Li, Q. (2012). NiuTrans: An Open Source Toolkit for Phrase-based and Syntax-based Machine Translation. In *Proceedings of the ACL 2012 System Demonstrations*, pages 19–24, Jeju, Republic of Korea.

Zens, R. and Ney, H. (2008). Improvements in Dynamic Programming Beam Search for Phrase-based Statistical Machine Translation. In *Proc. of the Int. Workshop on Spoken Language Translation (IWSLT)*, pages 195–205, Honolulu, HI, USA.

Zens, R., Ney, H., Watanabe, T., and Sumita, E. (2004). Reordering Constraints for Phrase-Based Statistical Machine Translation. In *COLING '04: The 20th Int. Conf. on Computational Linguistics*, pages 205–211, Geneva, Switzerland.

Zollmann, A. and Venugopal, A. (2006). Syntax Augmented Machine Translation via Chart Parsing. In *Proc. of the Workshop on Statistical Machine Translation (WMT)*, pages 138–141, New York City, NY, USA.

# Automatic Extraction of Turkish Hypernym-Hyponym Pairs From Large Corpus

Savaş Yıldırım and Tuğba Yıldız
Istanbul Bilgi University
Department of Computer Engineering
Engineering Faculty
savasy@bilgi.edu.tr, tdalyan@bilgi.edu.tr

ABSTRACT
In this paper, we propose a fully automatic system for acquisition of hypernym/hyponymy relations from large corpus in Turkish Language. The method relies on both lexico-syntactic pattern and semantic similarity. Once the model has extracted the seeds by using patterns, it applies similarity based expansion in order to increase recall. For the expansion, several scoring functions within a bootstrapping algorithm are applied and compared. We show that a model based on a particular lexico-syntactic pattern for Turkish Language can successfully retrieve many hypernym/hyponym relations with high precision. We further demonstrate that the model can statistically expand the hyponym list to go beyond the limitations of lexico-syntactic patterns and get better recall. During the expansion phase, the hypernym/hyponym pairs are automatically and incrementally extracted depending on their statistics by employing various association measures and graph-based scoring. In brief, the fully automatic model mines only a large corpus and produces is-a relations with promising precision and recall. To achieve this goal, several methods and approaches were designed, implemented, compared and evaluated.

KEYWORDS: hypernym/hyponym, lexico-syntactic patterns.

*Proceedings of COLING 2012: Demonstration Papers*, pages 493–500,
COLING 2012, Mumbai, December 2012.

# 1 Introduction

In this study, we describe how to acquire hypernym/hyponymy relations from a Turkish corpora (Sak et al., 2008) in a fully automatic way. The system extracts possible hypernym/hyponym pairs by using lexico-syntactic patterns, then it expands the hyponym list depending on semantic similarity.

The Hypernym/Hyponym relation is one of the semantic relations that play an important role for NLP. The terms hyponym and hypernym have the definition summarized as "hyponym is (a kind) of hypernym" (Miller et al., 1990). In recent years, many approaches have been developed to build semantic lexicons and extract the relations from a corpus or a dictionary. Hand-built lexicons, such as Cyc (Lenat et al., 1986) and WordNet (Miller et al., 1990; Miller, 1995; Fellbaum, 1998), are the most useful to provide resources for NLP applications. Some attempts (Markowitz et al., 1986; Alshawi, 1987; Jensen and Binot, 1987; Ahlswede and Evens, 1988) used patterns to extract semantic relation from a dictionary. Hearst was the first to apply a pattern-based method (Hearst, 1992, 1998). Several researchers have also used corpus-driven and pattern-based methods(Rydin, 2002; Cederberg and Widdows, 2003; Ando et al., 2004; Snow et al., 2004; Sang and Hofmann, 2007; Caraballo, 1999; Alfonseca and Manandhar, 2001; Etzioni et al., 2004; Ritter et al., 2009). Pattern-based methods have also been applied to web documents (Pasca, 2004; Kozareva et al., 2008; Kozareva and Hovy, 2010). There have been significant studies which present statistical and graph-based methods (Chodorow et al., 1985; Widdows and Dorow, 2002; Sumida and Torisawa, 2008; Imsombut and Kawtrakul, 2008).

Few studies have been published for Turkish Language, BalkaNet (Bilgin et al., 2004) is the first WordNet project for Balkan languages such as Turkish, although the project has not yet been completed. Some attempts used a Turkish Dictionary, TDK [1]. (Yazıcı and Amasyalı, 2011; Güngör and Güngör, 2007; Orhan et al., 2011; Şerbetçi et al., 2011) All studies of semantic relation are mostly based on a Turkish dictionary. Our study is the major corpus-driven attempt at integrating lexico-syntactic patterns and a bootstrapping approach.

# 2 The Methodology

Once the system has simply extracted possible hypernyms by using lexico-syntactic patterns from a Turkish corpus of 490M tokens, it incrementally expands the list by using a bootstrapping algorithm. It uses the most reliable pattern to determine the hypernym/hyponym pairs. For each hypernym, the most reliable candidate hyponyms (seeds) are passed to the bootstrapping algorithm. The algorithm incrementally expands the seeds by adding new seeds depending on a scoring function. The approach employs two different patterns; one is a lexico-syntactic pattern to obtain is-a pairs and the second is a syntactic pattern to compute co-occurrence of the words in a fine-grained way.

## 2.1 Candidate Hypernym/Hyponym

The most important lexico-syntactic patterns for Turkish are:

1. "NPs gibi CLASS" ( CLASS such as NPs),
2. "NPs ve diğer CLASS" (NPs and other CLASS)
3. "CLASS lArdAn NPs" (NPs from CLASS)
4. "NPs ve benzeri CLASS" (NPs and similar CLASS)

[1] The Turkish Language Association

The most reliable pattern is the first pattern that matched over 200,000 cases in the corpus from which 500 reliable hypernyms could be compiled.

## 2.2 Elimination Rules

Some incorrect hyponyms are extracted due to some factors. The objective of this step is to exclude these kinds of non-hyponyms and to acquire more reliable candidates. A partial exclusion can be performed as follows;

- In the first pattern,we observed that real hyponyms tended to appear in the nominative case. The rule implies if a noun was not in nominative case, it would be eliminated.
- If an item occurs only in a single match with the pattern, it will be eliminated. The assumption is that some matches to the pattern are accidental.
- The more general a word is, the more frequent it is. This rule is that, if a candidate hyponym has a higher frequency (df) than its hypernym, it will be ignored.

## 2.3 Statistical Expansion

Filtered hyponym list can remain some erroneous candidates. To improve precision, we can sort the candidates by their pattern frequency. The first K of these words can then be used as original seeds for expansion phase, where K can be experimentally chosen (e.g. 5). The system expands the seeds recursively by adding new seeds one by one. The algorithm will stop producing when it reaches sufficient number of items.

**Bootstrapping Algorithm:** The algorithm is designed as shown in FIGURE1-A. It first extracts hypernym/hyponym pairs and then applies bootstrapping with a scoring function, where a-scoring-f denotes an abstract scoring function for selecting new hyponym candidate. Our scoring methodologies can be categorized in two groups. The first is based on a graph model, the other simply uses semantic similarity between candidates and seeds. We call the former *graph-based scoring* and the latter *simple scoring*. All scoring functions take a list of seeds and propose a new seed.

**Graph-Based Scoring:** Graph-based algorithms define the relations between the words as a graph. Each word is represented as a vertex and the relation between the words is represented as weighted edge. Some researchers proposed a similar approach (Widdows and Dorow, 2002). Graph-based scoring was implemented as in FIGURE1-B in which each neighbor is compared not only with seed words but also with other neighbors to avoid infections. **Simple Scoring:** This method employs only the edge information between each candidate and the seeds. Therefore, the candidate which is the closest to the centroid of all seeds will be the winner. As shown in FIGURE1-C, the algorithm computes the similarity between a candidate and the seeds.

**Edge Weighting:** Both graph-based and simple scoring functions employ a similarity measurement to make a decision. Edge weighting schema that we used in the study are as follows:

1. **IDF/co-occur**: co-occurrence * inverse document frequency (IDF) of candidate.
2. **Binary**: If a seed and a candidate co-occur at least once in the corpus: 1, else 0.
3. **Dice**: $occur(i,j)/(freq_i + freq_j)$ where $occur(i,j)$ is the number of times the $word_i$ and $word_j$ co-occur together, and $freq$ is the number of times a $word$ occurs in corpus.
4. **Cosine similarity**: To compute the similarity between the words, a word space model in which words are represented as vectors is used.

```
Bootstrapping Algorithm (A)

Definitions:
INPUT: C, P
OUTPUT: hyponym/hypernym pairs

for each h: H
  cand<-empty
  for each hyponym:hyponyms(h)
     if(pass the elimination)
          cand  <- add hyponym;
  seeds <-take first K cand;
  while (insufficient)
      add-new-one(seeds, a-scoring-f);
  store(h, final-seeds);
```

```
Graph-Based Scoring (B)

Definitions:
INPUT: S
OUTPUT: new seed

for each n in N(S)
  for each m in N(S)
    if n != m
      score+= edge(n,m);
   assign(score, n);
 rank the N(S) by score
 return the best in N(S)
```

```
Simple Scoring (C)

Definitions:
INPUT: S
OUTPUT: new seed

for each n in N(S)
 for each seed in seeds
    score+= edge(n,seed);
 assign(score, n);
rank the N(S) by score
return the best in N(S)
```

Figure 1: Bootstrapping Algorithm and Scoring Functions, where C: Corpus, P: Pattern, H: Hypernym List, S: Seeds, N(S): Neighbors of S

**Building the Graph and Co-occurrence Matrix:** The words can be represented in a matrix. $cell_{ij}$ represents the number of times $word_i$ and $word_j$ co-occur together. The matrix is a simple representation of a graph. Co-occurrence can be measured with respect to sentences, documents, or a given window of any size. The conventional way to compute co-occurrence is to use all neighbors within a window by eliminating stop words. This approach has proved to be good at capturing sense and topical similarity (Manning and Schütze, 1999). For example, *train* and *ticket* can be found to be highly similar by this method. However, we need to apply more fine-grained methodologies to capture words sharing the same type such as train and auto or ticket and voucher.

To obtain such type similarity, the solution is to use syntactic patterns for computation of co-occurrence. For instance, nouns are considered similar when they are in particular patterns such as *"N and N"* or *"N,N,...,N and N"*. A similar approach was also used by (Cederberg and Widdows, 2003). Words (nouns) considered similar would either all be subject, or all object or all indirect object. This approach makes the model more fine-grained than other conventional ways of computing bi-grams.

## 3 Experimental Setup and Implementation

We implemented a utility program which can be used to verify and reproduce the results presented in the paper. We used a web corpus of 490M tokens and a morphological parser as language resources (Sak et al., 2008). The model parses the corpus and converts each tokens into the form of surface/lemma/pos. For the experiment and evaluation, the most frequently occurring hypernyms is selected. All settings are described as follows:

1. Lexico-syntactic pattern **(pattern)**: After extracting instances, some candidates are eliminated by elimination rules as described before.
2. Graph Scoring/binary **(gr-bin)**: All distance/edges of the graph are weighted in a binary way.
3. Graph Scoring/co-occurence **(gr-co)**: The edges of the graph are weighted by co-occurrence of words.
4. Simple Scoring/binary **(sim-bin)**: Distance between words is 1, if they co-occur; else 0.

5. Simple Scoring/dice **(sim-dice)**: Edges are weighted by dice coefficient.
6. Simple Scoring/co-occurrence**(sim-co)**: Edges are weighted by the co-occurrence frequency between words.
7. Simple Scoring/cosine **(sim-cos)**: The words are represented as vectors in a matrix. Edge is the cosine similarity between word vectors.

## 4 Results and Evaluation

For the evaluation phase, we checked the model against 17 selected hypernyms; **country, city, mineral, sport, illness, animal, fruit, bank, event, vegetable, newspaper, tool, profession, device, drink, sector and organization**. In order to measure the success rate, we manually extracted all possible hyponyms of all the classes.

| Category | # of output | pattern | gr-bin | gr-co | sim-bin | sim-dice | sim-co | sim-cos | avg |
|---|---|---|---|---|---|---|---|---|---|
| bank | 13 | 84 | 100 | 100 | 100 | 100 | 100 | 100 | 98 |
| mineral | 12 | 91 | 100 | 100 | 91 | 100 | 100 | 100 | 97 |
| news. | 21 | 90 | 52 | 42 | 57 | 47 | 61 | 61 | 59 |
| ... | ... | ... | ... | ... | ... | | | | |
| Average | 43 | 90 | 76 | 75 | 73 | 75 | 78 | 70 | 77 |

Table 1: Precision of the first experiment (# of output of the pattern module)

We tested the system within the seven different settings described above. The **pattern** extracted a number of hypernym/hyponym pairs. The expansion algorithms take the first five candidates as initial seeds (IS) suggested by the pattern module, then expands them to the size of the pattern capacity. Looking at TABLE 1, it seems that pattern module outperforms other expansion algorithms in terms of precision. In order to improve recall, we conducted a second experiment; the expansion algorithms expand IS to the size of actual hyponym list rather than the pattern capacity. And we eventually get a better recall value as shown in TABLE 2.

As third experiment, we incrementally altered the number of IS to investigate changes in recall. We used 10, 15, 20, 25, 30 and the pattern capacity as IS size. The pattern capacity is the number of the entire output proposed by the pattern. The average results are shown in TABLE 3. The results indicate that increasing IS gets better accuracy. This is because pattern module indeed gives promising results but it is limited. TABLE 1 shows that the average score of the pattern is % 90. Since this accuracy is reliable, the expansion algorithms can simply and reliably exploit the outputs of the pattern algorithm.

| Category | # of output | pattern | gr-bin | gr-co | sim-bin | sim-dice | sim-co | sim-cos | avg |
|---|---|---|---|---|---|---|---|---|---|
| country | 153 | 86 | 84 | 87 | 85 | 67 | 84 | 80 | 82 |
| city | 88 | 95 | 81 | 88 | 38 | 96 | 77 | 97 | 82 |
| ... | ... | ... | ... | ... | ... | ... | ... | | |
| news. | 32 | 59 | 46 | 28 | 50 | 34 | 50 | 53 | 46 |
| Average | 71 | 49 | 59 | 57 | 58 | 56 | 62 | 52 | 56 |

Table 2: Recall value of second experiment (# of output is the size of actual hyponym list)

There is no significant differences between the accuracy of the different expansion algorithms. **gr-bin**, **sim-bin** and **sim-co** seem to be the best scoring functions. The graph-based algorithms and cosine similarity weighting are costly and time-consuming. We computed the bi-gram information and weighted our graph by using specific syntactic pattern in a more fine-grained manner. It means only the words co-occurring in "N,N and N" pattern are accepted as bigram. Therefore *sim-co* or *sim-bin* which simply computes the relation are very successful. When looking a troublesome hypernyms having low accuracy in all tables, we face a classical word sense problem. Depending on the sense distribution, the expansion algorithm changes the direction of sense into frequently used senses.

## Conclusion

In this paper, we proposed a fully automatic model based on syntactic patterns and semantic similarity. We utilized two patterns: First, the most productive and reliable lexico-syntactic pattern was used to discover is-a hierarchy. We observed that hypernym/hyponm pairs are easily extracted by means of the pattern for Turkish Language. In order to get more precision, we designed some elimination criteria. It gave higher precision but a limited number of pairs with low recall. Second, syntactic pattern was used to compute co-occurrence and expand the list to get higher recall. To discover more hyponyms, we designed a bootstrapping algorithm which incrementally enlarged the pair list.

| # of IS | #out | pattern | gr-bin | gr-co | sim-bin | sim-dice | sim-co | sim-cos | average |
|---|---|---|---|---|---|---|---|---|---|
| 5 | 43 | **89,7** | 76,2 | 75,4 | 73,3 | 74,8 | 78,0 | 69,9 | 77,0 |
| 5 | 71 | 48,5 | 59,2 | 57,0 | 58,2 | 55,9 | **62,5** | 52,1 | 52,6 |
| 10 | 71 | 48,5 | 62,2 | 59,1 | 61,9 | 57,5 | **64,2** | 53,5 | 57,9 |
| 15 | 71 | 48,5 | **64,8** | 62,1 | **66,5** | 58,6 | **66,9** | 56,2 | 60,4 |
| 20 | 71 | 48,5 | **66,8** | 65,6 | **67,4** | 61,2 | **67,6** | 62,3 | 62,1 |
| 25 | 71 | 48,5 | **67,9** | **66,5** | **68,6** | 63,1 | **69,3** | 63,0 | 63,1 |
| 30 | 71 | 48,5 | **68,8** | **67,4** | **69,9** | 64,2 | **70,1** | 63,7 | 63,9 |
| all | 71 | 48,5 | **70,6** | 69,5 | **72,5** | 66,5 | **71,6** | 66,4 | 65,3 |

Table 3: Third experiment (IS: Initial Seed, all: all output from pattern)

In this modular system, we conducted several experiments to analyze is-a semantic relation and to find the best setup for the model. When we look at the third experiment as shown in TABLE 3, pattern algorithm gave promising results. This module successfully built initial seeds. In order to solve the recall problem, we improved the model capacity to discover new candidates. Both graph-based and simple scoring methodologies were applied and we observed that both approaches had a good capacity to get higher recall, such as 71.6 and 72.5.

A real application could be designed as follows: the all reliable candidates proposed by the pattern method might be used as initial seeds to make the model more robust. Moreover, the pattern module can be refined to obtain more secure candidates. For the sake of simplicity, a simple scoring method with binary weighting **(sim-bin)** would be the best setup with respect to the results.

The results showed that the fully automated model presented in the paper successfully disclose is-a relations by mining a large corpus. In future work, we will design a preprocessing phase in order to avoid the problems coming from polysemy and other factors.

## References

Ahlswede, T. and Evens, M. (1988). Parsing vs. text processing in the analysis of dictionary definitions. In *Proceedings of the 26th Annual Meeting of the Association for Computational Linguistics*, pages 217–224, Buffalo, New York, USA. Association for Computational Linguistics.

Alfonseca, E. and Manandhar, S. (2001). Improving an ontology refinement method with hyponymy patterns. In *Language Resources and Evaluation (LREC-2002)*, Las Palmas, Spain.

Alshawi, H. (1987). Processing dictionary definitions with phrasal pattern hierarchies. *Computational Linguistics*, 13:13–3.

Ando, M., Sekine, S., and Ishizaki, S. (2004). Automatic extraction of hyponyms from japanese newspapers. using lexico-syntactic patterns. In *LREC*. European Language Resources Association.

Bilgin, O., Çetinoğlu, Ö., and Oflazer, K. (2004). Building a wordnet for turkish. volume 7.

Caraballo, S. A. (1999). Automatic construction of a hypernym-labeled noun hierarchy from text. In *In Proceedings of the 37th annual meeting of the Association for Computational Linguistics*, pages 120–126.

Cederberg, S. and Widdows, D. (2003). Using lsa and noun coordination information to improve the precision and recall of automatic hyponymy extraction. In *In Proceedings of CoNLL*, pages 111–118.

Chodorow, M. S., Byrd, R. J., and Heidorn, G. E. (1985). Extracting semantic hierarchies from a large on-line dictionary. In *Proceedings of the 23rd Annual Meeting of the ACL*, pages 299–304, Chicago, IL.

Şerbetçi, A., Orhan, Z., and İlknur Pehlivan (2011). Extraction of semantic word relations in turkish from dictionary definitions. In *Proceedings of the ACL 2011 Workshop on Relational Models of Semantics*, pages 11–18, Portland, Oregon, USA. Association for Computational Linguistics.

Etzioni, O., Cafarella, M. J., Downey, D., Kok, S., Popescu, A.-M., Shaked, T., Soderland, S., Weld, D. S., and Yates, A. (2004). Web-scale information extraction in knowitall: (preliminary results). In *WWW*, pages 100–110.

Fellbaum, C., editor (1998). *WordNet: an electronic lexical database*. MIT Press.

Güngör, O. and Güngör, T. (2007). Türkçe bir sözlükteki tanımlardan kavramlar arasındaki üst-kavram İlişkilerinin Çıkarılması. volume 1, pages 1–13.

Hearst, M. (1998). WordNet: An electronic lexical database and some of its applications. In Fellbaum, C., editor, *Automated Discovery of WordNet Relations*. MIT Press.

Hearst, M. A. (1992). Automatic acquisition of hyponyms from large text corpora. In *In Proceedings of the 14th International Conference on Computational Linguistics*, pages 539–545.

Imsombut, A. and Kawtrakul, A. (2008). Automatic building of an ontology on the basis of text corpora in thai. *Language Resources and Evaluation*, 42(2):137–149.

Jensen, K. and Binot, J.-L. (1987). Disambiguating prepositional phrase attachments by using on-line dictionary definitions. *Comput. Linguist.*, 13(3-4):251–260.

Kozareva, Z. and Hovy, E. H. (2010). A semi-supervised method to learn and construct taxonomies using the web. In *EMNLP'10 in Proceedings of Conference on Empirical Methods in Natural Language Processing*, Boston.

Kozareva, Z., Riloff, E., and Hovy, E. H. (2008). Semantic class learning from the web with hyponym pattern linkage graphs. In *ACL'08: HLT in Proceedings of the 46th Annual Meeting of the Association for Computational Linguistics: Human Language Technologies*, pages 1048–1056, Columbus, USA.

Lenat, D., Prakash, M., and Shepherd, M. (1986). Cyc: Using common sense knowledge to overcome brittleness and knowledge acquistion bottlenecks. *AI Mag.*, 6(4):65–85.

Manning, C. D. and Schütze, H. (1999). *Foundations of Statistical Natural Language Processing*. The MIT Press, Cambridge, Massachusetts.

Markowitz, J., Ahlswede, T., and Evens, M. (1986). Semantically significant patterns in dictionary definitions. In *Proc. 24rd Annual Conf. of the ACL*, pages 112–119.

Miller, G. A. (1995). Wordnet: A lexical database for english. *Communications of the ACM*, 38:39–41.

Miller, G. A., Beckwith, R., Fellbaum, C., Gross, D., and Miller, K. (1990). Wordnet: An on-line lexical database. *International Journal of Lexicography*, 3:235–244.

Orhan, Z., İlknur Pehlivan, Uslan, V., and Önder, P. (2011). Automated extraction of semantic word relations in turkish lexicon. *Mathematical and Computational Applications, Association for Scientific Research*, (1):13–22.

Pasca, M. (2004). Acquisition of categorized named entities for web search. In *Proceedings of the thirteenth ACM international conference on Information and knowledge management*, CIKM '04, pages 137–145, New York, NY, USA. ACM.

Ritter, A., Soderl, S., and Etzioni, O. (2009). What is this, anyway: Automatic hypernym discovery. In *In Proceedings of AAAI-09 Spring Symposium on Learning*, pages 88–93.

Rydin, S. (2002). Building a hyponymy lexicon with hierarchical structure. In *Proceedings of the ACL-02 Workshop on Unsupervised Lexical Acquisition*, pages 26–33, Philadelphia, Pennsylvania, USA. Association for Computational Linguistics.

Sak, H., Güngör, T., and Saraçlar, M. (2008). Turkish language resources: Morphological parser, morphological disambiguator and web corpus. In *GoTAL 2008*, volume 5221 of *LNCS*, pages 417–427. Springer.

Sang, E. T. K. and Hofmann, K. (2007). Automatic extraction of dutch hypernym-hyponym pairs. In *Proceedings of the 17th Meeting of Computational Linguistics in the Netherlands*.

Snow, R., Jurafsky, D., and Ng, A. Y. (2004). Learning syntactic patterns for automatic hypernym discovery. In *NIPS*.

Sumida, A. and Torisawa, K. (2008). Hacking wikipedia for hyponymy relation acquisition. In *In Proceedings of IJCNLP 2008*, pages 883–888.

Widdows, D. and Dorow, B. (2002). A graph model for unsupervised lexical acquisition. In *In 19th International Conference on Computational Linguistics, COLING*, pages 1093–1099.

Yazıcı, E. and Amasyalı, M. F. (2011). Automatic extraction of semantic relationships using turkish dictionary definitions. volume 1, pages 1–13.

# Chinese Web Scale Linguistic Datasets and Toolkit

*Chi-Hsin Yu, Hsin-Hsi Chen*
Department of Computer Science and Information Engineering, National Taiwan University
#1, Sec.4, Roosevelt Road, Taipei, 10617 Taiwan
`jsyu@nlg.csie.ntu.edu.tw, hhchen@ntu.edu.tw`

ABSTRACT

The web provides a huge collection of web pages for researchers to study natural languages. However, processing web scale texts is not an easy task and needs many computational and linguistic resources. In this paper, we introduce two Chinese parts-of-speech tagged web-scale datasets and describe tools that make them easy to use for NLP applications. The first is a Chinese segmented and POS-tagged dataset, in which the materials are selected from the ClueWeb09 dataset. The second is a Chinese POS n-gram corpus extracted from the POS-tagged dataset. Tools to access the POS-tagged dataset and the POS n-gram corpus are presented. The two datasets will be released to the public along with their tools.

# 中文網路規模語言資料集和工具

網際網路提供研究人員巨量網頁進行自然語言處理研究，但是處理網路規模的文本不是件簡單的工作，而是需要大量的計算和語言資源。在本文中，我們介紹兩種加上中文詞性標記的網路規模資料集，以及易於將這些資源運用於自然語言處理應用的工具。第一種資料集選自於ClueWeb09的中文語料，並經過中文斷詞和詞性標記。第二種資料集是由上述詞性標記資料集中擷取中文詞性n-gram，所建立的語料庫。我們同時也提出搜尋詞性標記資料集和詞性n-gram語料庫的工具，這兩種資料集連同工具將提供研究人員使用。

---

KEYWORDS : Chinese POS n-gram, ClueWeb09, TOOLKIT
KEYWORDS IN $L_2$ : 中文詞性n-gram, ClueWeb09, 工具包

---

*Proceedings of COLING 2012: Demonstration Papers*, pages 501–508,
COLING 2012, Mumbai, December 2012.

## 1 Introduction

While using a large volume of data becomes a new paradigm in many NLP applications, preparing a web scale data collection are time consuming and need much cost. Recently, various versions of Gigawords which are comprehensive archive of newswire text data in Arabic, Chinese, English, French, and Spanish are distributed through LDC[1] to boost the researches. Besides newswire text, web n-grams in Chinese, English, Japanese, and 10 European languages created by Google researchers also released via LDC. Moreover, Lin et al. (2010) extend an English word n-gram corpus by adding parts of speech information and develop tools to accelerate the query speed.

In contrast to the web n-gram corpora, the ClueWeb[2] dataset developed by Carnegie Mellon University (CMU) contains a huge collection of raw web pages for researchers. It provides an alternative to construct corpora with fruitful context information rather than n-grams only. In this paper we extract the Chinese materials from the ClueWeb dataset, and develop two Chinese datasets, including a Chinese segmented and POS-tagged dataset called **PText**, and a Chinese POS n-gram corpus called **PNgram**. Besides, a toolkit is incorporated with these datasets.

This paper is organized as follows. Section 2 introduces the construction of the two Chinese corpora. Section 3 describes a Java-based tool for **PText**. Section 4 presents a user interface for the **PNgram**. Potential applications are also discussed in these two sections.

## 2 POS Tagging and N-gram Extraction

The ClueWeb09 dataset consists of about 1 billion web pages in ten languages. Based on the record counts, Chinese material is the second largest (177,489,357 pages) in ClueWeb09. Due to various charsets and encoding schemes, encoding detection, language identification and traditional Chinese-Simplified Chinese translation are indispensable preprocessing stages. Besides, enormous computational resources are needed for Chinese segmentation and part-of-speech tagging under this scale. The following sections show the procedures to construct two Chinese corpora and their basic statistics.

### 2.1 PText: A Chinese Segmented and POS-Tagged Dataset

Three tasks are described briefly as follows for the development of a Chinese segmented and POS-tagged dataset. The details can refer to Yu, Tang & Chen (2012).

(1) **Encoding detection and language identification.** Although the web pages in the ClueWeb09 dataset are encoded in UTF-8 encoding scheme, the correct encoding of a source page is still needed to be decided. In Chinese, web developers use many charsets and encodings to represent their web pages. For example, in traditional Chinese, there are charsets such as Big5, CNS 11643, and Unicode. In simplified Chinese, there are charsets such as GBK, GB2312, and Unicode. Furthermore, many ClueWeb09 web pages listed in Chinese category are actually in other languages such as Korean and Japanese. We must filter out those pages beforehand. Thus, encoding detection and language identification have

[1] http://www.ldc.upenn.edu/
[2] http://lemurproject.org/clueweb09.php/

to be done at the same time. Finally, 173,741,587 Chinese pages are extracted from the ClueWeb09 dataset.

**(2) Chinese segmentation.** A pure text in RFC3676 format is extracted from a web page for further linguistic processing. We translate all the web pages in traditional Chinese to simplified Chinese by using a character-based approach. Then, we split each Chinese web page into a sequence of sentences. The sentence boundaries are determined by full stop, question mark and exclamation mark in ASCII, full width and ideographic format. The new line characters '\r\n' are also used as a sentence boundary. Finally, we segment each sentence by using the Stanford segmenter (Tseng et al., 2005).

**(3) Chinese POS tagging:** The segmented sentences are tagged by using the Stanford tagger (Toutanova et al., 2003). The POS tag set of LDC Chinese Treebank is adopted. The tagger has been demonstrated to have the accuracy 94.13% on a combination of simplified Chinese and Hong Kong texts and 78.92% on unknown words.

The resulting dataset contains 9,598,430,559 POS-tagged sentences in 172,298,866 documents. In a document, we keep the original metadata such as title, the original TREC ID, and target URI in ClueWeb09. The encoding information in HTTP header and HTML header, and the detected encoding scheme are also preserved.

## 2.2 PNgram: A Chinese POS N-gram Corpus

For the extraction of the POS n-grams (n=1, …, 5), the first step is to determine the unigrams as our vocabulary. The minimum occurrence count of a unigram is set to 200, which is adopted in Chinese Web 5-gram (Liu, et al., 2010). After the unigram vocabulary is confirmed, the word *n*-grams (*n*=2, …, 5) are extracted. The minimum occurrence count of an n-gram (*n*=2, …, 5) is 40. After that, POS sequences for each word *n*-gram are extracted. The dataset format is like Google N-gram V2 (Lin et al., 2010). The following shows examples with their English translation.

*唸书 时间 VV NN 2 | NN NN 119*
*(read, time)*
*唸书 期间 NN NN 43*
*(read, period)*
*唸书 时期 VV NN 2 | NN NN 73*
*(read, period)*

Table 1 shows word n-gram statistics of the resulting PNgram corpus. There are 107,902,213 unique words in PText, and only 2.1% of unique words (2,219,170) with frequency larger than 200. For a word bigram, the minimum frequency is 40. Total 9.7% unique bigrams are selected. The ratio decreases roughly half when N increases.

| n-gram | #PText entries | # PNgram entries | Ratio |
|---|---|---|---|
| 1 | 107,902,213 | 2,219,170 | 2.1% |
| 2 | 645,952,974 | 62,728,971 | 9.7% |
| 3 | 4,184,637,707 | 200,066,527 | 4.8% |
| 4 | 10,923,797,159 | 294,016,661 | 2.7% |
| 5 | 17,098,062,929 | 274,863,248 | 1.6% |

TABLE 1 –Statistics of the word N-grams

Table 2 shows the statistics of the extracted PNgram corpus. The Stanford POS tagger (Toutanova et al. 2003) adopts LDC Chinese Treebank POS tag set in the trained Chinese tagger model. There is 35 POS tags plus one additional tag STM for sentence start mark <S> and stop mark </S>. We can see that the average POS patterns per word patterns are small. In other words, they range from 1.7 to 3.5 POS patterns.

| n-gram | Avg. POS patterns per word n-gram | Max. POS patterns of word n-gram |
|---|---|---|
| 1 | 3.5 | 20 |
| 2 | 2.5 | 301 |
| 3 | 2.3 | 2,409 |
| 4 | 2.1 | 9,868 |
| 5 | 1.7 | 7,643 |

TABLE 2 –Statistics of POS patterns in **PNgram**

## 3 Tools for the PText Dataset

The PText dataset are stored in Java serialization format which is easy to be manipulated by programmers.

### 3.1 Data Model and Tools

We briefly describe the data model and tools for the PText dataset as follows.

(1) **Data model.** The dataset contains 4,395 gzipped files. Each gzipped file contains a list of document objects, where a document contains a list of sentences, and a sentence contains a list of tagged words. In this way, it is very easy to traverse the whole dataset. There is no need to re-parse the data from plain texts.

(2) **Tools.** Java classes of data model are provided along with Java classes that are used to de-serialize the gzipped files. It is easy to traverse the whole dataset in parallel by programmers. Conversion tools are also provided for dataset users who want to convert the gzipped files to readable plain texts.

### 3.2 Applications with the PText dataset

The PText dataset is beneficial for many potential researches. We outline some interesting applications below.

(1) **Knowledge mining.** The PText dataset can be used as the source of OpenIE (Etzioni et al., 2008). In ReVerb, Fader, Soderland, and Etzioni (2011) use simple POS patterns to mine facts from the web texts in English. Similarly, researchers can extract facts from Chinese texts by specifying Chinese POS patterns. With the PText dataset, considerable pre-processing time can be saved for Chinese OpenIE researchers.

(2) **Sentiment analysis.** As shown by the papers (Wiebe et al., 2004; Abbasi, Chen, and Salem, 2008), parts-of-speech information is useful for many sentiment analysis tasks such as opinion classification and subjectivity analysis of web texts. With the large-scale PText dataset, researchers can investigate more rich phenomena in the web texts.

(3) **Basic NLP tasks.** Besides the new and interesting researches, the fundamental NLP tasks can also benefit from the PText dataset, e.g., the encoding detection and language identification in pre-processing Chinese web pages, the performance of Chinese word segmenters and POS taggers in large scale web texts, and so on.

## 4 A User Interface for the PNgram Corpus

Lin et al. (2010) provide source codes to search English POS n-gram data along with a Lisp-style query language. The query tool is powerful, but it is not intuitive for users of non-computer background. In this paper, we design an easy-to-use interface for users.

### 4.1 User Interface

Figure 1 shows the snapshot of the user interface to access the PNgram Corpus. At first, users input the length of the requested n-gram and the range of its frequency. By default, the minimum frequency is 40. Then system will provide suitable number of slots for users to write down the linguistic feature of each word. Users can fill in a wildcard * or a word, along with its lexical information specified in the constraint part. The possible constraints include a duplication form like AA for searching a duplication word 哈哈 (ha ha), and possible POS tags for filtering non-relevant patterns.

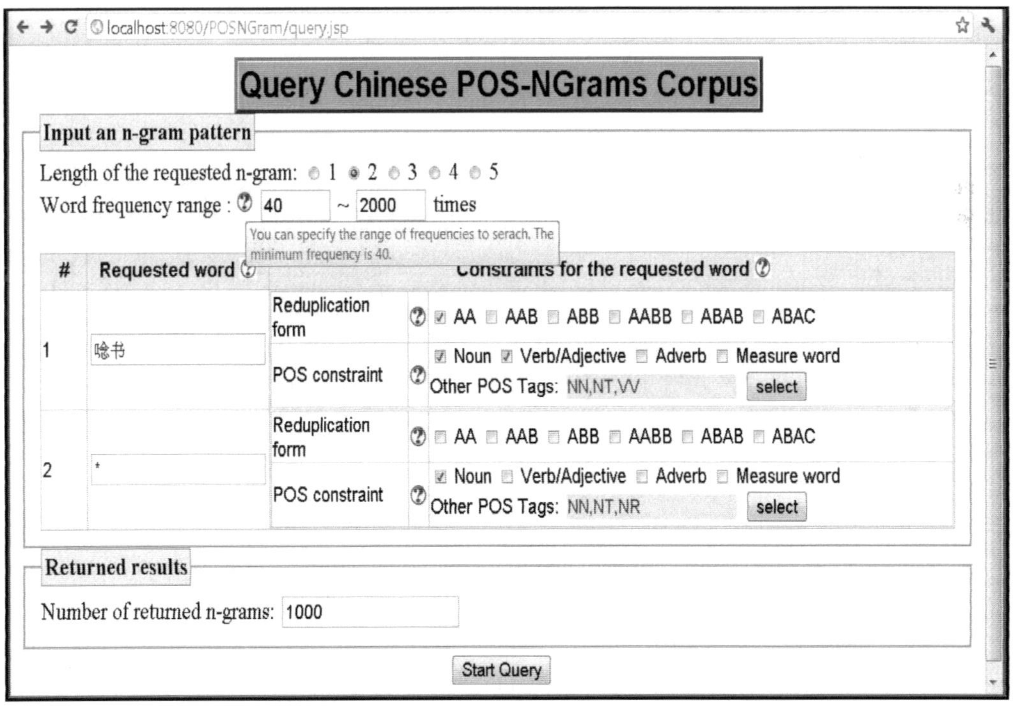


FIGURE 1 –A user interface to query the Chinese POS-NGram corpus

In Figure 1, users search bigram patterns. The first word is 啥书 (read), and it must be Noun, Verb/Adjective, or tags NN, NT, VV, which are selected in Figure 2. The second word can be any words with Noun, or NN, NT and NT tags. The word frequency is limited between 40 to 2,000 times. The returned POS n-gram results are similar to the examples shown in Section 2.2.

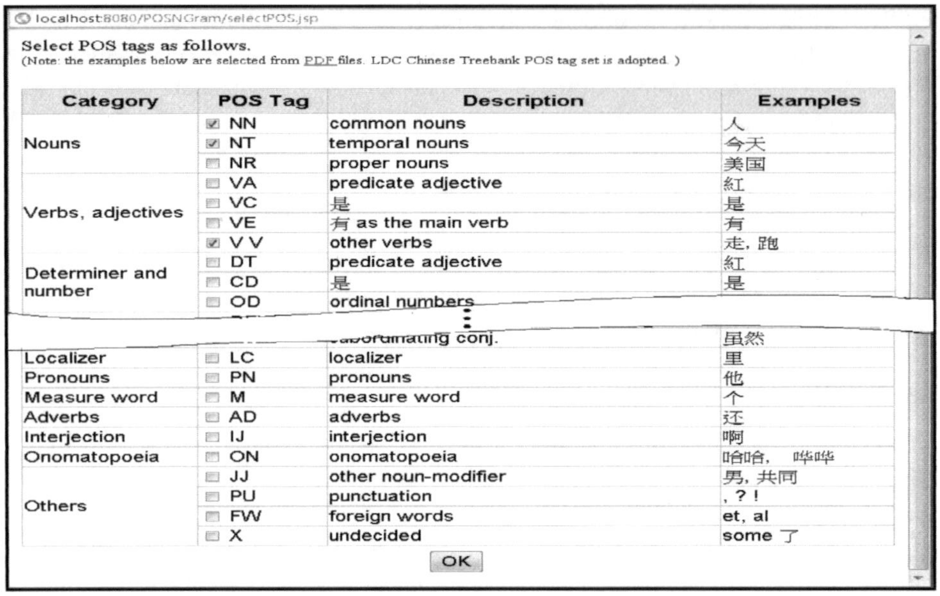

localhost:8080/POSNGram/selectPOS.jsp

Select POS tags as follows.
(Note: the examples below are selected from PDF files. LDC Chinese Treebank POS tag set is adopted. )

| Category | POS Tag | Description | Examples |
|---|---|---|---|
| Nouns | NN | common nouns | 人 |
| | NT | temporal nouns | 今天 |
| | NR | proper nouns | 美国 |
| Verbs, adjectives | VA | predicate adjective | 紅 |
| | VC | 是 | 是 |
| | VE | 有 as the main verb | 有 |
| | VV | other verbs | 走, 跑 |
| Determiner and number | DT | predicate adjective | 紅 |
| | CD | 是 | 是 |
| | OD | ordinal numbers | |
| | | : | |
| | | …subordinating conj. | 虽然 |
| Localizer | LC | localizer | 里 |
| Pronouns | PN | pronouns | 他 |
| Measure word | M | measure word | 个 |
| Adverbs | AD | adverbs | 还 |
| Interjection | IJ | interjection | 啊 |
| Onomatopoeia | ON | onomatopoeia | 哈哈， 哗哗 |
| Others | JJ | other noun-modifier | 男, 共同 |
| | PU | punctuation | , ? ! |
| | FW | foreign words | et, al |
| | X | undecided | some 了 |

OK

FIGURE 2 –Select specific POS tags for a word

## 4.2 Applications of the PNgram Corpus

The PNgram corpus along with the user interface is useful for many NLP applications. Yu and Chen (2012) employ it to detect Chinese word order errors. We outline some others as follows.

**(1) Language Learning.** In Chinese learning, we may be interested in what linguistic context some specific reduplication forms like "快快樂樂" (happy happy) appear. Through the interface, it is easy to collect their usages from the web data. Similarly, the uses of measure words in Chinese sentences are very common. The PNgram corpus along with the tool provides a flexible way to analyze the measure words for a specific word in web texts.

**(2) Pattern Identification for Information Extraction (IE).** In IE, a named entity usually ends with some specific characters such as 站/station in 雷达站/radar-station. But the character 站 /station can be a verb in word 站在/stand-in. The PNgram corpus and the accompanying tool can be used to collect similar NE patterns satisfying the POS criterion for NE rule extraction.

**(3) Chinese Noun Compound Corpus Construction**. As a concept is usually represented by a multiword expression, the structure of a noun compound is needed to be determined. We can specify a POS pattern to construct a noun compound corpus from the PNgram dataset, and use it to study the modifying structures of noun compounds.

# 5 Conclusion and Future Work

In this paper, we present the POS tagged dataset (**PText**) and the POS 5-gram corpus (**PNgram**). Besides, we provide tools for users to access these two resources. Researchers can collect sentences from the web-scale linguistic resources for their own specific research topics. For example, we will study the polarity of Chinese discourse markers based on these web-scale corpora. Sentences where discourse markers occur will be extracted, sentiment polarities of the discourse arguments connected by a discourse marker will be measured, and the relations between discourse parsing and sentiment analysis will be investigated.

## Acknowledgments

This research was partially supported by Excellent Research Projects of National Taiwan University under contract 101R890858 and 2012 Google Research Award.

## References

Abbasi, A., Chen, H., and Salem, A. (2008). Sentiment Analysis in Multiple Languages: Feature Selection for Opinion Classification in Web Forums. *ACM Transactions on Information Systems*, 26(3), 12:1–12:34.

Brants, T., and Franz, A. (2006). Web 1T 5-gram Version 1. Linguistic Data Consortium, Philadelphia.

Etzioni, O., Banko, M., Soderland, S., and Weld, D. S. (2008). Open Information Extraction from the Web. *Communications of the ACM*, 51(12):68–74.

Fader, A., Soderland, S., and Etzioni, O. (2011). Identifying Relations for Open Information Extraction. In the *Conference on Empirical Methods in Natural Language Processing (EMNLP '11)*, pages 1535–1545, Edinburgh, Scotland, UK.

Gao, J., Goodman, J., Li, M., and Lee, K.-F. (2002). Toward a Unified Approach to Statistical Language Modeling for Chinese. *ACM Transactions on Asian Language Information Processing*, 1(1):3–33.

Lin, D., Church, K., Ji, H., Sekine, S., Yarowsky, D., Bergsma, S., Patil, K., Pitler, E., Lathbury, R., Rao, V., Dalwani, K. and Narsale, S. (2010). New Tools for Web-Scale N-grams. In *the Seventh conference on International Language Resources and Evaluation*, pages 2221–2227, Malta.

Liu, F., Yang, M., and Lin, D. (2010). Chinese Web 5-gram Version 1. Linguistic Data Consortium, Philadelphia.

Toutanova, K., Klein, D., Manning, C. D., and Singer, Y. (2003). Feature-Rich Part-of-Speech Tagging with a Cyclic Dependency Network. In *the 2003 Conference of the North American Chapter of the Association for Computational Linguistics on Human Language Technology*, pages 173–180, Edmonton, Canada.

Tseng, H., Chang, P., Andrew, G., Jurafsky, D., and Manning, C. (2005). A Conditional Random Field Word Segmenter for Sighan Bakeoff 2005. In the *Fourth SIGHAN Workshop on Chinese Language Processing*, pages 168–171, Jeju, Korea.

Wiebe, J., Wilson, T., Bruce, R., Bell, M., and Martin, M. (2004). Learning Subjective Language. *Computational Linguistics*, 30(3):277–308.

Yu, C.-H., Tang, Y. and Chen, H.-H. (2012). Development of a Web-Scale Chinese Word N-gram Corpus with Parts of Speech Information. In *the Eighth International Conference on Language Resources and Evaluation*, pages 320–324, Istanbul, Turkey.

Yu, C.-H. and Chen, H.-H. (2012). Detecting Word Ordering Errors in Chinese Sentences for Learning Chinese as a Foreign Language. In *the 24th International Conference on Computational Linguistics*, Mumbai, India.

# Developing and Evaluating a Computer-Assisted Near-Synonym Learning System

*YU Liang-Chih HSU Kai-Hsiang*
Department of Information Management, Yuan Ze University, Chung-Li, Taiwan, R.O.C.
lcyu@saturn.yzu.edu.tw, s986220@mail.yzu.edu.tw

ABSTRACT

Despite their similar meanings, near-synonyms may have different usages in different contexts. For second language learners, such differences are not easily grasped in practical use. In this paper, we develop a computer-assisted near-synonym learning system for Chinese English-as-a-Second-Language (ESL) learners using two automatic near-synonym choice techniques: pointwise mutual information (PMI) and *n*-grams. The two techniques can provide useful contextual information for learners, making it easier for them to understand different usages of various English near-synonyms in a range of contexts. The system is evaluated using a vocabulary test with near-synonyms as candidate choices. Participants are required to select the best near-synonym for each question both with and without use of the system. Experimental results show that both techniques can improve participants' ability to discriminate among near-synonyms. In addition, participants are found to prefer to use the PMI in the test, despite *n*-grams providing more precise information.

KEYWORDS : Near-synonym choice, computer-assisted language learning, lexical semantics

*Proceedings of COLING 2012: Demonstration Papers*, pages 509–516,
COLING 2012, Mumbai, December 2012.

## 1 Introduction

Near-synonym sets represent groups of words with similar meanings, which can be derived from existing lexical ontologies such as WordNet (Fellbaum, 1998), EuroWordNet (Rodríguez et al., 1998), and Chinese WordNet (Huang et al., 2008). These are useful knowledge resources for many applications such as information retrieval (IR) (Moldovan and Mihalcea, 2000; Navigli and Velardi, 2003; Shlrl and Revle, 2006; Bhogal et al., 2007) and computer-assisted language learning (CALL) (Cheng, 2004; Inkpen, 2007; Ouyang et al., 2009; Wu et al., 2010). For instance, in CALL, near-synonyms can be used to automatically suggest alternatives to avoid repeating the same word in a text when suitable alternatives are available in its near-synonym set (Inkpen, 2007). Although the words in a near-synonym set have similar meanings, they are not necessarily interchangeable in practical use due to their specific usage and collocational constraints (Wible et al., 2003; Futagia et al., 2008). Consider the following examples.

(1) {strong, powerful} coffee (Pearce, 2001)
(2) ghastly {error, mistake} (Inkpen, 2007)

Examples (1) and (2) both present an example of collocational constraints for the given contexts. For instance, in (1), the word *strong* is more suitable than *powerful* in the context of "coffee", since "powerful coffee" is an anti-collocation. These examples indicate that near-synonyms may have different usages in different contexts, and such differences are not easily captured by second language learners. Therefore, this study develops a computer-assisted near-synonym learning system to assist Chinese English-as-a-Second-Language (ESL) learners to better understand different usages of various English near-synonyms.

To this end, this study exploits automatic near-synonym choice techniques (Edmonds, 1997; Inkpen, 2007; Gardiner and Dras, 2007, Islam and Inkpen, 2010; Wang and Hirst, 2010; Yu et al., 2010a; 2010b; 2011) to verify whether near-synonyms match the given contexts. Figure 1 shows an example of near-synonym choice. Given a near-synonym set and a sentence containing one of the near-synonyms, the near-synonym is first removed from the sentence to form a lexical gap. The goal is to predict an answer (i.e., best near-synonym) to fill the gap from the near-synonym set according to the given context. The *pointwise mutual information (PMI)* (Inkpen, 2007; Gardiner and Dras, 2007), and *n-gram* based methods (Islam and Inkpen, 2010; Yu et al., 2010b) are the two major approaches to near-synonym choice. PMI is used to measure the strength of co-occurrence between a near-synonym and individual words appearing in its context, while n-grams can capture contiguous word associations in the given context. Both techniques can provide useful contextual information for the near-synonyms. This study uses both techniques to implement a system with which learners can practice discriminating among near-synonyms.

**Sentence:** This will make the _____ message easier to interpret. (Original word: error)
**Near-synonym set:** {error, mistake, oversight}

FIGURE 1 – Example of near-synonym choice.

## 2 System Description

### 2.1 Main Components

**1) PMI:** The pointwise mutual information (Church and Hanks, 1991) used here measures the co-occurrence strength between a near-synonym and the words in its context. Let $w_i$ be a word in the context of a near-synonym $NS_j$. The PMI score between $w_i$ and $NS_j$ is calculated as

$$PMI(w_i, NS_j) = \log_2 \frac{P(w_i, NS_j)}{P(w_i)P(NS_j)}, \quad (1)$$

where $P(w_i, NS_j) = C(w_i, NS_j)/N$ denotes the probability that $w_i$ and $NS_j$ co-occur; $C(w_i, NS_j)$ is the number of times $w_i$ and $NS_j$ co-occur in the corpus, and $N$ is the total number of words in the corpus. Similarly, $P(w_i) = C(w_i)/N$, where $C(w_i)$ is the number of times $w_i$ occurs, and $P(NS_j) = C(NS_j)/N$, where $C(NS_j)$ is the number of times $NS_j$ occurs. All frequency counts are retrieved from the Web 1T 5-gram corpus. Therefore, (1) can be re-written as

$$PMI(w_i, NS_j) = \log_2 \frac{C(w_i, NS_j) \cdot N}{C(w_i)C(NS_j)}. \quad (2)$$

The PMI score is then normalized as a proportion of $w_i$ occurring in the context of all near-synonyms in the same set, as shown in Eq. (3).

$$\widetilde{PMI}(w_i, NS_j) = \frac{PMI(w_i, NS_j)}{\sum_{j=1}^{K} PMI(w_i, NS_j)}, \quad (3)$$

where $\widetilde{PMI}(w_i, NS_j)$ denotes the normalized PMI score, and $K$ is the number of near-synonyms in a near-synonym set.

**2) N-gram:** This component retrieves the frequencies of $n$ (2~5) contiguous words occurring in the contexts from the Web 1T 5-gram corpus.

## 2.2 System Implementation

Based on the contextual information provided by the PMI and N-gram, the system implements two functions: contextual statistics and near-synonym choice, both of which interact with learners. The system can be accessed at http://nlptm.mis.yzu.edu.tw/NSLearning.

**1) Contextual statistics:** This function provides the contextual information retrieved by PMI and N-gram. This prototype system features a total of 21 near-synonyms grouped into seven near-synonym sets, as shown in Table 1. Figure 2 shows a screenshot of the interface for contextual information lookup. For both PMI and N-gram, only the 100 top-ranked items are presented.

**2) Near-synonym choice:** This function assists learners in determining suitable near-synonyms when they are not familiar with the various usages of the near-synonyms in a given context. Learners can specify a near-synonym set and then input a sentence with "*" to represent any near-synonym in the set. The system will replace "*" with each near-synonym, and then retrieve the contextual information around "*" using PMI and N-gram, as shown in Fig. 3. For PMI, at most five context words (window size) before and after "*" are included to compute the normalized PMI scores for each near-synonym. In addition, the sum of all PMI scores for each near-synonym is also presented to facilitate learner decisions. For N-gram, the frequencies of the $n$-grams (2~5) containing each near-synonym are retrieved.

| No. | Near-Synonym sets | No. | Near-Synonym sets |
|---|---|---|---|
| 1 | difficult, hard, tough | 2 | error, mistake, oversight |
| 3 | job, task, duty | 4 | responsibility, burden, obligation, commitment |
| 5 | material, stuff, substance | 6 | give, provide, offer |
| 7 | settle, resolve | | |

TABLE 1 – Near-synonym sets.

Near-synonym set job task duty

| job | | | task | | | duty | | |
|---|---|---|---|---|---|---|---|---|
| Context | PMI_score | Frequency | Context | PMI_score | Frequency | Context | PMI_score | Frequency |
| teen | 1 | 1,816,316 | trivial | 1 | 78,286 | cycle | 1 | 342,491 |
| seekers | 1 | 1,479,452 | committees | 1 | 75,321 | breach | 1 | 336,947 |
| listings | 1 | 1,473,629 | pane | 1 | 52,660 | fiduciary | 1 | 325,983 |
| opportunities | 1 | 1,416,347 | privileged | 1 | 49,161 | tour | 1 | 240,835 |
| openings | 1 | 1,071,984 | force | 0.99 | 2,874,435 | stamp | 1 | 172,109 |

Near-synonym set job task duty N-gram 4 Submit

| job | | task | | duty | |
|---|---|---|---|---|---|
| to do the job | 438,769 | the task at hand | 172,859 | have a duty to | 202,441 |
| did a great job | 425,841 | with the task of | 167,026 | is the duty of | 191,024 |
| a good job of | 412,589 | not an easy task | 145,907 | be the duty of | 178,800 |
| do a better job | 357,618 | up to the task | 143,106 | shall be the duty | 161,951 |
| link to save job | 346,000 | of the task force | 122,120 | the line of duty | 160,011 |

FIGURE 2 – Screenshot of contextual statistics.

Near-Synonym set material stuff substance

It was found that the * of the matter and not only mere theory was to be regarded submit

Window size 3

| PMI | material | stuff | substance |
|---|---|---|---|
| found | 0.35 | 0.34 | 0.31 |
| that | 0.24 | 0.49 | 0.28 |
| the | 0.31 | 0.27 | 0.42 |
| of | 0.28 | 0.28 | 0.44 |
| the | 0.31 | 0.27 | 0.42 |
| matter | 0.15 | 0.08 | 0.77 |
| | 1.64 | 1.73 | 2.64 |

| | | | | | | |
|---|---|---|---|---|---|---|
| Bi-gram | the material | 7,488,173 | the stuff | 2,581,457 | the substance | 1,319,583 |
| | material of | 817,776 | stuff of | 392,805 | substance of | 848,188 |
| Tri-gram | that the material | 237,330 | that the stuff | 25,305 | that the substance | 52,803 |
| | the material of | 129,580 | the stuff of | 254,931 | the substance of | 545,206 |
| | material of the | 179,643 | stuff of the | 31,130 | substance of the | 341,962 |
| 4-gram | found that the material | 1,706 | found that the stuff | 211 | found that the substance | 623 |
| | that the material of | 3,082 | that the stuff of | 910 | that the substance of | 15,240 |
| | the material of the | 48,148 | the stuff of the | 9,307 | the substance of the | 242,832 |
| | material of the matter | 0 | stuff of the matter | 0 | substance of the matter | 6,205 |

FIGURE 3 – Screenshot of near-synonym choice.

## 3 Experimental Results

### 3.1 Experiment Setup

**1) Question design:** To evaluate the system, we designed a vocabulary test with near-synonyms as candidate choices. The vocabulary test consisted of 50 questions with a single correct answer for the 21 near-synonyms, where each near-synonym had at least two questions. The remaining eight randomly selected near-synonyms had three questions each. Each question was formed from a sentence selected from the British National Corpus (BNC). Figure 4 shows a sample question. For each question, the original word removed was held as the correct response.

| | |
|---|---|
| **Question:** | He wanted to do a better _____ than his father had done with him. |
| | A. job    B. task    C. duty |
| **Questionnaire 1:** | How much did you depend on the system to answer the question? |
| | ☐ 1 (Not at all dependent) ☐ 2 ☐ 3 ☐ 4 ☐ 5 (Completely dependent) |
| **Questionnaire 2:** | Which method did you use in the test? ☐ PMI ☐ N-gram |

FIGURE 4 – Sample question in the vocabulary test. The original word in the lexical gap is job.

**2) Test procedure:** In testing, participants were asked to propose an answer from the candidate choices, first in a pre-test without use of the system, and then in a post-test using the system. To obtain detailed results, participants were requested to provide two feedback items after completing each question, as shown in Figure 4. The first item is a 5-point scale measuring the degree to which the participant felt reliant on the system during the test, and reflects participants' confidence in answering questions. In the second item, participants were asked to indicate which method, PMI or n-grams (or both or none) provided the most useful contextual information.

## 3.2 Evaluation Results

A total of 30 non-native English speaking graduate students volunteered to participate in the test. Experimental results show that the participants scored an average of 44% correct on the pre-test. After using the system, this increased substantially to 70%. This finding indicates that the use of the system improved participants' ability to distinguish different usages of various near-synonyms. We performed a cross analysis of the two questionnaire items against the 1500 answered questions (i.e., 30 participants each answering 50 questions) in both the pre-test and post-test, with results shown in Table 2. The columns $C_{pre}/C_{post}$, $C_{pre}/\overline{C}_{post}$, $\overline{C}_{pre}/C_{post}$ and $\overline{C}_{pre}/\overline{C}_{post}$ represent four groups of questions partitioned by their answer correctness, where $C_*$ and $\overline{C}_*$ respectively denote questions answered correctly and incorrectly in the pre-test or post-test. The rows labeled Without_system and With_system represent two groups of answered questions partitioned according to participants' ratings on the first questionnaire item, where Without_system represents ratings of 1 and 2, and With_system represents ratings of 3~5.

For Without_system, around 36% (536/1500) questions in the post-test were answered without use of the system due to high confidence on the part of participants. As shown in Fig. 5, around 59% (315/536) of these questions were answered correctly in both the pre-test and post-test, while only 28% (151/536) were answered incorrectly in both the pre-test and post-test, indicating that participants' confidence in their ability to answer certain questions correctly was not misplaced. The remaining 13% of questions provided inconsistent answers between the pre-test and post-test. For With_system, around 64% (964/1500) questions answered using the system in the post-test. Of these questions, around 46% (448/964) were answered incorrectly in the pre-test but were corrected in the post-test, indicating that participants had learned useful contextual information from the system. Around 25% (244/964) of questions answered correctly in the pre-

| | $C_{pre}/C_{post}$ | $C_{pre}/\overline{C}_{post}$ | $\overline{C}_{pre}/C_{post}$ | $\overline{C}_{pre}/\overline{C}_{post}$ | Total | |
|---|---|---|---|---|---|---|
| Without_system | 315 | 21 | 49 | 151 | **536** | **1500** |
| With_system | 244 | 78 | 448 | 194 | **964** | |
| PMI | 91 | 51 | 239 | 100 | **481** | **824** |
| N-gram | 93 | 19 | 177 | 54 | **343** | |

TABLE 2 – Cross analysis of questionnaire items against answered questions.

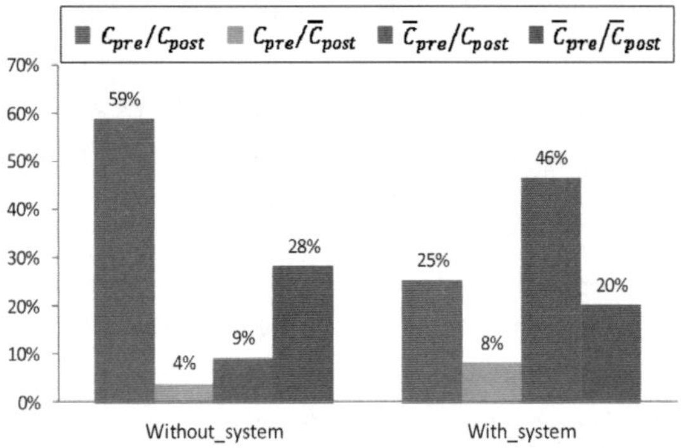


FIGURE 5 – Histograms of with and without system.

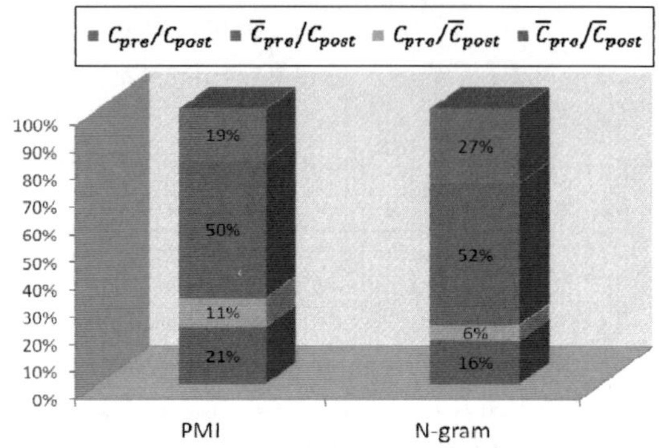


FIGURE 6 – Results of N-gram and PMI.

test were also answered correctly in the post-test because participants became more confident after double-checking their proposed answers with the system. Only 8% (78/964) of questions answered correctly in the pre-test were answered incorrectly in the post-test, and the remaining 20% of questions answered incorrectly in the pre-test were still incorrect in the post-test. A possible explanation is that the system does not always provide perfect results. In some cases, the system may provide ambiguous information, such as when the given context is too general. In such cases, participants may propose incorrect answers despite having used the system.

## 3.3 Comparison of PMI and N-gram

Table 2 shows that there were a total of 824 questions with feedback on the second questionnaire item, where 58% of questions were answered based on PMI, and 42% based on N-gram, indicating that participants had a preference for PMI in the test. But, in fact, previous studies have shown that the 5-gram language model has an accuracy of 69.9%, as opposed to 66.0% for PMI (Islam and Inkpen, 2010), thus N-gram provides more precise information. Evaluation results of 50 questions were consistent with this discrepancy, showing the respective accuracies of N-gram and PMI to be 68% and 64%. Figure 6 shows the comparative results of PMI and N-gram. The percentages of both $C_{pre}/C_{post}$ and $\overline{C}_{pre}/C_{post}$ for N-gram were higher than those for PMI, and the percentages of both $C_{pre}/\overline{C}_{post}$ and $\overline{C}_{pre}/\overline{C}_{post}$ for N-gram were lower than those for PMI. Overall, N-gram use resulted in a correct/incorrect ratio of 79:21 in the post-test, as opposed to 69:31 for PMI, indicating that N-gram can assist participants in correctly answering more questions and producing fewer errors caused by ambiguous contextual information.

## Conclusion

This study developed a computer-assisted near-synonym learning system using two automatic near-synonym choice techniques: PMI and N-gram, which can capture the respective individual and contiguous relationship between near-synonyms and their context words. Results show that both techniques can provide useful contextual information to improve participants' ability to discriminate among near-synonyms. While participants had a preference for PMI, *n*-grams can provide more precise information. Future work will be devoted to enhancing the system by including more near-synonym sets and incorporating other useful contextual information.

## Acknowledgments

This work was supported by the National Science Council, Taiwan, ROC, under Grant No. NSC100-2632-S-155-001 and NSC99-2221-E-155-036-MY3.

## References


Bhogal, J., Macfarlane, A., and Smith, P. (2007). A Review of Ontology based Query Expansion. *Information Processing and Management*, 43(4):866-886.

Cheng, C. C. (2004). Word-Focused Extensive Reading with Guidance. In *Proc. of the 13th International Symposium on English Teaching*, pages 24-32.

Church, K. and Hanks, P. (1990). Word Association Norms, Mutual Information and Lexicography. *Computational Linguistics*, 16(1):22-29.

Edmonds, P. (1997). Choosing the Word Most Typical in Context Using a Lexical Co-occurrence Network. In *Proc. of the 35th Annual Meeting of the Association for Computational Linguistics (ACL-97)*, pages 507-509.

Fellbaum, C. (1998). *WordNet: An Electronic Lexical Database*. MIT Press, Cambridge, MA.

Futagia, Y., Deanea, P., Chodorow, M., and Tetreault, J. (2008). A Computational Approach to Detecting Collocation Errors in the Writing of Non-native Speakers of English. *Computer Assisted Language Learning*, 21(4):353-367.

Gardiner, M. and Dras, M. (2007). Exploring Approaches to Discriminating among Near-Synonyms, In *Proc. of the Australasian Technology Workshop*, pages 31-39.

Huang, C. R., Hsieh, S. K., Hong, J. F., Chen, Y. Z., Su, I. L., Chen, Y. X., and Huang, S. W. (2008). Chinese Wordnet: Design, Implementation, and Application of an Infrastructure for Cross-lingual Knowledge Processing. In *Proc. of the 9th Chinese Lexical Semantics Workshop*.

Inkpen, D. (2007). A Statistical Model of Near-Synonym Choice. *ACM Trans. Speech and Language Processing*, 4(1):1-17.

Islam, A. and Inkpen, D. (2010). Near-Synonym Choice using a 5-gram Language Model. *Research in Computing Science: Special issue on Natural Language Processing and its Applications*, Alexander Gelbukh (ed.), 46:41-52.

Moldovan, D. and Mihalcea, R. (2000). Using Wordnet and Lexical Operators to Improve Internet Searches. *IEEE Internet Computing*, 4(1):34-43.

Navigli, R. and Velardi, P. (2003). An analysis of ontology-based query expansion strategies. In *Proc. of the Workshop on Adaptive Text Extraction and Mining (ATEM)*.

Ouyang, S., Gao, H. H., and Koh, S. N. (2009). Developing a Computer-Facilitated Tool for Acquiring Near-Synonyms in Chinese and English. In *Proc. of the 8th International Conference on Computational Semantics (IWCS-09)*, pages 316-319.

Pearce, D. (2001). Synonymy in Collocation Extraction. In *Proc. of the Workshop on WordNet and Other Lexical Resources at NAACL-01*.

Rodríguez, H., Climent, S., Vossen, P., Bloksma, L., Peters, W., Alonge, A., Bertagna, F., and Roventint, A. (1998). The Top-Down Strategy for Building EeuroWordNet: Vocabulary Coverage, Base Concepts and Top Ontology, *Computers and the Humanities*, 32:117-159.

Shlrl, A. and Revle, C. (2006). Query expansion behavior within a thesaurus-enhanced search environment: A user-centered evaluation. *Journal of the American Society for Information Science and Technology*, 57(4):462-478.

Wang, T. and Hirst, G. (2010). Near-synonym Lexical Choice in Latent Semantic Space. In *Proc. of the 23rd International Conference on Computational Linguistics (Coling-10)*, pages 1182-1190.

Wible, D., Kuo, C. H., Tsao, N. L., Liu, A., and Lin, H. L. (2003). Bootstrapping in a Language Learning Environment. *Journal of Computer Assisted Learning*, 19(1):90-102.

Wu, C. H., Liu, C. H., Matthew, H., and Yu, L. C. (2010). Sentence Correction Incorporating Relative Position and Parse Template Language Models. *IEEE Trans. Audio, Speech and Language Processing*, 18(6):1170-1181.

Yu, L. C., Chien, W. N., and Chen, S. T. (2011). A baseline system for Chinese near-synonym choice. In *Proc. of the 5th International Joint Conference on Natural Language Processing (IJCNLP-11)*, pages 1366-1370.

Yu, L. C., Shih, H. M., Lai, Y. L., Yeh, J. F., and Wu, C. H. (2010a). Discriminative Training for Near-synonym Substitution. In n *Proc. of the 23rd International Conference on Computational Linguistics (Coling-10)*, pages 1254-1262.

Yu, L. C. Wu, C. H. Chang, R. Y. Liu, C. H., and Hovy, E. H. (2010b). Annotation and Verification of Sense Pools in OntoNotes. *Information Processing and Management*, 46(4):436-447.

# Arabic Morphological Analyzer with Agglutinative Affix Morphemes and Fusional Concatenation Rules

*Fadi Zaraket*[1] *JadMakhlouta*[1]
(1) American University of Beirut, Lebanon
{*fz*11, *jem*04}@*aub.edu.lb*

Abstract

Current concatenative morphological analyzers consider prefix, suffix and stem morphemes based on lexicons of morphemes, and morpheme concatenation rules that determine whether prefix-stem, stem-suffix, and prefix-suffix concatenations are allowed. Existing affix lexicons contain extensive redundancy, suffer from inconsistencies, and require significant manual work to augment with clitics and partial affixes if needed. Unlike traditional work, our method considers Arabic affixes as fusional and agglutinative, i.e. composed of one or more morphemes, introduces new compatibility rules for affix-affix concatenations, and refines the lexicons of the SAMA and BAMA analyzers to be smaller, less redundant, and more consistent. It also automatically and perfectly solves the correspondence problem between the segments of a word and the corresponding tags, e.g. part of speech and gloss tags.

Title and Abstract in another language, $L_2$ (optional, and on same page)

# التحليل الصرفي لنصوص العربية بإستعمال قواعد صرفية اندماجية

المحللات الصرفية الاتصالية العربية المعاصرة تحسب اصل الكلمة وما يتعلق بها كمتعلق بادئ ولاحق باعتماد معاجم وقواعد اتصال للمكونات تحدد صحة اتصال البادئ واللاحق بالأصل أو ببعضهما البعض. المعاجم الحالية تحتوي الكثير من التكرار وتعاني من انعدام التناسق و تحتاج الى جهد يدوي ضخم في حال الحاجة الى اضافة متعلقات جزئية اليها. بخلاف الابحاث التقليدية، يعتبر منهجنا المتعلقات اندماجية ويمكن بناؤها من أكثر من مكون صرفي واحد. ويقدم منهجنا قواعد تصل متعلقين بادئين جزئيين لتكوين بادئ، وكذلك الأمر للمتعلق اللاحق. يشذب منهجنا معاجم BAMA وSAMA ليجعلها أصغر وأقل تكرارا وأكثر تناسقا. أيضا يحل منهجنا آليا وبشكل كامل مشكلة التلازم بين أجزاء الكلمة الصرفية والتعليقات الملحقة بها كمثل موقع المكون من الاعراب أو معناه.

---

Keywords: morphology; lexicons; computational linguistics; Arabization; affix.

Keywords in $L_2$: التحليل الصرفي؛ المعاجم؛ علم الألسنية الحسابي؛ التعريب؛ الملحق الاتصالي.

---

*Proceedings of COLING 2012: Demonstration Papers*, pages 517–526,
COLING 2012, Mumbai, December 2012.

Table 1: Partial prefix lexicon BAMA v1.2 معجم جزئي للملحقات الأمامية

| متعلق بادئ Prefix | مشكّل Vocalized | فئة Category | تعليق معنوي Gloss | موقع من الكلام POS |
|---|---|---|---|---|
| ف | فَ | Pref-Wa | and/so | fa/CONJ+ |
| ي | يَ | IVPref-hw-ya | he/it | ya/IV3MS+ |
| في | فَيَ | IVPref-hw-ya | and/so + he/it | fa/CONJ+ya/IV3MS+ |
| سي | سَيَ | IVPref-hw-ya | will + he/it | sa/FUT+ya/IV3MS+ |
| فسي | فَسَيَ | IVPref-hw-ya | and/so + will + he/it | fa/CONJ+sa/FUT+ya/IV3MS+ |
| ي | يَ | IVPref-hmA-ya | they (both) | ya/IV3MD+ |
| في | فَيَ | IVPref-hmA-ya | and/so + they (both) | fa/CONJ+ya/IV3MD+ |
| سي | سَيَ | IVPref-hmA-ya | will + they (both) | sa/FUT+ya/IV3MD+ |
| فسي | فَسَيَ | IVPref-hmA-ya | and/so + will + they (both) | fa/CONJ+sa/FUT+ya/IV3MD+ |
| و | وَ | Pref-Wa | and | wa/CONJ+ |
| وي | وَيَ | IVPref-hw-ya | and + he/it | wa/CONJ+ya/IV3MS+ |
| وسي | وَسَيَ | IVPref-hw-ya | and + will + he/it | wa/CONJ+sa/FUT+ya/IV3MS+ |
| وي | وَيَ | IVPref-hmA-ya | and + they (both) | wa/CONJ+ya/IV3MD+ |
| وسي | وَسَيَ | IVPref-hmA-ya | and + will + they (both) | wa/CONJ+sa/FUT+ya/IV3MD+ |

## 1 Short Summary in Arabic

## ملخص باللغة العربية

تحتاج تقنيات معالجة اللغات الطبيعية الى التحليل الصرفي لمعالجة نصوص العربية (Benajiba et al., 2007; Habash and Sadat, 2006) ، وذلك بسبب الغنى الصرفي للغة العربية الى جانب مصادر أخرى للغموض، منها غياب الحركات في أكثر النصوص. المحللات الصرفية المتواجدة حاليا للغة العربية تأخذ كلمة معزولة وتحسب مكوناتها الصرفية على شكل عدة حلول لكل منها تعليقات معنوية ونحوية مرتبطة بتشكيل كامل محتمل للكلمة الأصل. تعاني هذه المحللات من مشكلات عدة، أولها عدم قدرتها على عزل الكلمة، وثانيها، عدم قدرتها على حل مشكلة الكلمات المتصلة بدون فراغ بينها، وثالثها عدم قدرتها على المطابقة الدقيقة بين أجزاء الحل ومواقع الحروف في أصل الكلمة، ورابعها، خلل في الدقة في ربط المتعلقات المختلفة بأصول الكلمات.

المحللات الصرفية المعاصرة (Buckwalter, 2002; Kulick et al., 2010a) تعتمد على معاجم للمتعلقات البادئة، ولأصول الكلمات، وللمتعلقات اللاحقة وعلى قواعد اتصال تحكم صحة اتصال متعلق بادئ بأصل، واتصال أصل بمتعلق لاحق، واتصال متعلق بادئ بمتعلق لاحق. كما يبدو في الجدول 1 كل خانة في المعجم تحتوي على المكون الصرفي، وعلى تشكيله بحركات كاملة، وعلى فئته التي تحكم اتصاله بمكونات أخرى، وعلى تعليق يحدد موقعه في الكلام، وعلى تعليق يحدد معناه. تحتوي الخانات على متعلقات نهائية متكونة من متعلقات جزئية. مثلا، المكونان «فـ» و «يـ» يشكلان

متعلقات مستقلة قابلة للاتصال مباشرة بالأصل «لعب» لتكوين كلمتي «فلعب» و «يلعب». اضافة الى ذلك، يمكن للمكون «سـ» ان يتصل بـ «يلعب» لتكوين «سيلعب». بدوره المكون «فـ» يمكن أن يتصل بـ «سيلعب» لتكوين «فسيلعب». تحتوي معاجم BAMA و SAMA على كل المتعلقات الممكن تكوينها مما يؤدي الى المشاكل التالية.

أولا، يؤدي تكرار الخانات الى صعوبة الحفاظ على تناسقها وصيانتها.
ثانيا، يؤدي التكرار الى تضخم المعجم خاصة عندما نضطر الى اضافة مكون جديد اليه كهمزة الاستفهام.
ثالثا، تحتوي كل خانة على تعليقات معنوية مرتبطة بالمكون المركب. تركيب هذه التعليقات اتصالا يؤدي الى فقدان المطابقة الدقيقة بين مواقع الحروف في الكلمة الأم والتعليقات، وهو أمر هام جدا للتعلم الآلي.

في هذا البحث، نقدم المساهمات التالية.

أولا، نبني محللا صرفيا حديثا يعتمد المكونات الصرفية الاساسية ويصل بينها، كما يحدد قواعد لدمجها مستقاة من كتب الصرف العربية.
ثانيا، نحل مشاكل الاتساق بين المكونات في BAMA و SAMA وندرس أثر تصحيحاتنا.
وثالثا، نحل مشكلة المطابقة بين الكلمة الأم والتعليقات المعنوية، والتعليقات التي تحدد موقع الكلمة في النص.

المنهج الذي نعتمده في التحليل الصرفي يمكنه أن يعبر عن نفس الخانات في الجدول 1 باستعمال ٣ مكونات أساسية ومكون واحد جزئي و٣ قواعد اتصال جزئي. في الجدول، نحتاج الى اضافة ٥ خانات اذا أردنا اضافة حرف العطف كمكون مع قواعد اتصال خاصة بكل خانة، بينما لا يحتاج الأمر الا الى خانة واحدة باستعمال منهجنا.

في ما يلي نشرح تطبيق منهجنا في برنامج صرف آلي حديث للغة العربية ونعرض تقييمنا للنتائج. استطاع البرنامج تقليص المعاجم التي نحتاجها للتحليل الصرفي للغة العربية، واستطاع تصحيح اخطاء التناسق الموجودة في أدوات التحليل الآلي الحالية، كما استطاع أن يحل مشكلة المطابقة الحرفية بين الكلمة الأم ومكوناتها الصرفية في مقابل التعليقات وأجزائها.

## شكر.

نشكر المجلس الوطني اللبناني للبحوث لدعمه هذا العمل.

## 2 Introduction

*Natural language processing* (NLP) applications require the use of *morphological analyzers* to preprocess Arabic text (Benajiba et al., 2007; Habash and Sadat, 2006). Given a white space and punctuation delimited Arabic word, Arabic morphological analyzers return the internal structure of the word composed of several *morphemes* including *affixes* (*prefixes* and *suffixes*) and *stems* (Al-Sughaiyer and Al-Kharashi, 2004). They also return *part of speech* (POS) and other tags associated with the word and its constituent morphemes. For example, for the word فسيلعبون *fsylϑwn* (and/so they will play), the analyzer may return فسيـ *fsy* as a prefix morpheme with the POS tag `fa/CONJ+sa/FUT+ya/IV3MD` and with gloss tag `and/so + will + they (people)`, لعب *lϑ* as a stem with POS tag `loEab/VERB IMPERFECT` and with gloss tag `play`, and ـون *wn* as a suffix with POS tag `uwna/IVSUFF_SUBJ:MP_MOOD:I` and with gloss tag `[MASC.PL.]`. The alignment and correspondence between the original word and the several parts and tags of the morphological solution are essential to the success of NLP tasks such as machine translation and information extraction (Lee et al., 2011; Semmar et al., 2008).

Current concatenative morphological analyzers such as BAMA (Buckwalter, 2002) and SAMA (Kulick et al., 2010a) are based on lexicons of prefixes $L_p$, stems $L_s$, and suffixes $L_x$. As shown in Table 1, each entry in a lexicon includes the morpheme, its vocalized form with diacritics, a *concatenation compatibility category* tag, a part of speech tag (POS), and the gloss tag. Separate compatibility rules specify the compatibility of prefix-stem $R_{ps}$, stem-suffix $R_{sx}$, and prefix-suffix $R_{px}$ concatenations. The affixes in $L_p$ and $L_x$ contain final forms of generative affixes. For example, the affixes فـ *f* (and/so), and يـ *y* (he/it) in the above example are valid standalone prefixes, and can be concatenated to the stem لعب *lϑ* (play) to form فلعب *flϑ* and يلعب *ylϑ*, respectively. In addition, the morpheme سـ *s* (will) can connect to يلعب *ylϑ* to form سيلعب *sylϑ*. In turn, the morpheme فـ *f* (and/so) can form فيلعب *fylϑ* and فسيلعب *fsylϑ*. The BAMA and SAMA $L_p$ lexicons contain all the prefixes that can be generated from the three morphemes فـ, يـ, and سـ, as shown in Table 1. Several problems arise.

- The $L_p$ and $L_x$ lexicons contain redundant entries and that results in complex maintenance and consistency issues (Maamouri et al., 2008; Kulick et al., 2010b).
- Augmenting $L_p$ and $L_x$ with additional morphemes, such as أ *ʔa* (the question glottal hamza), may result in a quadratic explosion in the size of the lexicons (Hunspell, 2012).
- The concatenated forms in $L_p$ and $L_x$ contain concatenated POS and other tags. The segmentation correspondence between the prefix concatenated from several morphemes and the tags associated with it is lost. In several cases, this leads to missing correspondence between the tokens of the morphological solution and the segmentation of the original word.

In this paper we make the following contributions. More details about this paper and the supporting tools are available online [1].

- We build a novel Arabic morphological analyzer with agglutinative affixes and fusional affix concatenation rules ($R_{pp}$ and $R_{xx}$) using textbook based Arabic morphological rules as well as the concatenation rules of existing analyzers. Agglutinative affix morphemes can be concatenated to form an affix. Fusional affix concatenation rules state whether two affixes can

[1] `http://webfea.fea.aub.edu.lb/fadi/dkwk/doku.php?id=sarf`

Table 2: Example rules from $R_{pp}$

<table>
<tr><th>Category 1</th><th>Category 2</th><th>Resulting Category</th></tr>
<tr><td>NPref-Li</td><td>NPref-Al</td><td>NPref-LiAl</td></tr>
<tr><td colspan="3">substitute: r//ال||لل\\</td></tr>
<tr><td>Pref-Wa</td><td>{NOT "Pref-0" AND NOT "NPref-La"<br>AND NOT "PVPref-La"}</td><td>{$2}</td></tr>
<tr><td>IVPref-li-</td><td>{"IVPref-*-y*"}</td><td>{"IVPref-(@1)-liy(@2)"}</td></tr>
<tr><td colspan="3">substitute: d//he/||him/\\ d//they||them\\ … d//(+2)|| to\\</td></tr>
</table>

be concatenated and contain a regular expression that forms the resulting orthographic and semantic tags from the tags of the original morphemes (Spencer, 1991; Vajda).

- We solve 197 and 208 inconsistencies in the existing affix lexicons of BAMA and SAMA, respectively. We evaluate our approach using the ATBv3.2 Part 3 data set (Maamouri et al., 2010) and report on the effect of our corrections on the annotations.
- We solve the correspondence between the morphological solution and the morphological segmentation of the original text problem where we report perfect results, while a SAMA post-processing technique (Maamouri et al., 2008)reports 3.7% and MADA+TOKAN (Habash et al., 2009) reports 9.6% disagreement using the ATBv3.2 Part 3 data set (Maamouri et al., 2010).

## 3 Our method

Our method considers three types of affixes:

- *Atomic* affix morphemes such as ـي *y* (he/it) can be affixes on their own and can directly connect to stems using the $R_{ps}$ and $R_{sx}$ rules.
- *Partial affix* morphemes such as سـ *s* (will) can not be affixes on their own and need to connect to other affixes before they connect to a stem.
- *Compound* affixes are concatenations of atomic and partial affix morphemes as well as other smaller compound affixes. They can connect to stems according to the $R_{ps}$ and $R_{sx}$ rules.

We form compound affixes from atomic and partial affix morphemes using newly introduced prefix-prefix $R_{pp}$ and suffix-suffix $R_{xx}$ concatenation rules.

Our method, unlike conventional analyzers, considers $L_p$ and $L_x$ to be lexicons of atomic and partial affix morphemes only associated with several tags such as the vocalized form, the part of speech (POS), and the gloss tags. Agglutinative affixes are defined as prefix-prefix $R_{pp}$ and suffix-suffix $R_{xx}$ concatenation or agglutination rules. An agglutination rule $r \in R_{pp} \cup R_{xx}$ takes the compatibility category tags of affixes $a_1$ and $a_2$ and checks whether they can be concatenated. If so, the rule takes the tags of $a_1$ and $a_2$ and generates the affix $a = r(a_1, a_2)$ with its associated tags.

The tags of $r(a_1, a_2)$ are generated from the corresponding tags of $a_1$ and $a_2$ via applying substitution rules.Our rules are fusional in the sense that they modify the orthography and the semantic tags of the resulting affixes by more than simple concatenation.

We illustrate this with the example rules in Table 2. Row 1 presents a rule that takes prefixes with category `NPref-Li` such as ل *li-* (for) and prefixes with category `NPref-Al` such as ال (the).

The substitution rule replaces the ال with ل resulting in لل *li-*. The compound prefix لل corresponds to the fusion of two atomic prefixes and the fusion is one character shorter than the concatenation.

Row 2 states that prefixes of category `Pref-Wa` can be concatenated with prefixes with categories that are neither of `Pref-0`, `NPref-La`, and `PVPref-La` categories as denoted by the Boolean expression. The resulting category is denoted with {$2} which means the category of the second prefix. For example, و *w* (and) which has a category `Pref-Wa`, can be combined with ال *āl* (the) with the category `NPref-Al`, and the resulting compound prefix وال *wāl* has the category of the second `NPref-Al`. This category determines concatenation with stems and suffixes.

The third rule uses a wild card character '`*`' to capture substrings of zero or more characters in the second category. The in the resulting category, it refers to the $i^{th}$ substring captured by the wild cards using the '`@`' operator followed by a number $i$. Substitution rules for gloss and POS tags start with the letters *d* and *p*, respectively. The `+2` pattern in the substitution rule means that the partial gloss `to` should be appended after the gloss of the second affix.

Our method is in line with native Arabic morphology and syntax textbooks (Mosaad, 2009; AlRajehi, 2000b,a) which introduce only atomic and partial affixes and discuss rules to concatenate the affixes, and the syntax, semantic, and phonological forms of the resulting affixes. For example, Row 3 in Table 2 translates the textbook rule: `IVPref-li-` prefixes connect to imperfect verb prefixes and transform the subject pronoun (in the gloss) to an object pronoun. We built our rules in four steps.

1. We encoded textbook morphological rules into patterns.
2. We extracted atomic and partial affixes from the BAMA and SAMA lexicons.
3. We grouped the rest of the BAMA and SAMA affixes into rules we collected from textbooks.
4. We refined the rules wherever necessary, and we grouped rules that shared the same patterns.

We validated our work by generating all possible affixes and compared them against the BAMA and SAMA affix lexicons. This helped us learn inconsistencies in the BAMA and SAMA lexicons.

**Morpheme level segmentation.** (Habash et al., 2009) lists 13 different valid segmentation schemes. In 10 of those schemes, a word may be segmented in the middle of a compound affix. According to the latest ATB standards, the word وسيلعبها *wsylʿbhā* (and they will play it) should be segmented into ـو + ـسـ + يلعبـ + ها which separates the compound prefix وسـ into two morphemes. Our method is based on atomic and partial affix morphemes and enables all valid segmentations.

(Maamouri et al., 2008) reports that 3.7% of more than 300 thousand ATB entries exhibit discrepancy between the unvocalized input string and the corresponding unvocalized form of the segmented morphological solution. The analysis of the example للقضاء *llqḍāʾ*, `li/PREP + Al/DET + qaDA'/NOUN`, (for the justice) is segmented into two tokens: `li/PREP` and `Al/DET + qaDA'/NOUN`. Consequently, the best approximation of the unvocalized entry of each token is ل and القضاء, respectively, with an extra letter ا *ā*. This is not a faithful representation of the original text data and the segmentation does not correspond with that of the input text. Up until the release of ATB 3 v3.2, this correspondence problem between the unvocalized entries of segmented tokens and the input string resulted in "numerous errors" (Kulick et al., 2010b). Later work (Kulick et al., 2010b) provided an improved solution that is corpus specific as stated in further documentation notes (Maamouri et al., 2010) which also state that "it is possible that future releases either will not include extensive checking on the creation of these INPUT STRING tree tokens, or will leave out completely such tokens."

Our method provides a general solution for the segmentation correspondence problem since the valid compound affixes preserve the input text segmentation. In particular, a partial affix ال `Al/DET` connects to the atomic affix لِ `li/PREP` and resolves the problem.

**Redundancy and Inconsistencies.** Consider the partial affix lexicon in Table 1. Our method replaces the first five rows with three atomic affix morphemes and one partial affix morpheme in $L_p$ and three rules to generate compound morphemes in $R_{pp}$. In the original representation, the addition of the prefix يَ *ya-* (them/both) required the addition of four entries, three of them only differ in their dependency on the added يَ *ya-*. The addition of و *w* required the addition of five entries. In our method, the equivalent addition of يَ *ya-* (them/both) requires only two rules in $R_{pp}$ and the addition of و *w* requires only one additional entry in $L_p$. The difference in lexicon size is much larger when we consider the full lexicon.

We discovered a total of 197 and 208 inconsistencies in the affix lexicons of BAMA version 1.2 and SAMA version 3.2, respectively. We found a small number of these inconsistencies manually and we computed the full list via comparing $L_p$ and $L_x$ with their counterparts computed using our agglutinative affixes. Most of the inconsistencies are direct results of partially redundant entries with erroneous tags. We note that SAMA corrected several BAMA inconsistencies, but also introduced several new ones when modifying existing entries to meet new standards. SAMA also introduced fresh inconsistencies when introducing new entries. The full list of inconsistencies with description is available online 1.

## 4 Related work

Other morphological analyzers such as ElixirFM (Smrž, 2007), MAGEAD (Habash et al., 2005), and MADA+TOKAN (Habash et al., 2009) are based on BAMA and SAMA and use functional and statistical techniques to address the segmentation problem. (Lee et al., 2011) uses syntactic information to resolve the same problem. A significant amount of the literature on Arabic NLP uses the Arabic Tree Bank (ATB) (Maamouri and Bies, 2004) with tags from BAMA and SAMA for learning and evaluation (Shaalan et al., 2010; Benajiba et al., 2007; Al-Jumaily et al., 2011).

Several researchers stress the importance of correspondence between the input string and the tokens of the morphological solutions. Recent work uses POS tags and a syntactic morphological agreement hypothesis to refine syntactic boundaries within words (Lee et al., 2011). The work in (Grefenstette et al., 2005; Semmar et al., 2008) uses an extensive lexicon with 3,164,000 stems, stem rewrite rules (Darwish, 2002), syntax analysis, proclitics, and enclitics to address the same problem. We differ from partial solutions in (Maamouri et al., 2008; Kulick et al., 2010b) in that our segmentation is an output of the morphological analysis and not a reverse engineering of the multi-tag affixes.

TOKAN in the MADA+TOKAN (Habash et al., 2009) toolkit works as a post morphological disambiguation tokenizer. TOKAN tries to match the output of MADA, an SVM morphological disambiguation tool based on BAMA and the ATB, with a segmentation scheme selected by the user. We differ in that the segmentation is part of the morphological analysis and the segmentation can help in the disambiguation task performed later by the NLP task. We perform morpheme based segmentation, which subsumes all possible higher level segmentation schemes.

The morphological analyzer (Attia, 2006) divides morphemes into proclictics, prefixes, stems, suffixes and enclitics and supports inflections using alteration rules. We differ in that we support vocalization and provide glosses for individual morphemes.

Table 3: Lexicon size comparison.

| | $\lvert L_p \rvert$ | $\lvert R_{pp} \rvert$ | $\lvert L_x \rvert$ | $\lvert R_{xx} \rvert$ | $\Delta_L^{hmz}$ | $\Delta_R^{hmz}$ |
|---|---|---|---|---|---|---|
| **BAMA** | 299 | – | 618 | – | 295 | – |
| Agglutinative | 70 | 89 | 181 | 123 | 1 | 32 |
| With fusional | 43 | 89 | 146 | 128 | 1 | 32 |
| With grouping | 41 | 7 | 146 | 32 | 1 | 1 |
| **SAMA** | 1325 | – | 945 | – | 1,296 | – |
| Agglutinative | 107 | 129 | 221 | 188 | 1 | 38 |
| With fusional | 56 | 129 | 188 | 194 | 1 | 38 |
| With grouping | 53 | 18 | 188 | 64 | 1 | 1 |

## 5 Results

The $|L_p|$, $|L_x|$, $|R_{pp}|$, and $|R_{xx}|$ entries in Table 3 report the number of rules and the sizes of the affix lexicons needed to represent the affixes of BAMA and SAMA. The entries also report the effect of agglutinative affixes, fusional rules, and grouping of rules with similar patterns using wildcards on the size. Using our method, we only require 226 and 323 entries to represent the 917 and the 2,270 entries of BAMA and SAMA affixes with inconsistencies corrected, respectively. We observe that we only need 12 more entries in $L_p$, 42 in $L_x$, 18 rules in $R_{pp}$, and 64 in $R_{xx}$ for a total of 136 entries to accommodate for the transition from BAMA to SAMA. This is one order of magnitude less than 1,353 additional entries to SAMA. We also note that we detect most of the inconsistencies automatically and only needed to validate our corrections in textbooks and corpora.

**Segmentation.** We evaluate our segmentation under the guidelines of the ATBv3.2 Part 3, compared to a SAMA post processing technique (Maamouri et al., 2008), and to MADA+TOKAN (Habash et al., 2009). **Our automatically generated segmentation agrees with 99.991% of the entries.** We investigated the 25 entries for which our solution disagreed with the LDC annotation of the ATB, and we found out that both solutions were valid. SAMA+ (Maamouri et al., 2008) reports at least a 3.7% discrepancy after accounting for normalizations of several segmentation options. TOKAN disagrees with 9.6% of the words. It disregards input diacritics and performs segmentation based on the POS entries of the morphological solutions in a similar approach to (Maamouri et al., 2008). Since TOKAN is not concerned with the correspondence problem, it serves as a baseline.

**Augmentation.** The question clitic, denoted by the glottal sign (hamza أ *ʔa* ), is missing in BAMA and SAMA (Attia, 2006). $\Delta_L^{hmz}$ and $\Delta_R^{hmz}$ columns show that our method only requires one more atomic affix and one more fusional rule to accommodate for the addition of the question clitic whereas BAMA and SAMA need 295 and 1,296 additional entries, respectively, with more chances of inducing inconsistencies.

**Lexicon inconsistencies.** To evaluate how much lexical inconsistencies are significant we evaluated the presence of the detected inconsistencies in the ATBv3.2 Part 3 and found that 0.76% of the entries that adopted the SAMA solution were affected by the gloss inconsistencies. The rest of the entries have manually entered solutions. In total 8.774% of the words and 3.264% of the morphological solutions are affected by inconsistencies in gloss and POS tags. Finally, our analyzer automatically solves the 7 ATB occurrences of the question clitic.

**Acknowledgement.** We thank the Lebanese National Council for Scientific Research (LNCSR) for funding this research.

## References

Al-Jumaily, H., MartÃ■nez, P., MartÃ■nez-FernÃąndez, J., and Van der Goot, E. (2011). A real time named entity recognition system for Arabic text mining. *Language Resources and Evaluation*, pages 1–21.

Al-Sughaiyer, I. A. and Al-Kharashi, I. A. (2004). Arabic morphological analysis techniques: a comprehensive survey. *American Society for Information Science and Technology*, 55(3):189–213.

AlRajehi, A. (2000a). التطبيق النحوي *ālttibyq alnḥwy (The syntactical practice)*. Renaissance (nahda), first edition.

AlRajehi, A. (2000b). التطبيق الصرفي *ālttibyq alṣarfy (The morphological practice)*. Renaissance (An-nahda), first edition.

Aoe, J.-i. (1989). An efficient digital search algorithm by using a double-array structure. *IEEE Transactions on Software Engineering*, 15(9):1066–1077.

Attia, M. A. (2006). An ambiguity-controlled morphological analyzer for modern standard arabic modelling finite state networks. In *The Challenge of Arabic for NLP/MT Conference*. The British Computer Society.

Beesley, K. R. (2001). Finite-state morphological analysis and generation of Arabic at xerox research: Status and plans. In *Workshop Proceedings on Arabic Language Processing: Status and Prospects*, pages 1–8, Toulouse, France.

Beesley, K. R. and Karttunen, L. (2003). *Finite-State Morphology: Xerox Tools and Techniques*. CSLI, Stanford.

Benajiba, Y., Rosso, P., and Benedíruiz, J. (2007). ANERsys: An Arabic named entity recognition system based on maximum entropy. pages 143–153.

Buckwalter, T. (2002). Buckwalter Arabic morphological analyzer version 1.0. Technical report, LDC catalog number LDC2002L49.

Darwish, K. (2002). Building a shallow Arabic morphological analyzer in one day. In *Proceedings of the ACL-02 workshop on Computational approaches to semitic languages*.

Grefenstette, G., Semmar, N., and Elkateb-Gara, F. (2005). Modifying a natural language processing system for european languages to treat arabic in information processing and information retrieval applications. In *ACL Workshop on Computational Approaches to Semitic Languages*, pages 31–37.

Habash, N., Rambow, O., and Kiraz, G. (2005). Morphological analysis and generation for Arabic dialects. In *Semitic '05: Proceedings of the ACL Workshop on Computational Approaches to Semitic Languages*, pages 17–24, Morristown, NJ, USA.

Habash, N., Rambow, O., and Roth, R. (2009). Mada+tokan: A toolkit for Arabic tokenization, diacritization, morphological disambiguation, pos tagging, stemming and lemmatization. In Choukri, K. and Maegaard, B., editors, *Proceedings of the Second International Conference on Arabic Language Resources and Tools*, Cairo, Egypt. The MEDAR Consortium.

Habash, N. and Sadat, F. (2006). Arabic preprocessing schemes for statistical machine translation. In *Proceedings of the North American Chapter of the Association for Computational Linguistics(NAACL)*, pages 49–52.

Hajič, J. and Zemànek, P. (2004). Prague arabic dependency treebank: Development in data and tools. In *NEMLAR International Conference on Arabic Language Resources and Tools*, pages 110–117.

Hunspell (2012). Hunspell manual page.

Kulick, S., Bies, A., and Maamouri, M. (2010a). Consistent and flexible integration of morphological annotation in the Arabic treebank. In *Proceedings of the Seventh conference on International Language Resources and Evaluation (LREC'10)*, Valletta, Malta.

Kulick, S., Bies, A., and Maamouri, M. (2010b). Consistent and flexible integration of morphological annotation in the arabic treebank. In *International Conference on Language Resources and Evaluation*. European Language Resources Association.

Lee, Y. K., Haghighi, A., and Barzila, R. (2011). Modeling Syntactic Context Improves Morphological Segmentation. In *Conference on Computational Natural Language Learning (CoNLL)*.

Lee, Y.-S., Papineni, K., Roukos, S., Emam, O., and Hassan, H. (2003). Language model based arabic word segmentation. In *Association for Computational Linguistics*, pages 399–406.

Maamouri, M. and Bies, A. (2004). Developing an Arabic treebank: methods, guidelines, procedures, and tools. In *Semitic '04: Proceedings of the Workshop on Computational Approaches to Arabic Script-based Languages*, pages 2–9.

Maamouri, M., Bies, A., Kulick, S., Krouna, S., Gaddeche, F., and Zaghouani, W. (2010). Arabic treebank: Part 3 version 3.2. In *Linguistic Data Consortium,LDC2010T08*.

Maamouri, M., Kulick, S., and Bies, A. (2008). Diacritic annotation in the arabic treebank and its impact on parser evaluation. In *International Conference on Language Resources and Evaluation*.

Mosaad, Z. (2009). الوَجيز في الصَرف *alwağyz fy alṣarf (The Briefing of Morphology)*. As-Sahwa, first edition.

Semmar, N., Meriama, L., and Fluhr, C. (2008). Evaluating a natural language processing approach in arabic information retrieval. In *ELRA Workshop on Evaluation*.

Shaalan, K. F., Magdy, M., and Fahmy, A. (2010). Morphological analysis of ill-formed arabic verbs in intelligent language tutoring framework. In *Applied Natural Language Processing, Florida Artificial Intelligence Research Society Conference*. AAAI Press.

Smrž, O. (2007). Elixirfm: implementation of functional Arabic morphology. In *Semitic '07: Proceedings of the 2007 Workshop on Computational Approaches to Semitic Languages*, pages 1–8, Prague, Czech Republic.

Spencer, A. (1991). Blackwell Textbooks in Linguistics.

Vajda, E. J. Typology.

# SMR-Cmp: Square-Mean-Root Approach to Comparison of Monolingual Contrastive Corpora

*ZHANG HuaRui* [1,2] *HUANG Chu-Ren*[1] *Francesca QUATTRI* [1]
(1) The Hong Kong Polytechnic University, Hong Kong
(2) MOE Key Lab of Computational Linguistics, Peking University, Beijing, China
hrzhang@pku.edu.cn, churen.huang@polyu.edu.hk,
quattri.francesca@gmail.com

ABSTRACT

The basic statistic tools used in computational and corpus linguistics to capture distributional information have not changed much in the past 20 years even though many standard tools have been proved to be inadequate. In this demo (SMR-Cmp), we adopt the new tool of Square-Mean-Root (SMR) similarity, which measures the evenness of distribution between contrastive corpora, to extract lexical variations. The result based on one case study shows that the novel approach outperforms traditional statistical measures, including chi-square ($\chi^2$) and log-likelihood ratio (LLR).

KEYWORDS : Square-Mean-Root evenness, SMR similarity, corpus comparison, chi-square, log-likelihood ratio.

## 1 Motivation

Tools for detection and analysis of language variations are of foundational importance in computational/corpus linguistics. In general, most, if not all, NLP tasks (e.g. name entity recognition, disambiguation, information retrieval), are carried out based on distributional variations within the same text genre. On the other hand, distributional properties can be used to describe and account for language variations, such as the difference between two or more contrastive corpora. Such studies typically aim to locate and account for different lexical items in these contrastive corpora; but no satisfying quantitative ranking on the difference between the contrastive corpora is typically provided. In other words, there are no existent criteria to define what a meaningful ranking list of divergent words between contrastive corpora should look like. The ranking lists resulting from previous statistical comparisons have often been in conflict with intuition.

The same problem arises in the case of language learners who desire to learn significant words in a particular field. These categorical words are generally listed alphabetically and the list generated is often very long. We may ask - how could we assign a rank to the list so as to help foreign language beginners? In other words, how can we divide domain words into different levels of usefulness? Our research will also try to answer this question.

In the following, we first propose our solution based on Square-Mean-Root (SMR) evenness, then compare it with common statistical methods via a case study on American and British English.

## 2 Methodology

Our demo utilizes the novel statistical measure from Zhang et.al. (2004) and Zhang (2010).

### 2.1 Square-Mean-Root Evenness (DC)

The Distributional Consistency (DC) measure was proposed by Zhang et.al. (2004), and renamed as Square-Mean-Root evenness ($\text{Even}_{\text{SMR}}$) in Zhang (2010). SMR is the direct opposite of RMS (Root-Mean-Square) which is usually used in statistics. Gries (2010) provided a comprehensive comparison of dispersion measures, including DC.

SMR evenness captures the fact that if a word is commonly used in a language, it will appear in different parts of a corpus, and if it is common enough, it will be evenly distributed.

When a corpus is divided into *n* equally sized parts, SMR evenness is calculated by

$$\text{Even}_{\text{SMR}} = DC = \left( \sum_{i=1}^{n} \left( \sqrt{f_i} \right) \Big/ n \right)^2 \Big/ \left( \sum_{i=1}^{n} f_i \Big/ n \right)$$

where

$f_i$: the occurrence frequency of the specified word in the i$^{\text{th}}$ part of the corpus
$n$: the number of equally sized parts into which the corpus is divided
$\Sigma$: the sum of

When the whole corpus is divided into unequally sized parts, the formula becomes:

$$\text{Even}_{\text{SMR}} = DC = \left(\sum_{i=1}^{n}\sqrt{f_i C_i}\right)^2 \Big/ \left(\sum_{i=1}^{n} f_i\right)\left(\sum_{i=1}^{n} C_i\right)$$

with $C_i$ denoting the occurrence frequency of all words that appears in the i$^{th}$ part of the corpus

The SMR evenness will decrease when some parts are further divided ($n$ increases), however, this will not affect the effectiveness of comparison with the fixed number $n$.

## 2.2 Square-Mean-Root Similarity (bDC & mDC)

When comparing two contrastive corpora, there are two distributions $f$ and $g$. The SMR similarity is calculated by the following formula (Zhang, 2010):

$$\text{Sim}_{\text{SMR}} = bDC = \sum_{i=1}^{n}\left(\left(\sqrt{f_i} + \sqrt{g_i}\right)/2\right)^2 \Big/ \left(\sum_{i=1}^{n}(f_i + g_i)/2\right)$$

When comparing three or more contrastive corpora, the formula becomes (Zhang, 2010):

$$\text{Sim}_{\text{SMR}} = mDC = \sum_{i=1}^{n}\left(\sum_{f}^{m}\left(\sqrt{f_i}\right)/m\right)^2 \Big/ \sum_{i=1}^{n}\left(\sum_{f}^{m} f_i /m\right)$$

where $\sum_{f}^{m}\sqrt{f_i}$ means sum over $f$, if there are three distributions called $f$, $g$, $h$, then it expands to be $\sqrt{f_i} + \sqrt{g_i} + \sqrt{h_i}$.

## 2.3 Difference Measure

The difference measure is based on frequency and SMR similarity.

Here we propose the following formula:

$$\text{Diff} = \text{Freq} \times (1\text{-Sim}_{\text{SMR}})^2$$

This formula is comparable with chi-square in terms of dimension. But it is symmetric to both sides being compared while chi-square is not. Although there can be a symmetric version for chi-square, the result is not satisfying as our experiment shows.

# 3 Comparison with Chi-square ($\chi^2$) and Log-Likelihood Ratio (LLR)

In order to test the validity of our method, we extract the lexical difference between American English and British English via the Google Books Ngram dataset (Michel et al, 2010), which is the largest such corpus to the best of our knowledge. This enormous database contains millions of digitalized books, which cover about 4 percent (over 5 million volumes) of all the books ever printed. We utilize the American part and the British part during time span of 1830-2009 (180 years, $n$=180).

There have been various approaches to corpus comparison (e.g. Dunning, 1993; Rose and Kilgariff, 1998; Cavaglia, 2002; McInnes, 2004). We compare our result with more common approaches, including chi-square ($\chi^2$), as recommended by Kilgarriff (2001), and log-likelihood ratio (LLR) recommended by Rayson and Garside (2000).

In Table 1, the top 30 words by each criterion (SMR, $\chi^2$ & LLR) are listed. Almost every word in the list by our SMR measure is interpretable in the sense of being American or British except the word *cent* which demands further explanation.

From Table 1 we can see that there are large difference between the ranking of most biased words in AmE and BrE. On the left, almost every word in the list ranked by our method is obviously an American-dominant word or British-dominant word. In the middle, words in the list ranked by chi-square presents a mixture of biased words (e.g. £, *labour, centre, colour*) and unbiased common words (e.g. *which, you, of*), and both these example words appear in the top dozen. On the right, we can see somewhat similar or slightly better result in the list ranked by LLR.

It is interesting that *which* is ranked the 1st and 2nd position by $\chi^2$ and LLR, respectively. This suggests that *which* should be a very biased word. But from Figure 1 we can see the frequency distribution in AmE and BrE. The trend is so similar that we can hardly know whether *which* is more American or British.

In our approach, *which* is outside the top 100 words. Instead, *color* is ranked the second (as shown in Figure 2). This is clearly more reasonable by intuition.

Another example is *of* (as shown in Figure 3), whose frequency is almost the same (after smoothing) through 90 percent of the time span investigated, is yet ranked the 3rd position by both $\chi^2$ and LLR. By contrast, in our ranking by SMR, *of* is outside the top 1000 words.

Proportions of positive (in bold), vague, and negative (underline) contrastive words in three columns of Table 1:

SMR: **90%**; 10%; 0%. (vague: ", ", *cent.*)

$\chi^2$: **40%**; 10%; 50%. (top 3: *which, you, of*: all negative.)

LLR: **50%**; 10%; 40%. (top 3: *you, which, of*: all negative.)

The conclusion we draw is that SMR is more appropriate than $\chi^2$ and LLR for lexical difference detection between contrastive corpora.

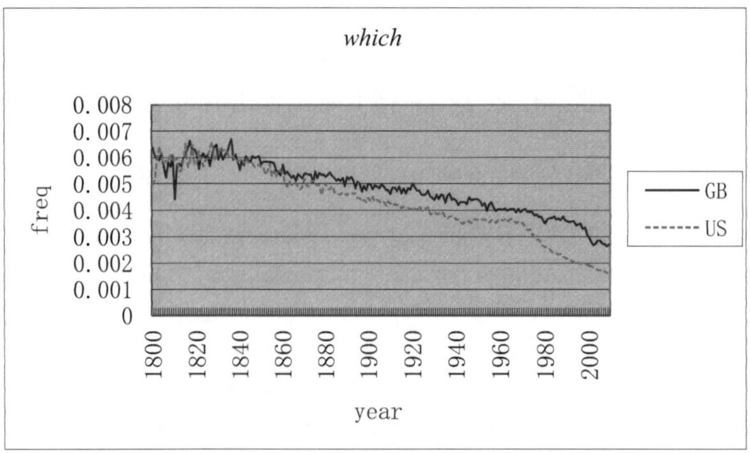


FIGURE 1 – *which*: with same trend in AmE and BrE, only different in quantity of use

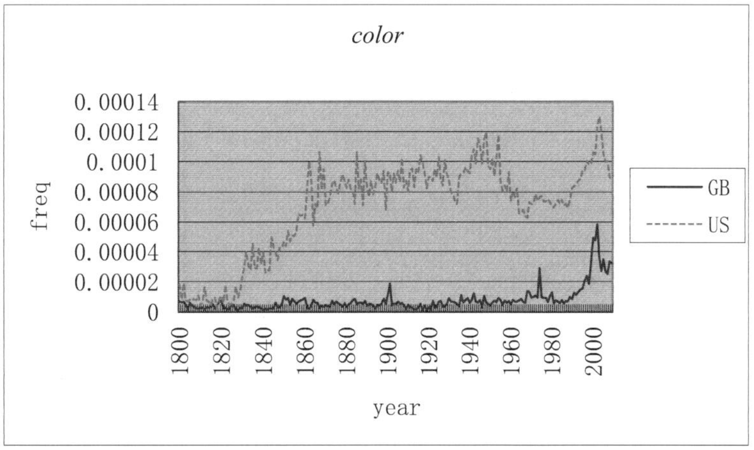


FIGURE 2 – *color* (AmE) is more frequent than *color* (BrE), although the latter experienced an increase in use around the year 2000

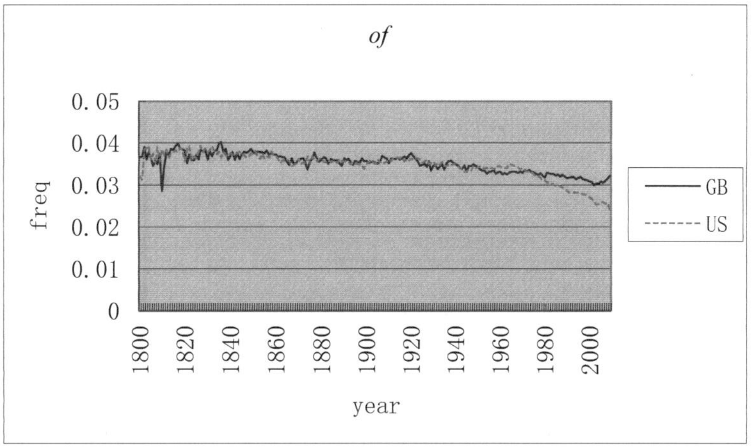


FIGURE 3 – *of*: Overlapping in AmE and BrE with a slight divergence from the 1980s on

## Conclusion and Future Work

The Square-Mean-Root (SMR) approach clearly outperforms chi-square ($\chi^2$) and LLR.

Future work includes the following :

(1) Exploring the theoretical nature of Square-Mean-Root (SMR)

(2) Extending to detection of lexical variation in Chinese, e.g. Mainland versus Taiwan

(3) Possible application in other NLP tasks, e.g. term extraction and document analysis

## Acknowledgments

Thanks to Adam Pease for his kind help. This work has been supported by RGC GRF(543512) and NSFC(91024009).

| No. | SMR rank | ratio: GB/US |
|---|---|---|
| 1 | labor | 0.1 |
| 2 | color | 0.1 |
| 3 | program | 0.16 |
| 4 | behavior | 0.17 |
| 5 | center | 0.11 |
| 6 | programs | 0.18 |
| 7 | labour | 3.88 |
| 8 | toward | 0.21 |
| 9 | favor | 0.1 |
| 10 | centre | 2.28 |
| 11 | colour | 4.04 |
| 12 | favour | 3.43 |
| 13 | £ | 3.22 |
| 14 | “ | 0.36 |
| 15 | ” | 0.35 |
| 16 | cent | 0.99 |
| 17 | percent | 0.16 |
| 18 | honor | 0.14 |
| 19 | colored | 0.07 |
| 20 | whilst | 2.82 |
| 21 | towards | 1.87 |
| 22 | defense | 0.12 |
| 23 | honour | 2.94 |
| 24 | behaviour | 5.14 |
| 25 | neighborhood | 0.08 |
| 26 | colors | 0.09 |
| 27 | railroad | 0.09 |
| 28 | defence | 1.9 |
| 29 | favorable | 0.09 |
| 30 | favorite | 0.11 |

| Chi-square rank | $\chi^2$ (x$10^6$) | ratio |
|---|---|---|
| which | 9.65 | 1.14 |
| you | 8.43 | 0.87 |
| of | 7.93 | 1.01 |
| £ | 7.6 | 3.22 |
| behaviour | 6.56 | 5.14 |
| cent | 6.52 | 0.99 |
| labour | 6.38 | 3.88 |
| t | 6.19 | 0.71 |
| centre | 5.79 | 2.28 |
| towards | 5.61 | 1.87 |
| her | 5.1 | 0.93 |
| colour | 4.79 | 4.04 |
| – | 4.54 | 0.9 |
| was | 4.48 | 1.07 |
| programme | 4.41 | 5.21 |
| et | 4.32 | 1.92 |
| toward | 3.97 | 0.21 |
| she | 3.79 | 0.9 |
| the | 3.73 | 1 |
| favour | 3.66 | 3.43 |
| is | 3.45 | 0.98 |
| labor | 3.41 | 0.1 |
| my | 3.38 | 1.08 |
| your | 3.25 | 0.9 |
| had | 3.18 | 1.09 |
| de | 3.11 | 1.5 |
| he | 3.1 | 1.04 |
| program | 3.07 | 0.16 |
| his | 2.92 | 1.05 |
| me | 2.83 | 1.04 |

| LLR rank | LLR (x$10^6$) | ratio |
|---|---|---|
| you | 9.43 | 0.87 |
| which | 8.87 | 1.14 |
| of | 7.71 | 1.01 |
| t | 7.19 | 0.71 |
| £ | 6.01 | 3.22 |
| her | 5.64 | 0.93 |
| toward | 5.23 | 0.21 |
| – | 5.1 | 0.9 |
| cent | 4.99 | 0.99 |
| labor | 4.9 | 0.1 |
| labour | 4.88 | 3.88 |
| behaviour | 4.84 | 5.14 |
| towards | 4.46 | 1.87 |
| program | 4.42 | 0.16 |
| was | 4.34 | 1.07 |
| centre | 4.3 | 2.28 |
| she | 4.23 | 0.9 |
| percent | 4.01 | 0.16 |
| color | 3.97 | 0.1 |
| et | 3.94 | 1.92 |
| colour | 3.84 | 4.04 |
| the | 3.68 | 1 |
| behavior | 3.67 | 0.17 |
| your | 3.65 | 0.9 |
| my | 3.53 | 1.08 |
| is | 3.37 | 0.98 |
| he | 3.23 | 1.04 |
| programme | 3.2 | 5.21 |
| center | 3.16 | 0.11 |
| had | 3.13 | 1.09 |

TABLE 1 – Comparison of ranking by our SMR(left), chi-square($\chi^2$, middle) and LLR(right)

## References


Cavaglia, G. (2002). Measuring Corpus Homogeneity Using a Range of Measures for Inter-Document Distance. *LREC 2002.*

Dunning, T. (1993). Accurate methods for the Statistics of Surprise and Coincidence. *Computational Linguistics.* 19(1): 61-74.

Google Inc. (2009). Google Books Ngrams (20090715 version). http://books.google.com/ngrams

Gries, S. Th. (2010). Dispersions and adjusted frequencies in corpora: further explorations. In Stefan Th. Gries, Stefanie Wulff, & Mark Davies (eds.), *Corpus linguistic applications: current studies, new directions*, pages 197-212. Amsterdam: Rodopi.

Kilgarriff, A. (2001). Comparing corpora. *International Journal of Corpus Linguistics*, 6(1):1-37.

Michel, J.-B., Shen, Y. K. et al. (2010). Quantitative Analysis of Culture Using Millions of Digitalized Books. *Science*. 331(6014):176-182. http://www.sciencemag.org/content/331/6014/176

McInnes, B. T. (2004). Extending the Log Likelihood Measure to Improve Collocation Identification. (Master of Science, Thesis). University of Minnesota.

Rayson, P. and Garside, R. (2000). Comparing Corpora using Frequency Profiling. *Proceeding of the workshop on Comparing Corpora. ACL 2000.*

Rose, T. and Kilgarriff, A. (1998). Measures of Corpus Similarity and Homogeneity between Corpora. *EMNLP 1998.*

Zhang, HR, Huang, C.-R. and Yu, SW. (2004). Distributional Consistency: As a General Method for Defining a Core Lexicon. *LREC 2004.*

Zhang, HR. (2010). Quantitative Measure of Language Information Concentrated on Square-Mean-Root Evenness. (PhD Thesis). Peking: Peking University.

# A Machine Learning Approach to Convert CCGbank to Penn Treebank*

Xiaotian Zhang[1,2] Hai Zhao[1,2†] Cong Hui[1,2]
(1) MOE-Microsoft Key Laboratory of Intelligent Computing and Intelligent System;
(2) Department of Computer Science and Engineering,
#800 Dongchuan Road, Shanghai, China, 200240
xtian.zh@gmail.com zhaohai@cs.sjtu.edu.cn huicong88126@gmail.com

## Abstract

Conversion between different grammar frameworks is of great importance to comparative performance analysis of the parsers developed based on them and to discover the essential nature of languages. This paper presents an approach that converts Combinatory Categorial Grammar (CCG) derivations to Penn Treebank (PTB) trees using a maximum entropy model. Compared with previous work, the presented technique makes the conversion practical by eliminating the need to develop mapping rules manually and achieves state-of-the-art results.

Keywords: CCG, Grammar conversion.

* This work was partially supported by the National Natural Science Foundation of China (Grant No. 60903119 and Grant No. 61170114), the National Research Foundation for the Doctoral Program of Higher Education of China under Grant No. 20110073120022, the National Basic Research Program of China (Grant No. 2009CB320901), and the European Union Seventh Framework Program (Grant No. 247619).

† Corresponding author

*Proceedings of COLING 2012: Demonstration Papers*, pages 535–542,
COLING 2012, Mumbai, December 2012.

## 1 Introduction

Much has been done in cross-framework performance analysis of parsers, and nearly all such analysis applies a converter across different grammar frameworks. Matsuzaki and Tsujii (2008) compared a Head-driven Phrase Structure Grammar (HPSG) parser with several Context Free Grammar (CFG) parsers by converting the parsing result to a shallow CFG analysis using an automatic tree converter based on Stochastic Synchronous Tree-Substitution Grammar. Clark and Curran (2007) converted the CCG dependencies of the CCG parser into those in Depbank by developing mapping rules via inspection so as to compare the performance of their CCG parser with the RASP parser. Performing such a conversion has been proven to be a time-consuming and non-trivial task (Clark and Curran, 2007).

Although CCGBank (Hockenmaier and Steedman, 2007) is a translation of the Penn Treebank (Marcus et al., 1993) into a corpus of Combinatory Categorial Grammar derivations, little work has been done in conversion from CCG derivations back to PTB trees besides (Clark and Curran, 2009) and (Kummerfeld et al., 2012). In the work of Clark and Curran (2009), they associated conversion rules with each local tree and developed 32 unary and 776 binary rule instances by manual inspection. Considerable time and effort were spent on the creation of these schemas. They show that although CCGBank is derived from PTB, the conversion from CCG back to PTB trees is far from trivial due to the non-isomorphic property of tree structures and the non-correspondence of tree labels. In the work of Kummerfeld et al. (2012), although no ad-hoc rules over non-local features were required, a set of instructions, operations, and also some special cases were defined.

Nevertheless, is it possible to convert CCG derivations to PTB trees using a statistical machine learning method instead of creating conversion grammars or defining instructions, and thus avoid the difficulties in developing these rules? Is it possible to restore the tree structure by only considering the change applied to the structure in the original generating process? Our proposed approach answers yes.

## 2 PTB2CCG and the Inverse

Let us first look at how CCG is derived from PTB. The basic procedure for converting a PTB tree to CCG described in (Hockenmaier and Steedman, 2007) consists of four steps:

1. Determine constituent types;
2. Make the tree binary;
3. Assign categories;
4. Assign dependencies;

Clearly, only step 2 changes the tree structure by adding dummy nodes to make it "binary", precisely, to make every node have only one or two child nodes.

Take the short sentence "Bond prices were up" in Figure 1(a) and 1(b) for example. As a preprocessing step, combine every internal node which has only one child with its single child and label the new node with the catenation of the original labels and #. That means to combine the shaded nodes in Figure 1 and obtain the corresponding new node. After the preprocessing, the node with a bold border in Figure 1(a) can be identified as "dummy" because the structure of CCG turns out to be the same as that of PTB if that node is deleted and its children are attached directly to its parent.

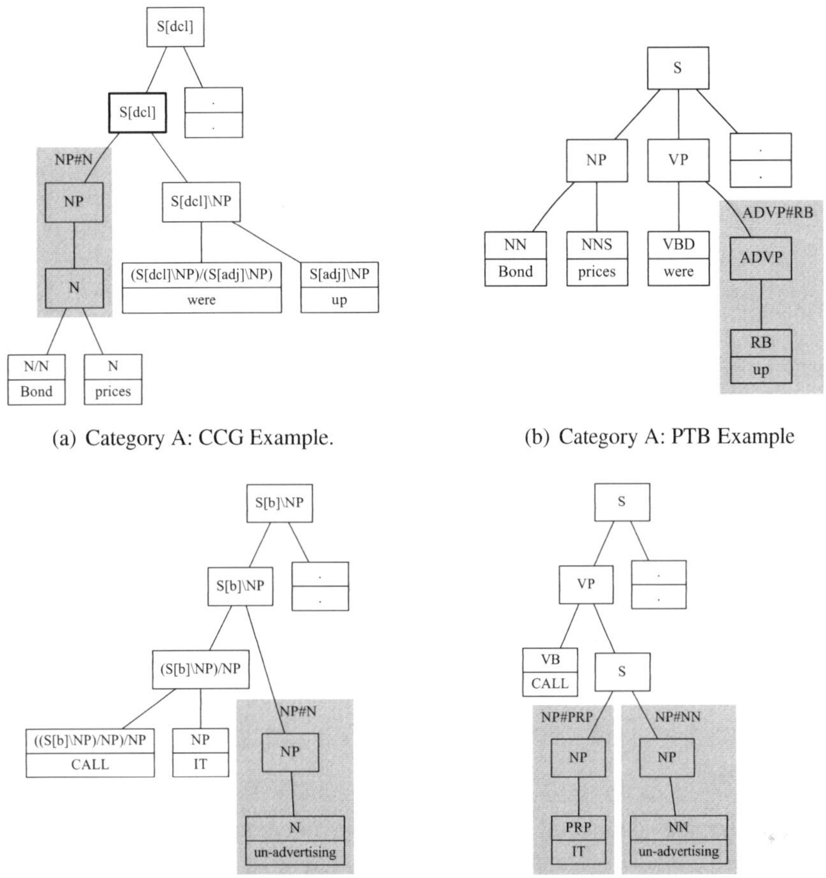


(a) Category A: CCG Example.

(b) Category A: PTB Example

(c) Category B: CCG Example

(d) Category B: PTB Example

Figure 1: CCG and corresponding PTB Examples of Category A and B. The grey shadow indicates the preprocessing that combines every internal node which has only one child with its single child. And the node with a bold border in Figure (a) is "dummy".

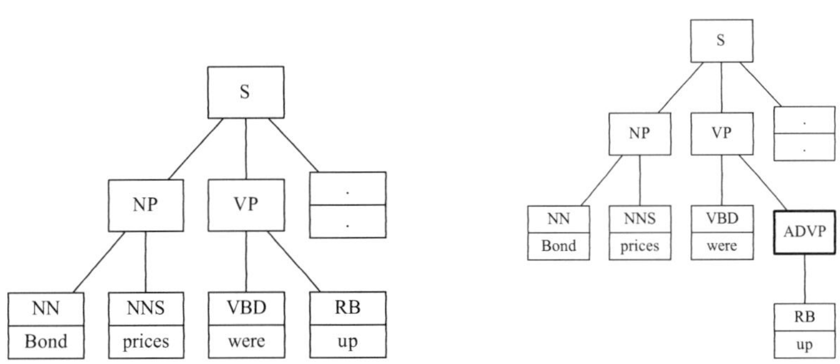


(a) Output PTB by $Classifier_1$

(b) Output PTB by $Classifier_2$

Figure 2: Output PTB by $Classifier_1$ and $Classifier_2$ when testing on the CCG sample in Figure 1(a). $Classifier_2$ corrects the output PTB of $Classifier_1$ by adding "ADVP", the node with a bold border, to dominate the leaf "RB".

However, it is more complicated in reality. There indeed exist CCG tree structures that can not be derived by just adding dummy nodes to the corresponding PTB trees, as shown in Figure 1(c) and 1(d), because actually a more sophisticated algorithm is used in the conversion from PTB to CCG. After investigation, all the cases can be grouped into two categories:

- Category A: The CCG tree structure can be derived from the PTB tree by adding dummy nodes, after the preprocessing step, as shown in Figure 1(a) and 1(b).
- Category B[1]: The CCG tree structure cannot be derived from the PTB tree by adding dummy nodes even if we perform the preprocessing, as shown in Figure 1(c) and 1(d).

The cases of Category B are less than 10% of the whole bank, so we simplify the problem by only focusing on solving the cases of Category A.

From the above discussion, after the preprocessing, one classifier is required to classify the CCG nodes into the target classes which are PTB labels and "dummy". However, preliminary experiments show that such a model still cannot handle the occasions in which a parent node occurs with a single child leaf in the PTB tree very well. For example, the S[adj]\NP node in the gold CCG tree (Figure 1(a)) tends to be classified as an RB node in the predicted PTB tree (Figure 2(a)) instead of the gold PTB label ADVP#RB (Figure 1(b)). So we use another classifier to predict whether each leaf node in the PTB tree produced by the first classifier has a parent dominating only itself and what the label of the parent is. This added classifier helps to identify the ADVP node (Figure 2(b)) in the above example and experiments show it increases the overall F-measure by up to 2%.

## 3 The Approach

Firstly, the training and test data need to be preprocessed as mentioned in Section 2. Then, classifiers are constructed based on the maximum entropy model[2]. As for the training process, the "dummy" nodes and the corresponding PTB labels could be identified by comparing post-order traversal sequences of each pair of CCG and PTB trees. And thus $Classifier_1$ can be trained. And based on the output of $Classifier_1$ tested on the training set and corresponding gold PTB trees, $Classifier_2$ can be trained.

When testing, there are two steps. Firstly, $Classifier_1$ is to classify the CCG labels into PTB labels and "dummy". The CCG tree is traversed in a bottom-up order and if the node is classified as "dummy", delete it and attach its children to its parent, otherwise replace the CCG label with the predicted PTB label. Then, an intermediate PTB tree is built. Secondly, $Classifier_2$ examines each leaf in the intermediate PTB tree and predicts whether a parent node should be added to dominate the leaf. The feature sets for the two classifiers are listed in Table 1.

## 4 Experiments

We evaluate the proposed approach on CCGBank and PTB. As in (Clark and Curran, 2009), we use Section 01-22 as training set[3], Section 00 as development set to tune the parameters and Section 23 as test set. Experiments are done separately with gold POS tags and auto POS tags predicted by Lapos tagger (Tsuruoka et al., 2011).

[1] According to our inspection, these cases always occur in certain language structures, such as complex objects, "of" phrases and so on.

[2] We use the implementation by Apache OpenNLP http://incubator.apache.org/opennlp/index.html

[3] Since the converter is trained on the gold banks, it doesn't have access to parsing output. And thus, the converting process is general and not specific to parser errors.

| **Feature Set 1** | **Feature Set 2** |
|---|---|
| *$Features_{CCGNode}$* | WordForm |
| Label | POS |
| ParentLabel | ParentLabel |
| LSiblingLabel | IndexAmongChildren |
| LSiblingWordForm | ParentChildrenCnt |
| RSiblingLabel | LSiblingLabel |
| RSiblingWordForm | LSiblingWordForm |
| Children | RSiblingLabel |
| ChildCnt | RSiblingWordForm |
| *$Features_{PTBNode}$* | LSiblingRightMostLabel |
| Children | RSiblingLeftMostLabel |
| LSiblingLabel | SecondRSiblingLabel |
| POS | SecondLSiblingLabel |
| $POS_{-1}$ | |

Table 1: Features Used by Two Classifiers ("LSibling", and "RSibling" represent "Left sibling" and "Right sibling". $POS_{-1}$ represents the POS tag of the previous word).

| POS Tag | P | R | F |
|---|---|---|---|
| Gold | 96.99 | 95.29 | 96.14 |
| Lapos | 96.82 | 95.12 | 95.96 |

Table 2: Evaluation on all the sentences of Category A in Section 23.

Firstly we leave out Category B and test on all the sentences belonging to Category A from Section 23. Table 2 shows our conversion accuracy. The numbers are bracketing precision, recall, F-score using the EVALB[4] evaluation script.

In order to compare with (Clark and Curran, 2009)[5], the approach is also tested on all of Section 00 and 23. The oracle conversion results are presented in Table 3. It shows the F-measure of our method is about one point higher than that of Clark and Curran (2009), no matter what kind of POS tags[6] is applied.

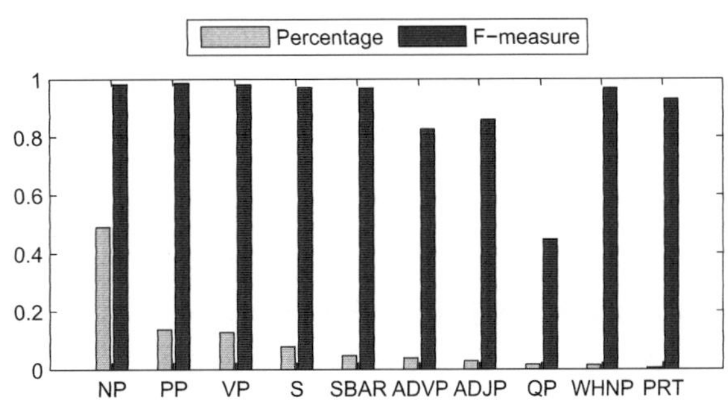


Figure 3: The conversion F-measure of top ten major kinds of phrases.

[4]http://nlp.cs.nyu.edu/evalb/

[5]We don't know which kind of POS tags, gold or predicted, was used in (Clark and Curran, 2009) as they did not report it in their paper.

[6]We have tried with different POS taggers and the results stay more or less stable.

| | Section | P | R | F |
|---|---|---|---|---|
| $Our_{gold}$ | $00_{all}$ | **96.92** | 94.82 | **95.86** |
| | $00_{len \leq 40}$ | **97.09** | 95.40 | **96.24** |
| | $23_{all}$ | **96.67** | 94.77 | **95.71** |
| | $23_{len \leq 40}$ | **96.69** | 94.79 | **95.73** |
| $Our_{lapos}$ | $00_{all}$ | 96.85 | 94.74 | 95.79 |
| | $00_{len \leq 40}$ | 97.03 | 95.34 | 96.18 |
| | $23_{all}$ | 96.49 | 94.64 | 95.56 |
| | $23_{len \leq 40}$ | 96.51 | 94.67 | 95.58 |
| Clark& Curran, 2009 | $00_{all}$ | 93.37 | **95.15** | 94.25 |
| | $00_{len \leq 40}$ | 94.11 | **95.65** | 94.88 |
| | $23_{all}$ | 93.68 | **95.13** | 94.40 |
| | $23_{len \leq 40}$ | 93.75 | **95.23** | 94.48 |

Table 3: Evaluation on all of Section 00 and 23.

| | -Simple | -Children | -Parent | -Sibling |
|---|---|---|---|---|
| F | 93.8 | 91.28 | 95.18 | **89.02** |

Table 4: Results on Section 23 using gold POS tags and features excluding one category each time.

To investigate the effectiveness of the features, we divide them into four categories[7], children, parent, sibling features and simple features (label, POS and wordform), and test using feature sets from which one category of features is removed each time. Table 4 shows that all the kinds of features have an effect and the sibling-related features are the most effective.

In error analysis, the conversion F-measure of each kind of phrases is examined (see Figure 3). As for the F-measure of the top ten major kinds, seven of them are over 90%, two around 80% while the worst is 44.8%. The high accuracy in predicting most major kinds of phrases leads to the good overall performance of our approach and there is still some room to improve by further finding effective features to classify QP phrases better.

## 5 Conclusions

We have proposed a practical machine learning approach[8] to convert the CCG derivations to PTB trees efficiently and achieved an F-measure over 95%. The core of the approach is based on the maximum entropy model. Compared with conversion methods that use mapping rules, applying such a statistical machine learning method helps saving considerable time and effort.

## References

Clark, S. and Curran, J. (2007). Formalism-independent parser evaluation with ccg and depbank. In *Proceedings of the 45th Annual Meeting of the Association of Computational Linguistics*, pages 248–255, Prague, Czech Republic. Association for Computational Linguistics.

Clark, S. and Curran, J. R. (2009). Comparing the accuracy of ccg and penn treebank parsers. In *Proceedings of the ACL-IJCNLP 2009 Conference Short Papers*, pages 53–56, Suntec, Singapore. Association for Computational Linguistics.

[7] Due to space limitations, we show the importance of every category of features instead of each individual feature.

[8] This software has been released, https://sourceforge.net/p/ccg2ptb/home/Home/.

Hockenmaier, J. and Steedman, M. (2007). Ccgbank: A corpus of ccg derivations and dependency structures extracted from the penn treebank. *Computational Linguistics*, 33:355–396.

Kummerfeld, J. K., Klein, D., and Curran, J. R. (2012). Robust conversion of ccg derivations to phrase structure trees. In *Proceedings of the 50th Annual Meeting of the Association for Computational Linguistics (Volume 2: Short Papers)*, pages 105–109, Jeju Island, Korea. Association for Computational Linguistics.

Marcus, M. P., Marcinkiewicz, M. A., and Santorini, B. (1993). Building a large annotated corpus of english: the penn treebank. *Computational Linguistics*, 19:313–330.

Matsuzaki, T. and Tsujii, J. (2008). Comparative parser performance analysis across grammar frameworks through automatic tree conversion using synchronous grammars. In *Proceedings of the 22nd International Conference on Computational Linguistics - Volume 1*, COLING '08, pages 545–552, Stroudsburg, PA, USA. Association for Computational Linguistics.

Tsuruoka, Y., Miyao, Y., and Kazama, J. (2011). Learning with lookahead: can history-based models rival globally optimized models? In *Proceedings of the Fifteenth Conference on Computational Natural Language Learning*, CoNLL '11, pages 238–246, Stroudsburg, PA, USA. Association for Computational Linguistics.

# Author Index